Secular By Design

Also by Alan W. Cecil

THE NOAHIDE CODE
THE NOAHIDE GUIDE TO MATTHEW

Secular By Design

A Philosophy of
Noahide Laws and Observances

Alan W. Cecil

Academy of Shem Press
Pompano Beach

First Edition 5771/2011
Second Edtion 5772/2012

ISBN: 978-0-9779885-4-9
www.academyofshem.com
Printed in the United States of America

Cover design by Layla Cecil

New Visigoth and Mercator fonts by Arthur Baker

For Jaiden and Charlotte

CONTENTS

⌒

PART ONE

THE PROTOCOLS OF THE ELDERS OF EDOM

PART TWO

THE RED, RED, WHITE AND BLUE

CHAPTER FIVE

CHAPTER SIX

∽

PART THREE

LESSONS FROM MORIAH

CHAPTER SEVEN

∽

Acknowledgments

I would like to thank my wife Teresa for her invaluable help with the manuscript, and whose love and support made this work possible. I wish to give special thanks to my daughter Marlena who helped proofread the manuscript and to my daughter Layla for her work on the cover and design.

I would also like to thank Dr. Ralph Peters for his invaluable assistance and suggestions. A special thanks also to the Atlanta Scholars Kollel, Rabbi Menachem Deutsch, Rabbi Yaakov Schwartz, Rabbi Dave Silverman, and Rabbi Menashe Goldberger.

Part One

&

The Protocols of the Elders of Edom

Overview

Intelligence works within the framework of limited but clearly stated goals, and may be quick to shear away questions of thought that do not seem to help in reaching them...intellect, on the other hand, is the critical, creative, and contemplative side of mind. Whereas intelligence seeks to grasp, manipulate, re-order, adjust, intellect examines, ponders, wonders, theorizes, criticizes, imagines. Intelligence will seize the immediate meaning in a situation and evaluate it. Intellect evaluates evaluations, and looks for the meanings of situations as a whole. Intelligence can be praised as a quality in animals; intellect, being a unique manifestation of human dignity, is both praised and assailed as a quality in men. When the difference is so defined, it becomes easier to understand why we sometimes say that a mind of admittedly penetrating intelligence is relatively unintellectual; and why, by the same token, we see among minds that are unmistakably intellectual a considerable range of intelligence.

— Richard Hofstadter[1]

THE INNOVATORS OF WESTERN CULTURE WHO CREATE THE CONCEPTS and ideologies which shape our society do not learn and develop their ideas in a vacuum. Our corporate executives, business leaders, professors, teachers, writers, artists, congressmen, judges, and lawyers—all of these individuals cultivate their ideas and ethics not only in the home and church but through an institutional education system designed to teach and support specific values and customs. These leaders, who influence much of the world economically, politically, and culturally are themselves influenced by the ideas of earlier men such as John Locke, Adam Smith, Thomas Jefferson, and Karl Marx. These are but a few of the men who have played a key and decisive role in the development of ideologies such as democracy, capitalism, and communism, and there are few people on the planet whose lives have not been affected by the concepts and doctrines developed by these men. These men of ideas, of keen analytical ability, once called "men of letters," we today call *intellectuals*.

Intellectuals in Western Culture deal with a diverse range of subjects, from politics, economics, religion, and history to the arts and

---

[1] Richard Hofstadter, *Anti-Intellectualism in American Life*. (New York: Vintage Books, 1963), 25.

entertainment. Intellectuals have an important function in our society as the supporters, expounders, and critics of education, government, business, and culture. Although in America the intellectual is most often associated with higher academics, historian Richard Hofstadter presented a broader concept based on the traditional meaning of "intellectual," asking: what separates the intellectual from the merely intelligent individual? We have all known intelligent people who, when faced with an abstract problem, idea, moral dilemma, or a political or ideological choice, never seemed to "get it." Despite their obvious intelligence, no matter how well you explained a position, what facts you presented, or how you defined your argument—they are unable to put the pieces of the puzzle together.

In his Pulitzer Prize winning book *Anti-Intellectualism in American Life*, Hofstadter explained the difference between being "intelligent" and being "intellectual." According to Hofstadter's definition, intelligent people know the rules and how to play the game. They may demonstrate great aptitude for learning, soaking up facts like a sponge, and they can be clever in their dealings with men. There is, however, something inflexible in their way of thinking, and they are unable to "think outside the box" as the cliché goes. The intellectual, however, not only questions the rules, but questions who made the rules, and questions why we should play the game in the first place. The intellectual is able to take the facts and reassemble them into new ideas and concepts, not to simply "play by the rules," for if the rules are faulty and the game is fixed, the intellectual understands that new rules are called for.

For many people, the term "intellectual" conjures up images of someone who is erudite and well-spoken, a person of broad culture, one who can think and speak about controversial topics with wit and aplomb, a person who does not resort to knee-jerk emotionalism: a person of reason.[2] For many others, however, the word "intellectual" evokes negative images: the "egghead," the "brain," the "grind," the "nerd," or the "geek," the person who often disdains the mores and values of polite society (and in fact may be trying to change the rules themselves), a snobby and cliquish left-wing bleeding heart liberal academic who is a vague but constant threat to a comfortably conservative and repetitious

---

[2] One common non-Hofstadterian definition of intellectual is that of an "expert," someone with highbrow credentials, such as a Ph.D. Those who often use the misnomer "pseudo-intellectual" abide by this definition.

way of life, particularly in matters of faith. In his review of Hofstadter's *Anti-Intellectualism in American Life*, Rush Welter observed that Hofstadter explained how "anti-intellectualism has permeated our religion and our politics, our economy and our education."[3]

In our educational system, the well-to-do in early nineteenth century America could send their children to academies to be taught "Latin, Greek, and mathematics, commonly supplemented by science and history,"[4] and the idea of intellectualism was grounded in a classical rather than a theological education. By the end of the nineteenth century, as public schooling became mandatory, the curriculum changed, as did the focus, and being able to reason and think logically was viewed increasingly as not simply unimportant, but detrimental to our expanding industrial economy. Business wanted schools that would turn out dependable and subservient workers for their factories, and thus the preference for professionals with academic credentials rather than philosophers.[5]

⁓⥈⁓

T HE MOST VISIBLE and continuing battleground for intellectuals has been the field of religion, especially the dominant religion in Western society—Christianity. The antagonism between intellectuals and Christianity goes back to the beginnings of Christian theology; the anti-intellectual foundation and framework of which is best summed up by the Latin saying *Credo quia absurdum*,[6] a phrase commonly attributed to Tertullian.[7] Christianity began as a movement among the

---

[3] Rush Welter, "Anti-intellectualism in American Life by Richard Hofstadter." *The Journal of American History*. Vol. 51, No. 3, (Dec., 1964), 482.

[4] Hofstadter, *Anti-Intellectualism in American Life*, 324.

[5] "A great deal of what might be called the journeyman's work of our culture—the work of lawyers, editors, engineers, doctors, indeed of some writers and of most professors—though vitally dependent upon ideas, is not distinctively intellectual...the heart of the matter—to borrow a distinction made by Max Weber about politics—is that the professional man lives off ideas, not for them." Hofstadter, *Anti-Intellectualism in American Life*, 26–27.

[6] "I believe because it is absurd."

[7] Tertullian was a Church father who lived during the late second and early third century of the Common Era. The idea that all Christian theology is simplistic is, of

simple and unlearned, developing a theology which often castigated knowledge, teaching that "heart knowledge" (emotionalism) was more important than "head knowledge" (intellectualism). This sentiment is based on teachings in the New Testament, such as Paul's First Epistle to the Corinthians: *Which things also we speak, not in the words which man's wisdom teacheth, but which the Holy Ghost teacheth; comparing spiritual things with spiritual* (1 Cor. 2:13). This is from the King James Version, and the archaic phrasing does not convey the meaning as well as a more modern translation such as the New International Version: *This is what we speak, not in words taught us by human wisdom but in words taught by the Spirit, expressing spiritual truths in spiritual words.* Even when the Church absorbed neo-Platonic[8] and neo-Aristotelian[9] elements into their theology in order to make it more appealing to men of learning, they were still bound by the teachings of the New Testament's attitude of conceptualizing ideas, not with enticing words of man's wisdom, but in demonstration of the Spirit and of power.[10] This teaching—"man's wisdom" versus "spiritual wisdom," or "heart knowledge" versus "head knowledge"— has been the firewall the Church has used against intellectualism, and as a result, Christianity has been perceived as the faith of the simple and slow of mind. Today, the majority of intellectuals in our culture do not take the Bible seriously, and most intellectuals relegate Scripture to the recycle-bin of mythological literature.

Even today, many of the leading intellectuals of popular Western culture—writers and lecturers such as Richard Dawkins, Christopher Hitchens, Daniel Dennett, Susan Jacoby, and Noam Chomsky—all believe in the equality of religion in the sense that they believe all religions are absurd, and these intellectuals named above are all

---

course, a broad generalization. There have been at various times both movements and individuals within Christianity who have championed intellectualism (within specific theological parameters) such as the early American Puritans. "Puritan society...had laid the foundation for a remarkable tradition of intellectual discipline." [Hofstadter, *Anti-Intellectualism in American Life*, 403]. These movements were, however, more the exception than the rule.

[8] Cf. the writings of Augustine of Hippo.

[9] Cf. the writings of Thomas Aquinas.

[10] New Testament, 1 Cor. 2:4.

virulently atheistic.[11] For these popular writers and speakers, to be an academic intellectual today one must forgo religion. These intellectuals portray religion as the antithesis of intellectualism, the enemy of enlightenment, the scourge of science, and the rival of reason. Religion is viewed academically as not only un-intellectual, but un-intelligent as well. This attitude is due in no small part to the role Christian theology has played in the formation of our cultural ideas and values.[12]

From the intellectual's viewpoint, the absurdities of Christian theology, while they might have worked in medieval times with an uneducated rabble, fail miserably in today's age of science and rationality. The Church's persecution of Galileo Galilei and the Scopes Monkey Trial are two familiar examples of the shortcomings of Christian theology. The Christian insistence that the Earth is only six thousand years old, that God created the fossils of prehistoric animals to test our faith, or that Jesus rode around on dinosaurs makes Christianity look as modern and as reasonable as the ancient Greek deities of Homer's *Odyssey*. This view of religion is one of the predominant themes in recent New York Times best sellers on religion, such as British evolutionary zoologist Richard Dawkins's *The God Delusion*, a book which brings a scientific approach to Dawkins's criticism of religion. Many of Dawkins's arguments often revolve around a scientific gene theory where he splices the science of genetics with his critique of creation. Another best-seller is British-born-and-bred American journalist Christopher Hitchens's *god* [*sic*] *is not Great*, where Hitchens's lush prose showcases his journalistic background, and his many anecdotes, quips, and proofs reveal a hostility to religion that has seemingly been bottled up and aged to a bitter potency. American writer Sam Harris's book *The End of Faith* expounds the dangers of religion to modern society, and, as the title suggests, the irrationality of faith.

---

[11] Although most intellectual writers are hostile to organized religion, Sam Harris is a tad more tolerant of personal beliefs, offering a mushy support for a benign atheistic form of Buddhism. "Mysticism is a rational enterprise. Religion is not." Sam Harris, *The End of Faith: Religion, Terror, and the Future of Reason*. (New York: W. W. Norton & Company, 2004), 221.

[12] Hofstadter touched on the role of this religion, where "anti-intellectualism must be sought out in the framework of our religious history…the patterns of modern thought, both religious and secular, are prefigured in our earlier religious history." Hofstadter, *Anti-Intellectualism in American Life*, 47.

These popular books have a similar theme in that they decry the evil perpetrated by organized religion, and all three books laud the positivism of science and the reason of philosophy (although both theology and philosophy had their origins in Ancient Greece). To be an intellectual in today's modern world, according to their argument, one should eschew religion and embrace atheism. The grand theme for these intellectual works is that religion "poisons" everything, as Hitchens repeatedly pointed out, whereas science and philosophy are the light of truth. Dawkins gleefully reveals that "more highly educated people are less likely to be religious,"[13] although he could have as easily said that most people who embrace Christianity are less likely to be educated, given Christianity's disdain for secular "book learnin'."

As far as organized religion's destructive effect on society, their arguments are difficult to refute. For the past seventeen centuries— through the Crusades, the Inquisition, the pogroms, the Holocaust, the intifada, and the countless wars which were fought in the name of Jesus or Muhammad—one would be hard pressed to find a more corrosive ideology than organized religion, particularly Christianity with its message of "love," and Islam, the religion of "peace." Certainly today, with the war in the Middle East, terrorism in Serbia, the unrest in Northern Ireland, the tension between Pakistan and India, the riots in France, the bombing of the World Trade Center, it would seem that the world would be a safer and saner place without organized religion.

One primary focus of these intellectual writers is the anti-intellectualism of religion. Dawkins explains that, "as a scientist, I am hostile to fundamentalist religion because it actively debauches the scientific enterprise.[14] It teaches us not to change our minds, and not to want to know exciting things that are available to be known."[15] These modern secular intellectuals believe that "reason," not "religion," should be the basis of morality,[16] that we should favor the "reason" that has its

---

[13] Richard Dawkins, *The God Delusion*, (New York: Mariner Books, 2008), 129.

[14] "Because nature is derivative and not ultimate, the knowledge of nature cannot be the paradigm of true knowledge." Paul Eidelberg, *Jerusalem vs. Athens: In Quest of a General Theory of Existence*. (Lanham: University Press of America, Inc., 1983), 12.

[15] Dawkins, *The God Delusion*, 321.

[16] "Success draws many kinds of camp-followers, and science, too, does not lack these. There is today a large movement which attempts to exploit science's prestige to propagate concepts outside its field of competence. Specifically, science is cited as validating, or at

roots in Greek philosophy rather than the "reason" based on theology and the Greek New Testament. Yet it seems that the only two choices given to us are Greek philosophy or Greek theology. The idea that there is another concept of "reason," one outside our culture's Greek system, one which is from a different cultural and ethical vantage point, is a theory these intellectual secularists are seemingly unable to grasp.[17]

◡◠◡

It IS NOT WITHOUT a touch of irony that the term "intellectual" was itself a creation of anti-Semitism.[18] The word "intellectual" came into its popular modern use during the Dreyfus[19] scandal in France (which began in 1894 and lasted well into the twentieth century) as a disparaging slur for Dreyfus's supporters. The accusations against the Jewish French military officer Alfred Dreyfus were transparently flimsy, but there was a sudden pandemic of anti-Semitism which infected the proceedings and divided the French over this issue; the intellectuals were outnumbered and Dreyfus was convicted and incarcerated. Throngs of the anti-Drefusards marched through the streets of Paris chanting *Death to the Jews*, and for one young Jewish reporter who was in Paris covering the Dreyfus affair for a Budapest

---

least endorsing, codes of morality and modes of conduct…these attempts, often termed scientism, are based either on a tacitly accepted definition of 'good' or on hypotheses outside the scope of science. Since science is concerned only with what was, what is, and what can be, it cannot possibly carry a message for a moral code which defines what should be, what is desirable, and what is justifiable." Yehudah Levi, *Torah and Science: Their Interplay in the World Scheme*. (Jerusalem: Feldheim Publishers, 2006), 3.

[17] "Science cannot supply the content of a moral code or even a rationale for one. The reason is inherent in the very nature of the scientific enterprise. To be effective and trustworthy, science must be free from value judgments, whether ethical or aesthetic." Robert Gordis, *Judaic Ethics For a Lawless World.* (New York: The Jewish Theological Seminary of America, 1986), 43.

[18] "The term *intellectual* first came into use in France. It was soon exported—at the time of the Dreyfus case, when so large a part of the intellectual community was aroused to protest against the anti-Dreyfus conspiracy and became involved in an ideological holy war on the French reactionaries. At that time the term came to be used by both sides—by the right as a kind of insult, by the Drefusard intellectuals as a proud banner." Hofstadter, *Anti-Intellectualism in American Life*, 38–39.

[19] Dreyfus, the only Jewish officer on the French General Staff, was accused of treason by passing French military secrets to Germany. The trial was marked by gross violations of judicial procedure as well as a lack of evidence. After two trials and many years of imprisonment, Dreyfus was completely exonerated of all charges.

newspaper, it was a clarion call that the Enlightenment had failed. Anti-Semitism had not been cured, it had only been in remission in Christian Europe, and the roots of anti-Semitism ran deeper into the European psyche than anyone had realized. It had become painfully obvious that the motto of *liberté, égalité, fraternité* that had seemed so promising a century earlier did not include the Jews.

Like so many of life's chance encounters, being at the right place at the wrong time, or the wrong place at the right time, can have life-changing consequences, and if the person is an intellectual of drive and energy, these consequences can ripple out into society. The blatant display of anti-Semitism in the streets of Paris was a shock to the young Jewish reporter, for he himself was a "secular" Jewish intellectual who had embraced the ideas and sentiment of the Enlightenment; like many others of his generation, he had shunned traditional Jewish education, acquiring a doctorate in law from the University of Vienna rather than a *semicha* at a yeshiva, and he, as did many other assimilated Jews, had assumed that the Christians of Europe had overcome anti-Semitism the same way they had overcome serfdom and slavery. For the troubled young Jewish reporter, the witnessing of the outpouring of anti-Semitism in the streets of Paris became a major turning point in his life.

And so the young Jewish journalist Theodor Herzl would leave Paris pondering where the Jewish people could find a safe haven away from the anti-Semitism that was once again spreading its poison throughout Europe. Dreyfus was convicted of treason and sent to Devil's Island in French Guiana, and from this sorry episode in Western history both the term "intellectual" and the modern state of Israel developed; none too soon, for in less than forty years—a Jewish generation—the concentration camp at Dachau would be open for business.[20]

The Dreyfus scandal marked the public re-emergence of anti-Semitism in Western Europe after a short "enlightenment" period when Christian Europeans, at the advice of their great thinkers and philosophers, gritted their teeth and tried to "be nice" to the Jews, letting them out of the ghettos and treating them, more or less, as real human

---

[20] "A hundred years almost to the day after the publication of [Hirsch's] *Horeb*, Jewish houses of Prayer and Study stood in flames throughout Germany, set on fire by a mad off-shoot of that very civilization which, in the view of the Reform Jewish of Hirsch's days, was to be the judge and arbiter of the morality of the Divine laws of the Torah." Dayan Dr. I. Grunfeld, introduction to Rabbi Samson Raphael Hirsch's *Horeb*, (New York, The Soncino Press, 1994), cxxx.

beings and fellow citizens. It might have worked, too, except that the "great thinkers and philosophers" of Europe had an ulterior motive— to destroy Judaism with kindness, separating Jews from the Law of Moses by enticement, attempting to make the Jews understand how much better the secular way of life was than to be yoked to the archaic Laws of the Torah.[21] It almost worked, too; a great many of the Jews of the nineteenth century did indeed give up Judaism, particularly in Western Europe. Try as they might, however, these emancipated and assimilated Jews never really fit in with "polite" European society; there was always something too *Jewish* about them. By the end of the nineteenth century, Christian Europe was losing patience with its "be nice to the Jews"[22] experiment, and the forced smile that it had held for nearly a century gradually turned into a snarling rictus.[23]

Of course, it was not only in France that anti-Semitism reestablished itself after decades of dormancy; throughout the continent, the old animosities towards the Jews would rekindle, often taking newer and subtler forms. One of the major works of anti-Jewish propaganda was first published in the early years of the twentieth century; during the very years of the bloody pogroms of 1903–1906, there appeared in Russia a short book entitled *The Protocols of the Elders of Zion*, a work plagiarized from earlier political writings (most notably from a satirical work about Napoleon III), and it was brought to the United States sometime

---

[21] "The Jews should be denied everything as a nation, but granted everything as individuals...it is intolerable that the Jews should become a separate political formation or class in the country...if they do not want this, they must inform us and we shall then be compelled to expel them...the existence of a nation within a nation is unacceptable to our country." From a speech by Count Stanislas de Clermont-Tonnerre in the French National Assembly, 1789, cited by Paul R. Mendes-Flohr and Jehuda Reinharz, ed., *The Jew in the Modern World.* (New York: Oxford University Press, 1995), 115.

[22] "By the end of the nineteenth century, after the liberal experiment had failed to dissolve the Jews in the pristine solvent of German tolerance, the erstwhile 'friends of the Jews' came to regard these strangers in their midst with the same loathing that their less idealistic contemporaries had nurtured all along." Harris, *The End of Faith*, 102.

[23] "The atmosphere in which the history of the exiles unfolds follows the pattern set by Antiochus...subjected to the pressures and the ridicule of crude force on the one hand, and the satanic smile of seductive temptation on the other, in the hope that they will be destroyed physically and morally at the same time." Rabbi Samson Raphael Hirsch, *Collected Writings*, Vol. II. (Jerusalem: Phillip Feldheim, Inc., 1997), 424.

during the aftermath of the Russian Revolution, where it was translated to English by the Russian anti-Semites in America.

The basic theme of *The Protocols of the Elders of Zion* can be summed up simply as *the Jews are plotting to take over the world.* Yet there is a question which no one has ever seemed to ask: exactly *who* are the Jews supposedly "taking over the world" *from*? It is simple logic that, if the Jews were plotting to take over the world, then there would have to be some other more *paranoid* group, a group of people who were (and are) in control of the world in order for it to be taken over.[24]

The *Protocols of the Elders of Zion* did attract the attention of many Americans, notably Henry Ford, who published it in his newspaper, *The Dearborn Independent* where it was re-titled as "*The International Jew: The World's Problem*." Ford's publication of *Protocols* in the *Dearborn Independent* would have a considerable effect on the racial and ethnic climate in America.[25] The greatest impact of Ford's publication, however, would be felt in Germany, a nation widely considered to be the most "civilized" nation on earth in the early twentieth century, where the Germans would develop a form of anti-Semitism that would prove to be deadlier than that which any previous culture had contrived. *The Dearborn Independent* caught the attention of many of Mr. Ford's great admirers in Germany, not the least of which was Adolf Hitler, who would incorporate many of its themes in his book *Mein Kampf.* This is a grim lesson we should take to heart: anti-Semitism can affect any nation, no matter how sapient their art and music, no matter how refined their customs or their cuisine, no matter how haughty their manners, and no matter how educated their intellectuals.

---

[24] One of the jokes which circulated during this time was of a rabbi coming across an old Jew reading a popular German anti-Semitic newspaper. "Why are you reading that?" the astonished rabbi asked. "Well," the old man replied, "when I read the regular news, it is all bad: Jews being beaten, synagogues burnt down, Jewish shops looted and vandalized, Jewish women and girls accosted. But in this paper, it is all good news! We Jews are in control of banking, business, media, and government—we are the ones running the world!"

[25] Ford's publication of *The International Jew* helped encourage support for the passing of the Johnson-Reed act of 1924, legislation which severely restricted Jewish immigration into the United States. This would lead to dire consequences for Jews in the years to come.

Sinners in the Hands of an Angry Intellectual

Scientists, being human beings of intelligence and sensitivity, have their attitudes and their points of view on all of these issues of values and goals...possessing greater intellectual capacity than the generality of men, scientists have a correspondingly greater responsibility to have their views made known and made effective. But when they do so, they function as citizens, not as scientists. Decision-making in the realm of public policy is not the province of science. By that token science cannot serve as the progenitor of ethics.

— Robert Gordis[1]

THE FLAW IN THE LOGIC OF THE INTELLECTUAL'S ARGUMENT IS THAT THEY treat the "fundamentalist monotheistic religions" of Judaism, Christianity, and Islam as three peas in a pod, indistinguishable from one another, all equally inane due to their nature of believing in a Divine Creator which, according to most secular intellectuals, does not exist.[2] As Hitchens points out, "the foundation story of all three faiths concerns the purported meeting between Moses and god [*sic*], at the summit of Mount Sinai."[3] But the Jewish faith stops there; there was no new revelation after Moses, at least not one that did not point back to Sinai as the pinnacle and foundation of Judaism. Christianity and Islam, on the other hand, added to the Jewish teaching, saying that their own prophets (Jesus and Muhammad) had a new and improved version of God's Word based on their additions to the Hebrew Bible, the New Testament and the Qur'an. This is an important point, that the two largest organized religions in the history of mankind felt the need to use the *Tanach*, or the Hebrew Bible, as the basis for their own faiths. It would seem reasonable, therefore, that the intellectual's attack would be at the heart of the problem—the Sinaic Revelation, the Torah of Moses.[4]

---

[1] Gordis, *Judaic Ethics for a Lawless World*, 44.

[2] "For most of my purposes, all three Abrahamic religions can be treated as indistinguishable. Unless otherwise stated, I shall have Christianity mostly in mind, but only because it is the version with which I happen to be most familiar." Dawkins, *The God Delusion*, 58.

[3] Christopher Hitchens, *god is not Great*. (New York: Twelve, 2007), 98.

[4] "Nothing is more sacred than the facts," Harris insists; "the litmus test for reasonableness should be obvious: anyone who wants to know how the world is, whether in physical or spiritual terms, will be open to new evidence." Harris, *The End of Faith*, 225.

This the secular intellectuals do not do. Although they attack the "Old Testament," their main targets are the theological teachings of the two offshoots of Judaism: Christianity and Islam. The secular attack on Judaism consists primarily of blaming Judaism for opening up the Pandora's Box of faith and being responsible for unleashing Christianity and Islam upon the world, and the bulk of atheist animosity is directed at the Christian and Islamic interpretations of the Hebrew Bible rather than Judaism itself. That Jewish interpretations might be fundamentally different from Christian or Islamic interpretations does not enter the intellectual's mind, and by attacking the New Testament and the Qur'an instead of the Torah proper, the secular authors mentioned above (Dawkins, Hitchens, and Harris) completely miss their target. Hitchens does ridicule Maimonides in passing on a few occasions, but other than a few oblique references to the Talmud, there is silence among these writers concerning the Jewish interpretation of their own Scripture, an interpretation that is different from the ones the intellectuals attack. The inability of these intellectuals to differentiate between Christian or Islamic theology and rabbinic interpretation makes their statements about the Torah sound as foolish as the teachings of the religionists the atheists themselves ridicule.

For example, Richard Dawkins questions the need for religion, arguing that we do not need religion to teach us to be moral. Dawkins insists that:

> We do not—even the religious among us—ground our morality in holy books…how, then, do we decide what is right and what is wrong?…one way to express our consensual ethics is as a 'New Ten Commandments'… here is one set of 'New Ten Commandments' from today, which I happened to find on an atheist website…[the first 'commandment' being] do not do to others what you would not want them to do to you.[5]

This is, in fact, a wonderful teaching: the "Golden Rule" of Christianity postulated in the negative. Dawkins, however, does not seem to realize that this is a teaching of rabbinic Judaism, a teaching that is over two thousand years old. In the Talmud (*Shabbos* 31a), there is a well-known story of a non-Jew who approached Rabbi Hillel and asked him to teach him the Torah while standing on one foot (i.e., quickly). Hillel replied: "What is hateful to yourself, do not do to another. This is the entire Torah, the rest is commentary. Go study it." Here is the essence of the Torah boiled down to one pithy saying, a

---

[5] Dawkins, *The God Delusion*, 298.

simple moral code for the non-Jew. What these secular intellectuals do not seem to understand is that Judaism has an entire branch of teaching for non-Jews, and their lumping together of Judaism, Christianity, and Islam obfuscates a concept that the secular intellectuals are unable to grasp; that, according to rabbinic Judaism, the Torah, which consists of the Five Books of Moses—Genesis, Exodus, Leviticus, Numbers, and Deuteronomy—has absolutely nothing to do with religion, at least as far as non-Jews are concerned.[6] Judaism teaches that there is a moral and legal code for all non-Jews, a code based on Jewish Law that is outside what we consider the sphere of religion.

For those brought up in Western culture, this sounds both astonishing and absurd. After all, the Bible is all about religious themes: the stories of Adam and Eve, Noah and the Ark, of Abraham, Isaac, and Jacob, the sojourn of Israel in Egypt, the story of Moses and the Ten Commandments, the teaching about prayer, sacrifices, the Sabbath, and God. These are the very things that, to the non-Jew, are all about "religion," at least as they define it. Yet this is what makes Judaism so very different from the two *mamzer* religions of Christianity and Islam that used the Hebrew Bible as the foundation for their organized faiths; Judaism is opposed to organized religion for non-Jews. Judaism has a universal teaching that the nations of the world are only to keep a moral and legal code, not to create organized systems of "religion" and "worship." This is why, unlike Christianity and Islam, the Jews do not proselytize every man, woman, and child they encounter. There is neither a "circumcise or put in a *mikvah* every man, woman, and child in the Name of *HASHEM*"[7] theology, nor a "Torah or the sword" mindset in Judaism. It is not by irrational theological teaching but by reason and rationality that the non-Jew should approach the "commentary" mentioned by Rabbi Hillel, the system of moral and legal laws known to the rabbis as the Seven Laws of Noah, or the Noahide Law. This law consists of prohibitions against idolatry and blasphemy (organized religion), murder, theft, illicit sex, the unnecessary harming of animals, and to make sure that courts of justice are set up in every society. These seven laws are the only laws of

---

[6] "The halakhic mind is not the religious mind, certainly not as the latter is portrayed by secularists and mystics." Paul Eidelberg, *Beyond the Secular Mind: A Judaic Response to the Problems of Modernity.* (New York: Greenwood Press, 1989), xiv.

[7] *HASHEM* is Hebrew for "The Name," the Holy Name of God.

the Torah that non-Jews, or Noahides, are commanded to keep.[8] The Noahide is neither commanded to observe the Sabbath nor to offer sacrifices, to have organized prayers at specific times, or to be circumcised or keep any Jewish "holy days." According to the rabbis, none of the commandments which we view as being "religious" have any bearing on the non-Jew. That Judaism forbids organized religion is a point missed by those still inside the box of Western culture who look at anything related to the Bible as "religious." To the Western mind, the paradigms of which were formed within the confines of a culture dominated by organized religion, the Bible is all about "religion" and "religious things." The Bible is about God, faith, and prayer, about holy days, feasts, and fasts; it is about the spiritual, not the secular.

The reason this teaching is unknown is because the Western scholar has been taught to disparage and ignore the teachings of the rabbis. The observant Noahide—that is, a non-Jew who follows the teachings of Judaism—is trained to be able to "think outside the box" of Christian culture and analyze our society and its institutions, its values and mores, from a Jewish rather than a Christian viewpoint; in other words, the Noahide is trained to reassess and question the meaning of what it means to be an intellectual. To both the Jew and the *Bnai Noah*, the Children of Noah, the Torah is not intrinsically anti-intellectual as the secularist critics would have you believe. The intellectual criticism levied at the Torah typically focuses on the "religious" elements instead of the teachings that pertained to the Jewish legal system as it applies to the non-Jew such as business and government—the Jewish teachings of what constitute our secular law, teachings that have been ignored by our non-Jewish culture. The secular view of the Torah—a view based on Enlightenment philosophy and science—has been overly concerned with "scientific" methodology. It is beyond the scope of this work to analyze in detail all of the different methodologies of the different academic disciplines such as philosophy and sociology; our focus will be the effect of modern anti-Semitism upon the study and transmission of the Torah in general and the Noahide Law in particular.

---

[8] "Only a limited part of this code shall one day become the common property of all of mankind...the teachings of right and social justice, of righteousness and love shall one day become part of the life of all mankind, without exception." Rabbi Samson Raphael Hirsch, *The Hirsch Psalms*. (Jerusalem: Feldheim Publishers, 1997), §i, 180.

F OR ALL OF their talk of "reason" and "logic," for all their talk about "empirical evidence," the Western intellectuals, like their Christian antagonists, have formed strong opinions concerning a subject— the Torah—they know little about. Grappling with the problems of terminology and the value-judgments of secular viewpoints and teachings about the Torah requires understanding of the terminology and language of the Torah itself.[9] To understand Noahide Law from an intellectual and rational perspective, one has to be familiar with the concepts in the Torah, and this requires a basic understanding of Hebrew. The translation of any foreign language to another has its own share of difficulties. For example, to translate the English sentence "he expected her for dinner" into French would require a degree of paraphrasing, since there is no word in French that exactly corresponds to the English word "expect." Likewise, in traditional Hebrew, there is no word or even a concept that is analogous to the English word "religion" in the meaning of an organized belief system separate from law and ethics. From the Torah viewpoint, there is no "religious" difference between the laws of a man selling a car and a Jew reciting the *Shemonei Esrai* or observing Shabbat. As Rabbi Adin Steinsaltz explains: "The Torah makes no essential distinction between 'matters between a man and his Creator'...and those 'between man and his fellowman'... because the structure of relationships between human beings is intimately connected to the relationship between man and his Creator."[10] This is why it is misleading to talk about "Jewish religion," for the Torah encompasses the entirety of Jewish culture in both what we call the "secular" and "religious" spheres, and differentiating between the two projects a false dichotomy onto the Torah and puts limits on our understanding.[11]

---

[9] The term "Judaism" came into vogue during the Enlightenment, when the secular academics wished to classify the Torah as a "religion."

[10] Rabbi Adin Steinsaltz, *Bava Metzia,* Vol. 1. (New York: Random House, 1989), 1–2.

[11] "Perhaps the most radical cure in a time of confusion and the loss of all values would be the—provisional—closing of all synagogues! Let such an idea not frighten the reader. The closing of all synagogues would not affect or alter the precepts of the Divine Law one iota...the closing of all synagogues through Jewish hands would constitute the loudest protest against the denial of the Divine Law in life and home; it would give the most drastic emphasis to the truth that Divine Judaism embraces and dominates the totality of Jewish life and does not find its fulfillment in the halls of prayer and worship." Hirsch, *Collected Writings,* Vol. I, 390–91.

To give an example, let us look at the religious term of "faith." In Christianity, faith is described as *the substance of things hoped for, the evidence of things not seen* (Hebrews 11:1). This is the definition that many of the intellectuals think of when they attack religion, such as in Sam Harris's best-selling tome *The End of Faith*. This definition, however, is not valid when applied to the Torah. To describe faith as "the substance of things hoped for, the evidence of things not seen" means to strongly believe in something you know little (if anything) about, to base your beliefs on something lacking in empirical evidence, which is the approach used in Christian theology. In Judaism, although the Hebrew word *emunah* is often translated as "faith," the best definition would be "trust." *Emunah* does not describe believing in the evidence of things not seen; *emunah* "signifies a state of mind one has not at the beginning, but at the end, of a process of observation and experience informed by rational contemplation, a process that results in clear-eyed and unwavering conviction and confidence."[12] At Sinai, the entire Nation of Israel was witness to the giving of the Decalogue, for they all saw the cloud and flame, and heard the Voice proclaim "I, HASHEM, shall be your God." Unlike other "religions," Judaism was not created by a single charismatic individual. Moses had none of the "charisma" that Max Weber spoke of; his speech defect and feelings of inadequacy for the role made him a very uncharismatic leader, in fact, the most uncharismatic leader in history.[13]

The Torah was written so that ancient Bronze Age shepherds would understand its basic principles, even though they did not have the knowledge of those living in today's modern society. The Torah is written simply so that people who were not blessed with high intelligence can understand it. Modern academics should grasp the science-fiction concept of looking at God being within a different dimension, a dimension beyond time and space. The "science fiction" approach is used by Richard Dawkins himself in his book *The God Delusion*; in the chapter *Why There Almost Certainly Is No God*, Dawkins waxes sublime about the creation of the universe, building up from the "big bang" to the

---

[12] Eidelberg, *Beyond the Secular Mind*, 54.

[13] It should be noted that Moses was at the foot of the mountain with the rest of Israel when God gave the Law (Exodus 19:25).

evolution of man.[14] Doubtless to say, trying to explain to the pastoral Hebrews of millennia past that "[Lee] Smolin's idea…hinges on the theory that daughter universes are born of parent universes, not in a fully fledged big crunch but more locally in black holes"[15] does not quite work as well as the plain and simple *In the beginning of God's creating the heavens and the earth*," which clearly and concisely teaches the main point: God is the Creator of the universe.

As far as the matter of "faith" is concerned, the intellectual claim that "atheists do not have faith"[16] is a misrepresentation of atheistic ideas. The atheist intellectual does have faith—faith in the human mind and in their own intellectual ability, the old Greek teaching that "man is the measure of all things," the faith in what they call "science" and "reason" to explain the mysteries of creation. Dawkins insists that "the whole point of religious faith, its strength and chief glory, is that it does not depend on rational justification."[17] Sam Harris said in his book *The End of Faith* that "our enemy is [*surprise!*] nothing but faith itself."[18] Yet, contrary to the postulations of both Christians as well as atheists, religious faith is not the focus of the Torah. As Rabbi S. R. Hirsch explained, "'*La Loi' und nich 'la fois' ist das Stichwort des Judentums'—the operative word in Judaism is not 'faith' but 'law'* (*Gesammelte Schriften*, Vol. II)."[19] The Torah is neither a history book nor a science book, nor is it primarily a book on religion. The Torah is, first and foremost, a book of law, and Judaism has always taught that, for the non-Jew, the Bible is not a book about "religion" but rather a book about a legal and moral code.

The Achilles' heel of the intellectual argument against the Torah is that the criticisms levied against the "Old" Testament are overwhelmingly criticisms of Christian theology, not rabbinic Judaism.

---

[14] "*The Origin of Species* became an oracle, consulted with the reverence usually reserved for Scripture." Richard Hofstadter, *Social Darwinism in American Thought*. (Boston: Beacon Press, 1992), 16.

[15] Dawkins, *The God Delusion*, 175.

[16] Ibid., 74.

[17] Ibid., 45.

[18] Harris, *The End of Faith*, 131.

[19] Grunfeld, introduction to *Horeb*, xxxvii.

The focus of the intellectual argument against "faith"[20] is misplaced when it comes to Judaism, for "faith" is a concept of non-Jewish organized religion. The conflict between science and Christianity is not a conflict between science and the Torah; it is a conflict between science and Christian theology. Non-Jews who are unfamiliar with Judaism assume that Jews have similar views[21] as the Christians, such as the world having been created just six thousand years ago. Yet, over two hundred years before Galileo Galilei was even born, Rabbi Isaac of Akko, a contemporary of the great sage Nachmonides, calculated the age of the universe to be 15,340,500,000 years old,[22] an estimate that is much closer to the modern scientific age of the universe than the age accepted by the Christian creationists. Rabbi Chisdai Crescas, a generation after Rabbi Isaac of Akko, expounded that there were many possible universes,[23] and that "there is nothing in Jewish theology to preclude the existence of life on other worlds."[24] This was centuries before Richard Dawkins postulated that "the suggestion…that Martin Rees himself supports, that there are many universes, co-existing like bubbles of foam, in a 'multiverse' (or 'megaverse,' as Leonard Susskind prefers to call it.)"[25] The Talmud, written over a thousand years before the Enlightenment began, spoke of the Earth being a sphere.[26]

---

[20] "There will remain four irreducible objections to religious faith: that it wholly misrepresents the origins of man and the cosmos, that because of this original error it manages to combine the maximum of servility with the maximum of solipsism, that it is both the result and the cause of dangerous sexual repression, and that it is ultimately grounded on wish-thinking." Hitchens, *god is not Great*, 4.

[21] "It has been widely assumed that, in posing a challenge to Christianity, science likewise represented a challenge to Judaism. The gratuitous borrowing of this premise has borne painful consequences." Nachum L. Rabinovitch, "Torah and Science: Conflict or Compliment?" *Challenge*. Aryeh Crmell and Cyril Domb, eds. (Jerusalem: Feldheim Publishers, 1976), 45.

[22] Aryeh Kaplan, *Immortality, Resurrection and the Age of the Universe*. (New York: KTAV Publishing House, Inc., 1993), 9.

[23] Rabinovitch, *Challenge*, 49.

[24] Aryeh Kaplan, *The Aryeh Kaplan Reader*. (Brooklyn: Mesorah Publications, Ltd. 1985), 171.

[25] Dawkins, *The God Delusion*, 173.

[26] *Avodah Zarah III*, Yerushalmi 42c.

Even with the creation of man, the Jewish view is vastly different than the Christian interpretation. The Sages of the Talmud taught that there were 974 generations of pre-Adamite man,[27] that modern man has been around for 44,731 years.[28] This is approximately the same time as the appearance of Cro-Magnon man, when "human history... took off around 50,000 years ago, at the time of what I have termed our Great Leap Forward."[29] Modern Cro-Magnon is quite different from his predecessors on the family tree—no brow ridges, smaller face, reduced internal nasal cavities, as well as differences in the limb skeleton: a new creation. The intellectuals of our Western Culture ignored these rabbinic insights, as they have ignored the teachings of the rabbis to this day. How did these rabbis know these things without "science"? Sam Harris can say that "there is no telling what our world would now be like had some great kingdom of Reason emerged at the time of the Crusades and pacified the credulous multitudes of Europe and the Middle East,"[30] but it is also true that had the teachings of the rabbis and sages of the Talmud been disseminated as had the teachings of the Greek philosophers or later Greek-influenced Renaissance scholars, their names would have been remembered with peers such as Galileo, Newton, and Darwin. Yet these rabbinic scholars remain unknown and unheralded[31] by the mainstream academics, and more often than not, ridiculed, even when the secular "intellectual" express views such as:

An intriguing version of the multiverse theory arises out of considerations of the ultimate fate of our universe.[32] Depending

---

[27] *Shabbat* 88, *Hagigah* 13b.

[28] 974 x 40 (the length of a Jewish generation) equals 38,960, plus 5771 (since Adam) gives us a sum of 44,731 years.

[29] Jared Diamond, *Guns, Germs, and Steel.* (New York: W. W. Norton & Company, 1999), 39.

[30] Harris, *The End of Faith*, 109.

[31] "As in all cases, the findings of science are far more awe-inspiring that the rantings of the godly. The history of the cosmos begins, if we use the word 'time' to mean anything at all, about twelve billion years ago." Hitchens, *god is not Great*, 57.

[32] "There is an insurmountable contradiction between eternally self-sustaining laws of nature and the second law of thermodynamics, that of energy decay or entropy. This law states that every system left to itself always tends to move from order to disorder,

upon the values of numbers such as Martin Ree's six constants, our universe may be destined to expand indefinitely, or it may stabilize at an equilibrium, or the expansion may reverse itself and go into contraction, culminating in the so-called 'big crunch.' Some big crunch models have the universe then bouncing back into expansion, and so on indefinitely with, say, a 20–billion-year cycle time...if bang-expansion-contraction-crunch cycles have been going on for ever like a cosmic accordion, we have a serial rather than a parallel, version of the multiverse. Of all the universes in the series, only a minority have their 'dials' tuned to biogenic conditions. And, of course, the present has to be one of that minority, because we are in it. As it turns out, this serial version of the multiverse must now be judged less likely than it once was, because recent evidence is starting to steer us away from the big crunch model. It now looks as though our own universe is destined to expand for ever.[33]

Dawkins dwells on the multiverse theory, yet he seems blithefully unaware that this same idea was put forth centuries before by Rabbi Chisdai Crescas. Why is the Torah viewed as non-academic, or that the followers of the Torah—both Jews and Noahides—presented as basing their religion on faith in myths and fairy tales? Fairy tales can take on many different forms, and the definition of faith often depends on your point of view. The secular atheists want you to believe that the universe—all the hundreds of billions of galaxies made up of hundreds of trillions of stars—came into being in a certain spot in space and time for no reason whatsoever;[34] it is by *faith* that you must believe

---

its energy tending to be transformed into lower levels of availability, finally reaching the state of complete randomness and unavailability for further work. When all the energy of the universe has been degraded to random motion of molecules of uniform low temperature, the universe will have died a 'heat death.' The fact that the universe is not yet dead is clear evidence that it is not infinitely old. And so, whereas the second law, that of energy decay, requires the universe to have a beginning, the first law, that of total energy conservation, precludes its having begun itself." Eidelberg, *Beyond the Secular Mind*, 71.

[33] Dawkins, *The God Delusion*, 174.

[34] The secular concept of the "Big Bang" is itself a violation of the law of causality. As Rabbi Soloveitchik wrote, "causality and creation are two irreconcilable antagonists." [Rabbi Joseph B. Soloveitchik, *Halakhic Man*. (Philadelphia: The Jewish Publication Society, 1991), 116.] The atheist and agnostic scientists have invented myriads of theories to explain this little problem of the causation of the universe, such as the "vacillating universe" theory, that the gravitational pull of the galaxies will eventually slow down their expansion and cause them to finally coalesce into a single mass,

in the "Big Bang" theory. Likewise, the religious Christian theologian wants you to believe—again by "faith"—that the world was created only six thousand years ago along with all creatures now existing. Modern science can explain what happened after the "big bang,"[35] but they cannot explain *why* or *how* it occurred.[36] Modern geneticists may be able to take DNA back to the first bacterium, but they cannot explain *why* or *how*[37] such a complex structure such as a DNA molecule (much less a bacterium) was formed in the first place.[38] "All you need is the right starting conditions and evolution[39] just has to happen"[40] Susan Blackmore says in her book *The Meme Machine*. What exactly are the "right starting conditions?" It seems that it would take a great deal of faith, as much faith as any Christian has, to believe that life

---

thereby causing a tremendous explosion, another "Big Bang" if you will. The problem with this theory is that the universe is expanding at an ever-increasing rate, and according to recent scientific study, there is not nearly enough matter in the universe for the gravitational pull needed for this to happen, which means that the creation of the universe was a one-time event. Of course, the atheists answer that there is indeed enough matter in the universe; it simply is invisible and undetected, and you simply have to believe the existence of this "invisible matter" by "faith." These and many more scientific theories unsupported by empirical evidence—such as theories about what came before the "Big Bang"—are based on the *pulling theories out of your tuchas* principle.

[35] "Maybe the 'inflation' that physicists postulate as occupying some fraction of the first yoctosecond of the universe's existence will turn out." Dawkins, *The God Delusion*, 185.

[36] "Nobody understands what goes on in singularities such as the big bang, so it is conceivable that the laws and constants are reset to new values." Ibid., 174.

[37] "It is a tedious cliché (and, unlike many clichés, it isn't even true) that science concerns itself with how questions, but only theology is equipped to answer *why* questions." Ibid., 80. (It should be noted that the *why* question is only tedious to those, such as Dawkins, who are unable to answer it.)

[38] "There are many disputes between evolutionists as to how the complex process occurred, and indeed as to how it began." Hitchens, *god is not Great*, 86.

[39] The Sages explain how the Torah hints at the creation of dinosaurs and evolution: "As Ramban wrote...the Torah's expression *and it was so* indicates that something was permanently established in its current state. Since the 'great sea-giants' did not remain in the state in which they were created, Scripture did not say *it was so* to describe the creations of the fifth day." Rabbi Yaakov Blinder, Commentary to *Ramban's Bereishis*. Rabbi Yaakov Blinder and Rabbi Yoseph Kamenetsky, trans. (Brooklyn: Mesorah Publications, Ltd., 2005), 67, n. 224.

[40] Susan Blackmore, *The Meme Machine*. (Oxford: Oxford University Press, 1999), 11.

spontaneously formed from some sort of magical "primeval soup."[41]
The atheist intellectuals give us only one of two choices[42] to accept: to
believe in the Christian theological view that the universe was created
six thousand years ago, or that life was created from a twelve ounce
can of *Darwin's Primeval Soup—now with 30 percent more RNA
replicators!* To think outside the box, the intellectual must entertain
the idea that there are other explanations and possibilities outside the
theological or secular realm.

---

[41] "This is the whole point of Darwin's inspiration—and what makes his theory so
beautiful—there is no master plan, no end point, and no designer...we now live
in a complex world full of creatures of all kinds and a few billion years ago there
was only a primeval soup." Blackmore, *The Meme Machine*, 13. Dawkins also used
the "primeval soup" allegory to describe memes; "In general memes resemble the
early replicating molecules, floating chaotically free in the primeval soup." Richard
Dawkins, *The Selfish Gene*. (New York: Oxford University Press, 2006), 196.

[42] "Whether or not man is able to find an adequate or correct explanation for the
natural laws governing any phenomenon of nature does not alter his moral calling...
this will never change, not even if the latest scientific notion that the genesis of all the
multitude of organic forms on earth can be traced back to one single, most primitive,
primeval form of life...Judaism in that case would call upon its adherents to give even
greater reverence than ever before to the one, sole God Who, in His boundless creative
wisdom and eternal omnipotence, needed to bring into existence no more than one
single, amorphous nucleus and one single law of 'adaptation and heredity' in order to
bring forth, from what seemed chaos but was in fact a very definite order, the infinite
variety of species we know today, each with its unique characteristics that sets it apart
from all other creatures. This would be nothing else but the actualization of the law
of *le-mino*, the 'law of species' with which God began His work of creation. This
law of *le-mino*, upon which Judaism places such great emphasis in order to impress
upon its adherents that all of organic life is subject to Divine laws, can accommodate
even this 'theory of the origin of species.' After all, the principle of heredity set forth
in this theory is only a paraphrase of the ancient Jewish law of *le-mino*, according
to which, normally, each member of a species transmits its distinguishing traits to
its descendants...Judaism should certainly be permitted to cite the existence of such
a theory as proof that so many of the theories confidently advanced by science to
disprove the Jewish concept of God and man are subject to change at any time...the
Rabbis have never made the acceptance or rejection of this and similar possibilities
an article of faith binding on all Jews. They were willing to live with any theory that
did not reject the basic truth that 'every beginning is from God.' In fact, they were
generally averse to speculation about what was in the past and what will be in the
future, because, in their view, such questions transgressed the limits of that which is
knowable to man, or, at best, they did not enhance man's understanding of his moral
function." Hirsch, *Collected Writings*, Vol. VII, 263–65.

Meme, Meme, Tekel Upharsin

It is time we recognized that the only thing that permits human beings to collaborate with one another in a truly open-ended way is their willingness to have their beliefs modified by new facts.

— Sam Harris[1]

ACCORDING TO ONE POPULAR THEORY, OUR BEHAVIORS ARE WHAT secularists have termed *memes*, self-replicating elements of cultural and social activities.[2] The word "meme" was coined by our good friend Richard Dawkins, who in his 1976 book *The Selfish Gene* proposed that the meme is "defined as an entity that is capable of being transmitted from one brain to another,"[3] a learned behavior that is taught and passed from one person to another as well as from one generation to succeeding generations.[4] Our thought processes, according to the secular intellectuals, are controlled by memes. The supporters of the *meme* theory even question whether we have free will; according to the theory, our very actions are the results of memes passed down from person to person in a particular culture, and these memes kick in whenever we are faced with a decision on how to act in a particular situation. Complex behaviors are what are termed "meme-plexes," or "groups of memes that are replicated together."[5] According to Dan Dennett, one of the more prominent and outspoken atheist intellectuals, the discipline of Memetics is supposedly "morally neutral," as Max Weber was "value-neutral" on the subject of Judaism.

---

[1] Harris, *The End of Faith*, 48.

[2] "I have heard people dismiss the whole idea of memetics on the grounds that 'you can't even say what the unit of a meme is.' Well that is true, I cannot." Blackmore, *The Meme Machine*, 53.

[3] Dawkins, *The Selfish Gene*, 196.

[4] "Everything that is passed from person to person in this way is a meme. This includes all the words in your vocabulary, the stories you know, the skills and habits you have picked up from others and the games you like to play. It includes the songs you sing and the rules you obey." Blackmore, *Meme Machine*, 7.

[5] Blackmore, *Meme Machine*, 19.

The idea that Memetics is "morally neutral" is itself morally sub-jective, a denial that a memeplex could come from outside the human experience. Judaism teaches otherwise; there is a memeplex which comes from outside the human experience, and this "memeplex" is what we call the Torah, six hundred and thirteen memes that are not of human origin, designed to replicate in their human hosts. Take a fairly common *meme-mitzvot*, such as "Thou shall not kill." This com-mandment applies not only to adults but to infants, even deformed and unwanted infants. In Greek and Roman[6] society (in most ancient cul-tures, in fact), infanticide was considered a way to get rid of unwanted children. Even Plato and Aristotle championed the idea of infanticide, not only for purposes of population control, but to keep society free of disfigured humans. The Torah teaches that every human life was pre-cious, even an infant born blind, or with a clubbed foot, or, as in many cultures even today, unwanted females. No other ancient culture or society had this "meme." It was neither the product of the human mind nor a "morally neutral" memeplex. It was a meme that was introduced into humanity by *HASHEM*, the Divine Meme-Maker.

Of course, many memes are harmful, such as anti-Semitism, which Dan Dennett[7] identified as a meme.[8] The anti-Semitic meme has in-fected academic and intellectual thought, corrupting the "scientific objectivity" of academic disciplines. The meme of anti-Semitism has followed a distinct pattern, such as the avoidance of Jewish primary

---

[6] One of the commandments of ancient Roman law was that "deformed infants shall be killed." *The Twelve Tables*, De Legibus, 3:8.

[7] "The claims about memes are meant (at least by Dennett) to be taken realistically. Memes that are truth bearers have contents that need to be construed Platonistically, or as Fregean senses. At some time, so the story goes, in a somewhat mysterious way, they acquired vehicles, occupied brains, and created human minds. But if all that is available to us is an intentional stance, then this is a myth, albeit a noble one; for there is nothing to content over and above the attributions made by our theory of interpretation. This indeed seems to be Dennett's own view: 'There are no real, natural, universal units of…semantic information.' Thus, there is a serious question whether there is available to Dennett a theory of meaning that would afford to memes the kind of robust status that memetics demands of them." David Holdcroft and Harry Lewis. "Memes, Minds and Evolution." *Philosophy*. Vol. 75, No. 292 (Apr., 2000), 182.

[8] "Still other [memes] are unquestionably pernicious, but extremely hard to eradicate: anti-semitism." Daniel C. Dennett, "Memes and the Exploitation of Imagination." *The Journal of Aesthetics and Art Criticism*. Vol. 48, No. 2 (Spring, 1990), 129.

texts, the use of theological arguments and influences, even by those supposedly non-religious, and irrational and illogical arguments based on emotion.[9]

To give an example, let us look at the debate over the creation of the universe. The secular viewpoint is that matter has always existed or was created in the event secularists call the "Big Bang." The concept of matter not being God's creation is a concept that has influenced the way our culture views the world. How is this, the concept of created or existing matter, the basis of pagan thinking?

First of all, there is the intellectual error of dealing with God using physical concepts, or thinking of God as part of the physical universe. The intellectuals maintain that "our belief is not a belief. Our principals are not a faith. We do not rely solely upon science and reason, because these are necessary rather than sufficient factors, but we distrust anything that contradicts science or outrages reason."[10] From the Torah perspective, God is a Singularity that is not a part of our physical universe. The concept that the One God is the Creator of all matter (as well as time and space itself) is a concept that is taught in the Torah. There is a part of every human being that interfaces with this dimension, and the Torah was given to us to attune this *ruach*, or "spirit," to the Other-Dimensional. It is not the Greek spirit-trapped-in-a-physical-body, but an essential part of our total being. The idea that God is part of the physical universe leads to errors such as Dawkins telling us that "Karen Owens has captured this witty little paradox in equally engaging verse:

> Can omniscient God, who
> Knows the future, find
> The omnipotence to
> Change His future mind?"[11]

The modern intellectual is also aghast at the idea that the God of such a massive universe would pay attention to the life crawling around on one of the small and seemingly insignificant planets within the vast cosmos.

---

[9] "While science can, at best, describe the natural processes, it cannot account for the ultimate forces that are responsible for their working, just as it cannot account for a first cause." Rabbi Joseph Elias, trans. and commentary. *Nineteen Letters by Rabbi Samson Raphael Hirsch*. (Jerusalem: Feldheim Publishers, 1996), 50.

[10] Hitchens, *god is not Great*, 5.

[11] Dawkins, *The God Delusion*, 101.

"Why should a divine being, with creation and eternity on his mind, care a fig for petty human malefactions? We humans give ourselves such airs, even aggrandizing our poky little 'sins' to the level of cosmic significance!"[12] Yet this very question was put forth long ago by King David:

> *When I behold Your heavens, the work of Your fingers,*
> *The moon and the stars, which you have set in place…*
> *What is the frail human that You should remember him?*
> *And what is the son of mortal man that You should be mindful of him?*[13]

This sentiment was much less poetically expounded by Dawkins: "Other sciences raise our consciousness in different ways. Fred Hoyle's own science of astronomy puts us in our place, metaphorically as well as literally, scaling down our vanity to fit the tiny state on which we play out our lives—our speck of debris from the cosmic explosion."[14] This was also the point made by Maimonides centuries ago: "Know that the major source of confusion in the search for the purpose of the universe as a whole, or even of its parts, is rooted in man's error about himself and his supposing that all of existence is for his sake alone. Every Fool imagines that all of existence is for his sake…but if man examines the universe and understands it, he knows how small a part of it he is." (*Morech Nevuchim* III:25). This is exactly what David sang about three thousand years ago, and he provided the answer to the question:

> *Yet you have made him only a little less than the angels,*
> *And crowned him with a soul and a splendor (Tehillim 8:6).*

Dawkins harps on the need for "scientific proof" of God. "I shall suggest that the existence of God is a scientific hypothesis like any other. Even if hard to test in practice…God's existence or nonexistence is a scientific fact about the universe, discoverable in principle if not in practice."[15] Dawkins's observation that "A God capable of calculating…values for the six numbers would have to be at least

---

[12] Ibid., 270.

[13] *Tehillim*, Vol. 1. Rabbi Avrohom Chaim Feuer, trans. and commentary. (Brooklyn: Mesorah Publications, Inc., 1995), 125, 127.

[14] Dawkins, *The God Delusion*, 143.

[15] Ibid., 73.

as improbable as the finely tuned combination of numbers itself, that that's very improbably indeed...I see no alternative but to dismiss [the problem at hand]"[16] is much less improbable as our complex DNA forming, by itself, out of a "primeval soup," or that the matter of the universe—making up the hundreds of trillions of stars within the hundreds of billions of galaxies—suddenly came into existence on its own for no reason whatsoever.[17] Dawkins ignores the great discontinuity of creation, and instead holds fast to his faith in the "leap of science."[18]

∽

To UNDERSTAND AND explain this concept further, we will look at the primary source, the beginning of *Bereishis* (Genesis), one of the most famous passages in the Bible:

1. In the beginning God created the heaven and the earth.
2. And the earth was without form, and void; and darkness was upon the face of the deep. And the Spirit of God moved upon the face of the waters.
3. And God said, Let there be light: and there was light.
4. And God saw the light, that it was good: and God divided the light from the darkness.
5. And God called the light Day, and the darkness he called Night. And the evening and the morning were the first day.
6. And God said, Let there be a firmament in the midst of the waters, and let it divide the waters from the waters.

This translation is from the venerable King James Version, probably the most well-known of all Bible translations, even if it is no

---

[16] Ibid., 171–72.

[17] "The spirit of the modern world...had led to the development of alternative theories for explaining the existence of our world, notably the theory of evolution, which ascribes the emergence of life in all its varied forms to the random operation of chance. In discussing the relationship of Torah and science, Rabbi S. R. Hirsch suggested that the believer in Divine creation can, in principle, accept the concept of evolution if (instead of remaining a vague and speculative hypothesis) it is universally accepted by the scientific world, with a clear understanding of how it works, and if, above all, it is not seen as a random process of natural selection but as a Divinely planned and instituted development." Elias, *Nineteen Letters*, 44.

[18] "If (which I don't believe for a moment) our universe was designed, and *a fortiori* if the designer reads our thoughts and hands out omniscient advice, forgiveness and redemption, the designer himself must be the end product of some kind of cumulative escalator or crane, perhaps a version of Darwinism in another universe." Dawkins, *The God Delusion*, 186.

longer the most popular. It is certainly the translation known best by those who were raised in a Christian culture whether they are atheist or religious. Chapter One of the Book of Genesis has also been a major battleground between the theologians and the secularists because of its account of creation; did God create the world in six days as the Christians claim, or is the universe billions of years old? Both atheist and Christian interpretations of these passages are based on a literal interpretation of the text. Yet there is another interpretation of the book of Genesis, an interpretation which both the atheists and Christians ignore: the Jewish interpretation.

To begin with, the Torah tells us that the universe began in a specific time and place. This concurs with the scientific concept of what is commonly known as the "Big Bang" when a singularity was formed in space. According to the Torah, all the matter and energy in the known universe was created at once, and we are talking about a lot of matter. The star Betelgeuse in the constellation Orion is a red giant, a star so massive that if it were where our sun is now, the orbit of Mars would be *inside* Betelgeuse. And Betelgeuse is not even the largest star known; stars such as VY Canis Majoris are even larger. When one realizes that there are hundreds of *billions* of stars in the Milky Way, our own modest-sized galaxy, and that there are hundreds of billions of galaxies, we are talking about a lot of matter.

But what *is* matter? This is not a facetious question, for it is the heart of the issue of idolatry: was matter created by God, did it spontaneously spring into existence, or was it always there? As Rabbi Samson Raphael Hirsch explained:

> That the Creator therefore acts only as the molder of preexisting matter has been the basis of pagan thinking to this very day—a most shameful denial of all freedom of will in both God and man, which would undermine the very foundations of morality. If matter had antedated Creation, then the Creator of the universe would not have been able to form a world that was absolutely 'good,' but only the best world possible within the limitations of the material given Him to shape. In that case, all evil, physical and moral, would be due to the inherent faultiness of the material available to the Creator, and not even God would be able to save the world from evil, physical or moral. Then man would be as little master over his body as God could be over the matter from which the world was made. Freedom would vanish from the earth, and all the world, including its God as well as the men who live upon it, would be propelled by a blind, immutable fate."[19]

---

[19] Rabbi Samson Raphael Hirsch, *T'rumath Tzvi*. (New York: The Judaica Press, 1986), 3.

So the questions of "what is matter?" and "where did it come from?" are necessary to understand the Torah's concept of idolatry. As most people know, matter is composed of atoms, usually depicted by little colored balls (protons and neutrons) in the center (the nucleus) while having smaller particles (electrons) orbiting around it. These colored "marbles" in the nucleus are not solid, but are themselves composed of even tinier particles such as *quarks* and *leptons*. According to the "Standard Model" of physics first proposed in the 1970s, there are four fundamental "forces" that influence these particles: the *strong force*, the *weak force*, the *electromagnetic force*, and the *gravitational force*. The *strong force* holds the nucleus of the atom together, the *weak force* holds the particles together in the protons and neutrons, the *electromagnetic force* holds atoms and molecules together, and the *gravitational force*, the weakest of the four fundamental forces, yet the force which causes particles of mass to be attracted to one another, and which is necessary to hold large objects such as stars and galaxies together.

The "Big Bang" started when an indescribable amount of these sub-atomic particles suddenly appeared (and we will have to suspend our understanding of the laws of causality[20] and entropy for a moment) in the first 10^{-43} second of the universe. Scientists speculate that all four fundamental forces were unified into one single force, and as the proto-matter expanded and cooled, the forces became separate. After a couple of minutes, the universe had cooled off enough to let the newly formed neutrons and protons to stick together, and after about ten thousand years, the universe cooled and expanded some more.

After about three hundred thousand years, the universe had cooled off enough for the electrons to be captured by the protons to form hydrogen, the most basic of matter. The electrons, to this point in time, had rendered the matter opaque due to their interaction with photons, but now, for the first time, light as we know it could be seen. This is how most of the scientists and physicists understand the beginnings of the universe and the creation of matter. How different, how modern this view is compared to the account from the King James Bible above! But now we turn to the Hebrew Torah, and the classical commentators of

---

[20] "The forces of cause and effect, which are god-like and therefore worshipped by men, were conferred by the Creator upon the realm of nature." Hirsch, *The Hirsch Psalms*, §ii, 420.

Judaism, many of whom explained creation long before the telescope was invented and long before secular science was able to explain the origins of the universe.[21]

Here are the first six verses of *Bereishis* (Genesis), with an English translation unfamiliar to the majority of non-Jews:

בראשית ברא אלקים את השמים ואת הארץ:

והארץ היתה תהו ובהו וחשך על־פני תהום ורוח אלקים מרחפת על־פני המים:

ויאמר אלקים יהי אור ויהי־אור:

וירא אלקים את־האור כי־טוב ויבדל אלקים בין האור ובין החשך:

ויקרא אלקים | לאור יום ולחשך קרא לילה ויהי־ערב ויהי־בקר יום אחד:

ויאמר אלקים יהי רקיע בתוך המים ויהי מבדיל בין מים למים:

1. In the beginning of God's creating space and matter—
2. when matter was without substance, and darkness was on the surface of the deep, and the Spirit of God hovered on the surface of the waters.
3. God said, "Let there be light," and there was light.
4. God saw that the light was good, and God separated the light from the dark matter.
5. God called to the light: 'Day', and to the darkness He called 'Night.' And there was evening and there was morning, one day.
6. God said, "Let there be a firmament in the midst of the seas, and let it separate between sea and sea."

To grasp how the beginning of Genesis can be translated this way from the original Hebrew, we need look no further than the explanations from the classical rabbinic commentators to the Hebrew text.

בראשית ברא אלקים את השמים ואת הארץ—*In the beginning of God's creating space and matter*. The beginning of the Torah is one of the most famous verses of the Bible, "In the beginning God created the heaven and the earth." This, or something similar such as "the heavens and the earth," is the familiar opening to Christian Bibles. The English translation in Jewish Bibles, on the other hand, phrases

---

[21] "The Torah harbors the General Theory for the Totality of Existence. Of course, we do not mean the Torah as ordinarily read or studied. We mean the Torah understood as written in code language, a language in which every letter has mathematical and ideographic significance. We mean the Torah whose narratives and precepts harbor hidden wisdom, the decodification of which requires the application of certain mathematical and logical rules on the one hand, and knowledge of the sciences on the other." Eidelberg, *Jerusalem vs. Athens*, xii.

it differently: "In the beginning of God's creating the heavens and the earth"[22] or "From the beginning did God create the heaven and the earth."[23] What this means is that God created all matter that exists in the universe. The word בראשית is often translated by non-Jews as an isolated phrase, "*In the beginning*, God created...," but this view is not held by many of the rabbinical commentators. Had the first word of Genesis meant *In the beginning*, it would not have been in the construct state and would have been written as בראשונה. It therefore attaches itself to the next word, "In the beginning *of*." The word ברא, *created*, is only used in the Torah when describing Divine activity. According to the Torah, all the matter in the universe, with its potential to form the stars and planets, was created in this first moment of time.

The Name אלקים, *Elokim*, is in the plural. The nineteenth century sage *Malbim* explained that this Name "signifies the many forces which spread throughout Creation. All these forces emanate from the One God, and in Him are found the sources of all forces in complete unity."[24] This parallels the view of the physicists who say that all four fundamental forces existed as one force in the first 10^{-43} second of Planck time. Also, *Ramban* explained (in the thirteenth century), "the word אלקים *Elokim* means 'the Master of all forces,' for the root of the word is *e-il*, meaning force, and the word *Elokim* is a composite consisting of the words *e-il heim*, as if the word *e-il* is in a construct state, and *heim*, [literally] 'they,' alludes to all other forces."[25] It should be mentioned that the sages also said there were four fundamental "forces" or "elements" that make up everything in the physical universe, a view which agrees with the "Standard Model" of physics.

That time itself was a creation of God is explained by the very first verse of *Bereishis*. The question of time and space was asked by Maimonides, the *Rambam*, in the twelfth century, "What determined 'the first day,' since there was no rotating sphere, and no sun?"[26] Also, by following Ibn Ezra's paraphrase *in the beginning of the creation of the firmament and the dry land*, we can translate the first verse of *Bereishis* as: *In the beginning of God's creating space and matter.*

---

[22] Artscroll *Chumash.*

[23] Rabbi S. R. Hirsch, *T'rumath Tzvi.*

[24] Rabbi Meir Zlotowitz, *Bereishis.* (Brooklyn: Mesorah Publications, Ltd., 2002), 33.

[25] *Ramban, Commentary on the Torah: Genesis.* (New York: Shilo Publishing House, Inc., 1999), 25.

[26] Maimonides, *Moreh Nevuchim*, II:30.

והארץ היתה תהו ובהו וחשך על־פני תהום ורוח אלקים מרחפת על־פני המים
*—when matter was without substance, and darkness was on the sur-
face of the deep, and the Spirit of God hovered on the surface of the
waters.*

"*When matter was without substance…*" According to the latest
scientific theory, when all the matter in the universe was created, particles had no mass. Then, as the particles cooled down, a mystical
and invisible energy field (dubbed the Higgs field) was created which
gave the particles mass. Rabbi Elie Munk renders the word חשך as
'*the opaque matter.*" This describes the time when matter was still
too hot to form atoms, and matter was "without form," a mass of protons and neutrons. *Ramban* stated that "with this creation, which was
like a very small point having no substance, everything in the heavens and on the earth was created."[27] This agrees with modern science,
that all the matter in the universe came from a very small point, and
it had no mass (or "substance") when it was created.

על־פני המים "Upon the surface of the deep." The Sages taught that this
"water" was different in form from the water on earth; "'On the face
of the waters,' does not refer to the waters which form the seas and
that part of the element 'water,' having received a particular form, and
being above the air, is distinguished from the other part which has
received the form of ordinary water."[28] Water, of course, is a molecule
that consists of one atom of oxygen and two atoms of hydrogen—the
simplest of all atoms, consisting of just one proton and electron.

ויאמר אלקים יהי־אור ויהי־אור—*God said, "Let there be light," and
there was light.* This primal light, before the stars were formed, is
why "the text does not say 'and it was so,' as it is said on other days,
because the light did not remain in this state all the time, as did the
other creations."[29] This light consisted of photons, and after the first
three hundred thousand years (as explained above) before this matter
cooled enough, the electrons (that were interfering with the photons)
were captured by the protons and neutrons.

[27] *Ramban, Commentary on the Torah: Genesis.* (New York: Shilo Publishing House,
Inc., 1999), 25.

[28] Ibid.

[29] Ibid., 28.

וירא אלקים את־האור כי־טוב ויבדל אלקים בין האור ובין החשך—*God saw that the light was good, and God separated the light from the dark matter.* The division between "light" and the "dark matter" and "dark energy." The theory of "dark matter/dark energy" is used to explain the gravitational effects seen in the rotation of galaxies by matter that emits no electromagnetic radiation, matter that cannot be seen. Scientists say that ninety–five percent of all matter in the universe is made of this invisible and unknown stuff. This is what is taught by "the commentators [who] point out, *darkness* is not merely the absence of light, but it is a specific object of God's creation."[30] Most astronomers now say that the universe is expanding at an ever-increasing rate, which is bad news to those who hold to an "oscillating universe" theory, that the universe has always expanded and contracted. There is not nearly enough matter for the universe to contract by gravitational forces, which means that the "big bang" was a one-time event, dispelling any notion that the universe is eternal.

ויקרא אלקים | לאור יום ולחשך קרא לילה ויהי־ערב ויהי־בקר יום אחד—*God called to the light: 'Day', and to the darkness He called 'Night.' And there was evening and there was morning, one day.* Here the Torah simply describes the function of the light and the darkness. The Talmud explains that the word ויקרא is better rendered as "summoned," as a king would summon his servants (*Yerushalmi Berachos* 8:6). By speaking in the language of men, the Torah explains the function of light and darkness.

As mentioned above, the words יום אחד "one day" do not mean one "day" as we know it; the Sages were aware that the six "days" of Creation were long epochs of time.

ויאמר אלקים יהי רקיע בתוך המים ויהי מבדיל בין מים למים—*God said, "Let there be a firmament in the midst of the [hydrogen] seas, and let it separate between sea and sea."* The root of רקיע [*firmament*, or *expanse*] is related to the word וירקעו in Exodus 39:3 [and they *hammered out*] as well as רקע [*spread out*] in Isaiah 42:5. This relates to the expansion of the universe of the past fifteen or so billion years, of the "space" between the great clouds of dust and gas which would form the stars and galaxies.

---

[30] Rabbi Meir Zlotowitz, *Bereishis*, Vol. I., 37.

ᘒ

THE FACT OF the matter—literally and figuratively—is that the Sages had some expert inside information on how the universe was formed. They also understood that this information, although illuminating to a scholar, was unnecessary to the layperson. All that needed to be known was that God had created the universe and everything in it. "In the beginning of God's creating the heavens and the earth" is all one really need know; there are more important matters to learn instead of dwelling on the mysteries of Creation, mysteries that modern science is still at a loss to explain. It is clear that the rabbinic interpretation is much closer to what modern science explains than the Christian theological interpretation, yet it is always the Christian theological interpretation used by the atheists to dismiss the Torah. The secular atheists say that the Bible is "anti-science," and should not be taught in schools. The problem is not that the Torah is anti-intellectual or anti-science; the problem is that the secular atheists are ignorant of the rabbinic commentary and the rabbinic interpretation of the Torah. In truth, the secular intellectuals are no closer to explaining how the universe began than the rabbis; in fact, unlike the rabbis, they really are not sure whatsoever, which is why they keep coming up with different theories about the origin of the universe every other week.

As wondrous and advanced as our technology and our science are, the Standard Model of physics is still incomplete. For all our scientific knowledge, scientists still do not understand what causes the fourth elemental force—gravity. For all our technological wisdom, we still do not know what gives particles mass. For several decades, the search has been on for the "Santa Claus" particle, the invisible, unknown particle that flies around the universe, giving mass to all the good little quarks and leptons. This particle (dubbed the Higgs Boson) is the reason billions of Euros are being spent on the LHC, the Large Hadron Collider, in the hope that its discovery will lead to new advances in particle physics. Atheists everywhere are hoping the LHC will be able to support the beliefs that they accept by faith, such as the existence of a powerful and invisible force that controls the galaxy. Yet even if the Higgs Boson is discovered, will we really be closer to understanding why the universe came into existence in the first place, or why the four fundamental forces exist? At the very best, the scientists may finally patch up the black hole in the Standard Model, and answer *how* gravitation works. They will still be unable to answer the *why*.

As Rabbi A. Crescas explained: "the mention in scripture of the Garden of Eden, the Tree of Life and the Tree of Knowledge, the description of Adam, his first condition and what he became later, the serpent, Eve, the naming of Adam's sons Cain and Abel, and all that long narrative, all refer to extremely deep matters which are inaccessible to the common run of humanity and were therefore given the form of an allegory."[31] The bottom line is that the ones who take the beginning of Scripture literally are Christians and secular atheists. Science has shown that the universe has not always existed, that it came into being at a certain point in space and time, that there are powerful and undetectable forces at work throughout the cosmos, that all humans alive today came from a single female, that there was a massive flood during the period after the end of the last Ice Age ten thousand years ago. These are all concepts that are taught in the book of *Bereishis*, or Genesis.[32]

The limitations of the "scientific method" are explained by Yehudah Levi in the beginning of his book *Torah and Science*: "All concepts of ethics and morality; ideals and desires; law, theology, and philosophy; art and beauty; even our personal feelings—love, hate, fear—are either not quantifiable or not observable at all."[33] What is the "reason" behind ethics and morality for the intellectual?[34] Today's intellectual

---

[31] Cited in Carmell & Domb, *Challenge*, 129. "Mystical symbols and conceptions, such as...*tzimtzum*...do not appeal to everyone. They are not, to use a Talmudical idiom, שוה לכל נפש—they are not congenial to everyone's frame of mind, and they would certainly not have fallen on fertile ground in the era in which Hirsch lived, when rationalism and shallow 'enlightenment' were the order of the day...the ethical thought-categories which Hirsch used in expounding the underlying ideas of our laws do appeal to the moral conscience and intellectual climate of all times and environments." Grunfeld, *Horeb*, cxxviii.

[32] "We do not view...the story of the Flood as derived from Babylonian sources, but, rather, we consider these sources faint echoes of primeval human experiences." Hirsch, *Nineteen Letters*, 24.

[33] Levi, *Torah and Science*, 1.

[34] "We...find that the serious ethical dilemmas are better handled by Shakespeare and Tolstoy and Schiller and Dostoyevsky and George Eliot than in the mythical morality tales of the holy books." Hitchens, *god is not Great*, 5.

is certainly aware of the need for morality.[35] The question put to us by Richard Dawkins, "if we reject Deuteronomy and Leviticus (as all enlightened moderns do), by what criteria do we then decide which of religion's moral values to *accept*?"[36] is best answered by studying the morality and protocols of the "enlightened moderns,"[37] and to see how these protocols have affected our society and culture.

The body of mis-interpretations of the Torah by non-Jewish theologians is what the secularists rage against, not the Torah itself. The Torah, from the viewpoint of rabbinic Judaism, does not have issues with modern science as does Christianity. Modern academics exclude the Torah because, as do the Christians, they form their arguments around theological motifs. This illogical fallacy is found in all secular academic disciplines such as history, philosophy, sociology, political science, and economics. As Susan Jacoby, the eminent writer and atheist explained:

> Free inquiry and the diffusion of knowledge…have always been the secular rays of hope in every vision of America's future…science—how deep a faith it inspired in the Enlightenment rationalists of America's

---

[35] "It is time for us to admit that not all cultures are at the same stage of moral development." Harris, *The End of Faith*, 143.

[36] Dawkins, *The God Delusion*, 81.

[37] "[The intellectual] must therefore try to scorn [Torah] in order to justify himself in his own eyes, for he must seek a position by virtue of which, as he imagines, he will be *above* these Torah-loyal people, a position which enables him to look down on them with scorn and contempt because they still confine themselves within the boundaries of the Divine Law…he must persuade himself that his sophisms, his brand of wisdom, and his apostasy constitute progress, that his dissoluteness constitutes freedom. He must convince himself that the Law was clearly not given to *him*; that it was not given to men of breeding and discernment such as he, nor to men of his social rank, nor to men who possess whatever other superb qualities he ascribes to himself. He must convince himself that the Divine Law would have no significance or value in the Olympian realms where his intellect dwells…there, he removes all 'drivel' from the Divine Law until it can be easily perceived that much of the Law is 'anachronistic,' until it is obvious that this 'irrelevant material' is valuable only for those who have not yet mentally escaped from under the Egyptian burden of bricks, or for those who still breathe the oppressive air of Galuth and medieval darkness. He declares that this 'irrelevant material' might have been beneficial and necessary in former times, but certainly cannot be of any use to free men…there, on the sublime heights, the intellectual rabble are separated from the intellectual patricians, and the Law which was dictated by God is left to the intellectually impoverished, the uneducated, and the ignorant…there, the superior man confers upon himself the diploma of 'rationalism,' 'enlightenment,' or whatever other beautiful terms are used to describe it. He stigmatizes those who are loyal to the Law, describing them disparagingly as 'living in darkness and superstition,' and is irrationally clinging to 'rigid religious formalism.'" Hirsch, *Collected Writings*, Vol. I, 356.

founding generation and their freethinking late nineteenth-century heirs!—can by itself provide no remedy for those who, out of ignorance or in servitude to an anti-rational form of faith, know little and care less about the basic principles that constitute the scientific method.[38]

Yet, what is an "anti-rational form of faith?" From the Noahide perspective, anti-rational forms of faith include both Christian theology and secular atheism. These two seemingly diametrically opposed viewpoints come from the same source: Greek thought and culture, and when it comes to Judaism and the Torah, they both too often influence and support each other.

༒

IT IS AT this point we must ask the secular intellectual: why did the most civilized, scientific, and cultured nation in the early twentieth century—a nation that led in the forefront of academics, reason, science, and philosophy—decide to mass-murder millions of innocent human beings? This nation decided to use science and reason to find the "exciting things that are available to be known" such as how best to dispose of millions of women and children that modern "science" deemed racially inferior, whose "reason" decided that their "inferior" morals needed to be expunged from the human race.

One intellectual who did try to answer this question was Daniel Goldhagen, a professor of social science at Harvard. Goldhagen's controversial book *Hitler's Willing Executioners* (1996) touched on this very theme: why the most "civilized" and "intellectual" nation on earth took it upon themselves to destroy the Jews. Goldhagen did not use the excuses so often repeated, that the Nazis were "non-Christian," or that their "science" and "reason" were faulty, or that the majority of Germans were duped by a small cadre of madmen; Goldhagen explained how the majority of the Germans—even if they did not personally pull the triggers or shove Jewish children into the gas chambers—supported the policies of the Nazis to rid Germany of Jews. Goldhagen recognized that "antisemitism has been a more or less *permanent* feature of the western world,"[39] and even though he noted that "throughout Western Europe in the nineteenth century… antisemitism shed much of its religious medieval garb and adopted

---

[38] Susan Jacoby, *The Age of American Unreason.* (New York: Pantheon Books, 2008), 308.

[39] Daniel Jonah Goldhagen, *Hitler's Willing Executioners: Ordinary Germans and the Holocaust.* (New York: Vintage Books, 1997), 42.

new, secular clothing,"[40] he placed the blame of the hatred of the Jews squarely on a people reared in an anti-Semitic Christian culture.

Christianity certainly had a major part in the German attitudes towards the Jews, but there were other variables which came into play. Why did the German intellectuals, even secular intellectuals, support Nazism? Why did the academic lovers of "reason" and "science" feel it necessary to murder women and children? Even among those intellectuals who did not support Hitler, most felt that the Jews were a "parasite" nation, sucking out the life-blood of the German economy and weakening the German state. Goldhagen pointed out that:

> The cognitive model of Nazi antisemitism had taken shape well before the Nazis came to power, and that this model, throughout the nineteenth and early twentieth century, was also extremely widespread in all social classes and sectors of German society, for it was deeply embedded in German cultural and political life and conversation, as well as integrated into the moral structure of society.[41]

Although at best the German intellectuals were against genocide and expulsion, they thought "the way in which Jews could renounce their Jewishness was to renounce their Judaism, because even those Germans who were secularly oriented understood the unwholesomeness of Jews to derive at least in large part from the tenets of Judaism, a religion asserted to be devoid of love and humanity by the German cultural judgment,"[42] therefore in order to destroy the Jews, they had to destroy Judaism itself. At least in this aspect they agreed with today's intellectuals, that Judaism—or more specifically, the Torah—"poisons everything."

What is it, exactly, that the Torah poisons? What are the "moral structures" in non-Torah society that the Torah affects? What are the "moral structures" of Western society based upon, and why are they supposedly superior to the "moral structures" of the Torah? How can intellectuals make value-judgments on the Torah when they appear to be woefully ignorant of its tenets and teachings? How thoroughly have our intellectuals and academic institutions reasonably and rationally analyzed the Torah? How has the meme of anti-Semitism affected secular academics? How legitimate are the arguments against the Torah? How has the anti-Semitic meme affected our culture and society? These are the interrelated questions that are worth closer examination.

---

[40] Ibid., 43.

[41] Ibid., 77.

[42] Ibid., 58.

CHAPTER ONE

Protocols of the Philosopher

Today...the most vicious ideas about Jews are primarily voiced not by downtrodden and disenfranchised fringe elements of society but by its most successful, educated and "progressive" members. This is true in the Islamic world, and it is even truer in the West. One is less likely to find anti-Semitism today in beer halls and trailer parks than on college campuses and among the opinion makers of the media elite.

— Gabriel Schoenfeld[1]

PHILOSOPHY HAS BEEN THE MAJOR REPLACEMENT SYSTEM FOR TORAH in Western culture, particularly in the field of ethics. Philosophy is from the Greek word meaning "the love of wisdom," the intellectual pursuit of knowledge based on systems of logical reasoning, although it would be better translated as "the love of Greek wisdom."[2] The list of philosophers who have influenced our social structure is a long and impressive one: Socrates, Plato, Aristotle, Augustine, Aquinas, Machiavelli, Descartes, Hobbes, Locke, Spinoza, Hume,

---

[1] Gabriel Schoenfeld, *The Return of Anti-Semitism*. (San Francisco: Encounter Books, 2004), 3.

[2] "'Know yourself,' said the Greeks, gently suggesting the consolations of philosophy." Hitchens, *god is not Great*, 283.

Kant, Hegel, Marx, Nietzsche, Wittgenstein, Heidegger—these are but a handful of the philosophers who have been instrumental in the development of Western Civilization's concepts of good and evil, right and wrong, truth and falsehood, beauty and ugliness, religious freedom and secularism, and political systems such as democracy and communism.

It is not only the systems of philosophy we need to question, but, more importantly, the results. How has philosophy, in lieu of Torah, contributed to the betterment of mankind? We must ask ourselves honestly: how far have we ethically progressed since the days of Plato and Aristotle? What are our standards of right and wrong? Is there less human misery in the world today than there was two thousand years ago? How has philosophy helped the human condition? Why do intellectuals feel philosophy is a superior guide to morality than the Torah? Have the philosophers themselves been good role models for the rest of humanity? Or is there a corruption in Western philosophy, a fatal flaw in Western logic and reasoning, no matter how grand and noble the ideas and logic, that keeps Western philosophy from being a successful system of ethics?

∽

THERE WERE TWO events in the early sixteenth century that accelerated the revival and interest of "classical" philosophy. The first event was the publication of the first Greek Bible printed in movable text (Erasmus's Greek version in 1516, the same year when the term "ghetto" was coined for the Jewish quarter in Venice where the Jews were forced to live). The second event was the rise of a neo-Gnostic movement in Christianity (which we call "Protestantism") in 1517, which began when Martin Luther nailed his ninety–five theses to the Wittenburg door. These two events meant that printed Greek texts were now widely available, and that the Catholic Church no longer had a monopoly on reading and interpreting the Bible, for the Protestant church encouraged every person to read it themselves. The interest in Greek flourished and, as the availability of inexpensive Greek and Latin texts of the New Testament increased, interest in other secular Greek and Latin works expanded, and "classical" learning—the ancient Greek and Roman literature—became popular in the West.

It was not only the concepts and teachings of the Greek philosophers that influenced the men of the Enlightenment, but also Greek attitudes about the Jews: "To the Greeks, to whom the idea of Sabbath was quite unknown, it seemed ridiculous…they made sport of the Jews and called them a foolish people."[3] This Greek anti-Semitism was easily accepted into a culture long accustomed to the anti-Jewish hatred of the Church. On top of this, the Enlightenment was a destructive force to many of the Torah-observant Jews, for "the revolution in Jewish thought and life caused by the emancipation of Jewry cannot be understood merely in the framework of the history of Jewish thought; account must also be taken of the history of the European mind by which the inner development of Jewish thought in the last century and a half has been—for good or for evil—so decisively influenced."[4] The philosophers of the Enlightenment believed that their man-made system of morals and ethics, based upon Greek "reason" rather than (as they perceived it) superstitious religion, was the key to happiness, and among the majority of the Enlightenment philosophers, the Bible was discarded as a guide to moral living.[5] As the Jews were released from centuries of sheltered ghetto life, "the contrast between the Hellenistic ideal of the search for individual power…and the simple, pious life which the scribes held up as the greatest good"[6] divided the Jews, and many of them cast aside the Torah in their endeavor to fit in with the Gentile nations who had given them the opportunity to join "civilized" society.

The focus of the Enlightenment was the dissolution of the ancient feudal system, a power struggle between the landed elite, royalty, and the Church on one side, and the growing merchant and intellectual class on the other. One of the important concepts developed during the Enlightenment was that of "freedom of the individual," a concept that is so often bantered about when talking about our government and social structures. Will Dudley, professor of philosophy at Williams College in Maine, looked at freedom from the philosophical viewpoint:

---

[3] Solomon Grayzel, *A History of the Jews.* (Philadelphia: The Jewish Publication Society of America, 1984), 43.

[4] Hirsch, *Horeb*, xx–xxi.

[5] "In sharpest divergence from the modern view, which regards intellectual attainments as a license for moral laxity and tends to make allowances for violators of God's moral law if they happen to be men of intellect, Judaism postulates that the higher the intellect, the greater must be the moral demands placed upon it." Hirsch, *T'rumath Tzvi*, 408.

[6] Grayzel, *A History of the Jews*, 51.

Not only is freedom poorly understood, but we are falsely confident
that we do understand it. This doubly unfortunate condition dissuades
people from undertaking needed investigations into the meaning of
freedom...because developments in the understanding of the concept
of freedom have an impact not only on the discipline of philosophy,
but also on the ways in which individuals and communities structure
their lives, freedom is a topic on which philosophers may do profes-
sionally respectable work while also entertaining the hope that their
labor may be of some relevance to the wider world. If philosophers
think about the meaning of freedom, and if such thinking improves our
understanding of the conditions of our social and political liberation,
then we all have a better chance of living more freely...if philosophers
think about the meaning of freedom, however, they will discover an
even deeper connection between freedom and philosophy. Thinking
about freedom reveals that its conditions of realization include not
only certain social and political developments but also the practice
of philosophy itself. In other words, philosophy is directly as well as
indirectly liberating: philosophy contributes indirectly to freedom by
articulating the social and political conditions of its realization; but
philosophy also contributes directly to freedom because freedom is
not only something about which philosophers think, but also something that is produced through philosophical thinking.[7]

Dudley makes several good points, not the least of which is that this
subject of "freedom" may give philosophy a chance to actually be of
some relevance to society, for philosophers such as Dudley to do right.
Obviously, according to Dudley, spending time thinking ("philosophiz-
ing") about freedom is liberating, since it frees you from having to think
about the mundane and dreary task of the practical aspects of actually
going out and doing something about the social and political conditions
of the modern world. He is correct, however, in that the subject of "freedom" is grossly misunderstood. To show how the concept of "freedom"
can be misapplied, we turn to Orlando Patterson, a professor of sociology
at Harvard. Patterson wrote a book entitled *Freedom in the Making of
Western Culture*, a book which is (according to philosopher Will Dudley)
one of the "preeminent examples"[8] on the topic of "freedom." In his book,
Patterson pays special attention to religious ideas, spending four entire
chapters on Christianity and its impact on "freedom," yet dismisses the
most famous story of freedom in the Bible with a single paragraph at the
beginning of his book:

---

[7] Will Dudley, *Hegel, Nietzsche, and Philosophy: Thinking Freedom.* (Cambridge:
Cambridge University Press, 2004), 1–2.

[8] Ibid., 2.

The best-known case in point is that of the Israelites. Their bondage, if that is the proper term for their sojourn in Egypt, was a collective one, and not slavery as we normally understand the institution. Quite apart from the fact that there is no extrabiblical reference to their flight from Egypt, the nature of the exodus is proof enough that the Israelites could not have been individually enslaved in Egypt, and this is borne out by what we know of Egyptian and related ancient Near Eastern slavery…its epic history, in which its Egyptian sojourn was retrospectively reinterpreted as slavery, has no special part in the history of individual freedom.[9]

Patterson's dismissal of the Torah's account of Israel's slavery in Egypt *in which its Egyptian sojourn was retrospectively reinterpreted as slavery*[10] has its philosophical roots in the retrospective theological interpretation of the *Tanach* by Pauline Christianity. The problem with Patterson's thesis is not only how the Christians developed the concept of "personal freedom," but why the Jewish concept of "freedom" was discarded and ignored. Patterson speaks of an *individual freedom*, or *individual salvation*, a decidedly Christian notion, while commenting that "freedom, in fact, was never a central value among the ancient Israelites and Jews."[11] Patterson instead identifies the "four phases in the development of early Christianity: the prophetic phase of Jesus and the Jesus movement; the primitive Palestinian sect; the Hellenistic phase of Jewish and gentile Christianity; and the culmination of this phase in the religion of Paul."[12] This view presupposes certain variables, namely that Jesus was a prophet and that the Jewish-led Palestinian sect was "primitive." Patterson identifies Paul as "the high point of creative Christian theology" and that "with the exception of the Johannie writings, Christian theology would take a downhill course for the next four hundred years."[13] Pauline theology became the basis of

---

[9] Orlando Patterson, *Freedom: Freedom in the Making of Western Culture.* (New York: BasicBooks, 1991), 33.

[10] "The foundation of our knowledge of God is the Exodus from Egypt…it is the event that with one blow overthrew the gods of Egypt, the god of Spinoza restriction, the god of Hegelian evolution, as well as the atheism of materialistic narrowness. It is the historic event which, more than any other, is designed to promote the understanding of God." Hirsch, *Collected Writings*, Vol. I, 39–40.

[11] Patterson, *Freedom*, 34.

[12] Ibid., 295.

[13] Ibid.

Christian theology which developed over the next four hundred years as the writings of the church fathers show. The problems with looking at the New Testament from this theological perspective are apparent in Patterson's statement that Jesus' miracles "demonstrated his divine powers"[14] ignored that other prophets had done the same miracles without claiming divinity. Patterson also says that "the injunctions 'Love your enemies and pray for those who persecute you' and 'To him who strikes you on the cheek, offer the other also' have no parallel in traditional Judaism"[15] shows a lack of understanding of Judaism. In Proverbs 25:21, it states that *If your foe is hungry, feed him bread; and if he is thirsty, give him water to drink.* This has traditionally been interpreted by the rabbis as doing kindness to your enemies. And Lamentations 3:30 says *Let one offer his cheek to his smiter* clearly shows that this teaching comes from the *Tanach.*

Patterson attempts to push the classic theological line that Jesus' teachings were "radically innovative" and "uniquely his own."[16] This is the basis for his claim that these "original" teachings of Jesus were the "precursors of the Christian preoccupation with freedom."[17] This follows the pattern among the social scientists to dismiss Israel, rabbinic teachings, and the Torah by disassociating Jesus from Judaism as can be seen in Patterson's statements such as "[Jesus'] most striking peculiarity was his attitude toward ritual purity. He ate what his more orthodox fellow Jewish considered unclean food, and enjoyed drinking wine to a degree that was offensive to any rabbi. Worse, he associated with riffraff and deviants of all sorts—prostitutes, publicans, and imperial tax collectors. His public informality with children and women was a great scandal to his fellow Jewish contemporaries" as well as his "critical attitude toward Jewish Law,"[18] all which are the character

---

[14] Ibid., 297.

[15] Ibid., 298.

[16] In *The God Delusion*, Richard Dawkins said that, "from a moral point of view, Jesus is a huge improvement over the cruel ogre of the Old Testament. Indeed Jesus, if he existed (or whoever wrote his script if he didn't) was surely one of the great ethical innovators of history. The Sermon on the Mount is way ahead of its time. His 'turn the other cheek' anticipated Gandhi and Martin Luther King by two thousand years." Dawkins, *The God Delusion*, 283.

[17] Patterson, *Freedom*, 298.

[18] Ibid., 298–99.

traits of a wicked person, as the *Tanach* and the Talmud point out. Patterson also spoke of Jesus' "new approach to the divine," that "Jesus felt that the *approach* of his fellow Jews to God…was wrong and in need of redefinition…people were not made free by Jesus to love God; they were commanded to do so."[19] But what kind of a "new" rule was this? It says in the *Shema*, the prayer said by every adult Jew every morning and every evening, to "love HASHEM, your God, with all your heart, with all your soul, and with all your resources."[20] It is difficult to understand how Jesus could have a "new approach to the divine" unless one understands the theology behind the message; "Christianity, alone among the religions of salvation, made freedom the doctrinal core of its soreria."[21] In Romans 7:6, Paul makes it clear about Christian freedom: *But now we are delivered from the law, that being dead wherein we were held; that we should serve in newness of spirit, and not in the oldness of the letter.* The central focus of Christian theology is that the basis of the doctrine of individual freedom—according to Paul—is the "gospel of freedom" from the Torah.

❧

J ESUS' TEACHING OF "freedom" is also redefined. Patterson points out that Rudolf Bultmann "emphasized that Jesus both denationalized and 'dehistoricized' the apocalyptic message of the Jewish prophets," and that "the dawning and coming kingdom of God did not entail a final phase in the history of the Jewish nation and of all nations culmination in a new and glorious Davidic kingdom but was directed at individuals."[22] This interpretation of Jesus' message follows the theological teaching that Jesus did not come to be an "earthly king" of the Jews, but the theological king of the Christian spiritual heaven.

In another example of Patterson's theological arguments forming the backbone of his thesis on "freedom," Patterson states:

> Jesus' originality inheres in precisely this combination of a traditionally Judaic God who demands with a new conception of what is demanded—not legalistic piety or social purity but complete inward purity of heart which, for him, constituted less a rejection of the law

---

[19] Ibid., 300.

[20] Deuteronomy 6:5.

[21] Orlando Patterson, *Freedom*, 294.

[22] Ibid., 300.

than a renewed and better realization of it. On this I find Bultmann thoroughly persuasive. Jesus' God will not be satisfied with a mere observance of the law which leaves people free to do as they please in those areas where the law is silent.[23]

It is clear that Patterson relies on the Christian interpretation of the Law; Patterson's statement that "freedom" from the Law, or freedom from the Torah, is a theological teaching. There is no "area where the Law is silent;" this is what makes the Torah different from any other "religious" system, for the Torah covers all areas of human endeavor. When faced with new concepts or problems, the flexibility of the Talmud allows the rabbis to make new rulings based upon similar cases. Patterson states: "This analysis makes it possible to recognize what was truly original in Jesus' most important sermon, that on the mount. Taken out of context, every one of these sayings can be traced back to contemporary reformist Judaism."[24] What does Patterson mean by "taken out of context?" The Sermon on the Mount was a speech delivered by a Jewish rabbi to a group of Jews, a sermon that dealt with the Jewish Law. It was the Christians such as Patterson who took it out of context, applying theological interpretations to the teachings of Jesus:

> The poor turning to God for justice was a hallmark of traditional Judaism, as was its tradition of almsgiving. But the traditional context was wholly honorific and hierarchical. No Orthodox Jew would have claimed this to be God's major concern...in breaking out of the honorific mold...Jesus arrives at the startlingly new conception of the traditional pieties. He proclaims love to be God's greatest demand... put simply: Love thy neighbor as thyself.[25]

To say that justice and charity were not "major concerns" of God, and that the "traditional context was wholly honorific and hierarchical" shows an amazing ignorance of the Torah. According to the Torah, justice and charity are indeed major concerns of God. To describe justice and charity as being "wholly honorific and hierarchical" is to impose non-Jewish concepts onto Judaism. There was no "hierarchical" system in Judaism; everyone, from the king on down, was equally under the Law. The rich turned to God for justice as did the poor.

Patterson's denial of the Jewish concept of "freedom" is at odds with rabbinic commentary.[26] The "proper term" for Israel's "sojourn"

---

[23] Ibid., 301.

[24] Ibid., 302.

[25] Ibid., 301–02.

[26] "'Order' in Egypt was not only the first duty of a citizen. It was his only duty. The

in Egypt is *avdut*, "enslavement." This was a step beyond *geirut* or "alienhood." In Exodus 1:13, it says that *The Egyptians enslaved the Children of Israel with crushing harshness*. The key phrase in Patterson's book about Israel is that "which its Egyptian sojourn was retrospectively reinterpreted as slavery," a statement which could only be supported by those who subscribe to the Wellhausen theory of Higher Criticism. This is how the most famous story of freedom in Scripture is discarded in favor of Patterson's own definition of "freedom," which is a theological definition of personal salvation. This definition of "salvation" was influenced, as one would expect, from scholars such as Max Weber:[27] "All religions of salvation were in one way or another involved with the problem of spiritual freedom or liberation... as Max Weber observed, 'in terms of 'what one wants to be saved from, and what one wants to be saved for.'"[28] The Christian concept of individual "freedom," or freedom from the Law, freedom from the "fleshy" and "earthy" material world, is a Christian concept alien to Judaism. The freedom sought by Israel was the freedom to live by the Law, and to be able to keep God's Law. The deliverance of Israel from slavery in Egypt is, according to Rabbi S. R. Hirsch, "the Divinely laid foundation of our entire Jewish essence...it is not limited to once each year with the return of its commemorative days...but it should, in fact, never depart from our thoughts, because it must form the root and the basis of all of our thoughts, feelings, and actions."[29]

The concept of "freedom" that is so dear to the hearts and minds of Americans developed from the opposition to the oppression of legal and economic constraints. Only by embracing and following the Noahide Law can a society become truly "free," and achieve "liberty" as the Torah verse inscribed upon the Liberty Bell says, to "proclaim liberty throughout the land" and ensuring that our society can free

---

stratified caste structure of the state was built according to an unchangeable plan. The resulting system completely destroyed man's God-given equality, the right to free self-development, self-sufficiency, and self-determination of the individual." Hirsch, *Collected Writings*, Vol. I, 32–33.

[27] It should be mentioned that Talcott Parsons, who translated Weber's *Protestant Ethic and the Spirit of Capitalism*, and was a major transmitter of Weberian ideas (such as in his 1937 work *The Structure of Social Action*), taught at Harvard from 1927 to 1973, and for many of those years was the head of the sociology department, leaving an indelible stamp on Harvard's sociology program.

[28] Patterson, *Freedom*, 294.

[29] Hirsch, *Collected Writings*, Vol. I, 57.

itself from Edomite class structure. This is made clear by the commentary of Rabbi Hirsch to this very verse—the Torah verse inscribed on the Liberty Bell (*Proclaim Liberty Throughout the Land*; Leviticus 25:10)—which in fact deals with "earthly matters," the freeing of slaves and the return of property to its rightful owner:

> The evils that beset the inner life of society due to social class differences and the unequal distribution of property, with the resultant sharp contrasts between opulence and misery, independence and dependence, etc., and the precarious situations that afflict nations in the course of their political relationships with other nations...Israel is to progress in this freedom and independence, within and without, which God bestows upon it again and again...until it reaches that ideal state in which it will become a bright and shining national entity in the midst of the nations. Then all the other nations will be drawn to it in order to learn from it the Divinely-established institutions which alone will guarantee freedom, justice and everlasting peace on earth.[30]

Here Rabbi Hirsch refutes Patterson's etymology on the meaning of *freedom* and *liberty*.[31] Freedom, personal or social, is determined by political and economic factors, not theological or spiritual ones. Only through the Divine Law can a society, and its individual members, become truly free, and it is the example of the nation of Israel that will eventually win over the nations to the idea of a system of justice for all mankind, not simply for one social class over another. Certainly the American slaves in the Deep Antebellum South did not need rabbinic interpretation to understand the clear meaning of the text of the Torah as they sung the slave spiritual *Go Down Moses*:

> *When Israel was in Egypt's land, Let my people go.*
> *Oppressed so hard they could not stand, Let my People go.*
> *Go down, Moses, way down in Egypt's land,*
> *Tell ole Pharaoh, let my people go.*[32]

---

[30] Hirsch, *T'rumath Tzvi,* 490.

[31] *Rashi*, in his commentary to Lev. 25:10, said, "Rabbi Judah said: What is the etymology (of the term "freedom")? 'As one who dwells in a dwelling,' etc., (i.e.,) one who dwells in any place which he desires, and is not under the authority of others (*Siphra: R. H. 9*)." Rabbi Abraham Ben Isaiah and Rabbi Benjamin Sharfman, *The Pentateuch and Rashi's Commentary: Vayikra*. (Brooklyn: S. S. & R. Publishing Company, Inc., 1977), 253.

[32] "The first stanza of this famous spiritual was published in October 1861 [by] the Reverend Lewis C. Lockwood in the New York-based National Anti-Slavery Standard newspaper." Steven Cornelius, *Music of the Civil War Era: American History Through Music*. (Westport, Conn: Greenwood Publishing Group, 2004), 118–19.

$\mathbf{A}$s the tyranny of the kings and the Church was gradually (and often violently) replaced by the tyranny of the state and the financial institutions such as bureaucratic governments, banks, and capitalist corporations, the philosophers redefined the concepts of "liberty" and "freedom." The concept of nationalism was developed, and fighting wars for Jesus gave way to fighting wars for patriotism and the state.[33] The "age of reason" of the Western nations was simply a transfer of power, and the moral code of the Torah was ignored in favor of the new moral code of the same Greco-Roman Christian culture that had ruled the West during the past seventeen centuries. The new "secular" ideas of John Locke[34] and Henry Bolingbroke influenced Enlightenment philosophers such as Voltaire and Rousseau, laying the moral groundwork for the new morality. The light of the Enlightenment was not grounded in the righteousness of Jacob, but the flame of the burning passion of Esau for domination and power. "Throughout the latter half of the eighteenth century, the writings of Diderot, Montesquieu, and Voltaire…although none of these writers were biblical scholars… their influence and popularity left an unmistakable impression that talmudic and midrashic interpretations of the Bible was at best amusing, at worst a grotesque perversion of the mind."[35] No one was more influential in instilling this concept into the mainstream of Western intellectual thought than the French philosopher Voltaire.[36]

---

[33] "In the field of politics, a revival of the Hellenic worship of idolized local states is, today, the dominant religion of the West and of a rapidly Westernizing world." Arnold J. Toynbee, *Hellenism: The History of a Civilization.* (Westport, Connecticut: Greenwood Press, Publishers, 1981), 253.

[34] "But it may be urged farther that, by the law of Moses, idolaters were to be rooted out. True, indeed, by the law of Moses; but that is not obligatory to us Christians. Nobody pretends that everything generally enjoined by the law of Moses ought to be practised [*sic*] by Christians; but there is nothing more frivolous than that common distinction of moral, judicial, and ceremonial law, which men ordinarily make use of. For no positive law whatsoever can oblige any people but those to whom it is given. 'Hear, O Israel,' sufficiently restrains the obligations of the law of Moses only to that people." John Locke, *A Letter Concerning Toleration*, 1689. William Popple, trans.

[35] Edward Breuer, *The Limits of Enlightenment*, (Cambridge, Massachusetts: Harvard University Press, 1996), 91.

[36] "An analysis of everything that Voltaire wrote about Jews throughout his life establishes the proposition that he is the major link in Western intellectual history between the anti-Semitism of classic paganism and the modern age." Arthur Hertzberg, *The French Enlightenment and the Jews.* (New York: Columbia University Press, 1990), 11.

The Dark Side of Enlightenment

The notion that the new society was to be a revocation of classical antiquity was the prime source of post–Christian anti–Semitism in the nineteenth century. The vital link, the man who skipped over the Christian centuries and provided a new, international, secular anti–Jewish rhetoric in the name of European culture rather than religion was Voltaire.

— Arthur Hertzberg[1]

FRANÇOIS MARIE AROUET DE VOLTAIRE[2] (1684–1778) LOOKED upon the Bible as an archaic relic of man's unenlightened past. Voltaire was a champion of Greek and Roman culture, and, to Voltaire, both Judaism and Christianity stood in the way of bringing Greek and Roman "enlightenment" to Western Civilization. Voltaire's acerbic opinions on the Jews and Judaism had more than simply a thin veneer of dislike towards the Jewish people: "Passing from the Greeks and the Romans to barbarous nations, let us only contemplate the Jews. Superstitious, cruel, and ignorant as this wretched people were, still they honored the Pharisees,"[3] and that "the Jewish people were, I confess, a very barbarous nation."[4] Voltaire's attack on the Bible was an attack on Christianity as well as Judaism, and the Christians in France, in defense of their religion, soon found themselves in the uncomfortable position of having to defend the Torah and, to a certain degree, Judaism.[5]

---

[1] Hertzberg, *The French Enlightenment and the Jews*, 313.

[2] "It is an ironic circumstance that the nickname of Voltaire in his own circle of friends was 'Goebbels.'" Hyam Maccoby, *Antisemitism and Modernity: Innovation and Continuity*. (London, New York Taylor & Francis Routledge, 2006), 59.

[3] Voltaire. *The Works of Voltaire: A Contemporary Version*,Vol. 7. William F. Fleming, trans. (New York: E.R. DuMont, 1901), 195.

[4] Ibid., 102.

[5] "While the traditional attacks on Jews and Judaism continued in Catholic Italy and Spain, the reverse occurred in France, where Catholics were so disturbed by the writings of Voltaire and others that they were forced to engage in the defense of Judaism." Maccoby, *Antisemitism and Modernity: Innovation and Continuity*. 59.

There have been many theories put forth on why Voltaire hated the Jews. One of the theories was that he had two unpleasant business dealings with them, causing him considerable financial loss. Others think it was his latent Christian theological conscience, a relic from his youth that led to his vehemence later in life.[6] Others said it was his anti-religious attitude and disdain towards the Bible, and since the Jews were responsible for the Bible, they naturally inherited a large part of the blame: "The essence of Voltaire's persistent attack on the Bible was that the religion of the Old Testament was most unreasonable."[7] None of these explanations are adequate, for Voltaire's *Hebrewphobia* bordered on the pathological.[8] The explanation "that Voltaire's attack on Jews and Judaism was…he was a hedonist"[9] makes sense; Voltaire did not want the Jews to inflict their morality on him or anyone else— if he wanted to go to an orgy in Paris, he did not want Biblical morality prohibiting him from doing so. Whatever the reasons, the bottom line was that Voltaire hated the Jews, and this hatred was well reflected in his writing. His influence among the intellectuals of his day was considerable,[10] and his anti-Semitic comments would often be echoed (if not outright quoted) by later philosophers, sociologists, and even theologians.[11]

---

[6] "The Christian idea that the religion of the Jews and their rejection of Christianity made them an alien element was still strong in Europe. It had now been reinforced by the pagan cultural argument that the Jews were by the very nature of their own culture and even by their biological inheritance an unassimilable element." Hertzberg, *The French Enlightenment and the Jews*, 11.

[7] Ibid., 256.

[8] "Though the Jews numbered fewer than 1 percent of France's population in the second half of the eighteenth century, Voltaire was obsessed with them. In his most important work, *Dictionnaire Philosophique*, 30 of his 118 articles dealt with the Jews, and described them in consistently deprecating ways." Dennis Prager and Joseph Telushkin, *Why the Jews?* (New York: Touchstone, 2003), 115.

[9] Hertzberg, *The French Enlightenment and the Jews*, 283.

[10] Needless to say, anti-Semitism was still rife among the common people of France. "It is most important to recognize that the new thinking that had begun in the 1670s and 1680s had not, even a hundred years later, conquered the majority even of educated Frenchmen. Education remained Catholic and every child in France was therefore taught that the Jews were Christ-killers who deserved their exile and low estate." Ibid., 33.

[11] "In his own time Voltaire's work encouraged anti-Semitism…for the next century he provided the fundamentals of the rhetoric of secular anti-Semitism." Ibid., 283.

Christopher Hitchens echoed the sentiments of many modern intellectuals when he said that "humanity began to grow up a little in the closing decades of the eighteenth century and the opening decades of the nineteenth,"[12] i.e., when "enlightened" secularism began its blitzkrieg on organized religion, replacing the ethical teachings of the Bible with those of the "enlightened" philosophers. The political consequences of the French Enlightenment and the teachings of philosophers such as Voltaire were a substantial influence that fueled the social turmoil which led to the French Revolution and the Reign of Terror, as well as the subsequent rise of Napoleon and of brutal warfare that convulsed Europe for two decades. To a lesser extent, the ideas of the Enlightenment affected the Colonies in America as well. Although the American Revolution was not nearly as bloody as the French Revolution, the conservative nature of the American Revolution was due to it being more over financial reasons rather than ethical ones (although the French certainly did have it out for the nobility and the upper class). The ethical Enlightenment philosophies such as freedom, liberty, and equality that so enamored the Founding Fathers of the United States did not seem to apply to people of different color. This created tension between the slave-holding South and the North later on which would indeed result in more bloodshed during the Civil War. Many of the "Founding Fathers" of the United States owned slaves, such as Benjamin Franklin and James Madison, the "Father of the Constitution." Thomas Jefferson, who penned the Declaration of Independence, not only owned over a hundred human slaves but, on occasion, used them to relieve his enlightened lust, as proved by the DNA sampling of Sally Heming's descendants. George Washington, the first president of the United States, had three times as many slaves as did Jefferson, and there were a few rumors about his cavorting with his black female slaves as well. As with Athens and Rome, a good part of the economy of eighteenth century United States depended on a large slave population, and the Constitution itself had a clause which stated that black slaves were only three-fifths of a person. The attitude toward the Native Americans was also a black spot on the early white settlers, for most Americans considered them barbarians and savages. There was, however, another difference between America and Europe; the Puritanical streak in America created a climate where the Jews prospered; "The

------

[12] Hitchens, *god is Not Great*, 66.

small number of Jews who were part of the generation of the Revolution were accepted as equals almost everywhere."[13] It was this Puritanical strain that made all the difference a century later when, at the close of the nineteenth century, the anti-Semitism of Europe that had heretofore been bottled up suddenly exploded with renewed vigor and venom[14] did not affect America to the degree it did Europe.

The British intellectuals followed the same pattern of Voltaire's anti-Semitism; the English writer and philosopher John Stuart Mill (1806–1873) had an attitude towards Israel which was not unlike Voltaire's:

> The Gospel always refers to a pre-existing morality, and confines its precepts to the particulars in which that morality was to be corrected, or superseded by a wider and higher; expressing itself, moreover, in terms most general, often impossible to be interpreted literally, and possessing rather the impressiveness of poetry or eloquence than the precision on legislation. To extract from it a body of ethical doctrine, has never been possible without eking it out from the Old Testament, that is, from a system elaborate indeed, but in many respects barbarous, and intended only for a barbarous people.[15]

After disparaging Israel and the ethics of the Torah, dismissing the Jews as "barbarous," ignoring the wealth of moral and legal teachings of the Talmud, Mill criticized Christianity for not having a workable moral and legal system. Mill highlights one of the major flaws of Christian theology, namely, its lack of a working system of ethics; Mill observed (correctly) that what ethical teaching the New Testament contained was taken from the Torah.

---

[13] Grayzel, *A History of the Jews*, 615.

[14] "The case of Voltaire and other Enlightenment antisemites (such as Baron d'Holbach and his circle) raises a very painful question. Why did anti-semitism survive the Enlightenment? This great movement of rationalism and science and liberalism dazzled the Jews with the prospect of toleration and acceptance and the end of prejudice and fanaticism. Many Jews welcomed the Enlightenment with delight and rushed to make their own intellectual contribution to it (Solomon Maimon, Moses Mendelssohn, for example). Yet in the heart of the Enlightenment (though by no means pervading it entirely) was vicious hatred and denigration of the Jews and of their religion and culture. Even the greatest thinker of the Enlightenment, Immanuel Kant, was affected by this specifically Enlightenment contempt for the Jews." Maccoby, *Antisemitism and Modernity: Innovation and Continuity*, 51.

[15] John Stuart Mill, *On Liberty and Other Essays*. (Oxford: Oxford University Press, 1991), 55.

The German historian Oswald Spengler gave one explanation for the reason for this omission, that "Jesus never lived one moment in any other world but this. He was no moralizer, and to see in moralizing the final aim of religion is to be ignorant of what religion is. Moralizing is a nineteenth-century Enlightenment, humane Philistinism. To ascribe social purposes to Jesus is a blasphemy."[16] Here Spengler paints Jesus as being opposed to not only the morality of the Torah, but of rabbinic Judaism itself:

> [Jesus] was born in the Classical Empire and lived under the eyes of the Judaism of Jerusalem, and when his soul, fresh from the awful revelation of its mission, looked about, it was confronted by the actuality of the Roman State and that of Pharisaism. His repugnance for the stiff and selfish ideal of the latter, which he shared with all Mandæanism and doubtless with the peasant Jewry of the wide East, is the hall-mark of all his discourses from first to last. It angered him that this wilderness of cold-hearted formulæ was reputed to be the only way to salvation. Still, thus far it was only another kind of piety that his conviction was asserting against Rabbinical logic.[17]

Again, it is the "cold-hearted formulæ" of "Rabbinical logic" that blocked the way to salvation, a decidedly theological viewpoint. What we need to compare is the logic of what Mill described as a "barbarous people" with the warm-hearted formulæ of John Stewart Mill's own values of humanistic morality, and Mill's role in one of the most tragic events that occurred at the height of the Age of Reason: Mill's support of the "civilized" British in regards to the Irish potato famine in the late 1840s, an event which resulted in the deaths of close to a million people due to starvation or disease caused by malnutrition.

∞

IRELAND IN THE 1840s had been under the domination of the British for centuries.[18] The power of the British oppression increased in the late seventeenth century, and Ireland was a country not unlike Judea under the Roman occupation, reducing the Irish to thralldom in their own land. The British hold on the passionate and smoldering Irish

---

[16] Oswald Spengler, *The Decline of the West*, Vol. 2. (New York: Knopf, 1932), 216–17.

[17] Ibid., 215–16.

[18] Ireland was first invaded by the Anglo-Norman army in 1169, and has never been totally free of foreign rule since that time.

was a tentative one, and the magnitude of the problem of the constant threat of uprising was such that "the Government of Ireland was admittedly a military occupation,"[19] the upshot of which was the British had to have a larger garrison of troops in tiny Ireland than they did in India. Most of the land was owned by the mainly absentee British landlords (which had increasingly been the custom since the late fourteenth century). Denied the "pursuit of property," the Irish were forced to rent their own land, and since (for most of the Irish) their sole source of income was farming or livestock, they were forced to live and subsist on very small plots of land. Ireland had a large population for such a small island; in 1845, Ireland had a population of well over eight million people on an island smaller than the state of Indiana (a state whose population in 2006 was just over six million people). Often large families were forced to feed themselves on plots of an acre or less. The only crop that could sustain them was the potato. It was cheap and abundant, and potatoes with milk or buttermilk provided practically all of the nutrients one needed; of course, a healthy young man had to eat a lot of potatoes to satisfy his dietary requirements.

Ireland had never been industrialized, and there were very few jobs available, so having a small plot of land to grow potatoes meant the literal difference between life and death for the desperately poor Irish. As a result, most of the Irish peasantry was impoverished, especially in the western part of Ireland. A family would often live in a crude cob hut with a thatched roof that had no windows and only one door, barely surviving off of its meager plot of land. Few had beds or even blankets, and furniture was considered a luxury. On top of this, the Irish had also operated for nearly a hundred and fifty years under the "Penal Laws," laws designed to destroy Catholicism, which was the religion of the vast majority of the Irish. This religious struggle between the Catholic Irish and their Protestant masters created a great deal of hostility on both sides.

In the summer of 1845, just as the potato crop was about to be harvested, a blight that had wiped out potato crops in both America and Europe struck Ireland. The effects were devastating, and entire fields were destroyed overnight. This blight would affect the potato crop for the next three years, and during that time nearly a million people died

---

[19] Cecil Woodham-Smith, *The Great Hunger: Ireland 1845–1849*. (London: Penguin Books, 1962), 19.

of starvation or disease. What made this disaster so disturbing was that there was a tremendous amount of food being produced in Ireland, and while the Irish were literally dropping dead in the streets from starvation, ships loaded with Irish grain and cattle were constantly being sent to England. During the famine, the British Parliament refused to repeal the Corn Laws (which put a high tariff on foreign grain) in order to ease the suffering of the Irish people.[20] This was due to the popularity of the concept of *laissez faire*, or letting the economy run without government interference, a philosophy John Stewart Mill supported. The irony of this was that it was the government policies themselves—laws protecting the British landlords and keeping the prices of foreign grain artificially high—that added to the grinding misery of the Irish.

Mill, siding with the British ruling class,[21] seemed to think that the Irish had every right to execute their personal freedom to starve to death, but not to cause harm to others, i.e., the English landlords or the grain and beef merchants in England who were selling Irish-grown crops to the poorly paid and overworked laborers who toiled in the textile mills of Britain. In a classic case of "blaming the victim," the English criticized the Irish for living like animals and foolishly depending on the potato when it was practically the only crop the Irish could feed themselves with on their miserably small leftover scraps of land allotted to them by their British overlords. This attitude of blaming the victim—which is similar to how the Jews were often blamed for their problems (such as being moneylenders when other forms of business were forbidden to them)—is summed up by Charles Edward Trevelyan, the head of the Treasury, who so poetically commented that "the great evil with which we have to contend [is] not the

---

[20] "The purpose of the Corn Laws was to keep up the price of home-grown grain. Duties on imported grain guaranteed English farmers a minimum and profitable price, and the burden of a higher price for bread was borne by the labouring classes, in particular by the millions of factory workers and operatives toiling in the great new industrial cities…it was asserted that if the Corn Laws were repealed all classes connected with the land would be ruined and the traditional social structure of the country destroyed, and…all interest in Ireland was submerged." Woodham-Smith, *The Great Hunger: Ireland 1845–1849*, 50.

[21] "Mill exerted a considerable influence on the educated public…the effects of his teaching…provided confirmation of the economic reasons usually put forward against the claims of the Irish peasantry." E. D. Steele, "J. S. Mill and the Irish Question: The Principles of Political Economy, 1848–1865." *The Historical Journal*. Vol. 13, No. 2 (June 1970), 217.

physical evil of the famine, but the moral evil of the selfish, perverse and turbulent character of the [Irish] people."[22] John Stuart Mill's own view of the Irish disaster was that "in any Continental complications, the sympathies of England would be with Liberalism; while those of Ireland are sure to be on the same side as the Pope—that is, on the side opposed to modern civilization and progress, and to the freedom of all except Catholic populations held in subjection by non-Catholic rulers."[23] Because the Irish were white, they got off relatively easy. Other countries the British conquered either militarily or economically were not so lucky, especially if the indigenous population was made of brown people—the indigenous populations of India, China, and the Australian aborigines to give but a few examples. This British attitude towards those of "inferior race" survived well into the twentieth century, and there is no better example of this attitude than England's "civilizing" mission in Kenya.

෴

In Kenya, during the late nineteenth century, the British pushed the indigenous peoples (mainly the *Kikuyu*) off of the land they had lived on for centuries, and by World War II, over 30,000 British "settlers" were living off the fat of the Kenyan land, producing cash crops such as coffee and tea. The Kenyan colony became even more important when India threw off the British imperial yoke, and Kenya became the new jewel in the rapidly-tarnishing British Crown. Of course, the ungrateful *Kikuyu* were becoming disgruntled about being the recipients of Mill's "greatest happiness principle," which of course meant the greatest happiness for the white British who had taken the best arable land and had resettled the *Kikuyu* into "reserves" or reservations, much as the Americans forced the Native Americans onto reservations during the nineteenth century. As conditions in the reserves deteriorated because of overcrowding, the *Kikuyu's* anger reached critical mass, turning into an armed rebellion known as the "Mau Mau War." The world-wide press at the time was wholly sympathetic to the brave British settlers who were defending themselves against the onslaught of the brutal and savage Mau Mau. It was many decades later when a much different picture began to develop, mainly due to the work of Harvard professor Caroline Elkins. Elkins spent many years in Africa interviewing the

---

[22] Woodham-Smith, *The Great Hunger*, 156.

[23] Bruce L. Kinzer, *England's Disgrace?: J.S. Mill and the Irish Question.* (Toronto: University of Toronto Press, 2001), 169–70.

Kikuyu and trying to uncover the truth about the Mau Mau war and its aftermath.[24]

The attitude of the British towards the *Kikuyu* was not only based on religious attitudes,[25] but on the enlightened views of "reason" and "science," that whites (particularly Englishmen) were physically and intellectually superior to non-whites, and that:

> To profit by Africans it seemed that whites must subvert them. On entering Kenya, therefore, settlers also entered a nineteenth-century South African debate on how to construct political security and morality on shifting sands. It was never resolved, whether in white opinion or in the priorities of the colonial state. Conservatives thought Africans inherently primitive, liberals that they were retarded children who promised well as modern men.[26]

Naturally, the *Kikuyu* resented this attitude:

> A wave of armed robberies, assassinations of government chiefs and increasing paranoia on the part of the European community led to the declaration of a State of Emergency in October 1952. Almost 100,000 squatters were repatriated en masse to the reserves, Central Province was 'closed' for seven years and British armed forces were brought in to suppress a revolt which in fact the Emergency had precipitated.[27]

---

[24] "At the beginning of the twentieth century the completion of the Uganda railway opened up the interior of Kenya for commercial exploitation. British government policy was to establish a settler economy capable of exporting produce in a quantity sufficient to justify high levels of investment, while at the same time ensuring that the indigenous population shared the financial burden of colonial government. To this end, by 1914, a system of African reserves with fixed boundaries was demarcated, together with an exclusive area of fertile land for European farming. The White Highlands stretch westwards from Nairobi, along the Rift Valley. The high altitude renders the climate suitable for a variety of crops, particularly tea, coffee and wheat. The introduction of hut taxation and the registration of adult males under the kipande pass law system was a double measure explicitly designed to raise revenue and force African participation in the labour market. African farmers were prevented legally from growing cash crops; this restriction consolidated the structural prerequisites for a dual economy premised on the reserves as a source of labour rather than produce." Maia Green, "Mau Mau Oathing Rituals and Political Ideology in Kenya: A Re-Analysis." *Journal of the International African Institute.* Vol. 60, No. 1 (1990), 70.

[25] "The Church never completely lost its association with colonial power. The expulsion of Gikuyu Christians from mission schools and churches in the 1930s in opposition to the practice of clitoridectomy at girls' initiation encouraged a perception of Gikuyu 'tradition' and 'religion' as objectifiable and valued entities." Ibid., 75.

[26] John Lonsdale, "Mau Maus of the Mind: Making Mau Mau and Remaking Kenya." *The Journal of African History*, Vol. 31, No. 3 (1990), 401.

[27] Green, *Mau Mau Oathing Rituals and Political Ideology in Kenya: A Re-Analysis* , 72.

As the British took on "the White Man's Burden" in Kenya,[28] many of the *Kikuyu* decided they had had enough of British Imperialism[29] and decided to fight for their land, and many secretly took the Mau Mau oath which revolved around two important aspects that Americans should recognize as "certain unalienable rights:" land and freedom. The Mau Mau were simply the *Kikuyu* who had armed themselves with machetes and clubs against the better armed and organized British veterans of the Second World War, and after hacking a few white settlers to pieces, the rebellion was quickly put down by the British. "The disparity in death is striking. On official data, Mau Mau (or Africans so described) lost 12,590 dead in action or by hanging over the four most active years of war; 164 troops or police died in the same period, most of them Africans. Mau Mau killed 1,880 civilians, nearly a third of them KG and all but 58 of them black."[30] Elkins's number of those killed was that:

> Officially, fewer than one hundred Europeans, including settlers, were killed and some eighteen hundred loyalists died at the hands of Mau Mau. In contrast, the British reported that more than eleven thousand were killed in action, though the empirical and demographic evidence I unearthed calls into serious question the validity of this figure. I now believe there was in late colonial Kenya a murderous

---

[28] "In the most coherent official version, Mau Mau was depicted as a savage, violent, and depraved tribal cult, an expression of unrestrained emotion rather than reason. It sought to turn the Kikuyu people back to 'the bad old days' before enlightened British rule had brought the blessings of modem civilization and development." Bruce J. Berman, "Nationalism, Ethnicity, and Modernity: The Paradox of Mau Mau." *Canadian Journal of African Studies / Revue Canadienne des Études Africaines*. Vol. 25, No. 2 (1991), 182.

[29] "The government also claimed that Mau Mau had emerged among a particularly unstable people who had difficulty adjusting to the strains of rapid social change and modernization. Playing upon their morbid fears and superstitions, Mau Mau turned the Kikuyu into savage and maniacal killers. Government intelligence reports dwelt on the 'insane frenzy' and 'fanatical discipline' of Mau Mau adherents. It had been deliberately organized, according to the government, by cynical and unprincipled leaders, seeking only to satisfy their own lust for power. Furthermore, officials repeatedly insisted that Mau Mau was not a response to economic deprivation and material grievances arising out of colonialism, but rather was an irrational rejection of the benefits of development. This view led them to stress repeatedly the essentially atavistic character of Mau Mau." Ibid., 182.

[30] Lonsdale, *Mau Maus of the Mind: Making Mau Mau and Remaking Kenya*, 398.

campaign to eliminate Kikuyu people, a campaign that left tens of thousands, perhaps hundreds of thousands, dead."[31]

Perhaps one of the most important and disturbing discoveries professor Elkins uncovered was that "the colonial government had intentionally destroyed many of these missing files [the 'countless documents pertaining to the detention camps'] in massive bonfires on the eve of its 1963 retreat from Kenya."[32] What Elkins revealed was that the British had good reason to destroy its files, for their treatment of the Kikuyu rivaled the Nazi excesses of the Holocaust[33] in spirit, if not in size. Alan Lennox-Boyd, who was appointed Colonial Secretary to Kenya in 1954, was "a master of disinformation" with a "high-minded sense of authoritarian righteousness."[34] To cover up the atrocities, "Lennox-Boyd did what he did best: he obfuscated the facts, skirted the issues, and lied. He shrouded violence and torture in the camps inside the garment of Britain's civilizing mission."[35] These "noble lies" can only be explained in terms of British morality, the same morality the British exhibited in Tasmania, in Gurkha, and in Ireland during the Irish potato famine.

⌒

IT WAS IN THIS brutal environment where the Torah-hating author Richard Dawkins spent his formative years.[36] A descendant of upper-middle class landed gentry, and a direct descendant of the Clinton family who held the Earldom of Lincoln, Dawkins spent his early childhood years in the imperialist British enclaves of Kenya, where "beyond such gentrified leisure, these privileged men and women

---

[31] Caroline Elkins, *Imperial Reckoning: The Untold Story of Britain's Gulag in Kenya.* (New York: Henry Hold and Company, 2005), xvi.

[32] Ibid., xii.

[33] "After years of combing through what remains in the official archives, I discovered that there was a pattern to Britain's cleansing of the records. Any ministry or department that dealt with the unsavory side of detention was pretty well emptied of its files, whereas those that ostensibly addressed detainee reform, or Britain's civilizing mission, were left fairly intact. This was hardly accidental." Ibid., xiii.

[34] Ibid., 138.

[35] Ibid., 332.

[36] Dawkins was born in 1941 in Nairobi, where he lived until 1949.

lived an absolutely hedonistic lifestyle, filled with sex, drugs, drink, and dance, followed by more of the same."[37] It is hard to imagine that Dawkins's formative years spent in the hedonistic and racist atmosphere of British-controlled Kenya did not have an effect on his mores and values. Even if Dawkins did not witness the brutality and immorality first-hand, he certainly was exposed to the prevailing British attitudes towards their ethnically-challenged subjects, the same attitudes the British displayed in Ireland, India, Australia, and South Africa. What is particularly ironic—if ironic is the correct word—is that one of the major criticisms Dawkins levies against the Jews is "the ethnic cleansing begun in the time of Moses...brought to a bloody fruition in the book of Joshua, a text remarkable for its bloody massacres it records and the xenophobic relish with which it does so."[38] What Dawkins misses is, as usual, the *why* question. The Canaanites[39] were the most hedonistic and unjust people in that time, and the only way to eradicate the memes they had created and spread was to eradicate the source—the Canaanites themselves. Dawkins chortled, "do not think, by the way, that the God character in the story nursed any doubts or scruples about the massacres and genocides that accompanied the seizing of the Promised Land,"[40] ignoring the fact that his own family was an important part of the system of British imperialism committing acts far worse than those he condemns the Israelites for doing.[41] In light of the British role in Kenya—which Dawkins's own family played an important part—it certainly puts an "enlightened" twist on Dawkins's

---

[37] Elkins, *Imperial Reckoning*, 11.

[38] Dawkins, *The God Delusion*, 280.

[39] "The land of Canaan at the time was occupied by the descendants of Cham, the most corrupt tribe among the Noachides." Rabbi Samson Raphael Hirsch, *The Hirsch Chumash: Bereishis*. Daniel Haberman, trans. (Jerusalem: Feldheim Publishers, 2006), 297.

[40] Dawkins, *The God Delusion*, 280.

[41] As the Kikuyu were evicted from their villages, they were "screened" by teams made up of "British district officers, members of the Kenya police force, African loyalists, and even soldiers from the British military forces" who used torture to acquire "confessions and intelligence." "If the screening team was dissatisfied with a suspect's answers, it was accepted that torture was a legitimate next resort. According to a number of the former detainees I [Elkins] interviewed, electric shock was widely used, as well as cigarettes and fire. Bottles (often broken), gun barrels, knives, snakes, vermin, and hot eggs were thrust up men's rectums and women's vaginas." Elkins, *Imperial Reckoning*, 66.

statements in *The God Delusion* such as: "The majority of us don't cause needless suffering...we don't cheat, don't kill, don't commit incest, don't do things to others that we would not wish done to us."[42] Of course, this was exactly what the Canaanites did; they cheated, killed, committed sexual perversions, and generally caused needless suffering such as sacrificing their own children to pagan gods.

The answer to Dawkins's question: "How, then, do we decide what is right and what is wrong?"[43] can only be understood in the context of Dawkins's own astonishing ignorance of the Torah. "My purpose has been to demonstrate that we (and this includes most religious people) as a matter of fact don't get our morals from scripture. If we did, we would strictly observe the Sabbath and think it just and proper to execute anybody who chose not to."[44] Dawkins's understanding of the Torah is clearly limited to a "religious" understanding—a Christian theological understanding.[45]

We need to point out the failure of secular philosophy to grasp the nature of the Torah ideal of "freedom" and "liberty." This can be seen in the above examples of John Stuart Mill's theoretical postulations on liberty and his views on the treatment of the Irish, or of Thomas Jefferson writing about "life, liberty, and the pursuit of happiness" while owning over a hundred slaves, or in Richard Dawkins's own family's involvement in the brutal repression and "needless suffering" of the *Kikuyu.* If we look closely at the morality demonstrated by the philosophers of the Enlightenment as well as the Western societies that nurtured these ideals, we can agree with Dawkins on his last point above—Western societies certainly did not get their morals from the Torah.

---

[42] Ibid., 298.

[43] Ibid.

[44] Ibid.

[45] Gentiles are not under Sabbath law. To infer that Gentiles would be held accountable for breaking laws which do not apply to them is a misrepresentation of Torah law. "How many literalists have read enough of the Bible to know that the death penalty is prescribed for...gathering sticks on the Sabbath and for cheeking your parents? If we reject Deuteronomy and Leviticus (as all enlightened moderns do), by what criteria do we then decide which of religion's moral values to accept?" Ibid., 81. This is an example of the problem with "enlightened moderns" trying to interpret the Torah without the Oral Law. "'There never was, nor will there ever be, such a thing as a "disobedient and rebellious son,"' a baraisa states. 'Why, then, this law? So that you may inquire into it and profit by your inquiry.'" (*Sanhedrin* 71a). Obviously, the "criteria" we need to decide is neither by "religion" nor secular philosophy, but by Torah law.

A Story Selden Heard

One may discern the link between Hellenism and the other worldliness of religion. For the Greeks, man is not the highest thing in the universe. This is why practical wisdom or politics, which is concerned with things human and variable, is inferior to philosophic wisdom. Therein is the dichotomy between the 'vita activa' and the 'vita contemplativa,' prompting certain sensitive types to abandon humanity for a more refined world. This dichotomy is foreign to the Torah, wherein man not only stands at the pinnacle of creation, but is charged (in Gen. **2:28**) with the duty of improving and perfecting it.

— Paul Eidelberg[1]

RETURNING TO MILL'S DESCRIPTION OF THE JEWS AS A "BARBAROUS people," we ask: what exactly makes a people "barbarous?" Mill's standard for civility was polite British culture and society, to play a fair game, tut-tut, tally-ho and all that.[2] Without an absolute moral system, the man-made rules of even the best-meaning of individuals are subject to the whims of the changing climate of human mores and values, and the moral system supported by philosophers such as Mill fell woefully short of the Torah ideal. Mill's view of Ireland, possibly influenced by the Fenian threat[3] to the British Union,

---

[1] Eidelberg, *Beyond the Secular Mind*, 134.

[2] This was the problem that Maurice Samuel wrote about when he commented on the difference between Jews and non-Jews, that "we have not of this joyous gamesomeness. We fight and suffer and die, even as we labor and create, not in sport and not under the rules of sport, but in the feeling and belief that we are part of an eternal process. We cannot have art such as you have, a free and careless lyrical beauty, songs and epics. Our sense of beauty springs from immersion in the universe, from a gloomy desire to see justice done in the name of God. Morality itself we take simply and seriously: we have none of your arbitrary regulations, your fine flourishes and disciplined gallantries; we only know right or wrong: all the rest seems to us childish irreverence." Maurice Samuel, *You Gentiles*, (New York: Harcourt, Brace and Company, 1924), 36.

[3] The Fenians were a secret society of Irish Nationalists founded in the mid-nineteenth century in America. After the Civil War, many of the hardened Irish veterans formed a military arm and launched a series of poorly-planned raids into Canada, and although their attempts failed, it alarmed the British who feared that the Fenians (who also

was that protection of the State of England (and hence, Great Britain) was the most important aspect. This hearkens back to the lesson of those who tried to build the great Tower of Babel, when the community (or state) asks the individual to serve the state instead of serving God, making the state "an end instead of merely as a means toward an end, then all of mankind's moral future is compromised."[4] Mill's idea of "personal liberty" obviously did not extend to those he felt were "on the side opposed to modern civilization and progress," i.e., opposed to the wealthy, classically educated British. Mill, as did many of his Enlightened contemporaries, disparaged the Jews at every opportunity.[5] Since Mill's influences were from the "classical" tradition, meaning from Greek and Roman sources rather than from the Torah, he believed that "what little recognition the idea of obligation to the public obtains in modern morality, is derived from Greek and Roman sources, not from Christian."[6] Mill, even though he was considered a secular humanist, could not escape the trappings of his Christian culture,[7] and the Christian teaching of personal salvation: "But religion, even supposing it to escape perversion for the purposes of despotism, ceases in the circumstances to be a social concern, and narrows into a personal affair between an individual and his Maker, in which the issue at stake is but his private salvation. Religion in this shape is quite consistent with the most selfish and contracted egoism."[8] Even as he criticizes religion, Mill cannot escape from its influence.

Mill ridiculed Judaism, calling it "barbarous;" he disparaged the Torah and the Commandments of God as being the ultimate "selfish and contracted egoism." Instead of Torah, Mill offered hedonistic

---

started using the term "Irish Republican Army") would invade Ireland itself, and lead a rebellion against Britain.

[4] Hirsch, *T'rumath Tzvi*, 55.

[5] "Christians…expanded from an obscure sect of the despised Hebrews into the religion of the Roman empire." Mill, *On Liberty and Other Essays*, 48.

[6] Ibid., 56.

[7] "When the legitimacy of infliction punishment is admitted, how many conflicting conceptions of justice come to light in discussing the proper apportionment of punishment to offences. No rule on this subject recommends itself so strongly to the primitive and spontaneous sentiment of justice, as the lex talionis, an eye for an eye and a tooth for a tooth." Ibid., 193.

[8] Ibid., 240.

pleasures of "happiness" as the greatest goal. It was against this traditionally liberal world-view that Rabbi Hirsch stated:

> The utilization of esthetics for the education of the uncultured is not the greatest good. A culture that affords man an ever-increasing measure of self-satisfaction as the sole standard by which to measure his life's activities but gives him no ideal outside himself, a culture that shines forth in its own light as the sole criterion for his conduct, cannot endure. Only an ideal capable of elevating man's spirit to a knowledge—and his emotions to an acknowledgment—of what is good and true can lead him toward the lofty plane of his true calling.[9]

Mill's "utilitarianism" pointed to "personal happiness"[10] as the ultimate goal for individuals (the "Greatest Happiness Principle").[11] Utilitarianism, with its Greek-epicurean philosophy on the "happiness of the individual," the liberal concept taught by Mill, showed that Judaism did not factor into the enlightened understanding of morality.[12] This attitude carried into the twentieth century, where Toynbee took a swipe at the Hebraic Christian movement of the seventeenth century: "It was an unfortunate perversity that led the founders of Protestantism in our modern Western Christendom to seek their main inspiration partly in the pre-prophetic books of the Old Testament."[13]

VOLTAIRE AND MILL'S criticism of the "barbarous people's (Jewish) pre-existing morality" was supported by the classically-trained philosophers of the Enlightenment, whose Greek morality included a love of hedonism, warfare, and the rich upper-class living a life of luxury and

---

[9] Hirsch, *T'rumath Tzvi*, 50.

[10] The subjective nature of "happiness" was noted by Rabbi S. R. Hirsch, who said that "is it so sure that happiness and perfection are the purpose for which man was created?...what would you answer the libertine, the criminal, to whom intoxication and momentary gratification of the senses outweigh every other happiness, temporal or eternal?" Hirsch, *The Nineteen Letters*, 14.

[11] Mill, *On Liberty and Other Essays*, 198.

[12] "If it be a true belief that God desires, above all things, the happiness of his creatures, and that this was [H]is purpose in their creation, utility is not only not a Godless doctrine, but more profoundly religious than any other." Ibid., 153.

[13] Arnold Toynbee, *A Study of History*, Vol. 1. (London: Oxford University Press, 1963), 211.

sloth on the forced labor of slaves or the working poor. To understand the practical application of Enlightenment philosophy, let us ponder the morality of another philosopher of the French Enlightenment, Jean-Jacques Rousseau (1712–1778), whose works influenced later philosophers such as Immanuel Kant and John Stuart Mill. Rousseau was not the anti-Semite that Voltaire was, yet his personal views and practices of morality raise some serious questions. Rousseau's morals were—as with the other Enlightenment philosophers—based upon Greek philosophy, and the way he treated his children shows us his adherence to the ancient Greek and Roman system of infanticide.

Rousseau had five children with his mistress, Thérèse Levaseur, who was ten years his junior. These newborns, none of which were even given a name, Rousseau snatched from the arms of his mistress, and immediately sent to a state orphanage whose record of infant deaths was so high that it was doubted that any of Rousseau's children survived infancy. Rousseau justified his actions by saying that having children running about the house would be a distraction and an annoyance. Rousseau thought his work was too important to let little things such as letting children constantly interrupt him, and that by getting rid of unwanted children he was only doing what Plato had advocated, "performing the act of a citizen and a father and I looked on myself as a member of Plato's Republic."[14]

This raises a disturbing theme of Plato's Republic, and we should question the sort of morality the Greeks were espousing. Infanticide was quite common throughout early Greek history[15] as well as in later Roman[16] culture. This attitude of disposable children influenced later liberal thought, and our modern society has also bought into this concept with its use of abortion as a means of disposing of

---

[14] Paul Johnson, *Intellectuals*, (New York: HarpePerennial, 1990), 23.

[15] "Abandonment of infants occurred to a greater or lesser degree throughout the Greek world from earliest times, and in the late Hellenistic Period became, it appears, an actual menace and evil." La Rue van Hook, *The Exposure of Infants at Athens. Transactions and proceedings of the American Philological Association*, Vol. 51 (1920), 144.

[16] "That…exposure and infanticide in other forms were not only practiced but also publicly recognized is clear not only from the evidence of Roman law, which has been mentioned, but also from Greek law, religion, and philosophy." A. Cameron, "The Exposure of Children and Greek Ethics." *The Classical Review*, Vol. 46, No. 3, (Jul., 1932), 108.

unwanted babies. The teachings of Rousseau (who was not about to let Jewish morality dictate the terms for his desire to live life the way he wanted it, which was to be unburdened by patriarchal duty) along with Voltaire's hedonism[17] makes thoughtful Noahides question the reasons behind the Enlightenment attack on Judaism. Is there a standard for morality, and if so, who dictates the terms? Are humans free to do what we feel is right in our own eyes, or is there a divine standard of conduct? Are men of learning and artistic ability free to make their own rules, in the words of the French painter Paul Gauguin, "the right to dare all"?

To rephrase the questions we asked earlier: why follow the philosophical teachings from men whose own personal morals concerning their own children were so abominable? Should men of great intellectual achievement be held up as standards of religious belief despite their moral paucity? Many atheist intellectuals crow about how Albert Einstein—the very name invoking genius—was an atheist despite his numerous references to God "inviting misunderstanding by supernaturalists eager to misunderstand and claim so illustrious a thinker as their own,"[18] and that Einstein's faith was not in God but rather in the "Enlightenment tradition" of philosophers such as "Kant and Goethe."[19] The atheists chortle about how this *übergenius*—the crown jewel of intellectuals—was firmly in the secular camp, and modern intellectuals thought Einstein was the best example of how a person of superior intelligence does not believe in God.

What the intellectuals ignore about Saint Albert was his personal morality. During Einstein's greatest period of intellectual achievement he was married to Mileva Marić, a homely but brilliant Serbian *shiksa* whom Albert considered his intellectual equal. She was pursuing a Ph.D. in physics at the Swiss Polytechnic in Zurich when she became pregnant with Albert Einstein's child, a girl named Lieserl. They married after Lieserl was born, but the child vanished a couple of years

---

[17] A famous quote attributed to Voltaire was "once a philosopher, twice a pervert." The setting for this quote is a little vague; one account says it was when Voltaire was invited to an orgy in Paris and declined to go a second time. The other account is Voltaire's experimentation with homosexuality. From the Noahide perspective, the statement should be: "once a pervert, twice a double pervert."

[18] Dawkins, *The God Delusion*, 34.

[19] Hitchens, *god is not Great*, 243.

later—whether she was put up for adoption, dumped in a home for handicapped children, or simply died we do not know—and although the Einsteins had two more children (both male), the loss of her only daughter haunted Mileva for the rest of her life. Mileva gave up her own career in science for the sake of her children and for her husband. There is evidence that much of Albert Einstein's greatest work—including his theory of relativity—was a joint creation with his brilliant wife. As his fame grew, Albert spent increasingly longer periods of time away from his family, and after his affair with Elsa Lowenthal, his own cousin whom he later married and subsequently cheated on as well, he abandoned his family entirely. In Albert Einstein's own words (in a letter written in 1916) he said that:

> Separation from Mitsa was for me a question of life. Our life in common had become impossible, even depressing, but I could not say why. So I am giving up my boys...during the two years of our separation, I have seen them twice...to my great sorrow I have found that my children do not understand my actions, that they feel a mute anger against me, and I find, although it hurts me, that it is better for them if their father does not see them any more...[Mitsa] is and will remain always for me a severed limb. I shall never again approach her; I shall finish my days far away from her.[20]

Einstein's children would doubtless have preferred a loving father who was faithful to his wife and family even if he had to take off his shoes to count to twenty. Comments by atheists such as Sam Harris, who wrote about how Einstein considered faith "nothing more than a eunuch left to guard the harem while the intellect was away solving the problems of the world" and that "Einstein robbed religion of the *truth* of its doctrine,"[21] makes one wonder what "truths" Einstein robbed. Albert Einstein, besotted by Western values and mores, was an atheist indeed.[22]

---

[20] Milan Popovic, *The Life and Letters of Mileva Marić*. (Baltimore: The Johns Hopkins University Press, 2003), 109–10.

[21] Harris, *The End of Faith*, 271.

[22] "Outside of Judaism we sometimes find the delusion prevalent that the requirements of moral law are valid only for men of the lower or middle social strata. According to that point of view, social prominence, and particularly intellectual prowess and genius constitute a license for indulgence in moral aberrations. Judaism does not share such views." Hirsch, *The Hirsch Psalms*, §ii, 192–93.

THE INTELLECTUALS IN Britain and France were not alone in their attitudes concerning the "barbarous" Jews.[23] By the end of the nineteenth century, with the wave of anti-Semitism erupting in France and spreading throughout Europe, it was clear that, from the Jewish viewpoint, the Enlightenment had failed. Neither Christian nor secular European culture could tolerate the Jews, and by the early twentieth century, great numbers of Jews (as had the Irish a generation earlier) fled Europe (particularly Eastern Europe) and settled in America. As the Spirit of the Enlightenment helped develop a system where the State took the place of the Church in many aspects; as the Industrial Revolution changed society and increased the wealth and power of Western states, wars became more and more bloody, culminating with the world wars of the twentieth century. As for the superior morality of the "enlightened" philosophers, the French Enlightenment produced the French Revolution, where during the Reign of Terror in 1793–1794, nearly 20,000 people were guillotined. When Ireland was hit by the potato blight, close to one million people died of starvation and disease. Here in America, our treatment of the Native Americans and the African Americans who were enslaved, and even long after they were freed, was just as bad. In Germany, a state that many considered to be the most civilized nation on earth in the early 20th century, the events of the 1930s and 1940s speak for themselves. The dream of society without religion and without the constraints of biblical morality—the sort of society which John Stuart Mill espoused (as well as today's atheistic intellectuals such as Richard Dawkins, Christopher Hitchens, and Noam Chomsky) was fulfilled in the regimes of the Soviet Union and China, where Stalin's "Command Economy" and "Great Purge" along with Mao Zedong's "Great Leap Forward" and "Cultural Revolution" created horrors that topped even Hitler's body count. Without the moral foundation of the Torah, the man-made systems of enlightened philosophical morality fell far short of achieving peaceful societies.

---

[23] "The enemies of the Jewish people, in justification of their own conduct, have pointed out many times that, from the very beginning of its history, this people had found no sympathy among the nations. Instead, they say, Israel has met with nothing but hostility and hatred throughout the world. Israel's enemies think this is sufficient reason for all future generations to cultivate and to transmit to their descendants the old hatred which the nations have long harbored against the Jews…it was not at the people of Israel, but at the ideals of Zion that this hatred had been aimed from the very beginning…the haters of the *ideals* represented by Zion became the enemies of the Jews." Hirsch, *The Hirsch Psalms*, §ii, 392.

The philosophers endeavored to replace the morality of the Torah with other moral systems derived from their own philosophical
"reason."[24] As we have seen, the non-Jewish philosophy developed
during the Enlightenment, no matter how elegant and erudite, so matter how sophisticated the methodology, did not provide the answers
to the primary questions of human behavior (where did the universe
come from, what is God, why are we here, what is good and evil,
etc.). No matter how grand and logical the teachings of the philosophers on the matter of ethics, there was a vast disconnect between their
personal beliefs and behavior and the teachings of the Torah.[25] The
questionable morality of the philosophers of the Enlightenment show
the influence of the Greeks and the Romans[26] and how their ideas were
combined and synthesized into a new academic model, a model that
has since affected practically all theological and historical study of
Israel by both the Church and secular academia. Practically every non-
Jewish commentary on the New Testament and every study on ancient
Judaism has been affected by it either directly or indirectly.[27]

The grand ideas and concepts such as "freedom" and "equality,"
as expounded by philosophers such as Voltaire, Rousseau, Kant, and
Hegel, influenced not only the historical schools of the Enlightenment, but all branches of the social sciences. Freedom, from the rabbinic viewpoint, is not simply another theological, philosophical, or
individualistic attribute or idea. "In order for a person to appreciate
freedom, he must value the freedom of others, just as he values his own

---

[24] "The accepted Jewish analysis of the problem is that apostasy does not start
in the rational, but that it is rather the result of a strong desire to commit certain
transgressions. These are later justified by a subservient intellect." Paul Forchheimer,
Maimonides' Commentary on Pirkey Avoth. (Jerusalem: Feldheim, 1983), 187.

[25] "Philosophies do not remold natures. What your radicals want is another form of the
Game, with other rules." Samuel, *You Gentiles*, 154.

[26] "Voltaire found his rationalization [of anti-Semitism] in history; he argued that the
Jews had always been despised, even before Christian times. He constantly adduced
pagan writers, such as Tacitus, Juvenal and Cicero, to prove this point." Hyam
Maccoby, *Antisemitism and Modernity: Innovation and Continuity*. (London, New
York Taylor & Francis Routledge, 2006), 54.

[27] "Reason transformed into prejudice is the worst form of prejudice." Allan Bloom,
The Closing of the American Mind. (New York: Simon & Schuster Inc., 1987), 253.

(*P'nei Yehoshua*)."[28] The Enlightenment concept of "freedom" was, on the other hand, "freedom" from the Torah.[29]

It was not that the philosophers were unaware of the Torah. We now come to the most damning evidence against the philosophers of the Enlightenment: the excision of the works and teachings of the Christian Hebraists, most notably John Selden.

～∂

DURING THE SEVENTEENTH century, just before the Enlightenment got underway, the Torah gained a brief but important toe-hold in the legal, religious, and philosophic thought of Europe, particularly in England and the Netherlands. The Christian Hebraists at the forefront of this movement were the Dutch scholar Hugo Grotius (1583–1645) and the British lawyer John Selden (1584–1654). Selden had studied the Talmud and the writings of Maimonides, and concluded that the Seven Noahide Laws were the Divine foundation of what then was being touted at the time as "natural law,"[30] and both Selden and Grotius taught that the Seven Laws not only provided the groundwork for national law, but international law as well.[31] Selden, one of the most erudite minds ever produced by Western Culture, did not agree with

---

[28] Rabbis Nosson Scherman and Hersh Goldwurm, *Vayikra*. (Brooklyn: Mesorah Publications, Ltd., 1990), 425.

[29] As Rabbi Hirsch observed: "These 'enlightened' ones make sure not to burden their children with knowledge of God, so that the children will without scruples, without trepidation, and without hesitation follow the footsteps which the irresponsibility of their fathers has marked out for them…it is better to entrust yourself and your child to the guidance of your God than to commit yourself and him to everyday sagacity of those thought of as 'intelligent,' whose sagacity in reality is blinded by the attractions of profit and pleasure." Hirsch, *Collected Writings*, Vol. I, 232.

[30] "The relationship between natural law and the seven Noahide laws was first elucidated by John Selden, the greatest English scholar of the seventeenth century, in his work *De Jure Naturali et Gentium juxta Disciplinam Ebraerum* (1640)—(Natural Law and Civil Law According to the Hebrews). He speaks of the 'laws of Noah' of universal obligation and application, and of the laws which are binding only on the Jews." Rabbi Elie Munk, *The Call of the Torah: Bereishis*. (Brooklyn: Mesorah Publications, Ltd., 1994), 35.

[31] "Grotius and Selden would view more positively the rabbinic tradition of a Noahide law that at least before the Sinai theophany provided a minimal set of moral laws that were divine and universally obligatory." Jason P. Rosenblatt, *Renaissance England's Chief Rabbi: John Selden*. (Oxford: Oxford University Press, 2006), 151.

the principle of "natural law" derived from reason, but of positive law,[32] a Law from the Supreme Lawgiver.[33] Selden came to this view from his study of the Talmud, and, unlike most of his contemporaries who felt that the teachings of the Noahide Code were little more than rabbinical flotsam in a sea of laws which Jesus had done away with, Selden saw the humaneness and reason in the rabbinical teachings that softened the often harsh legal pronouncements of the Written Torah. An example of this would be the penalty for sleeping with another man's wife; a person who violates this law is, technically to be put to death, yet for a man to be convicted of this punishment, the rabbis ruled that there would have to be a set of circumstances so precise that it would make the death penalty all but impossible: there would have to be two witnesses, and just prior to the violation, the law must be spoken to the potential violator *exactly* as it is written in the Torah. This would be like having two policemen giving the *Miranda* warning to a criminal just before he commits a crime, a scenario that would be highly unlikely.

Selden not only had a penchant for thinking "outside the box,"[34] but he championed the concept of the importance of primary sources,[35] as Charles A. Beard would comment, "one thing, however, my masters taught me, and that was to go behind the pages of history written by my

---

[32] "Natural law theory treats law essentially as the embodiment in rules and concepts of moral principles that are derived ultimately from reason and conscience. Positivism treats law essentially as a body of rules laid down ('posited') and enforced by the supreme lawmaking authority, the sovereign." Harold J. Berman, "The Origins of Historical Jurisprudence: Coke, Selden, Hale." *The Yale Law Journal*, Vol. 103, No. 7 (May, 1994), 1653.

[33] "[Selden] took the idea of man's natural freedom from moral laws a great deal further than Grotius, so far in fact that according to him the only way in which moral community could be understood was as an effect of God's positive imposition and enforcement of the moral law as promulgated in the precepts given to the sons of Noah." Knud Haakonssen, *Natural Law and Moral Philosophy: From Grotius to the Scottish Enlightenment.* (Cambridge: Cambridge University Press, 1996), 30.

[34] "Selden's most controversial uses of philology occur in his scholarly works, particularly in his treatises on Jewish law, where he explains disputed New Testament terms in the light of ancient Jewish institutions. This method is standard today: in the seventeenth century, it verged on heresy." Martha A. Ziskind, "John Selden: Criticism and Affirmation of the Common Law Tradition." *The American Journal of Legal History*, Vol. 19, No. 1 (Jan., 1975), 32.

[35] "One facet of Selden's critical attitude toward texts is his preference for primary over secondary sources." Ziskind, *John Selden: Criticism and Affirmation of the Common Law Tradition*, 35.

contemporaries and read 'the sources.'"[36] Selden's simple but profound reasoning led him to understand that since the Noahide Law was the original legal code God had given to mankind, and since the Jews were the keepers and transmitters of this ancient law, reason dictated that the Noahide Law as expounded by the rabbis should be the basis for all legal systems. Noahide Law pre-dated Roman law, and Selden believed that neither "the principles of natural law could be deduced wholly from the civil law of Rome, nor could a case be made for the universality of Roman law throughout history."[37] There were many elements of Roman Law in English common law, and even though "where national custom and Roman law came into conflict, national custom prevailed...Selden discusses in detail the triumph of the common law over efforts to establish Roman law as the law of England,"[38] Selden noted Roman law had an indelible and lasting impact on English Common Law (as can be seen in the use of Latin in English Law).

Following their expulsion in 1290, there had been no Jews in England (at least openly; a few Marrano refugees from Spain probably snuck in here and there, but they kept a low profile). For over three centuries, England had been devoid of Jews, which makes Selden's work all the more amazing. Selden "followed through on his longstanding hunch that ancient Jewish society had managed both a thoroughgoing social cohesion and an intimacy with the divine will."[39] His study of Maimonides led Selden to "transform the formidably complex Talmud and Mishnah into a finite number of precepts"[40] and to champion the Seven Noahide Laws as the basis for government.[41]

This was, to say the least, a remarkable achievement for someone who had neither met nor seen an orthodox Jew in his lifetime, for the Jews were not re-admitted into England until after Selden's death

---

[36] Charles A. Beard, *An Economic Interpretation of the Constitution of the United States*. (New Brunswick, N.J.: Transaction Publishing, 1998), xix.

[37] Ziskind, *John Selden: Criticism and Affirmation of the Common Law Tradition*, 37.

[38] Ibid.

[39] Reid Barbour, *John Selden*. (Toronto: University of Toronto Press, 2003), 13.

[40] Ibid., 218.

[41] "No one before Selden had so emphatically called attention to the analogy which Jewish law offers in this connexion [*sic*] with Greek and Roman jurisprudence." Rabbi Isaac Herzog, "John Selden and Jewish Law." *Journal of Comparative Legislation and International Law*. 3rd Ser., Vol. 13, No. 4 (1931), 238.

in 1654. The English jurist John Selden realized, by his own reason and intellect,[42] that the Noahide Law provided a link between God and non-Jewish society, a Divine Law that predated Islam, Christianity, and even Judaism. "This is not to say, however, that the ancient Jews segregated their society into matters sacred and profane. Nothing could be further from the truth as Selden sees it. God commanded the Jews to make the institutions of justice…justice itself was a natural and sacred dispensation."[43] Selden was not only influential among the seventeenth century philosophers[44] and scholars,[45] but also with the Puritans who were immigrating to America during his most productive years, bringing with them some of his ideas about the Hebrew Bible, not the least of which was that "Selden, throughout his writings, contrast[ed] the severity of the literal text of the Hebrew Bible with the humaneness of rabbinic interpretations of the text and of rabbinic law."[46]

Soon, however, the legal concepts from the Torah were replaced by a subtle shift in ideas and language among Western intellectuals. "Natural law" became "natural rights," and the light of the Torah that Selden and Grotius ignited among the Christians flickered only too briefly before it was extinguished. The intellectuals of Europe backslid into the anti-Semitic Greco-Roman philosophies that so enamored the Enlightenment philosophers such as Voltaire,[47] yet faint traces of

---

[42] "Selden stressed the importance not only of the covenantal, or contractual, nature of the Noachite obligations but also of God-given human reason in understanding them and of God-given human conscience in fulfilling them." Berman, *The Origins of Historical Jurisprudence: Coke, Selden, Hale*, 1699.

[43] Barbour, *John Selden*, 313.

[44] There is evidence that John Selden influenced the British philosopher John Locke, whose writings on natural law and liberty influenced later eighteenth century American intellectuals such as Thomas Jefferson. Cf. Rosenblatt, *Renaissance England's Chief Rabbi: John Selden*, 178.

[45] "Discussions of Noachide law in the seventeenth century that refer to Selden respectfully and often reverentially appear in the work of Isaac Newton, Henry Burton [an influential Puritan writer], John Lightfoot [Hebraist and Master of St. Catharine's College], Henry Stubbe [writer and scholar], Henry Hammond, Jeremy Taylor, James Harrington [political theorist], Edward Stillingfleet, John Toland, Samuel Pufendorf, Lancelot Addison (father of Joseph), and Sir John Vaughan, among many others. It is also clear that Selden's Hebrew scholarship influences Ben Johnson, John Milton, and Thomas Hobbes." Ibid., 169.

[46] Ibid., 179.

[47] "The crucial turn in the 1670s was that the debate about the Bible and the Jews, both ancient and modern, was essentially secularized." Hertzberg, *The French Enlightenment and the Jews*, 30.

philo-Semitism from Selden's work survived, for it was during the decade of the 1630s, when Selden wrote his most important works on the Noahide Laws, that waves of Puritan immigration from England floundered onto the shores of North America, primarily to Canada, the Caribbean, and New England, where over twenty thousand Puritans immigrated during this short but influential time. By the 1640s, during the English Revolution, the Puritan victory that meant they no longer needed to flee Britain, and the influx of Puritans to America gradually slowed to a trickle. As the intellectual ideas of the Enlightenment swept across Western Europe, where the ideas of Selden were ridiculed and then ignored, the Christian Hebraists who had been influenced by Selden had found a safe haven in America.[48]

◌

A<small>N IMPORTANT STEP</small> in the philosophical war against the Torah was the removal of academic discussion of the works of John Selden, who was considered the most learned man in England during the seventeenth century, the peer of Sir Isaac Newton and John Milton, an influence on Thomas Hobbes[49] and John Locke. Within decades, Selden's work had increasingly less impact on modern academia to the point where his teaching and influence became relatively unknown.[50] Selden's monumental work on the Noahide Law, *De Jure Naturali et Gentium juxta Disciplinam Ebraerum*, has yet to be translated into English (as of 2011) from the original Latin, and the topic of the Noahide Law was eventually banished from academic discourse. Even in the rare occurrence when Selden's works are mentioned, the subject of the Noahide Law is usually avoided.[51]

---

[48] "These Puritan emigrants, with their reliance upon the Book [Bible] and their wealth of scholarly leadership, founded that intellectual and scholarly tradition which for three centuries enabled New England to lead the country in educational and scholarly achievement...Puritanism, as a religion of the Book, placed a strong emphasis upon interpretation and rational discourse and eschewed ranting emotionalism." Hofstadter, *Anti-Intellectualism in American Life*, 60–61.

[49] "The context in which *livyatan* [leviathan] occurs in Chapter 27 of Isaiah clearly suggests that 'leviathan' is a metaphor for a powerful society in the midst of mankind." Hirsch, *Collected Writings*, Vol. II, 116.

[50] For example, the view that "historians have traced the origins of a doctrine that granted natural rights to all human beings either to John Locke in the seventeenth century or to William Ockham in the late Middle Ages." Kenneth Pennington, *The Prince and the Law, 1200–1600: Sovereignty and Rights in the Western Legal Tradition*. (Berkeley: University of California Press, 1993), 5.

[51] The treatment of Selden's writings on the Noahide Laws stood as a firm rebuttal against those who insist that the reason rabbinic scholarship has been ignored was

This was one of the consequences of the Enlightenment and the revival of Greek ideas[52]—the extinguishing of the ideas and influence of the Christian Hebraists, particularly the work of Hugo Grotius and John Selden.[53] The "Enlightenment" was the re-discovery and application of Greek philosophy and science, and although the age of the Enlightenment was from around 1650 to 1750 (some have it as late as 1850), we are, in many ways, still living in the Enlightenment age. For the intellectual and educated class—which is to say, those trained in the Greek way of thinking—the Enlightenment was mankind's glorious achievement leading men out of the dark ages of religion to a new age of reason and freedom. No more would mankind be held accountable by the morals and values of ancient religious myths and legends, but by modern methods of the new faith of positivism.

As we have seen, John Selden's work on the Noahide Law lost favor as the Industrial Age began, and one can only wonder how different British and American society would have been had Selden's teaching been heeded. There is no telling what the world might had looked like if the two mightiest Western empires of the past three centuries—Britain and America—had adopted the Noahide Law as the basis for both civil and international law, or at least incorporated it into their legal systems. Yet the most these two nations accomplished was to tweak the laws enough where the Jews did not have to live in constant worry that their houses would be burned down over their heads, their women raped, and their children bayoneted as the Western Europeans had been doing for centuries. As America, and then Britain, passed laws that enabled the Jews to live in society almost as equals, we patted ourselves on the back and beamed with pride at our new Constitution and laws, thinking of ourselves as a sublime example of humanity and reason. Besides, there were other races of men to exploit, humiliate, and

---

that it was only recently that rabbinic works have been widely available in a popular translation and unavailable to the general public.

[52] "Soon after 1730, there was a notable shift in New England ideology. The writings of John Locke and the works of Montesquieu and of other political thinkers of the Enlightenment often displaced the Bible as the center of interest." Milton R. Konvitz, *Torah & Constitution: Essays in American Jewish Thought.* Syracuse: Syracuse University Press, 1998, 15.

[53] "In the last few centuries, the Greco-Roman sources of natural law have continued to be cited, while the Judaic element has generally been ignored." Gordis, *Judaic Ethics for a Lawless World,* 65.

humble, men with brown or red skin. The Jews we could tolerate, as long as they behaved themselves and contributed to the economy.

Yet how reasonable is it to ignore a dissenting view, to disregard an entire school of learning and reason in lieu of its obvious relevance to Western thought? It is one thing to disagree with a particular view, but to dismiss it outright without looking at the evidence displays unreason. It was not that the Noahide Law was unknown to seventeenth century scholars—quite the contrary. Something else was at work, an underlying malaise that influenced the Enlightenment philosophers to ridicule, demean, and ignore the Torah. Even when the Torah was examined, with very few exceptions, the writings of the Sages and the responsa from the rabbis of their day was *treif* to the gentile Enlightenment scholars. From the Noahide perspective, this utter failure to accept anything Torah-related represented a step backward for Western culture, not a step forward, substituting a system of hedonistic Greek paganism for the system of theological paganism of the Church, and the flame that Grotius and Selden had lit in Western Europe was snuffed out by the Greek-loving intellectuals and philosophers of the Enlightenment.

THE PROTOCOLS OF the Enlightenment philosophers resulted in the development of systems of reason and logic that were neither based on Torah nor on rabbinic logic. As elaborate as these systems of philosophy were, they were ultimately used to justify any behavior—no matter how hedonistic—from the killing of unwanted babies to political ideologies such as Nazism. The philosophical secularization and polarization of religious morality and legalism was used to justify moral and ethical behavior which was against the teachings of Torah:

> Kant, with the consistency of thought which is the mark of a great philosopher, therefore puts the duties man has to himself ahead of the duties to others...the standard is neither the love of some neighbor nor self-love, but self-respect...moral conduct has nothing to do with obedience to any law that is given from the outside—be it the law of God or the laws of men.[54]

We now turn to these anti-Semitic memes that were passed from their classical and theological hosts, incubated in the minds of the philosophers, and then infected other academic scholars such as historians.

---

[54] Hanna Arendt, *Responsibility and Judgment*, ed. Jerome Kohn. (New York: Schocken Books, 2003), 67–68.

CHAPTER TWO

Protocols of the Historian

It used to be said that facts speak for themselves. This is, of course, untrue. The facts speak only when the historian calls on them: it is he who decides to which facts to give the floor, and in what order or context...it is the historian who has decided for his own reasons that Caesar's crossing of that petty stream, the Rubicon, is a fact of history, whereas the crossing of the Rubicon by millions of other people before or since interests nobody at all.

— Edward Hallet Carr[1]

IN OUR WESTERNIZED CULTURE, THE VERSION OF HISTORY THAT IS commonly taught can be summed up as follows:

For most of his existence, man dwelt in caves, living on nuts and berries along with what wild game he could catch. After thousands of years of hardscrabble existence, scrawling pictures of buffalo, deer, and bears on cave walls when he was not out hunting and gathering food, man finally learned how to farm, and then to write, and to build houses and form towns and communities. There were fights between towns, and many little kingships sprung up, and these kingships warred on other kingships. A few of the towns became cities, and a few of

---

[1] Edward Hallett Carr, *What is History?* (New York: Vintage Books, 1961), 9.

these cities became powerful city-states, and they built ziggurats and pyramids before being overthrown and seeing their cities destroyed and their people led off into slavery by more powerful city-states, who would themselves be overthrown. This state of affairs went on for a long time. Then, about twenty-five hundred years ago, in a little country called Greece, the people of a city named Athens invented philosophy, democracy and science, and they taught it to the people of Rome. The Romans added to the Greek teachings by establishing a complex civil law as well as impressive engineering feats such as public roads, viaducts, and sporting arenas. In the far eastern part of the Roman Empire, a man called Jesus invented Christianity, which quickly became the religion of the Greeks and Romans, and the Greeks and Romans spread their knowledge and religion far and wide, from Africa and Persia to the British Isles. Then the Western Europeans, who were so much wiser than everyone else, invented marvelous things such as oil painting, symphonies, telescopes, printing presses, guns, and—best of all—sailing ships that could navigate the oceans of the world. With these ships they sailed out from their ports to enlighten the backwards savages and barbarians that inhabited much of the world, and brought back the tribute given to them by the barbarians. This is how democracy, capitalism, and Christianity spread throughout the lands, and why the Western Europeans became the rulers of the earth.

This is a synopsis of the history that has been taught in our education system for generations, and it is an approximation of how Western Culture looks at mankind's journey from cave-dwellers to modern civilized society. As far as factual history, it is essentially correct, albeit from a Western European point of view; to call ancient and advanced civilizations such as the Sinic or the Aztec *backwards* is a symptom of Euro-centric subjectivity. There was evidence that other civilizations had found America long before Columbus, such as the Vikings, the Chinese, or perhaps even the Irish, but these events lacked physical evidence and written histories, or else what has been written has been ignored by scholars. Of course, there was a fine line between the difference between history and propaganda, and most histories were self-centered and self-serving; certainly the nations of antiquity can be excused, for before man learned how to safely navigate ships across seas and oceans, traveling to distant lands was a long and arduous task, and to someone who lived in Western Europe long ago, the rumors of lands such as China or Japan were tales which bordered on the mythological. This was one of the main criticisms about the Bible, particularly the early books of the Old Testament, that the biblical narrative was not "historically accurate," having been written before the development of modern (read: Greek) historical methods.

But what exactly *is* history? Is it a story, told from a particular point of view? Is it a bare assemblage of facts, *wie es eigentlich gewesen*? Or is it a mixture of both, a story told from a specific point of view, using such facts as the historian wishes to convey? Is history an objective science, or is history influenced by the historian's religion and politics, no matter how hard the historian tries to be objective? Who invented "modern historical methods," and how are they applied?

To better explain the problem, let us look at another example. Early in the year 1933, an event that would ultimately change the course of history occurred as a man with a spellbinding gift of oratory and a seemingly insatiable lust for power took control of the government of a powerful Western nation. His goal was to make his nation the most powerful on earth, but first he had to rebuild an economy shattered by a crippling depression by implementing national socialistic programs to get people back to work and jump-start the economy. He was widely popular, and his pictures adorned the walls of public buildings and schools, where school children stood every morning with their right arm fully outstretched, palm down in the ancient Roman salute,[2] bleating out their allegiance to the flag that was hung from a pole tipped with a grim metallic eagle. The citizens of this nation supported his programs, even when he led them into the greatest war mankind had ever known, and they continued to support him when he ordered the political "undesirables," those of an inferior race, to have their property taken away and have them thrown into newly-built concentration camps.[3] The citizens of the nation take little notice; after all, they had laws[4] which forbade those of inferior race to sit in the park benches or shop in the stores or eat in the restaurants of the Master Race, and there were signs put up to remind these inferiors not to eat, not to sit, not enter these establishments. The strain of leadership and the war drained him physically, however, and before the Great War ended, he

---

[2] The "Bellamy Salute," which was the original salute for the Pledge of Allegiance since the end of the nineteenth century, was the same "Roman" salute adopted by the German National Socialist Workers Party. In America, the Bellamy Salute was changed in 1942 to the now-familiar hand-over-the-heart due to the embarrassment of it being the formal salute of the Nazis.

[3] Cf. Executive Order #9066, signed February 19, 1942, p. 486–87 below.

[4] The "Jim Crow" laws in the South.

died in April, 1945, and although many thought he was a tyrant, there were others, even to this day, who considered him one of the great leaders of history.

The question is: who is this biography about, Adolf Hitler or Franklin Delano Roosevelt? This short biography can be accurately applied to either individual; Hitler and Roosevelt were two entirely different personalities, and which was the evil tyrant and which was the heroic leader depends entirely on one's subjective viewpoint, and which facts the historian calls upon.

There have been many books written about history and its various methodologies, its struggle for objectivity and truth. History today is a highly developed discipline, largely based on the German academic prototype developed in the mid-nineteenth century, since "German historical scholarship was an unavoidable model—and had the advantage of borrowed prestige."[5] The German school, following Hegel's philosophical approach, was at the time the most advanced and respected in the world of academics, and prided itself on being objective. The Germans were in the forefront of developing "scientific" methodologies for academic disciplines such as philosophy, history, and sociology.[6] When it came to the study of Judaism, however, these methodologies contained a good deal of subjective theological concepts. The question we need to ask is: how deeply does Christian theology affect the academic discipline of history? No one expects Christian theologians to be objective. But objectivity is expected of the professional and secular academician; that is one of their own criteria of what separates the professional from the amateur.[7] Unfortunately, the techniques of the historical profession

---

[5] Peter Novick, *That Noble Dream*. (Cambridge: Cambridge University Press, 1988, 21.

[6] "Our intellectual skyline has been altered by German thinkers even more radically than has our physical skyline by German architects…this is intended not as a know-nothing response to foreign influence, the search for a German intellectual under every bed, but to heighten awareness of where we must look if we are to understand what we are saying and thinking, for we are in danger of forgetting. The great influence of a nation with a powerful intellectual life over less well endowed nations, even if the armies of the latter are very powerful, is not rare in human experience. The most obvious cases are the influence of Greece on Rome and of France on Germany and Russia. But it is precisely the differences between these two cases and the example of Germany and the United States that makes the latter so problematic for us." Bloom, *The Closing of the American Mind*, 152–53.

[7] "The foundation of an historical profession—a community of the historically competent—was, by this influential contemporary criterion, an indispensable

have been influenced by theology as well as a virulent form of anti-Semitism developed by the Greeks, passed down to the Romans, and absorbed into both Christianity and secular culture, and the Western historian too often donned a pair of morose-colored glasses in which to view the history of the people of Israel. This problem of objectivity when dealing with all things Jewish, as we shall see, applies to other academic fields as well.

The job of the historian is to separate myth from fact, to determine what is "truth" and what is myth and legend. The historian then takes the facts and juggles them into some sort of useful narrative. But what is *Truth*? "Truth" is often described as conformity to fact or reality when addressing past events. Since the finding and understanding of "truth" was the object of many of the philosophers, it was not surprising that philosophers had gotten into the business of finding "truth" in history. Even the term "philosophy of history"—coined by the eighteenth century philosopher Voltaire[8] in the first part of his *Essai sur les Moeurs et L'Esprit des Nations*—suggested history was a logical and rational exercise into uncovering the facts of the past. Philosophers, after all, strove after "truth," and historical truth was certainly as important as any other truth. The problem was when you had philosophers writing about Jewish history, particularly philosophers who were Christian seminary-trained and educated, and had Christian theology obfuscate their objectivism. An example would be Immanuel Kant, the illustrious German philosopher of the late eighteenth and early nineteenth century. Kant wrote a historical essay in 1784 when the Enlightenment was in full flower, helping to influence the developing German school of history as well as the development of the modern university system.

This is a paragraph from Kant's essay:

> For if we start out from *Greek* history as that in which all other earlier or contemporary histories are preserved or at least authenticated, if we next trace the influence of the Greeks upon the shaping and misshaping of the body politic of *Rome*, which engulfed the Greek state, and follow down to our own times the influence of Rome upon the

---

prerequisite for the establishment, identification, and legitimation of objective historical truth…a related way in which professionalization served to consolidate the norm of objectivity was through its concentration of technique." Novick, *That Noble Dream*, 52.

[8] Carr, *What is History?*, 20.

Barbarians who in turn destroyed it, and if we finally add the political history of other peoples *episodically*, in so far as knowledge of them has gradually come down to us through these enlightened nations, we shall discover a regular process of improvement in the political constitutions of our continent. (Only an *educated public* which has existed uninterruptedly from its origin to our times can authenticate ancient history.[9] Beyond that, all is *terra incognita*; and the history of peoples who lived outside this public can begin only from the time at which they entered it. This occurred with the *Jewish* people at the time of the Ptolemies through the Greek translation of the Bible [i.e., the Septuagint], without which their *isolated* reports would meet with little belief. From this point, once it has been properly ascertained, their narratives can be followed backwards. And it is the same with all other peoples. The first page of Thucydides, as Hume puts it, is the only beginning of all true history.)"[10]

In this one paragraph, Kant succinctly expresses the view of the beginning of the history of Western Civilization, a view that fits in nicely with the short synopsis of Western History above. The beginning of Western European history is the history of the great achievements of the heroic kings and conquerors of Greece and Rome, powerful kingdoms and empires that left a legacy of culture of the sublime poetry of Homer, the philosophy of Plato and Aristotle, and the resplendent marble sculpture of ancient Greece that adorned its temples. The torch of High Civilization was passed to Rome, and Rome's magnificent architecture, literature, and law was passed down to the nations of Western Europe as the Empire of Rome engulfed Gaul, the Iberian Peninsula, and Britain. Beginning with Ancient Greece, the birthplace of Western Civilization, history proceeds in an unbroken march through Rome, and throughout Europe, and then on to the nations founded by Europeans, such as America and Australia. This has been the traditional view of the history of Western Civilization; even in our modern "politically correct" institutions of learning, where we give a brief nod to Sinic or ancient South American civilizations, the histories of other nations and cultures were inconsequential to the development of Western history either because they were *barbarian* cultures that had no written history, such as the aboriginal tribes of

---

[9] This is, ironically, the same argument the rabbis give for the validation of the Sinai event; that the uninterrupted history of the Jews from Sinai from an event witnessed by the entire nation validates its history.

[10] Immanuel Kant, *Kant: Political Writings*. H. S. Reiss, ed. (Cambridge: Cambridge University Press, 2005), 52.

America or Australia, or that they were marginal to the development of history until they were discovered and impacted by the Western exploration and imperialism, such as the "discovery" of China by Marco Polo or the "discovery" of the New World by Columbus. As American school children study the legacy of our world-shaping culture, we learn to appreciate its depth and richness, particularly when we compare it to the cultures of other less sophisticated societies.

Of all the known civilizations that had been touched by Greece and Rome, Kant chose to compare the Greco/Roman history with that of Israel, a small country on the Eastern Mediterranean coast that had seen its brief glory days long centuries before the Greeks started writing history. Why compare Greece and Rome with Israel? India, invaded by Alexander in 326 BCE, was an ancient civilization, more ancient than Greece; the *Rigveda* was already a thousand years old when Alexander was born. Egypt and Babylonia had hieroglyphic and cuneiform writings as well as art and architecture that were ancient before the Greeks assimilated its alphabet from the Phoenicians, let alone the literary works by which Greece would be famous for, yet it was Israel that Kant uses as an example of a non-Hellenistic nation whose history was "outside the public" and that whose "isolated reports" would have met with "little belief." Was there a reason, perhaps a subconscious theological reason, that made Kant draw attention to the tiny nation of Israel by comparing it to Greece?

This one seemingly innocuous comment about Israel could easily be overlooked, except for one small detail; it is not an isolated incident, but an example of a much larger pattern among historians, indeed throughout Western academia: the disparagement and slighting of Israel's written history, law, and religion. It should not come as any surprise that Christianity was hostile to Judaism, but across the broad scope of the social sciences—history, philosophy, economics, political science, and in sociology—a distinct model emerges. This model teaches that the gifts of the Jewish people to the West have been limited to the Hebrew Scriptures, preferably through the Greek Septuagint as a preamble to the New Testament. Western historians, even if not Christian, have been brought up in a Christian culture, and the Christian-influenced model ignores not only the Jews, but any kind of Jewish scholarship besides the Bible. The historical narratives which they feed us, from the historical hors d'oeuvres (such as Kant's historical morsel above) to the most sumptuous literary feasts, have all been seasoned with a generous dash of Christian theology.

The only era of Jewish scholarship that merits study (according to Western thought) was the era of the Prophets of Israel. This scholarly myopia was not limited to the historians, but, as mentioned above, to philosophers, sociologists, politicians, and even economists such as Adam Smith, who commented that "the Hebrew language having no connection with classical learning, and, except the holy scriptures, being the language of not a single book in any esteem."[11] When Smith said "classical learning," he was using it in the context of the Classical Western tradition, the histories, poetry, and philosophical writings of ancient Greece and Rome. But what made the learning of Greece and Rome "classical"? The learning and literature of the Jewish people had no small part in the shaping and foundation of Western culture, certainly no less than the Greeks.[12] Michelangelo may have been inspired by Greek sculpture, but his subject matter—David, Moses, and the ceiling of the Sistine Chapel—came from the Bible, not Thucydides. Much of the art of the Renaissance had biblical themes based on the *Tanach*, a book which had no little significance in the Western Cultural experience. And when you take into account that Jesus and his apostles were Jewish, this adds to the tremendous impact of Judaism on so many diverse elements of Western Culture such as Da Vinci's *Last Supper*, Handel's *Messiah*, or Milton's *Paradise Lost*. The great cathedrals of Italy, France, and England were not built to honor Demosthenes. Johannes Gutenberg's first printed book was the Bible, not Plato's *Republic*.

The Western historical view leaves out a critical element—the Jewish view and understanding of history. It is not that the nation of Israel has not been affected by or has affected Western history; its interaction with the West was deliberately excluded, an attempt to render the impact of Israel as insignificant or inconsequential. Even discounting the impact of the Hebrew Scriptures, when one looks at

---

[11] Adam Smith, *An Inquiry Into the Nature and Causes of the Wealth of Nations*. (Washington, D.C.: Regnery Publishing, Inc., 1998), 878.

[12] "Where among the spiritual treasures of modern nations and modern civilizations is there anything true and noble, good and beautiful, anything truly conducive to human happiness that cannot be traced back, directly or indirectly, to this sacred literature? Modern European civilization is the child of Hebrew and classic antiquity. Wherever we behold truth clothed in the beauty of form, we behold a joined product of Hebrew thought and Hellenic sensibility, Hebrew truth and Hellenic esthetics." Hirsch, *Collected Writings*, Vol. VII, 76.

the economic history of the Middle Ages, when "court Jews" were employed by barons and nobles since they were usually the only ones educated to read and write, or even in today's secular culture with the disproportionate number of Jews who have won the Nobel prize in areas such as science and mathematics, the importance of the impact of Jews on Western Culture goes well beyond their numbers.

‿

FOR MANY MODERN scholars, the Jewish people, the descendants of Abraham, Isaac, and Jacob, had little significance except when noticed or interpreted by the Greeks or Romans. Certainly the Talmud, which is certainly one of the most astounding literary achievements ever penned (to the Jew and observant Noahide it was certainly *the* most important piece of literature ever written; being dismissed by Adam Smith as one of the *unesteemable* books was an indication of how Western academics viewed this illustrious work of scholarship). According to Kant's view above, Jewish history only started to affect Western History with the translation of the *Tanach* into Greek. But why would Greek history, a history of a small group of isolated city states on a peninsula isolated from Western Europe, have a greater impact than Israel on the culture of Europe such as the Teutonic tribes of Germany or the Celts in Britain? When Rome spread its culture throughout its empire, and Christianity became the official religion of the Roman Empire, the tales of the *Tanach*, now a part of the Christian Bible, found their way to the distant shores of Western Europe. When Rome collapsed in the early fifth century and withdrew its legions from the West, Christianity and its Bible—three fourths of which was the translated Hebrew Scriptures, the history and literature of the Jewish people—remained behind. When the "Dark Ages" closed in on Western Europe, and the Classical Greek and Roman history and art was forgotten, the literature of the nation of Israel remained. Even when Western Europe rediscovered Greek and Roman culture during the Renaissance, the stories of the Holy Scriptures, of Abraham, David, Solomon, and Isaiah, the History of the Jews, were firmly entrenched into the culture and psyche of the West, and yet these important writings were not considered "classical."

An example of this "classical" myopia is the "Seven Wonders of the Ancient World." Since the times of Herodotus, people have made lists of the "greatest wonders of the world." In the Middle Ages, the list of the Seven Wonders of the Ancient World was canonized. It consisted of two tombs, two giant statues of pagan gods, a pagan temple, a palace with magnificent gardens, and a lighthouse. All of these structures were examples of brilliant engineering, art, and edifying symbols of the pagan cultures which built them. The Great Pyramid of Giza, the oldest and best known of the Seven Wonders (and the only one still existing), at nearly five hundred feet in height, was the tallest man-made structure in the world for over four thousand years. The Hanging Gardens of Babylon, as reported by Greek historians, was a massive terraced garden by the banks of the Euphrates. The Statue of Zeus was a spectacular forty foot statue wrought in ivory and gold. The statue was seated in the Temple of Zeus in Olympia in western Greece, not far from where the ancient Olympic games were held, and it was held in awe by travelers from other lands who came to the games. The Temple of Artemis at Ephesus, twice the size of the Parthenon in Athens, was considered to be the most beautiful building ever made. The Mausoleum at Halicarnassus was a marble crypt 140 feet high, decorated with magnificent statues, some of which survive today in the British Museum in London. The Colossus of Rhodes was a great bronze statue that stood at the entrance to the harbor at Rhodes, and was roughly the same size as the Statue of Liberty in New York. The Lighthouse of Alexandria was built on the small island of Pharos at the harbor entrance to Alexandria. It was a tower nearly four hundred feet high, sheathed in white marble. These awe-inspiring structures were all magnificent feats of art and engineering, and have stirred the imaginations of both artists and poets for millennia. The Great Pyramid of Giza has existed for most of human history. Yet, however wonderful and glorious these edifices were, they paled in comparison to the most remarkable building of the Ancient World, the greatest wonder of all time: the *Beis HaMikdash*, the Holy Temple in Jerusalem.

Why was the *Beis HaMikdash* left off of the list of the Seven Wonders? What other man-made "wonders" could possibly compete with the *Beis HaMikdash*, the most famous building in history, the spiritual center of the holiest city on earth, the place where the *Shechinah* dwelt between the cherubim in the Holy of Holies? Why would our culture focus on the achievements of pagan societies rather than the achievements of Israel, the keepers and teachers of God's Torah?

The question we must ask is: by what criteria do we judge what constitutes a "wonder?"[13] The *Bnai Yaphet*, the Children of Yaphet, son of Noah, were dazzled by external stimuli. The *Bnai Yaphet* saw only the glorious architecture, the stunning art and sculpture, and ignored the idols that abide within. Our cathedrals, basilicas, and churches are imposing structures, meant to impress and humble. The *Beis HaMikdash*, the Holy Temple, may not have been as awe-inspiring visually as the Pyramids, or the Hanging Gardens of Babylon, or even St. Peter's Basilica in Rome, but in it dwelt the Spirit of God.[14]

ᘯ

LET US REEXAMINE the words of Immanuel Kant, and his statement that "only an *educated public* which has existed uninterruptedly from its origin to our times can authenticate ancient history." When we place this concept within the proper context of the discontinuity of Greek history during the long centuries of the Middle Ages, a time when Greek history was forgotten among the *educated public* in Western Europe, we observe a flaw in Kant's logic and reason. Unlike the history of Greece, the history of Israel was kept uninterrupted not only by the Jews who were scattered throughout Europe and the Middle East, but with the non-Jewish Europeans themselves due to the inclusion of the "Old Testament" in the Christian Bible. Israel's history suffered no such interruption as did "Classical" Greek history. This clearly refutes Kant's idea that all history should "start out from Greek history" since there was a long span of time before Greek history and culture was reintroduced by way of Arabic scholars during the Renaissance.

We now turn our attention to the reasoning behind the Enlightenment version of history, of "which facts to give the floor, and in what order or context," particularly in the role Christian theology played in the retelling of historical events.

---

[13] "Yaphet...means 'beautiful' or 'attractive.' From that we get *Patai*, to be open to all external impressions, to let oneself be overwhelmed by them." Rabbi S. R. Hirsch, *Commentary on the Torah: Bereishis* Vol. I, (London: The Judaica Press, Inc., 1966), 137.

[14] "As to the temple which he built, and which the Jews believed to be the finest work of the universe, if the Bramantes, the Michelangelos, and the Palladios, had seen this building, they would not have admired it." Voltaire, *The Works of Voltaire: A Contemporary Version*, Vol. 7, 306.

All Roads Lead from Rome

The Jews were destined to be the eternal people of history, to wander the earth as the 'eternal Jew;' to stand at the cradle and grave of all nations; to undergo the evolutions and revolutions of history; to suffer in the catastrophes of nations. From the shipwreck of the past we were assigned the task of successfully savaging the eternal spiritual heritage of all of mankind. From the onset of history we were given stern notice: do not be dazzled by material might, no matter how brilliantly and meteorically it beckons on the historical firmament of nations. Do not tremble when sword-carrying nations subdue and brutalize the defenseless. Always be aware that the days of any power are numbered which fails to accept the certainty of the ultimate victory of man's spiritual and moral destiny.

— Rabbi Samson Raphael Hirsch[1]

T HE INFLUENCE OF CHRISTIANITY GOES FAR BEYOND COERCING Western academicians to date the historical events in Israel in accordance to Christian theology (such as the way we number the years; "BC" and "AD"—Before Christ and *Anno Domini*: "in the year of our lord"—which has to do with Christian interpretation and theology; few non-Jews understand that, according to the Jewish calendar, this is the year 5771, not 2011). Christianity influences how we look at history, its context, and the importance we give to certain events.

For an example of Christian influence, we will start with Edward Gibbon, whose *The Decline and Fall of the Roman Empire* (first published in the late eighteenth century) is considered to be one of the great histories ever penned. Gibbon stated that "a candid but rational inquiry into the progress and establishment of Christianity may be considered as an essential part of the history of the Roman empire."[2] Gibbon was vilified by many of his contemporaries for his criticism of Christianity, particularly in the role of the collapse of Rome. Gibbon's treatment of Christianity, however, was mild in comparison to his treatment of the Jews and Judaism. Even while being critical

---

[1] Hirsch, *Collected Writings,* Vol. II, 380.

[2] Edward Gibbon, *The Decline and Fall of the Roman Empire.* (New York: The Modern Library, 1995), 347.

about the role Christianity played in the decline of Rome, Gibbon describes Jews and Judaism from the perspective of Christian theology, using theological terminology and concepts, such as his comments on the early Jewish Church:

> Besides the general design of fixing on a perpetual basis the divine honours of Christ, the most ancient and respectable of the ecclesiastical writers have ascribed to the evangelic theologian a particular intention to confute two opposite heresies, which disturbed the peace of the primitive church. The faith of the Ebionites, perhaps of the Nazarenes, was gross and imperfect. They revered Jesus as the greatest of the prophets, endowed with supernatural virtue and power...but they obstinately rejected the preceding existence and divine perfections of the *Logos*, or Son of God, which are so clearly defined in the Gospel of St. John.[3]

From the Noahide perspective, there are several problems with Gibbon's statement. First of all, Gibbon pointed out the theology of the Ebionites and the Nazarenes was heretical. The Ebionites were in fact *the* "primitive church," the original church which all later Christian sects were directly descended from, the first and original Jewish Church that was based in Jerusalem, the church led by James and Peter. Gibbon himself pointed out the Jewish ties to the original Jewish church: "The Ebionites, or at least the Nazarenes, were distinguished only by their obstinate perseverance in the practice of the Mosaic rites...the insufficient creed of the Nazarenes and the Ebionites."[4] The original "Jewish" church's creed was "insufficient" because it did not contain the elements that were later developed by the Hellenistic Pauline sects, such as the "trinity," the "virgin birth," and the "incarnation." This is what made the Ebionites and Nazarenes "gross and imperfect:" they did not agree with the theology of the later-developed Catholic Church.

Gibbon ridicules the Ebionites and Nazarenes for "obstinately [rejecting] the preceding existence and divine perfections of the *Logos*, or Son of God, which are so clearly defined in the Gospel of St. John." According to the early church fathers, these early Jewish sects used a Hebrew manuscript of Matthew. Matthew, of course, is the most "Jewish" of the four gospels of the New Testament, and if these early Jewish Christians had a Hebrew version, there is good reason to believe that it was the original version. Why would the Jewish Christians, in

---

[3] Ibid., 594–95.

[4] Ibid., 1553.

possession of the original Matthew with its teachings in Jesus' native tongue, cast it aside for the later-written, more Gnostic-flavored Greek version of John? Gibbon could be excused in that he wrote his history in the late eighteenth century, when biblical textual criticism was in its infancy, and that he did not have the benefit of modern scholarship on the early Greek manuscripts of the New Testament.

But modern scholarship has done little to change the mainstream perception of Gibbon's point of view. There was a pattern that developed among historians; they choose the facts that suited their view of Judaism, the view of the Church, the viewpoint of Western Greco/Roman civilization. "The Jews are a peculiar phenomenon in world-history only so long as we insist on treating them as such"[5] wrote Oswald Spengler in his book *The Decline of the West*. Spengler, a product of the German historical school in the early 20th century, describes the task of the Western Historian in an attempt to prove that the Jewish people were really not all that special; their miraculous survival throughout the ages was simply an historical fluke. To portray the Jewish people as simply another group of people whose longevity was an oddity relegated to the status of an historical footnote was integral to a methodological system of denial that was applicable to the academic disciplines. This can be seen in Gibbon's incisive disdain of the Jews which pervaded his historical point of view:

> A single people refused to join in the common intercourse of mankind. The Jews, who, under the Assyrian and Persian monarchies, had languished for many ages the most despised portion of their slaves, emerged from obscurity under the successors of Alexander...the sullen obstinacy with which they maintained their peculiar rites and unsocial manners seemed to mark them out a distinct species of men, who boldly professed, or who faintly disguised, their implacable hatred to the rest of human kind. Neither the violence of Antiochus, nor the arts of Herod, nor the example of the circumjacent nations, could ever persuade the Jews to associate with the institutions of Moses the elegant mythology of the Greeks.[6]

This was the great affront to the Greeks and the Romans, that the Jews had so little respect for the culture and civilization which the

---

[5] Spengler, *The Decline of the West*, 205.

[6] Gibbon, *The Decline and Fall of the Roman Empire*, 348–49.

classical world thought superior, and that they stubbornly held onto their own "institutions of Moses." It did not occur to Gibbon (or the Greeks) that it was this very separation of the Jews from the nations of the world that enabled them to preserve these "institutions of Moses," or why the Jews thought that their Torah-based culture was superior to the "elegant mythology of the Greeks." Of course, from the Noahide perspective, Gibbon was looking through the wrong end of the telescope; it was mankind that refused to join the common intercourse of Israel, the "kingdom of priests and a holy nation," the keepers and teachers of the Torah. Most of the great body of rabbinic commentaries on the Torah are unknown to the non-Jew since they have been ignored by Western scholars for most of the past two thousand years. Christianity has only looked at the "superficial" themes of the Torah, such as the creation of the world, the fall of man, the flood, and the lives of the patriarchs. In fact, since the Enlightenment, the prevailing view among scholars of Biblical history, especially of Genesis, is that the Bible was looked upon as a series of fables and myths,[7] more suitable for bedtime stories for children than for serious historical scholars. Although many blame the heretic Jewish philosopher Baruch Spinoza[8] for first criticizing the authenticity of the Torah, his view was hardly original; in the second century CE, the Roman writer Celsus said that Genesis was a collection of ancient fables and myths, similar to what the Hellenized Jew Philo hinted at two hundred years earlier. Their criticisms were not unknown to the rabbis, who responded in depth, but the rabbis and their explanations to the problems with the text were ignored. Take, for example, the Jewish view that Rome was an extension of Edom, a view which was known to Gibbon:

---

[7] "Tales of a world-destroying flood are one of the most widespread and continuously evolving categories of stories in the world, and probably the most exhaustively studied by scholars over the centuries. The most thorough collections of such tales have described more than 300 examples drawn from every continent. Western studies of the flood across the centuries were dominated by the biblical tale of Noah, although versions of the myth were also known from ancient Greece and Rome." Mark Edward Lewis, *The Flood Myths of Early China*. (Albany: State University of New York Press, 2006), 4.

[8] "No one who has mastered, or at least has worked with the few who have mastered, the logical controls and hermeneutical rules of the Talmud, without which the Written Torah, long trifled with by outsiders, remains a closed book. No mere philosopher, Spinoza included, has entered this exclusive domain." Eidelberg, *Beyond the Secular Mind*, 53.

Their [the Jews] irreconcilable hatred of mankind, instead of flaming out in acts of blood and violence, evaporated in less dangerous gratifications. They embraced every opportunity of over-reaching the idolaters in trade; and they pronounced secret and ambiguous imprecations against the haughty kingdom of Edom [According to the false Josephus, Tsepho, the grandson of Esau, conducted into Italy the enemy of Æneas, king of Carthage. Another colony of Idumæans, flying from the sword of David, took refuge in the dominions of Romulus. For these, or for other reasons of equal weight, the name of Edom was applied by the Jews to the Roman empire].[9]

From the Jewish point of view, it was not simply that the descendants of Esau founded Rome. The Edomite spirit, the spirit of violence and war, permeated Roman culture. Along with this tendency for violence, to rule others by strength, Rome also inherited Esau's hatred for his brother Jacob. Along with adapting much of the Greek culture, Rome also adopted the Greek penchant for anti-Semitism. In the fourth century, when Christianity became the official religion of the Roman Empire, the theological hatred that Christianity had for the Jews fused with the deeper hatred of Esau. This is the theme that Maurice Samuel wrote about in his book *You Gentiles*, the difference between the focus of the implacable evil of Esau and the spirituality of Jacob.

ℴ

OTHER HISTORIANS FOLLOWED Gibbon's example, and described the Jews as a historical "fossil," a prehistoric and peculiar people pickled and preserved by their unswerving loyalty to archaic laws and customs that Jesus had graciously nullified, a religion whose only useful contribution to society—the preamble to the New Testament—had been made over two thousand years ago. There is no better example of this teaching than in the works of Arthur Toynbee, in his day a well-known British historian whose popularity has waned in recent decades. Toynbee viewed Judaism as an archaic leftover from bygone and primitive religions, that "Judaism is a fossil of the extinct Syriac Civilization."[10] This labeling of the Jews as being a "Syriac Civilization" was no doubt influenced by Voltaire, who said that "the Jews, who spoke a jargon half Phœnician and half Syriac, rhymed; therefore the great and powerful

---

[9] Gibbon, *The Decline and Fall of the Roman Empire*, 404.

[10] Arnold J. Toynbee, *A Study of History*, Vol. 2, 402.

nations, under whom they were in slavery, rhymed also. We cannot help believing, that the Jews—who, as we have frequently observed, adopted almost everything from their neighbors—adopted from them also rhyme."[11] The message here was that the Jews were unoriginal; they freely borrowed (or stole) from their neighbors ideas and literary devices; even their language was not their own. It is rare indeed that you see historians belittle the Greeks for stealing the alphabet and literary devices from the Phoenicians, but to belittle the Jews was a common occurrence.

Although arguably not as influential as Oswald Spengler in that Spengler published his work first, Toynbee's popularity during the middle of the 20th century wielded great influence in popular culture. Borrowing on Spengler's theme of cyclic civilizations:

> Toynbee's great work is written to illustrate the thesis that civilisations [*sic*] are born, grow, decay, and finally pass away. The process is there for all to see. But it may be interpreted differently, for a civilisation may be always dying yet always being reborn. For example, the old Graeco-Roman world, which 'died' and was succeeded by Western civilisation, may be viewed as slowly passing into the later phase, for most of our characteristic ideas and institutions have their roots in it. The Renascence (of ancient Mediterranean civilisation) is enough to prove this, and Western languages, politics, architecture, etc., all go back to Greece and Rome.[12]

Toynbee labeled Judaism as a "fossil," a religion clinging to its archaic and "fulfilled" Laws of Moses and not tossing them aside for Christianity, a cultural relic that had outlived its usefulness when Christianity arrived. Toynbee does not simply echo the Greek distaste for anything Hebrew; there are distinct theological motifs within his work.

Toynbee's attitude towards Judaism was not lost on Jewish scholars. Maurice Samuel wrote a critique of Toynbee's history during the height of Toynbee's popularity, criticizing Toynbee's attitude towards Jews and Judaism:

> When we collate the numerous and often repetitious passages on the Jews in *A Study of History* we discover, behind the arabesques of erudition, three familiar and rather shopworn ideas: 1. That there has been only one episode of value in Jewish history, the Prophetic;

---

[11] Voltaire, *The Works of Voltaire: A Contemporary Version,* Vol.7, 89.

[12] W. K. Lowther Clarke. *Concise Bible Commentary.* (London: SPCK, 1952), 303.

2. That the spiritually fatal mistake of the Jews was their rejection of Christianity; 3. That it was by this rejection that they condemned themselves to everlasting sterility.[13]

These themes were consistent with the common academic view of Judaism, not only for Toynbee and other historians and philosophers, but also sociologists, economists, and political scientists. Any Jewish criticism of these themes was ignored by non-Jewish scholars due to the anti-Jewish bias in secular academics.

For another example, here Toynbee describes one of the passages in the Tanach:

> Yet in these barren land-locked highlands, which were not of sufficient worldly importance to acquire even a recognized name of their own, there was immanent (to paraphrase Plato's language) a divine inspiration which made this uninviting country a means of grace to those who came to settle there. A Syriac fable tells how this divinity once tested a king of Israel with the most searching test that a God can apply to a mortal. 'The Lord appeared to Solomon in a dream by night; and God said: 'Ask what I shall give thee...' This fable of Solomon's Choice is a parable of the history of the Chosen People.[14]

Toynbee presents the Western secular view that many of the stories in the Tanach were little more than a collection of myths, and yet he views Jesus walking on water and raising the dead as viable historical events, such as Toynbee's treatment of a story in the Gospels:

> At that crucial moment, "when they which were about him saw what would follow, and they said unto him: 'lord, shall we smite with the sword?' And one of them smote the servant of the High Priest and cut off his right ear. And Jesus answered and said: 'Suffer ye thus far.' And he touched his ear and healed him."[15]

Toynbee labels Solomon's dream a "Syriac fable" and then gives historical credence to Jesus miraculously healing the ear of a servant of the High Priest, following the pattern by other scholars such as Gibbon and Wellhausen—stories in the *Tanach* are "fables" while the stories in the New Testament are historically authentic. This is also a continuing pattern among many Western academicians, to dismiss the *Tanach* as

---

[13] Maurice Samuel, *The Professor and the Fossil*. (New York: Alfred A. Knopf, 1956), 73.

[14] Toynbee, *A Study of History*, Vol. 2, 54–55.

[15] Ibid., Vol. 5, 73.

"fables" or "myths" and treat the events recorded in the New Testament as genuine, authentic, or at least unquestioned. Of course, there are also many secular academics that treat the stories of the New Testament as fables, but they lump them together with the stories in the "Old Testament," criticizing the Christian Bible as a whole.

Toynbee's haughtiness towards Judaism is apparent with many other comments such as "the most notorious historical example of this idolization of an ephemeral self[16] is the error of the Jews which is exposed in the New Testament,"[17] and that:

> In the drama of the New Testament a Christ whose epiphany on Earth in the person of Jesus is, in Christian belief, the true fulfillment of Jewry's long cherished Messianic Hope, is nevertheless rejected by a school of Scribes and Pharisees which, only a few generations back, has come to the front by taking the lead in a heroic Jewish revolt against the triumphal progress of Hellenization. The insight and the uprightness that have brought the Scribes and Pharisees to the fore in that previous crisis of Jewish history desert them now in a crisis of greater import for the destinies of Jewry and of Mankind.[18]

This brazen display of theology goes unnoticed by the Christian as well as the atheist or agnostic reader who was reared in a predominately Christian culture. The idea that "insight and uprightness" deserted the *Tannaim* is a slur not only on rabbinic interpretation, but on Jewish ethics and morals. This sort of subjectivity violates the rule that the historians themselves have made about the search for "objective truth" in history, teaching that "the objective historian's role is that of a neutral, or disinterested, judge; it must never degenerate into that of advocate or, even worse, propagandist."[19] Toynbee, however, was both advocate and propagandist for Christianity. Toynbee remarked that:

> The Israelites continued to live in obscurity until the Syriac Civilization had passed its zenith. As late as the fifth century before Christ, at a date when all the great prophets of Israel had already said their say,

---

[16] "Ignoring all the evidence in Scripture, the British sociologist and historian Arnold Toynbee (who in general regarded the Jews as a curious historical 'fossil') went so far as to denounce the 'idolization of an ephemeral self.'" Gabriel Sivan, *The Bible and Civilization*, (New York: Quadrangle/The New York Times Book Co., 1973),16.

[17] Toynbee, *A Study of History*, Vol. 5, 310.

[18] Ibid., Vol. 4, 246.

[19] Novick, *That Noble Dream*, 2.

the name of Israel was still unknown to the great Greek historian Herodotus and the Land of Israel was still masked by the Land of the Philistines in the Herodotean panorama of the Syriac World. When Herodotus wishes to designate the peoples of Syria as a whole, he calls them 'the Phoenicians and the Syrians in the Land of the Philistines'— Filastin or Palestine—is the name by which Erez Israel has continued to be known among the Gentiles down to this day.[20]

Again, this suggests similar views of Kant, Smith, and Spengler who view the historical impact of Judaism as having little significance except for the usurpation of the *Tanach* which was translated into Greek and added to the Christian Bible. To presume that Herodotus was granted the power to name people and lands fits in with Spengler's comment that "the Jews are a peculiar phenomenon in world-history only so long as we insist on treating them as such."[21] As long as Western Scholars call the land of Israel "Palestine," the Jewish people "a fossilized relic," and Judaism as having "no connection with classical learning," the Jews can be dismissed by treating them as such. As long as we give greater validity to Greek viewpoints, we can ignore the Jewish view. As long as we portray the Greek view as "secular, scientific, and objective" can we label the Jewish viewpoint as religious, mythological, and subjective. As Samuel pointed out, the pattern in Western social sciences has been one of theological subjectivity. As the West developed the social sciences in the late eighteenth and early nineteenth century, the higher academics were taught in seminaries. "The founding fathers of colonial education saw no difference between the basic education appropriate for a cleric and that appropriate for any other liberally educated man."[22] As the schools became increasingly secular, the theology remained—imperceptibly at times, but it remained.

Another literary historian, Gilbert Highet, a graduate from St. John's at Oxford who became professor of Latin and Latin literature at Columbia in the mid-twentieth century, explained the link between ancient Greece, Rome, and modern Western Civilization, and observed that "our modern world is in many ways a continuation of the world of Greece and Rome. Not in all ways—particularly not in

---

[20] Toynbee, *A Study of History*, Vol. 2, 54.

[21] Spengler, *The Decline of the West*, 205.

[22] Hofstadter, *Anti-Intellectualism in American Life*, 60.

medicine, music, industry, and applied science. But in most of our intellectual and spiritual activities we are the grandsons of the Romans, and the great-grandsons of the Greeks."[23] The "classical" education that was developed in Western Europe during the Enlightenment, not to mention the Christian connection, was the foundation of our modern culture, although Christianity (the Puritan strain of Protestantism in particular) arguably had a greater influence on modern American culture than it did in Europe. Both secularism,[24] as developed by philosophers in the seventeenth and eighteenth centuries, and the theology of the Church came from the same Greco-Roman source, and "classical literature, myth, art, and thought helped to produce the intellectual unity of Europe and the two Americas."[25] It was this foundation of Western culture, the culture of Greece and Rome, which was acutely anti-Semitic, and this has had considerable impact on both the secular intellectual community as well as the religious community. Highet's comment that "the example of Greco-Roman morality (particularly Stoicism)…to use classical literature and fine art as a moral restraint was well judged"[26] sums up the attitude of the intellectual Americans and Europeans. After all, what higher morality was there than the morality of the founders of Western Civilization, the Greeks?[27] For the Church, morality came from their Hellenized Greek New Testament, and the secular West based its morality on Greek philosophy and thought. They were two different branches of the same tree, two

---

[23] Gilbert Highet, *The Classical Tradition*. (New York: Oxford University Press, 1957), 1.

[24] "In the course of the history of Liberalism, the standard of justice became secularized. People no longer talked about God's Law, but about natural rights and the common good. But the secularization of the standard of justice does not alter the fact that when there is such a standard independent of individual belief the possibility of error appears." C. Dyke, "Collective Decision Making in Rousseau, Kant, Hegel, and Mill." *Ethics*, Vol. 80, No. 1, (Oct., 1969), 22.

[25] Highet, *The Classical Tradition*, 291–92.

[26] Ibid. 292.

[27] "The crucial distinction of modern Europe is the achievement of a way of life in which reason is recognized as supreme, in two forms: first, reason is now admitted to constitute the human essence, rather, than, say, faith or certain kinds of origins or natural qualities; secondly, no principle will be finally recognized in the modern state as the basis for politics and law other than that deriving from the concept of man as ultimately guided by a rational will." Donald J. Maletz, "History in Hegel's 'Philosophy of Right.'" *The Review of Politics*. Vol. 45, No. 2 (Apr., 1983), 227.

streams from the same source, two children from the same family, and they both looked askance at the morality of the Torah and its standard bearers, the Jews. Jewish morality has always had a corroding influence on the hedonistic Greek culture, since having a moral basis not founded upon the Torah was certainly recognized as a liability by Jewish scholars.[28]

It is hard to imagine how one could think that the secular attitudes towards the Jews could not help but be influenced by the ancient Greek and Roman anti-Semitism, attitudes such as: "It was about the same time that a committee of seventy-two rabbis was translating certain books of the Hebrew scriptures into Greek for the use of the Jews scattered beyond Palestine, who were forgetting Hebrew and Aramaic; but that version was not made for artistic purposes, and was not such a great milestone in the history of education."[29] If you add this sentiment to that of Adam Smith, "The Hebrew language having no connection with classical learning, and, except the holy scriptures, being the language of not a single book in any esteem," it appears the only contribution the Jews made to Western Culture was, according to Western Historians, limited to the development of a proto-Christian religion. The task of the objective historian was to gather the facts and tell the truth, and too many of the historians and sociologists believed the theological "truth" that Judaism[30] was a developed religion, and that Jesus was the "divine messiah."

---

[28] "The experience of the present epoch of history has shown that humanism without a religious basis—i.e., a humanism which denies that man was created in the image and likeness of God, will in the end destroy itself. Far from affirming man's self-confidence and creative power and thus elevating man, an irreligious humanism is bound to debase man by ceasing to read him as a being of a higher and Divine origin. Worldly humanism must in the end become not only anti-religious but anti-human. This remarkable phenomenon, which the Russian philosopher Berdyaev has called 'the self-destructive dialectic within humanism,' was clearly foreseen by Israel's Sages thousands of years ago when they uttered a warning against any attempt to base law and morality on anything else but a religious foundation." Dayan Dr. I. Grunfeld, intro. to *Horeb*, lxi.

[29] Highet, *The Classical Tradition*, 104–05.

[30] "Let us learn from our great teachers of Torah—among whom the *Ramban* certainly is one of the most outstanding—that we must never attempt to whitewash the spiritual and moral heroes of our past. They do not need our apologetics, nor would they tolerate such attempts on our part. *Emes*, truth, is the seal of our Torah, and truthfulness is the guiding principle of the Torah's great teachers and commentators." Hirsch, *Sefer Bereishis*, Daniel Haberman trans., 307.

A Foolish Consistency

The great political ideologies of the twentieth century include liberalism, socialism, anarchism, corporatism, Marxism, communism, social democracy, conservatism, nationalism, fascism, and Christian democracy. They all share one thing in common: they are products of Western civilization. No other civilization has generated a significant political ideology. The West, however, has never generated a major religion. The great religions of the world are all products of non-Western civilizations and, in most cases, antedate Western Civilization. As the world moves out of its Western phase, the ideologies which typified late Western civilization decline, and their place is taken by religions and other culturally based forms of identity and commitment. The Westphalian separation of religion and international politics, an idiosyncratic product of Western civilization, is coming to an end, and religion, as Edward Mortimer suggests, is 'increasingly likely to intrude into international affairs.' The intracivilizational clash of political ideas spawned by the West is being supplanted by an intercivilizational clash of culture and religion.

— Samuel P. Huntington[1]

POLITICAL SCIENTIST SAMUEL P. HUNTINGTON, IN HIS BESTSELLING book *The Clash of Civilizations*, argued that religion was a key component in his eight defined major civilizations.[2] Huntington points out that the secularized Greek/Roman legal system has dominated twentieth-century culture, while Eastern and Middle-Eastern religions have dominated world culture. Yet Huntington's view of Israel follows the typical Enlightenment pattern:

> What about Jewish civilization? Most scholars of civilization hardly mention it. In terms of numbers of people Judaism clearly is not a major civilization. Toynbee describes it as an arrested civilization which evolved out of the earlier Syriac civilization. It is historically affiliated with both Christianity and Islam, and for several centuries Jews maintained their cultural identity within Western, Orthodox, and Islamic civilizations.[3]

---

[1] Samuel P. Huntington. *The Clash of Civilizations and the Remaking of World Order*. (New York: Simon & Schuster Paperbacks, 1996), 54.

[2] "The central elements of any culture or civilization are language and religion." Ibid., 59.

[3] Ibid., 48.

This point of view was similar to Kant's view that "only an *educated public* which has existed uninterruptedly from its origin to our times can authenticate ancient history." Here we ask another question: exactly what was an *educated public*? To Kant, an *educated public* meant a public that had been educated in Greek and Roman culture and indoctrinated in Christian theology. This has had a profound impact on our view of history, both in the way it has been dated and the way it was interpreted. A people educated in Talmud and Torah, who have studied the *Mishna* and the *Gemara*, and the codes of Maimonides and Rabbi Yosef Caro, these people were, according to Western scholars, not part of an "educated public" because, to the Western mind, rabbinic Judaism and the Hebrew language were of little educational value. There was a reason that Jewish scholarship has not been "such a great milestone in the history of education;" it was deliberately excluded, and that "the history of Talmudic Judaism, since Hebrew philology became bound up in one specialism with Old Testament research, not only never obtained separate treatment, but has been *completely forgotten* by all the major histories of religions."[4]

☙

THUCYDIDES WROTE *The History of the Peloponnesian War* during the middle of the fifth century BCE. Yet most of the *Tanach* was written long before that: the Torah (the Five Books of Moses), the *Naviim,* and the *Chetuvim*. Ancient Greece had a tremendous impact on history, but was it truly greater than Israel's impact? When Adam Smith said that there was nothing written in Hebrew "of any esteem" other than the "Holy Scriptures," one wonders how he can ignore works such as the *Mishna* or the *Gemara*. What books of "esteem" did the Greeks produce in the early centuries before the Common Era that could rival the Talmud? Kant said that "only an *educated public* which has existed uninterruptedly from its origin to our times can authenticate ancient history." Yet what ancient people were more educated than the Jews, and what determining factor was there in what is considered "authenticated" history? Why are the Jews, who were spread out among the civilized nations of the Middle East, considered "isolated?" Why would Jewish reports be met with less belief than the Greek reports? Are the stories in Genesis and Exodus less believable than the stories of gods,

---

[4] Spengler, *The Decline of the West*, Vol. 2, 191.

magic, and monsters found in the *Iliad* and the *Odyssey*? Why would Jewish histories only be taken seriously after they were translated in the Greek Septuagint? How can one dismiss the Talmud, the *Midrash*, the writings of *Rashi*, Nachmanides, S. R. Hirsch, and countless others? To ignore the influence of the Jewish people, a people that have been involved in the history and culture of the West from the dawn of Western Civilization does not seem logical. Yet logic did not play a part in this attempt to belittle the learning and knowledge of a people that have done so much to shape the history of the world. The Greek language has no intrinsic superiority over Hebrew, nor do Greek ethics have any predominance over Jewish ethics; the reasons for the Greek derision towards anything Jewish have more to do with theology than reason or historical truth. Systems of Christian theology and Christian thought directly affect our view of history, and, to the untrained eye, often in subtle and imperceptible ways.[5]

The Jews also wrote about their history; in fact, they wrote about it long before the Greeks wrote about theirs, a fact not lost on some historians such as Mark T. Gilderhus:

> The Jews of ancient Israel developed a very different outlook. For them, history became more important than for any other ancient people...Hebrew historical writing was more the product of religious experience and faith than a manifestation of critical or rational inquiry. The Jews interpreted the events in the lives of their people according to intense convictions. Bias and inconsistency, to be sure, crept into their narratives. For example, Jewish writers sometimes incorporated different versions of the same events from diverse oral traditions. Nevertheless, they also displayed a capacity for hard-headed objectivity.[6]

Even when damning the Jews with faint praise, Gilderhus wrote in glowing prose that "the Greeks contributed something of immense significance in the development of historical thought: they invented critical history as a method of sorting out the true from the false... In the fifth century B.C., two geniuses, Herodotus and Thucydides,

---

[5] "The European Greeks who allowed themselves to feel superior to the Asiatic Greek contemporaries in the fifth century BC [*sic*] were at any rate free from that fanatical Judaic hallucination of being a 'chosen people.'" Toynbee, *A Study of History*, Vol. 8, 729.

[6] Mark T. Gilderhus, *History and Historians: A Historiographical Introduction.* (Upper Saddle River, New Jersey: Prentice Hall, 2003), 14.

brought about an intellectual revolution by employing rational techniques and creating the writing of history."[7] From the Torah perspective, we must question how "rational" the techniques of Thucydides
were. Thucydides, as did Herodotus, focused on warfare. The Greeks
gloried and reveled in warfare, as did most non-Jewish cultures,[8] but
the Greeks brought the love of war to a new art form. To the Jews,
war was a too-often necessary but dirty business, like having to take
out the garbage. To the Greeks, war provided the ultimate display
of their values of "honor," "strength," and "courage." Thucydides'
History of the Peloponnesian War was written in 431 BCE, long after
the *Tanach* had been written, and it detailed the war between Athens
and Sparta. Gilderhus states that "Thucydides, more than Herodotus, explained events in secular terms."[9] Gilderhus also pointed out
Thucydides "had historical figures deliver speeches in which they revealed their aims and intentions. Critics have attacked the use of such
monologues as false."[10] Yet when comparing the Jewish accounts,
"Hebrew historical writing was more the product of religious experience and faith than a manifestation of critical or rational inquiry," and
that "Jews interpreted the events in the lives of their people according
to intense [religious] convictions," Gilderhus implies that the history
written by the Jews, with their "bias and inconsistencies" that "crept
into their narratives" is somehow less honest than the "secular" Greek
history written by Thucydides, even though he invented long fictional
monologues as a narrative device.

This leads to yet another question—exactly what constitutes objective and critical historical writing? Why is separating the "secular" from the "religious" important to understand history? One of
the theological devices was to separate the fleshy from the spiritual,
the sacred from the profane. There is no division of "sacred" and

---

[7] Ibid., 15.

[8] "When you gentiles assert that you abhor war, you deceive yourselves...you hang out
your most gorgeous banners, you play merry music, your blood runs swiftly, happily,
your cheeks brighten and your eyes sparkle...it is not love of country which induces
this flood of happiness—it is combat, the glory of sport, the game, the magnificence
of the greatest of all contests." Samuel, *You Gentiles*, 53–54.

[9] Gilderhus, *History and Historians*, 17.

[10] Ibid., 17.

"profane" in Judaism.[11] Thucydides did not write from a religious perspective, for the religion of ancient Greece was replete with human-like gods and goddesses full of human emotional faults such as lust and envy, seducing and consorting with mortals—but he did write from a distinctly cultural perspective. Unlike the Jews, the Greeks glorified war and sports,[12] and this was reflected in their writings. Should not the glorification of war and sports be a factor in objectivity? Certainly the Jews thought so.

As mentioned above, the Torah is not a history book (as we define the term) because often the events described do not follow in a chronological order; for instance, the events in Genesis chapter fifteen occurred before the events mentioned in chapter twelve. Many events in the lives of the Patriarchs, for instance, are left out, and many seemingly unimportant details are discussed. What is important is not the exact chronological order, but the interpretation and lessons of history. To the non-observant, the subject of Noah and the ark usually conjures up images of popular children's books, cartoons, and animated features of a grandfatherly old man and his big boat full of warm, fuzzy critters. Few Gentiles have paid heed to the events that came after Noah and his family left the ark, and even fewer understood the importance of the covenant that God made with Noah. Yet the story of Noah takes up a full four chapters in Genesis. Since every word—indeed every letter—of the Hebrew Torah is important, having the Torah take up four chapters on one individual gives a hint as to his importance. After all, there was only one chapter that dealt with Lot, and he was the ancestor of the line of David and the kings of Israel as well as the future Messiah.

---

[11] "We [Jews] cannot conceive of a duality—religion and life, the sacred and the secular." Samuel, *You Gentiles*, 72.

[12] This love of sports by the Greeks continues to have a direct influence on Western culture. "Observers of American academia have often asked with some bitterness why athletic distinction is almost universally admired and encouraged whereas intellectual distinction is resented. I think the resentment is in fact a kind of back-handed tribute democracy pays to the importance of intellect in our affairs. Athletic skill is recognized as being transient, special, and for most of us unimportant in the serious business of life; and the tribute given the athlete is considered to be earned because he entertains. Intellect, on the other hand, is neither entertaining (to most men) nor innocent; since everyone sees that it can be an important and permanent advantage in life, it creates against itself a kind of universal fraternity of commonplace minds." Hofstadter, *Anti-Intellectualism in American Life*, 50–51.

There is also the problem with labels and with categorizing writing as "historical" or "religious" (it is also illuminating that Gilderhus uses "B.C."—the Christian term "Before Christ"—to date the era of his subject). To look at Greek history as being "critical history... sorting out true from the false" implies that Jewish history does not observe this distinction, for, according to the secular academics, Jews interwove "mythological" stories and accounts into their history, such as the story of Noah. The account of Noah and the flood[13] became a children's bedtime story, and the teachings of Noah regarding the Torah had been forgotten by the non-Jews during the long centuries of the Greek and Roman Empires. From the Noahide perspective, the Greeks had no Divine revelation as did the Jews. Their historical writings lacked this important element. For the Jews to ignore or be unaffected by their unique relationship with God is unrealistic; for the Jews, the Torah is the stamp of truth. The Church—and the West, breaking away from Jewish tradition—instead viewed past events from a Greek/Gnostic perspective. Christian religious elements and viewpoints crept into "secular" history, as we have seen in Gibbon and Toynbee, and these are ignored or overlooked. The message is: Christian religious viewpoints in "secular" history are permitted, but Jewish "religious" viewpoints are not.

The viewpoint of Enlightenment scholars such as Adam Smith and Immanuel Kant—that the only relevant literature that the Jews produced was the Hebrew Scriptures of the "Old Testament," and that the Hebrew "Old Testament" only became relevant when it was translated into Greek—was the Western teaching that the *Tanach* was only as important as its relevance to the Greek Bible of Christianity. The Hebrew Scriptures were merely a preamble to the Gospels, a foundation of the prophecies of Christ, and a backdrop to the Epistles of Paul. The Hebrew Scriptures are explained with theological terms and ideas, such as Irving M. Zeitlin's comment that "Paul's conception of Jesus as the sacrificial lamb whose death was expiatory is also distinctively Jewish: the Messiah was crucified and died of his own free will in order to atone by his blood for the sins of this world...in the Israelite sacrificial

---

[13] "Similar traditions are found in the Sumerian legend concerning Ziusudra. Other cultures that have a flood tradition, include India (Manu legend), China (Da Yu), Eskimo, and in the Western Hemisphere, American Indians (Iroquois), and Mexico (Maya— 'Creation')." Levi, *Torah and Science*, 176.

cult, the blood of the expiatory victim symbolizes life—a life offered to God as a substitute for another."[14] From the Noahide perspective, Zeitlin's idea of a "distinctively Jewish Messiah" was nothing of the sort; what Zeitlin describes was the theological Christian messiah. There is nothing Jewish about a human sacrifice atoning for the "sins of the world;" this was a Christian theological concept, not a Jewish one. The differences between Jewish and non-Jewish concepts were too often lost on secular historians. To give an example of Jewish thought, we turn once again to Rabbi S. R. Hirsch:

> When Scripture discusses the offerings, God does not characterize Himself as *Elokim*, for there He does not wish to be conceived in terms of the retributive, inexorable quality of His justice, as a deity that takes pleasure in sacrifices, one that, according to blasphemous pagan delusion, is a God of vengeance, accepting an animal's death struggle as a substitute for a forfeited human life. In the context of the offerings, He would rather be viewed as *HASHEM*, the loving God... the designation *HASHEM*, which is used in Scripture only in connection with offerings that are made to God by Jews, demolishes all the drivel of the scorners of the Law who would equate the majesty of the Jewish laws pertaining to offerings with a 'bloody sacrificial cult,' with the intention of dragging down what they call 'Mosaic' Judaism from the eternal lofty spheres of its Divine truth to the baseness of a long-outworn heathen notion.[15]

Yet Zeitlin's view was the norm in both secular and religious scholarship; this was the interpretation non-Jews had of the concept of "sacrifices," and the rabbinic interpretation was habitually ignored. This view was also consistent with the British historian Edward Gibbon, who wrote two centuries before Zeitlin:

> Christianity offered itself to the world, armed with the strength of the Mosaic law, and delivered from the weight of its fetters... the divine authority of Moses and the prophets was admitted, and even established, as the firmest basis of Christianity. From the beginning of the world, an uninterrupted series of predictions had announced and prepared the long expected coming of the Messiah, who, in compliance with the gross apprehensions of the Jews, had been more frequently represented under the character of a King and Conqueror, than under that of a Prophet, a Martyr, and the son of

---

[14] Irving M. Zeitlin, *Jesus and the Judaism of His Time*. (Cambridge: Polity Press, 1988), 177.

[15] Hirsch, *T'rumath Tzvi*, 372.

God. By this expiatory sacrifice, the imperfect sacrifices of the temple were at once consummated and abolished. The ceremonial law, which consisted only of types and figures, was succeeded by a pure and spiritual worship, equally adapted to all climates...the promise of divine favour, instead of being partially confined to the posterity of Abraham, was universally proposed to the freedman and the slave, to the Greek and to the barbarian, to the Jew and to the Gentile.[16]

Here we see Gibbon using theological language and the New Testament to describe and define historical events. He describes Christianity delivering mankind from "the weight of its [Jewish] fetters." This is a clear theological reference to Acts 15:10, when Peter whined to the council in Jerusalem: "Now therefore why do you tempt God, to put a yoke upon the neck of the disciples, which neither our fathers nor we were able to bear?" This verse has traditionally been used by Christians to "prove" that the 613 commandments of the Torah are not able to be kept by anyone, even the most scrupulously pious Jews.[17] Gibbon does not mention the Jewish view that mankind was not under the Jewish Laws of the Torah, but under the relatively simple and universal Seven Laws of Noah, a fact that Hebraists such as John Selden wrote about over a century before Gibbon. As far as the "gross apprehensions of the Jews" and their view of the Messiah, Gibbon again looks at Judaism from the perspective of a Christian theologian. The reason the Jews looked at the Messiah as a "King and Conqueror" was because that is exactly how the *Tanach* describes him. It was also from the view of Christian theology that the Jewish sacrifices were "imperfect," and that the sacrifice of Jesus was "expiatory." If the job of the historian is to separate myth from fact, then why are they seemingly unable to do it regarding religion? Zeitlin had two hundred years of scholarship on Gibbon, as well as access to many modern English translations of rabbinic commentary (such as the writings of Rabbi S. R. Hirsch), yet he failed to make use of rabbinic Jewish sources (with the exceptions of a few comments from assimilationist Jews such as

---

[16] Gibbon, *The Decline and Fall of the Roman Empire*, 351.

[17] Christian theology has traditionally taught that only Jesus was able to keep the entire Torah "perfectly." This view is refuted by the Jews who have kept the Torah from ancient times down to the present, and even the New Testament itself refutes this teaching (Luke 1:5–6). Keeping the entire Torah "perfectly" is absurd when you think about it; Jesus would have had to have kept the laws of the Kohanim, the laws of women's menstrual cycles, laws of wages and hiring, and many others that did not apply to him.

Heinrich Graetz, Leo Baeck, and Jacob Neusner) in his work on *Jesus and the Judaism of His Time*, preferring to have his Judaism distilled through theologians such as Joseph Bonsirven, W. D. Davies, and Jacob Jocz. To the secular academic, rabbinic writings are simply not "trustworthy" since they lack "objectivity."

In another example of Gibbon's bias, he wrote that:

> From the reign of Nero to that of Antonius Pius, the Jews discovered a fierce impatience of the dominion of Rome, which repeatedly broke out in the most furious massacres and insurrections. Humanity is shocked at the recital of the horrid cruelties which they committed in the cities of Egypt, of Cyprus, and of Cyrene, where they dwelt in treacherous friendship with the unsuspecting natives (In Cyrene they massacred 220,000 Greeks; in Cyprus, 240,000; in Egypt, a very great multitude. Many of these unhappy victims were sawed asunder, according to a precedent to which David had given the sanction of his example. The victorious Jews devoured the flesh, licked up the blood, and twisted the entrails like a girdle round their bodies.[18]

A generation after the destruction of Jerusalem in 70 CE, Trajan decided to follow Alexander the Great and invade the Middle East and possibly India. As the Roman legions marched into Mesopotamia, the Jewish people living in Parthia rebelled. Although many of these Jews did not experience the disastrous war in Judea, they were nevertheless affected by the destruction of Jerusalem. As Trajan emptied lands in the East Mediterranean region, the long-suffering Jews revolted in Cyprus, Cyrene, and in Egypt. Trajan's conquest of Parthia was put on hold as he made his general Turbo turn back to deal with the revolt. The Romans were ultimately successful in quashing the uprising, but at a terrible cost; this revolt marked the end of Roman expansion, and from then on the frontiers of the Roman Empire would slowly and steadily shrink. For the Jews, it was another disaster. The Jewish populations in Cyrene and Egypt were decimated, and the Jewish population in Cyprus was exterminated entirely. It should go without saying that Gibbon's account of the Jews "devouring flesh" and "licking up blood" was an exaggeration, yet this was the stigma that attached itself to the Jews, the "blood libel" that was popular in the Middle Ages, that the Jews required Christian blood, usually from a child, to make their matzos for Passover.

---

[18] Gibbon, *The Decline and Fall of the Roman Empire*, 403.

This treatment of the Jews contrasts greatly to Gibbon's treatment of the Romans, as Michael Parenti points out, that Gibbon's accounts of Rome reveal "not a word here about an empire built upon sacked towns, shattered armies, slaughtered villagers, raped women, enslaved prisoners, plundered lands, burned crops, and mercilessly over-taxed populations."[19] Gibbon was a member of the elite upper class (as were many other classical historians),[20] and his values were reflected in his historical outlook. When we understand that so much of our "history" has been distorted through the lens of class, culture, and Christianity, we can put into perspective the comments of Kant's statement that it was only through Greek history—the history of an "enlightened" and "educated public"—and that the protocols of the Edomite historian were to downplay the role of Israel and to highlight the role of Greece and Rome.

When we look at a map of the Western world, we notice two tiny specks representing the cities of Athens and Jerusalem. As Solomon Grayzel put it, "it is astonishing to realize that the culture of all the rest of the map is based on the contributions made by these two spots."[21] Although our culture is a synthesis of the teachings and legacy of these two cities, we clearly favor the Greeks, and it is the Greek conception of history that concerns us. What is the value of a classical education, an education limited to Greek and Roman studies? There is no argument that there are many things in classical Greek and Roman culture that are worthy of study, but there are also some serious shortcomings and limits to what a classical education can teach, particularly in the areas of morality and social structure. Our intellectual society has expended a tremendous amount of energy keeping Torah out of the public consciousness and academic dialogue. What can the Torah teach us about our society, and how to cure our social ills? How can our definition of

---

[19] Michael Parenti, *The Assassination of Julius Caesar: A People's History of Ancient Rome*. (New York: The New Press, 2003), 16.

[20] "Antiquity gives us numerous gentlemen chroniclers—Homer, Herodotus, Thucydides, Polybius, Cicero, Livy, Plutarch, Suetonius, Appian, Dio Cassius, Valerius Maximus, Velleius Paterculus, Josephus, and Tacitus—just about all of whom had a pronouncedly low opinion of the common people...Gibbon's view of history was not only that of all eighteenth-century English gentleman but of a whole line of gentlemen historians from bygone times, similarly situated in the upper strata of their respective societies." Ibid., 17–18.

[21] Grayzel, *A History of the Jews*, 2.

"intellectual" be expanded into one who incorporates the Torah into a framework and foundation for knowledge? Western society has modeled itself on the binary structure of secularism and religion, both of which are limited to the paradigm of Greek and Roman thought. Our educational, political, and economic system—in short, our entire culture—conforms to the culture of Ancient Greece and Rome; "Europe and the United States, after all, have a dual heritage—Judeo-Christian religion and ethics, Greco-Roman statecraft and law."[22] The problem with this view is that "there is little that is Judaic about Christian theology" and that the term "Judeo-Christian...was developed in the early twentieth century, [implying] a continuance (or at the least, a shared set of values) of the Judaic tradition in Christianity."[23] The underpinnings of Christian theology come from the same Greco-Roman sources as our secular "classical" knowledge; they are two branches of the same tree rooted firmly in the soil of ancient Greece and Rome.

∞

THE TORAH IS not primarily a book about history; the Torah is a book of law.[24] Often the Torah will talk about events that are out of sync with a linear timeline, such as telling us of the deaths of men such as Noah and Terach when their part in the Torah is finished, then speaking of events that occurred while they were still alive. This is a peculiarity of the Torah, and it is to teach us that there is something to be learned that is more important than simply a strict historical narrative. This is not to say that the Torah is ahistorical, but the history in the Torah is concerned with teaching morality and values, mores and values often different from those taught by the Greek and Roman histories. Unlike other ancient literature, the Torah often focuses on the mistakes made by even its greatest men and women showing the consequences of their actions.

---

[22] Morris Berman, *Dark Ages America: The Final Phase of Empire*. (New York: W. W. Norton & Company, 2006), 88.

[23] Alan W. Cecil, *The Noahide Code*. (Aventura: Academy of Shem Press, 2006), 33.

[24] "It is fundamental to a proper understanding of the Scriptural narratives that the Torah is not a history book and that whatever it records must have a halakhic or moral purpose." Rabbi Nosson Scherman, *The Stone Chumash*. (Brooklyn: Mesorah Publications, Ltd., 1994), 192.

The protocols of the historian resulted in downplaying the role of Israel in Western Civilization to the point where the Jews were presented as a fossilized archaic culture whose only contribution was to write the preamble to the New Testament. This resulted not only in how intellectuals viewed theology, but history as well. It is perhaps fitting that the hedonistic ideal of Greece was represented in the person of Alexander the Great who enjoyed a Sodomic and bacchanalian lifestyle as he spread Greek culture throughout the Middle East from Macedonia to India. After Alexander's death, his generals split up his massive empire; Ptolemy and Seleucus both claimed the land of Judea, but Ptolemy, in the words of Civil War general Nathan Bedford Forrest, "got there firstest with the mostest men." His capture of Jerusalem astonished his troops, for they simply marched into the city unopposed; since it was Sabbath, the Jews would not bear arms against them. The soldiers of Ptolemy "made sport of the Jews and called them a foolish people"[25] for not defending their city, thus underlying the Grecian culture's condescending attitude towards the Torah and strengthening the foundations of Greek anti-Semitism.

The Hellenistic empires founded by Alexander's generals, their borders constantly pulsing with battle, would last for two and a half centuries until the legions of Rome came knocking. The allure of Hellenistic culture attracted many of the Jews, and the tide of the Jewish Diaspora which had previously spread throughout Persia ebbed and flowed westward, bringing many of the Jews to the cities along the Mediterranean coast.

It was in Alexandria, a new commercial port built by Alexander and Ptolemy, where the Jewish presence was most keenly felt. The Jews of Alexandria were a sizable part of the population of the city, and it was in Alexandria where the Hellenistic Jewish culture had its greatest impact. It was here that the Torah was translated into Greek,[26] allowing the Hellenized Jews to hold on to their culture. This proved critical, for "almost all the ancient peoples whose names are mentioned in the Bible disappeared completely, early in the Greek period, swept away by the flood of Greek influence, the Jews remained steadfast in their own faith and their own manner of living."[27] Other books, such as *Ecclesiasticus*

---

[25] Grayzel, *A History of the Jews*, 43.

[26] Josephus, *Antiquities*, xii.

[27] Grayzel, *A History of the Jews*, 48.

and the *Wisdom of Sirach* were written at this time, and "these books of wisdom present the contrast between the Hellenistic ideal for the search for individual power"[28] and the Torah-based view of the Jews. Unlike most of the other civilizations and ancient peoples of the Middle East, the Jews were not pulled into the murky backwaters of history by the rip currents of Greek culture, even as Greek influence waxed among those Jews who wished to be like all other nations, and "Greek styles in dress, Greek names, the Greek language because stylish"[29] among the upper classes in Jerusalem. The clash of the two disparate cultures came to a head in the Maccabean revolt, and the Maccabean victory secured Judaism for another century. Unlike the revolt against the Seleucid Greeks, however, the revolt against Rome failed, and successive waves of revolt against Rome ended with the bitter and sanguinary defeat of Bar Kochba in 135 CE in a campaign which involved over half of the entire Roman army. Because of this, Emperor Hadrian renamed Judea "Palestine" after the enemies of the Jews, the Philistines, in order to humiliate the Jews and to forever blot out the memory of Israel.

The Greeks were the first to develop what is now looked upon as "anti-Semitism." The accusations of writers such as Manetho, Lysimachus, and the Roman Tacitus, who spoke of the Jews being "a leprous and scabby people"[30] and being driven out of Egypt because they were so "loathsome" would be echoed centuries later by Voltaire and Karl Marx, facilitated by the interest in Greek and Latin writing which was popularized by the religion of Christianity.

When Sam Harris said that "anti-Semitism is intrinsic to both Christianity and Islam,"[31] it somehow slipped his mind to mention that it was also intrinsic to Western Greek-based secular society as well, and this secular anti-Semitism was what has even influenced secularized Jewish intellectuals such as Noam Chomsky. The historians of the Enlightenment disparaged a nation that has seen the great kingdoms and empires of history come and go, a nation more than willing to share their collective wisdom with the rest of the world,

---

[28] Ibid., 51.

[29] Ibid., 55.

[30] Josephus, *Against Apion*, i:34–35.

[31] Harris, *The End of Faith*, 92.

teaching others what has made them so successful, why their culture, language, and their law, has survived when so many others throughout history have become extinct, a nation that has in fact broken just about every rule of history.[32] This was the "miracle" which the God told Israel He would perform in order to show the nations of the world that He is *HASHEM*.[33] There is no viable explanation for Israel to exist, and there is absolutely no other historical example of a nation that even compares to the survival of the Jews, a people who were not tucked away in some remote corner of the globe, on some isolated island or

---

[32] The American writer Mark Twain commented on this nation when he wrote: "If the statistics are right, the Jews constitute but one percent of the human race. It suggests a nebulous dim puff of star dust lost in the blaze of the Milky Way…properly the Jew ought hardly to be heard of, but he is heard of, has always been heard of. He is as prominent on the planet as any other people, and his commercial importance is extravagantly out of proportion to the smallness of his bulk. His contributions to the world's list of great names in literature, science, art, music, finance, medicine, and abstruse learning are also away out of proportion to the weakness of his numbers. He has made a marvellous fight in this world, in all the ages; and has done it with his hands tied behind him. He could be vain of himself, and be excused for it. The Egyptian, the Babylonian, and the Persian rose, filled the planet with sound and splendor, then faded to dream-stuff and passed away; the Greek and the Roman followed, and made a vast noise, and they are gone; other peoples have sprung up and held their torch high for a time, but it burned out, and they sit in twilight now, or have vanished. The Jew saw them all, beat them all, and is now what he always was, exhibiting no decadence, no infirmities of age, no weakening of his parts, no slowing of his energies, no dulling of his alert and aggressive mind. All things are mortal…all other forces pass, but he remains. What is the secret of his immortality?" Mark Twain, *The Complete Essays of Mark Twain*. (New York: Doubleday & Co., 1963), 249.

The answer to this question is supplied by Rabbi S. R. Hirsch: "'Our history should teach you to know the ways of God's Sovereignty,' Israel tells the nations. 'The Jewish people wander through the world without power and without arms, and yet all the nations of the world shall gradually gather beneath the Jewish banner, beneath the ideal which the Jewish people has held aloft and which has served it as its guiding star in its wanderings through time. What is the reason for this victory of the Jewish people? This victory will come about because we have left it to God to determine what our portion on earth should be…we have won the battle because we have taken pride in renouncing all personal grandeur and might, and this is the only kind of pride that finds favor in the eyes of the Lord…this is the pride in which the Lord delights because it derives from the proper understanding of the destiny of men and nations.'" Hirsch, *The Hirsch Psalms*, §i, 337.

[33] "The survival of the Jewish people, for the purpose of executing its Divinely assigned task, is predicted in the Torah, is reiterated by the prophets (for example, in *Yirmeyah* 5:15–18) and is presented as a lasting testimony to God's rulership (*Yeshayah* 43:10). This miraculous survival…is, indeed, the ultimate historical confirmation of the truth of Judaism." Elias, *Nineteen Letters*, 100.

peninsula, but a people who have been scattered from one corner of the earth to the other, who have been front and center in the annals of world history, and have interacted and influenced mankind to an astonishing degree despite Western attempts to eliminate them for over two thousand years.

The protocols of the historian (in regards to Israel) show a startling subjectivity. This subjectivity is based not only on the anti-Semitic teachings from Greek and Roman writings, but from the direct influence of Christian theology. How did theology manage to infect even the non-religious "secular" disciplines of our modern social sciences? It is this subject—the development and influence of "scientific" theology on secular academics—we will discuss next.

CHAPTER THREE

Protocols of the Theologian

Judaism very definitely does not want to give birth to a 'religion' from within...or for the soul of man...it seeks to implant religion into man's emotions through clear cognitive and intellectual perceptions based on the recognition and acceptance of Divine truths that have been objectively documented.

— Rabbi Samson Raphael Hirsch[1]

B Y THE NINETEENTH CENTURY, FUELED BY THE ENLIGHTENMENT fascination with Greek logic, concepts, and ideas, the idea that Greek "reason" could be applied to the social sciences gained a foothold in Western academics. When Charles Darwin's *The Origin of Species* (1859) was published, it created quite a stir in the scientific community, not only in biology, but among other scientists who tried to use the concept of evolution to understand the development of culture and society. "Social Darwinism," a phrase later made famous by historian Richard Hofstadter, described the newly emerging "social scientists"

---

[1] Hirsch, *Collected Writings*, Vol. II, 141.

who, taking a cue from Darwin, taught that societies evolved and grew, and the concept of "survival of the fittest" blended in nicely with the Edomite concept of power and strength. German scholars[2] such as Leopold von Ranke (1795–1886) tried to turn history into a science, or at least a discipline based on scientific methods. Ranke not only pioneered the emphasis on using primary sources, but also:

> Helped establish history as a separate discipline, independent from philosophy or literature…the determination to strip away the veneer of posthumous condescension applied to the past by philosophizing historians such as Voltaire and to reveal it in its original colors… Ranke introduced into the study of modern history the methods that had recently been developed by philologists in the study of ancient and medieval literature.[3]

Coming off of two hundred years of enlightenment re-discovery and re-application of Greek thought, philosophy, and science, the Prussian educational system swung into high gear during the latter half of the nineteenth century. As the academic obsession with science became more and more pronounced, methodology became increasingly important, and this focus on method became an infatuation, often obfuscating the reasons behind the study. Many scholars became so enamored with works of leading academics and their *modus operandi* that they failed to see the flaws in their reasoning and results, particularly when it came to Judaism. How did theology affect the social sciences? Why are intellectuals, despite all their cleverness, unable to perceive theological ideology used in their arguments about the Bible? To answer these questions, we must begin with the development of Christian theology itself.

⤳

IN THE SECOND CENTURY of the Common Era, after nearly seven decades of disastrous conflict with the Roman Empire starting with the destruction of the Second Temple and ending with the crushing of the Bar Kochba revolt in 135 CE, Judaism was in danger of extinction. The great rabbinic schools in *Eretz Yisrael* had been scattered or destroyed,

---

[2] "We are almost utterly dependant on our German missionaries or intermediaries for our knowledge of Greece, Rome, Judaism and Christianity; that, however profound that knowledge may be, theirs is only one interpretation; and that we have only been told as much as they thought we needed to know." Bloom, *The Closing of the American Mind*, 156.

[3] Richard J. Evans, *In Defense of History*. (New York: W. W. Norton & Company, 1999), 15.

the teaching of Torah had been outlawed, and as the great sages of the Torah, the living repositories of Jewish Law, died or were martyred by the Romans, and the knowledge of the Torah was being lost. As has happened many times in Jewish history as the flame of Israel began to flicker and die, a leader arose to fan the fire of the Torah; Rabbi Yehudah HaNasi, a direct descendant of the sages Hillel and Gamliel, took it upon himself to save the Oral Torah, the all-important explanation and commentary to the Written Torah that had been handed down from teacher to student in an unbroken transmission for over fifteen centuries. He began to collect the teachings of the great rabbis of the previous generations, writing down the knowledge before it was lost forever. At the end of the second century of the Common Era in the Jewish year 3960 (200 CE), after thirty years labor, Rabbi Yehudah HaNasi published the *Mishna*. A few hundred years later, the *Gemara*, the explanation to the *Mishna*, was completed.

The *Mishna* was written in Hebrew; the explanation to the *Mishna*, the *Gemara*, was written in Aramaic, a Semitic language similar to Hebrew, much like the similarities between the two Romance languages of Portuguese and Spanish. Together these two books make up the Talmud. In the Jewish Talmud, the material is divided into two groups; *halakha* and *aggada*. *Halakha*, literally meaning "going" as in "the way one should go" is the term for the legal teachings of the Law, covering sacrifices, government, business, kosher law, clothing, etc. There was no facet of human existence that the Talmud did not cover. The *aggadic* material is basically anything else in the Talmud that is not *halakhic* in nature such as homilies, history, and moral teachings. The Talmud contains the teachings of several thousand rabbis; it even has a quote from a wandering rabbi from Galilee: "I come not to destroy the Law of Moses, nor to add to the Law of Moses." (*Shabbat* 116b).

While Rabbi Yehuda HaNasi was writing the *Mishna*, a Hellenistic sect that was a spin-off from a small sect of Judaism was also creating a body of oral teachings and interpretations of the Tanach. Unlike the Hebrew *Mishna*, however, these writings were in Greek. Unlike Rabbi Yehuda HaNasi's *Mishna*, most of these books were written anonymously. Unlike the *Mishna*, which focused on correct behavior, this new oral teaching focused on correct theology, or belief. Unlike the *Mishna*, which has the teachings of well over a hundred of the Tannaim, these works were based primarily on the teachings of only two "rabbis," one named Saul of Tarsus, whom we call Paul. The other rabbi whose teachings were so prominent was the wandering rabbi from Galilee, the one quoted in the Talmud saying that his teachings had no effect whatsoever on the Torah of Moses: "I come not to destroy the Law of Moses, nor to add to the Law of Moses." Christians today, as they have for nearly two thousand years, call him Jesus.

Although there are a few similarities between Judaism and Christianity—belief in the God of Abraham, Isaac, and Jacob, recognition of Mosaic authority, as well as the authority of the Hebrew Scriptures—there are many important differences. Christians believe that Jesus was God incarnate, that God "came down" from heaven in the form of a human to teach mankind the "mysteries"[4] of things which were "kept secret since the world began"[5] such as the *trinity* and "original sin." Most importantly, Christianity teaches that believing that Jesus was God in the flesh was the only way to attain salvation, or spiritual everlasting life. According to Christianity, this salvation cannot be achieved by simply keeping the Mosaic Law; one had to accept the mystery teachings of Christianity, that you had to know Jesus in a "spiritual" sense.

These were not the teachings of the original Church, the Church of the Apostles, and they are certainly not teachings of Judaism. There is neither any teaching in the Torah about a new revelation from "heaven" (cf. Deut. 30:12) nor God coming down to earth in "human" form in order to correctly explain the Law. In fact, God told Moses that appearing in physical form was one thing He would never do (Deut. 4:9–19), and that if any human claimed otherwise, such as saying that they were God incarnate, they were to be put to death (Deut. 13:1–6). God also explained that there would not be anyone "coming down from heaven" to explain the Torah (Deut. 30:10–16). The Torah explains this in no uncertain terms: *God is not a man that He should be deceitful, nor a son of man that He should relent. Would He say and not do, or speak and not confirm?* (Num. 23:19). The question is: how did the theological teachings of Christianity find their way into the

---

[4] "How that by revelation he made known unto me the mystery; (as I wrote afore in few words, whereby, when ye read, ye may understand my knowledge in the mystery of Christ); which in other ages was not made known unto the sons of men, as it is now revealed unto his holy apostles and prophets by the Spirit." Ephesians 3:3–5.

[5] Romans 16:25.

small Jewish sect of the Jerusalem Church, supplanting the rabbinic teachings?[6] The answer comes from the actions of the one follower of Jesus who did not want to be a part of the Jerusalem Church, who did not even want to dwell in Jerusalem, much less the land of Israel. That man was Paul of Tarsus.

Paul, formally Saul of Tarsus, was a self-proclaimed "Pharisee" who had, oddly enough, been working for the Sadducee priests (Acts 9:1). After his hallucination on the road to Damascus and subsequent conversion to "Christianity," Paul made four missionary tours from 46 CE to around 62 CE. The first tour was through southern Asia Minor; starting at Antioch in 46 CE, Paul went south to Seleucla and sailed to Cyprus,[7] and from there swung through what is today south-central Turkey, returning to Antioch in 48 CE. Paul's second tour was far more ambitious, and he traveled from Jerusalem north to his hometown of Tarsus, revisiting some of the places he went to on his first journey such as Derbe, Lystra, and Antioch of Pisidea. From there he traveled to Troas on the Aegean coast where he then sailed to Thrace and then traveling down into Greece, stopping in Phillipi, Thessalonica, Berea, Athens, and Corinth before sailing back to Ephesus and then to Caesarea. Paul's third journey took roughly the same route, and his fourth journey Paul sailed to what is now Southern Turkey, Crete, Malta, Sicily, and then to Rome. It was here that the account in Acts suddenly ended, and a curtain of darkness descended on the history of the Church. Not until the beginning of the second century, with the writings of Clement of Rome, does the veil start to lift, and then only little by little. By the time the fog of history was lifted, the Jerusalem Church was no longer in control, and the Torah and the Noahide Law was discarded for another system of belief, one that was embraced by the Hellenistic (and increasingly Gentile-dominated) Church.

---

[6] In Acts 15, James, the brother of Jesus and the leader of the Jerusalem Church, ordered that the Gentiles who were coming into the Church not to convert to Judaism, but to observe the Noahide Law, including "the three absolute prohibitions of idolatry, adultery, and murder" [Alan W. Cecil, *The Noahide Guide to Matthew*. (Estero: Academy of Shem Press, 5769/2009), 11] along with Hillel's dictum "what is hateful to yourself, do not do to another." Hillel's quote is found in the Western Text families of the early New Testament manuscripts, as well as "the earliest quotation we have of Acts 15:20 [which] comes from the second-century church father, Iranaeus, in *Against Heresies*, book iii. 12:14, which quotes Hillel's maxim instead of the spurious 'and things strangled'" [ibid., 13].

[7] Acts 13:4.

This new Hellenistic Gentile sect of Christianity had many teachings that were not found in the Torah-oriented Jerusalem Church. The
focus was now on Jesus instead of the Law, and a plethora of different
Hellenistic Christian sects sprung up, all teaching different doctrines[8]
and each one claiming that *they* were the faithful transmitters of Jesus'
message. Correct theology became more important than correct actions
and correct behavior. By the beginning of the Second Century there
were many different branches of this new Hellenistic religion, but they
all shared major theological concepts, such as teaching that there was
an inseparable gulf between man and God, and that man was powerless
to save himself through the Torah. They taught that God was unreach-
able in "heaven," and the world was in the grip of a lesser but still
powerful evil god (often called the *Demiurge*,[9] or Satan). The theology
was structured in a strict dualistic language such as *saved* versus *lost*,
fleshy versus *spiritual*, and *light* versus *darkness*. The most noticeable
difference between the new faith and Judaism was that it focused on
personal salvation,[10] and that only by the *gnosis* (knowledge) of Jesus could one's soul escape the boundaries of this sinful materialistic
world and go to "heaven," as is taught in the Gospel of John: "No one
comes to the Father except through me. If you had come to the *gnosis*
of me (which, alas, you do not), you shall know my Father also. From
now on you have the *gnosis* of Him, and have seen Him."[11] These are
Gnostic teachings which focused on the *mysteries*[12] of Jesus' revelation, teachings such as the *trinity* and *original sin*. It was from this

---

[8] Cf. 1 Cor. 1:10–12, Gal. 1:6–9.

[9] "Even the idea of the demiurge in Plato's *Timeaus* does not capture the concept of
creation in its full sense as the Jewish people understand it." Soloveichik, *Halakhic
Man*, 163, n. 141.

[10] "In our [Jewish] religious ideology the selfish salvation of the individual soul is a
very minor theme. It is, I believe, an acquired dogma, and its irrelevance is proved by
its unimportance." Samuel, *You Gentiles*, 119.

[11] This translation of John 14: 6–7 follows the interpretation of Bruce Metzger,
A Textual Commentary on the Greek New Testament, (Stuttgart: Deutsche
Bibelgesellschaft, 2000), 207.

[12] "We might also note that historically Christianity has been unique among the
world religions in its emphasis upon paradox and mystery, features which, to be
sure, were attenuated within some major branches of the Protestant Reformation."
Roland Robertson, "On the Analysis of Mysticism: Pre-Weberian, Weberian and Post-
Weberian Perspectives." *Sociological Analysis*. Vol. 36, No. 3 (Autumn, 1975), 248.

word *gnosis*—the Greek word for "knowledge"—that the new religion got its name, which we call Gnosticism. A bitter power struggle between these Gnostic sects would ensue into the fourth century before one of them became dominant; the Gnostic sect we know today as the Catholic Church.

The Gnostic sect that became the Catholic Church—which all modern forms of organized Christianity are descended—survived by incorporating the Greek *Tanach* (the Septuagint) into the prologue of the New Testament, and the theological teaching which allowed this incorporation was the main difference between Catholic Christianity and the other Gnostic sects. Christianity has long been in denial about being Gnostic. To the Noahide (and certainly the Jew), the differences between rabbinic interpretation and Christianity's Gnostic interpretation of the *Tanach* are obvious. To the Noahide, the slight differences between the many early Gnostic sects are overwhelmed by their similarities (the focus on Jesus the "savior," personal salvation, mystery teachings, etc.). Many of these Gnostic sects proclaimed themselves the "true" Christianity, claiming that they were teaching the correct Pauline theology.[13] The differences between the various early Gnostic Christians were no greater than the differences between today's Christian sects. The differences between the Gnostic sects were nowhere near the differences between the Hellenistic Gnostic Christians and Judaism, or even the original Jewish Christians (who would later be known as the Ebionites). The Noahide perspective views modern Christianity—whether it is Protestant, Catholic, or Eastern Orthodox—as having Gnostic theological teaching as the foundation of its faith. After all, it certainly is not Jewish. The focus on Jesus of Nazareth as a "personal savior" was the major theme of all the Christian Gnostic religions. Christians point to the minor details in their theology in contrast to the other Gnostic sects—their favorite defense being the trite semantic argument that their theology is based on "faith" instead of "knowledge"—ignoring the major structural similarities that Christianity shares with other classical Gnostic Christian faiths of the early centuries of the Common Era. All the sects of Protestant, Catholic, and Eastern Orthodox Christianity focus on the person of the "divine" Jesus, his coming down from "heaven" to reveal God's plan of "salvation" and escape the clutches of Satan, the "god" of this

---

[13] "The Valentinians, in particular, allege that their secret tradition offers direct access to Paul's own teaching of wisdom and gnosis. According to Clement, 'they say that Valentinus was a hearer of Theudas, and Theudas, in turn, a disciple of Paul.'" Elaine Pagels, *The Gnostic Paul*, (Philadelphia: Trinity Press International, 1992), 1–2.

dualistic world. These concepts are so alien to Judaism and to the *Tanach*—there is clearly nothing in the *Tanach* about God coming down to earth at a later date in the human form of a divine savior named "Jesus" and committing suicide—that one has to "know" the theological (i.e., Gnostic) interpretations of the "prophecies" in the *Tanach* that point to Jesus. According to Christianity, without this "knowledge" of the Gnostic interpretations of the *Tanach*, a person cannot possibly understand that the entire *Tanach* is really all about Jesus. This is where the Christian argument of the semantics of "faith" rather than "knowledge" breaks down in lieu of the larger picture. If it is all about Jesus, then you know it is Gnosticism—there are simply no two ways about it. There is no "Jesus" in Judaism. Jesus is less useful and important to Judaism than a refrigerator is to an Eskimo living in an igloo.

The Gnostic's focus on *salvation*[14] cannot be over-emphasized. This was the main concern of Gnosticism; the spiritual salvation of the individual, the release of the soul from its earthy, fleshy, material body. Yet Gnosticism remains one of the least understood and least studied areas of Christianity. One would think that the pursuit of the origins of Christianity—a religion which evolved out of a morass of Gnostic faiths—would have had a detailed and exhaustive theological and academic treatment of Gnosticism. One of the problems has been a dearth of Gnostic material; when the Gnostic Catholic Church seized power, it systematically destroyed all of the early Gnostic writings it could get its hands on, and only a few scraps of Gnostic texts survived the purges of the Church. Most of our knowledge of Gnosticism came from the writings of the early church fathers, and these were decidedly one sided. This situation changed drastically in 1945, when a library of Gnostic writings—including some books that had been mentioned by second century church fathers and previously thought lost forever—were found in Nag Hammadi, Egypt. It has been over sixty years

---

[14] "Most of all, the Gnostic stock of concepts served to clarify the history of salvation. According to these concepts the Redeemer appears as a cosmic figure, the pre-existent divine being, Son of the Father (§ 12, 3), who came down from heaven and assumed human form and who, after his activity on earth, was exalted to heavenly glory and wrested sovereignty over the spirit-powers to himself. It is in this conception of him that he is praised in the pre-Pauline Christ-hymn which is quoted in Phil. 2:6–11. This 'mythos' is also briefly alluded to in II Cor. 8:9. The Gnostic idea that Christ's earthly garment of flesh was the disguise in consequence of which the world-rulers failed to recognize him—for if they had recognized him, they would not have brought about their own defeat by causing his crucifixion—lurks behind I Cor. 2:8." Rudolf Bultmann, *Theology of the New Testament*. (New York: Charles Scribner's Sons, 1951), §15, 175.

since the Nag Hammadi library was discovered, and over thirty since the last of the Nag Hammadi books had been translated into English, and yet relatively few books on Gnosticism have been written. It is as if the Church feared to peer too closely into its beginnings, particularly with a religion that was reviled by the early Church Fathers not because it was so different from "orthodox" Christianity, but because it was so similar. The few scholars who saw the Gnostic influence in the New Testament were largely ignored by the mainstream theologians.

The advanced Gnostic theology in the Gospel of John and the writings of Paul were a primary influence on Gnostic Christianity, for Paul and John were popular with the various Gnostic sects during Christianity's formative period. When the Roman Gnostic Church eliminated its Gnostic rivals and destroyed their literature, they felt the battle for control of Christianity had been won, and with the threat of Gnosticism silenced (forever, as the Church believed), the arguments and debates about Gnosticism were relegated to scholarly studies in the teachings of Ireneaus and Tertullian. However, with the discovery and translation of the Nag Hammadi texts, it became glaringly obvious that Christian theology had much more in common with Gnosticism than it did with Judaism, and that the main tenets of Christianity were recycled Gnostic concepts and ideas.

The influence of Gnosticism went far beyond religion and how we look at the Bible. Gnosticism has had a far-reaching effect on Western thought, but because of Christianity's reluctance to study Gnosticism, these effects have been overlooked. From Paul's teaching about "Law versus grace" in his Epistles, through Chrysostom's *Eight Sermons Against the Jews*, Augustine and Aquinas, to Martin Luther extorting Germans to "set fire to their synagogues" and "[raze and destroy] their houses,"[15] the Gnostic war on Judaism raged on. During the Enlightenment, the Gnostic teaching of its binary system of "spiritual" and "fleshy" helped foster the division of "religious" and "secular."[16]

---

[15] From Martin Luther's *On the Jews and Their Lies*, 1543.

[16] "It is no longer fashionable to avow a belief in Satan or his entourage of evil archons, but the fact is, nonetheless, that we are dualists. We have divided the world between God and ourselves. Part of what we consider our own, we are willing to turn over to Caesar, but—believing in civil liberties—part we retain as our private domain. Some are willing to share part of this domain with God, but some are very jealous of their privacy and exclude Him from it; they divide the world only between themselves and Caesar. The dualist is either a total or partial atheist. If he totally excludes God, then obviously he is an atheist. If he excludes God from a substantial part of the world, then to that degree he is an atheist." Konvitz, *Torah & Constitution*, 57.

The concept of "separation of church and state" as well as the Gnostic Christian "fleshy and spiritual" had their roots in the same Greek philosophy which also influenced scholars such as Thomas Jefferson and Immanuel Kant.[17] The fight against the Torah, however, subtly moved into new secular[18] battlefields, and the developing "secular" academic disciplines such as history, philosophy, and sociology all took up the theological sword of Gnostic interpretation to do battle with the Torah of Moses.

～⌒

IT WAS THIS concept that developed during the Enlightenment, the concept of *secular* and *religious*, or *sacred* and *profane*,[19] which was itself a Gnostic concept of the dualistic forms of *spiritual* and *material*. This Gnostic view has affected our concept of our own culture. We view Christian Gnosticism as a religious problem, but since there is no artificial separation between the religious and the secular in Judaism, the Noahide sees the problem going much deeper, a poison that has seeped into every aspect of our society. Our modern culture, with its division of "church and state," can be thought of in terms of being Gnostic secularism—the artificial division of the "religious" with the "non-religious." This non-Jewish teaching, that there are aspects of the world and of human existence which are outside the boundaries of God's domain, are themselves ideas that have been influenced by centuries of classical Gnostic thought transmitted through the Church and its seminaries and later through "secular" academic institutions.

---

[17] "Kant's notorious so-called 'dualism' was a classic statement invalidating, among other things, the traditional function of the natural law. This is hardly surprising, since his inspirations were Hume for his theory of knowledge and Rousseau for his ethics—the Hume who had denied the descriptive validity of law in nature and the Rousseau who had rejected the prescriptive validity of any intellectually known law for human action. Kant combined these piecemeal insights into a radical and systematic dialectic opposing knowledge to action and nature to morality, and undermining thereby the very foundations of the natural law as it had been previously conceived." Leonard Krieger, "Kant and the Crisis of Natural Law." *Journal of the History of Ideas*. Vol. 26, No. 2 (Apr.–Jun., 1965), 195.

[18] "Secularization theorists confidently averred that religious conflicts, along with their attendant tribal and ethnic animosities, would wither away with the advance of modernity. Social and economic development would bring the conditions for stable democratic government, and with democracy, society would be liberated from the dominance of religious symbols and institutions." Steven B. Smith, *Spinoza, Liberalism, and the Question of Jewish Identity*. (New Haven: Yale University Press, 1997), 1.

[19] The word "profane" is from the Latin *pro fano*—"outside the Temple."

Mercy at the expense of justice was also a hallmark of Gnostic Christian thought, the worship of *HASHEM*, the attribute of mercy, at the expense of *Elokim*, the attribute of justice. In traditional Judaism, these are two attributes of God, and you could not have one dominate at the expense of the other. Orlando Patterson, the "preeminent" writer on freedom, mentions the problem with Gnosticism, that "New Testament scholars seem particularly allergic to any demonstration of the influence of Gnosticism on the other Christologies."[20] Patterson stated that "had Christianity gone in the direction of Gnosticism, it would still have maintained the idea of spiritual freedom at the very center of its soteria"[21] without once considering that Pauline Christianity itself was Gnostic. Patterson ignores other scholars such as Hyam Maccoby and even Rudolph Bultmann who clearly recognized the Gnostic elements within Paul's writings: "Whatever one's opinion of Paul, no one would deny that Christianity was not only fundamentally shaped by his views but almost completely determined by them."[22] If Christianity is the religion developed by the Gnostic Paul, why do Christians teach that it is based on Jesus' teachings? Only by taking Jesus' teachings "out of context" and giving them a Gnostic interpretation can this be achieved.

Understanding and recognizing these problems with the theological interpretation of the New Testament—such as the Christian attempt to find the "historical Jesus"—cannot be disassociated with the problems of the traditional interpretation of those whom Gibbon calls "the race of Abraham…the obnoxious people."[23] The treatment of the Jews by secular scholars shows a remarkable conformity and consistency in their appraisal of Israel's contributions to Western Civilization's history and culture, a view unduly influenced by Gnostic theology.

---

[20] Patterson, *Freedom*, 312.

[21] Ibid., 313–14.

[22] Ibid., 316.

[23] Gibbon, *The Decline and Fall of the Roman Empire*, 414–15.

Higher Anti-Semitism

Even when deviating widely from its conclusions, all Old Testament study today is based on the splendid work of J. Wellhausen.

— Max Weber[1]

ONE OF THE LEADING PROPONENTS AND EARLY DEVELOPER OF scientific anti-Semitism was Julius Wellhausen (1844–1918), the son of a Lutheran minister. Wellhausen was a German scholar with a Ph.D.[2] in theology, and among his other accomplishments, a professor to the theological faculty at Greifswald. Wellhausen's contribution to both theology and the social sciences solved a problem that had been plaguing Christians for two hundred years— the Christian's defense of Judaism from the Enlightenment's relentless attack on religion and faith. Since the Christian Bible contained both the Hebrew as well as the Christian Greek Scriptures (the "Old" and "New" Testaments respectively), Christians were forced into the awkward position of having to defend Judaism from the secular Greek humanistic teachings of the Enlightenment philosophers. Because the Gnostic sect that became the Catholic Church had linked the Catholic New Testament to the *Tanach*, and that so much of Christianity's support came from their theological interpretations of the Hebrew Scriptures, having to defend the Torah also meant, to a degree, having to defend Judaism, and after sixteen centuries of attacking Judaism, this was a sore point among many Christians. If Judaism was exposed as merely myth and superstition, it would take Christianity down with it. The problem the theologians faced was: how could the Christians continue to attack Judaism while at the same time preserve Christianity unscathed? The answer to this problem was solved (to a large degree) by Julius Wellhausen, who took a cue from the Enlightenment philosophers and developed the "scientific" discipline of positivist theology known as "higher criticism."

---

[1] Max Weber, *Ancient Judaism*. Hans H. Gerth and Don Martindale, trans. (New York: The Free Press, 1952), 426.

[2] The Ph.D. as we know it today was another product of the nineteenth century German university system.

Wellhausen's theory was based upon the previous work of Christian theologians such as Wilhelm Martin Leberecht de Wette (1780–1849) and Karl Heinrich Graf (1815–1869). By mixing literary analysis along with a healthy dose of Social Darwinism and Hegelian[3] idealism, the crux of the Graf-Wellhausen theory was to deny Mosaic authorship of the Torah, "proving" the Torah had been written and edited long after Moses. Wellhausen argued that the ancient Hebrews were a nature-worshiping tribal cult that gradually centralized its power and religious focus over the centuries, culminating in the writing of the *Tanach*. This Darwinesque evolution of Judaism held sway over scholars for decades, and although it has fallen out of favor among theologians in the latter part of the twentieth century, its influence has remained.

Wellhausen's style was the typical nineteenth century German manner of heavy-handed pedantic prose, hundreds of scriptural references, and endless comparisons with other ancient religions, even religions from India and China which had nothing to do whatsoever with Judaism. Wellhausen contended that Judaism was a developed religion, and that Moses had little to do with its creation, and that the Torah was a compilation of many different scribes from the time of David down to the time of Ezra. According to Wellhausen, the Torah was written in four stages, which he labeled "JEDP." The "J" (or "Jehovah") text was the earliest, written sometime around the era of David and Solomon. It is represented by the use of the Holy Name of *HASHEM*, or the tetragrammaton. The letter "E" stood for Elohistic, from the name *Elokim*, used by a writer in the Northern Kingdom just after the "J" part was written. The "D" or Deuteronomic part was written after J and E, before the exile. The "P," or Priestly Code (most of Leviticus), was written after the destruction of the first Temple, after the Jews returned from Babylonia. Wellhausen also insisted that the "priests" also were the ones who edited the Torah into the form we

---

[3] The ideas of seminary-trained Hegel, as other philosophers before him such as Immanuel Kant, were affected by Protestant theology. Hegel, in his Science of Philosophy, said that "God in Christianity is conceived in his truth, and therefore as in Himself thoroughly concrete, as a person, as a subject, and more closely determined, as mind or spirit. What He is as spirit unfolds itself to the religious apprehensions as the Trinity of Persons, which at the same time in relation with itself is One." Georg Wilhelm Friedrich Hegel, J. Glenn Gray, ed., *On Art, Religion, and the History of Philosophy: Introductory Lectures* (New York: Harper & Row, 1970), 104.

know of today. This had the effect of turning the Torah from a primary source into a secondary source while, at the same time, maintaining the status of the Gospels as primary sources.

The concept of "primary" and "secondary" sources "was introduced above all by German scholars in the nineteenth century."[4] The Torah is Judaism's "primary source" since it records events that happened during the time of Moses. The main "primary event" was the giving of the Torah on Sinai. This event, which was witnessed[5] by the entire nation of Israel, was the foundation of Judaism. The goal of the German theologians was to make the Torah seem less reliable than the New Testament, thus presenting the Gospels as more authoritative. The theory behind this was dubbed the Graf-Wellhausen theory, which was known by many guises such as "Higher Criticism" or the Documentary Theory.

౼

WELLHAUSEN MADE TWO critically important comments in his book, one comment at the beginning, and the other at the end. Like theological bookends, they frame the content of the *Prolegomena* into a specific theological paradigm. Wellhausen's first comment stated:

> At last, in the course of a casual visit in Göttingen in the summer of 1867, I learned through Ritschl that Karl Heinrich Graf placed the Law later than the Prophets, and, *almost without knowing his reasons for the hypothesis, I was prepared to accept it*; [emphasis added] I readily acknowledged to myself the possibility of understanding Hebrew antiquity without the book of the Torah.[6]

In the very beginning of the *Prolegomena*, Wellhausen admitted to being predisposed to accept the concept of understanding the history of the Jews without the Torah. In other words, he was to design his theory to fit his preconceived notions that Judaism was a developed religion, and to pick and choose which "facts" were used to back up his thesis. In the first "bookend" comment, Wellhausen's work was designed to separate the Law from the land and people of Israel, unlocking the Torah

---

[4] Evans, *In Defense of History*, 81.

[5] The large *ayin* and *dalet* in the first verse of the *Shema* (Deut. 6:4) spell the word *Aid*, which means "witness."

[6] Julius Wellhausen, *Prolegomena to the History of Ancient Israel*. (Cleveland: The World Publishing Company, 1965), 3–4.

without the Talmud, and in place of rabbinic commentary, substituting a narrative filled with theological and literary constructs. Ignoring over two thousand years of Jewish scholarship, Wellhausen developed a theory designed not to shed light on the Torah and how it was written, but, as with the other liberal scholars of the Enlightenment, to undermine and destroy Judaism. No rabbinic sources, no conflicting opinions, no traditional rabbinic views were allowed into his one-sided approach. Wellhausen's system was to use modern "scientific" methods to find out how the Torah was written, and Wellhausen treated the Torah as simply a literary work instead of Divine Law, and he developed his thesis and arranged his facts in order to justify his theory instead of formulating a theory based upon an objective view of the Torah.

Wellhausen's attitude towards Jewish scholarship was much the same as Kant and Adam Smith: "The later Hebrew literature, which does not fall to be considered here, contributed very few new elements; in so far as an intellectual life existed at all among the Jews of the Middle Ages, it was not a growth of native soil but proceeded from the Mahometan or Latin culture of individuals."[7] Wellhausen certainly had access to Jewish scholarship, for Wellhausen published his *Prolegomena* in 1878, the very year Rabbi S. R. Hirsch published the final volume of his monumental *Der Pentateuch, übersetzt und erläutert von Samson Raphael Hirsch*. In this massive work (seven volumes), Hirsch had meticulously gone through each verse of the Torah, explaining the etymology of the Hebrew as well as the historical and halakhic context. Hirsch's work, although not written primarily as a refutation of Wellhausen's theory, does refute it in hundreds of places. Hirsch draws upon centuries of rabbinic scholarship, scholarship that Wellhausen "does not fall to be considered," to explain the meaning of the text of the Torah, elucidating the meaning of the Hebrew words and explaining (from a rabbinic point of view) many of the passages in the text that Wellhausen uses to prove his theory. To think that Wellhausen and the other German Christian theologians knew more about the Hebrew or Jewish history than a scholar such as Rabbi Hirsch is a matter of your point of view—whether you are a Christian or an observant Noahide or Jew.

Wellhausen had access to Hirsch, but obviously did not bother to read his work, preferring Christian scholarship when studying the Torah. Wellhausen did not include any commentary from Jewish sources,

---

[7] Ibid., 542.

except when they were taken from Christian works, and his disdain for Jewish scholarship can be seen in his comment about the kabbalah: "The Kabbala at most, and even it hardly with justice, can be regarded as having been a genuine product of Judaism. It originated in Palestine, and subsequently flourished chiefly in the later Middle Ages in Spain, and, like all other methodised [*sic*] nonsense, had strong attractions for Christian scholars."[8] It is clear from Wellhausen's work that it was not only the mystical writings of Judaism he considered "methodized nonsense," but any rabbinical writings, even the advanced etymology of Rabbi Hirsch, a scholar who understood the Hebrew language far better than Wellhausen.

∽

Wellhausen's theory of the Torah being spliced together from four different documents was based on five supporting factors: the different names of God, the variations of language and style of the Hebrew, contradictions of viewpoints, duplications and repetitions, and signs of composite structure.[9] From the end of the nineteenth century well into the twentieth century, this theory has been the staple of liberal Christian theologians whose objective was to discredit the Torah. Since World War Two, its value as scientific theory has tarnished even among theologians due to its obvious shortcomings, not the least of which is that there is absolutely no hard evidence to back up Wellhausen's claims, no manuscript evidence, no "smoking gun" such as Codex *Sinaiticus*[10] to show of textual corruption.

One of the areas of contention was that of the Hebrew language. As Wellhausen himself admitted, "the study of the history of language is still at a very elementary stage in Hebrew,"[11] meaning that the study of the history of the Hebrew language was at a very elementary stage

---

[8] Ibid.

[9] Rabbi Umberto Cassuto, *The Documentary Hypothesis*. (Jerusalem, Shalem Press, 2006), 17.

[10] "The era of modern NT editions began almost exactly a century ago, when Tischendorf's 'editio octava maior' broke new ground in this field." Kurt Aland, "The Greek New Testament: Its Present and Future Editions." *Journal of Biblical Literature*. Vol. 87, No. 2, (Jun., 1968), 179.

[11] Wellhausen, *Prolegomena*, 390.

for German Christian theologians.[12] Jews have been speaking Hebrew for thousands of years, and it would seem that Wellhausen would recognize that the rabbis would have valid insights into their own language. For example, Wellhausen says of the creation of woman, "Then he forms the woman out of a rib of the sleeping man,"[13] an obvious Christian interpretation. As Rabbi S. R. Hirsch points out, the word *tsalah* (side) never appears in the Tanach as "rib." *Rashi*, the eleventh century commentator *par excellence*, explained that Adam, being created in the image of God, had both masculine and feminine natures, and the woman (according to the Hebrew text) was taken from man's side; in other words, he was divided into two separate but equal beings.

Wellhausen's use of non-Jewish terminology (such as describing ancient Jewish religion as a "cult" or "cultus") is, in the words of Rabbi S. R. Hirsch:

> A dangerous phenomenon to which attention must be drawn with the greatest emphasis: the mistaken application of non-Jewish terminology to Jewish religious conceptions, which has caused great confusion and which to this very day blocks the proper understanding of authentic Judaism as an historical phenomenon. This wrong terminology carried from outside into the Jewish sphere mainly concerns the key terms 'religion' and 'religious ceremony,' which have been quite wrongly identified with Torah and Divine law...the Torah is One and Unique like God its Creator. It has nothing in common with other laws, teachings, systems and institutions. It is so unique that it can be compared only to itself, it is something *sui generis*; as soon as you describe it by names and terms taken from other spheres you falsify the essence of the Torah and bar the way to its real understanding.[14]

It was precisely this reason,[15] to reduce the Torah to a mere man-made

---

[12] "The rarity of Hebrew scholarship in Christendom during the millennium from Jerome to Johann Reuchlin is all the more astonishing...even before Jerome the 'language of the Jews' had come to be regarded increasingly by theologians as a symbol of the alien, the sinister, and the hostile." Pinchas E. Lapide, *Hebrew in the Church*. Errol F. Rhodes, trans. (Grand Rapids: William B. Eerdmans Publishing Company, 1984), 3.

[13] Wellhausen, *Prolegomena*, 300.

[14] Hirsch, *Horeb*, xx–xxi.

[15] "Let us imagine a language in which every expression gives only the real nature of the objects it describes and not merely our subjective relation with them. In this language, words dealing with law and morality, physics and metaphysics, would

system of religion, that Wellhausen developed and used this non-Jewish terminology.

As pointed out earlier, there is perhaps no better example of this than the term "religion." There is no word or concept in Hebrew for the English word "religion," which comes from the Latin *religiō*. This Latin word has a hazy etymology; some speculate it possibly came from the Latin verb *religare* meaning "to link" or "unite." The modern definition of "religion" as we use it today was created during the Enlightenment by the very people who were attempting to diminish the influence of the Church, and to install a "wall of separation" between the Torah and modern state governments and legal systems. The conceptual nature of the "religious" versus the "secular" parts of Western society is an artificial construct using non-Jewish ideas along with Edomite (Latin) language and definitions.[16] These literary slight-of-hand tricks developed by the Christians (and "secular" scholars such as Arnold Toynbee) were used to disparage the Torah, to describe and interpret it using non-Jewish words and concepts,[17] a practice which Wellhausen honed to a fine art.

---

have no other object than to tell us what their elements are and what they should represent for us. Such a language would create a uniform doctrine, a uniform view, of the world and existence. It would embrace universal wisdom; its breakdown would have the gravest consequences. For example, let us attempt to do without using the English word 'have.' Hebrew does not possess this word. 'Have' involves a physical idea, *habere, avere*, to languish after something, and when you possess it, you 'have' it. Imagine that this word did not exist and that one only considers his that which is allotted to him, לו, as Hebrew expresses it. Then even the very idea of 'mine' and 'yours' as distinct property does not exist, for it is inconceivable except in terms of the relationship of object to personality. Now, introducing the notion of 'have' into this conception would have no less than a revolutionary effect. It would transform a legal term into a notion of the law of the strongest (*R' S.R. Hirsch* develops analogous examples for Hebrew words concerning justice, virtue, religion, life, people, family, etc.)" Munk, *The Call of the Torah: Bereishis*, 147.

[16] This is a point to keep in mind when "secularists" bring up the "wall of separation" issue. The issue of a division between "religious" and "secular" is a pagan concept, and Western culture has been conditioned to this philosophy from centuries of Gnostic thought and theology. This dualistic concept of "secular" and "profane" is not a "fundamental truth" as the secularists and atheists wish to portray it. A secularist will push this point in order to define the argument on his own terms, using this non-Jewish vocabulary and non-Jewish definitions, just as a Christian is wont to do when he is insistent on using theological interpretations on the *Tanach*.

[17] "To claim epistemic privilege for a social discourse is to demand social authority not only for its social agenda but also for its producers and carriers. To assert that a social discourse speaks a universally valid language of truth confers legitimacy on its social values and its carriers. In a word, the politics of epistemology is bound up

To give another example, modern Christian theologians often use the term "sacrificial cult" when describing Israel during the time of Moses. This term conjures up images of bloody pagan sacrifices, and the word "cult" has become a disparaging term to denote hierarchical religious system. One can argue that Moses was hardly a power-mad leader, and more than once tried to beg off doing the job of leading Israel, and one can also argue about the sacrifices, but consider this; what if the term "bloody sacrificial cult" was applied to Christianity? From its earliest stages, the Christian religion has resembled a cult more than anything else, with its secret teachings and initiation rites such as baptism. It is certainly a cult based on sacrifice, a bloody human sacrifice at that. Any Christian would vehemently protest the use of the term "bloody sacrificial cult" in describing their religion, yet they continue to describe Judaism, particularly ancient Judaism, using that term.

As Wellhausen pioneered the use of non-Jewish terms to describe the Torah, his example was used by later scholars such as Max Weber who had a habit of using the word *taboo* to describe the negative prohibitions of the Torah. The word *taboo*—a Polynesian word that was popularized after Captain James Cook's visit to Tonga in the 1770s—could not possibly convey the meaning of the Hebrew words such as *chatah* (sin), *tumah* (unclean or defiled), or *toevah* (abomination). Likewise, Max Weber described Moses as an *aisymnetes*,[18] or tyrant. A comparison of the substitution of Hebrew terminology for theological terminology can be made with Arnold Toynbee and his labeling the Jews as "Syriac:"

> The Old Testament, of course, is only representative of the Syriac religious genius in its young and callow phase; and even in this phase, towards its latter end, there was an outburst of spiritual experience and spiritual creation—recorded in the Books of the Prophets—which points forward to the New Testament. It is in the New Testament, manifestly, that the Syriac religious genius is revealed at its zenith.[19]

Here we see Christian theology creeping into historical accounts. Toynbee does not identify the teachings of the Torah as Divine Law, instead calling it a "Syriac religious" element. Calling the Jews "Syrians" was but one of the methods used to disassociate Jews from being

---

with social struggles to shape history." Steven Seidman, "The End of Sociological Theory: The Postmodern Hope." *Sociological Theory*, Vol. 9, No. 2 (1991), 135.

[18] Max Weber, *Economy and Society*, Guenther Roth and Claus Wittich, eds. (Berkeley: University of California Press, 1978), 443.

[19] Toynbee, *A Study of History*, Vol. 1, 211.

Hebrews or Israelites. Describing the *Tanach* in terms of being "callow," or immature, Toynbee then explained that the "mature" phase of this religion was expressed in the New Testament, i.e., the teachings of Jesus. And it was not only the teaching of Jesus that Toynbee made a comparison with, but the events of the *Tanach* itself were brought into question for their reliability, and this was not unlike Wellhausen labeling Judaism as a "cult" or using theological language to describe the Tanach: "Instead of the Ecclesiastical History of the Hexatecuch, the Book of Judges forthwith enters upon a secular history completely devoid of all churchly character."[20] Even today, Wellhausian language and ideas are used by intellectuals such as Richard Dawkins's book *The God Delusion*, where Dawkins describes Judaism as "the oldest of the three Abrahamic religions, and the clear ancestor of the other two, is Judaism: originally a tribal cult of a single fiercely unpleasant God, morbidly obsessed with sexual restrictions, with the smell of charred flesh, with his own superiority over rival gods and with the exclusiveness of his chosen desert tribe,"[21] showing the effects of theological concepts even on the atheist Dawkins.

～

T HERE WAS, IN FACT, a great deal of opposition to Wellhausen's theory; many rabbis criticized Wellhausen's "scientific/literary" technique, and Torah scholars such as Rabbi David Hoffmann, Rabbi Umberto Cassuto,[22] and Rabbi Dr. Joseph H. Hertz pointed out the many errors and inaccuracies in Wellhausen's hypotheses, the unscientific methodology of his approach, and the hundreds upon hundreds of verses that refuted the documentary theory. The structural elements in the Torah text that Wellhausen finds fault with, as had others such as Spinoza[23]

---

[20] Wellhausen, *Prolegomena*, 127.

[21] Dawkins, *The God Delusion*, 58.

[22] "The more recent gigantic commentaries on Genesis by Benno Jacob (*Das Erste Buch der Torah*, 1933) and by Umberto Cassuto (*La Questione de la Genesi*, 1934) have never elicited the reaction they deserve. Both these Jewish scholars, while not considering themselves bound in any way by the orthodox viewpoint, have shown by competent scholarship, each in his individual way, how the methodology and conclusions of the documentary theorists were unscientific and untenable." Max Kapustin, article *Biblical Criticism: A Traditionalist View. Challenge.* Aryeh Carmell and Cyril Domb, eds. (Jerusalem: Feldheim Publishers, 2000), 426.

[23] "Long before Julius Wellhausen in the nineteenth century popularized the idea that the biblical text was composed by different authors living in different periods,

before him, had been pointed out and explained in detail by rabbis since Talmudic times, yet Wellhausen simply brushed aside the criticism, dismissing the rabbinic rebuttals as beneath his attention.[24] The rabbinic commentary and criticism have been constantly ignored by Christian scholars,[25] a centuries-old tradition that was passed from the Church to the modern secular universities with the help of Julius Wellhausen.

The criticism of the Wellhausen theory is succinctly summed up by Herman Wouk:

> Wellhausen starts by announcing his grand theme: the forging priests, the non-existent tabernacle, and the phony doctrine of central worship. Then he plunges into his main task: getting the Bible to retell its story according to Wellhausen, in its own words…his method is simple, but the working out in detail is grandiose. Whatever passages of Scripture support his thesis, or at least do not oppose it, are authentic. Wherever the text contradicts him, the verses are spurious. His attack on each verse that does not support him is violent. He shows bad grammar, or internal inconsistency, or corrupt vocabulary, or jerkiness of continuity, every time. There is no passage he cannot explain away or annihilate. If he has to change the plain meaning of Hebrew words he does that too. He calls this 'conjectural emendation'…early in the game he seems to realize that he will not quite be able to shout down one haunting question: how is it after all that hundreds and hundreds of Bible verses refute his theory in plain words? Wellhausen answers this challenge by unveiling an extraordinary hypothetical figure, the Interpolater, a sort of master forger. Seeing across a span of twenty-three centuries, this man (or men) obviously anticipated the Wellhausen theory, and went through all of Holy Scripture carefully inserting passages that refuted it!…with the discovery of the Interpolater, Wellhausen's difficulties were at an end. As a tool of controversial logic this figure is wonderful. Sections of the Bible that appear to contradict Wellhausen are not only shorn of their genuineness, they turn around to become arguments in his favor. Wellhausen, of course, does not name the Interpolater. He

---

Spinoza led the charge against the ascription of divine authorship to the Torah." Smith, *Spinoza, Liberalism, and the Question of Jewish Identity*, 56.

[24] "The 'Higher Critics'…merely seized upon apparent difficulties which have been well known for centuries to all Torah scholars and have explained them on the basis of their *a priori* assumption that the Biblical text is not inspired. There is nothing inherent in these 'difficulties' which cannot be explained." Rabinovitch, *Challenge*, 60.

[25] "Although Wellhausen's theory did not go unchallenged, the few dissenting voices raised in opposition to it, were ignored." Irving M. Zeitlin, *Ancient Judaism: Biblical Criticism from Max Weber to the Present*. (Oxford: Polity Press, 1984), 287.

does not even personify him as a single figure. He merely summons an interpolater, perhaps once on every other page, to do his duty. When all else fails Wellhausen—grammar, continuity, divine names, or outright falsifying of the plain sense of the Hebrew—he works an interpolater.[26]

In addition to these points made by Wouk, there is another important determining factor in Wellhausen's thesis: how Christian theology corrupted the "scientific" approach to the theory of "higher criticism," and Wellhausen's double standard in his treatment of the New Testament as opposed to the Torah.

[26] Herman Wouk, *This is My God.* (New York: Little, Brown and Company, 1988), 309.

Going to Wellhausen Once Too Often

This so-called historical-critical school has dreamed up a science of its own, which it uses as a basis for reforming Judaism; it changes Bible and tradition into their opposite and plays at will with texts and sources.

— Rabbi Samson Raphael Hirsch[1]

HOWEVER WELL THE RABBINIC SCHOLARS DECONSTRUCTED Wellhausen's theory, too often missing in the criticism of Wellhausen's theoretical shortcomings and methodology was Wellhausen's theological approach to the Torah. We must understand that it was Christian theology, and not logic or "science," which was the foundation of Wellhausen's theory, and this was a point that has seldom, if ever, been stressed.

Wellhausen interjected theological comments throughout his work. Christian theology flows like a swollen river throughout the *Prolegomena*, drowning the true meaning of the Hebrew text with Christological interpretations. This can be seen in Wellhausen's comments such as "in dogmatic theology Judaism is a mere empty chasm over which one springs from the Old Testament to the New,"[2] and "as to the Apostle Paul the Spirit is the earnest of the resurrection of those who are born again, so to our author the Torah is the pledge of the resurrection of Israel."[3] When a scholar peppers his work on the Torah with comments such as Judaism being an "empty chasm over which one springs from the Old Testament to the New" and talking about being "born again," it is a clear indicator of the scholar having Christological points of view. These are not the terms of science or of logic, but the terms used by theologians attacking Judaism. Many of Wellhausen's comments, such as "the Church, at first a substitute for the nation which was wanting, is affected by the same evils incident to an artificial cultivation as meet us in Judaism...the religious individualism of the Gospel

---

[1] Hirsch, *Collected Writings*, Vol. II, 348.

[2] Wellhausen, *Prolegomena*, 1.

[3] Ibid., 401.

is, and must remain for all time, the true salt of the earth"[4] would have felt right at home next to the works of Chrysostom, Augustine, or Luther. Although Jewish scholars such as Cassuto and Hertz have critiqued Wellhausen's theory, exposing its shortcomings, and even modern Christian theologians have (to differing degrees) abandoned many of Wellhausen's teachings, his underlying theological *modus operandi* has never been adequately understood or explained. This is understandable since the majority of rabbis and even secular scholars are not well versed in Christian theology, and many of Wellhausen's theological statements pass by unnoticed, disguised as "modern scientific method."

To illustrate this, we will juxtapose two passages from the *Prolegomena*, one on the Law, the other on the Gospels. Here is Wellhausen's view of the Law:

> The law thrusts itself in everywhere; it commands and blocks up the access to heaven; it regulates and sets limits to the understanding of the divine working on earth. As far as it can, it takes the soul out of religion and spoils morality. It demands a service of God, which, though revealed, may yet with truth be called a self-chosen and unnatural one, the sense and use of which are apparent neither to the understanding nor the heart. The labour [*sic*] is done for the sake of the exercise; it does no one any good, and rejoices neither God nor man. It has no inner aim after which it spontaneously strives and which it hopes to attain by itself, but only an outward one, namely, the reward attached to it, which might as well be attached to other and possibly even more curious conditions. The ideal is a negative one, to keep one's self from sin, not a positive one, to do good upon the earth; the morality is one which scarcely requires for its exercise the existence of fellow-creatures... there is no connection between the Good One and goodness.[5]

This critique stating that the Law "thrusts itself in everywhere... and blocks up access to heaven" and "sets limits to the understanding of the divine working on earth" is referring to theological concept that Christians are saved by grace and not "works." To imply that the Law "takes the soul out of religion and spoils morality" is a Christian teaching that the Law is simply suffocating legalism as opposed to the all-embracing "love of Christ." To say that the Law "does no one any

---

[4] Ibid., 513.

[5] Ibid., 509.

good" and that its aim is not to "do good upon the earth" can only be sustained by ignoring the vast mountain of rabbinic writing that has piled up in the past two millennia. "Doing good" in theological terms means spreading the *knowledge* of Jesus so people can be "saved," an obvious Gnostic focus on salvation.

This contrast between Wellhausen's attitude towards the Torah and his view of the New Testament is made clear by this statement dealing with the New Testament:

> Self-denial is the chief demand of the Gospel; it means the same thing as that repentance which must precede entrance into the kingdom of God. The will thereby breaks away from the chain of its own acts, and makes an absolutely new beginning not conditioned by the past. The casual nexus which admits of being traced comes here to an end, and the mutual action, which cannot be analysed, [*sic*] between God and the soul begins. Miracle does not require to be understood, only to be believed, in order to take place. With men it is impossible, but with God it is possible. Jesus not only affirmed this, but proved it in His own person. The impression of His personality convinced the disciples of the fact of the forgiveness of their sins and of their second birth, and gave them courage to believe it. He had in fact lost His life and saved it; He could do as he would...Jesus works in the world and for the world, but with His faith He stands above the world and outside it...He is the first-born of the Father, yet, according to His own view, a first-born among many brethren. For He stands in this relation to God not because His nature is unique, but because He is man; He uses always and emphatically this general name of the race to designate His own person. In finding the way to God for Himself He has opened it to all.[6]

This is not the language or logic of science or of academic literary analysis—it is the language and logic of a Christian Sunday-school sermon. Statements such as "entrance into the kingdom of God" and "with men it is impossible, but with God it is possible" (Luke 18:27) as well as commenting on Jesus being "first born of God" and having a "unique nature" are theological concepts, not "scientific" ones. It is a teaching of Gnosticism when Wellhausen describes Jesus as being "above the world and outside it." When Wellhausen says that "the law...blocks up the access to heaven" he is speaking in Gnostic termi-nology. What he is implying is that the teachings of Judaism block the

---

[6] Ibid., 510–11.

Christian belief in heaven, that doing "works" negates the theological concept of "grace," which is that the *gnosis* of Jesus will allow one salvation. His claim that Judaism "takes the soul out of religion and spoils morality" is a gross distortion of the teachings of the Torah; it is the traditional Christian claim that Judaism is nothing but dry and negative legalism that buries morality by the weight of its rabbinical (read: man-made) ordinances. This passage above is not an aberration of his thesis, for in the *Prolegomena* Wellhausen makes many theological statements: "Jesus is the revelation of God made man,"[7] "He is the first-born of the Father,"[8] and "Jesus works in the world and for the world, but with His faith He stands above the world and outside it. He can sacrifice Himself for the world because He asks nothing from the world."[9] Wellhausen's remark that "The ideal is a negative one, to keep one's self from sin, not a positive one, to do good upon the earth; the morality is one which scarcely requires for its exercise the existence of fellow-creatures" is in direct contrast to the genuine teachings of the Sages.

⌒

WELLHAUSEN'S *PROLEGOMENA* is not simply peppered with theological statements; despite its ostentatious display of faux-positivism, it is wholly a work of theology, and theology is the foundation of Wellhausen's grand theory. Wellhausen's theory was designed to show the superiority of Christianity over Judaism, or as he said above, to "understand Hebrew antiquity without the book of the Torah," which is another way of saying, "interpreting the Torah using Gnostic Christian theology." Even the most fervent of Wellhausen's devotees would have a difficult time explaining theologically-based passages such as:

> Jesus was so full of new and positive ideas that He did not feel any need for breaking old idols, so free that no constraint could depress Him, so unconquerable that even under the load of the greatest accumulations of rubbish He could still breathe...he did not seek

---

[7] Ibid., 401.

[8] Ibid., 511.

[9] Ibid.

to take away one iota, but only to fulfil...the Church is...but an inheritance from Judaism to Christianity.[10]

The rabbinic laws and ordinances, as well as the commentaries, what Wellhausen calls "the greatest accumulations of rubbish," gives a clear picture of how Wellhausen viewed rabbinic scholarship as well as the contrast of the "new and positive" teachings of Jesus and the "rubbish" of the rabbis.[11]

Another flaw in Wellhausen's approach was that he treated the gospels as primary sources; he did not question that the texts were written long after the apostles had died, or that the texts had been corrupted by later scribes. Since this was exactly the position he took on the Torah, one would think that his positivist approach would naturally have been applied to the New Testament as well. By Wellhausen's day there was enough empirical evidence by other scholars such as Tischendorf, Wescott, and Hort to show that the ancient Greek texts of the New Testament had been extensively tampered with, yet Wellhausen not only refrained from doing so, but he treated the New Testament as even "holier" scripture than the Torah. Thus Wellhausen developed the format for later generations of Biblical scholars, dismissing the Torah (and thus Judaism) as a patchwork of later texts, and instead spent considerable time on the many textual problems of the New Testament by giving complex apologetics.

This can be seen in the duplicitous manner in which the texts of the New Testament have been analyzed. The literary system used by Christian biblical scholars on the Torah is too often a different system than what is used on the New Testament; if the same system is used, it is with different methods and conclusions. For instance, none of the four Gospels are mentioned by the church fathers until the second half of the second century. This seems incredible, since not only is the *Septuagint* often quoted by the early church fathers, but many of Paul's letters as well. The few quotations of Jesus that are quoted by early second-century writers are, in the words of Bruce M. Metzger, "often difficult to identify and delicate to interpret."[12] The early Greek texts of the Gospels "developed freely...[they were] a 'living text'

---

[10] Ibid., 512.

[11] "What conscientious man can attach any weight to the opposite assertion of the Talmud?" ibid., 166.

[12] Bruce Metzger, *The Canon of the New Testament.* (Oxford: Clarendon Press, 1992), 40.

in the Greek literary tradition, unlike the text of the Hebrew Old Testament."[13] All evidence points to the early Gospel texts that the documentary theorists based their faith upon being oral traditions that were in the process of being written and edited, and it is precisely this evidence that Wellhausen ignored.

LET US EXAMINE one of Wellhausen's theological passages from the *Prolegomena* in detail:

> The Gospel develops hidden impulses of the Old Testament, but it is a protest against the ruling tendency of Judaism. Jesus understands monotheism in a different way from his contemporaries...this monotheism is not to be satisfied with stipulated services, how many and great soever; it demands the whole man, it renders doubleness of heart and hypocrisy impossible. Jesus casts ridicule on the works of the law, the washing of hands and vessels, the tithing of mint and cummin, the abstinence even from doing good on the Sabbath. Against unfruitful self-sanctification He sets up another principle of morality, that of the service of one's neighbour...just this natural morality of self-surrender does He call the law of God; that supernatural morality which ceases to be an art which the Rabbis and Pharisees understand better than the unlearned people which know nothing of the law. The arrogance of the school fares ill at the hands of Jesus; He will know nothing on the partisanship of piety or of the separateness of the godly; He condemns the practice of judging a man's value before God. Holiness shrinks from contact with sinners, but He helps the world of misery and sin; and there is no commandment on which He insists more than that of forgiving others their debts as one hopes for forgiveness himself from heaven. He is most distinctly opposed to Judaism.[14]

Wellhausen makes reference to Mark 7:8, which reads: *For laying aside the commandment of God, you hold the tradition of men, as the washing of pots and cups: and many other such like things you do.* The second part of this verse, *as the washing of pots and cups: and many other such like things you do.* This verse is not found in the most ancient Greek manuscripts of Mark, especially papyrus 45 which is dated to the beginning of the third century CE, and is the earliest version of Mark known. Later texts, such as Codex Bezae, have this part of the verse in two different places, at the beginning of the verse and at

[13] Kurt and Barbara Aland, *The Text of the New Testament.* Trans. By Erroll G. Rhodes. (Grand Rapids, MI: William B. Eerdmans, 1987), 69.

[14] Wellhausen, *Prolegomena*, 509–10.

the end of the verse. Since it is not found in the earliest texts, and was inserted later in two different places, it certainly arouses suspicion that it is a later addition to the text of Mark. Wellhausen's first sentence, *"The Gospel develops hidden impulses of the Old Testament, but it is a protest against the ruling tendency of Judaism"* smacks of Gnosticism, of the "hidden mysteries" of the Torah that Jesus revealed to his followers. The teaching that the Gospel is a "protest against the ruling tendency of Judaism" is a theological argument, discounting the many times where Jesus supports Judaism, such as Mark 12:29 or Luke 5:39 and 10:25–28. The famous "Sermon on the Mount" in Matthew chapters 5–7 supports the rabbinic teachings of the era, particularly those of Rabbi Hillel. The only way Wellhausen could make a statement such as this was that he was either ignorant of rabbinic teachings of that era, or he simply rejected them for theological reasons. Neither reason is satisfactory. The "ruling tendency" of Judaism that Wellhausen criticizes has much to do with Judea being an occupied country during the time of Jesus. Certainly the teachings of the Gospels speak of Jesus' rulership; in Matthew 20:21 and Acts 1:6 show that Jesus' followers clearly understood that Jesus would be the hoped-for messiah that would establish Jewish self-rule; in Matthew 20:29 Jesus departs Jericho for Jerusalem with an army of followers, and he deliberately rides into Jerusalem on two animals at the same time—certainly one of the more unappreciated miracles of Jesus (Matthew 21:7)—to make sure everyone understands his motives. After he rides into Jerusalem with his mob of followers hailing him as the messiah (Matthew 21:9), Jesus then proceeds to take over the Temple.[15] After taking over the Temple and refusing to answer legitimate questions about what authority he has to do such a thing (Matthew 21:27), Jesus then destroys some native vegetation (Mark 11:11–14) before teaching on several of his favorite topics such as revenge, murder, and killing (Matthew 21:33–44). The concept that Jesus came to found a brand new religion that superseded the Torah is a later theological and Gnostic concept.

---

[15] In one of the earliest of the Gospels, the *Gospel of the Nazaraeans*, there is a quote following Matthew 21:12 in a thirteenth century manuscript of the Aurora, by Peter of Riga that states, "In the Gospel books which the Nazarenes use it is written: From his eyes went forth rays which terrified them and put them to flight." In the *Midrash Sefer Otzar HaMidrashim* Volume 2 (557) it states that the original Christians were a violent group of political agitators, as hinted at in Matthew 26:51, Mark 14:47, Luke 22:50, and John 18:10.

The New Testament teaches that "Jesus Christ [is] the same yesterday, and to day, and for ever." Since Jesus was born a Jew, lived as a
Jew, was called "rabbi," and died being mocked as "King of the Jews"
makes one wonder why Christians think that Jesus had anything to do
with a religion that was diametrically opposed to Judaism, a religion
whose theological tenets were developed centuries after his death. The
enemies of Jesus certainly understood that Jesus supported "the ruling
tendency of Judaism" (Matthew 21:46; John 11:48).

Next Wellhausen stated that *"This monotheism is not to be satisfied
with stipulated services, how many and great soever; it demands the
whole man, it renders doubleness of heart and hypocrisy impossible.
Jesus casts ridicule on the works of the law, the washing of hands
and vessels, the tithing of mint and cummin, the abstinence even from
doing good on the Sabbath."* It is ironic that Wellhausen spoke of
"doubleness of heart and hypocrisy," and then went on to quote several passages of the New Testament that highlight the problems with
both the text of the New Testament as well as the interpretation. The
very passages that Wellhausen quotes, Mark 7:6–8, Matthew 23:23,
and Matthew 12:12 are themselves altered texts, and the charge of
"doubleness of heart and hypocrisy" can be levied against Christianity for altering these texts in the first place. The verse *Woe unto you,
scribes and Pharisees, hypocrites! for ye pay tithe of mint and anise
and cummin* is from Matthew 23:23. This chapter, one of the most
anti-Semitic chapters found in the New Testament, is a chapter of dubious origin. This chapter has many words that have been added or
deleted (such as verse 14, which is not found in the earliest Greek
manuscripts, as well as the Greek word αθειναι in verse 23). In the
verse Matthew 23:35, *that upon you may come all the righteous blood
shed upon the earth, from the blood of righteous Abel unto the blood
of Zacharias son of Barachias, whom you slew between the temple
and the altar,* spoke of an event that happened many years after Jesus'
death, an event described by Josephus.[16] The inclusion of this verse
is what makes the entire chapter suspect. It was probably written in
the early to mid-second century as a rebuke against the rabbis that the
later Gnostic church was debating.

---

[16] "And as they intended to have Zacharias the son of Baruch, one of the most eminent
of the citizens, slain…so two of the boldest of them fell upon Zacharias in the middle
of the temple, and slew him." (Josephus, *War of the Jews*, b. IV, ch. VII, v. II).

The verse quoted by Wellhausen, *the abstinence even from doing good on the Sabbath*, which Wellhausen claimed was a point being made by Jesus to "cast ridicule on the works of the law." The problem with this was that, in Matthew chapter 12, Jesus was using the "works of the law" to prove his point to the other Pharisees. The theological explanation of Matthew 12:1–8 is an example of misinterpretation due to the Christian theologian's lack of Torah knowledge.[17] Theologians have traditionally used these verses to show that Jesus did away with the observance of the Sabbath as required in the Torah. In the last part of the passage, Wellhausen stated:

> *Just this natural morality of self-surrender does He call the law of God; that supernatural morality which ceases to be an art which the Rabbis and Pharisees understand better than the unlearned people which know nothing of the law. The arrogance of the school fares ill at the hands of Jesus; He will know nothing on the partisanship of piety or of the separateness of the godly; He condemns the practice of judging a man's value before God. Holiness shrinks from contact with sinners, but He helps the world of misery and sin; and there is no commandment on which He insists more than that of forgiving others their debts as one hopes for forgiveness himself from heaven. He is most distinctly opposed to Judaism.*

Wellhausen stated that Jesus was "distinctly opposed" to the Judaism of his day. Jesus was a Jew, and his whole life revolved around the Torah. His language, his family, his entire culture was based on Torah. To be "distinctly opposed" to Torah means that Jesus was distinctly opposed to himself and that which defined him. It would also mean that Jesus was a false prophet and a false teacher according to the Torah itself.[18] What Wellhausen meant, in theological terms, was that Jesus the Jew was theologically opposed to Judaism. Yet Jesus was not a Christian. He did not convert to a religion that did not exist in his lifetime, nor did he cease being a Jew. He often disagreed with other rabbis (Pharisees), but rabbinic disagreements were certainly not unusual then or now. The person who is "distinctly opposed to Judaism" is Wellhausen himself, and he projects his own prejudices onto Jesus. Wellhausen's statement that "*Against unfruitful self-sanctification He sets up another principle of morality, that of the service of one's neighbour*" begs one to ask: why is self-sanctification unfruitful? Wellhausen is

---

[17] Cf. Deut. 13: 1–6. Cecil, *The Noahide Guide to Matthew*, 94–95.

[18] Cf. Deut. 13: 1–5.

making a value-judgment here. In Judaism, one sanctifies himself by helping one's neighbor, paying tithes, and observing the Sabbath.

As with the historians, economists, and philosophers noted above, Wellhausen disparaged the Jew's own written history:

> It is not the case that the Jews had any profound respect for their ancient history; rather they condemned the whole earlier development, and allowed only the Mosaic time along with its Davidic reflex to stand; in other words, not history but the ideal. The theocratic ideal was from the exile onwards the centre of all thought and effort, and it annihilated the sense for objective truth, all regard and interest for the actual facts as they had been handed down. It is well known that there never have been more audacious history-makers than the Rabbins. But Chronicles affords evidence sufficient that this evil propensity goes back to a very early time, its root the dominating influence of the Law, being the root of Judaism itself.[19]

In this passage, as Wellhausen rewrites the history of Israel, he chastises the Jews for not being "objective" or having any "profound respect for their ancient history." Yet, throughout his work, Wellhausen only treats verses that support his theory as "authentic," while treating the New Testament by a different standard: "It might most fitly be compared with the Logos of the prologue of John, if the latter is understood in accordance with John x. 35, an utterance certainly authentic."[20] That the gospel of John was not mentioned until 170 CE by the Gnostic Heracleon, or that the first gospel mentioned was the gospel of Luke sixteen years earlier, and that the gospels of Mark and Matthew were not mentioned until the late Second Century CE creates certain historical difficulties for the theologian.

The early Church Fathers, such as Clement of Rome, often quoted from the Tanach, "frequently introduced by such well-known formulas as

---

[19] Wellhausen, *Prolegomena*, 161.

[20] Ibid., 401. The Gospel of John, a second-century Gnostic work, is entirely paraphrased (the same author of John also wrote the epistle of 1 John, which helps explain why Jesus' monologues in John are diametrically different than those found in the synoptic Gospels). The verse Wellhausen mentions, John 10:35, says "If he called them gods, unto whom the word of God came, (and the scripture cannot be broken)." The last phrase, "and the scripture cannot be broken" is an editorial comment from the writer of the Gospel. Also, in the previous verse, John 10:34, it says "Jesus answered them, Is it not written in your law, I said, Ye are gods?" Jesus' use of the second person pronoun "your" when speaking to the Jews about the Torah (Jesus himself was a Jew and under the Law) shows that this passage is most likely unauthentic.

'the Scripture says'…'it is written'…'that which is written.'"[21] Clement also quotes from a number of Paul's epistles. The few quotations of Jesus' teachings, however, are from the oral tradition, not from the written gospels. Ignatius, another early Second Century Church Father, also quotes from the oral tradition when attributing sayings of Jesus. It is not until the latter part of the Second Century when the Church Fathers begin to attribute Jesus' sayings to a written text, and even these early sayings are widely divergent, suggesting that they too came from an oral tradition.

Although there is evidence of an early Hebrew version of a number of Jesus' sayings, there is also evidence that the earliest versions of both Matthew and Luke did not contain the first two chapters (the "Virgin Birth" story), and that the early versions of the text state that Joseph was Jesus' father (texts which were later changed) as well as the silence of the early Church Fathers (as well as Paul) about the miraculous "Virgin Birth" make the accounts of Jesus' birth in both Matthew and Luke highly suspect. More importantly, out of the over five thousand Greek manuscripts of the New Testament, no two are in complete agreement, and the further back you go (to the end of the Second Century CE), the more variances in the text. All of the evidence points to an editing process culminating in the two major text-types first seen in the late third/ early fourth century, the Alexandrian and the Byzantine.

The empirical evidence of the early papyri as well as the extant work of the early Church Fathers all point to one inescapable conclusion; the Gospels were all written no earlier than the middle of the Second Century, and that the teachings of Jesus were orally transmitted for over a century. Wellhausen, however, ignored this evidence as did the theologians who followed him, even to the present day.

⁓

At the beginning of the previous section (p. 144, above) we mentioned the first of two comments that framed Wellhausen's work, his comment in the opening pages of the *Prolegomena*. "At last, in the course of a casual visit in Göttingen in the summer of 1867, I learned through Ritschl that Karl Heinrich Graf placed the Law later than the Prophets, and, almost without knowing his reasons for the hypothesis, I was prepared to accept it; I readily acknowledged

---

[21] Metzger, *The Canon of the New Testament*, 41.

to myself the possibility of understanding Hebrew antiquity without the book of the Torah." Wellhausen then proceeds to develop his "literary theory" to back up his desire to separate the Jews from the Torah. In his last statement of his work, he then gives the reason for doing so:

> The Jews, through their having on the one hand separated themselves, and on the other hand been excluded on religious grounds from the Gentiles, gained an eternal solidarity and solidity which has hitherto enabled them to survive all the attacks of time. The hostility of the Middle Ages involved them in no danger; the greatest peril has been brought upon them by modern times, along with permission and increasing inducements to abandon their separate position...the persistency of the race may of course prove a harder thing to overcome than Spinoza has supposed; but nevertheless he will be found to have spoken truly in declaring that the so-called emancipation of the Jews just inevitably lead to the extinction of Judaism wherever the process is extended beyond the political to the social sphere. For the accomplishment of this centuries may be required.[22]

For the accomplishment of "this"—the extinction of Judaism, and by association, the Jews themselves—*centuries may be required.* If there were any lingering doubts about Wellhausen's motives, he erases them at the ending of his work. The theory of "Higher Criticism" was Julius Wellhausen's scholarly contribution to the goal of the annihilation of Judaism. This was the goal not only of Christian theologians, but of the Greek-influenced philosophers of the Enlightenment, as exemplified in Immanuel Kant's statement[23] that the Jews should be led "to the final end...we can consider the proposal of Ben David, a highly intelligent Jew, to adopt publicly the religion of *Jesus* [presumably with its vehicle, the *Gospel*], a most fortunate one... the euthanasia of Judaism is pure moral religion, freed from all the ancient statutory teachings."[24] The aim of both the Christian theologian as well as the liberal Enlightenment scholar was the eradication

---

[22] Ibid., 548.

[23] "The description of Israel's future predicts that, over the centuries to come, nations and statesmen will not devote thought and effort to finding ways of dealing justly and humanely with these exiles in their midst, promoting their prosperity, affording them a livelihood, and aiding them in their pursuit of happiness. Instead, the aim of the nations and their leaders will be...'to destroy them,' to diminish them, to wear them down until they cease to exist." Hirsch, *Collected Writings*, Vol II, 423.

[24] Immanuel Kant, *The Conflict of the Faculties*. (Lincoln: University of Nebraska Press, 1992), 95.

of Judaism, if not by destroying the Torah, then by the conversion of Jews to Christianity. The only Jews that the Enlightenment tolerated were those that forsook the Torah, the "secular" Jews who would hopefully (in the eyes of the Enlightenment) assimilate themselves out of existence. Wellhausen was not a seeker of truth, but an expositor of theology; as with the other "enlightened" scholars of the nineteenth century, he was trying to destroy Judaism, not explain its origins.

The protocols of the theologians are the same as their secular academic counterparts, to destroy Judaism and eradicate the Jews, and with the support of other Enlightenment scholars, Julius Wellhausen developed new tools in which to perform this task. Wellhausen's documentary hypothesis would probably have ended up a minor theological theory except for one thing: it was adopted and used by secular academicians. The Graf-Wellhausen theory has been the tool of not only theologians, but also of historians such as Arnold J. Toynbee and sociologists such as Max Weber and Irving M. Zeitlin, for even as the Wellhausen theory slowly fell out of favor with theologians during the twentieth century due to its untenable methodology, it was repackaged into new forms of social theory.

CHAPTER FOUR

Protocols of the Sociologist

> If one had to name the single most important intellectual influence from the social sciences it would surely be Max Weber, whose work entered the mainstream of American academic discourse only after World War II.
>
> — Peter Novick[1]

THE ANALOGOUS THREADS OF GREEK-FUELED ANTI-SEMITISM OF THE Enlightenment philosophers and historians were bolstered with the implacable animosity of Christian theology, and this strain of anti-Semitism found its intellectual apogee in the work of Max Weber (1864–1920). Weber was the scholar most responsible for disseminating the Wellhausen theory throughout the social sciences (and to a lesser extent, the humanities), and it was through Weber's influential work, rather than Wellhausen's *Prolegomena*, that "Higher Criticism" or the "Documentary Hypothesis" was generally accepted among non-Jewish academicians.[2]

---

[1] Novick, *That Noble Dream*, 383.

[2] "Weber was most concerned with the problem of values, the role of religion in their formation, and community...Weber [was] part of that great pre-Hitlerian German classical tradition, which everyone respected." Bloom, *The Closing of the American Mind*, 148–49.

Weber not only made substantial contributions to the academic study of religion, economics, history, and political science, but he is recognized as one of the founders of the academic discipline of sociology.[3] Weber's transdisciplinary feats developed in an era when the paradigms of the social sciences were not as solidly fixed as they are today. In fact, it was Weber himself who provided the theory of *rationalization*[4] to explain that, as the social sciences became more complex and the amount of information increased, people would increasingly specialize in certain areas of each academic discipline. From the early decades of the 20th century on, academic disciplines have become separated as the knowledge base increases, and today the amassed knowledge in any one field is almost too much for any one scholar to handle, let alone master other fields. Thus Weber was one of the last of a vanishing breed, a polymath who had tremendous influence on the social sciences and the humanities, and even today many scholars speak in hushed, reverential tones when talking about *Saint Max*, an intellectual *par excellence*.

Sociology has always had an odd and indelible relationship with Judaism; two of its "Big Three" scholars credited for the creation of the science of Sociology, Karl Marx and Emile Durkheim,[5] were secular, assimilated Jews, products of the Enlightenment that swept through Western Europe in the nineteenth century. The third, Max Weber, was not Jewish, but, as Voltaire, obsessed with Judaism.

---

[3] Sociology is the youngest of the social sciences; it is the study of social groups, from the smallest group (such as the dynamics of a family) to the study of entire cultures. As with philosophy, which the Greek culture developed as an ethical and moral guide in lieu of Torah, so Sociology is the West's developed science to study and understand human interactions. The Sociologist, like the character Chance the Gardner in Jerzy Kosinski's *Being There*, just likes to watch. The Sociologist is supposed to be "value-free" or "value-neutral," which is sociological jargon for looking at the subject objectively. Weber has long been considered the paragon of objectivity.

[4] *Rationalization* has been described as the "organization of life through a division and coordination of activities on the basis of exact study of men's relations with each other, with their tools and their environment, for the purpose of achieving greater efficiency and productivity." [Julian Freund, *The Sociology of Max Weber*, (New York: Vintage Books, 1969), 18.] Or, as Jerome Karabel explained it, rationalization is "the process whereby emotion and tradition are increasingly replaced by knowledge-based rational calculation." Jerome Karabel, *The Chosen: The Hidden History of Admission and Exclusion at Harvard, Yale, and Princeton.* (New York: Houghton Mifflin Company, 2005), 610, n. 54.

[5] Durkheim's *anomie* comes from the Greek word *anomian*—usually translated as "lawlessness." In Matthew 7:23 *anomian* literally translates to "against the Jewish Law."

Before the Enlightenment, the hatred of the Jews was fueled by Christian theology; by the late nineteenth century, this burning hatred was intellectualized by the Enlightenment and stoked by the rediscovery of the concepts of Greek anti-Semitism. During this period, there began a series of writings (such as the *Protocols of the Elders of Zion* mentioned above) which helped perpetrate the concept that the Jew was manipulating the banking and financial markets of Europe, that it was the Jew who was in financial control of the European states, bribing governments, financing wars, and enticing revolution. Christian Europe looked at the Jews, who constituted less than one per-cent of society, as the prime motivators of social discord and political and economic upheaval, the aim of which was the Jewish domination of the world. Weber's work helped provide a scientific groundwork of the "myth of the Jewish aspiration for world domination found in the *Protocols of the Elders of Zion*, disseminated during the Weimar period"[6] which would have grave consequences for the Jews of Germany in the years following the collapse of the Weimar Republic. Weber's contributions to intellectualized and institutionalized anti-Semitism have, by and large, been ignored or overlooked.

As did Wellhausen, Weber grew up with a devoutly Lutheran parent. In Weber's case, it was his mother, whom Weber remained close to throughout his life, and this Lutheran upbringing doubtless influenced the cultural and theological framework for Weber's later temper concerning the Jews.[7] The anti-Semitic theology of German Lutheranism[8] had substantial influence upon the German Grand Theorists (Weber in particular), and influenced the research techniques of the later 20th century American social sciences.[9] Max Weber's proto-Nazi theories

---

[6] Gary A. Abraham, *Max Weber and the Jewish Question.* (Chicago: University of Illinois Press, 1992), 18.

[7] "It is almost certainly impossible to appreciate Max Weber's sociology without fully recognizing not only the salience of this theme, but also its relationship to Lutheranism." Roland Robertson, "On the Analysis of Mysticism: Pre-Weberian, Weberian and Post-Weberian Perspectives." *Sociological Analysis*, Vol. 36, No. 3 (Autumn, 1975), 245.

[8] "For centuries, the Lutheran Church disseminated some of the most toxic ideas in the history of anti-Semitism" Schoenfeld, *The Return of Anti-Semitism*, 81.

[9] "The withdrawal into systematic work on conceptions should be only a formal moment within the work of social science. It is useful to recall that in Germany the yield of such formal work was soon turned to encyclopedic and historical use.

on Judaism were the unfortunate culmination of transdisciplinary anti-Semitic teachings from the great German schools of history, philosophy, and—most notably—Christian theology.[10] Weber, more than any other scholar of the past two hundred years, was responsible for much of the anti-Jewish ethos in Western (particularly American) academia.[11] It is imperative, therefore, that we should take a hard and close look at Max Weber, who wielded great influence on the social sciences.

ᴄᴧ

Wᴇʙᴇʀ's ɪɴᴛᴇʀᴇsᴛ ɪɴ classical learning was evident at an early age; when the precocious thirteen-year-old Weber "wrote an essay on 'The Roman Empire from Constantine to the Teutonic Migrations,'"[12] he had already developed a fierce nationalism that would often resurface in later years, placing "the glory of the nation and the power of the state above all else."[13] It was this nationalism—another product of the Enlightenment, the secular West's attempt to replace values lost during its purge of religion—that exposed the limits of German academic objectivity. It was the reaction to this German nationalism that the American scholars—still partially inoculated by the Hebrew Puritanism—were able to keep this virulent strain of anti-Semitism at bay:

> On one issue American historians had been united since the summer of 1914: they were appalled at the prostitution of academic standards, and particularly historical scholarship, in all of the belligerent powers.

That use, presided over the ethos of Max Weber, was the climax of the classic German tradition." C. Wright Mills, *The Sociological Imagination.* (New York: Oxford University Press, 1959), 48.

[10] "In reflecting upon the rise of Nazism, some writers began to view Weber, not so much as a direct Nazi forerunner, but as a symptom of things to come." Guenther Roth, "Political Critiques of Max Weber: Some Implications for Political Sociology." *American Sociological Review.* Vol. 30, No. 2. (Apr., 1965), 220.

[11] "One of the most profound intellectual developments of the modern period has been the genesis of a specifically historical worldview, attentive not only to changing events and circumstances, but also to the subtly changing ways by which human understanding structures its world as a coherent unity. Between the late eighteenth and early twentieth centuries, when principles of historical understanding received their deepest conceptual foundation, this worldview gave rise to the conviction, most profoundly expressed in Germany, of the essentially historical character of human existence." Jeffery Andrew Barash, *Martin Heidegger and the Problem of Historical Meaning.* (New York: Fordham University Press, 2003), xvii.

[12] Weber, *Economy and Society*, xcvii.

[13] Raymond Aron, *Main Currents in Sociological Thought*, v.2., translated by Richard Howard and Helen Weaver. (New York: Basic Books Inc., 1967), 242.

The first dramatic example of the cooperation of scholars in wartime propaganda was 'To the Civilized World,' a 1914 manifesto signed by virtually every leading German scholar[14] and scientist—Albert Einstein was the sole important exception—endorsing the most outrageously false German official assertions on the origin and conduct of the war.[15]

Although Weber himself did not sign this manifesto, it is clear that he accepted many of its tenets. In historian Wolfgang J. Mommsen's book *Max Weber and German Politics 1890–1920*, Mommsen comments on part of an essay written by Weber in 1917 near the end of the Great War:

> This and the following passages were omitted from *Pol. Schr.* with the justification that they do not contribute 'anything to the issue' (p. 227). One asks: *which* issue? We can deplore the fact that Max Weber ever could have penned such sentences and even viewed it as scarcely possible. But is it right, especially in a scholarly edition, to hide one's head in the sand? It is impossible to avoid the fact that it is part of the picture of Max Weber as a 'heroic nationalist' that in extreme situations he did not hesitate to seize upon extreme means or extreme phraseology. We therefore offer [Max Weber's] relevant passage here verbatim:
>
> "But then *sheer scoundrels and adventurers* are at the head of some of the enemy powers—as is proved by the tone of their official statements, in contrast to those of the Germans. They are incapable of speaking about us except in the form of unworthy and at the same time clever insults, charge us with malicious imputations that *no people with a sense of honor* could bring themselves to utter. They speak of the war with the phrases of a prize fighter, and above all they forcefully repress the yearnings for peace of their own people, those of their allies, and those whom they subjugate. They do all this exclusively because they have to fear *their own* personal days of reckoning after the peace in view of the totally unrealizable fruits of war they have promised (in contrast to the German government). They therefore postpone the peace in the illusion that the German people's will for survival can yet collapse. As long as they maintain this illusion, *there will be no peace*. The German people alone know what fate would be prepared for them. The enemy armies are composed *increasingly of barbarians*. On the western frontier, the flotsam of African and Asiatic savages and all of the robbers and rabble of the world are fighting *with* them.

---

[14] There were more than a few theologians who signed the manifesto, including Adolf von Harnack.

[15] Novick, *That Noble Dream*, 114.

They are ready to devastate the German countryside the moment our army is no longer adequately supplied with the means of war. The bestial abomination that the undisciplined Russian hordes committed during their temporary advance in a region inhabited in part by their own *racial comrades*, recalls the medieval Mongol period. A part of the dominant classes of the enemy countries seem to have become completely *insane with hate*. An educated large landlord who was previously war minister of the Russian revolutionary government openly recommended the use of the knout against unarmed prisoners. In France, students have joined in the practice of spitting at unarmed foes that elsewhere has been characteristic only of prostitutes. No one can therefore doubt what would await the German people if there is any decline in war preparedness, all the more so because the enemies openly discuss, without dispute, plans for the systematic looting and permanent enslavement of Germany."[16]

In this telling passage, we get a glimpse of Weber's rabid nationalism which clouds his objectivity—here Weber sounds more in keeping with the later Nazi propagandists than from a "value-neutral" sociologist. Weber's nationalism and his attitude towards the "scoundrels and barbarians" of the Allied forces in contrast to the "honorable Germans" should be kept in mind when observing his attitude in his writings about the Jews.

Many hundreds of books and papers have been written about Weber and his methods; however, few scholars look at the role that Christian theology played in the development of Weber's theories.[17] American historians admired the Germans and copied their methods, yet the American mind-set was fundamentally different from the European. Even today, Americans have a puritanical streak that separates them from the Old World academia. It was through Weber's influence, particularly after World War II, that many of these European anti-Semitic ideas and concepts would filter into American academia.

W E SHOULD TAKE a moment to explain how the Jews have often been blamed for not being "patriotic" to their host countries, a charge

---

[16] Wolfgang J. Mommsen, Michael S. Steinberg, trans., *Max Weber and German Politics 1890—1920*. (Chicago: The University of Chicago Press, 1990), 263.

[17] "An exposition of Weber's views on methodology may be not merely incomplete but even misleading if it makes no reference at all to his substantive views on history and politics." W. G. Runciman, *A Critique of Max Weber's Philosophy of Social Science*. (Cambridge: Cambridge University Press, 2002), 4.

which, like so many others, is simply not true. The Jew is simply non-nationalistic. This has to do with Jewish identity; every non-Jewish nation on earth views their nationality on their country of birth. You are a German because you were born in Germany, you are American because you were born in America, and so on. The Jews—unlike every other nation—became a nation in the wilderness of Sinai long before they had a country. Being a Jew does not depend on where you were born. It does not matter that your parents were not themselves born Jewish,[18] for if they converted before you were born, you are considered a Jew, no matter if your skin is black or your hair is blonde and your eyes are blue. Even if your parents were Gentiles, if you convert, you are considered a Jew in every respect, a member of the nation of Israel. This is not to say that the Jews do not love the land of Israel; it was a gift to them from God, and what son does not love a treasured heirloom given to him by the father he loves?

It should also be pointed out that the attribute of nationalism is not a Torah virtue. The artificial value modern society places on nationalism was commented on by Rabbi Hirsch:

> Now if the community declares, 'We want to demonstrate the powers that are inherent in the community. We want to join forces so that we may establish ourselves'; if the community does not summon the individual to serve God but only to serve the community; if the community considers itself as an end instead of merely as a means toward an end, then all of mankind's moral future is compromised. The result will be that…men will perceive their own powers…and come to believe that the community can do without God and His moral Law…the creation of the idol of vacuous purpose, one which will bring no happiness but for the sake of which the individual is expected to give up his existence and the community is expected to renounce its allegiance to the moral law…the individual will believe that he has lived long enough if he sacrifices his life for the community even if it is for a vain cause, as long as that cause will promote the fame of his community, a quest for fame which cares nothing for the cost in human life.[19]

Judaism teaches that one should honor and be faithful to his host country and pray for the welfare of the state and its leader; from the

---

[18] Israel is the only nationality which is determined by the mother. If the mother is Jewish, her offspring are Jewish. If the mother is not Jewish, neither are her children, no matter what the pedigree of the father is.

[19] Hirsch, *T'rumath Tzvi*, 55.

Noahide perspective, a Noahide's first allegiance should be to God and His Torah, not the man-made boundaries of a political entity. After all, the state which a Noahide resides in is HASHEM's state, and every Noahide community is responsible for supporting a Torah-based system of law.

∽

ALTHOUGH ONE COULD argue that Weber was not a "practicing" Christian, he certainly had great interest in religion.[20] Weber was influenced by theologians such as Rudolph Sohm, who developed the concept of the "charismatic" individual,[21] as well has his close personal friend Ernst Troeltsch[22] and his cousin Otto Baumgarten, the professor of practical theology in Kiel. Weber was involved with the Evangelical-Social Congress, where he developed friendships with the theologians Gaul Göhre and Friedrich Naumann.[23] Weber was also influenced by the Neo-Kantian philosophy of scholars such as Heinrich Rickert,[24] and it is this influence that helped shape his views on Judaism. In his book *The Coming Crisis of Western Sociology*, Alvin W. Gouldner stated that "Weber was less hypocritically pious about morality and more 'realistic.'"[25] Weber was also less hypocritically anti-Semitic—he may have had a tolerance for assimilated Jews, but it was obvious he had little tolerance for orthodox Judaism, or little else that was different from his Aryan-Protestant culture. That many modern sociologists believed that Weber was not a Christian, such as Steven Seidman's claim that "I know of no evidence that indicates that Weber was a Christian

---

[20] Max Weber's wife, Marianne Weber, wrote that "[Max Weber] always preserved a profound reverence for the Gospel and genuine Christian religiosity." William H. Swatos, Jr. and Peter Kivisto, "Max Weber as 'Christian Sociologist.'" *Journal for the Scientific Study of Religion*. Vol. 30, No. 4, (Dec., 1991), 347.

[21] Thomas Ekstrand, *Max Weber in a Theological Perspective*. (Leuven, Belgium: Peeters, 2000), 167.

[22] Ibid., 36.

[23] Ibid., 34–35.

[24] Ibid., 24.

[25] Alvin W. Gouldner, *The Coming Crisis in Western Sociology*. (New York: Equinox Books, 1970), 388.

in either the sense of Church affiliation, espousal of Christian beliefs, or obeying a regimen of daily life organized around or legitimated by Christianity,"[26] a view which shows a lack of understanding of the theological themes in Weber's sociology.[27]

Weber has traditionally been the standard of consummate objectivity in his observations, yet when it came to the subject of Judaism—no small subject in his works—there was a marked theological subjectivity that permeated his theories of religion, economics, and history. When faced with Judaism, Weber lapsed into theological arguments in place of "objective" sociological theory. For example, compare Weber's view of the *Tanach* with his treatment of the New Testament. Weber said that "the entire written tradition then existing and the Levitical Torah were correspondingly revised...the tradition has then, during the fifth century, received its present form,"[28] and "the absolute prohibition of mixed marriages was practically the most important point...it is more probable that one and all of the prohibitions represent late theological constructions of formalist minded priests occasioned by the tabooing of 'mixture with Gentiles' and 'the cultic Decalogue.'"[29] Here we see Weber import the theological theories and language of Wellhausen into his "objective" and "scientific" approach to the Jewish Scriptures, using Wellhausen's theological theories of an "edited" Torah to subtly undermine Judaism. Weber's view of the New Testament, however, was that "the New Testament accounts bear the stamp of full trustworthiness in the decisive points."[30] This was the contrast that Weber made throughout his works: the Jewish Scripture—the Torah in particular—

---

[26] Steven Seidman, "Weber's Turn to Sociology: A Reply to Horst Helle." *Canadian Journal of Sociology / Cahiers canadiens de sociologie*. Vol. 10, No. 2, (Spring, 1985), 202.

[27] This also shows a discontinuity with Seidman's own postmodernist theories: "How can a knowing subject, who has particular interests and prejudices by virtue of living in a specific society at a particular historical juncture and occupying a specific social position defined by his or her class, gender, race, sexual orientation, and ethnic and religious status, produce concepts, explanations, and standards of validity that are universally valid?" Steven Seidman, *The Postmodern Turn: New Perspectives on Social Theory*. (Cambridge: Cambridge University Press, 1998), 123.

[28] Max Weber, *Ancient Judaism*, 350.

[29] Ibid., 351.

[30] Ibid., 421.

was not trustworthy, while the New Testament bore the "stamp of full trustworthiness." This attitude would later impact Weber's development of social theories by his use of the New Testament as a primary source when explaining the ethical morality of the Jews.

Since Weber's economic, political, and religious theories on Judaism were based on the work of Wellhausen, Weber's work was dependent on the continuing relevancy of the Wellhausen theory, a problem that has rarely been addressed. Besides the obvious problem of the anti-Semitic nature of the Christian point of view, the field of Sociology of Religion requires a great deal of remedial knowledge, and few "secular" social scientists have made the connection that Weber's work on ancient Judaism was based on the relevance of Wellhausen's "Documentary Theory."[31] Weber's reliance on Wellhausen is seen from examples such as "the newer wording (Lev. 19:9f.) ritualizes this in a manner typical of the priestly version...the older wording of the prescription is of superstitious origin,"[32] and that "the collection of Deuteronomy, dating from the time of kings, has been interpolated,"[33] as well as "it is highly probable...that the Sabbatical year was an interpolation from priestly law into the Book of the Covenant."[34] These passages show the Wellhausen influence on Weber's thesis of the development of "Israelite religion." Weber structured his thesis on the Graf-Wellhausen theory, and without it, his comparative theory of the development of Israelite religion falls apart. Weber's use of broad, sweeping generalizations too often goes unchallenged ("[in] the manner of the priestly version," etc.) What is Weber's "ideal-type" of the "priestly manner"? This is not what Judaism taught about itself, it is what Weber's theology has projected onto the Torah. Weber's assertions, such as "the older wording of the prescription is of superstitious origin,"[35] were made without his understanding of the Hebrew text, the subtle nuances in the original language, and certainly

---

[31] "Weber did little more than elaborate a number of theories of Julius Wellhausen." Abraham, *Max Weber and the Jewish Question*, 12.

[32] Weber, *Ancient Judaism*, 47.

[33] Ibid., 48.

[34] Ibid., 49.

[35] Ibid., 47.

without the understanding of the Oral Law. For example, without an understanding of the *halakha* for damage of sacred objects or property (cf. *Bava Kamma* 6b), one can miss the point of the written text entirely,[36] which is something Weber did quite often.

⌒

Weber's underlying thesis in *Ancient Judaism* was based on theological constructs, teaching that Judaism was a developed religion while Christianity was a revealed religion. For instance, Weber stated:

> The present legal norms of Deuteronomy may well have originated in the pre-exilic times of the city kingdoms, but they are certainly revised by the theologians in Exile. Presumably this also holds for the so-called 'Holiness Code' only that here the contribution of the Exile theologians was substantially greater. The social prescriptions found in this collection like those in the so-called 'Priestly Code' originated entirely in Exile.[37]

That Weber's theories on Judaism were substantially based on Wellhausen is readily apparent in his statements such as "the Deuteronomic work was probably completed near the time of what Wellhausen called the 'Jehovistic' fusion of the Yahwistic and Elohistic revisions of the ancient patriarchial legends and Levitical Moses traditions."[38] Not only Weber's ideas, but even his terminology[39] which he served up when

---

[36] "That as far as this law is concerned, a person could have smashed the holy Ark of the Covenant, rent the holy Curtain, destroyed the Temple vessels and indeed all the treasures of the Temple, and yet there would have been no judge on earth authorized to make him pay so much as one penny in damages…this state of affairs is certainly unique among all the world's legal systems, and we cannot help pointing out that already this one fact proves most cogently that Jewish Law is not the work of men, much less the product of a priestly hierarchy…priests or hierarchs would have branded the perpetrators of such a sacrilege as criminals guilty of a most flagrant offense and would have directed the secular officials of the government to serve first and foremost as protectors and avengers of their treasures." Hirsch, *T'rumath Tzvi*, 294.

[37] Weber, *Ancient Judaism*, 70.

[38] Ibid., 248.

[39] Weber often uses theological terms such as *liebesakosmismus*, or "world-denying love," a decidedly Gnostic concept. "The euphoria produced by salvation religion, related to a 'direct feeling of communion with God,' can incline the believers toward 'an objectless world-denying love' (einen objektlosen Liebesakosmismus)." Robert N. Bellah, "Max Weber and World-Denying Love: A Look at the Historical Sociology of Religion." *Journal of the American Academy of Religion.* Vol. 67, No. 2, (Jun., 1999), 283.

describing the Torah—generous helpings of words such as "cultic" and "taboos" accented with plenty of "so-called," "highly probables," and "most likelies"—show a subjectivity that is too often ignored by other sociologists, even when they were aware of Weber's reliance on Wellhausen.[40] Weber constructed his theory of the development of the Torah in *Ancient Judaism* using the foundation of Wellhausen's theological theory, and the validity of Weber's entire thesis (of Judaism as a developed religion) was wholly dependant on the validity of Wellhausen's *Prolegomena*—a fact too often overlooked by sociologists falling over themselves in their rush to praise Weber's work. The thought that basing a sociological theory on Wellhausen's "Higher Criticism" might be analogous to basing the theory of human evolution on the Piltdown Man seems to have been ignored.

By using theological language and concepts combined with the Wellhausen theory, such as using the word "legends" to describe the patriarchs, Weber paints the patriarchs as the forerunners of the "crafty Jew," saying that "their commercial ethic is questionable," and that "they characterize the ethic of a pariah people," and that "they lack all traits of personal heroism" as "they are characterized by trusting, devout humility and good nature admixed with a cunning shrewdness."[41] When Weber suggested that circumcision was "the one Israelite rite diffused from Egypt,"[42] Weber was taking a page from Voltaire, who claimed that "the Jews borrowed these customs from the Egyptians, as every ignorant and barbarous nation endeavors to imitate its learned and polite neighbors; hence those Jewish festivals, those dances of priests before the ark, those trumpets, those hymns, and so many other ceremonies entirely Egyptian."[43] Also, Weber's antipathy of rabbinical interpretations and viewpoints led to statements such as "the obvious proverbial turns of phrase with *Elokim* represent old Canaanite language usage. The use of *Elokim* in late writings is of course due to

---

[40] "Weber basically accepts Eduard Meyer's and Wellhausen's 'higher criticism' of the biblical texts…with 'higher criticism' Weber shares distrust in the great age of much of the patriarchal legends." Hans H. Gerth and Don Martindale, *Preface to Weber, Ancient Judaism,* xvi.

[41] Weber, *Ancient Judaism,* 51–52.

[42] Ibid., 92.

[43] Voltaire, *The Works of Voltaire: A Contemporary Version,* Vol. 19, 152.

shyness opposite the tetragrammaton."[44] The problem here was that Weber seemed to have no idea what the difference in the different Names of God represented. The rabbinical explanation of the use of the two Names is that *Elokim* is the Name of the attribute judgment, and the tetagrammaton, or *HASHEM* (the Name), is the attribute of mercy. For instance, the name *Elokim* is never used with Jewish sacrifices in the Torah, which goes against the pagan notion of sacrifices being necessary to appease the wrath of an angry God. To Weber, this view of the rabbis was either unknown or ignored, and his use of the qualifier "of course" sounds forced.

Weber's scholarship was no better than the philosophers, historians, and theologians which he based his theories upon, and, as we shall discuss, when it came to Judaism these theories were highly subjective. As with most other German academics, Weber not only continued the practice of ignoring the Jewish primary sources in his approach to the study of ancient Judaism but he took it to a new extreme. Weber made clear his attitude on rabbinic scholarship:

> For ancient Israelite religion, modern Protestant, especially German, scholarship is acknowledged to be authoritative to this day. For Talmudic Judaism, on the whole the considerable superiority of Jewish scholarship is unquestionable.[45]

What is questionable is that Weber not only ignored the rabbinic scholarship of ancient Jewish history, but he did not use Jewish scholarship when discussing the Talmudic and post-Talmudic period, a subject which he spoke of extensively in his major work *Economy and Society*. It is hard to conceive a situation such as this, where the most erudite and literate scholars of the subject being discussed are not consulted or rarely quoted. To dismiss Jewish scholarship on the subject of their own history and religion because it is "not authoritative" is an indicator of the subjectivity of Weber's approach, which is that the Jewish point of view is entirely ignored in favor of a Christian theological point of view. In *Ancient Judaism*, when explaining the role of the rabbi, Weber uses New Testament references such as, "the conditions presupposed by the Gospels indicate" and "the accounts of the Gospels indicate."[46] When explaining the role

---

[44] Weber, *Ancient Judaism*, 449.

[45] Ibid., 425.

[46] Ibid., 392.

of miracles in Judaism, he gives as his example "the Gospels had the Jews and also, expressly, the scholars and the Pharisees, demand a 'sign' from Jesus."[47] Weber, following Wellhausen, used the New Testament as his primary source for portraying the Pharisees and the rabbis of the late Second Temple era, and he relied on "modern Protestant, especially German" scholarship to interpret the text of the *Tanach*.

In the introduction to Max Weber's *Sociology of Religion*, Talcott Parsons wrote that when Weber "turned his studies toward religion, his focus was not upon religion 'as such,' as the theologian or church historian conceives it."[48] This is, however, exactly what Weber did, approaching Judaism "as the theologian and church historian" conceived it, and the use of theological language and concepts affected Weber's theory of religion—one of the foundational theories of sociology, a theory that "is generally the most difficult to grasp: the influence of certain religious ideas on the development of an economic spirit, or the ethos of an economic system."[49] This theory has been viewed as a normative model of the influence of ideas upon society, opposed to Marx's thesis that "values and beliefs [were] by-products of class or material interests."[50] The theological ideas that affected Weber's viewpoint and analysis of the development of religious ethics, and the concept of keeping the viewpoint "scientific," and not as "the theologian or church historian conceives it," removed critical viewpoints and ideas from sociological theory, ideas which were absolutely necessary for the understanding of concepts such as Weber's concept of *rationalization*. If sociologists think that inclusion of a religious point of view sullies the pure scientific thought of the "objective" sociologist, how can they be cognizant of theology in fundamental sociological theory if they are not aware that these ideas exist? The point is that a sociologist believes that he is approaching the subject "objectively" by viewing the structural evidence not as the theologian or church historian conceives it. To approach a subject such as religion from a different religious vantage point can make a difference, not just in theological understanding, but in determining even which structural evidence to present and how it is interpreted. Therefore, in claiming

---

[47] Ibid., 394.

[48] Talcott Parsons, introduction to Max Weber, *The Sociology of Religion*. Ephraim Fischoff, trans. (Boston: Beacon Press, 1991), xxx.

[49] Max Weber, *The Protestant Ethic and the Spirit of Capitalism*. (New York: Charles Scribner's Sons, 1958), 27.

[50] Frank Parkin, *Max Weber*. (New York: Routledge, 1991), 40.

themselves to be objective and at the same time omitting an important structural and normative perspective, sociologists actually limit their objectivity rather than enhance it.

◌

Max Weber's method of comparative sociology in his book *Ancient Judaism*[51] starts off by analogizing the Jews to the Indian caste system, specifically the pariah class. He uses terminology that defines the uniqueness of the Jews in a decidedly negative light, saying that "sociologically speaking, the Jews were a pariah people."[52] The Jews, the keepers and teachers of the Torah, the moral and ethical leaders of mankind, the nation of priests and a "holy people," were—in Weber's eyes—the untouchables of Western Civilization, and he makes that point in the very beginning of his book. His comparison with the pariah caste of India and the application of the term to Israel set the tone of Weber's thesis,[53] and it follows the pattern of other Western scholars in describing the Jews in depreciating terms, from Gibbon's "obnoxious" Jews to Voltaire and Mill's "barbarous" Jews, Toynbee's "fossilized" Jews, and finally to hit the bottom as the "pariah" class of Weber's *Ancient Judaism*.[54] According to Weber, it was the pariahism of the Jews that separated them from the rest of humanity. Basing his thesis on the theological theory of Wellhausen,[55] Weber laced his theory with

---

[51] "[Weber's] work on Judaism was dedicated to his mistress, who was the wife of a Jewish colleague and friend." Arnaldo Momigliano, "Two Types of Universal History: The Cases of E. A. Freeman and Max Weber." *The Journal of Modern History*, Vol. 58, No. 1 (March 1986), 244.

[52] Weber, *Ancient Judaism*, 3.

[53] "Believing Jews never gave up their sovereign rights and never admitted to being without political institutions of their own. This excludes that subjective acceptance of an inferior, non-political, status which seems to be essential to Weber's definition of the Jews as pariahs." Arnaldo Momigliano, "A Note on Max Weber's Definition of Judaism as a Pariah-Religion." *History and Theory*. Vol. 19, No. 3 (Oct., 1980), 316.

[54] It should be remembered that by the time of Weber's writing in the early twentieth century, the Jews had been "liberated" from the ghettos and had obtained—from a legal standpoint at least—full citizenship in Germany and thus were technically no longer "pariahs."

[55] "Because Weber possessed only a limited command of Hebrew, his study of ancient Judaism depended heavily on the secondary analyses of Wellhausen and his followers, the range of which he mastered to an outstanding degree." Tony Fahey, "Max Weber's Ancient Judaism." *The American Journal of Sociology*. Vol. 88, No. 1 (Jul., 1982), 78–79.

theological statements, saying that "the world-historical importance of Jewish religious development rests above all in the creation of the *Old Testament*, for one of the most significant intellectual achievements of the Pauline mission was that it preserved and transferred this sacred book of the Jews to Christianity as one of its own sacred books," and by doing so, eliminated "all those aspects of the ethic enjoined by the *Old Testament* which ritually characterize the special position of Jewry as a pariah people."[56] So Weber's readers do not miss the theological importance of this interpretation of the Hebrew Scriptures, Weber adds that "these aspects were not binding upon Christianity because they had been suspended by the Christian redeemer."[57] The problem, from the Noahide perspective, that Jesus was neither a Christian nor a redeemer was a point which seemed to elude Max Weber.

Weber recognized that it was the acceptance of the Hebrew Scriptures that allowed the Gnostic sect that became the Catholic Church to emerge triumphant over the other Gnostic Christian sects, but he does not grasp that the theological motifs of Christianity were themselves Gnostic: "Pharisaic and older Judaism were unfamiliar with the dualism[58] of 'spirit' and 'matter,' or spirit' and 'body,' or 'spirit' and 'flesh,' or divine purity and the corruption of the 'world,' dualisms which Hellenistic intellectualism had elaborated."[59] Weber interprets the *Tanach* from the same German Lutheran viewpoint as did Julius Wellhausen, saying that "the unique promises of the great unknown author of exilic times who wrote the prophetic theodicy of sufferance (Isaiah 40–55)— especially the doctrine of the Servant of Yahwe who teaches and who without guilt voluntarily suffers and dies as a redeeming sacrifice"[60] meaning, of course, salvation in Jesus, which is, needless to say, not a Jewish concept. Weber further elaborates on the Gnostic concepts of Christianity, such as its focus on the salvation of the individual, by

---

[56] Weber, *Ancient Judaism*, 4.

[57] Ibid.

[58] "The Rabbis insisted on the corporeality of human essence and on the centrality of physical filiation and concrete historical memory as supreme values. Consistent with their rejection of dualism in anthropology, they also rejected dualist theories of language." Daniel Boyarin, *Carnal Israel: Reading Sex in Talmudic Culture*. (Berkeley: University of California Press, 1995), 235.

[59] Weber, *Ancient Judaism*, 400.

[60] Ibid., 5.

saying that "with the salvation doctrine of Christianity as its core, the Pauline mission in achieving emancipation from the self-created ghetto, found a linkage to a Jewish—even though half buried—doctrine derived from the religious experience of the exiled people."[61] Viewing Judaism from a decidedly Christian foundation and using the Documentary Hypothesis, the theological motifs of Weber's argument provide the structure necessary for his thesis of "how did Jewry develop into a pariah people."[62] Weber maintains that the "emancipation from the ritual prescriptions of the Torah, founding the caste-like segregation of the Jews, the Christian congregation would have remained a small sect of the Jewish pariah people,"[63] which is another theological argument.

The problem with this argument was that Noahides did not have to be "emancipated" from "the ritual prescriptions of the Torah" simply because they were not under them to begin with. The Noahides had only to keep the Seven Laws—a fact Weber obviously did not understand; in his book *Ancient Judaism* Weber wrote that "the '*ger-sha'ar*' (proselyte of the gate) was, according to theory, the old metic under Jewish jurisdiction. He vowed before three members of the brotherhood to honor no idols. The seven Noachidic commandments, the Sabbath, the taboo against pigs, the ritualistic fasts were binding on him, but not circumcision."[64] Although Weber knew of the Seven Laws, his understanding was obviously incomplete, and was doubtful that he wanted to understand it, since it was a teaching of rabbinic Judaism.[65] Had Weber truly taken the time to research the Noahide Law, he might not have believed that "emancipation from the ritual prescriptions of the Torah, founding the caste-like segregation of the Jews, the Christian congregation would have remained a small sect of the Jewish pariah people." Weber also neglects to grasp that if the reforms of Constantine's nephew Emperor Julian "the Apostate"[66] had

---

[61] Ibid.

[62] Ibid.

[63] Ibid., 4–5.

[64] Ibid., 419.

[65] Concerning the context of Weber's remark that "for Talmudic Judaism, on the whole the considerable superiority of Jewish scholarship is unquestionable," it is obvious that Weber did not regard the "superior" Jewish scholarship on this issue.

[66] "So far from being the monster of iniquity represented by the Church Fathers, Julian was one of the very few rulers of the Roman world who extended the hand of

taken effect (he ruled for only two years—361–63 CE), such as his decree to rebuild the Temple in Jerusalem—thus reversing the work of his uncle—the Noahide Code might have been the dominant faith in the Roman Empire instead of Christianity, and the Jews would not have been "pariahs" but rather co-religionists with the people of the Empire. It should also be pointed out that the early Church in Jerusalem—the Church led by James the brother of Jesus—was itself using the Noahide Law as the basis for including the Gentiles coming into the nascent Christian sect. This can be adduced by the inclusion of Hillel's maxim "what is hateful to yourself, do not do to another" in Acts 15:20 that is found in many of the earliest Greek manuscripts of Acts as well as in the earliest quotation of this verse by the Church Father Irenaeus.[67] That this verse (and subsequent theological teaching) was altered by the later Church brings into question the idea that the "emancipation from the ritual prescriptions of the Torah" was the work of the "Christian redeemer" or the teaching of the early Jerusalem Church.

This is an important point, since the Jew's stubborn adherence to the Law was a primary variable in Weber's *pariah* thesis, which supports his theory of *ressentiment* (which we will deal with below). According to Weber, had the Christians not "emancipated" themselves from the Law, they too would have been infected with *pariahism*, just like the Christian doctrine of Adam being infected with "original sin." Concerning Weber's analysis, Jesus did not "suspend" the Law, nor did the Christians "emancipate" themselves "from the ritual prescriptions of the Torah, founding the caste-like segregation of the Jews." The Jerusalem Church, later known as the Ebionites, eventually died out on its own a few centuries later from continual persecutions from their "stubborn" allegiance to the Torah, as well as their realization that Jesus was obviously not the promised Messiah. The Gnostic Jesus cult was a wholly new and different organism, based on the Gnostic teachings of Paul and others such as Marcion who came after him. The "Christianity" which became the established Church centuries later was a child of Greek Gnosticism, adopted by Rome/Edom, the enemy of Israel. Weber, following the Gnostic interpretations, ascribes Divine approval to Christological interpretations instead

---

friendship and good-will to the scattered race of Israel." Michael Adler, "The Emperor Julian and the Jews." *The Jewish Quarterly Review*. Vol. 5, No. 4 (Jul., 1893), 592.

[67] Irenaeus, *Against Heresies*, book iii.,12:14.

of the original teachings of the Jewish Church which was hijacked by Gnostics; Weber's "analysis" consisted of endless comparisons of Israelite to other pagan cultures, and always within the Wellhausen framework of Judaism being a developed religion. Concepts such as charity that are taught in the Torah were not from God's revelation to Moses, but "presumably the development of old Israelite charity was influenced by Egypt directly or by way of Phoenicia."[68] Weber endlessly compares Judaism with Greek, Egyptian, Babylonian, and even Christian religions. As with Wellhausen, Weber even compared Judaism with religions that Israel had little or no contact with in those days, such as the religions of China or India. Judaism was presented as a developed religion, soaking up the religious practices of its neighbors as the centuries progressed. It is a one-way transfer of ideas; it was the Jews that absorbed pagan religious concepts, and then changed them to fit their own idiosyncrasies. With his theme of pariahism, Weber came close to describing Israel as the "parasite nation," as the German propagandists would paint them just a few decades after *Ancient Judaism* was published.

❧

I<small>N</small> *E<small>CONOMY AND</small> S<small>OCIETY</small>,*[69] Weber builds upon the argument which was "expounded by Nietzsche"[70]—the attitude of *ressentiment*, derived from passages in the "Old Testament," most notably in the Psalms—that "the unequal distribution of mundane goods is caused by the sinfulness and illegality of the privileged, and that sooner or later God's wrath will overtake them."[71] The Psalms, more than any other part of the Hebrew Scriptures, have been revered by Christians since the beginning of Christianity; indeed, next to the New Testament, the Psalms were the most popular part of the Christian Bible. Even today, many "pocket" New Testaments include the Psalms. Therefore, if the Psalms had an influence upon Judaism (and therefore Jews), logic

---

[68] Weber, *Ancient Judaism*, 258.

[69] Weber's *Economy and Society* was a rebuttal to Werner Sombart's *The Jews and Modern Capitalsim*, which itself was a rebuttal to Weber's *Protestant Ethic and the Spirit of Capitalism*. The core of all three books revolved around the argument of whether Jews or Calvinists were responsible for the development of Capitalism.

[70] Weber, *Economy and Society*, 494.

[71] Ibid.

would dictate that they also had an influence upon Christianity (and therefore Christians) since Christianity holds these same Hebrew texts to be sacred.

To determine the factors in Weber's theory where *ressentiment* is reflected in the "pariah" culture[72] of the Jews, or if the dominant Christian culture also has produced the *ressentiment* ethic, one has to understand Weber's theological argument that the ethic of *ressentiment* of the Jews was a dependant variable of their pariah status, and that the scriptural passages which speak of "vengeance" were written after the loss of political autonomy of the Jews. Christianity, however, has used these same passages for the development of Christian "replacement" theology which teaches that, since the Jews denied Jesus as the Messiah, or Christ, God removed all of the promises which He made in the Old Testament[73] from Israel, and that the "church," i.e. Christianity, was the "New Israel" and that all of the wonderful promises and terrible "vengeance" against its enemies which God had promised would now be applied to Christians, not Jews. It was the Jews, therefore, that became the recipients of the wrath of God, and not the Christians. Weber therefore developed a model where the Scriptural *ressentiment* passages could be used against the Jews.

If you look at the way the Psalms were interpreted by the Jews, particularly the "resentment" Psalms, you can see the dichotomy[74] in

---

[72] "In our usage, 'pariah people' denotes a distinctive hereditary social group lacking autonomous political organization and...additional traits of...political and social disprivilege and a far-reaching distinctiveness in economic functioning." Ibid., 495.

[73] In the "ressentiment" Psalms, "the hope is entertained that ultimately the wrath of God will finally have been appeased and will turn itself to punishing the Godless foes in double measure, making of them at some future day the footstool of Israel." Ibid.

[74] "Why should such terrible suffering be imposed on nations in punishment for what seems to imply an ethical shortcoming? Their glee, blameworthy and reprehensible as it was, did not contravene any of the seven Noachic laws. Why then, should the punishment be so severe? This question calls into focus the very essence of the Torah's perception of the gentile nations and their relationship to God and Israel. The Torah stresses repeatedly that no special expectations of reward set Israel apart from the other nations. The promise of *life* for walking in God's statutes is to *man* in general (*Leviticus* 18:5), not to Israel in particular; Heaven's gates are exhorted to open for any *nation* of enduring loyalty (*Isaiah* 26:2). All righteous people will enter God's gates (*Psalms* 33:1). Nor will God's kindness be bestowed upon Israel exclusively. All who are good and straightforward in their hearts (*Psalms* 125:4) will merit it (*Yalkut, Leviticus* 591). Israel is distinguished not in privileges but in responsibilities...it is to be the כהנים ממלכת, kingdom of priests (*Exodus* 19:6), who...are to lead the whole

the scholarship of the Jews and the Christians. Here is an example of one of the Psalms (2:8–12) where Weber's "resentment" is found:

> You ask of Me that I let the nation of the earth be your [the Jews] inheritance, and the ends of the earth your possession. But if you must break them with a rod of iron, then you will smash them to pieces like potter's vessels. And now, O kings, comprehend this; chastise yourselves, O judges of the earth! Serve the Lord with fear and rejoice greatly with trembling. Grid yourselves with purity,[75] lest He be angry and you perish on the way, for His wrath might be kindled soon! Only those stride forward who will put their trust in Him.

The interpretation and commentary on this Psalm by Rabbi S. R. Hirsch explains the Jewish perspective:

> It can be clearly seen from Verses 10–12 that the terms "inheritance" and "possession" as used here cannot be construed to mean the conquest and subjugation of the nations under the sovereignty of rulers. Homage to God and to His moral Law, joyous devotion to Him and to His will, and girding oneself with purity are the demands made upon the rulers of the nations through the fact of the existence of the Kingdom of David. נחלה and אחזה, therefore, denote only the spiritual and ethical conquest, the fact that the ideas and attitudes of nations will fall to the spirit and doctrine of David.[76]

---

of mankind to God just as a kohen within Israel is assigned to strengthen the bond between God and His people. Since God's lofty purpose for the nations of the world can be realized only by their willingness to be led by Israel, their right to existence must depend on the degree to which they are willing to learn from Israel and her fate. Indeed, the one nation which will obstinately and unbendingly refuse to accede to Israel's role—Amalek (see *Yalkut, Exodus* 268)—*is for that reason* condemned to ultimate, total destruction. (See *Pachad Yitzchak* to Purim, ch. 1). The destruction of Temple and land had been planned as a lesson to mankind. *Deuteronomy* 29:23 describes how the nations were to realize that Israel's terrible fate resulted from its forsaking of God and His covenant. Had the nations learned this lesson and related to Israel and her situation according ot God's plan, they would thereby have justified their existence. However, Israel's neighbors were far from being sobered by the holocaust. Instead, they mindlessly rejoiced at the downfall of their enemy. They were condemned to destruction, therefore—not in punishment for their unethical reaction, but because their attitude revealed that they could never fulfill the purpose of their existence." *Yechezkel*. Rabbi Moshe Eisemann, translation and commentary. (Brooklyn: Mesorah Publications, Ltd., 1994), 429–30.

[75] Many Christian Bibles have deliberately mistranslated this part of the verse as "Kiss the Son" in an attempt to make this a "prophecy" about Jesus.

[76] Hirsch, *The Hirsch Psalms*, §i., 12.

This interpretation is vastly different from the picture painted by Weber (and Wellhausen) that portrayed the Jews as a vengeful people that wished to dominate and rule the rest of mankind. "In no other religion in the world do we find a universal deity possessing the unparalleled desire for vengeance manifested by Yahweh...the religion of the Psalms is full of the need for vengeance...in the mind of the pious Jew the moralism of the law was inevitably combined with the aforementioned hope for revenge."[77] Yet if Christians themselves had the ethic of *ressentiment* (as described by Weber), then they would somehow have to describe themselves as the "disprivileged" group to fit their theology of being the "New Israel" in with the Scriptures. Since Christians of the past five centuries (during the formative period of capitalism as explained by Weber) did not exactly fulfill the requirements laid out by Weber to be a "pariah" people, we must find examples of how the Christians were able to portray themselves as the biblically disprivileged group, or the "New Israel" who suffered at the hands of their oppressors, the Jews, and how Weber's concept of *ressentiment*—"the unequal distribution of mundane goods...caused by the sinfulness and illegality of the privileged"—can be applied to the Christians.

The first example is the commodity that was "unequally" distributed in the New Testament, which is the major commodity of the Church: salvation. Throughout the New Testament, the major theme of Christian *ressentiment* was that the Jews had a monopoly on salvation, and Jews taught that salvation came from the Law and not from "grace" or "faith in Jesus." The greatest fear of the Christians (not only theologians but scholars such as Wellhausen and Weber) was that the Jews would spread the Torah throughout the world, and by so doing not only eradicate Christianity, but nationalism as well: "[The Jews] dreamed not only of a restoration of the old kingdom, but of the erection of a universal world-monarchy, which should raise its head at Jerusalem over the ruins of the heathen empires."[78] Here we see the paranoia of Esau, the concept taught by the Sages of "*The might shall pass from one regime to the other*."[79] It was this fear of losing

---

[77] Weber, *Economy and Society*, 495.

[78] Wellhausen, *Prolegomena*, 503.

[79] "They will never be both strong at the same time; when one falls, the other will rise." *Rashi*, commentary on *Bereishis* 25:23.

power that fuels the hostility towards Judaism, and the portrayal of the Jews as a power-mad people bent on world domination: "As the heathen empires stood in the way of the universal dominion of Israel, the whole of them together were regarded as one power, and this world-empire was then set over against the kingdom of God, i.e., of Israel."[80] The next example has to do with Weber's reasons that the Jewish pariahism was not the result so much of external factors, but of internal ones; not only does Weber treat the ethic of *ressentiment* of the Jews as a dependant variable of their pariah status, but also that of a so-called double ethical standard. Weber stated that the Jews "as a pariah people, they retained the double standard of morals which is characteristic of primordial economic practice in all communities: what is prohibited in relation to one's brothers is permitted in relation to strangers."[81] According to Weber's thesis, not only Jewish *ressentiment* but the "double moral standard" are dependant variables of the Jew's pariah status, and are two premises which Weber uses to support his principle of Jewish "pariahism."

In Weber's section of Chapter VI; xii; 4. in his *Economy and Society*, the sub-section on *Religious Ethics, Economic Rationality and the Issue of Usury*, Weber's use of comparative sociology—where he had previously been comparing Judaism to Christianity, Islam, Buddhism, Hinduism, and whatever other religions he could come up with—was tossed aside. In the entire section on *usury*, Weber did not compare the Jewish laws on usury with other legal systems, and only mentioned the Jews twice in passing, saying that "among the Jews, collecting usury from 'members of the tribe' (Volksgenossen) was prohibited"[82] and that "emergency loans for businesses at fixed rates of interest were provided during the Middle Ages by allocating this function to the Jews."[83] Yet, in the very next chapter, Weber brings up the issue of usury as a moral imperative, saying:

> Even in antiquity the Jews almost always regarded strangers as enemies. All the well-known admonitions of the rabbis enjoining honor and faithfulness toward Gentiles could not change the impression

[80] Wellhausen, *Prolegomena*, 507.

[81] Weber, *Economy and Society*, 614.

[82] Ibid., 583.

[83] Ibid., 587.

that the religious law prohibited taking usury from fellow Jews but
permitted it in transactions with non-Jews...in fine, *no proof is required*
[emphasis added] to establish that the pariah condition of the Jews,
which we have seen resulted from the promises of Yahweh, and the
resulting incessant humiliation of the Jews by Gentiles necessarily led
to the Jewish people's retaining different economic moralities for its
relations with strangers and with fellow Jews.[84]

Instead of "comparative sociology," Weber uses his theological argument of *ressentiment* and the "pariah" status of the Jews as the root
cause of their law of *usury*. What Weber is saying is that the Jews
"almost always" looked upon strangers as enemies, this gave the impression that they employed a double standard, and that "no proof is
required" to establish that the "primordial economic ethic"[85] [read:
business ethics] which the Jews employ is the direct result of their
understanding of the promises of Yahweh found in the scriptures.

Rabbinic commentary offers a different perspective. The basis of
Jewish law regarding "usury," or interest on loans, is found[86] in *Shemos* (Exodus) 22:24: "If you lend money to My people, to the poor
man who is with you, you shall not behave toward him like a creditor; you shall not impose interest upon him." Here we see the biblical
law of a Jew being forbidden to charge interest on a loan to a fellow
Jew. What needs to be pointed out is that this verse must be taken in
context; the previous three verses speak of charity towards the widow
and the orphan, and instruct the nation of Israel to stand up for the
most powerless in their society. And in the preceding verse, 22:20, it
says: "But you shall not grieve a stranger who has come over to you,
or oppress him, because you [yourselves] were strangers in the land of
Mitzrayim." According to the rabbis, there is a reason these verses are
linked together, and that is because the prohibition of usury for fellow
Jews has to do with *tzedakah*, or charity. It has nothing to do with regarding Gentiles as "enemies" as Weber maintains, but the command
to help fellow Jews in need.

U NDERSTANDING WEBER'S concept of Jewish *ressentiment* and
their "pariah" status is the key to Weber's most famous theory on

---

[84] Ibid., 615.

[85] Ibid.

[86] It is also found in *Vayikra* (Leviticus) 25:36–37.

economics, which he outlined in his work *Protestant Ethic and the Spirit of Capitalism*, where Weber maintained that the Calvinists produced the ethic which enabled modern capitalism to flourish according to the evidence and thesis which Weber provides, and then developed more fully in his later work *Economy and Society*.

From the Noahide perspective, it was the Calvinists who were guilty of a double ethic as Weber claims the Jews were. Weber's theology influenced his identification of the variable factors supporting his analysis of both Christian and Jewish ethics, for these same scriptures on charging interest are in the Christian "Old Testament," and they were used by the Calvinist Church. Following this line of reasoning, if the Christian religion was also affected by the same "promises of Yahweh," then Christians would not only have an ethic of *ressentiment*, but also employ a "double standard" of ethics as described by Weber.

Comparative Anti-Semitism

The transfusion of this religious mythmaking or value-positing interpretation of social and political experience into the American bloodstream was in large measure effected by Max Weber's language.

— Allan Bloom[1]

SINCE MAX WEBER'S ESSAYS ON ANCIENT ISRAEL HAVE BEEN THE MOST decisive and influential secular academic work on the subject of Judaism—Weber's *Economy and Society* being the culmination of a century and a half of historical, philosophical, and theological anti-Semitism—it is necessary to go into some detail about Weber's underlying theological structures and arguments.

One of Weber's most influential supporters was Talcott Parsons, who was arguably the most well-known sociologist in the United States during sociology's heyday in the 1950s and 60s. Not only did Parsons translate Max Weber's *Protestant Ethic and the Spirit of Capitalism* from German to English in 1930, Parsons outlined the concepts Weber used in the formulation of the theory behind *Protestant Ethic and the Spirit of Capitalism*, the "two crucial foci" which Weber used: the "ideal type" analysis in which "the investigator attempt[s] to put himself in the actor's place," and the concept of *Sinnzusammenhänge*, or "systems of meaning,"[2] or the interests of the actor. Yet, by means of comparative analysis, when you contrast Weber's thesis on the "ethos of an economic system" with the thesis of one of Weber's contemporaries, Werner Sombart (whose reputation in social science in the early part of the twentieth century was as great—if not greater—than Max Weber's), you see a difference in their conclusions, a point Parsons missed.

Sombart's *The Jews and Modern Capitalism,* published in 1911, in which he responded to the thesis of Weber (that Calvinism provided the values foundation which allowed modern capitalism to grow) with his own thesis that it was the Jews, and not the Calvinists, who had

---

[1] Bloom, *The Closing of the American Mind*, 208.

[2] Weber, *Sociology of Religion*, xxxiii.

developed rationality into a lifestyle, affecting not only their business practices but all phases of Jewish life. Sombart's book was written in direct response to Weber's *Protestant Ethic and the Spirit of Capitalism*, which Weber had written in 1905. In answer to Sombart's criticism of his thesis, Weber responded with his *Economy and Society* which was left unfinished by his sudden death in 1920 at the age of fifty-six.[3] Yet Weber has gone on to become one of the great figures of sociology, while Sombart has drifted into sociological obscurity.

Sombart has often been criticized in comparison with Weber. In the introduction to Weber's *Economy and Society*, Guenther Roth wrote about Weber with glowing tribute:

> With his customary realism, [Weber] stressed the compensatory functions of religion...Weber had a much more profound sense than Marx for the meaning of ethical conduct...[then] Weber turns to an examination of all major social strata and their affinity to religion [which] provides a comparative frame for assessing the Puritan bourgeoisie...after this tour de force in the sociology of knowledge Weber balances his analysis of status tendencies with an investigation of religious intellectualism.[4]

With uncustomary realism, we will now analyze Weber's "analysis of status tendencies" to see if his "investigation of religious intellectualism" is a tour de force or a tour de farce.

It should be pointed out from the outset that Sombart was certainly no friend to the Jews; Sombart's works had a hefty dose of anti-Semitism, yet Sombart did not let his own anti-Semitism keep him from looking at the primary sources from both the Jews and the Christians to obtain a broader perspective.[5] This is something which Weber did not do, and the sheer volume of Weber's research cannot make up for his theological viewpoint and dependence on Wellhausen's documentary theory. When you explore the substance of Weber's "customary realism" and

---

[3] "Although the essays go back, in all important respects, to much earlier studies of mine, I need scarcely emphasize how much their presentation owes to the mere existence of Sombart's substantial works, with their pointed formulation, even—and especially—where they diverge from them" Weber, *Economy and Society*, lxxvi.

[4] Guenther Roth, introduction to *Economy and Society*, lxxviii.

[5] "Werner Sombart...pointed to the material and intellectual preeminence of Jews in modern capitalist culture with a mixture of admiration and alarm." Robert S. Wistrich, *Laboratory for World Destruction: Germans and Jews in Central Europe* (Lincoln: University of Nebraska Press, 2007), 19.

his grasp of "religious intellectualism," to understand Weber's "much more profound sense...for the meaning of ethical conduct" and see if it was profound enough—indeed more profound enough or even ultimately much more profound than the thesis presented by Sombart. To challenge the idea Talcott Parsons introduced, that Weber "turned his studies toward religion, his focus was not upon religion 'as such,' as the theologian or church historian conceives it," but that Weber did in fact have a theological viewpoint which influenced his thesis on "the influence of certain religious ideas on the development of an economic spirit, or the ethos of an economic system,"[6] and it was this theological framework which provided the foundations for his theory of "rationalization" (and most especially for its reconstituted variant—Parson's secularization theory).

Sombart came from the same school of German historical economics and had access to the same empirical evidence as did Weber. Critics claim that Sombart did not employ the exhaustive investigation into the historical aspects of ancient religions as Weber: "Where Sombart merely glanced [at other major civilizations, such as the Chinese, Indian, or ancient American], Weber proceeded to the comparisons of *Economy and Society* and, immediately afterwards, the studies as China, India, and Ancient Judaism."[7] Although Sombart did not do a thorough comparative analysis of other religions, he certainly glanced at the one source that counted—Judaism. In fact, Sombart did more than "merely glance" at Jewish scholarship; Sombart cited works by Jewish Rabbis such as Samson Raphael Hirsch, the champion of Orthodox Judaism in nineteenth-century Germany. In contrast to this, Weber, in his prolix *Ancient Judaism* and *Economy and Society*, listed not a single source from orthodox Jewish writers—all of Weber's sources were either theologically or culturally Christian sources. Weber developed his theories from one point of view: the theological point of view. This leads to suspicions why Sombart has been academically dismissed for "merely glancing" at different cultures as opposed to the admiration for Weber's sheer volume of research. Was Werner Sombart—ironically, since he would later become a member of the Nazi party—a victim of academic anti-Semitism? There is no denial that Weber's

---

[6] Weber, *The Protestant Ethic and the Spirit of Capitalism*, 27.

[7] Roth, intro. *Economy and Society*, lxxiii.

range of economic, historical, and political factors is impressive. Yet, the criticisms leveled at Sombart seem to be based in the sociologist's (the German sociologist in particular) peculiar love of sheer volume of research and empirical evidence, of modes and systems of analysis, without questioning the relevance of the research in question. Sociologists (as well as other social scientists) seemed more impressed with methods than results as well as in the quantity instead of the quality of Weber's scholarship, particularly in the one area of major disagreement between Weber and Sombart—the role played by the Jews in the development of modern capitalism. It seems that with all of his vast accumulation of empirical evidence, Weber could not escape the boundaries of his own Christian culture, and therefore his thesis was flawed by his own subjective Western theological viewpoint.[8] The inability of Weber to "think outside the box" is a prime example of the limits of classical intellectualism. Weber's preference for "Protestant German scholarship" and ignoring rabbinic scholarship limited his objectivity. In comparison, Sombart explained:

> To comprehend the spirit of the Talmud it is necessary to read the text itself…the Talmud has this characteristic: that although the sections follow each other in some fixed order, yet not one of them is strictly limited as regards its subject matter. They all deal with practically the whole field of Talmudic subjects. Hence by studying one or more of the (63) Tractates, it is comparatively easy to obtain a fair notion of the contents of the whole, and certainly, to find one's way about in the great sea. Specially to be recommended is the Tractate *Baba Mezia* and its two sister tractates [*Baba Kama* and *Baba Bathra*].[9]

Sombart, unlike Weber, recognized that rabbinic scholarship was invaluable in order to understand both ancient and modern Judaism.

∝

STARTING WITH THE twelfth century crusades and throughout the Middle Ages, the Jews of Europe came under increasingly severe

---

[8] "[Weber's] *Ancient Judaism*…shows no interest in the consequences of Israelite religion on the economic life or thought of Israel. *Ancient Judaism* very explicitly has a different focus—the specification and explication of those characteristics of Judaism which enabled the formation and preservation of a geographically dispersed and ritualistically segregated Jewish congregation after the destruction of the states of Israel and Judah." Fahey, *Max Weber's Ancient Judaism*, 73.

[9] Werner Sombart, *The Jews and Modern Capitalism*. (Brunswick, NJ: Transaction Books, 2006), 388–89.

economic and political strictures in their Christian host countries. Up to that time, Jews had been successful merchants, the go-between in trade with Christian Europe and the Muslim Middle East. As the Christian merchants replaced the Jews as international traders, they also denied the Jews access to the guilds, and the Jews were forced into finding new ways to make a living. One of the few (and often only) means for the Jew to earn a living was that of the occupation of moneylending, a trade for which they were demonized.[10] Weber ignored the structural reasons for the Jews not being involved in the process of the development of organized labor, resorting instead to anti-Semitic jargon that the closure was due to the Jew's "ancient and medieval business temper...the will and the wit to employ merci-lessly every chance of profit."[11] Weber built an impressive case for the Calvinists, a "tour de force in the sociology of knowledge,"[12] to support his thesis, supplying evidence from Oriental and Occidental cultures, showing why it was the Protestants of Western Europe who developed the ethic which enabled capitalism to flourish. Yet when Weber gave his reasoning of why the Jews did not develop the ethic which influenced the growth of modern capitalism, Weber discarded all pretense of objectivity and instead attacked the Jews with irratio-nal anti-Semitic slurs and theological jargon, ignoring the economic and legal barriers which prevented the Jews from developing orga-nized labor.[13]

---

[10] "At the beginning of the nineteenth century, when German liberals inspired by French revolutionary ideals were agitating the Prussian monarchy for a constitution, the status of Jews throughout the kingdom was no different from what it had been during the Middle Ages. Jews were not citizens in Germany. Under the law, they were not even human. They existed as servi camerae, 'serfs of the chamber'...like other serfs, Jews could not move from one town to another, marry, or have more than one child without permission." Dennis K. Fischman, *Discourse in Exile: Karl Marx and the Jewish Question*. (Amherst, Mass. University of Massachusetts Press, 1991), 26.

[11] Weber, *Economy and Society*, 614.

[12] Ibid., lxxviii.

[13] To quote once again that "the ultimate theoretical reasons for this fact, that distinctive elements of modern capitalism originated and developed quite apart from the Jews, are to found in the peculiar character of the Jews as a pariah people and in the idiosyncrasy of their religion...also of fundamental importance was the subjective ethical situation of the Jews. As a pariah people, they retained the double standard of morals which is characteristic of primordial economic practice in all communities: what is prohibited in relation to one's brothers is permitted in relation to strangers." Ibid., 614.

Weber compared the ethical practices of the Jews, particularly in the realm of economics, to other groups such as the "Jains and Parsees in India" and the Puritans of early North America. "Jewish economic ethic was quite different...since Antiquity, Jewish pariah capitalism, like that of the Hindu trader castes, felt at home in the very forms of state- and booty-capitalism along with pure money usury and trade, precisely what Puritanism abhorred."[14] Ignoring the state-sponsored usurping of Native American lands which influenced Calvinist capitalism, Weber also ignores or dismisses the social closure which forced the pariah status upon the Jews in the first place, such as the ordinance legislated at Augsburg in 1434 which forced upon the Jews to wear apparel at all time which would be distinct from that of their Christian neighbors, the infamous "Jew badge." In Barvaria, a new code called *Schwabenspiegel* "hemmed in the Jews with new, humiliating restrictions. Jews were, for one thing, no longer permitted to bear arms."[15] Jews did not have the same legal status as did Christians, and were often forced to live in "ghettos," cramped areas of towns, often a single street, which was blocked off. Their very access to the rest of the town was limited. The social closure did not stop with economic and legal restrictions; it was prevalent in the art and folklore of Europe, where Jews were depicted in statues and engravings as familiars of Satan, suckling on a sow or eating her excrement, and using Christian children as sacrifices, to give but a few examples. One wonders if Weber—had he lived a couple of more decades—would also have said the Jews "felt at home" wearing the "Jude" yellow star on their clothing during the late 1930s and early 1940s.

Weber asks the question, "how does one explain the fact that no modern and distinctively industrial bourgeoisie of any significance emerged among the Jews to employ the Jewish workers available for home industry, despite the presence of numerous impecunious artisan groups at almost the threshold of the modern period?"[16] Weber then answers his own rhetorical question, that the reasons "that the distinctive elements of modern capitalism originated and developed quite apart from the Jews, are to be found in the peculiar character of the

---

[14] Weber, *Ancient Judaism*, 345.

[15] Ruth Gay, *The Jews of Germany*. (New Haven: Yale University Press, 1992), 23.

[16] Weber, *Economy and Society*, 614.

Jews as a pariah people, and in the idiosyncrasy of their religion."[17] This view, which "does not allow the pressures from the Jews' socio-political environment, rather than Judaism, determine the incidence of types of segregation,"[18] was disputed by Werner Sombart, who had a more realistic grasp of the structural barriers which the Jews faced. Sombart observed:

> A still greater obstacle in [the Jews] path were the laws regulating their position in public life. In all countries there was remarkable uniformity in these; everywhere the Jew was shut out from public offices, central or local, from the Bar, from Parliament, from the Army, from the Universities. This applied to the States of Western Europe—France, Holland, England—and also to America.[19]

With this statement Sombart gives sound opposition to Weber's "ultimate theoretical reasons for this fact, that distinctive elements of modern capitalism originated and developed quite apart from the Jews;" instead of blaming the Jews for their "pariah" status, Sombart correctly points out that the Jews did not have any political, legal, military, or academic power, and that more than nullified whatever economic power the Jews had, a fact which was proved time and time again, for "when Jews were forced to set themselves up as moneylenders, it was possible to impose very heavy taxes upon them and later to confiscate whatever property they possessed."[20] Without the political or legal power, how could Jews wield the necessary influence to build and develop the organization of industrial production? Weber ignores the structural factors which restricted the Jews in Christian societies,[21]

---

[17] Ibid.

[18] Abraham, *Max Weber and the Jewish Question*, 9.

[19] Sombart, *The Jews and Modern Capitalism*, 181.

[20] Grayzel, *A History of the Jews*, 390.

[21] "Laws were passed which required a Jewish father to die before his son would be allowed to earn a living, a Jewish man to die as the condition for sparing the life of his brother. These laws said that only one section of the family could succeed to the family estate, while the others were condemned to want and poverty...most lawful means of supporting themselves were forbidden. The means of support legally permitted to Jews were so sub-paragraphed and sub-claused in the legal codes, that the dexterity of a tightrope walker was necessary in order to walk upon the narrow, unsteady tightrope of 'lawfulness,' without losing balance and toppling to the right or to the left into the waiting arms on an avenging 'justice'...no technical skill, no imaginative genius, no knowledge or insight had any value to society when demonstrated by a Jew...all laws which society enacted governing the Jew...said to the Jew: Pursue money. That is the

offering instead vacuous generalizations about the Jews, such as "no proof is required to establish that the pariah condition of the Jews, which we have seen resulted from the promises of Yahweh."[22] The theology behind this kind of reasoning is clear—to those who can look at sociological theory "as the theologian or church historian conceives it." In replacement theology, the Jews, who obstinately cling to the "old Law," are clearly shown to be punished by God for their rejection of Jesus by their misfortunes and miserable lifestyle, i.e., their "pariah status" among the gentile nations, and "no proof is required," given the absence of these structural arguments, to show that Weber was influenced by theological concepts.

⁓

IN THE MATTER of the ethics of *ressentiment* and of the "double standard" as it applied to Jews, in light of Weber's own arguments, the Calvinists did in fact have a double standard of ethics—one for themselves, another for the Jews. What we need to ask at this juncture is: what were Weber's limitations, or criteria, for what constitutes a "double ethical standard?" Weber described the double standard as "what is prohibited in relation to one's brothers is permitted in relation to strangers."[23] Weber expands his concept of the "double ethical standard" by saying:

> It is certain that economic behavior was not the realm in which a Jew could demonstrate his religious merit…in economic relations with strangers…never were they infused with positive ethical value…this is the basis of whatever factual truth there was in the observations concerning the inferior standard of economic legality among Jews… it would still have been difficult for the Jew to demonstrate his ethical merit by means of characteristically modern business behavior.[24]

This view of Judaism is opposite to the *halakha* of Jewish business practice and the teaching of the Talmud, which lays great stress on "economic behavior" and "ethical merit." To cheat Gentiles in monetary matters would be to the Jews a matter of *chillul HASHEM*,

---

only thing for which we value you. Whether you are an artist, a poet, or a philosopher, you remain a Jew." Hirsch, *Collected Writings*, Vol. I, 144–45.

[22] Weber, *Sociology of Religion*, 251.

[23] Weber, *Economy and Society*, 614.

[24] Ibid., 614–16.

a desecration of God's Name, and was halakhically forbidden.[25] To imply that "it is certain that economic behavior was not the realm in which a Jew could demonstrate his religious merit" shows a significant deficiency in the understanding of Jewish law. It is true that there are some opinions in the Talmud from rabbis saying it is permissible to cheat Gentiles, but—like all other matters discussed in the Talmud—you will find many different opinions on every subject, many of them harsh. These opinions were left in the Talmud to show that the issue was disputed from every angle, and every argument that could come up later had been covered. The trick was to know the *halakha*,[26] the ultimate legal decision on the issue, and regarding the issue of economic behavior, it was prohibited to cheat anyone, Jew or Gentile.

Weber's "double standard" criteria can be described as follows:

- Differentiation in business practices when dealing with social groups other than your own.
- Looking at the business realm as not being a proper forum for "demonstrating religious merit."
- In dealing with "strangers;" i.e., those outside one's social group, not having business dealings "infused with positive ethical value."

These are the limitations of the general principle of a "double standard" as described by Weber as they were applied to Jews. Now we shall see if they also apply to Christians as well.

Weber's analogy between the Jew's ethical standard and the Protestant Christian's ethical standard is striking:

> The pious Puritan…could demonstrate his religious merit through his economic activity because he did nothing ethically reprehensible, he did not resort to any lax interpretations of religious codes or to systems of double moralities, and he did not act in a manner that could be indifferent or even reprehensible in the general realm of ethical validity…no really pious Puritan—and this is the crucial point—could have regarded as pleasing to God any profit derived from usury, exploitation of another's mistake (which was permissible to the Jew), haggling and sharp dealing, or participation in political or colonial exploitation."[27]

---

[25] "The first thing a person is asked when he is brought for his final judgment is, 'Did you do business honestly?'" (*Shabbos* 31a). Rabbi Yoel Schwartz, *Kosher Money*, David Weiss, trans. (Jerusalem: Feldheim Publishers, 2004), v.

[26] "We consequently find in [the Talmud] a vast collection of opinions, some of which are mutually opposing and contradictory. Only the final results of these discussions have binding authority; they have been set down systematically in our codes of Jewish law." Hirsch, *Collected Writings*, Vol. VII, 213.

[27] Weber, *Economy and Society*, 614–16.

In this excerpt (ignoring for the moment in the context of the "pious Puritan" dealing with the Native Americans), Weber deals with criteria #2 and #3, which deal with the religious merit involved in business, but he fails to deal with criteria #1, differentiation in business practices when dealing with social groups other than your own. As shown above, the Christians of Europe, Calvinists included, did in fact employ a double ethical standard when dealing with "strangers," in this case, Jews. The Jews were not equal citizens with any Christian in any country in Europe during the formation of "modern capitalism." The major trade which they were involved in—moneylending— was not the trade of choice for many of the Jews; they simply had no other alternatives. Even moneylending was a "perilous territory, for the repayment of loans was never a certainty—Jews did not have the same status in law courts as did Christians—and persecution or expulsion could bring disaster."[28] To state that the "pious Puritan" did nothing "ethically reprehensible" simply because he broke no law or ethic which already severely handicapped the Jews in all areas of business activity throws the validity of criteria #2 and #3 into doubt also, for the very existence of these laws showed that there was a double standard already entrenched in Western law and culture. To understand Weber's observation that the "pious Puritan" did not participate "in political or colonial exploitation," we need to briefly overview Weber's framework for describing the various types of capitalism.

It seems as though Weber makes his point about the origins of the modern capitalism; the Puritans did in fact develop the modern, rationalistic methods for capitalism. However, this can only be possible if one accepts Weber's classifications of capitalism. Weber looked upon traditional, or ancient capitalism, as "the type of large-scale undertaking found in all civilizations from the earliest times. These undertakings were usually set up for specific and limited ends."[29] The categories of booty capitalism and pariah capitalism (as Weber describes them) seem to be too rigid and custom made, as if the purpose of these categories is to make sure Weber's concept of rational capitalism is more tightly defined. It is not Weber the structuralist we are taking to task, but Weber the normative theorist, and the problems with Weber's structural concepts of booty capitalism.

---

[28] Chaim Potok, *Wanderings: Chaim Potok's History of the Jews*. (New York: Fawcett Crest, 1978), 414.

[29] Parkin, *Max Weber*, 41.

One of the problems with Weber's structural argument is that he drastically downplayed the role of colonialism in his theory of modern capitalism, regulating it to the role of booty capitalism, "a manner of acquiring wealth and riches by way of war, plunder, and speculative adventures."[30] Weber did not explore the links between colonialism and modern capitalism, for he categorized the different kinds of capitalism, maintaining that booty capitalism did not have a significant impact on modern capitalism. Weber ignored that the European countries which developed modern capitalism were the same countries which colonized the New World and later Africa, Asia, Australia, and the Pacific. Weber also ignored structural reasons why neither Spain nor Portugal developed modern capitalism, which had to do with the detrimental effects of too much gold and silver and neglect of labor and manufacturing, whereas Holland and Great Britain used their colonies for raw materials and goods such as lumber, tobacco, cotton, rubber, and sugar. Another important element was the exploitation of the natural resources of the colonies as well as colonial produced goods or "cash crops" which were then shipped back to the mother country providing the cheap raw materials for the capitalist industries (such as cotton for England's textile industry). The link can be made between this exploitation of colonial resources, as can be seen in historical models such as Germany's industrial capitalism growing at the same time of her colonial expansion in the late nineteenth century, England's fall from being a world economic power with the loss of British colonies following World War II, and as recently as to the detrimental effect to both the United States and Western Europe's economy with the loss of the exploitation of the Middle East's inexpensive petroleum. The focus should be with the normative factors behind the modern capitalist's exploitation of the land and peoples of the New World and other non-European colonies, or the protestant ethic and the spirit of booty capitalism.

In respect to the Puritans in America, it seems that the only way which the Puritans could morally justify the genocide of the American Indians was for they themselves to use the concept of *ressentiment*. Puritan preachers lectured from the pulpit about the concept of God being on the side of the Christian, portraying the European Christians as the "brave pioneers" picturing themselves as the underdogs outnumbered by "savages" in a hostile new land, who had a "manifest

---

[30] Ibid.

destiny" to destroy these "infidel" occupying the land in the New World, land that was "rightfully theirs." The Puritan's "double ethical standard" which they applied to the Native Americans (and African slaves) certainly fits into the category by Weber's own standards. As mentioned above, understanding Weber's statement, that "the pious Puritan…could demonstrate his religious merit through his economic activity because he did nothing ethically reprehensible, he did not resort to any lax interpretations of religious codes or to systems of double moralities, and he did not act in a manner that could be indifferent or even reprehensible in the general realm of ethical validity,"[31] is difficult to digest along with Weber's statement of the "pious Puritan…not act[ing] in a manner that could be indifferent or even reprehensible in the general realm of ethical validity" in light of the Puritan's treatment of the Native Americans. It seems that the European Calvinists simply transferred the theological reasoning of ethically reprehensible double moralities from the Jews to the American Indians. One Christian sect (the Mormons) even went so far as to identify the American Indians with the lost ten tribes of Israel,[32] making their ethic of *ressentiment* even more theologically sound (this is also something which many of the Puritans believed). There is also the matter of the Puritan Calvinists being influenced by the ideas of Selden and Grotius, and what effect this had on the rationality of the Puritan development of capitalism. How can Weber say the Jews did not influence the development of capitalism when they had an influence on the Hebraic Calvinists?

IT IS TRUE THAT Sombart came nowhere close to Weber in establishing the negative model for the western capitalistic system, contrasting Oriental with Western European models. It is also true that Sombart had no theological restraints before he did the research for *The Jews and Modern Capitalism*. These two factors, that Sombart did not demonstrate the same level of scholarship that Weber did in this particular field and that Sombart—unlike Weber, who had studied theology—had no religious or theological predispositions before researching his book, were factors in Sombart's analysis. Sombart certainly was no friend of the Jew; his own early Marxist tendencies influenced his penchant to

---

[31] Weber, *Economy and Society*, 616.

[32] This belief continues among many Mormons even today, despite DNA proof to the contrary.

blame the Jews for inflicting capitalism upon the world.[33] After Hitler's rise to power, when Sombart embraced the Nazi philosophies[34] and became critical of socialism, he then blamed the Jews for the development of socialism as well. Sombart's own negative attitudes towards Judaism led to several misconceptions; his analysis of Judaism is far from perfect, yet his antipathy for the Jews had a racist and nationalistic foundation, not a theological foundation. This meant Sombart could look at the Jewish religion without having to worry that his faith would be compromised by discovering something in Judaism which might affect his own Christian beliefs.

Sombart, as did Weber, accepted the new and popular Graf-Wellhausen theory of Judaism being a developed religion, and this also affected his understanding of Talmudic Judaism, which he looked at as "Jewish religion—which, by the way, must not be confused with the religion of Israel."[35] Despite these limitations, it should be noted that Sombart, unlike Weber, understood and explained the corpus of Jewish Law—the written Torah, the Talmud, and the Codes. Sombart not only understood the difference between *halakha* and *haggada*, but he understood the problem with taking quotations from the Talmud out of context:

> Does, for example, the Talmudic adage, 'Kill even the best of the Gentiles,' still hold good? Do the other terrible aphorisms ferreted out in Jewish religious literature by Pfefferkorn, Eisenmenger, Röhling, Dr. Justus and the rest of that fraternity, still find credence, or are they, as the Rabbis of to-day indignantly protest, entirely obsolete?…in other words, it is possible to 'prove' absolutely anything from the Talmud, and hence the thrust and counter-thrust between the anti-Semites and their Jewish and non-Jewish opponents from time immemorial…there

---

[33] "To a large extent, Sombart is sympathetic with Jews—and he certainly differentiated himself from the Jew-as-passionate-lecher stereotypes that surrounded him. But there are strong anti-Semitic currents that course through his thought, largely by implication." Johnathan Freedman, *The Temple of Culture: Assimilation and Anti-Semitism in Literary Anglo-America*. (New York: Oxford University Press (US), 2000), 234–35.

[34] "I took advantage of the opportunity to raise the question of Sombart's antisemitism and reported Nazi sympathies. Baron responded that he thought that what people say about his becoming a Nazi was not true. 'He was a little bit of an opportunist.' 'Sombart was not an antisemite in the normal sense,' and *Jews and Capitalism* was definitely not an antisemitic book." Robert Liberles, *Salo Wittmayer Baron: Architect of Jewish History*. (New York: New York University Press, 1995), 395.

[35] Sombart, *The Jews and Modern Capitalism*, 206.

is nothing surprising in this when it is remembered that to a great extent the Talmud is nothing else than a collection of controversies of the different Rabbinical scholars.[36]

In contrast to Sombart, Weber—with his limited knowledge of Judaism and his disdain for rabbinic scholarship—eschewed the primary sources of Judaism, turning instead to the New Testament in his explanation of rabbinic Judaism: "The conditions presupposed by the Gospels indicate…one consulted men who actually legitimized themselves through charismatic knowledge of the law and the art of interpretation," and "the accounts of the Gospels indicate…the formally charismatic authority of the rabbinical teacher was supported solely by education and schooling and found its analogies in many similar phenomena from the Roman jurisconsul…to the Indian gurus."[37] It is difficult to understand how Weber could come to this conclusion regarding the "formally charismatic authority of the rabbinical teacher" by limiting his scholarship to the Christian Gospels and then comparing them to Indian gurus. For some reason, this sort of logic impressed later sociologists, unlike Sombart's study of the primary sources of Judaism which did not seem to impress sociologists at all.

In another example, Sombart described the mission of the Jew as "how holiness and legalism are connected; they show that the highest aim of Israel still is to be a kingdom of priests and a holy nation; and that the path to that end is a strict obedience to God's commandments."[38] Sombart's understanding of Judaism was no doubt influenced by his study of rabbinic scholars such as Rabbi S. R. Hirsch, for example in Sombart's statement:

> The Torah is as binding to-day in its every word as when it was given to Moses on Sinai. Its laws and ordinances must be observed by the faithful, whether they be light or grave, whether they appear to have rhyme or reason or no. And they must be strictly observed, and only because God gave them. This implicit obedience make the righteous, makes the saint…obedience to the behests of the Torah is the surest ladder on which to climb to higher and higher degrees of holiness.'"[39]

∽

---

[36] Ibid., 203.

[37] Weber, *Ancient Judaism*, 392.

[38] Sombart, *The Jews and Modern Capitalism*, 224.

[39] Ibid., 223–24.

IN SHARP CONTRAST to Sombart, Weber's work echoes the theological thought of Kant and Adam Smith, that the only thing the Jews
did that was culturally or intellectually important was to write the
preamble to the New Testament:

> The world-historical importance of Jewish religious development
> rests above all in the creation of the *Old Testament*, for one of the most
> significant intellectual achievements of the Pauline mission was that it
> preserved and transferred this sacred book of the Jews to Christianity
> as one of its own sacred books. Yet in so doing it eliminated all those
> aspects of the ethic enjoined by the *Old Testament* which ritually
> characterize the special position of Jewry as a pariah people.[40]

Here is distilled the difference between the two; Sombart called
the Jews "a kingdom of priests and a holy nation," while Weber continually used his pariah reference in describing the Jews. With Weber,
the purpose for Israel's existence was based upon theological premises; Judaism was merely the precursor to the founding of Christianity, even while saying that "empirical research, of course, treats the
data and sources of Israelite-Jewish-Christian religious developments
impartially. It seeks to interpret the sources and to explain the facts
of the one by the same principles it applies to the other."[41] Weber
re-told the history of Israel by distinctly non-Jewish principles. For
instance, Weber said that "it has been generally assumed, and rightly,
that Jeremiah is not the author of Jer. 17:19f."[42] This passage spoke
of keeping the Sabbath, which, according to the Wellhausen theory,
was a later addition; Weber assumes wrongly, as we have seen with
his acceptance of the literary integrity of the New Testament.

In Weber's analysis of the "*ressentiment*" scriptures, he focused
upon the impact they had upon Jewish beliefs but neglects the impact
they had upon Christian beliefs and ethical conduct. The Christians
feared the "*ressentiment*" passages for reasons stated by Weber and
therefore kept the Jews in a "pariah" state for religious reasons, since
the Bible does in fact teach that Israel will rise above all other nations
in the end times, and to prevent this, the Christian countries employed
numerous economic, political, and social barriers (much like the "Jim

---

[40] Weber, *Ancient Judaism*, 4.

[41] Ibid., 426. As we have seen from Wellhausen, this is, of course, not true. The Torah
and the New Testament have been treated by two very different standards.

[42] Ibid., 455.

Crow" laws in the Southern United States which kept blacks "in their place"). This link Weber totally ignores, thus missing the reasons for the social closure and the "pariah" status of the Jews of Europe as well as ignoring the Christian's double-standard of morality.

∞

ANOTHER CONCEPT WHERE Sombart differed from Weber was the Jewish view of God. The Jews understood God to be the ultimate in rationality and reason; with our limited abilities and human emotions, the only way Jews could understand God's methods and motives was to ascribe emotions to them such as anger, jealousy, and love. Because God is the ultimate in rationality and objectiveness, the Jews taught that He was the model to emulate, as opposed to any mere human. This is not to say that emotions are "bad," for as a part of the human experience they are both necessary and natural. The ancient sages made it clear that the singular difference between man and all other animals was that we are rational creatures, and our reason and rationality could overcome emotions. The rabbis emphasized that, for finite human minds, there was no such thing as pure objectivity; it was a model to constantly strive towards, but ultimate objectivity was impossible to obtain, except for God. To Sombart, the Jew's emulation of God led to the complete rationalization of all of life's experiences, which of course include economic activity:

> The effect of the rationalization of the whole of life on the physical and intellectual powers of the Jew...to a mode of living contrary to (or side by side with) Nature and therefore also to an economic system like the capitalistic, which is likewise contrary to...Nature. What in reality is the idea of making profit, what is economic rationalism, but the application to economic activities of the rules by which the Jewish religion shaped Jewish life?[43]

To the Christian, or one who was reared in a Christian culture, all sensual satisfactions which do not have to do with religion lead away from God. To the Jew, sensual satisfactions such as sex are fine as long as one partakes of them in moderation and at the proper times and places. To the Jew, sensual satisfactions do not lead away from God; rather they are a natural part of life and must be controlled

---

[43] Sombart, *The Jews and Modern Capitalism*, 237–38.

(or "rationalized"). Weber's thesis was an example of how a square Christian theological concept could be hammered into a round Jewish hole, for theological Christian concepts to have been superimposed onto Old Testament or Jewish teachings. The effect of this, besides giving a completely distorted view of Judaism, was to support the concept of the so-called "Judeo-Christian" tradition, that what the Christian believed, the Jew believed also. Thus, instead of using Judaism as a contrast or a negative model to Christianity, which (according to Christian theology) Judaism was in most aspects, this system could use Judaism to either support or contrast a "Judeo-Christian" theological concept at the whim of the theologian.

Christians employed an ethic of *ressentiment* which could not be explained by any structural models except for theological ones, and the Calvinists definitely employed a "double standard" toward "strangers," in this case Native Americans and Jews, whom the Calvinists did not consider their Christian "brothers." Weber's definition of Jews being a "pariah" people was therefore incorrect, since their political and economic stratification was the direct result of Christian "differentiation in business practices when dealing with social groups other than your own." Weber's blaming the Jew for his troubles, implying that they "resulted from the promises of Yahweh" was also incorrect, since his definitions of *ressentiment* and an ethical "double standard" applied to Calvinists. Since these two factors were of critical importance in Weber's foundational thesis that Calvinism and not Judaism (as Sombart maintained) was responsible for the "ethic" which helped produce capitalism, "no further proof is required" to show that Weber's theory was, in effect, theological theory. The concept behind Weber's thesis—that the Calvinists developed capitalism to accumulate wealth as proof that they are "saved" (while maintaining their Gnostic disdain for the "earthly" love of money) ignores the Jewish view that mere accumulation of wealth is not a sign of Divine favor; it is what the person does with the wealth that matters, whether a person uses his wealth to help others or simply hoards it for self indulgence and expensive toys—or to simply "prove" that God favors him and that he has salvation. Weber's thesis of Protestant Calvinism being the vehicle that produced modern capitalism is embedded in his thesis on Judaism, and Weber supported the same thesis of scholars such as Wellhausen and Kant; that the pariah nation of Israel should become extinct through assimilation and the religion of Judaism, an anachronistic fossil, removed from mankind.

Weber ends his book *Ancient Judaism* with these words:

> The goal of the conversion of Jews has been pronounced very often by Christendom…the missionary endeavor as well as the compulsory conversions have always and everywhere remained equally inconsequential…all of this makes the Jewish community remain in its self-chosen situation as a pariah people as long and as far as the unbroken spirit of the Jewish law, and that is to say, the spirit of the Pharisees, and the rabbis of late antiquity, continued and continues to live on.[44]

This seems to be the goal of Max Weber; to break the spirit of the "Pharisees" and rabbis by destroying the validity of the Law.[45]

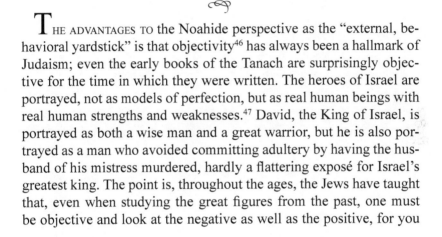

THE ADVANTAGES TO the Noahide perspective as the "external, behavioral yardstick" is that objectivity[46] has always been a hallmark of Judaism; even the early books of the Tanach are surprisingly objective for the time in which they were written. The heroes of Israel are portrayed, not as models of perfection, but as real human beings with real human strengths and weaknesses.[47] David, the King of Israel, is portrayed as both a wise man and a great warrior, but he is also portrayed as a man who avoided committing adultery by having the husband of his mistress murdered, hardly a flattering exposé for Israel's greatest king. The point is, throughout the ages, the Jews have taught that, even when studying the great figures from the past, one must be objective and look at the negative as well as the positive, for you

---

[44] Weber, *Ancient Judaism*, 424.

[45] "Despite the fact that Weber often expressed tolerance of Jews, his scholarly and extrascholarly utterances on Judaism and the Jews, when taken as a whole and placed in their appropriate contexts, suggest that he was, like many other liberal nationalist Germans, less than happy with the prospect of the continued existence of the Jewish group." Abraham, *Max Weber and the Jewish Question*, 7.

[46] "Jewish Law is the only system of laws that did not emanate from the people whose constitution it was intended to be. Judaism is the only 'religion' that did not originate from the human beings who find in it the spiritual basis for their lives. It is precisely this 'objective' quality of Jewish Law and of the Jewish 'religion' that makes them both unique, setting them apart clearly and explicitly from all else on earth that goes by the name of law or religion…all other 'religions' and codes of law have originated only in the human minds of a given era; they merely express the conceptions of God, of human destiny, and of their relationship to God and to one another held by a given society at a specified period in history." Hirsch, *T'rumath Tzvi*, 279.

[47] "[Scripture] teaches us how far removed Jewish ideology is from the cult of the idealization of our great men, from endowing them with superhuman perfection. Under the glaring light of this truth [shows us] the weakness and errors of our giants, as well as their virtues." Ibid., 64.

can learn from both. This is different from the Christian portrayal of Jesus, insisting that he was "perfect" and "without sin," since Christians believe him to be divine, and refuse to accept anything less, no matter what kind of evidence is presented. In the Talmud, the rabbis questioned every law and every custom, arguing against it from every conceivable angle, using complex and sophisticated systems of logic to try to find any weaknesses in their arguments. The Christians, on the other hand, did not use logic in the formation of their theology; any arguments against their religion or which contradicted their dogmas were suppressed, and the most damaging testimonies against their faith were ignored. In place of rational discussion about the problems in the way Christians interpreted the Bible, the Christians responded irrationally by burning books, burning synagogues, and even burning the people who were critics of their religion. Their logic seemed to be: as long as there was no one to argue against Christianity, and as long as there were no arguments against Christianity, then Christianity must be right. This kind of "rationality" deeply affected theology, and in turn, affected the Christian philosophers such as Augustine and Aquinas who in turn influenced the later theologically-trained philosophers such as Kant and Hegel.[48] Intellectuals such as Marx and Weber,[49] while studying these philosophers, inadvertently received a heavy dose of theology along with the philosophy. When later sociologists used the work of Marx and Weber to develop sociological theories, they unwittingly infested these theories with Christian theological concepts and attitudes, yet presented the theories as to be objective and religion-free.

Weber's own nationalism and religious background unduly influenced his thesis as he peered into the religions of other cultures. But

---

[48] "In establishing the view that history could be made theoretically intelligible, and an essential element of political philosophy, he produced a concept of historical progress which is free of utopian idealism, distinguishable from theologically inspired precursors, compatible with freedom (indeed, history becomes the story of the realization of freedom), and an alternative to a quite different form of historicism which thought insight into history would justify antirationalist realism or subjectivism." Maletz, *History in Hegel's "Philosophy of Right,"* 209–10.

[49] "Although it is readily conceded that Weber seemed to use Marx as a focal point in certain aspects of his work, the interesting fact remains that, in spite of Weber's concern to avoid both materialism and the excesses of nineteenth century idealism, his stance toward Marx inevitably involved, consciously or not, the resurrection of some Hegelian themes." Roland Robertson, *On the Analysis of Mysticism: Pre-Weberian, Weberian and Post-Weberian Perspectives,* 241.

the religion of Judaism he treated much differently, and in Weber's arguments against the Jews we find an emotional theology in place of his alleged cool empiricism, as well as hiding behind the theological works of his Christian peers (such as his friend Ernst Troeltsch) instead of grappling with Judaism one-on-one and reading the Jewish primary sources for his information. There is no other logical explanation for the difference in the approaches between Sombart and Weber except for Weber's own Protestant ethic, namely, to ignore anything from a Jewish perspective while embracing theological viewpoints. You can argue about Weber not being "religious" and not being a "practicing" or a "believing" Christian, but there is no other rational explanation for the irrationality in the theological arguments which he employs to formulate his thesis on the Jewish ethic.

Weber's *Ancient Judaism* dealt with the development of the people of Israel, from their beginnings to the end of the first century of the Common Era when the second Temple was destroyed. The religion which was developed by the rabbis, what we call Judaism, was forged out of the ashes of the Israelite civilization, and developed over the centuries. Its growth roughly coincided with that of Christianity from the first century onwards. Weber pointed out that neither early Christianity nor the Catholic Church developed the ethic which was conducive to the development of capitalism, yet he doesn't allow for the changes which Judaism underwent during this same time period. To suggest that the religion of the Jews in the sixteenth and seventeenth centuries was the same as the Judaism nearly two thousand years earlier was ludicrous and insulting to the intelligence of the reader; although the Torah does not change, the structure of Jewish Law was flexible enough to adapt to changing times and circumstances. But because Weber limited himself to "modern Protestant, especially German, scholarship," he ignored the teachings of Judaism during the crucial time in which capitalism developed. Weber kept his view strictly Protestant-Christian, myopically focusing upon the ancient Jewish civilization through the anti-Semitic lens of German scholarship:

> All over the world, for several millennia, the characteristic forms of the capitalist employment of wealth have been state-provisioning, the financing of states, tax-farming, the financing of military colonies, the establishment of great plantations, trade, and moneylending…one finds Jews involved in just these activities, found at all times and places but especially characteristic of antiquity…the Jews evinced the ancient and medieval business temper which had been and remained typical of all primitive traders"[50]

---

[50] Weber, *Economy and Society*, 614.

It is disturbing that statements such as these are ignored or over-looked by sociologists. Conditioned by the "Great is Diana of the Ephesians!"-type mantra of the supremacy of classical Western schol-arship, Western academicians—like Wellhausen—were, almost with-out knowing the reasons for the hypothesis, prepared to accept that the Jews were an inferior money-grubbing culture, and whose writings and scholarship were of no account.

࿇

I~N A SPEECH given at Munich University in 1918, Weber said:

> Integrity, however, compels us to state that for the many who today tarry for new prophets and saviors, the situation is the same as resounds in the beautiful Edomite watchman's song of the period of exile that has been included among Isaiah's oracles: *He calleth to me out of Seir, Watchman, what of the night? The watchman said, The morning cometh, and also the night: if ye will enquire, enquire ye: return, come.* The people to whom this was said has enquired and tarried for more than two millennia, and we are shaken when we realize its fate. From this we want to draw the lesson that nothing is gained by yearning and tarrying alone, and we shall act differently. We shall set to work and meet the 'demands of the day,' in human relations as well as in our vocation.[51]

Weber seemed to miss the point that the "yearning and tarrying" was the result of the Edomite keeping the Israelite out of his land by force. But Weber was correct on one thing: the Germans would certainly act differently in just a few years down the road.

In direct contrast to Weber, Sombart's understanding of Judaism was different: "Now what of the contents of the ordinances? All of them aim at the subjugation of the merely animal instincts in man, at the bridling of his desires and inclinations and at the replacing of impulses by thoughtful action; in short, at the 'ethical tempering of man.'"[52] Despite his own personal shortcomings, Sombart grasped the nature of Judaism as well as the main conflict within the historical context that both Sombart and Weber dealt with, namely, which group provided the ethos for capitalism, the modern system of organized production, the Jews or the Puritans? Seen on a superficial level, by using the methodology of his "ideal type" analysis in which Weber

---

[51] H. H. Gerth and C. Wright Mills (trans. and eds), *From Max Weber: Essays in Sociology*, (New York: Oxford University Press, 1946), 156.

[52] Sombart, *The Jews and Modern Capitalism*, 227.

built his "historical types of concerted action,"[53] he did not contrast with the opposing "subjective" view, the Judaic viewpoint, and instead compared Judaism with other unrelated religions and faiths. The historical context in which Weber operated was a purely Christian one. Sombart, on the other hand, utilized Judaic scholarship, and grasped the understanding that the modern Jew had in ethics, rather than the traditional Christian viewpoint which Weber based his analysis:

> These words show clearly enough how holiness and legalism are connected; they show that the highest aim of Israel still is to be a kingdom of priests and a holy nation; and that the path to that end is a strict obedience to God's commandments. Once this becomes apparent, we can imagine the importance the Jewish religion has for the whole of life. In the long run, external legalism does not remain external; it exercises a constant influence on the inner life, which obtains its peculiar character from the observance of the law.[54]

∿

To conclude this analysis of Max Weber's theories on Judaism, we need to point out, again, that it was in fact the Calvinist societies which developed the modern capitalistic system as described by Weber. What can be disputed are Weber's normative reasons of why the Calvinists and not the Jews developed it. It seems as though later sociological theorists, apparently over-impressed by the amount of Weber's research, made the simple mistake of scrutinizing and analyzing Weber's theoretical methods without bothering to first look into the possibility that Weber's theories might have been negatively affected by his theological beliefs and ethics. All subsequent sociologists, from Parsons on down the line, obviously disregarded Weber's own thesis "which is generally the most difficult to grasp: the influence of certain religious ideas on the development of an economic spirit, or the ethos of an economic system."[55] In this case, it was the influence of religious ideas upon a certain German sociologist which was too difficult to grasp, since, as Parsons himself stated, the sociologists did not focus upon religion "as the theologian or church historian

---

[53] Guenther Roth, introduction to *Economy and Society*, xxxvi.

[54] Sombart, *The Jews and Modern Capitalism*, 224.

[55] Weber, *The Protestant Ethic and the Spirit of Capitalism*, 27.

conceives it." The result of this oversight was that sociologists looked at Max Weber's work from every conceivable angle except the one which was the most important: from a Jewish or Noahide viewpoint. The result was that Weber's theory was much more subjective than its supporters knew, since it came from a decidedly Christian viewpoint, using Christian concepts in its foundations in the mistaken belief that to be "objective" one must not use a "religious" viewpoint to augment the development of sociological theory. Sombart, on the other hand, grasped that the Jewish view of what constituted "religion" was vastly different from the Christian who confined "the worship of [God] to certain places, times and occasions, to temples, churches, synagogues, festivals and special ceremonies of life."[56] The bottom line was that Werner Sombart, the future Nazi, was more objective and sympathetic to Judaism than Max Weber, the paragon of sociological objectivity.

Max Weber was the best the secular academic social sciences had to offer, whose "rich empirical studies of the world's great historical religions…[and] extraordinary combination of erudition in the social sciences, disinterested and impartial observation,"[57] and his "superb penchant for the architectonic construction of sociological categories"[58] led to his work on *Ancient Judaism* and Judaism's role in the development of the spirit of capitalism, and whose analytical acumen was described in glowing reverential terms as "the hand of the master… evident in the ordering of immense masses of scholarly material from various disciplines."[59] Max Weber, the renowned economic historian with his broad background in, among other things, German Law and German Economic history, and whose *Sociology of Religion* is said to be "the most crucial contribution of our century to the comparative and evolutionary understanding of the relations between religion and society, and even of society and culture generally."[60] Despite these impressive accolades, we see that Max Weber gave Julius Wellhausen's documentary theory a false credibility, and that his moral and

---

[56] Hirsch, commentary to *Psalms*, §i. 51.

[57] Ephraim Fischoff, trans., *Sociology of Religion*, xxiii.

[58] Ibid, xxiv.

[59] Ibid.

[60] Talcott Parsons, Introduction to Weber's *Sociology of Religion*, lxxvii.

ethical analysis of Judaism was based on a theological foundation. Max Weber's theology played a major role in his theories and the subsequent secularization theory of Talcott Parsons, influencing the way the social sciences viewed Judaism[61] in the twentieth century, paving the way to a rationalization of Nazism[62] and other anti-Zionist and anti-Judaic philosophies which influence Western academia to this day,[63] endlessly citing works of earlier scholars who themselves cited earlier theological works—particularly German—quoting secular or Christian "experts" on Judaism. This chain of academic anti-Semitism invariably goes back to the theologians such as Martin Luther, Thomas Aquinas, and Augustine of Hippo, and ultimately the authors of the New Testament.

---

[61] "There is 'Oriental philology,' a kind of 'Biblical archaeology' supported by reports brought back by modern explorers of the Orient. The expounders of this 'comparative philology' seek to apply their interpretations of the linguistic and cultural phenomena of the non-Jewish Orient to the history, language and culture of Judaism. They do not consider that the unique character of God's Law, which dominates the life, the thoughts, the emotions, the words and the actions of an entire nation in the spirit of pure monotheism, makes it possible that this Law of God could, and we may indeed safely say, should, have exerted such a unique creative influence on the language and culture of the Jewish people that our sacred literature can be studied only 'out of itself,' without attempting to compare it with the literary products of other civilizations." Hirsch, *Collected Writings*, Vol. VIII, 320–21.

[62] "The most famous legal theorist of Nazism, Carl Schmitt, drew heavily upon Weber's thinking when developing his theories about the *Führerstaat*." Thomas Ekstrand, *Max Weber in a Theological Perspective*, 131.

[63] "The historical study of the Holocaust has proved beyond reasonable doubt that the Nazi perpetrated genocide was a legitimate outcome of rational bureaucratic culture." Zygmunt Bauman, "Sociology after the Holocaust." *The British Journal of Sociology*. Vol. 39, No. 4 (Dec. 1988), 469.

Mad Max: Beyond Theology

Max Weber adopted the concept of 'ideal-type' as a basic element of his sociological method. The so-called 'ideal-type' is an intellectual construct in which one brings together all the characteristic features of a given cultural phenomenon, thereby defining its basic nature.

— Irving M. Zeitlin[1]

THE IMPACT OF WEBER'S THEOLOGICAL THEORIES ABOUT JUDAISM AND the Torah has continued to have a substantial effect on the social sciences throughout the twentieth century, and the "Old" Testament has been scrutinized for well over a hundred years by literary textual criticism, usually described with language such as "cult" or "primitive." Christianity, on the other hand, is hardly ever described with these words, or any words that carry a negative connotation. The Torah is textually analyzed, and differences in the wording of events or differences and apparent contradictions "prove" that it was written by different people over a period of time. The New Testament is treated differently; the textual differences, the disagreeing genealogies, the differences in the stories (was Jesus born in Nazareth or Bethlehem?) are explained by saying that the author in question (Matthew, Mark, Luke, or John) simply wanted to give a different side or spin to the same exact event or teaching. The Graf-Wellhausen supporters use an elaborate explanation to "prove" that the Torah was written much later than Moses' time, while using a different but equally elaborate system to "prove" that the Gospels were indeed written in the first century by the apostles whose names appear on the title of the books. The evidence of the documentation of the creation of the New Testament—the writings of the early church fathers as well as the papyri and vellum parchments that have been recovered—is ignored, and the teachings in the Gospels are presented as authentic. The Torah is compared to other ancient religious writings, again "proving" that the Torah is a collection of stories and laws assimilated from surrounding cultures. Christianity is not presented in this way; it is not compared to Marcionism, Valentinism, Theodotianism, or Manicheism to

---

[1] Zeitlin, *Ancient Judaism*, 1.

show its links to classical Gnosticism. Christianity is inadvertently and consistently presented as a "unique" religion, a true religion with a unique and true savior, and the effects of Christianity on sociology have remained even to the early twenty-first century—indebted to a great degree to Max Weber's theology used in his theories on Ancient Jewish religion—and there is a continuing impact of the theological values upon sociological theory to this day.

For example, one popular modern sociologist dealing with the subject of Judaism is Irving M. Zeitlin. In Zeitlin's *Ancient Judaism: Biblical Criticism from Max Weber to the Present*, Zeitlin begins by talking about elements of the Canaanite religion [Deut. 18] that God explicitly told Israel not to emulate. Zeitlin draws on the *Ras Shamra* tablets which date to around the year 1200 BCE. Zeitlin says that "what the Ras Shamra evidence shows beyond doubt is that the Canaanites did in fact have an influence upon the culture of Israel. The only question is not whether such an influence existed, but rather its nature, and how and when it occurred."[2] From the rabbinic point of view, the influence of Canaanite culture on Israel was all negative,[3] basically, the Canaanites were an example of what *not* to do. Zeitlin, however, continued the sociological practice of using German Protestant theologians such as Albrecht Alt[4] and Jewish assimilationist sources such as Hermann Gunkel, which led to his view that "Israel's culture is a syncretic product of the prolonged interaction with the Canaanites,"[5] and that "magical forces according to pagan mythology reside in the idols, is something which the Bible never succeeds in grasping."[6] Zeitlin ignores the rabbinic teaching that the Canaanites were "disgorged" from the Land of Israel because of their abominable culture, and that many of the laws in the Torah were to prevent the

---

[2] Ibid., 19.

[3] Early Israelite religion was monotheistic. Israel had neither male and female prostitutes in the Temple, nor did they sacrifice children by burying them alive. Any similarities between the two are vague and forced; there were good reasons that the Canaanites and their immoral memes were eliminated.

[4] "'Secular history,' writes Alt, 'provides no grounds for believing that the ancestors of Israel lived for a time in Palestine, then went away, and finally returned to establish themselves.'" Zeitlin, *Ancient Judaism*, 64.

[5] Ibid., 23.

[6] Ibid., 34.

Jews from synthesizing the Canaanite culture with their own (cf. Lev. 18:24–29). As for Zeitlin's statement that the Bible "never grasped" the idea that pagans believed their idols had magical powers shows an unfamiliarity of the teaching that God is the source of all power (cf. Isaiah ch. 44) and that idols are powerless. Even today, with very rare exceptions, when interpreting the Torah, rabbinic scholarship and viewpoints are still disregarded in favor of non-Jewish viewpoints and scholarship. Zeitlin makes observations based on the documentary hypothesis saying that "the theory that the Pentateuch consists of diverse sources or authors is almost universally accepted by modern biblical scholars."[7] What needs to be emphasized is that the "theory…accepted by modern biblical scholars" is only accepted by non-Jewish scholars who ignore rabbinic scholars. If Jewish scholars are used, it is typically non-observant Jewish scholars who reinforce the Wellhausen thesis. Had Zeitlin used authentic rabbinic sources, he would not have made such fundamental mistakes such as stating that "in Genesis, or the patriarchal 'straum' of the tradition, Egypt plays a central role. Both Abraham and Isaac find their way there because of the famine in Canaan."[8] Isaac did not go to Egypt. In Genesis 26:2, God forbids Isaac to go to Egypt since, according to *Rashi*, he had been placed on the altar of the *Akeidah*, and was considered an unblemished offering. Again, Zeitlin states that "the fear of Isaac [Gen. 31:42] may have derived from the appearance of a deity that terrified Isaac. 'Fear' is often a term for god in other religions. However, W. F. Albright has suggested that *pahad* should be rendered as kindred or kinsman since in other Semitic languages it means 'clan.'"[9] Had Albright read the commentary of Rabbi S. R. Hirsch, whose grasp of Hebrew was *nonpareil* in comparison with the secular scholars, he would have seen that Hirsch translated the Hebrew *Pachad Yitzchak* as the "Dread of Isaac."[10] These fundamental mistakes are typical of the academic who disregards rabbinic scholarship.

Over one hundred years after its publication, and its thorough rebuttal by rabbinic scholarship, Zeitlin still uses the theological

---

[7] Ibid., 284.

[8] Ibid., 67.

[9] Ibid., 63.

[10] "*Pachad Yitzchak* is not a name for God, but refers to that dread moment of the Akeda, when Isaac felt the knife already drawn at his throat." Hirsch, *T'rumath Tzvi*, 145.

Wellhausen theory in explaining the Torah: "Genesis, then, is a folk-book in so far as it relates popular traditions that originated in the earliest memories of the people. The traditions were transmitted from generation to generation until they were written down in much their present form in the tenth century BC."[11] This statement, along with others such as "one important issue is whether Abraham, Isaac, Jacob, Joseph, Ishmael, Esau, *et al.* are individuals or personifications of tribes. For Gunkel, the names referred to the tribes themselves"[12] and "whereas J uses [HASHEM] throughout Genesis, that is, throughout the pre-Mosaic period, not so E and P"[13] show the influence that Wellhausen had long after his theory was in vogue. Zeitlin explains his reliance upon the Wellhausen theory, even though "Wellhausen's theory did not go unchallenged, the few dissenting voices raised in opposition to it, were ignored"[14]—apparently even by Zeitlin himself.

Zeitlin elaborates upon the concept of the Torah as a developed religion, saying that "while it is most likely that the patriarchs were polytheists, they were nevertheless pioneers in intuiting a religious idea that could be built upon later."[15] This reflects a theme expressed by Toynbee:

> In this picture Christianity stands, not side by side with Judaism, but on its shoulders, while they both tower above the primitive religion of Israel…before and below the Prophets, the Biblical tradition presents us with a Moses, and before and below Moses with an Abraham. These dim figures are regarded by one school of modern Western "higher critics" as mere creatures of a primitive mythopoeic imagination, and by another school as at least partially authentic historical persons who have left their marks upon "folk memory."[16]

It is little wonder that, when studying biblical interpretation, beginning with the idea that the stories in the *Tanach* are "mythopoeic" will lead one to conclusions not in agreement with rabbinic commentary. To call Abraham, Isaac, and Jacob "polytheists" is a denial of one of the great themes of the Torah; the singularity of God.

---

[11] Zeitlin, *Ancient Judaism*, 38.

[12] Ibid.

[13] Ibid., 58.

[14] Ibid., 287.

[15] Ibid., 69.

[16] Toynbee, *A Study of History*, Vol. 5, 119.

Another modern sociologist, Jeffrey Kaplan, a professor at the University of Wisconsin at Oshkosh, wrote a book entitled *Radical Religion in America: Millenarian Movements from the Far Right to the Children of Noah*. This book talks about some of the most radical and violent Christian groups such as the Christian Identity and the National Socialist Party of America as well as pagan religions such as Odinism and Ásatrú (Kaplan devotes an entire chapter to the German/Norse Odinism as well as Ásatrú, two religions that have much less in common with Christianity than does Islam). He also includes a chapter on the *Bnai Noah* as one of his "millenarian" movements, portraying the *Bnai Noah* as a fringe religious group instead of it being a teaching of mainstream orthodox Judaism. The absurdity of this is not lost even on Kaplan; he opens his chapter on the *Bnai Noah* with an apologetic "the inclusion of the philo-Semitic B'nai Noah or Children of Noah may at first glance seem incongruous in a book devoted largely to racialist and anti-Semitic belief systems."[17] There is a reason for this, obviously, although not the one which he presents. Dr. Kaplan is a professor of Islamic studies, a Fulbright lecturer in Hebron (in the West Bank) during the late 1980s. He has also taught in Iran, Saudi Arabia, and Indonesia—all militant Islamic countries. So it is perhaps no surprise that Dr. Kaplan, who is immersed in Islamic culture and religion, would take a negative approach to the *Bnai Noah* and author a book trying to tie the Noahide movement in with "radical" and "dangerous" movements.

Although Kaplan ties the *Bnai Noah* in with the "millenarian" movements because of their expected hope of the Messiah, one must understand that the Messiah the *Bnai Noah* is expecting is the Jewish Messiah, not the Christian one. Kaplan describes the *Bnai Noah* as "no less radically contra-acculturative...than are the most outspoken of racialist millenarians."[18] According to Kaplan, it is the hatred of the right-wing Christian groups that ties the *Bnai Noah* in with them. In actuality, the reason the groups Kaplan lists in his book hate the *Bnai Noah* is precisely because they hate Judaism and Jews. Radical Muslims also hate Jews, so it would make sense that Kaplan would have included Islam in his list of "radical religions" as well. After all, a religion that glories in the terrorist massacre of innocent civilians by strapping bombs to women and children certainly seems to

---

[17] Jeffrey Kaplan, *Radical Religion in America: Millenarian Movements from the Far Right to the Children of Noah.* (Syracuse: Syracuse University Press, 1997), 100.

[18] Ibid.

fit the moniker of "radical religion." (It should be noted that there is a disparate body count; radical Muslims have murdered nearly three thousand American citizens in the United States alone, and "radical" Noahides have, to date, not murdered anyone.) Once again, we see theological themes sneaking their way into sociological theory; one problem with Kaplan's thesis is that the concept of the "millenarian movement" is a Christian concept, not a Jewish one.

～∞～

A DISTINCT PATTERN developed in the German school[19] of the social sciences starting in the late eighteenth century with Kant and progressing through the nineteenth century with Hegel, Wellhausen, and Weber—particularly Weber's theories of *ressentiment* and *pariahism*, which supported the academic foundation for the later policies of the Nazi regime.[20] Were the Germans intrinsically evil, as Goldhagen postulated in his book *Hitler's Willing Executioners*? Were the Germans any more evil in nature than the Poles or the Lithuanians, whose citizens also turned on the Jews? Were the Germans less moral than the British, with their deplorable treatment of the Irish, the Kenyans, or the people of India? Or even the Christian Americans, whose Jim Crow laws in the South, with "colored only" signs on benches and water-fountains, lynching and beatings of black Americans, internment of Japanese-Americans in our own concentration camps, and our attempted genocide of Native Americans (which was only a generation or two removed from World War Two) which mirrored the atrocities of the Nazis? Were the German people destined for *Götterdämmerung*,

---

[19] "The unresolved problem of classical antiquity is the task of bringing the liberation inherent in individuality and knowledge to some fruitful embodiment in the world. In this task, the Germanic realm, combining as well as modifying the influences of classical antiquity and Christianity, builds up the groundwork of the modern state. The Germanic realm is itself originally pervaded by a division between faith and reason, church and state, and Hegel suggests that these seem for a long time to be two opposed realms (§§ 359–60). But there is nevertheless an implicit unity, which is brought to light in the genesis of the nineteenth-century state. In fact the new principle is less a harmonious combination of these opposing forces than the victory of reason and the state over faith and the church" Maletz, *History in Hegel's "Philosophy of Right"*, 227.

[20] "The theme of Jewish parasitism was also central to the societal conversation about Jews in Weimar and during the Nazi period...the common view in Germany echoed Hitler's: The Jews were parasites whose working lives were devoted to feeding on the blood of the industrious German people...getting a Jew to work, for those beholden to the prevailing German model of Jews, was an expressive act, was, to use Weber's term, value rational." Goldhagen, *Hitler's Willing Executioners*, 284–85.

as Herman Wouk suggested, when Arminius in 9 CE defeated three Roman legions in the Teutoburg Forest east of the Rhine, securing forever a refuge for German barbarism? The Holocaust was no mere aberration of history or of a modern military regime in the hands of a madman; it was Western Europe putting into practice the Christian teachings and interpretations of the past nineteen centuries, teachings of men such as John Chrysostom and Martin Luther, and a culmination of centuries of Christian crusades, inquisitions, and pogroms against the Jews. Although there were a small number of Christians who risked their lives to save Jews during the Holocaust, the sad fact is that, overwhelmingly, the German man-in-the-street (as well as the Polish, Lithuanian, French, etc.) was either a participant or turned a blind eye to the massacre of an entire people. In the early 20th century Germany was considered the most cultured, civilized, and advanced society in Western Culture. The Germans took the anti-Semitic lessons gleaned from "classical" sources that were popularized from the "Age of Enlightenment," where science and reason captured the attention and imagination of the greatest minds of Western Culture, and wove them into a systematic model of Biblical interpretation that influenced Western academics, politics, and public opinion. In the nineteenth century, Germany led the way in scholarship as well as development of the modern university system (and secondary schools as well). During the nineteenth century, the movement away from "religion" and towards positivism became an intellectual weapon in the hands of German scholars, and the reasons behind German eugenics[21] and the medical experiments of German doctors such as Josef Mengele were considered (at the time) scientifically sound. This leads to the question: how does one in our modern culture expand the paradigms of intellectualism, not simply as a social class or academic elite, but in the tools and resources used in

---

[21] The "science" of eugenics was based on the earlier work of Enlightenment philosophers such as Hume, Kant, and Hegel. "The superabundance of the iron particles, which are present in all human blood, and which are precipitated in the reticular substance through evaporation of the acids of phosphorus (which make all Negroes stink) cause the blackness that shines through the superficial skin ... in short, the Negro is produced, well suited to his climate; that is, strong fleshy, supple, but in the midst of the bountiful provision of his motherland lazy, soft and dawdling." Immanuel Kant, *Of the Different Races of Man. Race and the Enlightenment: A Reader.* Emmanuel Chukwudi Eze, ed. (Oxford: Blackwell Publishers, Ltd., 2000), 46.

intellectual thought, to balance science and reason with justice and morality without eschewing the lessons taught in the Torah?

Guenther Roth, in his introduction to Weber's *Economy and Society*, explains how Weber "builds a sociological scaffolding for raising some of the big questions about the origins and the possible directions of the modern world."[22] A few other questions come to mind, however, such as why sociologists have failed to explain the theological scaffolding in their "scientific" theories on Jewish culture and religion, and why, despite the complex methodology and erudition, they continue to use these theological constructs in their approach to Judaism.

The mystery of why the more highly educated people in our society are less religious is really no mystery at all. It has little to do with innate intelligence, logic, or reason; it has to do with the modern intellectual's foe, the religion of Christianity, whose Gnostic theology is ill-equipped to deal with science or reason, and exacerbated by Greek and Roman anti-Semitism, whether in its theological or positivist form, along with the exclusion and ridicule of genuine Torah in our colleges and universities. To limit intellectual thought to Greek and Roman culture where the intellectual is little more than the field agent of the army whose commander-in-chief is the philosopher (as Ayn Rand put it) limits our intellectual activity. To be able to "think outside the box," to have an "external, behavioral yardstick," to question the limits of intellectual thought that are based on Greek and Roman secular and religious disciplines taught in our institutions of higher learning is why the Noahide perspective is so vitally important.

The intellectual damage of the teachings of men such as Max Weber went far beyond the academic institutions; for over a hundred years the men (and increasingly, the women) who would become our nation's political and economic leaders were exposed to these subtle (as well as the not-so-subtle) anti-Semitic teachings. From every school, from every college, from every university, we find the teaching that the Jews were a fossilized race clinging to a repugnant and barbaric theology that was even more detestable than Christianity, and the book they based their claims upon was at best a crude mythology, and at worst a complete fabrication. Any claims the Jews had as a separate people or a sovereign nation were, as taught by our "enlightened" academic institutions, based on fairy tales and folklore and

---

[22] Guenther Roth, introduction to *Economy and Society*, xxxv.

could therefore be dismissed. These ideas were carried from the class-room into the halls of Congress, the Supreme Court, and ultimately into the White House itself. The intellectuals who made the decisions for our society would be guided by these principles, and this would severely impact the world's political and economic climate throughout the twentieth century.[23]

⁓

THE PROCESS OF developing a logical and rational intellectual ap-proach to the Torah is fraught with difficulties. As we have seen, al-though there are academic disciplines that discuss the Torah, they de-liberately misrepresent the Torah and the teachings of the rabbis. The path of rationality and level-headed objectivism of our modern edu-cational system runs into a cliff of emotional and illogical arguments when confronted with the Torah, and few can scale its heights without being properly equipped with the knowledge, the tools of Torah, and an understanding of rabbinic logic.

The first step is to understand the observation Sam Harris made[24] about having our beliefs modified by new facts. In a quote apocry-phally attributed to John Maynard Keynes, when asked why he had changed his position on a certain topic, Keynes reportedly said: "When the facts change, I change my mind. What do you do, sir?" When this question is put to the secular intellectuals, when it comes to the Torah, the answer is that they either ignore or distort the facts. This might seem like a sweeping generalization to some, but the facts are incontrovertible. There is no discipline or academic institution that has or even supports a system that teaches Torah to non-Jews. In fact, our schools, colleges, and universities employ a system designed to distort, misrepresent, and demean the Torah.

---

[23] "In the wake of the political upheavals that accompanied and followed the French Revolution, many profound changes occurred in the moral and social conditions of Europe's intellectual structure. These affected practically all cultural institutions and standards of ethics. No wonder that "religion" and its tenets—alleged to be at the root of a bankrupt social system, one of the main causes of the tremors which shook the civilized world—could not cope any longer with the new Europe which emerged from decades of war and revolution. Then a new political order became apparent, which undertook to restore the old structure of Europe under a new alliance of nations while retaining the cultural achievements of the Revolution. 'Religion,' as it had been known, remained however the opprobrium of the time of 'Enlightenment.'" Hirsch, *Collected Wrtitings*, Vol. 138–39.

[24] Epigraph p. 35 above.

In order for those living in Western society to, as Sam Harris put it, "collaborate with one another in a truly open-ended way," the intellectuals[25] of our society must be open to new facts—in this case, that the Torah has been blocked from academic discourse for reasons not based on logic or reason.[26] Those who are in political and financial control of our society do not want the Torah to have a fair representation in the court of public opinion. To understand the reasons behind this we must look at our political and economic systems, not from a liberal or conservative viewpoint, but from the Noahide perspective.

---

[25] "One thing we know from history is that political mobilization is impossible without an intellectual mobilization to clear the way." Daniel Lazare, *The Velvet Coup: The Constitution, the Supreme Court, and the Decline of American Democracy*. (London: Verso, 2001), 133.

[26] "There is nothing that is hidden or obscure in Judaism. Anyone who wishes to obtain a clear view of Jewish thinking and Jewish life can do so without difficulty. Jewish scriptures are not mysterious hieroglyphics; the Jewish Bible is available and accessible to every man, woman and child...yet almost no subject of scholarly research is less understood and more misinterpreted than Jewish life and thought... From Tacitus—whose writings usually reflect a clear-thinking, razor-sharp mind but who maintains that Jews worship donkey heads—down to the most recent 'experts' on Judaism, almost everything that is said and written about things Jewish amounts to pure caricature." Hirsch, *Collected Writings*, Vol. VIII, 249.

Part Two

❦

The Red, Red, White and Blue

Overview

When you step back and pose the civilizational question about Rome—On balance, who prevailed?—it's not at all clear that the Romans were driven from the field. The religion of the Romans, Christianity, became the religion of the newcomers, and to this day the language of the Romans is, in a sense— *mutatis mutandis*—spoken by their descendants. The people in the Roman lands remained drinkers of wine. Their architectural designs and building techniques became standard. Their towns and cities are still inhabited, and their seasonal rituals, under different names, still celebrated. Their attention to law and to legal systems spoke powerfully to America's own Founders, and Roman law remains foundational in Europe to this day.

— Cullen Murphy[1]

THE CLOSEST THING JUDAISM HAS TO A CREED WOULD PROBABLY BE the *Shema* from Deuteronomy 6:4, "Hear O Israel: HASHEM is our God, HASHEM is the One and Only!" The Noahide "creed" would no doubt be Rabbi Hillel's injunction "what is hateful to yourself, do not do to another." The Edomite creed is summed up best by the popular bumper-sticker from the 1980s: "He who dies with the most toys wins!"[2] The Edomite is consumed by consumerism, by material delights, by possessions. The Edomite is egocentric, with a *what is mine is mine and what is yours is yours*[3] attitude that permeates our

---

[1] Cullen Murphy, *Are We Rome?* (New York: Houghton Mifflin Company, 2007), 183–84.

[2] "The psalmist [Psalm 49, verses 7–9] now speaks of those who know no fear not because they have faith in God but because they place their trust in their material possessions. They measure the value of their lives, that is, 'the emanation of their personalities,' only in terms of the abundance of their tangible wealth. They use their possessions only for selfish purposes and not as a means toward the end of fulfilling their duty." Hirsch, *The Hirsch Psalms*, §i, 349.

[3] America's attitude towards the poor, its attitude towards poor immigrants, and the recent beatings of the homeless draws unpleasant comparisons to Sodom. "The maxim שלי שלי שלך שלך, 'I keep what is mine, you keep what is yours' stamps being necessitous as a crime, and reliving it as folly and a crime against the public welfare. Under the regime of Sodomite justice, where only achievement but not necessity, is

economy, our government, and especially our legal system.[4] Even the majority religion of Edomic civilization—Christianity—is a religion based on individual salvation without regard to the community.[5] Of all of the evil deeds by Edom, however, "the absence of justice is the most serious, bringing about the destruction of civilization in its wake." [*Redak*, from *San.* 108a][6] This difference on the philosophical outlook in life between Israel and Edom was the subject of a book written by Maurice Samuel titled *You Gentiles.*

Maurice Samuel was a Romanian-born Jewish intellectual who emigrated to the United States at the beginning of World War I and who published *You Gentiles* a decade later. The theme of *You Gentiles* is about the difference in Gentile and Jewish "character," about the fundamental differences between Esau and Jacob. In his book, Samuel explained that the distinction between nations and peoples is a spiritual distinction, that the difference between a Frenchman or an Englishman or an American, or even a Westernized Arab or Asian is much less than the difference between a Jew and a Gentile. Samuel said, in the beginning of his book, that "I have long pondered this question of Jew and gentile it is because I suspected from the first dawning of Jewish self-consciousness that Jew and gentile are two worlds, that between you gentiles and us Jews there lies an unbridgeable gulf."[7] He then goes on to describe this great spiritual gulf, the difference in the mindset of the Jew and the Gentile:

---

considered as a ground for a claim, poverty and wretchedness are despised; at most, strangers who are prospective profit-bringing rich men, like Lot, may be admitted, but 'begging is prohibited', and improvident hungry unfortunates are treated as criminals and can only expect 'jail and being moved on.'" Hirsch, *Commentary on the Torah: Bereishis*, 321.

[4] "We have seen how the Civil Law of Rome and the Common Law of England have extended their influence over a great part of the inhabited globe." R. W. Lee, "The Civil Law and the Common Law: A World Survey." *Michigan Law Review.* Vol. 14, No. 2 (December 1915), 94.

[5] "Gnostic theology is basically self-centered, as can be seen by the Gnostic theology on social responsibility: '*Judge not, that you not be judged*' (Matthew 7:1, Luke 6:37). This teaches that your responsibility only begins and ends with yourself. The Gnostics say you are to forgive, they teach you should be merciful, and you should do good works—only to bring reward to yourself. The Gnostic message is *save yourself.*" Cecil, *The Noahide Code*, 103.

[6] Rabbi A. J. Rosenberg, *Isaiah,* Vol. *2.* (Brooklyn: The Judaica Press, Inc., 2004), 468.

[7] Samuel, *You Gentiles*, 9.

To you life is a game and a gallant adventure, and all life's enterprises partake of the spirit of the adventurous. To us life is a serious and sober duty pointed to a definite and inescapable task. Your relations to gods and men spring from the joy and rhythm of the temporary comradeship or enmity of spirit. Our relation to God and men is dictated by a somber subjection to some eternal principle. Your way of life, your moralities and codes, are the rules of a game—none the less severe or exacting for that, but not inspired by a sense of fundamental purposefulness. Our way of life, or morality and code, do not refer to temporary rules which govern a temporary and trivial pastime...to you morality is 'the right thing,' to us morality is "right." For all the changing problems of human relationship which rise with changing circumstances you lay down the rules and regulations of the warrior, the sportsman, the gentleman; we refer all problems seriously to eternal law. For you certain acts are 'unbecoming' to the pertinent ideal type—whether he be a knight or a 'decent fellow.' We have no such changing systems of reference—only one command.[8]

For Samuel, the rules that Gentiles create for themselves are rules of a game. Take "honor" for example. In Gentile society, "honor" is held in highest regard. Duels have been fought over it, people have died for it. But there is no sense of what is right or wrong with "honor," such as "honor between gentlemen" and "honor among thieves and pirates." Non-Jews spend inordinate amounts of time with things that, from the Noahide perspective, are meaningless at best and at worst morally destructive, as Samuel pointed out:

Wars for Helen and for Jenkins' ear; duels for honor and for gambling debts, death for a flag, loyalties, gallant gestures, a world that centers round sport and war, with a system of virtues related to these; art that springs not from God but from the joyousness and suffering of the free man, a world of play which takes death itself as part of the play, to be approached as carelessly and pleasantly as any other turn of chance, cities and states and mighty enterprises built up on the same rush of feeling and energy as carries a football team—and in the same ideology—this is the efflorescence of the Western world."[9]

The Jews have routinely been criticized for their "nitpicky attention to the minutiae of the Law."[10] Yet our Western society has its own

---

[8] Ibid., 31–32.

[9] Ibid., 35.

[10] "It has been contended that Judaism based on the Halachah rests on an arid legalism with its sole concern for religious rites and observances, devoid of

nitpickiness when it comes to law, too often in matters that so baffled Jews such as Maurice Samuel. While criticizing the Jews and their Oral Law, the Gentiles fill their minds with meaningless laws and rituals. For example, let us look at the game of baseball, the Great American Pastime, a game which is made up of insignificant nitpicky laws.

The origins of the game (or "sport") of baseball go back to the nineteenth century (there is a legend that modern baseball was a creation of Abner Doubleday, who commanded the First Corps at Gettysburg after General John F. Reynolds was killed), and it consists of grown men in funny-looking outfits hitting a little ball with a wooden stick and running around in circles touching bags anchored in the ground while other grown men chase after them and try to touch them with the ball. There are many laws dealing with the ball itself. The ball is to be made of cork, rubber, and yarn; it is then covered with cowhide (before 1974, horsehide). The laws of this game stipulate that the ball must be nine inches in circumference and weigh five ounces, and must retain its shape after being subjected to a 65 pound force and distort less than 8/100ths of an inch under compression as well as it registering a rebound of 54.6% of the original velocity when hit with the stick. There are similar laws concerning the other equipment and tools for this game, such as the wooden sticks used to hit the ball, the oversized leather gloves used to catch the ball, and the costumes worn by the men.

The ball is put in play by what is called a "pitcher" who gets to stand on a mound of dirt. This is no ordinary mound of dirt, however; the dirt has to be piled up to exact specifications. The mound of dirt must be exactly eighteen feet in diameter, and no more than ten inches higher than the flat playing field. The top of the mound is a level area which must be five feet wide and thirty–four inches deep, and there is a thick rubber "plate" twenty-four inches wide and six inches deep that is exactly eighteen inches from the dead center of the mound. The slope of the mound starts six inches from the front of this plate, and it has to slope one inch for each foot of the mound. There are many other laws involving what the pitcher can or cannot do, including one of the most important—not to drool on the ball, which is considered a very serious infraction indeed. The pitcher can be ejected from the game if he drools on the ball.

---

spiritual significance." Dayan Dr. Myer S. Lew, *The Humanity of Jewish Law*. (London: The Soncino Press, 1985), 1.

The object of the game is for the "pitcher" to throw the ball to the man with the stick, called the "batter." There are all sorts of laws about the stick, which is called the "bat." A few of these laws include that a "bat" cannot be longer than forty–two inches long and no wider than two and three-quarter inches wide at its widest part, it has to be made out of solid wood, and a prohibition on putting gooey tree sap more than eighteen inches up from the end of the handle of the stick.

The pitcher tries to throw the ball past the man with the wooden stick, and the man with the stick tries to hit the ball with the stick. The batter stands next to a five-sided slab of whitened rubber called the "plate" which is exactly seventeen inches long with two of the sides set at an angle to make a point. The pitcher has to throw the ball over this "plate" in order for it to count. Once the man with the wooden stick hits the ball, he must run around in a square that has three fifteen inch stuffed square bags in the corners of the square, touching them with a part of his body (usually his foot, but also his hands or what-ever part of the body he can make contact with). The stuffed bags must be exactly 90 feet from one another, and exactly 127 feet 3 3/8 inches from the opposite diagonal bag, and the field must conform to other exact dimensions. There are many other rules that involve the man with the wooden stick as well as the men in the field that try to catch the ball that the man with the wooden stick hits, the men who run around the square field touching the stuffed bags, as well as the "umpires," men who are the paid legal "experts" that stand around in various parts of the field to ensure that all of these laws are upheld.

For over a hundred years, many of these men who have a higher than average ability to hit the little ball with the wooden stick have become cultural heroes[11] to the public at large. Detailed statistics of their performance are kept, often down to a ten-thousandth of a deci-mal point; how many times a man with the wooden stick hits the ball, or how many times he does not get to hit the ball, the percentage of how many times he hits the ball versus the attempts to hit the ball, how many times he gets to run to the first stuffed bag, how many times he gets to run to the second stuffed bag or the third stuffed bag, and

---

[11] "Hero worship" is another oddity of Western Culture. There is an entire industry built on "hero worship," and the youth of the West admire and emulate many of our cultural "heroes" despite the dubious moral turpitude of many of these so-called "heroes."

so on. Statistics are kept on the man who throws the ball to the man with the wooden stick; how many times he throws the ball and the batter misses hitting the ball, how many times he throws the ball and the batter hits it, etc. These statistics are well-known to the "fans" of the game, the people who pay enormous sums of money to go to the multi-million dollar coliseums that are built specifically for this game, and these statistics are often discussed and debated among the public, many whom consider these statistics important. Even the Supreme Court has spent time ruling on this "game" in cases such as *Federal Baseball Club v. National League* (1922), *Flood v. Kuhn* (1972), and *Major League Baseball Players Association v. Steve Garvey* (2001).

There are many other "sports" that are equally as important to other Western nations, sports that involve running around kicking a ball, or throwing a ball through a round metal hoop or running around in the grass or mud with a ball, or hitting a little ball with a stick to make it go into a small hole in the ground, racing around a track on foot, on horseback, or with machines. All of these "sports" have hundreds of similar laws ruling the games they play, and the nitpicky minutiae of the number of these laws and the seriousness with which they are applied are amazing, to say the least.[12]

Many of these coliseum events are dangerous (particularly the ones involving people racing around a track on machines). There are many

---

[12] The love of nitpicky rules and regulations are not limited to games; another example is "dining etiquette." When eating out at a fancy or expensive restaurant or a formal dinner at someone's home, there are extensive and complicated rituals and rules governing proper dining behavior. There are rules about the procedures of sitting down, of the utensils used, and even about the "napkin," a small cloth used to wipe off any stray food. There are rules about when one must unfold the napkin, where one puts the napkin while dining, how to use the napkin properly, what to do with the napkin if you have to be excused momentarily, and what to do with the napkin after your meal.

There are rules on when to start eating. There are rules about forks, spoons, knives, plates, bowls, and glasses; which different knife, fork, spoon, plate, bowl, or glass one should use at what time in the meal and with what food or drink. There are rules about how the knives, forks, spoons, plates, bowls and glasses are to be presented, and how to set them on the table. There are rules about how to hold your utensils, what to do with them when you are eating, what to do with them when you are finished eating, and what to do with them if you have to be excused for a moment. There are rules about serving food, and rules about passing food around the table. There are rules about how to eat your food, and which utensils should be eaten with which food. There are rules about table manners such as how one should sit, or what parts of the body should or should not be on the table (such as elbows) as well as rules about how much one should eat, how quickly one should eat, and what to do after eating. These rules are taken very seriously by many, particularly the upper class.

of these "sports," however, that regularly have occasional fighting, particularly the one where the "players" wear big padded costumes and are forced to play on a slippery field of ice using special shoes with a metal blade attached on the bottom. This is so they can maneuver around the ice with long, curved sticks so they can hit a rounded and flattened chunk of vulcanized rubber into a net. The intermittent fights that break out during the game are highly enjoyed by the "spectators." Of course, for those who enjoy more sanguinary entertainment there are always the ancient Greek standbys—boxing and wrestling—and these events are often held in large coliseums. This love of coliseum sporting events featuring fighting and death is one of the West's more obvious social patterns inherited from Rome.

It was this emphasis of sports on our culture—particularly by those who sneer at Judaism being full of nitpicky laws—which led Maurice Samuel to observe that the Gentile's "ideal morality is a sporting morality."[13] The value our culture has put on sports has led to the ethos of "sportsmanship," which can be summed up as "it is not if you win or lose, but how you play the game." When one ponders the way our society has treated the Jews and the Torah, it is no wonder that Samuel said that "compared with each other, you are gentlemen, warriors, democracies: set side by side with us, you are bullies and cowards and mobs."[14]

Those who think this an unfair exaggeration must understand how international politics, with politicians who were run through the academic mill of Western culture, have treated Israel. The nations of the world criticize Israel for their treatment of the Palestinians, for their occupation of the West Bank and Gaza,[15] yet who drew the geopolitical lines designating these areas? The United States has embassies in every nation's capital but one: Jerusalem. Israel has named Jerusalem the capital, yet nearly every nation on earth has their embassies elsewhere, and do not recognize Jerusalem as the capital of Israel. What reasons do the nations of the world have to dictate to Israel—a sovereign state—the terms of which city is the capital of their own nation?

---

[13] Samuel, *You Gentiles*, 42.

[14] Ibid., 129.

[15] As can be seen in statements such as "the painful history of the Israeli occupation of the West Bank and Gaza." Harris, *The End of Faith*, 109.

Here, in the political arena, we see that the rules of "sportsmanship" do not apply to Israel, and the "great gulf" spoken of by Maurice Samuel manifests itself in the way the Western Nations treat Israel differently from other sovereign nations.

୧

Hᴏᴡ ʜᴀᴠᴇ ᴛʜᴇ ʜɪsᴛᴏʀɪᴄᴀʟ, philosophical, and sociological attitudes regarding the Jews influenced modern politics in regards to the modern state of Israel? At the end of World War I, after nineteen centuries of continuous foreign rule by the Romans, Byzantines, Arabs, Crusaders, Mamelukes, and the Ottomans, the iron grip of Edom on *Eretz Yisrael*, the Land of Israel, began to loosen. On November 2, 1917, a letter was sent to Lord Rothchild from Arthur James Lord Balfour:

> Dear Lord Rothchild,
> I have much pleasure in conveying to you, on behalf of His Majesty's Government, the following declaration of sympathy with Jewish Zionist aspirations which has been submitted to and approved by, the Cabinet.
> "His Majesty's Government view with favour the establishment in Palestine of a national home for the Jewish people, and will use their best endeavours to facilitate the achievement of this object, it being clearly understood that nothing shall be done which may prejudice the civil and religious rights of existing non-Jewish communities in Palestine, or the rights and political status enjoyed by Jews in any other country."
> I should be grateful if you would bring this declaration to the knowledge of the Zionist Federation.
> Yours sincerely,
> Arthur James Balfour.[16]

Oddly, it seems that no one ever stops to ask the question: what exactly gave Britain the "right" to grant Jews the right to live in their own ancient homeland? At the end of World War I and the defeat of the Central Powers (Germany, Austria-Hungary, and Turkey), the victorious militaries of Britain and France occupied the Middle East, and they decided to carve up the former Ottoman Empire into nations populated with the indigenous wandering Arab desert tribes. The French and British decided to name the new states using quaint

---

[16] Walter Laqueur and Barry Rubin, ed. *The Israeli-Arab Reader: A Documentary History of the Middle East Conflict.* (New York: Penguin Books, 1984), 18.

Biblical names such as Syria, Jordan, and Lebanon. They also thought it would be prudent (seeing how it was getting close to Jesus' two thousandth birthday) to return the Jews to the ancient land of Israel in order to facilitate "Christ's return."

Problems with the plan, however, began almost immediately. Hussein ibn Ali, the Hashemite and *sharif* of Mecca, was unhappy about the situation, and tried in vain to negotiate with the British to create "not self-determination for the Arabic-speaking subjects of the defunct Ottoman Empire but the formation of a successor empire, extending well beyond the predominately Arabic-speaking territories."[17] The spoke in Hussian's wheel was the plan for a Jewish homeland in Israel, for "the core of the pan-Arab rejection of the Jewish right to statehood [was] no concern for the national rights of the Palestinian Arabs but a desire to fend off a perceived encroachment on the pan-Arab imperial patrimony…Palestine was not perceived as a distinct entity deserving of national self-determination but as an integral part of a unified regional Arab order."[18] Attacks on Jews by Arabs occurred in Jerusalem, Jaffa, and Hadera; synagogues were destroyed, and there were murders, rapes, and beatings of Jews. Thus began the Arab's war of terror on the Jewish population of Israel.

We need to point out that, contrary to popular belief, there had always been a Jewish presence in the Land of Israel since the Bar Kochba revolt in the early second century. No Edomite Empire, for nearly two thousand years, had managed to eradicate the Jews totally from the land. We should also point out that, during the first years of the "partition plan," that "the 'historic rights' of the Arabs to Palestine, allegedly existing for a thousand years, had not yet been discovered."[19] This was because there had never been a state, nation, or country called "Palestine." The term "Palestine" to denote the Land of Israel was invented by the Romans (after the Bar Kochba revolt was crushed in 135 CE) as an insult to the Jews; it was derived from the Greek word "Palestini," or "land of the Philistines," the Biblical enemies

---

[17] Efrain Karsh, *Islamic Imperialism*. (New Haven: Yale University Press, 2007), 133–34.

[18] Ibid., 140.

[19] Samuel Katz, *Battleground: Fact & Fantasy in Palestine*. (New York: Taylor Productions, Ltd., 2002), 42.

of Israel who lived along the coast (roughly from Jaffa to Gaza) and had long since vanished. The Arabic term "Filistine" comes from this Edomite word, and was not generally used until after the 1967 Six Day War; "Filistine" is a political designation, not a word used to describe nationality. The language, cultural or ethnic differences between the "Filistine" Arabs and the Arabs of surrounding states was no greater than, say, the differences between the American citizens of Tennessee and those in Illinois or Oregon.

The British interest in "Palestine" was not only about theological concerns, but to secure the flank of the Suez Canal, the important water route to their Empire. The officials who were in charge of the British "mandate" in "Palestine" did not share the lofty ideals of Lord Balfour and were mainly concerned with keeping order. To keep the "peace," they caved in to Arab demands, first by lopping off the entire area of Eastern "Palestine" (which the British had promised earlier to Israel) and giving it to the Arabs, an area which would later be named "TransJordan." Of course, there were plenty of anti-Semites in high positions, such as assistant secretary Ernest T. Richmond. Richmond finagled to have Haj Amin el Husseini appointed as Mufti of Jerusalem and de-facto leader of the "Palestinian" Arabs, a post he would hold onto until World War II. Husseini's credentials were perfect for the job: Husseini had served in the Ottoman Military, fighting the British, and hated Jews with a passion, and he had been one of the ringleaders in the riots in Jerusalem in the spring of 1920.[20] Also, Husseini would later become a close friend and advisor to Adolf Hitler, supporting Hitler's plans for the "Final Solution." Among Husseini's duties as Mufti were to spread anti-Jewish propaganda and to organize attacks on Jewish settlers.

As the lukewarm British support for the Balfour declaration cooled, the British started restricting Jewish immigration into the land they had promised them while, at the same time, allowing a great deal of Arab immigration. This became official policy with the drafting of the Passfield White Paper in October of 1930 (following the Arab pogroms of the previous year). In the White Paper of 1939, there was even more revision on the Balfour Declaration, stating that "His Majesty's Government believe that the framers of the Mandate in which

---

[20] The British Court of Inquiry would sum up this attack as "The Jews were the victims of a peculiarly brutal and cowardly attack, the majority of the casualties being old men, women and children." Ibid., 64.

the Balfour Declaration was embodied could not have intended that Palestine should be converted into a Jewish State against the will of the Arab population of the country."[21] Thus the British slammed the door shut on Jewish immigration to Israel during the Holocaust.

We pause here to ask a few questions. The first is, if the British were so concerned about protecting the Suez Canal, why would they support a population of Arabs that were decidedly pro-Nazi? Secondly, why were the British so concerned about the "rights" of the "indigenous Arab population" of "Palestine" when British attitude concerning the rights of other indigenous populations in countries which they controlled (Kenya and India, for example) were exactly the opposite? Why would the British be concerned with protecting "the civil and religious rights of existing non-Jewish communities in Palestine" when Jews living in Arab states were constantly being stripped of their rights?[22] And finally, why would anyone think that the British, or any other Western nation, would behave any differently towards a people that have been portrayed in academia as a "fossilized, barbarous, and pariah" nation, a nation whose only claims to the land were from a book and religion that Western scholarship had endeavored to show was false and corrupted?

On November 29, 1947, when the enormity of the Holocaust had shamed even the most jaded Christian, the United Nations General Assembly passed Resolution 181, dividing the Land of Israel (after nearly eighty per cent of what Britain had promised to the Jews was taken away to create "Jordan") into separate Jewish and Arab homelands, with Jerusalem as an "international city." This proposition

---

[21] Laqueur and Rubin, *The Israeli-Arab Reader*, 66.

[22] Many of the Jews living in neighboring Arab lands were driven out of communities which they had lived in for centuries, too often the Jews were forced to leave with only the clothes on their back. "Israel has not found sympathy anywhere. Those who harbored hostile feelings against Israel were in the overwhelming majority. But, what was even worse, the reins of power were in the hands of those who actively desired to paralyze Israel, to hinder it in its every movement, to render it powerless while it was yet alive. It was for this purpose that they came forward against Israel with trumped-up charges. It was their intention to force Israel 'אז' in this manner, to restore 'all that which it had actually acquired by honest and legal means' as if Israel had obtained such possessions by 'robbery.' In generally, the Jews were denied the right to existence. Everything that a Jew possessed, even if he had acquired it by unimpeachably honest means, was viewed, or at least treated, as loot which had been amassed by robbing other nations." Hirsch, *The Hirsch Psalms*, §i, 473.

was accepted by the Jews but rejected by the Arabs. The day after Israel declared its independence on May 14, 1948, the larger and better-equipped Arab armies invaded Israel, aiming to "drive the Jews into the sea." After Israel defeated the Arabs, the West Bank was controlled by Jordan and the Gaza by Egypt. No attempt or even dialogue was made to take these areas away from Jordan and Egypt to create a "Palestinian Homeland," a fact too often overlooked by intellectuals today.

By May of 1967 the countries of Egypt, Syria, and Jordan had been rearming themselves for a war against Israel. Egyptian President Gamal Abdel Nasser was explicit in his aims—to drive the Jews into the sea and destroy the nation of Israel. Egyptian, Syrian, and Jordanian troops began massing on Israel's borders, and on May twenty-second, Egypt closed the Straits of Tiran to all Israeli shipping, an obvious act of war. On the fifth of June, Israel attacked in what is now known as the "Six Day War," taking Gaza and the Sinai from Egypt, the West Bank from Jordan, and the Golan Heights from Syria. Since that time, these areas (except for Sinai, which was returned to Egypt twelve years after the war) have been depicted on Western maps as "occupied territories" even though these areas were part of the original "Jewish homeland" promised under the original British Mandate after World War I and part of the ancient and traditional Jewish homeland. The nonsense we hear almost daily in the Western press about "the painful history of the Israeli occupation of the West Bank and Gaza"[23] ignores that Egypt and Jordan occupied these areas for two decades (1948–1967) without a hint of setting up an independent "Palestinian State" for the "refugees," and that this land had been promised to Israel before Britain reneged on the deal.

In order to understand the context of the Arab's claim to these lands, we have to keep in mind that none of the Arab states that border Israel existed before 1920—all were carved out of the Ottoman Empire, and none of them had existed as independent states for over a thousand years, yet the West regards this Israeli "appropriation" of Arab lands a violation of their "sovereignty." The West is constantly bemoaning the fate of the hundreds of thousands of "Palestinians" who were "driven" from their "homeland," while ignoring the plight of the hundreds of thousands of Jews driven from Arabic nations—from communities where Jews have lived for centuries—forcing Jews to leave their

---

[23] Harris, *The End of Faith*, 109.

property behind. The West also ignores that "Jordan"—the area that was originally supposed to be part of the Jewish homeland promised by Britain—is where the "Palestinian" Arabs have a "homeland."[24] As author Eugene Narrett explained:

> The discussions of strange, otherwise unfathomable political alliances and pressures, diplomatic initiatives and dicta, economic, strategic, and Intelligence failures of the West become comprehensible when seen in relation to the unvarying pole star of the oligarchies that control western policies to facilitate, encourage, even to take pride in attrition against the Jewish people until the heartland of Israel is cleansed of Jews and Jewish sovereignty.[25]

Britain and France, conquerors of the Ottoman Empire in the First World War, claimed the right to say who lived where in the Middle East, what nations should be formed, and what they should be named. The Jews, on the other hand, had no right to say what should be done with the same lands they conquered militarily, even when they were part of the ancient homeland of Israel. What we see are the Edomite memes in action—the hatred of Israel, Jews, and the Torah that overrides every other political and economic concern, even going so far as to back the supporters of Adolf Hitler and of Nazism.[26]

THE STRUCTURAL DYNAMIC of the Western double-standard in regard to Israel[27] makes it clear that the rules of "sportsmanship" and "fair play" do not apply to the Jews in politics, economics, or any other social activity. This double standard, seen in the way scholars have treated the Torah, the way historians have treated Israel, and the way

---

[24] "The solution was, obviously, to create two states side by side ... and so it would have been, decades ago, if the messianic rabbis and mullahs and priests could have been kept out of it." Hitchens, *God is not Great*, 24.

[25] Eugene Narrett, *Israel and the Endtimes: Writings on the Logic and Surface Turbulence of History.* (Bloomington: AuthorHouse, 2006), ix.

[26] For example, in David's Psalm (Ps. 144) of victory over his enemies is explained by Rabbi S. R. Hirsch: "[David] knows that war is necessary because of the perfidy of the nations with which no dependable covenant of peace can be made, and whose insidious politics makes constant preparedness for war imperative." Hirsch, *The Hirsch Psalms*, §ii, 462.

[27] Because of this double-standard, we can also dismiss the claim that there is a difference between *anti-Zionism* and *anti-Semitism*; anti-Zionism is merely a different form of anti-Semitism.

sociologists treated Judaism, cannot be blamed solely on Christianity, for it goes far beyond the bounds of religious intolerance. The protocols of Edom are to eliminate the Jews, to eliminate Israel,[28] and to eliminate the Torah from existence, for as long as Israel survives it is a threat to Edom's power.

The characteristics of the Roman/Edomite culture and nation are a self-aggrandizing lust for power[29] (political, economic, and military) coupled with a hatred of the norms and values of the Torah which are embodied in Israel. In the Edomite society, the economy is structured upon a large slave/serf/low-paid worker society, and wealth and property flow from the bottom working class to the cadre of the Ruling Class who are constantly consolidating their wealth and power. Although the Edomite may trade peacefully with its neighbors, it often relies on *hamas* (the Hebrew word for violence and robbery)—particularly by warfare which it is most adept—to steal resources from weaker nations. In this way it acquires the raw materials it needs: coal, lumber, metals, oil, or more animal or human labor. As its resources run out (often with the destruction of the environment), the economy and the society collapse, and are swallowed up by another Edomite nation. At the end of the fifteenth century, the Spanish and Portuguese (both speaking *Romance*—i.e., Latin-based—languages) invaded and plundered the Americas. The Dutch, the French, and the British followed their example, and by the early twentieth century, most of the

---

[28] "In the final analysis, the fight of Israel's enemies is not directed against us but against 'Thee'; that is, against God Himself. God stands in the way of men and nations with His absolute power as a ruler and with the absolute requirements of His moral law, for both of which He has sent Israel as a memorial and messenger among the nations. Judaism, with its concept of the invisible God and its idealistic views of the world and of life as a whole, has always been thoroughly hated by those who capitalize upon the degeneracy and corruptibility of man...the advent of 'Israel' as...a nation among nations, bare of all those things upon which the other nations base their existence, represents such a protest against the entire social and political structure of the rest of the world that the nations would desire nothing more than the elimination of Israel from their midst, so that its very name...and the fact of its persistent survival should no longer proclaim the ultimate and universal supremacy of God's rule." Hirsch, *Psalms*, §ii, 94–95.

[29] "The men of the East India Company, the Spanish conquistadors, the investors in South African mines and the slave traders knew very well what they wanted. They wanted to be rich. Colonial empires were exploited ruthlessly as sources of cheap raw materials and cheap labour, and as monopolized markets." Anthony Brewer, *Marxist Theories of Imperialism: A Critical Survey*. (London, New York Taylor & Francis Routledge, 1990), 2.

world's nations had fallen under the influence, if not the direct political and economic control, of Western Edomite civilization.[30]

---

[30] "The key to the Westerners' success in creating the first truly global empires between 1500 and 1750 depended upon precisely those improvements in the ability to wage war which have been termed 'the military revolution.' The Expansion of the West was also facilitated by the superiority in organization, discipline, and training of its troops and subsequently by the superior weapons, transport, logistics, and medical services resulting from its leadership in the Industrial Revolution. The West won the world not by the superiority of its ideas or values or religion (to which few members of other civilizations were converted) but rather by its superiority in applying organized violence. Westerns often forget this fact; non-Westerns never do." Huntington. *The Clash of Civilizations and the Remaking of World Order*, 51.

Reflexive Intellectualism

In Talmudic sources and in Midrashic literature the names Esau–Edom are often identified with Rome. *Rashi* echoes these traditions when he connects the 'fatness of the earth,' mentioned in Isaac's blessing to Esau, with Italy (27:39; cf. *Rashi* to Numbers 25:19). Later, when Rome adopted Christianity, the same appellation was conferred upon the whole of the Christian world. Flavius Josephus records that Tz'fo, a grandson of Esau (Genesis 36:11), was the founder of Rome, which eventually became the center of Christianity (*Ramban* on 49:31). Since then, it has become traditional to consider the Christians as representative of Esau's offspring and the Jews as descendants of Jacob. The antagonism between Jacob and Esau is thus symbolic of that between Rome and Jerusalem; and the reasons underlying this antagonism are also applicable to the Jewish and Christian worlds. One can therefore conclude that the hostility of Christian anti-Semites is not based on religious, political, or economic grounds; nor is it based on any other definite motive. It is of an irrational nature, for it goes back to the prenatal stage. It was already manifest in the womb, where an unrelenting struggle was carried on between two brothers representing two worlds with a deep gulf separating them. Note that it has never been possible to discover and identify the true motives of anti-Semitism through logical analysis, despite the countless studies devoted to it.

— Rabbi Elie Munk[1]

T HE WORLD-HISTORICAL CONFLICT BETWEEN JACOB AND ESAU, OR ISRAEL and Edom, was a rivalry which would define Western Civilization.[2] To better understand this concept, we need to explore the complex nature of Edom in our culture. The influence of Edomite ideals and ideas[3]

---

[1] Munk, *The Call of the Torah: Bereishis*, 337.

[2] "[Edom was] unlike Israel and Ishmael or Israel and Canaan. Israel's destiny would not be linked of necessity to that of the other nations. The world could have fifty powerful empires without in the least affecting Israel. In the same prophecy which assured Abraham of the greatness awaiting Isaac's offspring, he was told that Ishmael would be a great and powerful nation. Israel and Ishmael can coexist as easily as can Israel and China. Geographical 'proximity' need not necessarily be a hindrance to either. But Jacob and Esau cannot rise independently of one another…the history of the world would be played out in the rivalry between the philosophies of good and evil as represented by them." Scherman, *Bereishis*, 1024.

[3] "There is another dimension to Edom, one that carries it beyond its territorial boundaries and places it squarely at the center of world history. Edom is the last, and

has gone far beyond the confines of organized religion.[4] Our government is based on an unhealthy mix of Greek democracy and Roman Republicanism, our military culture is based on the Greek and Roman love of the art of war.[5] Our nation is full of examples of classical art and architecture, such as our statues and government buildings[6] in Washington D.C. Our music is based upon Greek modes and scales. Our calendar, holidays, and weeks are organized around the Christian

---

most vicious, of the Four Monarchies destined to subjugate Israel in its road through history…it is no coincidence that Edom plays this pivotal role in Israel's history. At the very dawn of Israel's beginnings, God had decreed that it whom He was to love (Malachi 1:2) would, until the End of Days, have its fate intertwined with a balancing force of evil which would embody everything hateful to God (Malachi 1:3). Two nations were within Rebecca's womb, and two irreconcilable world views of peoplehood were to diverge from within her (Genesis 25:23). Never would these two be able to coexist. One would always be in the ascendant; the other, in decline (Rashi, there, based on *Pesachim* 42b, *Megillah* 6a)." *Yechezkel*. Translation and Commentary by Rabbi Moshe Eisemann, 542.

[4] "Europe and the United States, after all, have a dual heritage—Judeo-Christian religion and ethics, Greco-Roman statecraft and law." Berman, *Dark Ages America*, 88. Cf. n. 22, p. 125 above.

[5] "Among the people they ruled the Romans aggressively displayed the symbols of their power—like the well-known fasces, the wooden rods bundled around an ax and tied up with red straps…as symbols, the fasces today seem relatively innocuous, the bundled rods often given the anodyne interpretation 'strength in unity.' They were adopted as a republican symbol by a young America. Look behind the president when he gives the State of the Union address, and you'll see fasces on the wall of the House chamber. You'll see them on the massive marble seat Abraham Lincoln occupies in his memorial. But historians remind us what the fasces originally were: 'a portable kit for flogging and decapitation.'" Murphy, *Are We Rome?*, 128–29.

[6] For example, the Supreme Court building, completed in 1935, is a modern recreation of pagan Greek and Roman temples. As were the ancient pagan temples, the Supreme Court building is sheathed in white marble with free standing columns, and the building is raised on a podium and a wide and formal staircase leading up to the main entrance. In front of the Supreme Court building is the sculpture named "The Contemplation of Justice," a representation of *Themis*, the Greek goddess of justice. The name "Justice" comes from *Justicia*, which was one of the four Roman virtues depicted in the form of a woman. The bronze doors of the main entrance to the building are seventeen feet high and weigh thirteen tons (this is another attribute of pagan temples; bronze doors also graced the Roman senate and the pantheon). The frieze panels on the doors show scenes from ancient Greek and Roman times. The eight bas-relief panels include a scene from the *Iliad*, a Roman praetor, Julian (Roman law instructor), the publishing of the Justinian Code, the Magna Carta, the Westminster Statute, Lord Chief Justice Coke and King James I, and Chief Justice John Marshall and Associate Justice Joseph Story. These panels show the story of how American law was descended from Greek and Roman law.

Sabbath. The days of the week are named after pagan gods such as Saturn, Odin, and Thor. Our government, schools, and businesses run according to Christian Sabbaths and holidays. Rome has been popular in literature,[7] drama,[8] and, most recently, motion pictures.[9] We enjoy "sporting" events in large coliseums modeled after the original Coliseum in Rome, and every four years the world watches the Olympic games, another cultural albatross from Ancient Greece.

Even our language bears the stamp of Rome. Not only does Latin make up a good fifty percent of modern English,[10] but Latin serves as the language of academia;[11] Latin is the language of science, medicine, and most importantly, law.[12] Latin often adorns the architecture of our courthouses, government buildings, and universities, and practically every single adult carries samples of Latin with them on their person, for we have Latin on all of our coin and paper money. Observe at the back ("tails") of a Lincoln penny, specifically a penny made

---

[7] Popular novels such as *Quo Vadis* and *I, Claudius* were based in Ancient Rome.

[8] Shakespeare had an affinity with Ancient Rome; *Titus Andronicus, Coriolanus, Julius Caesar* and *Antony and Cleopatra* were all set in Classical Rome.

[9] Roman-themed motion pictures such as *Cleopatra*, *Spartacus*, and *Gladiator* were all multiple-Oscar winners and popular with the public.

[10] "When the Norman Conquest brought French into England as the language of the higher classes, much of the Old English vocabulary appropriate to literature and learning died out and was replaced later by words borrowed from French and Latin." Albert C. Baugh, Thomas Cable, *A History of the English Language*. (Englewood Cliffs: Prentice-Hall, Inc., 1993), 53.

[11] "Classical western political theory arose out of city-states in ancient Greece...the root for the words city and citizen is the Latin civitas, as developed in Roman law. The ideas of the city and citizen are of earlier origin, in the polis and polites of ancient Greece. The Roman conception leads towards the liberal idea of citizenship as the possession of civil rights by an individual against the state (and potentially as part of a universal society). The Greek conception is more communitarian, stressing collective membership and individual participation in political office." Nancy L. Schwartz, "Communitarian Citizenship: Marx & Weber on the City." *Polity*. Vol. 17, No. 3 (Spring, 1985), 531.

[12] In a letter to John Brazier, Thomas Jefferson commented that "the lawyer finds in the Latin language the system of civil law most conformable with the principles of justice of any which has ever yet been established among men, and from which much has been incorporated into our own." Louis B. Wright, "Thomas Jefferson and the Classics." *Proceedings of the American Philosophical Society*. Vol. 87, No. 3 (Jul. 14, 1943), 227.

from 1959 to 2009. What you have on the penny is a pagan temple, and the words *E Pluribus Unum*[13] and "One Cent,"[14] words of Latin, the language of Rome.[15] The entire structure of our culture bears the unmistakable imprint of Edom/Rome. Our glorification and slavish mimicry of Roman art, architecture, economics, and legal ideology has made us culturally little more than ancient Romans in business suits. Many would agree with "the neoconservative writer Max Boot, arguing that America must become the successor empire to Britain (which once saw itself as the successor empire to Rome)"[16] that the United States is the latest and most successful embodiment of Rome to date, an embodiment which has permeated all aspects of our culture. Our entire culture reeks of Rome.[17]

But, we argue, is this necessarily a bad thing? Are not the civilizations of Greece and Rome worthy of emulation? Did not the Greeks lead us out of barbarism, teaching us that there is beauty in the world?[18]

---

[13] "Out of many, one." This motto is disturbingly similar to "Ein Volk, ein Reich, ein Führer."

[14] From the Latin word *centum*, "hundred."

[15] As opposed to the "heads" side of the penny, which has the words "In God We Trust," "Liberty" (from Leviticus 25:10), and a bust of a man named Abraham.

[16] Murphy, *Are We Rome?*, 7.

[17] "Separation of powers, checks and balances, government in accordance with constitutional law, a toleration of slavery, fixed terms in office, the presidential 'veto' (Latin for 'I forbid')—all of these ideas were influenced by Roman precedents. John Adams and his son John Quincy Adams often read Cicero and both spoke of him as a personal inspiration. The architects of the new American capital were so taken with Rome that they even named the now filled-in creek that flowed where the Mall is today the 'Tiber River.' Alexander Hamilton, James Madison, and John Jay, in writing the Federalist Papers to argue for the ratification of the Constitution, signed their articles with the pseudonym 'Publius Vlerius Publicola'—who was the third consul of the Roman Republic and the first to personify its values." Chalmers Johnson, *Nemesis: The Last Days of the American Republic*. (New York: Metropolitan Books/Henry Holt and Company, 2006), 59.

[18] "Hellenistic thought stimulates mind and soul and aims to develop, through joy in knowledge and pleasure in all that is noble, harmony and beauty as weapons to suppress brutish outbursts of passion. It makes him responsible to himself, and expects him to ennoble himself by self-control, by doing away with all that is evil and vulgar, attributes that disturb the divine harmony in character and in sentiment, in speech and in deed. The Hellenistic spirit creates civilized, gentle, joyful and free men... the Hellenistic spirit appeals to the Godly spark in the human breast and encourages the human mind to perfect his self-perception, to the recognition of the greatness of intellectual pursuit and science, and guarantees man's spirit of individual freedom." Hirsch, *Collected Writings*, Vol. II, 202.

Did the Romans not create order out of chaos? Should we not cherish the cultural gifts which Greece and Rome bequeathed to Western Civilization as we cherish the nectar of the fruit and the honey of the bee?

The problem is that fruits have pits and bees have stings, and there is a downside to Greek and Roman culture[19] that has a negative impact on Western society.[20] According to the Torah, *Yavan* (Greece), the son of *Yaphet*, was to be the developer of culture, art, and beauty. The descendants of *Yaphet* were to decorate the tent of Shem, whose "tent" was the framework of the moral and legal laws that provide the structure of society.[21] A legal system based on the Torah is a system based on justice for all, not a system which favors the wealthy such as an oligarchy or a system that discriminates against those with property such as communism. We have built a society that aspires to sit at the summit of Mount Seir instead of the foot of Mount Moriah, a civilization that strives to be the head of foxes rather than the tail of lions. In order to understand the problems inherent of having a non-Torah based legal system and government, we must critically analyze our current political and economic structure. The difficulty is that Americans have been conditioned to love democracy with a visceral patriotic fervor, touching off an emotional response when someone says something negative about the Constitution, capitalism, or democracy.[22] There is hardly a tremor in these same

---

[19] "That the Sages consider Rome to be Edom is unquestionable. References to the present exile as Galus Edom are too numerous to need mention. *Rambam (Sefer Geulah* ch. 3., p. 284, ed. Chavel) believes that because the Edomites were the first to accept the Nazarene's creed and they brought the cult to Rome, where it later became the state religion." Rabbi Hersh Goldwurm, *Daniel.* (Brooklyn: Mesorah Publications, Ltd., 1998), 105.

[20] "The dichotomies of Western civilization are not merely philosophical conundrums; they are denials of the God of Abraham." Eidelberg, *Beyond the Secular Mind*, 153.

[21] "'God will open minds to the influence of Japhet, but He will dwell in the tents of Shem.' (Gen. 9:27)...the cultural education of the nations of Japhet was essentially directed to give them an emotional appreciation of grace and beauty, and to accustom people to judge their own appearance according to the beauty and harmony around them, as well as to apply the same measure to their moral actions and way of life... but there was still a higher standard...human affairs must be so ordered as to make it possible for God to dwell in our midst." Hirsch, *Collected Writings*, Vol. IV, 122–23.

[22] "The discovery of a pathological aspect of democracy may appear blasphemous, at least to those who exalt democracy's contribution to the alleviation of human misery. But the true friend of democracy does not transform it into a religion immune to questioning...unfortunately, the Churchillian adage that democracy is not the best form of government but all others are worse, has become a refuge for intellectual

people when the Torah is disparaged. Likewise, we have been taught that the importance of the Bible is relative; the Bible is only important to those who believe in its "myths," and should garner no more respect than other "ancient works of fiction."

From the Noahide perspective, the Torah gives us a broad overview of world history, and the world-historical importance of the Family of Abraham: Ishmael, Jacob, and Esau,[23] each respectively representing Arab/Muslims, the Jews, and Western Christendom. Since the descendants of Abraham play such a prominent role in current events, it would seem that understanding their development from the primary source of the Torah would be of no little importance, and that the keepers and teachers of this great body of work—a work whose beginnings go back to the time of the Trojan War and the reign of Tutankhamun—should be listened to and respected. It is a work that has profoundly affected world culture, history, art, music, literature, religion, and politics. Yet it is still a work shrouded in mystery, because of a rivalry that stretches back nearly four thousand years.

The result of this rivalry is the irrational hatred of the Jews, a hatred which is exemplified by the intellectuals of the "Enlightenment." They patted themselves on the back for their wonderful idea of government by law, or social contract (*bris*).[24] They spoke of how "all men are created equal, that they are endowed by their Creator with certain unalienable Rights" etc. while denying these rights to Jews. Even the release of the Jews from the ghettos and letting them become "citizens" had an ulterior motive—to eliminate Judaism, and therefore, the Jews.

Our heritage from Greece and Rome is not only in the arts, music, philosophy, science, government, and law; it is in the mores and values of Edom, the selfish "what's yours is yours and what's mine is mine" mindset, the lust for wealth and power, the idea that he who steps on others to reach the top has excellent balance. Christianity has played an important part in the transmission of these ideas, not only in the language and law it helped preserve, but in the theology itself, of

---

complacency." Paul Eidelberg, *Demophrenia: Israel and the Malaise of Democracy.* (Columbia: Prescott Press, Inc., 1994), 12.

[23] In his commentary to *Bereishis* 14:1, *Ramban* explains that the last of the four kings, "Tidal, king of Goiim—this is this Evil Kingdom [Rome]…which conscripts soldiers from all the nations of the world" [or, "alternatively, 'which collects tribute from all the nations.'"] *Ramban, Bereishis*, Vol. I, 319.

[24] The Torah is, in fact, a social contract between man and his Creator.

its doctrine of "individual salvation" being the most important goal.[25]

For the past two millennia,[26] organized religions—particularly Christianity and, to a lesser extent, Islam—have been the major carriers and transmitters of Edomite mores and values, the *anopheles gambiae* or *ixodes scapularis* of Greek and Roman ideas, laws, and culture, infecting entire societies throughout with the virus of Edom.[27] Christianity was infected from the very beginning, when Rome became the political center of the Church. After Christianity spread its theology and Justinian's Code throughout Western Europe, a thousand years of *Pax Romana* dissolved into a thousand years of darkness. During this time, the Arabic scholars kept the Greek philosophy alive during the Middle Ages, incubating the Edomite virus, and the re-infection of these Edomite ideas occurred during the Renaissance and throughout the Enlightenment when the Edomite memes became full-blown. Hitchens's statement that "religion poisons everything" is not too far from the truth; however, it might more accurately be said that "Edomite religious theology poisons everything," even our "secular" academic disciplines.[28]

As glorious and glittering as the accomplishments of the Enlightenment were, in the end Western intellectual culture only traded one Greek/Roman way of thinking (theology) for another (scientism),

---

[25] The "save yourself" theology of the church has conditioned Americans to the Edomite philosophy that is reflected in our society's belief that they can do whatever was "good in their own eyes," justifying this attitude with words such as "freedom" and "liberty."

[26] "For two thousand years the Jewish people were governed by law—the Halakha—without the coercive agency of any state. This phenomenon is not only unique, but virtually incredible. It confounds and confutes all the political philosophers and political scientists. For ever since Polemarchus and his companions compelled Socrates to join them on the way to the home of Cephalus (in The Republic), it has been the unanimous contention of serious students of mankind that coercion, in contradistinction to persuasion, is an essential and inevitable ingredient of political life. This may be construed to mean that authentic Judaism is incompatible with politics." Eidelberg, *Beyond the Secular Mind*, 165.

[27] Dawkins wrote about "ideas that catch on and propagate themselves...by jumping from brain to brain, likened them to parasites infecting a host, treated them as physically realised [*sic*] living structures." Blackmore, *The Meme Machine*, 6.

[28] "During the last century, we became intimately familiar with the right wing variety [of anti-Semitism]; with its racialist and religious roots: the variety that found its most extreme expression in the Nazi era. Today, with that form of anti-Semitism utterly discredited, it is another tradition—anti-Semitism of the Left—that is gaining respectability and momentum. The roots of this strain can be traced back to the Enlightenment." Schoenfeld, *The Return of Anti-Semitism*, 4.

and what little Torah was taught was filtered and sterilized through Edomite theology and philosophy. For a brief time in the seventeenth century, there was a glimmer of open-mindedness with the work of intellectuals such as Grotius and Selden, but the door to the Torah was slammed shut by the later intellectuals of the Enlightenment, led by Voltaire and the French *philosophes*. Later in the nineteenth century, the German[29] school took the lead, assaulting the Torah with a faux-positivism that would not only filter into Western academia, but it would give structure to the brutal Edomite political philosophy which manifested itself in Germany during the 1930s and 1940s.[30]

The United States of America, the flagship of Edom, cannot endure within the current paradigm of its current economic, political, and social structure. Our nation has gone through a subtle sea change in our governmental philosophy during the past few decades, an increasing attitude from *what's mine is mine and yours is yours* to the more psychopathic *what's mine is mine and what's yours is mine*. We can see it with the bailing out of our banks and corporations while we cut social programs to the poor. The bills Congress pass are often filled with hidden agendas, tax cuts, and goodies for the wealthy (there is a reason we use the non-kosher term *pork* to describe this). Our society is running out of gas and will soon coast to a stop, and since there are no more Indias or Kenyas left to subjugate, to keep the good ship America afloat will require the increased domination and forced labor of the lower classes. As the increasing poverty crushes the poor, there will no doubt be social unrest. The government of the United States, along with the Constitution, will in all probability be overthrown by force, or, more than likely, a military coup under the pretext of "social order." Eventually America will collapse under the pressures of its failed economic and social policies.[31] The cliché that democracy is

---

[29] "It is Germany, the mother of that modernized Jew, that gave birth, with him, to modern anti-Semitism...when modernization removed the old, superstitious form of expression, the professor replaced the priest, science religion." Samuel, *You Gentiles*, 137.

[30] "The era of Western history that began with the French Revolution ended in Auschwitz." Hertzberg, *The French Enlightenment and the Jews*, 5.

[31] "Academic lawyers fight over constitutional principles just as academic philosophers fight over political principles. Libertarians and socialists, democrats and elitists disagree about the meaning of the Constitution, the proper method of interpreting the Constitution, and the function of the judiciary in the constitutional system. What unites their theories is their mutual assumption that similar, if not identical, conclusions follow from both constitutional and political theory." Mark A. Graber, "Our (Im)Perfect Constitution." *The Review of Politics*. Vol. 51, No. 1 (Winter, 1989), 87.

the best form of government we have tried runs afoul of the logic that
it really does not matter what form of government one has as long as
the legal system is based on Torah.[32] This is the true battleground for
our society—the cultural foundations of Edom that have perpetuated
the hedonism of Greece and the oppressive legalism of Rome. This is
where the short-sightedness of our intellectual community manifests itself, such as Sam Harris's statement that "we need a world government.
How else will a war between the United States and China ever become
as unlikely as a war between Texas and Vermont? We are a very long
way from even thinking about the possibility of a world government, to
say nothing of creating one. It would require a degree of economic, cultural, and moral integration that we may never achieve."[33] What Harris
forgets is that there *was* a sanguinary war between Texas and Vermont
only a hundred and fifty years ago (and another war between Texas and
Mexico just twenty–five years before that), and given the current political climate between the "red states" and the "blue states," we must at
least entertain the possibility there could be another war between the
two (not to mention between the United States and China) as long as our
culture remains in the grip of Esau.

Harris's statement also belies another example of the short-sightedness of our intellectual's inability to see out of the box of Greco/
Roman culture. Our legal system was here before the Constitution was
written, and it will doubtless be here when the Constitution is tossed
aside unless we do something about it. In Plato's time, it was the ruler
or too often the tyrant who dictated the law, and this state of affairs
lasted until modern times. With a body of law that was impermanent
and changeable, it was important to have a specific form of government. With the Torah as the basis of law, democracy could certainly
work as long as an "educated public," in the words of Kant, understood Torah principles; for example, that even the leaders of government were under Torah Law, and had to follow Torah guidelines.

For over three thousand years, the Jews, the Nation of Israel, the
descendants of Abraham, Isaac, and Jacob, have developed and refined a Law that was given to them by the Creator of the Universe for
the purpose of teaching it to the rest of mankind. They were told, three

---

[32] "So far as the Torah is concerned, it is perfectly acceptable for a people to live under
a kingship, a republic, or a mixed regime, and to have a capitalist, a socialist, or a
mixed economy." Eidelberg, *Beyond the Secular Mind*, 150.

[33] Harris, *The End of Faith*, 151.

millennia ago, that their nation would miraculously be preserved in order to accomplish this mission regardless of whether they deserved it or not. They were told, millennia ago, that the nations of the world would finally accept this Law when all other forms of human government have been tried and failed miserably. The time has come—long past due, actually—for this Law to at least have some serious attention paid to it. The intellectuals of the West are out of excuses for excluding Torah from their academic curriculum.

The excuse heard most often against using the Torah as a basis for law is the fear of establishing a theocracy. The negative view of theocracy has to do with the past and current abuses from the organized religions of Christianity and Islam. The intellectual must understand that the Torah observant Noahide-based state is a *theonomy*, not a *theocracy*. The Torah supports a law-based state that puts limits on political power. The model the Torah gives us, first of all, is a separation of powers, particularly an independent judiciary. In Jewish law, the Sanhedrin is the most powerful branch of the government. A "separate and independent judiciary interpreting and enforcing an independent legal system cannot be overemphasized, and it plays an important role in controlling government power."[34] This concept, of a powerful and independent judiciary, is a relatively new idea in Western democracies,[35] an institution to protect the rights of the minorities.[36]

Of course, for most of American history, the power of the independent judiciary was applied to protect the rights of one specific minority: the Ruling Class. Any time the Supreme Court deviated from this mission—such as during the tenure of Franklin Roosevelt or the Warren Court—there was intense political pressure to elect a conservative head of state to appoint justices who would restore the status quo.

---

[34] Rabbi Dr. Warren Goldstein, *Defending the Human Spirit: Jewish Law's Vision for a Moral Society*. (Jerusalem: Feldheim Publishers, 2006), 60.

[35] Judicial review of the Constitution was an afterthought. It did not really begin until *Marbury v. Madison* in 1803, and it was mainly the result of the forceful personality of Chief Justice John Marshall.

[36] "A clear picture emerges from Madison, Hamilton, Jefferson and de Tocqueville. Democracy, for all its positive features, contains within it the potential for harm, specifically harm inflicted by the majority on the rights of minorities. An independent judiciary with the power to interpret and apply the constitution and specifically the human rights provisions is one of the most important mechanisms for controlling the excesses of majority rule." Goldstein, *Defending the Human Spirit*, 79.

The ultimate breakdown in our "democratic" system of an independent judiciary occurred in 2000, when the Supreme Court voted along strictly "conservative" lines (i.e., supporting the minority "rights" of the Ruling Class) to install a president who lost the "democratic" vote, yet a president who would appoint justices who would be counted upon to interpret the Constitution according to pro-corporate agenda.

One of the greatest problems with Western regimes of the past (especially theocracies) is that the sovereign—be it king, emperor, or czar—has too often wielded supreme authority in matters of law.[37] The Torah puts severe limitations on the leader of a state, such as the abuse of "executive privilege" for a president, king, or whatever sort of leader a Noahide government chooses. In a theonomy, a leader is under the Torah and can be prosecuted as any other citizen. The head of state is chosen by the judiciary, not the other way around as it is in Western nations. Abarbanel's suggestion—that kings (and any other heads of state) should be given term limits to prevent abuses of power—was thought of centuries before the idea became in vogue with Western intellectuals.

≈

Constitutional law, limits on political power by individuals such as kings or presidents, laws against the oppression of women,[38] and personal liberty—these are some of the concepts which characterize the Torah. For all our technological advances, for all our art and science, our music and architecture, our impressive (if wasteful) use of fossil fuel, our culture, our society is no more morally advanced than it was two thousand years ago. We are a culture pickled in Roman vinegar, and for all the posturing of our modern intellectuals,[39] we are faced with the unpleasant reality that our "enlightened" moral and ethical system is no more advanced than the morality and ethics of the

---

[37] "In Judaism, righteous laws are about, among other things, protecting vulnerable people from oppression at the hands of the powerful. In a pre-law state of nature, it is the fittest and strongest who survive. From a Jewish law perspective, the purpose of a legal system is not to entrench the natural order, but to redeem it by seeking to eliminate the injustices that result from the law of the jungle." Ibid., 8.

[38] Until the late twentieth century, it was legal in both England and America for a husband to rape his wife, something which has always been prohibited under Torah Law. According to Torah law, women have always been allowed to own and inherit property as well as being allowed to run a business, ideas which are recent Western innovations.

[39] "But what modern moralist would wish to follow him [Abraham]?" Dawkins, *The God Delusion*, 274.

ancient Greeks and Romans. We have put them on a pedestal, thinking that their ideas, mores, and values were the highest achieved by man.

This is, of course, the intellectual's argument, that Greek and Roman thought and culture was the highest form achieved by man. The Torah, however, is not a product of man. This is the difference. The simple observation that these two legal systems, Roman Law and the Torah, have different values and objectives should be enough to convince us that there is a higher goal than protecting the property of the upper class, or, in the other extreme, taking by force the property of the upper class, or having an "upper class" to begin with. Is it the law that stratifies the classes, or is it the class system that creates the law which enables it to lord it over the "rabble"?

Of course, there are many who rail against the Torah, those whose paranoia derives from losing their idol-worshiping organized religion, their love of hedonism, or their "freedom" of doing what is good in their own eyes. They claim that the Jews are plotting to take over the world, a claim that has been made for generations against the nation that has been the most defenseless and powerless of all nations. Do these people stop and consider that the Jews are also under this same Law, that in fact they have many more of the laws of the Torah they have to observe and fulfill? It is not the kingship of the Jews that the Torah represents, but the Kingship of God.[40] The structure of society, what we perceive as the "secular" legal system, is to be based on the Torah. The decorations of culture are to be provided by *Bnai Yaphet*, the art and music of Greece, but the tent—the legal, political, and economic structure—is to be provided by *Bnai Shem*.

The complaint among many is about this view of the legalistic nature of the Noahide Law. As mentioned above, "it has been contended that Judaism based on the Halacha rests on an arid legalism with its sole concern for religious rites and observations, devoid of spiritual significance."[41] This is, of course, not true; the Noahide Laws are

---

[40] "When that time comes Israel will not merge with nations of the world, but rather the nations will merge with Israel...the Jewish people will return to their land not in order to set up a state on the principle adopted and copied from other countries and cultures. They will return as the people of God, ready to put into practice the Torah and fulfill the Word of God as a nation of priests. Mankind will then derive its culture and values from the Divine Torah and the Word of God which flows out from the land of Israel...this future will not be the ultimate victory of 'belief,' but the victory of Law." Hirsch, *Collected Writings*, Vol. IV, 227–28.

[41] Lew, *The Humanity of Jewish Law*, 1.

themselves "spiritual," for in keeping these laws mankind is fine-tuning itself spiritually to the Will of the Creator. It is our warped view of what is "spiritual" and "secular" that has caused the problem. We ourselves are to blame for choosing the ways of Esau over the ways of Jacob, and we cling tenaciously to a system of law and observance that has failed miserably for the vast majority, and contrary to the postulations of the secular atheists, humanity did not "grow up" during the Enlightenment. What society did do was to take anti-Semitism to a higher level, to repackage it in a new intellectual box and wrap it with "reason" to make it more fashionable as well as embracing the destructive Edomite memes which have wreaked havoc with Western culture:

> Only a fraction of Shem's teaching was successfully conveyed to mankind. Even this portion was garbled, confused and weakened to suit the Japhetic whim, leaving the enlightenment of mankind as an unfinished goal. Only the theory was revealed to mankind while the "Law" was omitted; the one factor was withheld on which the redemption and the harmonious organization of all mankind is based... theory, even in its purest, unmutilated form, only enlightens the mind; it is unable to redeem the "tents" of earthly existence and to achieve the perfection and purity of life itself.[42]

Understanding the concept of Torah as social and legal theory (as opposed to the theory of Noahide Law being a "religion" for individuals and personal salvation) is only the first step; we must put the Torah into practice. This means developing a society based on Torah Law, particularly the laws dealing with government, courts, and economics.[43] We just take a hard look at our political and economic system from a Noahide perspective instead of simply comparing it to other Esavian systems past or present.

---

[42] Hirsch, *Collected Writings*, Vol. II, 205.

[43] "Woe unto him who builds a house without justice or righteousness; who pilfers the strength of this fellow man and fails to pay his wages; who focuses on profit, participates in the shedding of innocent blood, and flippantly resorts to violence." Ibid., 286.

CHAPTER FIVE

Esavian Politics

In the long run, we are going to need a science of social change. We have applied scientific knowledge to virtually all of the practical areas of life except government and economics—two areas still dominated by myths and ideology.

— Charles A. Reich[1]

U NTIL NOW, WE HAVE PRIMARILY FOCUSED ON THE THEORETICAL ASPECTS of Edomite intellectualism. We now turn to the practical application of Edomite philosophy, and how the secular and religious Edomite memes have come together in the interrelated areas of politics and economics. It is here that the dearth of Torah logic and morality is most keenly felt as our academic institutions churn out our civic, economic, and political leaders who transfer the anti-Semitic memes from Enlightenment-influenced philosophers, historians, theologians, and sociologists and develop them into political and economic constructs. This transference of classical ideals, mores, and values from Greek and Roman thought from the intellectuals of Western culture to the cream of our political and economic leadership has been the primary task of our educational system, and many of our most influential civic leaders have had

---

[1] Charles A. Reich, *Opposing the System*. (New York: Crown Publishers, Inc., 1995), 7.

their ideals and values formed in elite boarding schools such as Groton,[2] Milton,[3] St. Mark's,[4] and St. Paul's[5] as well as the top universities such as Harvard, Yale, and Princeton.[6] As our political leaders went through the Edomite educational system, they learned the lessons and concepts which had been formulated by the philosophers, historians, and sociologists of the Enlightenment.[7] Thus the problems we face in political science and economics are not that we lack a "science of social change" but that, in fact, we have applied "science," rather than Torah, to both areas. The term "science" is used in the traditional sense, the same Greek-inspired use of human reason and logic which we have seen used in the fields of philosophy, history, religion, and sociology. This "science" can be seen in models such as Social Darwinism, eugenics, and *laissez-faire* economics which support the Edomite memes[8] of power and self-gratification.

∽

W HEN POLITICAL PHILOSOPHER Francis Fukuyama's New York Times best-selling *The End of History* was first published in 1992, it generated both a good deal of both praise and controversy. The premise of Fukuyama's argument (which was first published as an article of

---

[2] A few noted alumni of Groton include Franklin D. Roosevelt, Sumner Welles, Richard Whitney, George Herbert Walker III, Joseph M. McCormick, and C. Douglass Dillion.

[3] Alumni include Robert and Ted Kennedy, Elliot Richardson, and James A. Perkins.

[4] Alumni include Ben Bradlee, Robert Christopher, Tim Forbes, Harold Stirling, and William Kissam (II) Vanderbilt.

[5] Alumni include John Jacob Astor IV, Archibald Cox, William Randolph Hearst, John Kerry, J. P. Morgan, Jr., Lewis Thompson Preston, and Charles Scribner III.

[6] Thirteen out of forty-four presidents—a solid thirty percent—went to these three universities.

[7] "Educational and cultural ideals, Max Weber once observed, are always 'stamped by the decisive stratum's…ideal of cultivation.' In the United States in the late nineteenth century, the 'decisive stratum' was the WASP upper class and its ideal, that of the cultivated 'gentleman' along British lines." Karabel, *The Chosen*, 25.

[8] "The longer man lies complacently in satisfying circumstances, the more his origins recede into the past, the more he readily forgets his very beginnings and their conditions. But whether conscious to man or not, he carries with him the commitment to the past which he owes the present and his future. None, be it an individual or a people, can bury the memory and with it the legacy of the original calling without endangering and finally losing the very identity, the very meaning of human existence that are the marks of man as an individual or as a group." Hirsch, *Collected Writings*, Vol. I, 374–75.

the same title in 1989) was that, with the fall of communism, liberal democracy had triumphed, and was (in Fukuyama's humble opinion) the "final form of government," the very best type of government that humanity has and can achieve, thus "the end of history." Basing his theory on the works of German philosophers such as Kant and Hegel, Fukuyama postulated that our accrued knowledge in science and technology "confers decisive military advantages on those countries that possess it" and that "modern natural science establishes a uniform horizon of economic production possibilities" while "technology makes possible the limitless accumulation of wealth, and thus the satisfaction of an ever-expanding set of human desires."[9]

Fukuyama's *The End of History* pays homage to liberal democracy. According to Fukuyama, democracy has won the battle of the "survival of the fittest" in defeating other forms of government such as fascism and communism; democracy is (again according to Fukuyama) mankind's glorious political *magnum opus*, the final form of government that is destined to become the *de facto* form of government for all nations, although not all at once. Fukuyama, who follows the same pattern which we have seen with our academicians and intellectuals, bases his theories on strictly Western philosophies and ideas, particularly the German political philosophies of Kant and Hegel. This is not the only problem in Fukuyama's book; while he champions liberal democracy, he dismisses "Periclean Athens" from being a "true democracy" because "it did not systematically protect individual rights,"[10] ignoring the minor detail that the United States itself is not a true democracy.[11] As with Toynbee before him, Fukuyama has many critics, and yet even his staunchest critics cannot seem to bring themselves to criticize the object of Fukuyama's adoration, our precious liberal democracy.

Among many secularists, the word *democracy* has the same sort of meaning the phrase "kingdom of heaven" has for Christians; *democracy*[12] represents an ethereal, other-worldly, utopian sort of status

---

[9] Francis Fukuyama, *The End of History and the Last Man*. (New York: Free Press, 2006), xiv.

[10] Ibid., 48.

[11] Our government, "despite what it says in the high-school civics texts…is not a democracy…it is an eighteenth-century republic that has come to resemble a democracy in certain respects, but which at its core remains stubbornly pre-democratic." Lazare, *The Velvet Coup: The Constitution, the Supreme Court, and the Decline of American Democracy*, 9.

[12] "The decency and civility still visible in contemporary democracy have nothing to do with democracy itself. They derive from the morality of the Bible and of the urbanity of Greek philosophy, especially the former. Neither democratic equality

that brings the citizen salvation as long as they *believe*. We worship the Athenians in our temples of higher education, those wonderful Greeks who invented democracy, and we have been taught that this form of government is the best mankind has to offer. After all, the Greeks produced some of the greatest minds in human history, great thinkers such as Plato and Aristotle, and the Greeks were the inventors of Western art, music, science and culture, and so why not think that their system of government would not be worthy of emulation as well?

This teaching was what Plato called "the Noble Lie,"[13] and it was only when you actually study their works that you found that neither Plato[14] nor Aristotle[15] were particularly keen on democracy as a form of government.[16] To Plato and Aristotle, mob rule, particularly when a large portion of the mob was on the wrong side of the Bell Curve, was not conducive to able and just government.[17] Plato thought it best

---

nor democratic freedom provide any moral standards as to how man should live." Eidelberg, *Demophrenia*, 28.

[13] Plato's "Noble Lie" is what we would call "propaganda" today. For example, the United States is not really a true democracy but rather a Federal Representative Republic, and yet we are constantly bombarded with messages of praise for our wonderful "democracy."

[14] "Plato left no room for a combination of wisdom and law, for compromise, for accommodation, for an order of society, institutions, and thought based on both law and morals." Konvitz, *Torah & Constitution: Essays in American Jewish Thought*, 80.

[15] "[Aristotle] presupposed, as a more or less permanent condition of man, an economy based on scarcity. Slaves would therefore be necessary to perform household chores and other menial tasks to enable gentlemen of leisure, the rulers of the best regime, to cultivate intellectual and moral excellence. Therein is the reason why persons engaged in manual occupations (the large majority) are excluded from citizenship in Aristotle's best regime—kingship or aristocracy—which alone can cultivate men of high quality as a matter of public policy." Eidelberg, *Beyond the Secular Mind*, 134.

[16] "Aristotle...disliked the power that he thought the expansion of democracy necessarily gave the poor...Plato, an outright opponent who condemned democracy as rule by the unfit and advocated instead a perennially appealing system of government by the best qualified." Robert Alan Dahl, *Democracy and Its Critics*. (New Haven: Yale University Press, 1989), 14.

[17] "Hellenistic culture is a protector of rights and freedom. These concepts, however, are applied only to those who are educated; they are subject to an arrogance which claims that the rights of human beings begin only after they have attained a certain level of culture. Therefore, sensitivity and concern regarding one's own self, and those close to oneself, are paired with an enormous callousness, with an utmost cruelty, which assumes that the inferior 'uneducated masses' lack genuine feelings of honor or a sensitivity for of freedom or human rights. Attica, so vainglorious

that political power should be in the hands of the intelligent, not the ordinary, and certainly not the feeble-minded. Plato explained that "unless...the philosophers rule as kings or those now called kings and chiefs genuinely and adequately philosophize, and political power and philosophy coincide in the same place...there is no rest from ills for the cities...nor I think for human kind."[18] The point which Plato made was that the majority of common men—the non-philosophers who were neither trained in philosophic thought nor smart enough to grasp philosophical principles—were simply too unintelligent to make democracy work. Plato felt democracy was inherently self-destructive because it gave the unintelligent and uneducated the freedom to vote and be a part of the political process, electing unintelligent leaders, or worse, a tyrant. To Plato, the idea that the ignorant and the unlearned were running the government and making the laws was not only an unpleasant idea, but a threat to society.[19]

It has been said that tyrannies rule by might and democracies rule by propaganda—the manipulation of the public will. One reason democracy is so popular among the Ruling Class[20] is because it is conducive to supporting a class stratification based on wealth and political power (enabled by the relative ease in convincing the gullible masses that we *all* "agreed" to our "democratic" system of law and government; cf. p. 476, n. 2). To indoctrinate the simple-minded in the cherished values of democracy has been one of the main tasks of both our public education system as well as the mass media. Early media pioneers such as William Randolph Hearst found that "Noble Lies" spread through

---

about its rights and liberties, saw no contradiction to the fact that three-quarters of its inhabitants lived in servitude and slavery. Thus, history teaches us that the 'educated' were able to tolerate public tyranny and accept the rules of force, provided it was applied only to the lower 'uneducated' masses and left the rights of the 'cultured' untouched." Hirsch, *Collected Writings*, Vol. II, 203.

[18] Plato, *The Republic,* Allan Bloom, trans. (New York: Basic Books, 1991), 153.

[19] "Plato attacks democracy precisely for its freedom and variety (557b–558c). He even goes so far as to suggest that, in an ideal state, those whose power of reason is weak should, for their own good, be enslaved to those in whom it is strong (590c–d)." R. F. Stalley, "Plato's Doctrine of Freedom." *Proceedings of the Aristotelian Society, New Series*, Vol. 98 (1998), 145.

[20] What Charles A. Reich called "the System," what C. Wright Mills called "the Power Elite," and what Karl Marx described as the "Ruling Class," are all different terms for the same concept—the small cadre of individuals whose political and economic power enabled them to create and operate the legal system and government to further their own interests, a distinctly Esavian philosophy.

print—and later radio and television—could have a profound effect on those who were not trained to reason and think logically. Since the institutions of our media have been owned and controlled by wealthy and powerful individuals and corporations such as Hearst, Rupert Murdoch, and Disney,[21] it was not hard to guess which class their economic sympathies were allied, and the media has become a conduit of Noble Lies designed to influence the majority of citizens into a unified mass of drooling, patriotic, flag-waving, pro-democratic capitalists. To understand, from the Torah point of view, that democracy could be as structurally unsound as communism, has been a difficult concept to grasp for those indoctrinated in our democratic Edomite culture.[22]

The first point we need to address is that democracy itself was founded upon a slave system which was part of a severe class structure.[23] The foundation of the fifth-century Athenian economy was "a surplus-generating slave population [which was] indeed important... the rich silver mines of south Attica were especially lucrative."[24] Karl Marx gleefully observed that "Greek society was founded upon slavery, and had, therefore, for its natural basis, the inequality of men and of their labour powers."[25] This is the legacy of our "democratic" tradition, the influence of the Athenian model, where slaves:

> In Attica...were kept at work only in order to increase the revenues of a democracy...it is all the more remarkable, therefore, that in the

---

[21] Most of today's major book publishers are owned by just a handful of corporations. For instance, the German corporation Bertelsmann AG owns Random House, the world's largest publisher of trade books (Bertelsmann also owns Europe's largest broadcasting network as well as the largest magazine publishing company). Bertelsmann also owns Ballantine, Del Ray, Fawcett Books, Dell, Bantam, Knopf Publishing, Doubleday, Anchor, and Golden Books. CBS owns Simon & Schuster, Scribner, Fireside, Touchstone and Free Press, who published Fukuyama's *The End of History* as well as Max Weber's *Ancient Judaism*. Rupert Murdoch's News Corporations owns HarperCollins (formally Harper & Row), Quill Trade Paperbacks, Avon, and Zondervan among many others.

[22] "The word 'democracy' literally means the 'rule of the people,' or popular sovereignty. Clearly this notion clashes with the Torah which proclaims the sovereignty of God." Eidelberg, *Beyond the Secular Mind*, 66.

[23] Communism goes one step further in presupposing a severe class structure as the basis of its teaching; only in an Edomite society can communism claim to have any sort of validity.

[24] Josiah Ober, *Mass and Elite in Democratic Athens: Rhetoric, Ideology, and the Power of the People*. (Princeton: Princeton University Press, 1989), 30.

[25] Karl Marx, *Capital*. (London: Penguin Books, 1990), 25.

works of Greek thinkers we meet with no recognition of the unjust basis upon which the political structure of Athens was reared...for they were unable to conceive that a State could have any other industrial basis than slavery. Their view was that a State should be composed on the one hand of free citizens, whose main business was to be self-cultured, and on the other of a great inarticulate enslaved mass, who should be the means of creating the national wealth.[26]

Although there were some later grumblings about this system, "the protest of the later philosophers came far too late for the generations of slaves whose labour lay at the foundation of Athenian greatness,"[27] and this observation has, by and large, been ignored or overlooked.

The main reason that the Greek philosophers did not like democracy was not because of slavery, but that democracy was susceptible to tyranny. Plato listed four types of government: timocracy, oligarchy, democracy, and tyranny, and explained the merits and problems with each. When it came to democracy, Plato recognized a weakness in democracy, that it could easily succumb to tyranny. This fear was shared by many of the Framers, as well as observers such as de Tocqueville.

TAKING ITS CUES from the Greeks, Rome developed the model of social and economic class stratification[28] that we are familiar with today—the rich, the middle class, the poor—which (to varying degrees, at least in respect to the upper and lower classes) has been the structural societal model of Western Civilization throughout its history (although the existence of the middle class has been a tentative one at best; usually it has been a large lower class of slaves, serfs, or indentured workers toiling under the rule of a small propertied upper class). Certainly in America, this class system has continued where, as with the Romans, "Americans accept enormous disparities of wealth, and allow the gap to widen."[29] As with Ancient Rome, it was the small and powerful elite, the Ruling Class, that ran the government and created

---

[26] W. Romaine Paterson, *The Nemesis of Nations*. (New York: E. P. Dutton & Co., 1907), 196.

[27] Ibid., 198.

[28] "The hollowness of the Roman achievement was revealed in the wretchedness of its homes, the barbarousness of its leaders, the oppression of its lower classes." Hirsch, *Collected Writings*, Vol. I, 261.

[29] Murphy, *Are We Rome?*, 15.

and enforced the laws of the state.[30] Class conflict—rich versus poor, bourgeoisie versus proletariat—has been a major theme of conflict theorists for the past one hundred and fifty years. Although it has often been analyzed, the reasons for our passive acceptance of this class structure have, for the most part, been ignored, and we assume this is simply the "natural order of things." For those who have been brought up in a society with such a class structure, having a classless society[31] seems hard to imagine.[32] [What needs to be emphasized here is that the Torah does not support this sort of class structure based upon wealth and power. The Levites, the Priestly Class, owned no property. All of the Children of Israel—from the King of Israel to the humblest Jew—were forbidden to amass wealth for its own sake.[33] The Jewish attitude towards money is different from the Edomite ideal in that "the Sages frowned upon all class distinction and ostentation."[34] The Torah ideal behind power and wealth is different, as is what is expected of Israel's leaders.[35]]

---

[30] "The small top group, consisting of the aristocracy of the municipia and of the towns in the provinces, dominated the political, cultural and economic life of these places...these were the groups that would provide the senators under the principate." David Johnston, *Roman Law in Context*. (Cambridge: Cambridge University Press, 1999), 34.

[31] "What was the spirit that prevailed in the [Jewish] ghettoes? The inhabitants enjoyed a complete equality among themselves; the poor man walked side by side with the rich as his equal, knowing no aristocracy and no serfdom; they enjoyed a communal autonomy whereby all authority came from a free congregation ruled by Law, governing everyone equally. They had associations of free benevolent societies, where the work of human love was done by volunteers, thus permitting no proletariat in the Jewish streets. They upheld the 'Din Torah'—their own system of Jewish jurisprudence—that knew nothing of endless lawsuits which devour litigants together with their assets. Their law was accessible to everyone equally, and even the most complicated lawsuits were decided quickly, justly, and practically free of cost. That was the spirit that prevailed in the ghettoes when all around there was only brute force, barbarism and depravity; and freedom and light were the privilege of only a select few." Hirsch, *Collected Writings*, Vol. I, 181–82.

[32] "Strictly speaking...a Torah community is devoid of classes in the socioeconomic or political sense of the term." Eidelberg, *Beyond the Secular Mind*, 81.

[33] Cf. *Devarim* 8:11–14. The Torah does not condemn wealth. The Torah ideal is much different than the Edomite ideal; acquiring wealth to help those less fortunate is praised, but to obtain wealth for power, personal glory, and to lead a life of avarice is prohibited.

[34] Lew, *The Humanity of Jewish Law*, 186.

[35] Obviously, this does not apply to the modern political leaders of today's secular state of Israel who are enamored with Western Edomite values. As Rabbi Hirsch

The Roman class structure was enforced and maintained by its complex[36] legal system.[37] This system was developed in the early days of the Roman Republic, where "it was stipulated by the leges Liciniae Sextiae in 367 [BCE] that one of the two consuls had to be a plebeian, the dividing line between patricians and plebeians hardly existed any more: from then on the main distinction was simply between rich citizens and poor citizens…three orders can be distinguished: the senatorial aristocracy, the equites[38] and the middle and lower classes."[39] In the Roman model, wealth was the key to obtaining (and keeping) political power.[40] In perfecting their political and economic model, Rome was greatly influenced by the legal and economic structures from Greece,[41]

---

pointed out: "You, too, [O Israel,] will feel the need for national unity in order to obtain the greatest good for yourself, but [as distinct from the other nations] you deem this good to lie solely in the most complete possible realization of the Law of God in your own midst. For this purpose, you, too, will feel that you need a king [but the function of your king will be different from that of the kings of the other nations]. The function of your king will be to stand out as the first among all Jews loyal to the Law—to shine forth personally in all the moral nobility of this allegiance to the Law. Himself imbued with the spirit of your mission, he will deem it his task to win the hearts and minds of all his subjects for this spirit, in thought, word and deed, and to utilize the power of his word, his personal example and his personal prestige to combat anything that would violate this spirit…a Jewish king who glories in building up a mighty military force is guilty of a two-fold sin. He commits a direct transgression, because his true calling lies elsewhere…his first act on ascending the throne shall be to write out for himself, with his own hand, a copy of the Torah. By this act he acknowledges that the Law was given to him before all others; that he is not above the Law, but rather that the Law must be the immutable guideline for all his life." Hirsch, *T'rumath Tzvi*, commentary to *Devarim* 17:16–18, 733.

[36] "Rome's complex system was made even more complex by the class struggle embedded in its society." Johnson, *Nemesis*, 62.

[37] "Class distinctions and social status determined an individual's fate and privileges in ancient Mesopotamia. The same was broadly true of the laws of Rome, both in regard to the rights of aliens and to those of citizens." Sivan, *The Bible and Civilization*, 115.

[38] The *equites* were Roman horseman, or "knights," the second tier in the Roman pecking order, the direct ancestor in rank and social class to the British "knighthood" (Sir So-and-So, Dame Such-and-Such).

[39] Johnston, *Roman Law in Context*, 33.

[40] "Government is necessarily a tool of the ruling class because its chief function is to maintain order…the order to be preserved is the order in which the ruling class enjoys a strategic advantage over other classes." Edward Bryan Portis, *Reconstructing the Classics: Political Theory From Plato to Marx*. (Chatham: Chatham House, 1998), 176.

[41] "It is generally accepted that Roman legal science began in the second century BC, under the influence of the Greek philosophers." Johnston, *Roman Law in Context*, 60.

particularly Athens which had a small, male, elite ruling class whose main economic support was the large class of slaves laboring in the silver mines at Laurium producing a majority of the wealth that was the foundation of their economic and political power. The importance of the economic support from the slave class[42] was obvious, for when the mines in Attica closed, the era of Athenian dominance[43] ended. It was this slave society which the Greeks developed that was the economic foundation for Athenian "democracy," the forced labor of a slave class allowing the "citizens" the leisure time to develop the arts and sciences that Western Culture finds so alluring. Although (for obvious embarrassing reasons) this has been largely ignored by most Western writers and historians, it was a point noticed by both Karl Marx[44] and Friedrich Engels[45] and more recently by Sir Moses I. Finley who noted that "the cities in which individual freedom reached its highest expression—most obviously Athens—were cities in which chattel slavery flourished."[46] This connection between economic freedom and indivicual freedom has too often been overlooked (cf. p. 62, n. 30 above).

Although there has been slavery throughout human history, the Greeks created the first slave society, and the Romans expanded it to a

---

[42] Although there was slavery in the Torah, this was on an individual basis; there was no slave class as with the Greeks or Romans. The Torah has strict controls on the treatment of slaves, as well as their manumission every seven years. Although the law on non-Jewish slaves is different (Leviticus 25:44-46), and the non-Jewish slave does not have to be freed during the Jubilee year (where it states in Leviticus 25:46 לעלם בהם תעבדו, that you can keep them permanently as bondsmen), it is considered a *mitzvah* (good deed) "for reasons of general morality" to give them their freedom, and according to the Talmud, you had "no right to mishandle them, to hurt their feelings, or put them to shame" (*Nidda* 47a). Hirsch, commentary to Lev. 25:46, 774–75.

[43] "By the third century BCE the silver mines in the hills of Attica were spent, and so was the energy of the Hellenistic world." Robert Raymond, *Out of the Fiery Furnace: The Impact of Metals on the History of Mankind.* (University Park, PA: Penn State Press, 1986), 83.

[44] "Greek society was founded upon slavery, and had, therefore, for its natural basis, the inequality of men and of their labour powers." Marx, *Capital*, Vol. 1, 152.

[45] "Without slavery, no Greek state, no Greek art and science; without slavery, no Roman empire...no modern Europe." Quote from Friedrich Engels's essay, Herr Eugen Duhring's *Revolution in Science* (Anti-Duhring), cited in M. M. Bober, *Karl Marx's Interpretation of History* (New York: Norton, 1965), 50.

[46] Moses I. Finley, *Was Greek Civilization Based on Slave Labor?* Moses I. Finley, ed., Slavery in Classical Antiquity: Views and Controversies (Cambridge: W. Heffer, 1960), 3.

continental scale.[47] During the Principate, "the number of people who could not earn their own living rose considerably, they moved to the large towns and became part of the urban proletariat. Because the lower classes constituted a potential threat to political stability, food was distributed regularly and games and impressive spectacles were organized. This 'bread and games' treatment was meted out to the urban proletariat in Rome as well as in the other large towns of the empire."[48] The "bread and circuses" approach helped quash revolutionary fervor by placating the lower classes with food and entertainment, and it worked so well at suppressing unrest that it became a model in modern cultures with the welfare state and preoccupation with entertainment such as television, motion pictures, theatre, and "sporting events."[49]

As social structures during the last few centuries of the Roman Empire became more rigid, the "emperors increased the influence of the state, for instance by obliging the citizens to perform all kinds of tasks for the benefit of the state, by making these tasks hereditary and by creating a huge bureaucracy to try and keep things under control."[50] Dr. Hugh J. Schonfield observed that in ancient Rome:

> There was a vast gulf between the extremes, the patricians and the plebs. The Roman commons, where poverty and misery was acute, especially under urban conditions, had to be kept under control.

---

[47] "So it was through the Romans that the Greeks would set the style of the new world. Even if it was still based on what was only an Iron Age economy, dependent on slavery for the production of goods, it was enough to support the corresponding, new intellectual and political elites, with their polished cultural and intellectual structures. Athens, in particular, lucky enough to find its own rich vein of silver at the mines of Laurium, was able to grow to become a city of an unprecedented 35,000 people, making it then by far the world's largest city. Even after building the all-important warships, Athens still had money to spare, which the city wisely spent on making itself the most beautiful in the world. And Athens spawned more than just magnificent buildings. It produced a sophisticated and politically active citizenry who delighted in poetry, music, theatre, and, of course, philosophy. It is these intangible investments by the ancient Greeks that left a legacy of thought, first amongst them the writings of Plato, which has yet to be exhausted." Martin Cohen, *Political Philosophy: From Plato to Mao*. (London: Pluto Press, 2001), 6–7.

[48] Johnston, *Roman Law in Context*, 70.

[49] "The most interesting thing about fighting as a sport is the form in which various peoples institutionalize it and what they reveal about themselves in so doing." Michael B. Poliakoff, *Combat Sports in the Ancient World*. (New Haven: Yale University Press, 1987), 2.

[50] Johnston, *Roman Law in Context*, 112.

> When the support of the plebs was needed in the name of democracy
> this was found to be obtainable by timely gifts of food and money and
> lavish free entertainments.[51]

This was a pattern that would manifest itself in American society, particularly in the last century with the Federal income tax, where much of the middle and lower class works a percentage of the year to pay for Government projects such as military operations and subsidies for corporations as well as providing the public funding for the arenas for their own "bread and circuses" to keep themselves entertained, and "steam could be let off by witnessing cruel sports, shows and dangerous games, the more bloody and bizarre the better."[52] It also provides the template for the modern welfare state, to keep the poor sated with enough "bread" to keep them from revolting. As the Romans had learned long ago, this system works reasonably well, as long as there is enough public funding to keep providing the "bread and circuses."

The System is not only stratified by wealth and power, but by culture and education. Those on the wrong side of the Bell Curve (besides being on the wrong side of the economic curve) should not be allowed to make decisions regarding law and government. It is "the Smart Man's Burden" to shield the unintelligent masses from themselves, and rulership in any society must be by the intelligent. There is another function of the "bewildered herd," however; it is the worker caste, the ones who produce the wealth of the state. As the Western Roman Empire disintegrated in the early fifth century, the legacy of Rome's agricultural slavery was modified to become serfdom, where the lower classes were forced to work the land owned by the small but powerful group of landowners, the "specialized class" of the Middle Ages.[53]

---

[51] Dr. Hugh J. Schonfield, *Those Incredible Christians*. (New York: Bantam Books, 1969), 6.

[52] Ibid., 7.

[53] "The Romans had Christianized the office of emperor; the early Middle Ages moved his center of authority from Rome to Northern Europe. Even though the empire in its medieval form never achieved the unity that theory described, the rediscovery of Roman law in the eleventh century reinforced its claims of universal power in the twelfth century. In addition, the revival of Roman law did much more than create a jurisprudential doctrine of lordship in Europe. It excited the inconclusive thoughts surrounding the nuclei of monarchy and sent off highly charged ideas in all directions. These ideas, embedded in the dense margins of medieval law books, impacted on

Our glorified image of ancient Greek and Roman civilizations too often fails to take into account that they were composed of a small wealthy ruling class and a disproportionably large slave and servant class. This disparity is not brought out in our "history" books; the glorified image of Greece and Rome is glamorized in our culture, our motion pictures, and in our theater. The brutality of the legal system that kept the lower classes in check is ignored,[54] and we are left with the image of the "noble Roman." We are taught that this is the "natural" order of things, the Social Darwinistic strata of human society (the Edomite "law of the jungle") where the rich and powerful subjugate the poor and the weak.

ᘐ

O F ALL THE cultural foundations we have inherited from Rome, none is more salient to the obstruction of social justice than the Roman legal system,[55] the true arm behind the "invisible hand" on the market forces, the false weights on the scale of Lady Liberty, the yoke on the necks of the poor, the orphan, and the widow.[56] The study of

---

medieval governing institutions at every level: the empire, the Church, the national monarchies, principalities, city-states, and local corporations of clerics and laymen." Pennington, *The Prince and the Law*, 3.

[54] "The Roman nobility reacted fiercely when their interests were infringed upon, especially their untrammeled 'right' to accumulate as much wealth as possible at the public's expense...the nobles were less devoted to traditional procedures and laws than to the class privileges those procedures and laws were designed to protect." Parenti, *The Assassination of Julius Caesar*, 82.

[55] "Even as Rome fell, her spirit triumphed over those that had defeated her, and before long, the spirit of Rome had placed a double yoke of domination over the necks of the nations. For centuries the Roman law which went forth from the City of the Seven Hills imposed upon the peoples of Europe that absolute order which dictated their relations with one another and their relationship with their God. To this day, the talons of the Roman eagle, grasping this double bolt of lightning, terrestrial and celestial, maintain a firm hold on the political and religious life of civilized nations. Would not the Roman spirit of Esau be right to consider itself the Divinely-appointed master of this earth...justified in regarding itself as the heir to the blessing and the covenant which God had once bestowed upon the nation of Jacob, a nation which He Himself had subsequently driven from its homeland and which He Himself, through His 'law' and His 'church,' had debarred for centuries from human rights and Divine grace?" Hirsch, *Collected Writings,* Vol. II, 435.

[56] "When people see their leaders acting in accordance with the highest standards of rectitude, not using public office for personal advancement but rather caring for the poor, the orphan, and the widow, friendship will indeed be the bond of the community. And when everyone is taught the unalterable laws of the Torah, laws that define and delimit the duties and privileges of the leaders themselves, leaders who can be called to account by any humble Jew, the envy, discontent, and cynicism that rack all

how Roman law began and how it was inherited by the Church and spread throughout the lands of Western Europe would require another substantial work in itself, but a brief background of Roman law's influence on English common law (as well as European Civil Law) is necessary to understand this link in the evolution of American law.[57]

Rome's legal and governmental system was developed over a period of nearly a thousand years from the first code (the "Twelve Tables" in 450 BCE) to the final code written under Emperor Justinian in the beginning of the sixth century CE. This legal code, as well as Rome's governmental structure, has been the template for both the government and legal systems of Western Civilization. Coupled with Christianity and the plastic arts of Greece, this synthesis of law, religion, and culture provided the foundation for Western Civilization. Roman law, however, was different than Torah Law in many aspects. For instance, according to Roman law, in Roman society an adult male was not truly "free" until his father died:

> In the long history of Roman law, the father of a family retained many of his ancient despotic rights over his wife and his adult children even in the final codification made, by the orders of the Emperor Justinian, in the sixth century of the Christian Era, at a date when Roman law had been exposed for seven hundred years to the humane influence of Hellenic philosophy, and for two hundred years to the gentle influence of Christianity. During the greater part of the course of Roman history, an adult male Roman citizen had been virtually his father's slave till his father's dying day.[58]

The wealthier the father, the more power he wielded. In Rome, the more wealth, the more legal power one had. A debtor in Rome was legally no better off than a son; in Rome during the time of the Twelve Tables, a debtor could be not only sold into slavery, but be killed and hacked up into pieces at the whims of the plaintiffs.[59]

As the Roman Empire crumbled, Western Europe became bereft of Roman jurisprudence. Echoing the words of Gibbon, Barbara W. Tuchman wrote:

Esavian regimes can gain no foothold in the hearts and minds of men." Eidelberg, *Beyond the Secular Mind*, 160.

[57] "By the beginning of the 18th century, however, this 'Law of God' had given way to the Common Law of England." Sivan, *The Bible and Civilization*, 136.

[58] Toynbee, *Hellenism: The History of a Civilization*, 52.

[59] Peter Stein, *Roman Law in European History*. (Cambridge: Cambridge University Press, 2005), 6.

In those dark ages between the fall of Rome and the medieval revival, government had no recognized theory or structure or instrumentality beyond arbitrary force. Since disorder is the least tolerable of social conditions, government began to take shape in the Middle Ages and afterward as a recognized function with recognized principles, methods, agencies, parliaments, bureaucracies. It acquired authority, mandates, improved means and capacity, but not a noticeable increase in wisdom or immunity from folly.[60]

After the fall of Rome in the early fifth century, Western European nations, part of the old Roman Empire, found that it was simpler to adopt the Roman Law as their legal system: "the Visgothic Roman law [was] the main source for western vulgar law in the last century of the western empire. It also became the main source for Roman law in the kingdoms which replaced the empire from the sixth century to the eleventh."[61] It was through the influence of Christianity, however, that the Roman law was spread throughout Western Europe. "The main custodian of the Roman legal tradition was the Church" that carried "knowledge of Roman legal notions even to remote parts of Europe, where Roman institutions had disappeared after the end of imperial rule."[62] By the beginning of the twelfth century, there was renewed interest in Roman law from the rediscovery of Justinian's Digest.[63] As the first Western universities developed in France and England, the study of Roman law became part of the curriculum along with the study of theology:

Romano-canonical procedure, ultimately derived from the late-Roman professional procedure, was developed in the Church courts and in arbitrations conducted by churchmen. By the thirteenth century it was ready to be used in secular courts…eventually an entirely written procedure was created, which, as it became more technical, needed professional advocates to operate it. If they were university trained, it was natural that they would cite the civil law that they had learned, where it advanced their argument. The adoption of the learned procedure was thus the first step to adopting parts of the civil law.[64]

Since the language of the Church [Latin] was also the language of Roman law, "Roman civil law became, together with canon law and theology, part of a common Christian learned culture shared by those

---

[60] Barbara W. Tuchman, *The March of Folly*. (New York: Ballantine Books, 1984), 16.

[61] Stein, *Roman Law in European History*, 32.

[62] Ibid., 40–41.

[63] "It is difficult to overrate the significance of the rediscovery of the Digest." Ibid., 44.

[64] Ibid., 59.

who occupied positions of authority, both lay and ecclesiastical."[65]
The "technical superiority"[66] of Roman law supplied the structure of
the legal systems of Western Europe, and this would have a world-
wide affect when European legal models were adapted during the
European[67] colonization period. Like a "diving duck,"[68] Roman law
would resurface now and again as states and empires rose and fell.
This would have important consequences in the formation of American government and law as Western Europe colonized the New World,
bringing their Roman-based legal system along with them. With the
Roman-based legal system firmly entrenched in our society, our new
nation developed a constitutional government which operated under
the banner of "democracy," and the advantages of a democratic system were emphasized while the disadvantages were ignored.[69]

---

[65] Ibid., 66.

[66] Ibid., 61.

[67] R. Daniel Kelemen and Eric C. Sibbitt, "The Globalization of American Law."
International Organization. Vol. 58, No. 1 (Winter, 2004), 105, n. 9.

[68] "Then the enduring life of Roman law, which, like a diving duck, hides itself from
time to time." Johann Wolfgang Von Goethe, *Conversations of Goethe*. (Whitefish,
MT: Kessinger Publishing, 2005), 389.

[69] "Now, when opinion rules, as it does in any democracy, it is only necessary to
examine, not its truth, but the number of those who express this opinion. It is not even
necessary to examine whether any individual who expresses this opinion is serious or
frivolous, whether his opinion is the result of reflection or impulse, whether it is an
abiding conviction or a passing fancy. As a consequence, wherever the quantification
of opinions rules rather than truth or the verification of opinions, people are less apt to
take opinions seriously. Hence, they will be less likely to develop the habit of critical
thinking or of making logical and moral distinctions. Feelings or the emotions thus
will end to supplant bivalent logic. The symmetrical logic at work at the base of the
emotions then will overwhelm the asymmetrical logic of scientific thought. People
will become more susceptible to propaganda whose target is the emotions." Eidelberg
Demophrenia, 149.

Dysfunctional Democracy

The twentieth century is also the century of triumphant democracy. As the century draws to a close, however, enlightened friends of democracy see signs of decay. Allan Bloom's compelling critique, *The Closing of the American Mind*, may readily be extended to the democratic mind: America is nothing if it is not democratic. Bloom, a distinguished professor of political philosophy, paints a dismal picture. Democracy, which enlarged freedom of expression, is witnessing an appalling decline of intellectual standards. Democracy, which elevated the principle of equality, is undergoing a leveling of all moral distinctions. Democracy, which championed human dignity, is now yielding to abject vulgarity. All this Bloom largely attributes to the university-bred doctrine of moral or value relativism. It is this doctrine that has closed the American mind: closed it to the possibility that human reason can discover objective or universally valid standards of how man should live. It is this doctrine that renders all "life-styles" morally equal, for it denies any rational grounds for preferring the way of life of a Socrates to that of a Marquis de Sade. As a consequence, higher education undermines the quest for the Good, the True, and the Beautiful on one hand, and fosters nihilism on the other.

— Paul Eidelberg[1]

A S INFLUENTIAL AS INTELLECTUALS SUCH AS PLATO, MACHIAVELLI, John Locke, and Adam Smith were in providing the ideas which influenced Western nations and states, no two men have done more to shape modern world politics than Thomas Jefferson, an aristocratic slave-owner and political leader who was born into privilege, and Karl Marx, the Jewish-born political exile who battled poverty much of his adult life and whose financial support came from a close friend whose father was a wealthy textile manufacturer. The political and economic systems of these two men polarized much of the world during the twentieth century;[2] Jefferson we associate with America and capitalism, and ideals such as "freedom" and "liberty," and Marx we associate with coercive communist regimes such as the Soviet Union and

---

[1] Eidelberg, *Beyond the Secular Mind*, ix.

[2] The economics of these two systems—democracy and communism—are deeply intertwined with their respective political systems.

Castro's Cuba, of gulags and repression. As far apart as these men seem in their ideologies and as disparate the political systems they represent, we look at them from the Noahide's "outside the box" perspective and see how their ideas are viewed compared to the Torah.

It does not matter if the political framework of a state is democratic or communistic, it does not matter if its beginnings were based on the lofty visions and ideals of a Jefferson or Marx—the Edomite meme manages to become the dominant value in determining economic and political policy as well as law. Here we have social movements, influenced by men such as Jefferson and Marx; although there were many others who contributed ideas, it was Jefferson and Marx who became the two poster-boys for democracy and communism. These two intellectuals had synthesized their ideas from the works of previous thinkers (Locke and Hegel, for example), but it was their works that set the stage for the political and economic drama of the twentieth century.

There was doubtless no one in American history who better exemplified Plato's idea of the "philosopher-king" than Thomas Jefferson. Born during the height of the Enlightenment, Jefferson came from a relatively well-to-do family. He was classically educated, meaning that "the literature of Greece and Rome was the core around which all other studies were grouped."[3] Jefferson's classical education contained "the preponderance of classical authors in his reading during the formative period of his life…Homer, Herodotus, Euripides, Anacreon, Virgil, Cicero, Horace, and Terence."[4] Besides the influence of philosophers such as Locke and Voltaire, "Jefferson's ethical views were a fusion of classical and Christian ideals, a synthesis of the best that he could extract from Epictetus, Epicurus, and Jesus."[5]

Although well read in the classics, the Torah played no part in Jefferson's philosophy, and doubtless the teachings of philosophers such as Voltaire colored Jefferson's view of Judaism. Although revered by Jews for promoting religious tolerance and alleviating the religious repression they had encountered in Europe, this feeling was not reciprocated by Jefferson, who said that "the Jews…although believing in one God only, had degrading and injurious ideas about Him, and followed

---

[3] Wright, *Thomas Jefferson and the Classics*, 225.

[4] Ibid., 227.

[5] Ibid., 228.

an imperfect ethical code 'often irreconcilable with the sound dictates of reason and morality,' and 'repulsive and anti-social, as respecting other nations,'"[6] a decisively Esavian philosophy.

ᑫᑰ

İf Max Weber was, in the words of historian Peter Novick, the "single most important intellectual influence from the social sciences," then Karl Marx would certainly be a close second. Marx's detailed analysis of capitalist systems of production has been the subject of hundreds (if not thousands) of books and articles. Although routinely demonized by capitalists, much of Marx's idealism was motivated by the plight of the working poor. In *Das Capital*, he spoke of the children forced to work long hours in the factories, such as "William Wood, 9 years old, was 7 years and 10 months when he began to work...he came to work every day in the week at 6 A.M., and left off about 9 P.M....fifteen hours of labour for a child 7 years old!"[7] A few pages later, Marx mentions "Josiah Wedgwood, the inventor of modern [industrialized] pottery, himself originally a common workman, said in 1785 before the House of Commons that the whole trade employed from 15,000 to 20,000 people,"[8] including many children as young as eight. (This is the same Josiah Wedgwood who was the grandfather of Charles Darwin, and it was the wealth that Darwin inherited from his grandfather that allowed him to live a life of leisure looking at bugs and birds while trying to discredit the Torah.)

As with Jefferson, Marx kept Jewish scholarship off the intellectual menu, gorging his mind instead with Greek and Roman philosophy.[9] In his work *Capital*, Marx cited Aristotle, Francis Bacon, Charles Comte, René Descartes, Georg Hegel, Thomas Hobbes, John Locke, Martin Luther, John Stuart Mill, Plato, Jean Rousseau, Adam Smith, and Thucydides among many others. No Jewish sources were cited,[10] and the few comments about the Jews were depreciatory, such

---

[6] George Harmon Knoles, "The Religious Ideas of Thomas Jefferson." *The Mississippi Valley Historical Review*, Vol. 30, No. 2 (Sep., 1943), 191.

[7] Marx, *Capital*, 354.

[8] Ibid., 378.

[9] "Plato...treats division of labour as the foundation of which the division of society into classes is based." Ibid., 487–88.

[10] "[Marx] never made the slightest effort to acquaint himself with Jewish history or culture. He was a polymath, who covered the whole range of philosophy, history, and

as "pharisaical capitalist"[11] and "the Shylock-law of the Ten Tables,"[12] where Marx mixed his metaphors with the distinctly different Roman law and Judaism.[13]

In matters of personal morality, Marx also relied on the Greek and Roman philosophical models. Marx's father, descended from a long line of rabbis, was a successful lawyer who had abandoned Judaism in the heady early years of the Enlightenment, and little Karl was baptized as a Lutheran. The precocious Marx was "a brilliant, spoiled child, who bullied his younger sisters and taunted his schoolmates with sarcastic witticisms."[14] His university years were uneventful; Marx enjoyed a bohemian lifestyle drinking and carousing, and his self-indulgence led him to be "sued several times for non-payment of debts"[15] which exasperated his father. Marx's egomania led him, as it did Rousseau, to believe that the world owed him a living, and would continue to blame his economic problems "on other people...Marx repeatedly denounced creditors who insisted on collecting what he owed them."[16] Marx's most productive period came when he was in exile in England, and as he wrote incessantly on the evils of capitalism, he and his family were being supported by his friend and communist compatriot Friedrich Engels, who himself held a lucrative managerial job working for his wealthy textile-industrialist father. Ironically, Marx's great work *Capital* was written with the financial support of the textile-industrial capital he so vigorously denounced in his work.

Most Westerners tend to think of Marx as the enemy of such nebulous concepts as "liberty" and "freedom" along with the violations of Torah concepts such as private property[17] and the importance of the

---

science; the one total gap in his knowledge was Judaism." Maccoby, *Antisemitism and Modernity: Innovation and Continuity*, 64.

[11] Marx, *Capital*, 519.

[12] Ibid., 400.

[13] For a glimpse of Marx's level of understanding of Judaism, one need look no further than to his 1844 essay *On the Jewish Question*.

[14] Thomas Sowell, *Marxism: Philosophy and Economics*. (New York: William Morrow and Company, Inc., 1985), 165.

[15] Ibid., 166.

[16] Ibid., 175.

[17] The violation of Torah principles in Marx's work has no greater example than in the concept of the abolition of private property espoused by Marx: "In this sense the theory of the Communists may be summed up in the single sentence: abolition

family, particularly teaching one's own children. Marx often seemed concerned for the plight of children in industry; in another part of *Capital*, Marx talks about the conditions in the mining industry, and how "the Inquire Commission of 1840 had made revelations so terrible, so shocking, and creating such a scandal all over Europe, that to salve its conscience Parliament passed the Mining Act of 1842" prohibiting "the employment underground in mines of children under ten years of age and females."[18] From a later (1866) report, Marx excerpts a few complaints from the miners about employment of children and women (above ground), inspections of the dangerous working conditions, and the use of false weights and measures used to cheat the miners out of their proper quota. Yet Marx's own attitude towards children should be viewed in light of how he treated his own illegitimate son Freddy Demuth, the product of Marx sleeping with his long-suffering maid Helene Demuth:[19] "Marx...did not love the boy; he did not dare to do anything for him, the scandal would have been too great,"[20] an excellent example of Marx's adherence to the Greek and Roman value system.

Because both Jefferson and Marx were trained and educated in classical literature and philosophy, their works shared common Edomite interests. The writings of these two men were widely read by other intellectuals, and their ideas taught in colleges and universities, influencing intellectual thought throughout the world, even in non-Western cultures such as Japan, China, and Korea. The men who went to the top universities not only became leaders in government, but in business and finance. In the complex world of ideas implanted in the carefully controlled petri dish of academic society, the concepts of the

---

of private property." Karl Marx and Friedrich Engels, *The Communist Manifesto*. (New York: Pocket Books, 1964), 82. Unlike the Edomite philosophy, where the accumulation of private property is the avenue to power and control, under Torah law owning property gives the person the opportunity to practice the *mitzvah* of charity, to help those less fortunate.

[18] Marx, *Capital*, 626.

[19] "Only a few friends knew of the child's birth, he was sent away to be raised by a working class family, and there was no father's name on the birth certificate. Marx's wife was told that Engels—a bachelor—was the father, but long after the death of Marx and his wife, it came out that in fact the father was Karl Marx...Freddy...was sacrificed first to Marx's convenience, then to Marx's image." Sowell, *Marxism*, 176.

[20] David McLellan, *Karl Marx: His Life and Thought*. (New York: Harper & Row, Publishers, 1973), 272.

Torah have been kept out of intellectual discourse, and this has had a substantial effect on modern academia, particularly with the Marxist doctrine of conflict theory, which states that social problems have to do with the economic clashes between the upper and lower classes, a distinctively Esavian characteristic. As with the division between "religious and secular," as well as the Greek and Roman flavored Christianity and Greek-based science and philosophy, Jeffersonian Democracy and Marxism were two branches of the same Edomite tree that grew out of the tailings of the silver mines of Laurium.

∝

Despite the good intentions of the Framers of the Constitution in creating the best possible government,[21] their reliance on Greek and Roman models maintained the inherited Roman-based class structure (along with its system of chattel slavery) and a supporting legal system based on English common law, a system where *stare decisis* (rendering judgment based on previous cases) was the rule. This is why, even though the United States fought a revolution in order to change its government to a constitutional system, the legal structure was, by and large, unaffected by the Framers when they drafted the Constitution.[22]

Producing a fairer and just legal system was not the primary aim of the Framers.[23] In his influential book *An Economic Interpretation of the Constitution of the United States* (first published in 1913), Charles A. Beard explained that the Framers were guided by economic

---

[21] In a "letter to Edward Carrington, August 4, 1787," Jefferson wrote about the Articles of Confederation, saying "with all the imperfections of our present government, it is without comparison the best existing or that ever did exist." Max Farrand, *The Federal Constitution and the Defects of The Confederation*. The American Political Science Review, Vol. 2, No. 4 (Nov., 1908), 533.

[22] "Because of Thomas Jefferson's historical studies in English law, and his acquaintance at first or second hand with Roman legal principles, it is not surprising that in the field of law he was aware of certain influences of Roman on the English law only recently enunciated." Henry C. Montgomery, "Thomas Jefferson and Roman Law." *The Classical Weekly*. Vol. 37, No. 15 (Mar. 6, 1944), 162.

[23] "Conservative delegates among the Framers—later the core of the Federalist Party—had feared that if ordinary people were given ready access to power they would bring about policies contrary to the views and interests of the more privileged classes." Dahl, *How Democratic is the American Constitution?* (New Haven: Yale University Press, 2003), 24.

self-interest.[24] Of the members of the Convention, "a majority of the members were lawyers by profession…[and] were immediately, directly, and personally interested in the outcome of their labors at Philadelphia, and were to a greater or less extent economic beneficiaries from the adoption of the Constitution."[25] It was the protection of property that concerned the framers, and although they wanted basic "human rights" to be supported for the lower classes (to minimize the chances of revolution), these classes were not represented at the Constitutional Convention in 1787.[26] The Constitution was designed not to facilitate change for the betterment of society, but to prevent change, and to uphold the Roman model of class distinction, keeping the power in the Ruling Class.[27]

That the Constitution was designed to protect the economic interests of the upper class[28] should be of no surprise; after all, the Revolution was fought on the colonist's unhappiness with Britain's economic

---

[24] "That all states are primarily animated by material interests is the unanimous conclusion of political theorists from Plato to the present…having given themselves their own laws—laws dependent of the shifting opinions, passions, and interests of men—it is only natural for Esavian nations to engage in frequent conflict with each other, and to succumb, so easily, to hatred of the one nation that did not give itself its own laws." Eidelberg, *Beyond the Secular Mind*, 110.

[25] Beard, *An Economic Interpretation of the Constitution of the United States*, 149.

[26] "In an examination of the structure of American society in 1787, we first encounter four groups whose economic status had a definite legal expression: the slaves, the indented servants, the mass of men who could not qualify for voting under the property tests imposed by the state constitutions and laws, and women, disfranchised and subjected to the discriminations of the common law. These groups were, therefore, not represented in the Convention which drafted the Constitution, except under the theory that representation has no relation to voting." Ibid., 24.

[27] "The Founders…created a system in which the three branches of government were suspended in almost perfect equipoise so that a move by one element in any one direction would be almost immediately offset by a countermove by one or both of the others in the opposite direction…a counterdemocratic system dedicated to the virtues of staying put in the face of rising popular pressure." Daniel Lazare, *The Frozen Republic: How the Constitution is Paralyzing Democracy.* (New York: Harcourt Brace & Company, 1998), 3.

[28] "The 'Beardian' view of the American political system presented a quite compelling critique to many intellectuals. The argument gleaned from Beard's writings was that the Constitution systematically aimed to protect the property and power of the capitalist elite. Moreover, the constitutional checking function of judicial review claimed for the courts by Federalist Justice John Marshall in Marbury v. Madison was designed to frustrate the democratic will of legislative majorities." Pope McCorkle, "The Historian as Intellectual: Charles Beard and the Constitution Reconsidered." *The American Journal of Legal History.* Vol. 28, No. 4 (Oct., 1984), 315.

principles[29] such as the protest against the Stamp Act of 1765, the Town-shend Acts of 1767, or the events that led to the Boston Tea Party (such as the government subsidies that were given to the East India Company, allowing them to undercut the prices from the tea-smugglers and law-breakers such as John Hancock). Beard noted that:

> Most of the law (except the elemental law of community defense) is concerned with the mere defense against violence (a very considerable portion of which originates in forcible attempts to change the ownership of property) because of relatively less importance, and property relations increase in complexity and subtlety…inasmuch as the primary object of a government, beyond the mere repression of physical violence, is the making of the rules which determine the property relations of members of society, the dominant classes whose rights are thus to be determined must perforce obtain from the government such rules as are consonant with the larger interests necessary to the continuance of their economic processes, or they must themselves control the organs of government.[30]

Without going into the morass of arguments for or against Beard's thesis,[31] we should look at the founding of our government, and the reasons behind it. The first place to start should be the Declaration of Independence, which "only became an object of reverent exege-sis in the early nineteenth century, when a civil religion of national patriotism sanctified it as 'American Scripture,' a status it has held consistently and continuously only since the Civil War."[32] There is,

---

[29] "The crowning counterweight to 'an interested and over-bearing majority,' as Madison phrased it, was secured in the…use of the sanctity and mystery of the law as a foil to democratic attacks." Beard, *An Economic Interpretation of the Constitution of the United States*, 161.

[30] Ibid., 12–13.

[31] "The Beardian view of the formation of the Constitution has been dismissed for the wrong reasons and with little, if any, empirical backing. A careful reading of Charles Beard's *An Economic Interpretation* suggests the Beardian view is that political institutions are not formed purely on the basis of political or ideological principles, but the self-interest of individuals involved in the formation of new institutions will influence the character of those institutions." Robert A. McGuire and Robert L. Ohsfeldt, "Economic Interests and the American Constitution: A Quantitative Rehabilitation of Charles A. Beard." *The Journal of Economic History*. Vol. 44, No. 2 (Jun., 1984), 516.

[32] David Armitage, "The Declaration of Independence and International Law." *The William and Mary Quarterly*. Third Series, Vol. 59, No. 1 (Jan., 2002), 40.

however, no better rebuttal against the critics of Beard's thesis than the tax revolt known as Shays Rebellion, the fledgling nation's first crisis.

～∾

THE CREATION OF the Declaration of Independence and the Constitution was the result of a series of political and economic events starting with Britain's Seven Years War[33] with France, part of which was fought on North American soil. To pay off the enormous war debt, Britain decided to tax the colonies. This was only logical since the debt accrued was, in a large part, from protecting the colonies from the French. This raised the ire of the wealthy colonial merchants (who felt that the colonies did not owe the Mother Country anything, since the colonists had done their fair share of the fighting), and an armed rebellion soon broke out as well as the destruction of private property, i.e., the tea belonging to the British East India Company. These actions resulted in sanctions against Boston merchants.[34] As the rebellion broke out, the famous "minutemen," the armed farmers of Massachusetts, fired the "shot heard 'round the world" at the British regulars, followed by many more shots, and the rebellion against "unfair taxation" was on. The War of Independence,[35] which meant the war against unfair taxation without representation, along with the stories of Valley Forge, Bunker Hill, Washington crossing the Delaware, has since taken on a mythological aura.

Not long after the war for American Independence ended, the nascent Colonial government of Massachusetts found itself over fourteen million dollars in debt, and to pay off its war debts decided to tax its citizens. Keep in mind that the state government

---

[33] Known on the American continent as the "French and Indian War."

[34] "The 342 chests of tea—over 90,000 pounds—thrown overboard that night were… valued by the East India Company at 9,659 pounds sterling or, in today's currency, just over a million U.S. dollars…in response to the Boston Tea Party, the British Parliament immediately passed the Boston Port Act stating that the port of Boston would be closed until the citizens of Boston reimbursed the East India Company for the tea they had destroyed…[the War of Independence was largely] triggered by a transnational corporation and its government patrons trying to deny American colonists a fair and competitive local marketplace." Thom Hartman, *Unequal Protection*. (New York: Rodale, 2004), 63.

[35] The Revolutionary War began as "the war between the American colonists and their opponents, the governors and soldiers of the East India Company and its British protectors." Ibid., 121.

of Massachusetts was run by the same "patriots" who, fifteen years earlier, were clamoring for independence from Britain since, among other things, unfair taxation that was eating into their profits. Yet the "state extraction took the form of direct taxes on property and polls, which placed a disproportionate burden on farmers with small holdings. Duties were imposed on land regardless of its value, and almost forty percent of tax revenue came from a head tax, with equal amounts due from rich and poor."[36] The farmers were being squeezed by the same men who incited them to rebellion with words like "liberty," "freedom," and, ironically, "no taxation without representation." Their livestock was taken from them, then their farms, and not a few faced debtor's prison. These farmers felt that they had done their share for the new nation by fighting the British, and they had plenty of experience in dealing with governments trying to impose unfair taxation upon them, and they also knew how to rectify the situation. Led by Daniel Shays, a veteran of battles such as Bunker Hill and Ticonderoga, the farmers once again took up arms and started to rebel against unfair taxation to repay the Massachusetts war debt, and their main objective was to take over the courthouses across the state in order to halt the legal proceedings against them. When well-known patriots such as Samuel Adams condemned the rebellion and called for Shays and the other rebels to be caught and hung (shades of King George III), Governor Bowdoin realized something had to be done, but since the state was out of money and the Articles of Confederation had no provisions to deal with such a contingency:

> The governor turned to wealthy men from the Boston area who contributed the necessary funds. On January 25, 1787, the rebels attacked the federal arsenal at Springfield, where they were repelled by the troops, suffering four fatalities. The largest military action of Shays' Rebellion occurred one week later at Petersham and involved 1,900 rebels and 3,000 troops; the rebels fled and 150 were arrested. From March until June, collective action became more scattered. The rebellion ended by June, broken primarily by force.[37]

The question begging to be asked is: why was Shays' Rebellion against unfair taxation any less moral than the reasons the wealthy

---

[36] Rachel R. Parker, "Shays' Rebellion: An Episode in American State-Making." *Sociological Perspectives*. Vol. 34, No. 1 (Spring, 1991), 99.

[37] Ibid., 101.

merchants fought England, unless it was simply a matter of protecting the economic interests of the wealthy and upper-class of the colonies?[38] Although not the primary cause of the American aristocracy wanting a stronger central government, Shays' Rebellion was certainly a contributing factor.[39]

What the Ruling Class of Massachusetts wanted was a Federal army to put down any sort of interstate rebellions that threatened their power and economic security. So it was that the leaders of the new nation, its merchants, lawyers, businessmen, landowners, decided to meet one more time, and in May of 1787 they headed to Philadelphia to create a new government. Not a government "by the people, for the people," but an immovable and inflexible system[40] that ensured the status quo's hold on power,[41] a system resistant to sudden changes by the "tyranny of the majority" (i.e., the poor) yet pliable in the hands of the Power Elite, the Ruling Class, who were able to change the law at their will and pass legislation which would benefit their economic interests. A semblance of "democracy" was put in place so that the unwashed masses, the "bewildered herd,"[42] could vote and elect the interchangeable cogs[43] of government (the politicians),[44] but the structural system of government and,

---

[38] The event of Shays' Rebellion supports Charles A. Beard's thesis that the primary motivation of the leaders of the American Revolution were driven by economic concerns rather than the crepuscular and oblique concepts of "freedom" and "equality."

[39] "[James] Madison identified Shays' Rebellion as a significant occurrence between the Annapolis and Philadelphia meetings, a 'ripening event.'" Parker, *Shays' Rebellion*, 107.

[40] "Government in America doesn't work because it's not supposed to work." Lazare, *Frozen Republic*, 5.

[41] The framers of the Constitution "as practical men…were able to build the new government upon the only foundations which could be stable: fundamental economic interests." Beard, *An Economic Interpretation of the Constitution of the United States*, 151.

[42] A term coined by American propagandist Walter Lippmann. "Lippmann took a jaundiced view of the public's ability to grasp complex affairs of state. Far better to leave such matters to experts, such as Lippmann himself." John V. Denson, *The Costs of War: America's Pyrrhic Victories*. (New Brunswick: Transaction Publishing, 1999), 312.

[43] According to Marx, the politicians are merely interchangeable cogs, and it mattered little who is elected, since "democratic capitalism is merely a matter of 'deciding once in three or six years which member of the ruling class was to misrepresent the people in parliament.'" Sowell, *Marxism*, 144.

[44] "Now there are two 'functions' in a democracy: The specialized class, the responsible men, carry out the executive function, which means they do the thinking and planning and understand the common interests ['how do they get into the position where they

more importantly, the existing legal system, would be unaltered. In this respect, the Framers succeeded in establishing a government that was nearly impervious to change from the lower classes.

~∾

For over two thousand years governments have come and gone. We continually strive for better and more effective governments, but our legal system has kept its Roman foundations, and has stayed basically the same even if certain laws have been tweaked here and there due to advances in economics, technology, and political philosophy. The Greek and Roman models of government and class structure work best with an uninformed and uneducated public, or else a public which can be controlled with "Noble Lies," i.e., propaganda supported by our state-run educational system and corporate-owned media. Even among the educated, it is imperative that the educational paradigm stays within certain boundaries, making sure that nothing is taught that would lead people to question the status quo, and the arguments against this system have been kept within a certain paradigm, that is, the Greek and Roman model, which is why there has not been a workable solution to the problems facing our society. Our intellectual leadership, while critical of certain aspects of the system, has not proposed any solutions from outside carefully defined parameters.

The American legal system follows the Roman principle of *what's mine is mine and what's yours is yours*.[45] This is an attitude of selfishness the Talmud describes as being wicked, the attitude of Sodom and Edom. Practically every major government today has been affected by

---

have the authority to make decisions…by serving people with real power…the ones who own the society']. Then, there is the bewildered herd, and they have a function in democracy too. Their function in a democracy, [Lippmann] said, is to be 'spectators,' not participants in action. But they have more of a function than that, because it's a democracy. Occasionally they are allowed to lend their weight to one or another member of the specialized class. In other words, they're allowed to say, 'We want you to be our leader' or 'We want you to be our leader'…that's called an election." Noam Chomsky, *Media Control: The Spectacular Achievements of Propaganda.* (New York: Seven Stories Press, 1997), 12–14.

[45] "Esavian regimes may be described as follows. Tyrannical states (religious as well as secular) are instruments of force and fraud designed to facilitate expansion and conquest. Their diplomacy conforms to the precept 'What's mine is mine and what's yours is negotiable.' In contrast, liberal and social democratic states are designed to facilitate self-indulgence and 'peace' (recall Munich), which may require one democracy to sacrifice another. Esau sacrificed his birthright for potage. Today the democracies would sacrifice Israel for petroleum." Eidelberg, *Beyond the Secular Mind,* 109.

this Greek/Roman system of law, whether it is democratic, Marxist, or Islamic. Having a court system based on this legal structure is not a system of courts of justice as the Torah dictates, to neither discriminate against the poor as in our capitalistic system, nor to discriminate against those who are successful in business, as does communism.

What is important to understand about the Constitution was that it was simply an outline for government—it did not change the underlying legal system of our society. The local courts did not cease, for people still committed crimes and went to trial, and people still did business. The laws for theft, property, and murder did not fundamentally change. It was simply an establishment of government by the Power Elite, those who made the Rules.

The colonial rebellion which flared into a civil war became revolutionary in character with the drafting of the Articles of Confederation and the Constitution. This was a decisively new form of government, a government which was based on a social contract. There is no denying that, at the time, the Constitution was a milestone in human government. There is also no denying that the Constitution neither altered the existing structure of government nor the legal system of Roman-influenced English common law, and that the Constitution has become an antiquated political relic unsuited to the needs of the people it holds under its sway.

The Constitution of the United States, the oldest working constitution in the world, has risen to near-scriptural[46] status and reverence among Americans, inerrant and above reproach. It was written during the days of the Holy Roman Empire, when Kaisers and Czars[47] ruled, when only white men could vote, and African-Americans were considered to be only three-fifths human.[48] "The problem with the Constitution lies not with any single clause or paragraph, but rather with the concepts of balance and immutability, indeed with the very idea of a holy, all-powerful Constitution."[49] The Constitution is a sparse and imperfect document, designed primarily for the organization

---

[46] Likewise the Declaration of Independence; "The Declaration was at first forgotten almost entirely, then recalled and celebrated by Jeffersonian Republicans, and later elevated into something akin to holy writ." Maier, *American Scripture*, 14.

[47] Both these terms, Kaiser and Czar, come from the Latin "Caesar."

[48] Cf. Article I, Section 2 of the Constitution.

[49] Lazare, *The Frozen Republic*, 3.

of government.[50] The great bulk of our case law was inherited from the British courts, in which Roman law played a significant part,[51] and, as we have noted, there was a great difference between Roman law and Talmudic Law.[52]

When the Constitution became our framework for government, it was immediately yoked to the existing system of English common law that was the basis of the legal system in the colonies. Instead of changing the law, the Framers developed a government that would fuse itself to the existing common law and to be bound up with it—a government that would be impervious to change by what John Adams called "the rabble."[53] The ancient Constitution of England, on the other hand, had never been written down—it consisted of oral traditions that had been handed down throughout the generations—and these oral traditions were inherited by the United States as well as their Roman-influenced system of lawyers, and both these institutions have influenced our government from the very beginning.[54] How odd that our nation,

---

[50] "In the American colonies in the eighteenth century, 'constitution' signified the design, structure, and composition of government." Herman Belz, *A Living Constitution or Fundamental Law? American Constitutionalism in Historical Perspective.* (Lanham, Md.: Rowman & Littlefield, 1998), 2.

[51] "The most important and distinctive legal source in US law is the US Constitution of 1787. It is brief and incomplete, often unclear, and antiquated (Dahl, 2002): it has only seen 27 amendments since its drafting, ten of which—the Bill of Rights—by 1791. Despite, or perhaps because of, all this, the US Constitution is still the founding document of national and legal identity to the same degree as the French Civil Code in France, a testament to the respective importance of public and constitutional law in the United States, compared to that of private law in Continental Europe. The Constitution is comparable to the Code in another sense: it provides a superior normative framework for legal development. Large areas of US law are still based on case law, developed by the courts through the system of precedent. Courts, in deciding a case, will look at previously decided cases as authority and guidance." *Elgar Encyclopedia of Comparative Law*, Jan M. Smits, ed. (Cheltenham, UK: Edward Elgar Publishing Limited, 2006), 68.

[52] Adding to the disparity between the systems of Roman/British/American law and the Torah was how the law was interpreted. The courts, the Supreme Court in particular, were given the power to interpret the law. As we shall see, the Constitutional system allowed the Ruling Class to mold the law according to its own Edomite desires. "[American] law is not usually understood as a coherent and systematic whole, but rather as a hodgepodge of court decisions and statutes; therefore systematic arguments carry little weight ... court decisions are the result of the better argument made by the winning party, not by logical deductions from a coherent system of law." Ibid., 71.

[53] "The men who signed the Constitution were schooled in English law and simply wanted to rid the colonies of arbitrary enforcement of laws they had no voice in shaping." Peter H. Irons, *A People's History of the Supreme Court.* (New York: Viking, 1999), 3.

[54] "Congress has been dominated by lawyers from its inception." Lazare, *Frozen Republic*, 16.

looked upon in modern times by the rest of Western nations as being the most fundamentally Christian, is so firmly entrenched upon a written law and its system of lawyers. It is as if the lessons of the Church about the Oral Law, Pharisees, and the Jewish lawyers that have been criticized from the beginning of Christianity had been forgotten. Yet the idea from men such as Henry Boilingbroke, whose "rejection of human sovereignty and his neomedieval concept of law as something over and above society, which society was eternally required to obey, became the cornerstone of the American theory of government"[55] was the right idea. They simply used the wrong sources for the Law, rejecting the Torah for the Greek and Roman systems.

The real reasons of the Revolution were that the American upper class wanted the power to war, to control commerce, and to set up their own markets. It was not an unjust law that the colonists rebelled against, for the early colonists "decided to adopt the legal system of their mother country and to establish a continuing union with it by submitting themselves to 'the same common sovereign.'"[56] That the colonial leaders of the Revolution had, at its source, economic reasons for dissolving the bonds of government with Great Britain can be seen in the previous declaration written two years earlier.[57]

༄

SINCE THE BEGINNING of the Enlightenment, every legal system and government of every nation has either sacrificed the rights of the individual (such as Communism) or, as Allan Bloom pointed out, eroded community values with the dogma of "equality." The Torah is the only legal system which can successfully balance the rights of the individual with the welfare of the community. The Torah is the only legal system which protects the economic rights of the poor while, at the same time, protects the property and business interests of the wealthy. The Torah is the only legal system that holds the economically and politically powerful to the same standards of conduct as the lowest pauper. Most importantly, the Torah is also the only legal system which has been routinely ignored by Western political theorists.

---

[55] Ibid., 29.

[56] Maier, *American Scripture*, 112.

[57] Cf. below; Appendix, *Declaration and Resolves of the First Continental Congress, October 1774*, p. 507.

Supreme Nonsense

Bring forth for yourselves, i.e. choose and out of your midst, name to me...men who know the given laws...who have the ability to draw the right conclusions and decisions from the facts given to them in the case before them...whose characters are known to you.

— Rabbi Samson Raphael Hirsch[1]

T
HE FRAMERS OF THE CONSTITUTION WERE REGARDED BY THE succeeding generations as the greatest collective genius America has produced, and for generations the Supreme Court has often been guided by the "intent of the Framers" in deciding legal cases.[2] The Framers, as we have seen, were schooled in Greek and Roman thought, which, for the Noahide, leads to a conflict of interest: should we decide law by the rules of Rome and the philosophy of Greece, or by the Torah? The Constitution is only a framework (and an incomplete framework at that) for federal government, and there are two major problems with the Constitution that exacerbate the problem of justice and which are beyond repair. One was that our Constitution was permanently linked to the existing common law which was inherited from Britain and descended from Roman law. The second problem was that the laws were interpreted and fitted into this framework by the work of much lesser men, men neither elected democratically nor held accountable by any democratic process.[3] We also must remember that

---

[1] Hirsch, commentary on *Devarim* 1:13, 11.

[2] "A belief that the Constitution is nearly flawless not only underlies the so-called fundamental values strand of constitutional thought but also those strands of constitutional argument based on conceptions of the democratic process or the original intentions of the framers." Mark A. Graber, *Our (Im)Perfect Constitution*. The Review of Politics, Vol. 51, No. 1 (Winter, 1989), 86.

[3] "Most often when one speaks of the United States Constitution, or when journalists editorialize about the Constitution, the reference is to a specific document, adopted in 1789, supplemented by relatively few amendments...the fact is, however, that by 1994 there were over 500 massive published volumes of the opinions and decisions of the Court. Although many of these cases did not involve constitutional questions, many thousands of them did involve constitutional issues—questions of constitutional interpretation and construction. In many cases there are multiple opinions, concurring

the main body of Common Law inherited from Britain remained in place, with only a handful of "rights" (albeit important rights, to be sure) elaborated by the first ten Amendments which put certain limits on the pre-existing law. This law is linked to the Constitution, which is considered *fundamental and permanent* law.[4] Here is where the debate between the two schools of thought—legal realism versus legal formalism (as postulated by Paul Eidelberg)—comes into focus.[5]

ॐ

COMPARING AND CONTRASTING the Constitution with the Torah (as far as "fundamental" or "permanent law" is concerned) will give pause to anyone who has canonized the Constitution. We need to recognize that for over two hundred years the Constitution has been portrayed as "American Holy Scripture" while the Torah has been attacked (often by the same group of scholars) as man-made rules that were produced

---

and dissenting, and this is especially true in case of constitutional law that have wide and deep significance for the American people...the Constitution under which Americans live encompasses a great deal more than the written document—precisely as the Torah is infinitely more than the scroll that is in the ark of the temple or synagogue. The United States Constitution includes the opinions and decisions in the hundreds of volumes of the Supreme Court reports. It includes the ideals and values towards which the Supreme Court decisions reach out and only sometimes grasp." Konvitz, *Torah & Constitution*, 7–8.

[4] "The judiciary, no less than the Senate and the executive, was instituted, in part, to limit the operation of the democratic principle embodied in the House of Representatives, but especially should that principle come to dominate the legislature as a whole. It is in this light that we are to understand the idea of limited government and with it the doctrine of judicial review. Briefly stated, limited government is that which restricts the legislative (but not only the legislative) power by fixed or permanent laws. These fixed or permanent laws are contained in what is called the 'fundamental law,' namely, the Constitution. Ordinary law, to be ultimately valid, must be consistent with the Constitution. Under a limited government, it cannot be the prerogative of those who make (or execute) the laws to be the ultimate judge of their constitutionality." Paul Eidelberg, *The Philosophy of the American Constitution*. (Lanham, MD: University Press of America, 1986), 203.

[5] "What the realists rejected, and quite rightly, is the naïve notion that judges, in deciding whether a law is consistent with the Constitution, are merely involved in a problem of legal or formal logic. Looking more closely at the judges/pronouncements, the realists saw, and continue to see, not logic but rhetoric...beneath the pronouncements of the Court they see the personality or personal preferences of individual judges; they see considerations of expediency or of public policy; they see accommodations to the dominant morality or sentiments of the times; and all this judiciously couched in language conveying the meaning of the Constitution and for the intentions of the Founders." Ibid., 220–221.

at specific times for narrow events and customs as taught by the secular academic disciplines of history, sociology, philosophy, political
science, economics, and whatever other disciplines wished to jump on
the Constitutional bandwagon.

One of the great differences in the Torah system was that the Sanhedrin Court was made up of men of upright ethical character, men who
not only knew the Law but also the condiments to wisdom such as mathematics and chemistry, men who were chosen because of their superior
moral and intellectual ability, not from how wealthy they were or how
high and noble their lineage. In contrast to the qualifications for the Sanhedrin, the members of the early Supreme Court only had to be staunch
and wealthy Federalists. The early court was unremarkable in its role as
the supreme arbitrator of Constitutional law; in Peter Iron's *A People's
History of the Supreme Court*, Irons gives a background to some of the
men who were appointed (not elected) to the bench of what was to become the world's most powerful court.

The first court was an unremarkable collection of political appointees, loyal Federalists, and sots such as John Rutledge. John Jay, tapped
by Washington himself, was the first Chief Justice. Jay set the tone for
the justices who followed, as "his favorite maxim was that 'those who
own the country ought to govern it,'" as well as advocating "stringent
property qualifications on voting."[6] Oliver Ellsworth, "an extremely
wealthy, arrogant, and aristocratic man,"[7] was the second Chief Justice
"whose four year tenure as Chief Justice was marked only by his success in persuading the Court to abandon the practice of separate opinions in each case."[8] Samuel Chase, one of the early Supreme Court Justices, had been "forced to resign from Congress in disgrace for trying
to corner the flour market by corrupt means."[9] Chase was a supporter of
the Alien and Sedition Acts, and as a circuit judge in 1800 prosecuted
John Fries, a Pennsylvanian cooper who led a militia group of about
sixty men to forcibly keep tax assessors from counting windows for tax
purposes.[10] The similarities with Fries and Shays's Rebellion—as well

---

[6] Irons, *A People's History of the Supreme Court*, 87.

[7] Ibid., 95.

[8] Ibid.

[9] Ibid., 97.

[10] Because of the Jay Treaty (the same John Jay who was the first Chief Justice) with
England, it was feared that France would go to war with the United States. In order to

as rebellions such as the "Boston Tea Party"—are obvious. Section One of the Sedation Act said that:

> Be it enacted by the Senate and House of Representatives of the United States of America, in Congress assembled. That if any persons shall unlawfully combine or conspire together, with intent to oppose any measure or measures of the government of the United States, which are or shall be directed by proper authority, or to impede the operation of any law of the United States, or to intimidate or prevent any person holding a place or office in or under the government of the United States, from undertaking, performing, or executing his trust or duty: and if any person or persons, with intent as aforesaid, shall counsel, advise, or attempt to procure any insurrection, riot, unlawful assembly, or combination, whether such conspiracy, threatening, counsel, advice, or attempt shall have the proposed effect or not, he or they shall be deemed guilty of a high misdemeanour, and on conviction before any court of the United States having jurisdiction thereof, shall be punished by a fine not exceeding five thousand dollars, and by imprisonment during a term of not less than six months, nor exceeding five years; and further, at the discretion of the court, may be holden to find sureties for his good behaviour, in such sum, and for such time, as the said court may direct.[11]

---

raise money in anticipation for war, Congress authorized a House Tax on slaves and property. Since many Northern states such as Pennsylvania had few slaves, the tax was directed towards private property. To judge the size of a dwelling, tax assessors were sent to count the number of window panes in houses.

[11] When one compares this with the Administration of Justice Act of the "Intolerable Acts" passed by Parliament that helped spark the American Revolution, the similarities are striking: "Whereas in his Majesty's province of Massachuset's Bay, in New England, an attempt hath lately been made to throw off the authority of the parliament of Great Britain over the said province, and an actual and avowed resistance, by open force, to the execution of certain acts of parliament, hath been suffered to take place, uncontrouled and unpunished,...and whereas, in the present disordered state of the said province, it is of the utmost importance...to the reestablishment of lawful authority throughout the same, that neither the magistrates acting in support of the laws, nor any of his Majesty's subjects aiding and assisting them therein, or in the suppression of riots and tumults,...should be discouraged from the proper discharge of their duty, by an apprehension, that in case of their being questioned for any acts done therein, they may be liable to be brought to trial for the same before persons who do not acknowledge the validity of the laws, in the execution thereof, or of the magistrate in support of whom, such acts had been done: in order therefore to remove every such discouragement from the minds of his Majesty's subjects, and to induce them, upon all proper occasions, to exert themselves in support of the public peace of the province, and of the authority of the King and Parliament of Great Britain."

During Fries trial for "treason," Chase "was so determined to punish Fries that he dispensed with even the rudiments of fair trial."[12] Chase's conduct on the bench was so appalling that he would later be impeached, although (unlike Federal Judge John Pickering who was impeached for similar reasons) Chase was not removed from office.

Another early Supreme Court Justice, James Wilson, was actually jailed for debts incurred from reckless land and finance speculation. As Irons pointed out, "contract law became a crucial issue during the first third of the nineteenth century because of the frenzied land speculation,"[13] speculation which was exacerbated due to the Edomite penchant for breaking legitimate treaties with the Native Americans and forcibly pushing them off their land. Contracts between white Christian men were serious business; contracts between the government and the Native Americans were simply a matter of convenience[14] (Section 10 of Article I of the Constitution is the provision that "No State shall...pass any Bill of Attainder, ex post facto Law, or Law impairing the Obligation of Contracts"). In the 1810 case of *Fletcher v. Peck*, which involved Wilson's 1795 land speculations, purchasing land that the Georgia legislature had sold through contracts "obtained through bribery and fraud."[15] Marshall, in writing his opinion to the case, ignored the fraudulent means by which the land was obtained, and "Marshall's refusal to examine the real issue—whether a law enacted through widespread bribery could be repealed by subsequent legislation—struck most observers as judicial evasion of duty."[16]

It was not until the appointment of John Marshall as Chief Justice that the Supreme Court became the powerful third branch of

---

[12] Irons, *A People's History of the Supreme Court*, 99.

[13] Ibid., 112.

[14] "The federal government was so determined to take Indian lands that it defied a ruling in 1831 by Chief Justice Marshall that Indian tribes were 'dependent domestic nations' with rights to lands they did not voluntarily cede to the United States. After the Court issued its decision in *Worcester v. Georgia*, President Andrew Jackson reportedly answered, 'John Marshall has made his decision; now let him enforce it.'" [Ibid., 111.] Jackson ordered troops to remove the Indians off of their native lands, resulting in the famous "Trail of Tears" in 1838 where they were driven from Georgia into Oklahoma territory during harsh winter conditions. Thousands of Indians—a majority of them women and children—perished due to exposure, disease, and hunger.

[15] Ibid., 113.

[16] Ibid., 115.

our government. Marshall was a Virginian lawyer who "specialized in representing the owners of landed estates and used his legal fees to purchase a large chunk of the Fairfax estate, which made him a wealthy man in land and slaves."[17] This estate was the center of the complex case of *Martin v. Hunter's Lesse* in 1813. The Fairfax estate, which consisted of "300,000 acres of prime tobacco-growing land,"[18] had been seized from the British loyalist Lord Fairfax and given to the good citizens of Virginia. Denny Martin, Lord Fairfax's nephew (and a British Subject), had been legally willed this land by his uncle, but during the last years of the Revolutionary War, David Hunter "obtained a grant of eight hundred acres" but was prohibited from possessing the land by Denny's brother (and Virginia citizen) Thomas Martin which he based on a law passed by the Virginia legislature in 1779. The legality of Hunter's claim was further compounded by Jay's Treaty with Britain in 1783 which recommended that the States return confiscated land to the Loyalists, a recommendation which Virginia ignored. The case was ruled in favor of Martin, based mainly on a "strained reading of the Jay Treaty."[19] The real winner in this case was John Marshall and his brother James Marshall, who "had brought Denny Martin's claim to the Fairfax estate" and who "stood to make a fortune if Martin's claim to the land was upheld by the courts."[20] Before it reached the Supreme Court, the "suit between Martin and Hunter dragged on for years in the Virginia courts," and in his ruling for Hunter, "Spencer Roane, the state's chief justice, ruled in 1810 that John Marshall and his brother Thomas had violated 'the principles of justice' in pressing Martin's claim" and that, in his written opinion, "came close...to accusing the Marshalls of fraud and unethical behavior."[21] Thus Marshall would set the standard for Esuvian Justices, taking his rightful place on the bronze doors of the Supreme Court Building.

◦

O NE OF THE RARE glimpses of the mechanics and thought-processes of the Supreme Court can be found in Bob Woodward and Scott Armstrong's *The Brethren*, where "most of the information"

---

[17] Ibid., 103.

[18] Ibid., 117.

[19] Ibid., 119.

[20] Ibid., 117.

[21] Ibid.

was gathered from interviews with "more than two hundred people, including several Justices, more than 170 former law clerks, and several dozen former employees of the Court."[22] In this equally amusing and disturbing book, Woodward and Armstrong gave a detailed account of the early Burger court and exposed the arbitrariness and politics that too often influenced Supreme Court decisions. That Chief Justice Warren E. Burger "declined to assist us [Woodward and Armstrong] in any way"[23] should not be surprising, for the book gives an unflattering portrait of the man who was chosen to lead the highest court in the land, a man who had previously no trial experience whatsoever, for Burger was nominated by Nixon for his political views, not his legal acumen. It was not just that Burger was a political appointee who would decide cases supportive of the administration which was in power at the time—all Supreme Court Justices are political appointees to some degree—but many believed Burger was intellectually unfit to be on any court, let alone the court that decided Constitutional law. "It was not just the Chief's intellectual inadequacies or his inability to write coherent opinions that bothered [Justice] Powell"[24] but that "the Chief provided no intellectual leadership. In fact, when it came to legal analysis, he was grossly inadequate."[25] His draft opinions were often "confused, rambling"[26] accounts, and three times early in his first term (1969), Burger's "published orders had incorrectly identified cases that had been accepted for full review…[Burger's] secretary and law clerks had tried to help [but]…he was still making mistakes. 'Any dumb ass could pick it up' the Chief's secretary once remarked privately."[27] One of Burger's former clerks "had observed Burger in action at the District of Columbia Court of Appeals the previous year. He had sent early and repeated warnings to [Justice] Stewart, characterizing Burger as petty, unpleasant, and dishonest."[28] For example,

---

[22] Bob Woodward and Scott Armstrong, *The Brethren*. (New York: Simon and Schuster, 1979), 3.

[23] Ibid.

[24] Ibid., 257.

[25] Ibid., 256.

[26] Ibid., 54.

[27] Ibid., 64.

[28] Ibid., 71.

one of the perks of being Chief Justice was that he could determine who would write the majority opinion since "by tradition, the senior Justice in the majority at conference selected the Justice who was to write the Court opinion for the majority. Since the Chief was considered senior to all the others, he made the assignments when he was in the majority, Burger was careful, in his first term, to make sure that he was in the majority most of the time—even if he had to adjust his views"[29] and that "[Burger often] changed his ground in a case three or four times. Legal arguments couldn't reach him…he would go out of his way—bend the law, overlook earlier Court decisions—to hold a majority."[30] For Chief Justice Burger, the overriding concern was political power, not justice.

In *Griggs v. Duke Power Co.*, Burger "assigned the opinion to himself. One of his clerks did virtually all of the research and drafting. Stewart was surprised by Burger's draft. It was well-written with first-rate reasoning. He was staggered, however, by the sweeping language of the opinion"[31] [as opposed to drafts which Burger had written himself].[32] Another problem was that "Burger was much too concerned with appearances"[33] and spent much of his time in such pursuits as taking "great interest in the proper refurbishing" of the Ladies Dining Room, making sure it was stocked with "newly acquired antiques" which "were selected by the Chief with great care."[34] Burger "accepted too many social, speaking and ceremonial engagements, and exhibited too little affection for the monastic, scholarly side of the Court's life,"[35] showing that Burger was more of a showman than a legal scholar.

Justice Harry Blackmun, who wrote the majority opinion in the famous *Roe v. Wade* case, the Supreme Court decision that made abortions legal, did not come across much better than Burger. Blackmun's *Roe v. Wade* draft "by mid-May, after five months of work, Blackmun was still laboring over his memorandum. Finally, he let one of his clerks look

---

[29] Ibid., 64.

[30] Ibid., 72.

[31] Ibid., 122–23.

[32] "Burger's double-spaced typewritten draft was hand-delivered to each chamber. Stewart read it carefully. It was an appalling effort." Ibid., 103.

[33] Ibid., 89.

[34] Ibid., 153.

[35] Ibid., 174.

over a draft. As usual, he made it clear that he did not want any editing. The clerk was astonished. It was crudely written and poorly organized. It did not settle on any analytical framework, nor did it explain on what basis Blackmun had arrived at the apparent conclusion that women had a right to privacy, and thus a right to abortion."[36] Of course, there were occasionally men of great intellect and morality on the Court, but too often Supreme Court Justices were picked not out of their intellectual ability or their knowledge of Constitutional Law, but that they could be counted upon to uphold the current administration's position be it liberal or conservative. Most importantly, Supreme Court justices were often selected because of their economic viewpoints, supporting the Ruling Class on matters of economic law. This factor alone would have substantial consequences for our society.[37]

The capriciousness of the system of interpretation of American Constitutional law is unlike Jewish Law, which:

> Like science, deals with logically and experientially controlled concepts, concepts that are often subject to quantitative and probabilistic delimitations. Jewish law thereby minimizes judicial arbitrariness on the one hand, and facilitates public understanding and accountability on the other. The simplistic dichotomy of 'judicial activism' and 'judicial self-restraint' that plagues American constitutional law is foreign to Jewish jurisprudence.[38]

To BETTER UNDERSTAND how "judicial arbitrariness" affects our legal system, let us examine two cases specifically involving Constitutional verses Torah law (the appellants in both cases being Orthodox Jews). These two cases, handed down the same day in 1961, show the "logic" employed by the Justice System in "secularizing" religious arguments, a point explained by Justice William O. Douglas in his excellent (and lone) dissent.

<hr />

[36] Ibid., 183.

[37] One of the most notable examples is the Supreme Court's decision in the recent ruling *Bush v. Gore* when the Supreme Court—in a 5–4 decision which went along strict party lines—overruled the "democratically" elected Al Gore in favor of George Bush.

[38] Eidelberg, *Beyond the Secular Mind*, 162–63.

McGowan v. Maryland, 366 U.S. 420 (1961)
No. 8
Argued December 8, 1960
Decided May 29, 1961
366 U.S. 420

Syllabus

Appellants, employees of a large department store on a highway in Anne Arundel County, Md., were convicted and fined in a Maryland State Court for selling on Sunday a loose-leaf binder, a can of floor wax, a stapler, staples and a toy, in violation of Md.Ann.Code, Art. 27, § 521, which generally prohibits the sale on Sunday of all merchandise except the retail sale of tobacco products, confectioneries, milk, bread, fruit, gasoline, oils, greases, drugs, medicines, newspapers and periodicals. Recent amendments now except from the prohibition the retail sale in Anne Arundel County of all foodstuffs, automobile and boating accessories, flowers, toilet goods, hospital supplies and souvenirs, and exempt entirely any retail establishment in that County which employs not more than one person other than the owner. There are many other Maryland laws which prohibit specific activities on Sundays or limit them to certain hours, places or conditions.

Held: Art. 27, § 521 does not violate the Equal Protection or Due Process Clause of the Fourteenth Amendment or constitute a law respecting an establishment of religion, within the meaning of the First Amendment, which is made applicable to the States by the Fourteenth Amendment. Pp. 366 U. S. 422–453.

Mr. Chief Justice Warren[39] delivered the opinion of the Court.

The issues in this case concern the constitutional validity of Maryland criminal statutes, commonly known as Sunday Closing Laws or Sunday Blue Laws.[40] These statutes, with exceptions to be noted hereafter, generally proscribe all labor, business and other commercial activities on Sunday[41]...Appellants are seven employees of a

---

[39] Earl Warren, "as governor [of California] he had strongly supported the internment of Japanese-Americans during World War II. As district attorney, he had authorized offshore searches of questionable legality outside the three-mile limit." Woodward and Armstrong, *The Brethren*, 26.

[40] The "Blue Laws" were originally laws to keep people from working on the Christian "Lord's Day" as is explained in greater detail below.

[41] For all the criticism the Jews have had over the years about Judaism being "nitpicky legalism," it is difficult to imagine something more nitpicky than this law, as shown below.

large discount department store located on a highway in Anne Arundel
County, Maryland. They were indicted for the Sunday sale of a three-
ring loose-leaf binder, a can of floor wax, a stapler and staples, and a
toy submarine in violation of Md. Ann. Code, Art. 27, § 521. Generally, this section prohibited, throughout the State, the Sunday sale of
all merchandise except the retail sale of tobacco products, confectioneries, milk, bread, fruits, gasoline, oils, greases, drugs and medicines,
and newspapers and periodicals[42]...applicants further allege that §
521 is capricious because of the exemptions for the operation of the
various amusements that have been listed and because slot machines,
pin-ball machines, and bingo are legalized and are freely played on
Sunday[43]...applicants here concededly have suffered direct economic
injury, allegedly due to the imposition on them on the tenets of the
Christian religion[44]...Appellants contend that the statutes violate the
guarantee of separation of church and state in that the statutes are laws
respecting an establishment of religion contrary to the First Amendment, made applicable to the States by the Fourteenth Amendment.[45]
The essence of appellants' "establishment" argument is that Sunday is
the Sabbath day of the predominant Christian sects; that the purpose of
the enforced stoppage of labor on that day is to facilitate and encourage church attendance; that the purpose of setting Sunday as a day
of universal rest is to induce people with no religion or people with
marginal religious beliefs to join the predominant Christian sects; that
the purpose of the atmosphere of tranquility created by Sunday closing is to aid the conduct of church services and religious observance
of the sacred day[46]...Although only the constitutionality[47] of § 521, the

---

[42] What was the intrinsic difference between a three-ring loose-leaf binder (a school
notebook) and a periodical (magazine)? Or the difference between a can of floor wax
and oils and greases? Why was buying tobacco or gambling legal, yet purchasing a
stapler or selling a toy submarine for a child considered unconstitutional?

[43] An excellent point brought up by the appellants; this law was firmly based on the
Christian "Sabbath."

[44] This is one of the reasons for the "Blue Laws"—to inflict economic injury on Jews
and other non-Christians. This legal tradition goes back to Roman times.

[45] As we have seen, the Constitution was written with economic goals in mind, not
moral ones. This is why the court ruled against the Jewish appellants in this case.

[46] This is exactly the reason for the "Blue Laws" as Justice Warren himself admits
below.

[47] What exactly is "constitutionality"? The common definition is a law that is in accordance
with the Constitution. Our laws are declared "constitutional" or "unconstitutional"
depending on how the Supreme Court defines certain words. The problem is that the
Constitution is an often poorly worded, inexact document. The case of *McGowan
v. Maryland* hinges on the first sentence of the First Amendment: "Congress shall
make no law respecting an establishment of religion, or prohibiting the free exercise

section under which appellants have been convicted, is immediately before us in this litigation, inquiry into the history of Sunday Closing Laws in our country, in addition to an examination of the Maryland Sunday closing statutes in their entirety and of their history, is relevant to the decision of whether the Maryland Sunday law in question is one respecting an establishment of religion. There is no dispute that the original laws which dealt with Sunday labor were motivated by religious forces.[48] But what we must decide is whether present Sunday legislation, having undergone extensive changes from the earliest forms, still retains its religious character.

Sunday Closing Laws go far back into American history, having been brought to the colonies with a background of English legislation dating to the thirteenth century.[49] In 1237, Henry III forbade the frequenting of markets on Sunday; the Sunday showing of wools at the staple was banned by Edward III in 1354; in 1409, Henry IV prohibited the playing of unlawful games on Sunday; Henry VI proscribed Sunday fairs in churchyards in 1444 and, four years later, made unlawful all fairs and markets and all showings of any goods or merchandise; Edward VI disallowed Sunday bodily labor by several injunctions in the mid-sixteenth century; various Sunday sports and amusements were restricted in 1625 by Charles I. Lewis. The law of the colonies to the time of the Revolution and the basis of the Sunday laws in the States was 29 Charles II, c. 7 (1677). It provided, in part:

"For the better observation and keeping holy the Lord's day, commonly called Sunday: be it enacted…that all the laws enacted and in force concerning the observation of the day, and repairing to the church thereon, be carefully put in execution; and that all and every person and persons whatsoever shall upon every Lord's day apply themselves

---

thereof." When the Constitution was written, Christianity had long been established. There were few (if any) Moslems (the first mosque in America was not established until 1915), and even fewer (if any) Buddhists, Confucianists, Zoroastrians, etc. The "establishment clause" had to do with Christian denominations, and the establishment of one denomination over another (such as the Anglican Church). The First Amendment specifically states that "Congress shall make no law respecting an establishment of religion," and not "Congress shall make no law respecting an establishment of religious denominations." The problem is that, to Christians or those raised in a Christian culture, Christian denominations are perceived as different "religions." The upshot was that Supreme Court's decision did in fact make a law respecting the establishment of Christianity, as Justice Douglas pointed out in his dissent.

[48] Here Justice Warren admits that the basis of the "Blue Laws" was to uphold the Christian religion.

[49] This is a prime example of how our legal system is merely a continuation of English Common Law, which was based on Roman/Edomite Law.

to the observation of the same, by exercising themselves thereon in the duties of piety and true religion, publicly and privately; and that no tradesman, artificer, workman, laborer, or other person whatsoever, shall do or exercise any worldly labor or business or work of their ordinary callings upon the Lord's day, or any part thereof (works of necessity and charity only excepted);...and that no person or persons whatsoever shall publicly cry, show forth, or expose for sale any wares, merchandise, fruit, herbs, goods, or chattels, whatsoever, upon the Lord's day, or any part thereof..."[50]

Observation of the above language, and of that of the prior mandates, reveals clearly that the English Sunday legislation was in aid of the established church.

The American colonial Sunday restrictions arose soon after settlement. Starting in 1650, the Plymouth Colony proscribed servile work, unnecessary travelling, sports, and the sale of alcoholic beverages on the Lord's day and enacted laws concerning church attendance. The Massachusetts Bay Colony and the Connecticut and New Haven Colonies enacted similar prohibitions, some even earlier in the seventeenth century. The religious orientation of the colonial statutes was equally apparent. For example, a 1629 Massachusetts Bay instruction began, "And to the end the Sabbath may be celebrated in a religious manner..." A 1653 enactment spoke of Sunday activities "which things tend much to the dishonor of God, the reproach of religion, and the profanation of his holy Sabbath, the sanctification whereof is sometimes put for all duties immediately respecting the service of God..." These laws persevered after the Revolution and, at about the time of the First Amendment's adoption, each of the colonies had laws of some sort restricting Sunday labor.[51]

But, despite the strongly religious origin of these laws, beginning before the eighteenth century, nonreligious arguments for Sunday closing began to be heard more distinctly and the statutes began to lose some of their totally religious flavor. In the middle 1700's, Blackstone wrote, "The keeping one day in the seven holy, as a time of relaxation and refreshment as well as for public worship, is of admirable service to a state considered merely as a civil institution. It humanizes, by the help of conversation and society, the manners of the lower classes; which would otherwise degenerate into a sordid ferocity and savage

---

[50] As Mr. Warren himself admits, the basis of the "Blue Laws" was Christianity, the religion of the majority of American citizens.

[51] Once again we see how the legal system of the United States did not fundamentally change after the drafting of the Constitution.

selfishness of spirit; it enables the industrious workman to pursue his occupation in the ensuing week with health and cheerfulness."[52] The preamble to a 1679 Rhode Island enactment stated that the reason for the ban on Sunday employment was that "persons being evil minded, have presumed to employ in servile labor, more than necessity requireth, their servants..." The New York law of 1788 omitted the term "Lord's day" and substituted "the first day of the week commonly called Sunday." With the advent of the First Amendment, the colonial provisions requiring church attendance were soon repealed.

More recently, further secular justifications[53] have been advanced for making Sunday a day of rest, a day when people may recover from the labors of the week just passed and may physically and mentally prepare for the week's work to come.[54] In England, during the First World War, a committee investigating the health conditions of munitions workers reported "if the maximum output is to be secured and maintained for any length of time, a weekly period of rest must be allowed...on economic and social grounds alike this weekly period of rest is best provided on Sunday." The proponents of Sunday closing legislation are no longer exclusively representatives of religious interests.[55] Recent New Jersey Sunday legislation was supported by labor groups and trade associations..."A Bill for Establishing Religious Freedom" was passed in 1785. In this same year, Madison presented to Virginia legislators "A Bill for Punishing...Sabbath Breakers," which provided in part: "If any person on Sunday shall himself be found labouring at his own or any other trade or calling, or shall employ his apprentices, servants or slaves in labour, or other business, except it be in the ordinary household offices of daily necessity, or other work of necessity or charity, he shall forfeit the sum of ten shillings for every such offence, deeming every apprentice, servant, or slave so employed, and every day he shall be so employed as constituting a distinct offense..."[56]

---

[52] It is important in Edomite society to keep the "lower classes" from degenerating "into a sordid ferocity and savage selfishness of spirit," and making sure that "it enables the industrious workman to pursue his occupation in the ensuing week with health and cheerfulness." The reasons, given by Warren, are based on "secular" economic factors.

[53] In other words, non-Torah based justifications. Justice Warren relies on a vapid interpretation of "secularism" to decide what is or is not permitted to do on the "sabbath" created by Christianity.

[54] Warren seems to forget that this idea originally came from the Torah, as well as Sunday being the first day of the week.

[55] What are the "economic and social grounds" for having Sunday being the day the "Blue Laws" are enacted except that it is a tradition from British Common Edomite Law and Christianity?

[56] The Supreme Court has traditionally relied heavily on the writings of Madison and Jefferson in their interpretation of the Constitution. One should note that Madison's law is about "[Sunday] Sabbath-Breakers," not "secular-day-of-rest" breakers.

The First Amendment, in its final form, did not simply bar a congressional enactment establishing a church; it forbade all laws respecting an establishment of religion. Thus, this Court has given the Amendment a "broad interpretation[57]... in the light of its history and the evils it was designed forever to suppress..." Everson v. Board of Education, supra, at pp. 330 U. S. 14–15. It has found that the First and Fourteenth Amendments afford protection against religious establishment far more extensive than merely to forbid a national or state church.[58] Thus, in McCollum v. Board of Education, 333 U. S. 203, the Court held that the action of a board of education permitting religious instruction during school hours in public school buildings and requiring those children who chose not to attend to remain in their classrooms to be contrary to the "Establishment" Clause...

In light of the evolution of our Sunday Closing Laws through the centuries, and of their more or less recent emphasis upon secular considerations, it is not difficult to discern that, as presently written and administered, most of them, at least, are of a secular, rather than of a religious, character, and that presently they bear no relationship to establishment of religion as those words are used in the Constitution of the United States...[59]

Throughout this century and longer, both the federal and state governments have oriented their activities very largely toward improvement of the health, safety, recreation and general wellbeing of our citizens. Numerous laws affecting public health, safety factors in industry, laws affecting hours and conditions of labor of women and children, weekend diversion at parks and beaches, and cultural activities of various kinds, now point the way toward the good life for all.[60] Sunday Closing Laws, like those before us, have become part

---

[57] Unlike Jewish Law, there are no rules of interpretation for the Supreme Court justices. Their methods are not unlike the way Christians interpret the "Old" Testament, by simply making things up to make sure the interpretations of the *Tanach* conform to their theology. Likewise, the Supreme Court justices too often based their "interpretations of the Constitution" on emotional, economic, or theological whims that had nothing to do with any system of interpretation.

[58] The Fourteenth Amendment was also the basis for a corporation to be a "person."

[59] Again, the problem is the wording (or rather, the lack of wording) of the Constitution. Changing the term "Lord's Day" to "Sunday" and re-baptizing certain elements as "secular" as opposed to "religious" does not negate the simple fact the "Blue Laws" have a Christian basis, or that they form an unbroken tradition going back to the Christian laws of medieval England.

[60] "If there is any principle that is distinctively biblical it is the bias of righteousness in favor of the poor and helpless." [Konvitz, *Torah & Constitution*, 64.] Warren's defense ignores the fact of the Supreme Court consistently ruling in favor of the wealthy corporations (as opposed to the working class) over the years.

and parcel of this great governmental concern wholly apart from their original purposes or connotations. The present purpose and effect of most of them is to provide a uniform day of rest for all citizens; the fact that this day is Sunday, a day of particular significance for the dominant Christian sects, does not bar the State from achieving its secular goals.[61] To say that the States cannot prescribe Sunday as a day of rest for these purposes solely because centuries ago[62] such laws had their genesis in religion would give a constitutional interpretation of hostility to the public welfare, rather than one of mere separation of church and State.[63]

We now reach the Maryland statutes under review. The title of the major series of sections of the Maryland Code dealing with Sunday closing—Art. 27, §§ 492-534C—is "Sabbath Breaking"; § 492 proscribes work or bodily labor on the "Lord's day," and forbids persons to "profane the Lord's day" by gaming, fishing et cetera; § 522 refers to Sunday as the "Sabbath day." As has been mentioned above, many of the exempted Sunday activities in the various localities of the State may only be conducted during the afternoon and late evening; most Christian church services, of course, are held on Sunday morning and early Sunday evening. Finally, as previously noted, certain localities do not permit the allowed Sunday activities to be carried on within one hundred yards of any church where religious services are being held. This is the totality of the evidence of religious purpose which may be gleaned from the face of the present statute and from its operative effect.

The predecessors of the existing Maryland Sunday laws are undeniably religious in origin. The first Maryland statute dealing with Sunday activities, enacted in 1649, was entitled "An Act concerning Religion." It made it criminal to "profane the Sabbath or Lords day called Sunday by frequent swearing, drunkennes or by any unciville or disorderly recreation, or by working on that day when absolute necessity doth not require it…" But it should be noted that, throughout the Judefind decision, the Maryland court specifically rejected the contention that the laws interfered with religious liberty and stated that the laws' purpose

---

[61] The very arbitrariness of judicial decisions is seen here in how the Supreme Court can simply re-word the law from being "religious" to "secular."

[62] Warren conveniently ignores that his ruling violates the principle of *stare decisis*, not to mention the Torah itself, which sees no separation of what is "religious" and "secular." Business, which is what this ruling is all about, is covered by the laws of the Torah and applicable to the Noahide, therefore, under Torah Law, business should be considered a "sacred" venture.

[63] The concept of separation of "Church and State" came after enactment of the Blue Laws.

was to provide the "advantages of having a weekly day of rest, from a mere physical and political standpoint..."[64]

But this does not answer all of appellants' contentions. We are told that the State has other means at its disposal to accomplish its secular purpose, other courses that would not even remotely or incidentally give state aid to religion. On this basis, we are asked to hold these statutes invalid on the ground that the State's power to regulate conduct in the public interest may only be executed in a way that does not unduly or unnecessarily infringe upon the religious provisions of the First Amendment. See Cantwell v. Connecticut, supra, at pp. 310 U. S. 304-305. However relevant this argument may be, we believe that the factual basis on which it rests is not supportable. It is true that, if the State's interest were simply to provide for its citizens a periodic respite from work, a regulation demanding that everyone rest one day in seven, leaving the choice of the day to the individual, would suffice.

However, the State's purpose is not merely to provide a one-day-in-seven work stoppage. In addition to this, the State seeks to set one day apart from all others as a day of rest, repose, recreation and tranquility—a day which all members of the family and community have the opportunity to spend and enjoy together, a day on which there exists relative quiet and disassociation from the everyday intensity of commercial activities, a day on which people may visit friends and relatives who are not available during working days.[65]

Obviously, a State is empowered to determine that a "rest one day in seven" statute would not accomplish this purpose; that it would not provide for a general cessation of activity, a special atmosphere of tranquility, a day which all members of the family or friends and relatives might spend together. Furthermore, it seems plain that the problems involved in enforcing such a provision would be exceedingly more difficult than those in enforcing a "common day of rest" provision.

---

[64] "It is only a perverse blindness that makes it possible for us to see the law of God in the Bible but only the law of Caesar in the statutes enacted by Congress or by the state legislatures or in the decisions and opinions of our courts." Konvitz, *Torah & Constitution*, 63.

[65] Here is the problem defined. The prevailing Christian culture views the Torah Sabbath (the seventh day of the week) as the day of Torah violation, of shopping, partying, and enjoying any and all non-Torah based activities. This is where a paradigm shift in our culture would help in attuning our society to Torah-based values.

Moreover, it is common knowledge that the first day of the week has come to have special significance as a rest day in this country.[66] People of all religions[67] and people with no religion regard Sunday as a time for family activity, for visiting friends and relatives, for late sleeping, for passive and active entertainments, for dining out, and the like. "Vast masses of our people, in fact, literally millions, go out into the countryside on fine Sunday afternoons in the Summer..." Sunday is a day apart from all others. The cause is irrelevant;[68] the fact exists. It would seem unrealistic for enforcement purposes and perhaps detrimental to the general welfare to require a State to choose a common day of rest other than that which most persons[69] would select of their own accord. For these reasons, we hold that the Maryland statutes are not laws respecting an establishment of religion.[70]

JUSTICE **W**ILLIAM **O. D**OUGLAS, in his lone dissent, said that:

If the 'free exercise' of religion were subject to reasonable regulations, as it is under some constitutions, or if all laws 'respecting the establishment of religion' were not proscribed, I could understand how rational men, representing a predominantly Christian civilization, might think these Sunday laws did not unreasonably interfere with anyone's free exercise of religion and took no step toward a burdensome establishment of any religion...I do not see how a State can make protesting citizens refrain from doing innocent acts on Sunday because the doing of those acts offends sentiments of their Christian neighbors.

---

[66] This is entirely due to Christianity, and the theological teaching that the Sabbath was "changed" from Saturday to Sunday. What needs to be challenged is the legality of this theological alteration of Torah.

[67] This is, of course, not true at all. Sunday is, for Jews, the first day of the workweek.

[68] Actually, the cause is quite relevant. The Christian Church changed the Sabbath from Saturday to Sunday, and the laws of Sunday being the official day of rest are wholly theological in origin.

[69] So much for the "intent of the Framers" in protecting the rights of a minority against the "tyranny of the majority." A fine example of how the Supreme Court Justices understood the intent of the Framers when it came to economic versus religious matters.

[70] The problem was that the religion (Christianity) was already established. That organized religions are permitted at all, religions that influence our legal system, forming laws used to desecrate the Sabbath and persecute Torah-keeping Jews, should convince any observant Noahide that our Constitutional system violates Torah law.

The institutions of our society are founded on the belief that there is an authority higher than the authority of the State; that there is a moral law which the State is powerless to alter; that the individual possesses rights, conferred by the Creator, which government must respect...yet why then can it make criminal the doing of other acts, as innocent as eating, during the day that Christians revere?

Sunday is a word heavily overlaid with connotations and traditions deriving from the Christian roots of our civilization that color all judgments concerning it. This is what the philosophers call 'word magic.' For most judges, for most lawyers, for most human beings, we are as unconscious of our value patterns as we are of the oxygen that we breathe.

The Court picks and chooses language from various decisions to bolster its conclusion that these Sunday laws, in the modern setting, are 'civil regulations.' No matter how much is written, no matter what is said, the parentage of these laws is the Fourth Commandment,[71] and they serve and satisfy the religious predispositions of our Christian communities. After all, the labels a State places on its laws are not binding on us when we are confronted with a constitutional decision. We reach our own conclusion as to the character, effect, and practical operation of the regulation in determining its constitutionality Carpenter v. Shaw, 280 U. S. 363, 280 U. S. 367-368; Dyer v. Sims, 341 U. S. 22, 341 U. S. 29; Memphis Steam Landry v. Stone, 342 U. S. 389, 342 U. S. 392; Society for Savings v. Bowers, 349 U. S. 143, 349 U. S. 151; Gomillion v. Lightfoot, 364 U. S. 339, 364 U. S. 341-342.

It seems to me plain that, by these laws, the States compel one, under sanction of law, to refrain from work or recreation on Sunday because of the majority's religious views about that day. The State, by law, makes Sunday a symbol of respect or adherence. Refraining from work or recreation in deference to the majority's religious feelings about Sunday is within every person's choice. By what authority can government compel it?...These laws are sustained because, it is said, the First Amendment is concerned with religious convictions or opinion, not with conduct. But it is a strange Bill of Rights that makes it possible for the dominant religious group to bring the minority to heel because the minority, in the doing of acts which intrinsically are wholesome and not antisocial, does not defer to the majority's religious beliefs...the State can, of course, require one day of

---

[71] It should be pointed out that Noahides are forbidden to observe the Sabbath "in the manner of the Jews."

rest a week: one day when every shop or factory is closed. Quite a few States make that requirement. Then the "day of rest" becomes purely and simply a health measure. But the Sunday laws operate differently. They force minorities to obey the majority's religious feelings of what is due and proper for a Christian community; they provide a coercive spur to the "weaker brethren," to those who are indifferent to the claims of a Sabbath through apathy or scruple...when these laws are applied to Orthodox Jews, as they are in No. 11 and in No. 67, or to Sabbatarians, their vice is accentuated. If the Sunday laws are constitutional, kosher markets are on a five-day week. Thus, those laws put an economic penalty on those who observe Saturday, rather than Sunday, as the Sabbath. For the economic pressures on these minorities, created by the fact that our communities are predominantly Sunday-minded, there is no recourse. When, however, the State uses its coercive powers—here the criminal law—to compel minorities to observe a second Sabbath not their own, the State undertakes to aid and 'prefer one religion over another'—contrary to the command of the Constitution. See Everson v. Board of Education, supra, 330 U. S. 15.

༄

IN THE CASE of Braunfeld vs. Brown, handed down the same day:

Braunfeld v. Brown
No. 67
Argued December 8, 1960
Decided May 29, 1961
366 U.S. 599

Appellants are members of the Orthodox Jewish Faith, which requires the closing of their places of business and total abstention from all manner of work from nightfall each Friday until nightfall each Saturday. As merchants engaged in the retail sale of clothing and home furnishings in Philadelphia, they sued to enjoin enforcement of a 1959 Pennsylvania criminal statute which forbade the retail sale on Sundays of those commodities and other specified commodities.[72] They claimed that the statute violated the Equal Protection Clause of the Fourteenth Amendment and constituted a law respecting an establishment of religion, and that it interfered with the free exercise of their religion by imposing serious economic disadvantages upon

---

[72] It should be noted that the sale of commodities on Sunday is allowed in the Torah.

them if they adhere to the observance of their Sabbath, and that it
would operate so as to hinder the Orthodox Jewish Faith in gaining
new members.

Held: the statute does not violate the Equal Protection Clause of the
Fourteenth Amendment, nor constitute a law respecting an establishment of religion, Two Guys from Harrison-Allentown, Inc. v. McGin-
ley, ante, p. 366 U. S. 582, and it does not prohibit the free exercise
of appellants' religion, within the meaning of the First Amendment,
made applicable to the States by the Fourteenth Amendment. Pp. 366
U. S. 600-610.

[Again handed down by Warren]

Certain aspects of religious exercise cannot in any way be restricted or
burdened by either federal or state legislation. Compulsion by law of
the acceptance of any creed or the practice of any form of worship is
strictly forbidden. The freedom to hold religious beliefs and opinions
is absolute...

However, the freedom to act, even when the action is in accord with
one's religious convictions, is not totally free from legislative restrictions. Cantwell v. Connecticut, supra, at pp. 310 U. S. 303-304, 310
U. S. 306. As pointed out in Reynolds v. United States, supra, at p.
98 U. S. 164, legislative power over mere opinion is forbidden, but it
may reach people's actions when they are found to be in violation of
important social duties or subversive of good order, even when the actions are demanded by one's religion. This was articulated by Thomas
Jefferson when he said:

'Believing with you that religion is a matter which lies solely between
man and his God, that he owes account to none other for his faith or
his worship, that the legislative powers of government reach actions
only, and not opinions, I contemplate with sovereign reverence that
act of the whole American people which declared that their legislature
should 'make no law respecting an establishment of religion, or prohibiting the free exercise thereof,' thus building a wall of separation
between church and State. Adhering to this expression of the supreme
will of the nation in behalf of the rights of conscience, I shall see with
sincere satisfaction the progress of those sentiments which tend to restore to man all his natural rights, convinced he has no natural right in
opposition to his social duties.'

And, in the Barnette case, the Court was careful to point out that:

'The freedom asserted by these appellees does not bring them into col-
lision with rights asserted by any other individual. It is such conflicts

which most frequently require intervention of the State to determine where the rights of one end and those of another begin…It is…to be noted that the compulsory flag salute and pledge requires affirmation of a belief and an attitude of mind.'

But, again, this is not the case before us because the statute at bar does not make unlawful any religious practices of appellants; the Sunday law simply regulates a secular activity[73] and, as applied to appellants, operates so as to make the practice of their religious beliefs more expensive. Furthermore, the law's effect does not inconvenience all members of the Orthodox Jewish faith, but only those who believe it necessary to work on Sunday.[74] And even these are not faced with as serious a choice as forsaking their religious practices or subjecting themselves to criminal prosecution. Fully recognizing that the alternatives open to appellants and others similarly situated—retaining their present occupations and incurring economic disadvantage or engaging in some other commercial activity which does not call for either Saturday or Sunday labor—may well result in some financial sacrifice in order to observe their religious beliefs, still the option is wholly different than when the legislation attempts to make a religious practice itself unlawful…[75]

To strike down, without the most critical scrutiny, legislation which imposes only an indirect burden on the exercise of religion, i.e., legislation which does not make unlawful the religious practice itself,[76] would radically restrict the operating latitude of the legislature. Statutes which tax income and limit the amount which may be deducted for religious contributions impose an indirect economic burden on the observance of the religion of the citizen whose religion requires him to donate a greater amount to his church; statutes which require the courts to be closed on Saturday and Sunday impose a similar indirect burden on the observance of the religion of the trial lawyer whose religion requires him to rest on a weekday…"

---

[73] The Supreme Court rules that, on the basis of Thomas "the Jews followed an imperfect ethical code [and are]…repulsive and anti-social" Jefferson's views on the Torah, that the secular Constitution overrules the Torah.

[74] The implication here is that Orthodox Jews should not cling to their ancient and obsolete Torah Law.

[75] The Supreme Court is ruling that there is a difference between "business" and "religion," a decidedly non-Torah view.

[76] Operating a business on the Sabbath is, for Jews, prohibited by Torah Law.

J USTICE WARREN'S BLITHE dismissal of Torah Law based on the "common knowledge that the first day of the week has come to have special significance as a rest day in this country. People of all religions and people with no religion regard Sunday as a time for family activity" goes against the common knowledge that, for both Jews and Noahides, Sunday is the first day of the work week, not the Sabbath. Likewise, Justice Warren's statement that "the cause is irrelevant" is illogical; it was Christianity, the established religion of American society, which changed the Sabbath from the last day of the week to the first day of the week. The "secular" argument given by Justice Warren, based on Jefferson's statement "that religion is a matter which lies solely between man and his God, that he owes account to none other for his faith or his worship, that the legislative powers of government reach actions only, and not opinions," underlines the fact that the secularists establish the concept of "faith-based" religion, a view which relegates religion as simply a system of beliefs and not actions. This logic is as much a product of Greek thought as the theology which preceded it. As we have noted earlier, the only two choices we are given are those of Greek-based theology or Greek-based philosophy; the Torah-based view is ignored completely.

The law of our society, based on Greek organized religion and Greek philosophy, too often violates Torah law. It was clear that the "intent of the framers" was to base our government and legal system on Greek philosophy as well as the Roman legal system.[77] Bolstered by an educational system that indoctrinated the public into believing the opinions of the Framers was "holy writ," a mythology was created about the Constitution, along with an ever-swelling bureaucracy that both fed off of and supported this system.

The disdain for what John Adams called "the rabble," the common people, is best exemplified by Chief Justice Oliver Wendell Holmes in his 1927 opinion in *Buck v. Bell*, 274 U.S. 200 (1927):

> We have seen more than once that the public welfare may call upon the best citizens for their lives. It would be strange if it could not call

---

[77] "*Pesharah* [arbitration] differs strikingly from its application in Roman or modern civil law. The latter regard arbitration as contradictory to juridicial action and as an extra-legal procedure...that pesharah is very much a legal procedure is attested to by the strict halakhic requirements which govern its operations; it is not an informal and arbitrary agreement." Rabbi Abraham R. Besdin, *Reflections of the Rav: Lessons in Jewish Thought.* Vol. I. (Hoboken: KTAV Publishing House, Inc., 1993), 54.

upon those who already sap the strength of the State for these lesser sacrifices, often not felt to be such by those concerned, in order to prevent our being swamped with incompetence. It is better for all the world if, instead of waiting to execute degenerate offspring for crime or to let them starve for their imbecility, society can prevent those who are manifestly unfit from continuing their kind. The principle that sustains compulsory vaccination is broad enough to cover cutting the Fallopian tubes. Jacobson v. Massachusetts, 197 U.S. 11. Three generations of imbeciles are enough.

AMERICANS ARE CONDITIONED to support a type of government based on a model invented nearly two and a half thousand years ago in Ancient Greece.[78] Our Constitutional government, whose economic foundation was initially based on slavery, was wedded to a legal system which supported a severe class structure, making sure the lower classes stay in their place by giving them a limited role in government, a role which created the illusion that they, the lower classes, had some semblance of control over the government, and, at the same time, protecting the political and economic power of the wealthy Ruling Class. This form of government, which is called by the misleading name of "democracy," which, as we have noted, has several inherent flaws built into its system, not the least of which are the concepts of "freedom" and "equality," which are defined, as Allan Bloom pointed out, by a leveling of all moral distinctions.

The greatest challenge we face is that the legal system of America is the direct descendent of the legal systems of Europe, which are based on (or at least heavily influenced by) Roman Law.[79] It is a legal system which favors the wealthy, a legal system which is maintained by a Constitutional government resistant to democratic change from the bottom while at the same time is able to be easily manipulated by the Ruling Class. The protocols of the politicians have been to keep this system in place, and convince the lower classes of the myth that there is no better system that has been devised by man.

---

[78] "Jerusalem versus Athens remains as ever the paramount issue of mankind." Eidelberg, *Beyond the Secular Mind*, 119.

[79] "For many centuries the Law of Rome has occupied a foremost place in the universities of the continent of Europe. The study of the Common Law has in recent years made famous the law schools of America. In the English universities the Civil Law and the Common Law are studied side by side." R. W. Lee, "The Civil Law and the Common Law: A World Survey." *Michigan Law Review*. Vol. 14, No. 2 (Dec., 1915), 89.

CHAPTER SIX

Esavian Economics

Today the great American corporations seem more like states within states than simply private businesses. The economy of America has been largely incorporated, and within their incorporation the corporate chiefs have captured the technological innovation, accumulated the existing great fortunes as well as much lesser, scattered wealth, and capitalized the future. Within the financial and political boundaries of the corporation, the industrial revolution itself has been concentrated. Corporations command raw materials, and the patents on inventions with which to turn them into finished products. They command the most expensive, and therefore what must be the finest, legal minds in the world, to invent and to refine their defenses and their strategies.

— C. Wright Mills[1]

WHEN FRIEDRICH ENGELS GAVE HIS EULOGY AT THE GRAVESIDE OF HIS close friend and comrade Karl Marx, Engels said that "Marx discovered the law of development of human history: the simple fact, *hitherto concealed by an overgrowth of ideology*, [emphasis added] that mankind must first of all eat, drink, have shelter and clothing, before it can pursue politics, art, science, religion, etc."[2] Had Marx been

---

[1] C. Wright Mills, *The Power Elite*. (New York: Oxford University Press, 1956), 124.

[2] Sowell, *Marxism*, 63.

more literate in Talmud rather than Hegel, he would have "discovered" this idea that was such a major part of Torah law, the importance of economics in a civilized society.

From the Noahide point of view, there is no greater example of Torah observance than the economic laws of a society. The Sages give us the example of the contrast between the generation of the Flood and the generation of the Tower of Babel: the generation of the flood was destroyed because of robbery; the generation of the Tower of Babel, who rebelled against God, were merely dispersed after their language was confounded. The difference between the two was that the Generation of the Tower of Babel cooperated with one another and did not steal. Theft, particularly of the property of the poor by legal means, was the hallmark of an evil society.

Out of the 613 *mitzvot* in the Torah, over 100 of these commandments deal (in some form) with business and economics.[3] Dealing with the protocols of economics in our society could easily take up an entire book in itself; indeed, many of the books we have mentioned— works of prominent intellectuals such as Adam Smith's *The Wealth of Nations*, Karl Marx's *Capital*, and Max Weber's *Economy and Society*, just to name a few—have had a world-historical impact on the economics and politics of the past century. As the slogan for Bill Clinton's 1992 presidential campaign said, "It's the economy, stupid."

From the Noahide perspective, the slogan for Western culture should be, "*It's the Torah, stupid.*" Western mores and values about wealth come from the same Greco-Roman paradigm as our legal system. The attitude which we inherited from Edom, as explained by Michael Parenti, was that "in Rome's Late Republic…it was a disgrace to be poor and an honor to be rich. The rich, who lived parasitically off the labor of others, were hailed as men of quality and worth; while the impecunious, who struggled along on the paltry earnings of their own hard labor, were considered vulgar and deficient."[4] This is another of the defining characteristics of Edom, certainly the defining characteristic of Esavian economics. Wealth in Esavian culture is, and always has been, the key to power, and the more wealth one had (or had political control of), the more power one wielded. In contrast to

---

[3] Larry Kahaner, *Values, Prosperity and the Talmud: Business Lessons From the Ancient Rabbis*. (Hoboken: John Wiley & Sons, Inc., 2003), xvii.

[4] Parenti, *The Assassination of Julius Caesar*, 32.

the Esavian view of wealth, many of the Sages of the Talmud[5] earned a meager living from hard labor, yet were honored and respected even in their lifetimes as men of great wisdom.[6] Wealth, according to the Torah, was neither an indicator of character or worth, nor was it a factor for inclusion in the Great Sanhedrin, the highest court in Israel. Rather, it was what one did with their wealth that was the indicator of character and worth, if you used your wealth to help others less fortunate or avariciously hoarded it for luxuries, power and self-aggrandizement in the manner of Esau.

≈

THERE IS PERHAPS no greater embodiment of Edom in our modern society than the entity known as the corporation,[7] the defining economic structure of modern times. Our food, clothing, medicines, homes, furniture, media,[8] transportation, finance, educational

---

[5] "The Talmudic view is often not what you would expect. For example, the Talmudic rabbis view money and profit not as sources of evil, as in some religions, but as opportunities to do good works, in general raising people's standard of living so they can spend more time with their families, study important works of wisdom, and enjoy life's pleasures." Kahaner, *Values, Prosperity and the Talmud: Business Lessons From the Ancient Rabbis*, xx.

[6] "Nowhere in the world is honest work to gain an independent living held in such high esteem and honour as was the case in ancient Jewish circles. Our greatest spiritual heroes, whose light still illuminates us, and to whom their age and all ages looked up to, and still look up to full of respect and honour, a Hillel, a Rabbi Jehoshua, a R. Chanina and R. Auchio, a R. Huna all lived in the most straightened circumstances and earned their living as woodchopper, cobbler, porter, drawer of water, and by their example taught the maxim 'live no better on Sabbath than on the rest of the week and be independent.'" Hirsch, commentary to *Devarim* 15:11, 275.

[7] "The corporate mystique is a set of cherished beliefs and illusions at the very heart of American culture…[it] dictates how we think about not only what corporations are and the importance of their roles in our lives, but what government and markets, business and democracy, and the good life are all about…the corporate mystique is, at heart, an ideology, which for decades has effectively disguised the rising power of corporations in our lives…the rise of a new weakened form of democracy in which the powers of average Americans are being transferred to vast institutions with diminishing public accountability." Charles Derber, *Corporation Nation: How Corporations are Taking Over our lives and What We Can Do About It*. (New York: St. Martin's Griffin, 1998), 2–3.

[8] "The closer a story gets to examining corporate power the less reliable our corporate media system is as a source of information that is useful to the citizens of a democracy." John Nicholes and Robert W. McChesney, *It's the Media, Stupid*. (New York: Seven Stories Press, 2000), 22.

system—indeed, our economy and government are dominated by the corporation, and our "commons" have become corporate enclaves, such as the great shopping malls, sports arenas, and theme parks. The size of large corporations is staggering; out of one hundred of the world's largest economies, over half of them are corporations. In fact, the corporation has become so powerful that it has been able to change its status and become, according to the Supreme Court, not simply a mere business, but a "person" with Constitutional rights.[9] This raises a disturbing point: if the corporation is a "person," what sort of person would it be? In Joel Bakan's book *The Corporation*:

> [Bakan] asked Dr. Robert Hare, psychologist and internationally renowned expert on psychopathy…to apply his diagnostic checklist of psychopathic traits (italicized below) to the corporation's character, he found there was a close match. The corporation is *irresponsible*, Dr. Hare said, because "in an attempt to satisfy the corporate goal, everybody else is put at risk." Corporations try to "*manipulate* everything, including public opinion," and they are *grandiose*, always insisting "that we're number one, we're the best." A *lack of empathy* and *asocial tendencies* are also key characteristics of the corporation, says Hare—"their behavior indicates they really don't concern themselves with their victims"; and corporations often *refuse to accept responsibility for their own actions* and are unable to feel remorse.[10]

Rabbi Elie Munk described a similar personality in the Torah, a personality who acted in "maliciously, craftily…underhanded ways,"[11] a personality who used "brute strength…to treat men and animals ruthlessly,"[12] a personality who had "no scruples when it [came] to pursuing his goals."[13] That personality was Esau.

---

[9] "Through a bizarre legal alchemy, courts had fully transformed the corporation into a 'person,' with its own identity, separate from the flesh-and-blood people who were its owners and managers and empowered, like a real person, to conduct business in its own name, acquire assets, employ workers, pay taxes, and go to court to assert its rights and defend its actions…[and that] corporations should be protected by the Fourteenth Amendment's rights to 'due process of law' and 'equal protection of the laws,' rights originally entrenched in the Constitution to protect freed slaves." Joel Bakan, *The Corporation: The Pathological Pursuit of Profit and Power*. (New York: Free Press, 2004), 16.

[10] Ibid., 56–57.

[11] Munk, *The Call of the Torah: Bereishis*, 339.

[12] Ibid., 341.

[13] Ibid., 368.

To subjugate others and to feed his lust for power was the purpose that drove Esau. In *Bereishis* 25:28 it says that Isaac loved Esau for game was in his mouth. The literal interpretation was that Esau supplied his father with venison (wild game). The *Midrash* interprets this, however, that Esau ensnared Isaac with words; that is, he used his mouth to deceive Isaac (*Rashi*). *Or HaChaim* interprets this as Esau deceiving his father in order to obtain his blessings. Likewise, the religion of Christianity has deceived its followers in implying that the Church is the "New Israel" which would reap all of the blessings that the *Tanach* speaks of for Israel. This was accomplished by giving a Gnostic interpretation of the Hebrew text. Christians, as did Esau with Isaac, honor the "Father" (i.e., God), yet they continue the tradition of Esau by eschewing Torah values, squandering their strength by plundering, murdering, and throwing away their birthright simply to fill their bellies for the moment, ignoring the spiritual, legal, and moral path of Torah in order for immediate physical and spiritual gratification.

This is the basis for the irrational and illogical anti-Semitism of Western Christian civilization. The poison of Esau pulsed in the veins of the Church, and as the Church spread throughout Europe and into the New World, it carried this venomous hatred of the Torah with it,[14] as well as the Esavian lust for wealth and power. This is the poison that has entered the veins of our legal, economic, and political systems, and there is no greater example of this than the corporate mentality,[15] the economic embodiment of Esau.

It is this "person"—the corporation—that has become the tyrant which Plato warned us of in his criticism of democracy, the soulless *golem*, the "person" who, by means such as manipulation of

---

[14] "Balaam further saw the rising of the wicked empire [Rome], which would subdue great kingdoms, and [he saw that] its destruction would be brought about by the hand of the Messiah. Thus, it is said, 'But ships will come from the coast of Kittim.' [Numbers 24:24]. [The latter] are the Romans, according to the words of the Targum [Onkelos]." *Ramban, The Book of Redemption*. Rabbi Dr. Charles B. Chavel, trans. (New York: Shilo Publishing House, Inc., 1986), 17.

[15] "The problem of the corporation is at root one of design. Corporations are not structured to be benevolent institutions. They are structured to make money. Under the prevailing interpretation of corporate law, corporations have one primary duty: to make money for shareholders...in the pursuit of this one goal, they will freely cast aside concerns about the societies and ecological systems in which they operate." Lee Drutman and Charlie Cray, *The People's Business: Controlling Corporations and Restoring Democracy*. (San Francisco: Berrett-Koehler Publishers, Inc., 2004), 3.

the media[16] and its economic muscle to influence political campaigns as well as legal and governmental decisions, has taken over our government, economy, and culture. As with Esau, the corporate mentality is driven to dominate others, to conquer and acquire by force or guile.[17]

⤺

THE FIRST MODERN corporations were not the behemoths we think of today. Even the early British trading companies, such as the East India Company, were "different from modern corporations in that they were quasi-governmental institutions chartered by the crown for specific purposes, such as grabbing as much wealth as possible from the East Indies and bringing it back to England."[18] These same corporations (such as the Virginia Company) had a hand in the development of the United States, and it was the abuse of their power (such as the very same East India Company's tax on tea that led to the "Boston Tea Party" in 1773) as well as "European feudalism in general [that] made the Founding Fathers wary of any large concentrations of wealth and power because they knew where such concentrations could lead"[19] that put strict limits on what corporations could and could not do according to state charters.

It should be pointed out that, despite what many believe, corporations are not intrinsically evil.[20] Having investors pool their capital in

---

[16] Corporations may not be able to tell people what to think, but they are certainly effective at controlling what people think *about*. "Corporations...have assumed unprecedented power to delimit, directly and indirectly, what takes place in the realm of public discourse." Carl Boggs, *The End of Politics: Corporate Power and the Decline of the Public Sphere*. (New York: The Guilford Press, 2000), 70.

[17] "Over the last three hundred years, corporations have amassed such great power as to weaken government's ability to control them...the corporation now dominates society and government." Bakan, *The Corporation*, 8.

[18] Drutman and Cray, *The People's Business*, 16.

[19] Ibid., 18.

[20] One of the problems the Noahide faces is dealing with issues that lack precedent in *halakhic* sources, such as laws that cover the modern corporation. According to some interpretations of Oral Law, the *halakhic* status of the corporation is that it *could* be viewed as a separate entity, although certainly not to the extent of today's modern corporations. Under Torah law, for instance, a non-locally owned and run corporation (for example, a corporation which had its headquarters relocated to a place outside the United States—such as Bermuda—in order to avoid paying taxes) would neither be allowed to open a store in a community that would severely affect smaller retailers, putting them out of business and destroying the livelihood of the owners by selling items below cost, nor use its political muscle to have legislators pass laws that would give it an unfair

order to form corporations can be beneficial for a society. In the early decades of the United States, for instance, there were many corporations that were formed for "needed turnpikes and banks and canals and insurance and other enterprises that were too massive and risky for individual businessmen to undertake themselves."[21] To keep corporations from abusing their power, each state kept "close legislative control of the chartering process" where the state charters made sure that "strict limits were placed on corporate enterprises through rules on capitalization, debt, land-holdings, and sometimes even profits."[22] These laws were needed to make sure that the corporation served the public good, and not the other way around. For over a hundred years after the nation's founding, this system would work to the advantage of a growing and youthful America. By the end of the nineteenth century, starting with the precursor to the internet, the telegraph, and the creation of the steam locomotive,[23] whose humble beginnings began a century earlier, the situation had changed.

In 1698, just ten years after John Locke had first published *Two Treatises of Government*, an English inventor with a fondness for mechanics named Thomas Savery patented the first steam pump. A decade and a half later, another Englishman, blacksmith Thomas Newcomen, improved Savery's design with an engine "that combined for the first time a piston-in-cylinder arrangement and a basic motive principle involving the formation of a vacuum within the cylinder through the induced condensation of steam."[24] The goal of these

---

advantage over smaller retailers by or getting large tax-breaks and subsidies from local city, county and state governments, effectively making local businesses pay extra taxes in order for a corporation to move in and undercut their own businesses (since the owners and beneficiaries of the corporation—the shareholders—rarely live in the communities themselves, and do not have to pay local taxes). "The nontaxpaying outsider should therefore be denied entry [into a marketplace] even if no cost advantage will result for him if he is allowed to enter." Aaron Levine, *Moral Issues of the Marketplace in Jewish Law*. (Brooklyn: Yashar Books Inc., 2006), 107.

[21] Drutman and Cray, *The People's Business*, 18.

[22] Ibid., 19.

[23] "Cheap coal, the cheap steel it made possible, and the telegraph brought dramatic changes to the landscape of America...by 1860, largely through government subsidies to the new rail companies, over 30,000 miles of track were in regular use in the United States, and the railroads were the largest and most powerful corporations the nation had ever seen." Hartmann, *Unequal Protection*, 83.

[24] F. M. Sherer, "Invention and Innovation in the Watt-Boulton Steam-Engine

inventors was to create an engine that they could market to England's coal industry. Although coal has a relatively low energy density compared to petroleum, it is more efficient than wood. Coal burned at much higher temperatures, making it ideal for the smelting of metals and the production of commodities such as brick and glass. There was plenty of coal in Britain; the problem was the vast majority of coal was deep underground where it could only be obtained by extensive underground mining, and the problem with deep shaft mining was that the shafts quickly filled with water which had to be manually pumped out, making large-scale coal mining unprofitable (as well as dangerous). The Newcomen steam engine was the first truly efficient steam engine, and it provided access to the vast seams of coal buried beneath Wales, Scotland, and North and Central England.

In 1765, a Scottish engineer named James Watt was given the job of repairing a Newcomen engine. Watt started tinkering, working on a design to improve the engine's efficiency, and four years later, Watt patented an engine with a separate condenser that was connected to the boiler by a valve, vastly improving efficiency over the Newcomen engine. When Watt's patent ran out in 1800, the rush to use the coal-fired steam engine for industry began.[25] Steam engines were put on ships, they were given wheels and put on rails, and they were put in factories to drive machines.

The telegraph also had a tremendous impact on the economy. On May 24, 1844 Samuel Morse sent the first telegraph message from Washington D.C. to Baltimore,[26] and the modern age of telecommunications began with a sputtering and sparking of electro-magnetic energy. In the span of a single generation, James Watt's coal-fueled water pump had suddenly allowed industry to produce more, faster, and cheaper; they could ship more goods in hours when it used to take days, days when it used to take weeks, and weeks when it used to take

---

Venture." *Technology and Culture.* Vol. 6, No. 2 (Spring, 1965), 166.

[25] "The 1769 patent was successfully defended against charges of invalidity, persons exploiting inventions that infringed the separate-condenser principle were prosecuted...Watt's refusal to issue licenses allowing other engine-makers to employ the separate-condenser principle clearly retarded the development and introduction of improvements." Ibid., 185–86.

[26] Ironically, Morse's first message was, "What hath God wrought," a quote from Numbers 23:23 in the English King James Bible—"Surely there is no enchantment against Jacob, neither is there any divination against Israel: according to this time it shall be said of Jacob and of Israel, What hath God wrought!"

months. With the telegraph, they could make same-day business transactions with distant towns and countries, taking orders and confirming deliveries. Britain was blessed with abundant coal, iron, copper, and other resources, allowing the British to take full advantage of its fossil fuel windfall, and the British had the will to use and develop them, and their world-wide imperial markets[27] produced a flow of capital that allowed it to build its military, particularly its navy, to a size undreamt of by the Athenians. America, with vastly greater resources, was slower to develop this coal-based technology. In the North, although some industries were using coal-based steam engines, water and animal power were still preferred, while in the South, human slaves provided the cotton that was used in Britain's growing textile industry.

As economic conditions changed during the beginning of the Industrial Revolution, there was a change in the views and attitudes towards serfdom and slavery. There was a new slave to do the heavy work: fossil fuel. The energy produced by a coal-fired steam engine could easily do the work of a hundred slaves or laborers. The Ruling Class realized that slaves were more expensive than freedmen (and certainly more expensive than coal, which could be bought for mere shillings a ton); the cost of housing, feeding, medical care—not to mention replacing those slaves who died—was greater in the long run for a slave.[28] Slaves had a tendency to eat as much as they could and

---

[27] At its imperialist peak, England—a country the size of Alabama—ruled over a quarter of the earth.

[28] "The fund destined for replacing or repairing, if I may say so, the wear and tear of the slave, is commonly managed by a negligent master or careless overseer. That destined for performing the same office with regard to the freedman is managed by the freeman himself. The disorders which generally prevail in the economy of the rich, naturally intrude themselves into the management of the former; the strict frugality and parsimonious attention of the poor as naturally establish themselves in that of the latter. Under such different management, the same purpose must require very different degrees of expense to execute it. It appears, accordingly, from the experience of all ages and nations, I believe, that the work done by freemen comes cheaper in the end than that performed by slaves." Adam Smith, *An Inquiry Into the Nature and Causes of the Wealth of Nations*, 34.

In regards to slavery being "immoral" and how we have become wise enough and moral enough to outlaw it, it is foolish to think that, even today, we have so "morally progressed" as many of the events of this past century have shown, particularly with that most civilized and advanced of peoples, the Germans, who used slave labor during the Nazi era. The discovery of fossil fuel being a more efficient form of energy than the backs of slaves no doubt had an impact on why chattel slavery was outlawed in the West. The process which Adam Smith described has been ongoing; for example,

do as little work as possible, making them an inefficient use of man-power. If the production of a worker was tied to his ability to eat—say, paying a worker a "minimum wage" or basing his pay on his produc-tion—then the worker's efficiency would be increased. The Enlighten-ment philosophers took the moral high road, condemning slavery, yet the working poor did not see their condition improve, and the choice between working twelve hours a day in a factory six days a week sim-ply to eke out a marginal existence was the reality of what the working class faced during the Industrial Revolution.

ᴄᴇᴏ

THE RAILROAD GREW into the first great modern corporation, helped by enterprising lawyers who wanted to milk the cash cow. In 1853, one eager young attorney from Illinois came up with an idea that would have grave repercussions in our economic history while he was involved in the lawsuit by the Illinois Central Railroad Company against McLean County of Illinois.[29] Although the young lawyer sympathized with the state, the railroad corporation offered him more money, so he went to work defending the railroad. When the case ended up in the Illinois Supreme Court, the young lawyer came up with a brilliant and novel defense; he claimed that "Section Two, Article Nine of the Illinois State Constitution of 1847 required 'uniform taxation' of all 'persons using and exercising franchises and privileges'"[30] and he claimed that the railroad was a "person" and therefore exempt from taxation. Although he lost the case, the enterprising young lawyer's idea took hold, and the argument for corporate personhood would continue. As for the young attorney, he continued his successful career as a corporate lawyer. Dur-ing this time, he befriended some of the employees of the Illinois Cen-tral Railroad, such as the Vice President and Chief Engineer George B.

---

having modern factory workers being "laid off" because their jobs have been taken over by new technologies such as robots. Robots are much cheaper to repair and replace than their temporary human counterparts. The laid-off worker is "free," unlike the slave. The corporation has no responsibility for him, and he can use his freedom to apply for food-stamps, free to move to a much smaller residence (since his home was probably repossessed), free to go without medical care since he and his family no longer have insurance, etc.

[29] "Illinois Central Railroad Company chose not to pay its property taxes to McLean County, Illinois, and sued the county in Circuit Court to prevent collection." Hartmann, *Unequal Protection*, 84.

[30] Ibid., 85.

McClellan as well as the treasurer, Ambrose E. Burnside. He also met a down-on-his luck veteran from the Mexican war who was looking for a job with the railroad, a man named Ulysses S. Grant.[31] When this enterprising lawyer was elected President in 1860, he would later offer these men jobs working for the Federal Government.

By the end of the Civil War, after being helped considerably by government subsidies, the corporate railroads had swollen into multi-state behemoths. Dodging federal and state regulations, they were able to charge customers whatever they wished, and they used their newly-acquired wealth to influence the state and federal legislatures and courts. Laws such as the "Contract Labor Law, which allowed employers to exchange a year's low-cost or free labor for passage and immigration from a foreign nation to the United States" had the desired effect of "[breaking] up strikes and [lowering] labor costs."[32] The Contract Labor Law also enabled the railroads to legally abscond on having to pay employees who terminated their contracts with the railroad,[33] and these pro-corporate legal victories were precursors of the manipulation of our legal system by corporate wealth.

During the last couple of decades of the nineteenth century, the character and the nature of the corporation started to change. The basis of this change was due to changes in corporate law as well as its interpretation. States realized the enormous potential of large corporations to fill state coffers through corporation fees and tax revenues, and they began a "reform" of the laws dealing with corporate charters. In 1891 New Jersey:

> Became the first state to allow corporations to buy and sell stock or property in other corporations and issue their own stock as payment, creating 'holding companies' that were crucial to the functioning of trusts…but the real watershed came in 1896, when New Jersey enacted its General Revision Act, an embarrassingly permissive law that effectively signaled the end of states' ability to regulate and control corporations through tier charters.[34]

---

[31] Ibid., 87.

[32] Ibid., 89.

[33] The Contract Law said that a corporation which broke a contract with another corporation had to pay restitution; this was not the case between a corporation and an individual, an individual who thought that they were entering into a contract as equals. "You should be extremely careful not to deceive your fellow man…the first question a person is asked when he is brought before the [Heavenly] Court is: 'Have you [always] been honest in your dealings?'" *Kitzur Shulchan Aruch*, 62:1.

[34] Drutman and Cray, *The People's Business*, 24.

Other states, rushing to get on the corporate revenue bandwagon, changed their corporate charter laws as well to entice corporations to locate in their taxable jurisdiction. Delaware won the race by passing the most lax corporate charter laws in the nation, and today "more than 308,000 companies, including 296 (59.2 percent) of the Fortune 500 largest corporations in the United States, are incorporated in Delaware"[35] providing "\$500 million a year in incorporation fees (which accounts for roughly one-quarter of state revenue)."[36] The state laws of Delaware have become, in effect, the national law as far as corporate control is concerned.

We should pause and reflect on an important point, that it was our legal system that allowed corporations to acquire the enormous political and economic clout they now enjoy, and it is our legal system which should be the focus of the problem. The first changes in the law were harbingers of things to come. In the case of *Dartmouth College v. Woodward* (argued March 10–12, 1818, decided February 2, 1819) the Dartmouth corporate charter (which had been granted by King George III in 1769) was the focus of a legal battle beset with partisan politics: "New Hampshire's newly elected Jeffersonian-Republican governor, William Plumer, and the Republican-dominated legislature determined to transform Dartmouth College by ousting what they regarded as a self-perpetuating Federalist hierarchy among the college's trustees and replacing it with trustees appointed through the political process"[37] and that "Thomas Jefferson, writing to Plumer from Monticello, supported his move; the notion 'that institutions, established for the use of the nation, cannot be touched nor modified' struck Jefferson as 'most absurd.'"[38] Yet the Supreme Court sided with Dartmouth, "establishing the sanctity of the corporate charter and striking a blow against the ability of states to repeal and revise corporate charters."[39] Dartmouth hired one of its most famous graduates, Daniel Webster, to represent their case before the Supreme Court, and "Webster's justly renowned eloquence reached new heights

---

[35] Ibid., 26.

[36] Ibid., 33.

[37] *The Oxford Guide to United States Supreme Court Decisions*, Kermit L. Hall, ed. (New York: Oxford University Press, Inc., 1999), 71.

[38] Irons, *A People's History of the Supreme Court*, 127.

[39] Drutman and Cray, *The People's Business*, 23.

and he larded his remarks with Latin phrases,"[40] most of which went over Marshall's head. The Supreme Court, led by Chief Justice John Marshall, voted five to one in favor of Dartmouth. In writing his opinion based on his personal interpretation of Article I, Section 10 of the Constitution which states that "no State shall…pass any…Law impairing the Obligation of Contracts," Chief Justice Marshall said that "it can require no argument to prove…the circumstances of this case constitute a contract."

There was an excellent counter-argument, but it was dismissed by Marshall. John Holmes, the lawyer for New Hampshire, argued that "the Contract Clause 'did not extend to grants of political power; to contracts concerning the internal government and police of a sovereign state'" such as marriage or charitable contracts, and although "there was some legal substance to this argument, and little precedent to support [the] claim that corporate charters were contracts between the state and the granters of such charters," Marshall ignored his own ruling fifteen years earlier in *Head & Amory v. Providence Insurance Company* that "a corporation 'is a mere creature of the act to which it owes its existence; its powers are only those which the legislature granted to it.'"[41] We see that, early in the court's existence, they would interpret the Constitution as protecting the rights of "those who provided capital for America's expanding corporations from political meddling in their business."[42] The rights of the lower classes—not to mention blacks, women, and children—were not as important as the rights of men of capital and property. Marshall was "pragmatic and flexible in reading the Constitution" with "Bible-thumping certitude" when the wording of the Constitution suited him, and retreating to "'general principles' of law—drawn from English common law—to justify his opinions."[43] This trend of "corporate-friendly" Supreme Court justices continued, and "Supreme Court nominations during the 'Gilded Age' in American history went to men, regardless of party, whose legal experience and

---

[40] Irons, *A People's History of the Supreme Court*, 128.

[41] Ibid.

[42] Ibid.

[43] Ibid., 131.

judicial philosophy favored the interests of business and industry"[44] including many who had themselves been corporate lawyers.

⌐∕

T HE TIPPING POINT came with the landmark decision in the relatively minor case [*Santa Clara County v. Southern Pacific Railroad Company*, 118 U.S. 394 (1886)] that forever changed the legal status of the corporation. The Supreme Court ruled:

> In an unusual preface, entered before argument, Chief Justice Morrison R. Waite[45] observed that the Court would not consider the question 'whether the provision in the Fourteenth Amendment to the Constitution which forbade a state to deny to any person within its jurisdiction the equal protection of the Constitution, applied to these corporations. We are all of the opinion that it does' (p. 396). It followed that corporations enjoyed the same rights under the Fourteenth Amendment as did natural persons.[46]

Since the members of the board of trustees could be replaced as they died or retired, the corporation could theoretically live forever, and thus acquired a power over the mere mortals of the middle and working classes. The only threat to the corporation was insolvency, and so the corporation would pursue power and wealth at whatever cost to society to insure its survival.

The most astonishing thing about the infamous *Santa Clara County v. Southern Pacific Railroad Company* case of 1886 was that it was an obscure court reporter (J. C. Bancroft Davis) who added the note to the opinion that said, "the defendant corporations are persons within the intent of the clause in section 1 of the Fourteenth Amendment in the Constitution of the United States, which forbids a State to deny to any person within its jurisdiction the equal protection of the laws." This was neither a formal ruling of the Supreme Court nor part of its decision, yet many corporate legal decisions since 1886 have revolved around this statement.[47] It was this added footnote by a mere court

---

[44] Ibid., 217.

[45] "Chief Justice [Morrison Remick Waite]...a graduate of Yale University and formerly a lawyer out of Toledo, Ohio, Waite had specialized in defending railroads and large corporations...Waite had never before been a judge in any court." Hartmann, *Unequal Protection*, 96.

[46] *The Oxford Guide to United States Supreme Court Decisions*, 274.

[47] "Of the 307 Fourteenth Amendment cases brought before the Supreme Court in the years between Waite's proclamation and 1910...288 were suits brought by corporations seeking the rights of natural persons." Hartmann, *Unequal Protection*, 105.

reporter that gave the corporations their status as a "person," and the argument that Abraham Lincoln had proposed several decades before, that a corporation was a "person," became the de-facto law of the land.

As Drutman and Cray pointed out, "one of the oddities of our corporate law system is that though most of our large corporations conduct business on national and international levels" and since "they are charted at the state level, and state laws define their operating governance,"[48] it would be a relatively easy task to control corporate behavior by threatening to revoke their state charters. However, state governments, which rely on the tremendous amount of revenue (as well as the politicians who benefit from the campaign funding from these same corporations), refuse to do so. It is easy to blame the corporations and "Big Government" for the problem, but the blame should be put where it belongs—upon our Esavian legal system that allows the corporations to wreak such financial havoc with the middle and lower classes.[49]

In the nineteenth century, when the Supreme Court was packed with former corporate lawyers or corporate-friendly judges who, unlike the judges of the Sanhedrin that followed strict halakhic guidelines for determining legal rulings, followed no such system; the Supreme Court would determine what was "Constitutional" based on their own logic, logic that was too often influenced by theological and Esavian economic concerns. As religion was replaced by "reason" during the Enlightenment, the Esavian concepts of power and domination took on new forms, and the rule by "divine right" of Christian kings morphed into the nearly-divine legal rights of a new "person:" the corporation, a wholly legal entity created by the Supreme Court.

◦◦◦

T HE 1919 CASE OF *Dodge v. Ford Motor Co.* [170 N.W. 668 (Mich. 1919)] was a landmark decision which has determined "shareholder primacy" for the past century. In this famous case, "brought by the Dodge brothers, minority owners in Ford Motor Company who challenged majority owner Henry Ford's decision not to issue a special

---

[48] Drutman and Cray, *The People's Business*, 33.

[49] "The major change taking place is a shifting of burdens off the super rich and onto everyone below them. It is a shift that began with the Democrats in 1983 and that has been increased dramatically since the Republicans won control of the House in 1995." David Cay Johnston, *Perfectly Legal: The Covert Campaign to Rig Our Tax System to Benefit the Super Rich—and Cheat Everybody Else.* (New York: Portfolio, 2005), 17.

dividend but to instead put the money back into the business to help out workers."[50] Ford explained to the court that "my ambition…is to employ still more men; to spread the benefits of this industrial system to the greatest possible number, to help them build up their lives and their homes. To do this, we are putting the greatest share of our profits back into the business." The court, however, ruled against Mr. Ford, saying:

> A business corporation is organized and carried on primarily for the profit of the stockholders. The powers of the directors are to be employed for that end. The discretion of directors is to be exercised in the choice of means to attain that end, and does not extend to a change in the end itself, to the reduction of profits, or to the nondistribution of profits among stockholders in order to devote them to other purposes.

With this ruling, exactly one hundred years after *Dartmouth College v. Woodward*, our Esavian legal system completed its transformation of the corporation from a benign economic institution into a "person" who was to maximize profits at all costs, even if it led to reducing families to poverty by laying off workers so it could outsource jobs to nations with a cheaper labor pool, pollute the environment, destroy public land, and wipe out entire communities. According to our legal system, a corporation was to maximize profits at the expense of the common good of the public.

The latest power grab came in January of 2010 in the case of *Citizens United v. Federal Election Commission*, when the Supreme Court struck down the ban on corporate limits on spending for campaign advertising. Upholding "First Amendment Rights" for the corporate "person," the Supreme Court, in a partisan 5–4 decision, allowing corporations to pay for advertising for the candidate of their choice. This gives the corporation, often with budgets in the hundreds of millions of dollars, to pay for political advertising, giving corporations a great advantage in the political process. The question is, how will corporations use this advantage? Will the corporations be benevolent, using their great economic and political power to help the less fortunate in society? Or will the corporations use their immense power to continue to influence political and thus military doctrine in order to acquire more wealth and power? Understanding the Esavian memes that influence corporate behavior as well as our legal system, it is not a difficult question to answer.

---

[50] Drutman and Cray, *The People's Business*, 111.

The Sacred and the Propane

Once upon a time, you could trace the spread of imperialism by counting up colonies. America's version of the colony is the military base; and by following the changing politics of global basing, one can learn much about our ever more all-encompassing imperial "footprint" and the militarism that grows with it...the total of America's military bases in other people's countries in 2005, according to the official sources, was 737...interestingly enough, the thirty-eight large and medium-sized American facilities spread around the globe in 2005—mostly air and naval bases for our bombers and fleets—almost exactly equals Britain's thirty-six naval bases and army garrisons at its imperial zenith in 1898. The Roman Empire at its height in 117 AD required thirty-seven major bases to police the realm from Britannia to Egypt, from Hispania to Armenia. Perhaps the optimum number of major citadels and fortresses for an imperialist aspiring to dominate the world is somewhere between thirty-five and forty.

— Chalmers Johnson[1]

SINCE THE BEGINNING OF THE INDUSTRIAL REVOLUTION, CHANGES IN economics have influenced (and been influenced by) the great political revolutions and social convulsions which occurred during this same time period along with the favorite Western Esavian economic and political pastime: war. War is vitally important to Esavian societies in many ways; it provides economic stimulus to the nations in both the booty that is taken from the losing side, as well as the fortunes made not only for financing the war with creative debt (such as Lend-Lease) but also the sale of armaments and munitions, the production and availability of which was greatly increased by the Industrial Revolution. This lesson was driven home by the American Civil War, where American industries and railroad companies made vast fortunes supplying the materials and weapons of warfare. "The Civil War demonstrated to industrialists and financiers how a standardized population trained to follow orders could be made to function as a reliable money tree...the coal-driven society was welcomed...for its potential as a wealth-maker."[2] Although America had larger coal reserves

---

[1] Johnson, *Nemesis*, 138–39.

[2] John Taylor Gatto, *The Underground History of American Education.* (New York: The Oxford Village Press, 2006), 150.

than did Great Britain, it never developed a coal economy as did the British, for America had a fossil fuel source that was more abundant, more energy efficient, and easier to produce: petroleum. This amazing substance would define the economics of not only America, but the entire world throughout the next century.

∞

In the century spanning the halcyon days between Waterloo and the first Battle of the Marne,[3] Western Esavian states reached their zenith, controlling most of the planet militarily and economically. The aggressive imperialism of Western European nations helped pave the way for the destructive wars of the twentieth century, events which eventually led to the United States becoming the dominant economic and political power (as well as the standard-bearer of Edom) during the second half of the twentieth century. Esavian hegemony was the goal that precipitated the two world wars, the true prize that the Western nations had been jockeying for position during the past few centuries: which Esavian nation would dominate and rule the earth. First Spain and Portugal, with their booty they looted from the New World, then the upstart Dutch played their hand, superseded by the English and the French, and finally, the Germans. By the end of World War II, the European Esavian nations had beaten each other bloody, and America picked up the banner that had fallen amongst their prostate Esavian brethren, and the United States marshalled its political and economic might in order to keep the banner as long as it was able. Its only competition was the Soviet Union, a state that had itself been infected with the toxic Esavian memes of Christianity and Marxism. The ideological battle between the two camps reached a crescendo in the fifty or so years following World War Two when the world writhed between these two superpowers, each with its own economic and political doctrine; one based on Marxism, the other on Jeffersonian ideas. Even the initials of the two nations—the "SU"[4] and the "US"—had an oddly tweedledee-tweedledum aspect to it.

∽

---

[3] With the exception of a few relatively localized military engagements such as the Crimean War and the Franco-Prussian debacle, the West enjoyed a relatively peaceful century (ignoring, of course, the imperial conquests overseas). The conflagration in America during the first half of the 1860s was limited to the United States.

[4] The "SU" standing for the "Soviet Union" rather than the more familiar and official "USSR," the "Union of Soviet Socialist Republics."

A̲t̲ t̲h̲e̲ e̲n̲d̲ of World War Two, the United States found itself in a position unique in world history; it was the dominant economic, political, and military power over the entire earth, exceeding even Rome during the height of its empire. Not only did the United States have a land rich in natural resources, but it was relatively untouched by the devastating war that had ground the industrial capabilities of much of Asia and Europe to powder. The American Navy had nearly complete control of the shipping lanes of the oceans, which meant it had access to all the raw materials and markets for its finished goods that it could ever dream of. Plus, America had a psychological edge; it had the ultimate weapon: the Atom Bomb.

As with other Esavian societies and states, the allure of power proved to be too great to resist, and it initiated programs designed to keep itself on top. In the early months of 1950, Paul Nitze of the National Security Council drafted a Top Secret[5] document titled NSC 68 that laid the foundation for American economic and political policy for the next several decades. Based on the paranoia of the Soviet Union's newfound nuclear capabilities,[6] NSC 68 argued for the justification of a military buildup during a time without war as preventive measures against supposed Soviet aggression.[7]

---

[5] NSC 68 was declassified in 1975.

[6] NSC 68 stated that "the issues that face us are momentous, involving the fulfillment or destruction not only of this Republic but of civilization itself."

[7] One of the major reasons the Soviet Union was paranoid about American military aggression and imperialist aims was due to the little-known, seldom-spoken-of, and hardly-ever-taught-in-the-public-school-system American invasion of Russia to support the anti-Bolshevik White Army forces during the Russian Civil War. In the closing months of World War I, elements of the U.S. Army's 85th Division (primarily the 339th Infantry) invaded Russia at Archangel, a Russian port on the White Sea about six hundred miles north of Moscow. Driving south while fighting the Bolshevik (Red army) forces, the Americans battled towards Moscow. In January of 1919, the Bolsheviks finally stopped the advance, defeating the American forces in a sanguinary battle at Shenkursk which halted the American invasion. About the same time as the Archangel invasion, another American Expeditionary force, the 27th Infantry, landed at Vladivostok in the Eastern coast of Russia, and after joining up with White Army forces, fought the Bolsheviks along the Trans Siberian Railroad. This two-pronged attack on the Red Army ended in early 1920, when American forces were finally recalled. Unlike their American counterparts, Soviet memories of this American invasion of Russia after the end of World War I were still fresh in the minds of Soviet leaders during the early years of the Cold War.

NSC 68 described "the fundamental purpose of the United States" as it "is laid down in the Preamble to the Constitution…'to form a more perfect Union, establish Justice, insure domestic Tranquility, provide for the common defense, promote the general Welfare, and secure the Blessings of Liberty to ourselves and our Posterity.' In essence, the fundamental purpose is to assure the integrity and vitality of our free society, which is founded upon the dignity and worth of the individual." After sixty years of hindsight, the true interpretation of the Constitution's preamble should have been: "To form a more perfect Military, establish technological supremacy, insure domestic obedience, provide for the uncommon defense, promote general Warfare, and secure the Blessings of Liberty to ourselves but especially our Corporate Stockholders."

In contrast to "the idea of freedom" in the United States was the purpose of the Kremlin (the Soviet government) and their opposition to "freedom." The concept of freedom was described by NSC 68 as:

> The most contagious idea in history, more contagious than the idea of submission to authority. For the breadth of freedom cannot be tolerated in a society which has come under the domination of an individual or group of individuals with a will to absolute power. Where the despot holds absolute power—the absolute power of the absolutely powerful will—all other wills must be subjugated in an act of willing submission, a degradation willed by the individual upon himself under the compulsion of a perverted faith. It is the first article of this faith that he finds and can only find the meaning of his existence in serving the ends of the system. The system becomes God, and submission to the will of God becomes submission to the will of the system. It is not enough to yield outwardly to the system—even Gandhian non-violence is not acceptable—for the spirit of resistance and the devotion to a higher authority might then remain, and the individual would not be wholly submissive.

These were powerful sentiments, yet we must look at them from the Noahide perspective. The United States is itself an Esavian culture, and although it might appear benign compared to the brutal Soviet regime, America comes up ideologically short of the Torah ideal. For example, the same year NSC 68 was drafted was the beginning of the McCarthy "witch hunts," the forced "submission to the will of the system." It also would have been difficult to find many African-Americans enthusiastic about such abstract concepts as "freedom;"

the blacks in the South who lived under the Jim Crow laws dealing with segregation (and signs everywhere saying "White Only" or "Colored Only" reminded blacks that lynching was a very real possibility if they stepped out of line) and that they were little better off than the Jews living in Nazi Germany. Even the glowing accolade given to the Constitution belied that, when the Constitution was drafted, not all in America were free; the United States in the late eighteenth century was, like democratic Athens, a slave state, and the black slaves were only considered three-fifths of a person according to the Constitution. One could argue that the Stalinist regime had massacred millions of its own people in the 1930s, but (albeit on a smaller scale) the United States had pursued similar policies in exterminating the Native American population during the nineteenth century. Seen in this light, the moral superiority trumpeted in NSC 68 was on shaky ground.

The objectives in NSC 68 made it clear that Americans "must make ourselves strong, both in the way in which we affirm our values in the conduct of our national life, and in the development of our military and economic strength. We must lead in building a successfully functioning political and economic system in the free world," or, in other words, to undertake a massive military buildup to protect the political and economic interests of the United States. The transformation of the economy of the United States into a permanent military-based economy after World War II was unprecedented in American history. With the Great Depression still on the minds of the politicians, the allure of a military-based economy (which the economists believe pulled the United States out of the Depression) proved too hard to resist.[8] As stated in NSC 68, *"a large measure of sacrifice and discipline will be demanded of the American people. They will be asked to give up some of the benefits which they have come to associate with their freedoms."* This reflects the "intent of the Framers," that economic concerns are decidedly more important than the nebulous concepts of ideas such as "freedom" and "liberty." The idea that "the rules on which we founded this nation sought, imperfectly for sure, to create individual freedom with equal justice and opportunity for all"[9] has

---

[8] "It is no secret that the billions of dollars demanded by the Pentagon for the armaments industry are necessary not for 'national security' but for keeping the economy from collapsing." Hanna Arendt, *Responsibility and Judgment*, Jerome Kohn, ed. (New York: Schocken Books, 2003), 272–73.

[9] David Cay Johnston, *Free Lunch: How the Wealthiest Americans Enrich Themselves at Government Expense (and Stick You With the Bill)*. (New York: Portfolio, 2007), 13.

turned out to be a pipe dream in a culture based on an Esavian legal and economic system. It is to the structural dynamics of this system that we now turn.

౿

AFTER ADAM SMITH and Karl Marx, the most influential figure of twentieth century economics was John Maynard Keynes, a British economist whose 1936 book *The General Theory of Employment, Interest, and Money* rivaled the popularity and impact of Adam Smith's *The Wealth of Nations* a century and a half earlier. Keynes's theory, simply put, was for governments to take a more proactive approach to the state economy[10] by using deficit spending to create jobs and boost the economy in order to reduce recessions, and to pay off the debt when the economy was robust. This system seemed a good idea at the time when oil production and manufacturing were increasing every year; as long as the nation was producing wealth, it could weather occasional deficit spending as well as keeping the wolf of economic depression and the bear of communism from the door.

In July of 1944, in the Mount Washington Hotel in Bretton Woods, New Hampshire, over seven hundred delegates from the Allied nations came together to develop a post-war economic policy. Keynes, who headed the British delegation, had a great deal of influence on the proceedings, where "during these 3 weeks and in subsequent meetings, the attendees hammered out the Bretton Woods Agreement, which created the International Monetary fund (IMF), the World Bank, and laid early foundations of the General Agreement on Tariffs and Trade (GATT), which gave birth to the World Trade Organization (WTO)."[11] As treaties were signed between the Western industrialized nations, they became the law of the land.[12] This provision was enacted under Article VI of the Constitution, where it states that "this Constitution, and the Laws of the United States which shall be made in Pursuance

---

[10] "Although Keynes's *General Theory* had immense influence on policy, orthodox economists...continued to cherish the idea that governments should not interfere with the price system." Robert Kuttner, *The End of Laissez-Faire*. (New York: Alfred A. Knoff, 1991), 4.

[11] Hartmann, *Unequal Protection*, 137.

[12] "The industrial democracies are today effectively linked in a web of binding legal agreements which regulate their mutual economic interactions." Fukuyama, *The End of History*, 283.

thereof; and all Treaties made, or which shall be made, under the Authority of the United States, shall be the supreme Law of the Land; and the Judges in every State shall be bound thereby, any Thing in the Constitution or Laws of any State to the Contrary notwithstanding." This is one of the main reasons how the Roman/Esavian law tightened its grip on international economic law, and our domestic corporations took full advantage, eventually moving our manufacturing base into countries where workers were paid a fraction of what American workers were paid. This increased corporate profits while at the same time reducing the earning capacity of American domestic workers.

Since the early 1970s, as the availability of well-paying factory jobs disappeared, it meant that both parents were forced to work longer hours for less pay in order to support their family, and this had an effect on an entire generation of "latchkey" children who often came home from school to an empty house. In the span of just a single generation, we have seen that many families have had to resort to both parents entering the workforce simply to make ends meet, and yet "once they have paid the mortgage, the car payments, the taxes, the health insurance, and the day-care bills, today's dual-income families have *less* discretionary income—and less money to put away for a rainy day—than the single-income family of a generation ago."[13] In other words, the two-income family of today makes less in real earnings than the father alone made in 1970. The loss of a living wage, forcing mothers into the marketplace to help support their families, is one of the major causes of the breakdown of our families. Men who feel that they cannot support a family, even working three low-paying jobs, will hedge at keeping a marriage together; financial quarrels are a major factor in the high divorce rate in America. This has been one of the main reasons for the recent corrosion of the family unit, the foundation of a moral and stable society.

The corrosive effect which this new "globalization" had on the family was only part of the problem; because of these new international treaties, many laws of sovereign nations were overturned:

> [Laws] banning imports of products that were manufactured with slave or child labor…laws in England and France restricting the use of asbestos…Asian laws that barred the marketing of tobacco products… laws of several European countries restricting the import of lumber

---

[13] Elizabeth Warren & Amelia Warren Tyagi, *The Two-Income Trap: Why Middle-Class Parents are Going Broke.* (New York: Basic Books, 2003), 8.

cut from old-growth forests or by environmentally destructive clear-cutting…laws proposed to reduce automobile emissions by cars… laws banning the importation of genetically modified organisms… European laws, passed by elected legislatures, that banned beef laced with hormones…were all thrown out.[14]

As we have seen, the end result was that these treaties became the law of the land, brushing aside environmental and other concerns as well as enabling the malignancy of Esavian law to spread into other non-Western nations.

Another major result of Bretton Woods was that it made the American dollar the world's "reserve currency."[15] Since the United States was relatively untouched by the carnage of World War II, America became the reigning superpower. The dollar was the most stable currency at the time, and America had the most modern and strongest military (along with atomic weaponry), the greatest economy backed by the largest gold reserves, and tremendous access to raw materals, particularly petroleum. This state of affairs ran smoothly for the next two decades; Western European nations, Japan, and Korea were markets for America's massive and diverse manufacturing base (in part thanks to the Marshall Plan, where we let war-torn Western Europe have plenty of dollars so they could turn around and buy American goods), and the extra dollars these nations accumulated could always be redeemed in gold.

By the late 1960s the first cracks appeared in the Bretton Woods system. As the United States started falling deeper into debt trying to fund both the Vietnam War as well as President Johnson's "Great Society" programs, Britain devalued the pound sterling in 1967, and foreign central banks from the now-recovered West started a run on America's gold reserves (particularly France, which as early as 1963 cashed in their surplus dollars at the rate of about thirty tons of gold a month),[16] depleting the reserves to an alarming degree, so much so that

---

[14] Hartmann, *Unequal Protection*, 147.

[15] An historic plaque at the site was erected by the state of New Hampshire. It read "In 1944 the United states government chose the Mount Washington Hotel as the site for a gathering of representatives from 44 countries. This was to be the famed Bretton Woods Monetary Conference. The Conference established the World Bank, set the gold standard at $35.00 an ounce, and chose the American dollar as the backbone of international exchange. The meeting provided the world with a badly needed post war currency stability."

[16] Kuttner, *The End of Laissez-Faire*, 61.

in 1971 then-president Nixon forsook the Bretton Woods agreement and slammed shut the "gold window." Instead of having a powerful reserve currency backed by gold, the Bretton Woods agreement was replaced by a system of floating currencies.[17] Soon after this occurred, however, the United States brokered a secret deal with Saudi Arabia (in exchange, no doubt, with continuing US reassurance to keep the House of Saud in power) to have all international purchases of petroleum made exclusively with American dollars. In other words, if nations such as Germany or Japan wanted to buy oil from Saudi Arabia, they had to pay for it with American currency. This is what kept the demand for the dollar high, and petroleum—the new "black gold"—replaced real gold in backing the dollar.

This put added pressure on America's military; not only were the United States armed forces needed for self-defense, but they had to keep the oil flowing through the overseas trade routes, protecting our economy as well as the rest of the "free" world, insuring the dollar's supremacy. The role of the military after World War II had always been to make sure the world was safe for "democracy," meaning American business. The colossal American military machine, the largest in world history, with military expenditures that cost more than the next ten largest nations expenditures combined, was put to work for corporate interests and forcibly funded by the American taxpayer.

∽

As the cost of American hegemony mounted, the tax-cuts for the corporations and the wealthy since the 1980s meant that the financial burden fell increasingly upon the working class, one of the "sacrifices" mentioned in NSC 68. This use of income tax to fund a massive military and a bloated government was, as mentioned above, unprecedented in American history. Until the Civil War, the Federal government was able to run on excise taxes and customs duties. The first income tax was a result of the Revenue Act passed in 1861, and it was a simple flat tax of three percent on all incomes over $800 a year. A year later it was modified into a two-tier system with a three percent

---

[17] "In this phase, large international banks, such as Citibank, Chase Manhattan, or Barclays Bank, in effect privatized control over monetary policy." William R. Clark, *Petrodollar Warfare: Oil, Iraq and the Future of the Dollar.* (Gabriola Island, BC: New Society Publishers, 2005), 20.

rate for incomes under $10,000, and a five percent rate for everything above. The revenue generated by this tax helped fund the Civil War; it was repealed after ten years, but the idea of using an income tax to fund military expenditures remained.

In 1890 Robert Percival Porter, the Superintendent of the census, "closed" the frontier (since there was no longer a "frontier line" that had been moving steadily westward since the end of the Civil War) and the people of the United States, for the first time in three-hundred years (when the British waded ashore at Roanoke), had run out of room. Certainly there were a few nooks and crannies here and there, but they had long been behind the frontier line, and the expansion was halted at the cool green waters of the Pacific Ocean. As with other Esavian nations, the desire to expand and conquer proved too great a temptation;[18] in less than ten years America started its imperial conquests in the aftermath of the Spanish-American War in which Esavian America wrested from Spain the control over Cuba, Puerto Rico, and the Philippines.[19] Only a few years before, the Supreme Court had struck down Congress's attempt to resurrect the income tax, but Congress outmaneuvered the Court when they passed the Sixteenth Amendment in February of 1913, allowing the taxing of income (cf. p. 500, below). In addition, 1913 saw the passing of the Federal Reserve Act later in the year, resulting in the creation of the Federal Reserve Banking System.

Despite what many people think, the Federal Reserve is not part of the Federal Government; it is owned and controlled by our corporate banking system.[20] Our nation's monetary policies are in the hands of men who are neither elected nor held accountable by our "democratic"

---

[18] "When Manifest Destiny had run its course and there was no more contiguous land to buy, annex, or conquer—the root impulse got channeled into overseas expansion." Berman, *Dark Ages America*, 103.

[19] "The centerpiece of the foreign policy strategy of William McKinley, Theodore Roosevelt, William Howard Taft, Woodrow Wilson, and Warren G. Harding [according to Charles A. Beard]…was economic expansion—exporting our economic surpluses…pushing open the doors of trade and investment everywhere, whether by polite coercion or by military force." Ibid., 101.

[20] "Since 1913, the 12 Federal Reserve Banks that handle the nation's money supply have been owned by commercial corporations (the member banks), as are all other U.S. banks, and the Federal Open Market Committee—which sets the nation's interest rates—does not allow the public into its meetings, does not publish transcripts of its meetings, and is responsible only to itself for its own budget." Hartmann, *Unequal Protection*, 40.

system; American financial control is in the hands of private corporate interests. To briefly explain the control the Federal Reserve has over the economic system, we first need to ask: what exactly is money, other than being a claim on labor and resources? If you look closely at a dollar bill (or any denomination of United States paper currency) you will see, printed across the top, "Federal Reserve Note." In smaller print on the front of the bill are the words, "This note is legal tender for all debts, public and private." This piece of paper is money simply because the Federal Government says it is, and everyone accepts it, even other nations. This is what we call *fiat* currency; money that has no intrinsic value of its own, as opposed to commodity money such as gold or silver coins. Until the mid 1960s, dimes, quarters and half-dollars were still ninety percent silver, and you could still get a dollar's worth of silver with a Federal Reserve Note (and before 1935, gold). Beginning in 1965, however, dimes and quarters were made with a nickel-copper alloy, and the silver content of the half-dollar was reduced to less than half of the content of the coin (silver dollars had not been minted since the mid–30s) until 1970, when it too was converted into a nickel and copper alloy. As Gresham's Law kicked in, the bad money replaced the good, and the silver coinage disappeared from circulation. This system of fiat currency worked fine as long as the United States had plenty of oil and a strong manufacturing base to go with its gold reserves, and the dollar was what the American government said it was: a unit of wealth.

How, then, is this wealth created? First, the Treasury Department prints up a batch of Treasury Bonds. For example, if you bought a Treasury Bond worth one hundred dollars with a stated fixed interest rate of ten percent, you would get back one hundred ten dollars in a year. These bonds are sold to other large foreign banks (such as the banks in China, Japan, the United Kingdom, Brazil, and Germany). These bonds are bought back by the Federal Reserve, which simply sends the bank with the bonds credit for the bonds. When the Fed needs currency, it sends an order to the Treasury Department to print more money. There is over eight hundred billion dollars in American currency, most of which is held by foreign banks. To pay the interest on the Treasury Bonds, the Fed simply has the Treasury Department print up more money.

On the local scale, the system of what are called "money multipliers" kicks in. After the fiat money is printed up, you then deposit money (government debt) in a bank, and under Federal law the bank can loan out up to ninety percent of your deposit. In other words, if you deposit one hundred dollars, the bank can create a loan for ninety dollars, or two loans for forty-five dollars, or three loans for thirty dollars, etc. This loan is spent, for example, on buying a ring from a jeweler, who then puts the recycled ninety dollars in the bank. Then the bank can make another loan for eighty-one dollars, or ninety percent, and that gets spent and re-deposited, and the bank makes another loan for seventy-two dollars and ninety cents, and so on. At the end of the cycle, the bank has "created" one thousand dollars—all from a one hundred dollar deposit. This is the magic of fractional reserve banking—creating money out of debt.[21] When the loans get paid back, the money "disappears." The hitch to this little scheme is that the banks charge interest on a loan, which means that there is not enough money to pay back all the loans, which means more fiat money is needed, which the Federal Reserve has printed up, which means more money to deposit, and so on. This is why our economy has to grow each year at a percentage that will allow us to create the "wealth" to pay off our interest for the Federal debt, a great deal of which is from military spending and entitlement programs.

$\sim$

F OR NEARLY ONE HUNDRED years, our Esavian economic system has tightened its grip on our beleaguered society, resulting in the transference of wealth from the bottom ninety–nine per cent of the population to the top one per cent; the economic machinery was oiled by our Esuvian legal system, allowing our gold and silver coin to be replaced with Federal Reserve Notes (corporate IOU's), the creation of the Internal Revenue Service (the Income Tax police), and slowly shifting the tax burden onto the working class. As the corporation continued its inexorable takeover of all phases of American business, the corporate workers were forced to subsidize the very corporations who were cutting their benefits, destroying their unions, and outsourcing their jobs to overseas markets. This was accomplished by the compulsory acquisition of a percentage of the working class's earnings. Our current tax

---

[21] This vast amount of money created out of thin air also calls into question the banking system's abominable practice of charging outrageous sums for overdrafts; legally, a bank can charge thirty dollars or more if you go fifty cents over the limit on your account from purchasing a three-dollar latte with a debit card.

laws have the bracket of a family making \$68,000–\$137,300 having to pay twenty-five percent of their income to the Internal Revenue Service. This means that for an average of three months out of the year, a family has to work simply to pay the government, mainly for military, past military, deficit, and entitlement programs which come to nearly three-fourths of the Federal Budget. This form of modern serfdom requires that the lower and middle classes are forced to pay for the government's massive military expenditures, the bulk of which are not so much for "defense" but to keep and maintain access to foreign markets and trade.

Because our "money" is simply debt, a claim on future labor and resources, this bodes ill for a nation that is running out of labor and resources. As the baby-boomer generation ages and retires, the outlays for Social Security and Medicare will increase to unsustainable levels since there are fewer people whose labor can be taxed. When you add the problem of our eroding manufacturing base with the tightening of credit for new business, the loss of meaningful jobs—the sort of jobs that can ensure the repayment for the claim on future labor and resources—this means that we can only sustain our economy by borrowing more "money" from other nations. This necessitates an increased military presence to assert our hegemony, and this added expense, along with our recent bail-outs to the finance sector and the automobile industry, which will supposedly be paid for with even greater taxpayer revenue down the road, will ensure that this tax burden will increase, not diminish.

The only alternatives we have to this economic conundrum are defaulting on the Federal debt or having the Fed print up more and more money triggering a steady devaluation of the dollar along with a subsequent inflation of the price of commodities. Unfortunately, the plug is about to be pulled on the continuous growth the system requires to make it work, and our economy is about to come to a screeching halt. We are heading into an event that will inevitably signal the end to the Industrial Revolution, globalization, the corporate dominance of the past century, in fact, our entire Ponzi economy: the depletion of the world's fossil fuel reserves.

Crude, Food, and Socially Unacceptable

Industrial societies have been flourishing for roughly 150 years now, using fossil energy resources to build far-flung trade empires, to fuel the invention of spectacular new technologies, and to fund a way of life that is opulent and fast-paced. It is as if part of the human race has been given a sudden windfall of wealth and decided to spend that wealth by throwing an extravagant party...but soon the party itself will be a fading memory—not because anyone decided to heed the voice of moderation, but because the wine and food are gone and the harsh light of morning has come.

— Richard Heinberg[1]

AS MENTIONED ABOVE, MUCH OF THE SOCIAL UPHEAVAL IN THE PAST two and a half centuries has been in direct correlation to the acceleration of economic output. During the period of the Industrial Revolution, Western society has been transformed from a largely agrarian into an urban industrial society. Modern intellectuals like to think that the explosive growth in technology, science, and medicine had to do with the Enlightenment throwing off the yoke of "religion" and letting "science," "reason," and "logic" guide our intellectual growth. What has actually fueled our economic boom, starting with the "industrial revolution," has been the tremendous surplus of energy provided by our use of fossil fuels such as coal, petroleum, and natural gas. The "industrial revolution" could better be described as the "fossil fuel revolution." With the creative technological uses of hydrocarbons—the blessings of cheap energy, the ability to do work—has meant that for the past three hundred years we have seen unprecedented economic growth. The advent and use of this cheap energy meant that mankind was able to create world-wide markets for the first time in its history. As world population swelled to nearly seven billion people, our markets have increased dramatically. This naturally brought about the changes in international economic law mentioned earlier.

For most of human history, the use of fuel has largely been limited to relatively inefficient sources such as wood, peat, and animal dung.

---

[1] Richard Heinberg, *The Party's Over: Oil, War and the Fate of Industrial Societies.* (Gabriola Island, BC: New Society Publishers, 2003), 6.

Although coal had been used as a fuel since the twelfth century in England, it was not until the invention of the steam engine that coal would be put to a practical industrial use. The use of the steam engine for manufacturing of textiles and the smelting of iron as well as subsequent modification for use as transportation (locomotives and steamboats) revolutionized industry. Modern machinery (in Marx's words) "is intended to cheapen commodities"[2] and that "Claussen's circular loom...though a tool when worked by hand, would, if worked by steam, be a machine...in 1735, John Wyatt brought out his spinning machine and began the industrial revolution of the eighteenth century."[3] It is the "machine, which is the starting point of the industrial revolution...constructed to be driven both by human and by purely mechanical motive power."[4] It was the invention of machines that "by the consumption of coal and water...that was urban and not, like the water-wheel, rural; that permitted production to be concentrated in towns instead of, like the water-wheels, being scattered up and down the country."[5] It was the power of fossil-fuel machines which allowed the capitalist to change the value of commodities such as cotton and linen into greater profits; the laborer who spun cotton by hand could then operate a machine that would produce many times the amount of fabric, even if the laborer was paid the same.

The idea for using distilled petroleum in the steam engine greatly accelerated its productivity, and the creative uses for this petroleum engine had a tremendous impact on modern civilization. The politics and economics of modern states are directly correlated to how these states are able to exploit fossil fuels, whether for industry, agriculture, or transportation of commodities. Our modern society revolves around the use of fossil fuels, and the use of hydrocarbons impacts every aspect of our culture.

In his book *Collapse*, Jared Diamond explained that "unintended ecological suicide—ecocide—has been confirmed by discoveries made in recent decades by archaeologists, climatologists, historians, paleontologists, and palynologists," and that the ecological damage

---

[2] Marx, *Capital*, 180.

[3] Ibid., 181.

[4] Ibid., 183.

[5] Ibid., 184.

that caused the collapse of many ancient societies can be listed into eight categories: "deforestation and habitat destruction, soil problems (erosion, salinization, and soil fertility losses), water management problems, overhunting, overfishing, effects of introduced species on native species, human population growth, and increased per-capita impact of people."[6] Diamond points out that there are other "contributing factors" that affect the collapse of a society such as "climate change, hostile neighbors, and friendly trade partners," it is "society's responses to its environmental problems" that proves "significant" to the demise of any human society.[7] One of the most gripping tales in Diamond's book is the story of the Easter Islanders, Polynesians who settled "somewhat before 900 A.D."[8] and by 1722 had managed to have chopped down every single tree on the island,[9] depleting their source of fuel and leading to the collapse of their small civilization.

The unpleasant question few dare to ask is: how sustainable is our modern culture? In 1859,[10] when the first oil well was drilled by Edwin Drake in Northwestern Pennsylvania, world population was about one and a half billion people. Current estimates of world population based on sustainable fertilizing techniques would put the top end of world population at perhaps two billion people, give or take a few hundred million. Estimates of today's (2011) world population are nearly seven billion, or over three times the amount that non-artificially fertilized food production could efficiently sustain. In 1798, the British economist Thomas Malthus published *An Essay on the Principle of Population* in which he argued that human population would someday outstrip food production. "The notion, still widespread today, that we can promote human happiness *merely* by increasing food production,

---

[6] Jared Diamond, *Collapse*. (New York: Viking, 2005), 6.

[7] Ibid., 11.

[8] Ibid., 90.

[9] Easter Island was the home to the (now extinct) largest palm tree known, a monster of a tree that had a trunk seven feet in diameter. "Most radiocarbon dates on the palm nuts themselves are before 1500, suggesting that the palm became rare or extinct thereafter." Ibid., 107.

[10] Coincidentally, 1859 was also the year that Darwin published his book *Origin of the Species*.

without a simultaneous reining-in of population growth, is doomed to end in frustration—or so says Malthus."[11] What Malthus had no inkling of was the impact of the role fossil fuels would play in the greatest population explosion in recorded history.[12]

～∽

T O PUT THE limitations of the fossil-fueled Industrial Revolution into perspective, we turn to the empirical work of Dr. M. King Hubbert, a geophysicist who taught at Stanford and MIT, and, more importantly, worked for the Shell oil company during the heyday of Big Oil. In June of 1956 Hubbert published a paper titled *Nuclear Energy and the Fossil Fuels*. In his paper, Hubbert stated that:

> The fossil fuels, which include coal and lignite, oil shales, and tar and asphalt, as well as petroleum and natural gas, have all had their origin from plants and animals existing upon the earth during the last 500 million years...when we consider that it has taken 500 million years of geological history to accumulate the present supplies of fossil fuels, it should be clear that, although the same geological processes are still operative, the amount of new fossil fuels that is likely to be produced during the next few thousands of years will be inconsequential.[13]

Hubbert based his observations on the depletion of oil fields in Ohio and Illinois, of how after a certain period from their discovery[14] and initial drilling, the oil fields would increase in production, level off, and then start to irreversibly decline. Hubbert demonstrated his theory of ultimate production-versus-time with a formula[15] which led

---

[11] Diamond, *Collapse*, 312.

[12] "Malthus was certainly correct, but cheap oil has skewed the equation over the past hundred years while the human race has enjoyed an unprecedented orgy of nonrenewable condensed solar energy accumulated over eons of prehistory." James Howard Kunstler, *The Long Emergency*. (New York: Atlantic Monthly Press, 2005), 7.

[13] M. King Hubbert, "Nuclear Energy and the Fossil Fuels." *Drilling and Production Practice*. Publication no. 95 (1956), 5.

[14] Hubbert showed that the average field peaked about forty years after discovery. Since United States oil field discovery peaked in 1930, this was the basis of his prediction for American Peak Oil around 1970. World oil field discovery peaked in the mid-1960s—forty-five years ago. There has not been a major oil field discovery in over thirty years. There are many smaller fields that have not been discovered, but they are woefully inadequate to support our growing thirst for oil.

[15] Hubbert, *Nuclear Energy and the Fossil Fuels*, 15.

him to demonstrate the rise, peak, and decline of oil fields with a bell-shaped graph.[16]

Hubbert did not say that the United States would run out of oil, but that once roughly half of the reserves (what was estimated to be in the ground) were taken out, then it would become harder and more expensive to remove the remaining oil, and that the decline of production would roughly mirror the production phase. Hubbert stated that "with due regard for these considerations, it is almost impossible to draw the production curve based upon an assumed ultimate production of 150 billion barrels…if we suppose the figure of 150 billion barrels to be 50 billion barrels too low…then the ultimate potential reserve would be 200 billion barrels…then the date of culmination is retarded only until about 1970."[17] Hubbert was mocked and his theory criticized[18] by oil company experts, politicians, and economists—in short, just about everyone. During the middle of the twentieth century the United States was awash in oil; not only was the United States the world's largest oil producer during this time, but up until the late 1940s the United States was the world's largest oil exporter, and the idea that production would go into irreversible decline in just fourteen years seemed ridiculous. Fourteen years later, the laughter stopped; Hubbert, unfortunately, was correct, and United States production did in fact peak in 1970, just as Hubbert had predicted. Rarely, if ever, has a scientist gone from crackpot to sage in so short a time.

More disturbing was Hubbert's later prediction for world-wide oil reserves,[19] that world-wide oil production would peak sometime around the year 2000, and this scenario is the reality we are living with today. The largest oil field in the world—the granddaddy of them all, Saudi Arabia's Ghawar[20]—is close to its peak, if it has not

---

[16] Dr. Hubbert first graphed his linear curve of peak petroleum in 1949.

[17] Hubbert, *Nuclear Energy and the Fossil Fuels*, 23–24.

[18] The criticism of Hubbert's theory was similar to the criticism of Robert H. Goddard's 1919 paper *A Method of Reaching Extreme Altitudes* where Goddard first proposed that a liquid fueled rocket could go into outer space and return to earth.

[19] "Ultimate world crude-oil production based upon initial reserves of 1250 billion barrels." Hubbert, *Nuclear Energy and the Fossil Fuels*, 32.

[20] "Ghawar is the greatest oil-bearing structure the world has ever known." Matthew R. Simmons, *Twilight in the Desert: The Coming Saudi Oil Shock and the World Economy*. (Hoboken: John Wiley & Sons, Inc., 2005), 151. Ghawar first started producing in 1951,

peaked already. The next three largest fields—Cantarell[21] (Mexico), Burgan[22] (Kuwait), and Da Qing[23] (China)—are all in decline, having peaked in the past few years. These four represent nearly 11% of all world oil production, which is (as of 2008) about 84 million barrels a day.

This might sound like unimportant trivia to some, but it has (and will continue to have) a titanic impact on our economy and culture. As we follow the curve of Hubbert's bell graph, in less than twenty years—2030—we will only be able to produce as much oil as we did in 1990; in 2040 we will have as much oil as we did in 1980, and so on. The problem is that our population today is much larger than it was in 1980, and, in many areas across the globe, is still growing at an exponential rate. This means the demand for oil is also greater than it was in 1980 due to the expanding economies of other large nations such as China and India. The key issue is not when Peak Oil arrives, rather, it is the inevitability of Peak Oil. It does not matter if petroleum peaks this decade or next; Peak Oil is inevitable, and the decline will be irreversible. As oil declines and demand grows, the competition for the remaining oil will undoubtedly be fierce.

The greatest impact will be on the oil-dependent economies of the West. As oil becomes increasingly more expensive and scarce, and the cost of fuel skyrockets, diesel-powered trucks will stop delivering (as independent truckers go out of business), shipping cheap electronics, toys, and clothes from the far East will become too expensive to maintain, air travel will slow to a trickle, and even that symbol of Americana, the private automobile, will be too pricey to run for all but the wealthy.

The problems with Peak Oil go far beyond gasoline being more expensive and harder to come by; many of our manufactured goods are products of petroleum. The list of products made from petroleum is staggering: most of our plastics such as ball point pens,

---

which means it is sixty years old and well past its prime. This one field accounts for well over half of Saudi Arabia's total output.

[21] Cantarell was discovered in Mexico's Bay of Campeche in 1975. It is the last of the giant (over one million barrels a day) fields ever discovered. It peaked in 2003, and its decline was spectacularly rapid; it now produces a quarter of the oil it did at its peak.

[22] Burgan, once the second largest oil producing field in the world, is in steady decline after six decades of production.

[23] Da Qing has been in production since 1960, and latest reports say its production for 2011 will drop four percent.

disposable diapers, bandages, umbrellas, synthetic cloth such as polyester, toys, furniture, car battery cases (and car interiors), fishing rods and lines, CVC pipes, trash bags, insulation for electric wiring, computer keys and casing—the list goes on and on. Practically all of our (sans canned) food comes wrapped or contained in some sort of plastic, as do other goods such as shampoo, medicine, cleaners, petroleum jelly (a petroleum product in a petroleum container), etc. It is hard to imagine a modern world without plastic. Plastic is just one product we get from hydrocarbons; petroleum is invaluable for things such as asphalt for our roads, medicines, fresh water supply and purification, insecticides, and fertilizers.

More devastating than the loss of petroleum products will be the loss of our modern agricultural system. As noted above, in 1859, when the first oil well was drilled in Pennsylvania, the world population was about a billion and a half people. This is close to the carrying capacity of the earth's ability to feed people without the aid of chemical fertilizers (such as ammonium nitrate) derived from natural gas, which comes from the same source as oil. Right now, the population of the world is nearing seven billion people, a result of our being able to produce artificial fertilizers to increase productivity as well as to process and transport the food to where it is needed. In the coming decades, we will lose the ability to feed billions of people around the world.

The link between fossil fuels, food production, industrialization and the creation of wealth is not a new topic by any means. In 1865—just six years after Drake discovered oil in Pennsylvania—a British economist named William Stanley Jevons wrote a prophetic book titled *The Coal Question*. Jevons, sounding a good deal like the modern writers on Peak Oil[24] such as Dr. Colin Campbell and Matthew R. Simmons, analyzed British coal production and depletion, and his book was peppered with statistics, charts and graphs on British coal consumption and expected reserves. In *The Coal Question*,

---

[24] "The social and political consequences to ourselves and to the world of the partial exhaustion of our mines are of a far higher degree of uncertainty than the event itself, and cannot be made the subject of argument...are we wise in allowing the commerce of this country to rise beyond the point at which it can be long maintained?" William Stanley Jevons, *The Coal Question: An Inquiry Concerning the Progress of the Nation, and the Probable Exhaustion of Our Coal-Mines*. A. W. Flux, ed. (London: Macmillan and Co, Limited, 1906), 454.

Jevons explained the importance of coal to the British economy,[25] its limited availability,[26] and the inevitable peak in which there would be an irreversible decline.[27] As with the geophysicists today, Jevons had problems with contemporary economists and politicians who soothed public fears with assurances Britain had plenty of coal for the future.[28]

Jevons was of course correct, and British coal production peaked in the early twentieth century. As with Athens and the silver mines of Attica, the peaking of Britain's coal signaled the slow and painful reversal of fortunes of the British Empire. So too with America; the quality of life in the United States for the working class has slowly deteriorated since America hit Peak Oil in 1970[29] when, after about one hundred years, real wages for working Americans stopped rising, the first result of Peak Oil which has caused serious disruption to our society.

⟋⟍

ONE OF THE painful realities we need to face is that there are no viable alternative fuels we can use to replace oil. There is nothing that comes close to the energy-rich hydrocarbons found in petroleum. As the popular example goes: think about the effort and energy required

---

[25] "Coal in truth stands not beside, but entirely above, all other commodities. It is the material source of the energy of the country—the universal aid—the factor in everything we do." Ibid., 2.

[26] "For once it would seem as if in fuel, as the source of universal power, we have found an unlimited means of extending our command over nature. Alas! No! The coal is itself limited in quantity...so that each year we gain our supplies with some increase of difficulty." Ibid., 198.

[27] "I must point out the painful fact that such a rate of growth will render our annual consumption of coal before long comparable with the total supply. In the increasing depth and difficulty of coal mining we shall meet that vague but inevitable limit which will stop our progress." Ibid., 200.

[28] "Geologists...were long ago painfully struck by the essentially limited nature of our main wealth. And though others have been found to reassure the public, roundly asserting that all anticipations of exhausting are groundless and absurd, and 'may be deferred for an indefinite period,' yet misgivings have constantly recurred to those really examining the question." Ibid., 2–3.

[29] "By 1968 income distribution was not more unequal than it had been in 1776. This all changed after 1971. Data from the Congressional Budget Office show that from 1973 to 2000, the average real income of the bottom 90 percept of American taxpayers fell by 7 percent." Berman, *Dark Ages America*, 59.

in having to push an SUV one mile. How much energy, or how many calories, would it take for you to push a car, even over level ground, for ten miles? One gallon of gas, which you can purchase for only a few dollars, can push a two ton vehicle at sixty miles an hour for ten miles. There are those who tout a hydrogen-based fuel system; unfortunately, hydrogen is not a viable replacement for petroleum since there is more hydrogen in a gallon of gas than there is in a gallon of liquid hydrogen. Moreover, as with electricity, hydrogen is a fuel carrier, not a fuel source; it takes more energy to produce hydrogen than you can get out of it. This is what is known as EROEI—Energy Return on Energy Invested. This is the problem with the touted alternatives to liquid petroleum such as oil sands, oil shale, or ethanol; if it takes one barrel of oil to produce one barrel of alternative fuel (the gas and diesel needed for mining, extraction, and transport) it is useless as a fuel source. We have hydro-electric plants, wind farms, and solar power, but you cannot fly planes or drive trucks with these energy sources, and at any rate, even if we built thousands of wind farms and solar-powered generators, it would not be nearly enough to close the energy deficit created by the peak of our fossil fuel depletion. Besides, it takes massive amounts of petroleum-based trucks and machinery to build dams, windmills, and silicon chips. It may be that our boffins and scientists will miraculously develop an alternative fuel source, say, cold fusion, but so far they have been unable to do so. Are we willing to gamble our future on such a large "*if*"?

Globalization is certain to be a short-lived concept as well. Soon it will be too expensive to ship those cheap plastic doo-dads from China and other places where they pay the workers forty-five cents an hour. We will have to do without grapes and peaches from Chile in the middle of January as food production becomes more localized. Our globalized economy is based on the availability of inexpensive non-renewable fuel such as oil, gas, and coal, and we are nearing the end of the "limitless" supply of these fuels. Yes, there are many Peak Oil deniers who say that there is plenty of oil out there "somewhere," we just have to find it, or pump more of it.[30] This train of thought is contrary to

---

[30] Many believe there are vast oil reserves in North America just waiting to be tapped if only the "environmental lobby" would allow it. The geologists disagree; no place on earth has been explored for oil more than North America, and there are simply no more great oil fields waiting to be discovered. There has also been a great deal of talk about reserves from the Alberta Oil Sands and the Bakken Oil field. These non-traditional reserves do contain vast amounts of oil, but our current technology makes their extraction expensive

the geologists who have combed the world over looking for the specific geological formations that contain oil, and this is why we are having to now drill in places such as the Arctic and in the deep ocean—there simply are no more large oil fields on terra firma to be found. Certainly there are many small ones, but building a three-million dollar oil rig to produce two million dollars in oil is simply not cost-productive. And this is all that is left out there—smaller and smaller oil fields. There have not been any large discoveries in decades,[31] and the oil companies are closing oil refineries[32] and not building more—the oil companies are well aware the end of the oil age is near. Peak Oil does not mean the end of oil, but the end of cheap oil, and with it, cheap energy as well as the ability to produce cheap electricity. Dams, coal-mining equipment, power plants and power stations, the entire physical structure of our power grid with its thousands of miles of power cables, transformers, etc., requires petroleum to build and maintain. Rolling brownouts will become more and more common, and one day the lights will go out and they will not come back on.[33] This means no more amenities such as refrigerators, air conditioning, internet, or cell phones. The Industrial Revolution has relied on several factors:

---

and difficult. Oil sands have to be dug up, transported, steam-washed (which uses a tremendous amount of energy), and the EROEI (Energy Returned on Energy Invested) ratio is, at best, very poor. Likewise the Bakken; the oil is in shale deposits rather than in sandstone. It is possible, with new drilling techniques (i.e., horizontal drilling and fracking) to extract the oil, but it is much more difficult and costly. It has been surmised that we could get as much as 500,000 barrels of oil a day from the Bakken, but considering the United States uses about twenty million barrels of oil a day, that represents only five percent of our current needs. To continue our current standard of living, America needs to find three or four Ghawar-sized oil fields to maintain the standard of living we are accustomed to, an event which is, to put it mildly, highly unlikely.

[31] Oil field discovery peaked in the mid-1960s and has been declining ever since; we are now using over six barrels of oil for every one barrel discovered.

[32] Nearly one hundred oil refineries have been taken offline in the past twenty five years, and no new refineries have been built.

[33] Dr. Richard C. Duncan introduced a theory twenty years ago called the "Olduvai Theory" which predicts that the Industrial Age will only last one hundred years, from 1930 when energy-use hit 37 percent per person, and then peaking in the late 1970s. Since then it has remained on a steady plateau, but with the immanent decline in world oil production we will soon be on the downside of the Olduvai curve. According to Duncan, electricity is the "crucial end-use energy for industrial civilization," and as blackouts become more frequent, the grid will finally come down and not come back up, signaling the end to the Industrial Age. According to Duncan, this event will occur in the next twenty to fifty years.

cheap labor, cheap resources, but most important of all, cheap energy. The implications for our society and our nation are mind-boggling. How can a complex and large nation-state such as the United States survive without the continual economic growth provided by cheap energy? How will our government and military function? What will happen to our education system or our health care system? How will our cities, with their sprawling suburbs and people living miles away from their place of employment and food production, survive?

∽

THE CIVILIZATION-CHANGING effects of Peak Oil will call for a reassessment of modern economic theory.[34] Among economists, there seems to be a lack of understanding between the correlation between an economy supported by cheap fossil fuels and economic growth, particularly the consequences of Britain's peak coal production in the early twentieth century and America's peaking in petroleum production in 1970.[35] American economic dominance in the second half of the twentieth century was not a result of our wonderful Constitution, our democratic system, or the "superior" American way of life. As with Athens and the silver mines of Laurium, our economic advantage and high standard of living had to do with the vast amount of "black gold" we were able to obtain at very little cost. In 1950, when the United States had less than seven percent of the world's population and fifty percent of the world's wealth, America was not only the world's major oil producer, it was the world's major oil exporter. For the next two decades, this steady stream of wealth and energy allowed the government to have

---

[34] "We live today in a world completely dominated by energy. It is the bedrock of our wealth." Paul Roberts, *The End of Oil*. (New York: Mariner/Houghton Mifflin Company, 2004), 5–6.

[35] "Only twice in the history of industrial capitalism has a national economy that dominated international economic affairs entered into a relative decline...the first nation to undergo this experience was Britain after achieving its peak of supremacy in the third quarter of the nineteenth century. The second was, or rather is, the United States after its turn at the top in the quarter century following World War II...the academic debate over the explanation of Britain's relative decline is far from settled." William Lazonick, "Industrial Organization and Technological Change: The Decline of the British Cotton Industry." *The Business History Review*. Vol. 57, No. 2. (Summer, 1983), 195–96.

the public subsidize the military while at the same time maintaining the highest standard of living for the working class.[36] This was the era of peak hegemony, when America was unrivaled in both economic and military power, and the main reason for this was our wealth derived from our petroleum reserves.

Of course, this largesse from our energy bonanza did not extend to minorities, but at least the blacks in the South were able to fight for their "freedom," such as the freedom to drink out of a nice refrigerated water-fountain and to order a sandwich at a restaurant as the white Edomites could do. Those living in the third-world countries that the United States was using as their new sources of food and raw materials such as oil, lumber, and bananas were not so lucky. In many of these countries—Guatemala, Iran, Chile, and Nicaragua, for example—America overthrew the governments (often democratically elected ones, at that) who dared defy Edom; i.e., they wanted to use their own land and resources for their own people, and the United States set up brutal dictatorships in order to keep their peasants in line (so much for "freedom" and "liberty;" if there was one thing America cannot tolerate in Third-World nations, it was democracy). Of course, these developments were lost on the average Americans happily dwelling in Leave-it-to-Beaverland. Americans were engrossed in raising families in the new shiny suburbs, watching television, and following their favorite sports teams, all the time fed a steady diet of "Noble Lies" about those *other* evil Esavian civilizations in Eastern Europe and Asia who wanted to take away our "freedoms," which was why we had to make economic sacrifices in order to protect the "American Way."

~

WHEN AMERICAN OIL fields peaked in 1970, our economy—already strained from funding the Vietnam War and Lyndon Johnson's social programs—took a hit when the Middle Eastern oil spigots were closed in 1973 and 1979 due to political problems.[37] When the last of the great American oil fields (Prudhoe Bay, discovered in 1968) started to

---

[36] An example would be the Federal-Aid Highway Act of 1956, a twenty-six billion dollar public works project designed to facilitate military movement within the United States. This massive project was funded through taxes on gasoline as well as taxes on other items such as automobiles and tires.

[37] The 1973 oil "crisis" was yet another example of how anti-Semitism affects us; the Arabs embargoed oil to America over its role in helping Israel in the Yom Kippur War.

pump at full capacity, our economy received a boost in the early 1980s as oil prices plummeted. This boost was deceptive, however; with the election of Ronald Reagan, the energy-conservation measures that were put in place by his predecessor Jimmy Carter were ignored or tossed out. Further long-term economic damage was done with the systematic destruction of unions (beginning with the emasculation of the Air Traffic Controllers Union by Reagan in 1981) as well as the dismantling of our manufacturing base.[38] Tax cuts for the wealthy (and more importantly, the corporate interests) shifted an ever increasing amount of the tax burden to the working class while at the same time plunging the nation into enormous debt by massive borrowing from foreign nations.[39] America's debt went from nine hundred billion when Reagan took office to four and a half trillion after twelve years of the Reagan-Bush presidencies, and now stands at an unbelievable fifteen trillion dollars with no sign of it reducing anytime soon, if ever.

One of the "Noble Lies" propagated by the Reagan-Clinton-Bush era was the myth of *laissez-faire* capitalism,[40] the idea of an economy that "regulates itself" without government interference.[41] The gospel of "supply-side" economics[42] was all the rage, and Reagan and his

---

[38] "In official statistics, the finance, insurance, and real estate (FIRE) sector of the U.S. economy swelled to 20 percent of the gross domestic product in 2000, jumping ahead of manufacturing, which slipped to 14.5 percent." Kevin Phillips, "*American Theocracy*. (New York: Viking, 2006), 245.

[39] In regards to ancient Rome, Parenti said that "rather than contributing to the commonweal, the wealthy fed off it. They avoided paying rents for the public lands they or their forebears had expropriated…the money they lent to the state was paid back to them with interest from funds the state raised by taxing less privileged populations at home and abroad. This system of deficit spending—of borrowing from the rich and paying them back by taxing poor commoners—amounted to an upward redistribution of income much like the kind practiced by indebted governments today, including our own." Parenti, *The Assassination of Julius Caesar*, 52–53. The debt incurred by the United States government in the past thirty years—now over fifteen *trillion* dollars—is the result of massive borrowing and spending while at the same time cutting taxes for the rich.

[40] Even Max Weber described capitalism as a system of "masterless slavery." Cf. Weber, *Ancient Judaism*, xi; Weber, *Economy and Society*, 1186.

[41] "The promised solution was to get government out of the way—to let business operate largely free of public oversight in the form of government programs, rules and regulations…'government is not the solution,' Reagan famously declared as the battle cry of his revolution. 'Government is the problem.'" Johnston, *Free Lunch*, 9.

[42] "The supply-siders preached an odd mixture—an almost Keynesian gospel of growth stimulated by lower taxes, along with an extreme faith in the genius of unregulated markets." Kuttner, *The End of Laissez-Faire*, 84.

obedient Congress busied themselves with tax cuts, military build-up, and cutting social programs. The problem with *laissez-faire* is that it goes against the teaching of the Torah;[43] that since the economy is dominated by those who have property and capital, the idea of *laissez-faire* is euphemistic of letting those with wealth and power dictate what the economy does,[44] and the Torah puts strict controls on wages and prices[45] to ensure that abuses of economic power do not materialize.[46]

The result of the Reagan/Bush-style economic philosophy that has held America in sway was, as with Roman model, wealth redistribution from the bottom ninety-nine percent of the population to the top one percent that has gone unabated in the past three decades. The legal fleecing of middle and lower-class America from "a quarter century of tax cuts has produced not trickle-down economics, but Niagara-up."[47] American society at the beginning of the twenty-first century

---

[43] "Even before the publication of Adam Smith's *Wealth of Nations* in 1776, various Protestant denominations had advocated the separation of morality from economics. With these inducements to laissez-faire, greed was given a moral license." Eidelberg, *Demophrenia*, 22.

[44] "We do not live in a laissez-faire economy in which there is no interference from government and people are allowed to do as they please, operating the economy by making contracts with one another. We have rules…the richest Americans and the corporations they control shaped and often wrote these new rules and regulations under which our economy now functions." Johnston, *Free Lunch*, 13.

[45] "The Rabbis regarded the raising of prices above their actual value as a serious threat to the economic welfare of the public. They explained that the Psalmist's prayer 'Break the arms of the wicked' [Psalm 10:15] had reference to those who raised prices and thereby oppressed the poor [cf. *Megillah* 17b, *Bava Batra* 90b]." Lew, *The Humanity of Jewish Law*, 184.

[46] "Amid business dealings and the exchange of goods and products, the Law extends love and love's requirements. It forbids the strict carrying on of right where this could lead to oppression and cruelty, or even to the enslavement of free men who possess little or no wealth. It forbids the creditor to seize the widow's goods. It forbids the invasion of privacy and the seizure of work tools. It commands the creditor to behave with kindness and consideration in the administration of the laws governing debts." Hirsch, *Collected Writings*, Vol. I, 219.

[47] Johnston, *Perfectly Legal*, 2. The problem our form of debt/wealth creation is that there is a constant drain of wealth due to the structure of our modern corporate economy. Back in the pre-corporate day, local businesses would deposit money in local banks, which served local customers. Now, with corporate headquarters far removed from local cities and towns, the "money" spent at corporate chain stores flows out of the community and into the coffers of corporate accounts far away, so that "money" is not recycled in the community.

is beginning to resemble, albeit in a more complex way structurally, the feudal system of the Middle Ages in Europe. The American working class has been transformed into an economic serfdom by means of the Federal Income Tax, which is used to collect a portion of the American worker's income to fund its military expenditures as well as to subsidize corporate interests. The tax brackets run from ten to thirty-five percent, which means that, depending on your income, anywhere from five to eighteen weeks of the American serf's yearly labor are taken by the government, much like the Medieval serf who had to spend a good portion of his time working his landowner's fields or giving a portion of his income to the landowner. Most of the services we associate with taxes—schools, waste and sewage, road and highway maintenance, etc.—are from state and other local taxes such as property taxes, sales taxes on commodities such as gasoline, state taxes, and so forth.

To give a recent example of how our Esavian legal system is different from the Torah, in early 2010 seventy–four teachers and nineteen school administrators (including the principal) were fired at Rhode Island's Central Falls High School for their refusal to work longer hours with little extra pay. The issue is not that the teachers in Rhode Island are among the highest paid in the country (average pay is $54,000) but that the law allows the school board to fire teachers—many of whom have their own families to support[48]—for refusing to work extra hours for nothing, a clear violation of Torah law.[49] This is symptomatic of the plight of the American working class; as wages for the bottom ninety percent of Americans have remained stagnant (or have actually fallen due to inflation and higher costs

---

[48] "According to a Talmudic ruling the workman's wages must be adequate for his family's needs. (Keuboth 105a)" Lew, *The Humanity of Jewish Law*, 144.

[49] "Workmen's wages were fixed by the authorities who safeguarded the employees' standard of life. There were also regulations as to the hours of labour and other rights. In some communities rules were laid down by unions of artisans who were permitted to call a period of rest (strike) in defense of their rights. (Tosefta Baba Metzia 11,25; Baba Metzia 77a) The working hours were also fixed. The time taken up by the workman in going to the place of labour was included in the working hours but not the time needed by the labourer to return to his home. (Baba Metzia 63b) Even if the employer paid the workman more than the usual rate of wages he was not allowed to make him work longer hours. If longer hours were specially agreed it implied that the increase was for his skill in executing better work and not in respect of longer hours. (ibid. 83a)" Ibid., 143–44.

in areas such as medical expenses), they are forced to work longer hours for the same pay.[50]

⁓

Iғ Peak Oil is such a major issue, why have we not heard more about it? The answer is that our corporate-owned media does not want people to know about Peak Oil. If knowledge of Peak Oil was more widespread, people would be reluctant to purchase those SUV's and suburban dream homes, since the vast majority of these people would be taking out loans to buy these items, the creation of wealth would be curtailed and our economy (i.e., the corporations) would suffer. Since our media (television, radio, newspapers, magazines, etc.) get most of their revenue from corporate advertising, corporate reticence on the issue of Peak Oil is not surprising.[51]

As noted above, the Peak Oil crisis will soon force us to rethink popular economic theories such as those of Marx and Keynes. As energy becomes more expensive, markets will shrink, production will dwindle, and capital will melt away as our increasing and overwhelming debt puts an end to continuous economic growth. Since we took the dollar off the gold standard and hooked its fortunes to the oil pump, the repercussions of Peak Oil will have a devastating effect on our economy when the other nations stop buying oil with dollars and start dumping greenbacks on the market. As the dollar dances down the happy trail of devaluation, America's massive foreign debt will suddenly make its treasury bonds look unattractive to foreign investors, and America's creditors will start selling them off (as China has already started to do) in an international going-out-of-business sale.

We have seen that Peak Oil (as well as peak coal, peak uranium, peak phosphate, and so on) is not too far off in the future if it is not here already; crude oil production has hit a plateau since 2005, and we can expect a permanent and irreversible decline very soon.[52] Our

---

[50] "The work year for the typical American has lengthened by 184 hours since 1970... an additional 4½ weeks on the job." Hartmann, *Unequal Protection*, 265.

[51] "Businesses spent some $214 billion in the United States on advertising in 1999—some 2.4 percent of the GDP—and almost all of this money ended up in the hands of some media firm." Nichols and McChesney, *It's the Media, Stupid*, 31.

[52] World oil production peaked in July of 2008 at 84 mbd (million barrels a day) when oil was $147 a barrel, and OPEC and other oil producers were pumping full-tilt to take advantage of the high prices. Production a year later had fallen to 82 mbd.

fiat-currency, debt-fueled, military-industrial economy is based on the future productivity of working Americans, and that does not bode well for a nation lacking the energy for continuous growth. America will become less and less able to support and sustain its opulent lifestyle, let alone pay back its massive debt. As the Industrial Age eventually winds down, we will eventually be forced back to a pre-industrial level of society, and the capitalistic factory system which Marx based his theories on will be a thing of the past, a mere blip in the long saga of human history.[53] There are no more virgin continents to plunder. We have dug up most of the gold, platinum, copper and other metals we need for our industrial and economic way of life, paved over great swaths of farmland with petroleum goo, drained our aquifers, replaced our natural diversity of grains and vegetables with Monsanto frankenberries, and depleted our once abundant fish stocks such as cod and tuna (and what fish we have left we have poisoned with petroleum, pesticides, and mercury). As economic collapse intensifies, the coming end of the fossilized fuel economy will impact us on a global scale, particularly in food production. Since our planet cannot support more than a billion and a half people—two billion tops—without the cheap fossil fuel fertilizers we depend on to grow our crops, humanity will be culled, and there will doubtless be wars fought over the shrinking resources of our tiny planet.[54] We could go the way of the Easter Islanders and chop down the last available timber and dig up the last of the coal, but that will only buy us a few decades and make the planet unlivable for future generations. This is not the gloom and doom "end of the world" hysteria that has been propagated by religious quacks, but the glum realities postulated by our scientists, realities ignored by our economists and politicians who simply want the fossil fueled party to continue, oblivious to the problems caused by our squandering of finite resources. We are not only faced with change we can believe in,

---

[53] Conflict theory is only applicable to the Esavian class conflict whose value structure is based on wealth; in a classless society such as one based on the Torah, conflict theory does not apply.

[54] "We like to think that our human intelligence and moral codes set us apart from other organisms. When other creatures gain an energy subsidy, they instinctively react by proliferating: their population goes through the well-studied stages of bloom, overshoot, and die-off...so far we have reacted to the energy subsidy of fossil fuels exactly the way rats, fruit flies, or bacteria respond to an abundant new food source." Heinberg, *The Party's Over*, 240.

but change that will be forced upon us in many nasty unpleasant ways. We will come to the realization that our experiment with our modern version of capitalism is about to come to an end. For all of our talk about how much we have progressed since the Enlightenment, of how wonderful our scientific advances have been, about how proud we are to have such a fine democratic system, we need to look at it from a Torah perspective. For all our achievements, who truly has benefitted? Most of the world toils in poverty, living in crude huts without access to fresh water, subsisting on just a few dollars a day. The lifestyle of the industrialized West has long been different from the lifestyle of those living in Haiti, or in the Indian states of Orissa and Bihar, or in the mountains of Nicaragua, or the dry plains of Ethiopia, but that will soon change.

～

W HAT THE REPERCUSSIONS of "peak energy"[55] mean for us is that the Torah is about to become relevant again (not that it was ever irrelevant, it was simply perceived so). We are about to revert back to an agrarian society, not out of choice, but out of necessity. The laws in the Torah dealing with livestock, plowing, reaping, harvesting, land boundaries, life revolving around the family and the community with small farms and craftsmen—all of these things that we look as quaint and outmoded in our modern lifestyle are about to re-introduce themselves. Our wealth will soon be measured in goats and sheep, in grain and flax.

Intellectuals do not take into account the problems facing our modern culture. Sam Harris glibly prophesized that "two hundred years from now, when we are a thriving global civilization beginning to colonize space…"[56] making one question who are the ones that are putting their faith into myths; Harris should spend less time watching *Star Trek* and more time watching *Soylent Green*. The same goes for intellectuals such as Fukuyama who said that "democracies do not fight one another, then a steadily expanding post-historical world will be more peaceful and prosperous"[57] and that "the fundamentally unwarlike character of liberal societies is evident in the extraordinarily

---

[55] Peak oil (which is, according to some geologists, already upon us), peak coal (not too far down the road), and peak electricity (which is dependent on oil and coal). We will be in a permanent energy decline sometime in the next few decades.

[56] Harris, *The End of Faith*, 47.

[57] Fukuyama, *The End of History*, 280.

peaceful relations they maintain among one another."[58] We shall see just how un-warlike modern Esavian democracies are when the oil spigots start going dry and the nations start to scramble for the last remaining barrels of oil.

What are we, the American people, going to do about this situation? The bad news is, there really is not much we can do. Without any viable solutions being presented to our imminent energy depletion, we are fast running out of options. Many of those who talk about the coming economic meltdown are saying things such as "buy gold!" Unfortunately, for the majority of working Americans who live check to check and hand-to-mouth, this is not a realistic option. As our economy slowly shuts down (or quickly, depending on unforeseen variables such as war, terrorist attacks, or some natural catastrophe) the United States as we know it will cease to be. Certainly our opulent, energy-rich lifestyle will forever be a memory, but when our government goes bankrupt, it will have to lay off most of its employees. We will be without police, fire departments, sanitation crews, water works, schools for our children and a host of other things which we take for granted.

T HE MOTTO OF the "supply-side" economist can be summed up as "production is based on demand." Actually, production is based on cheap fossil-fuel energy, something which is not going to be around too much longer no matter how much we demand it. We are on the brink of a Depression that will be much worse than the "Great Depression" of the 1930s, the main reason being that peak oil discovery in America was in 1930 when we were on the upside of the energy curve. The forty years of cheap oil that America was able to produce from 1930 to 1970 is what fueled our recovery and led to America becoming the economic powerhouse of the twentieth century. We are now on the wrong side of the energy curve, not only here in America, but in every industrialized nation on earth which will have to deal with ever-dwindling supply of oil. We could switch to coal for a time, but that too is a finite resource, and increasing coal use will no doubt exacerbate environmental problems such as climate change.

We must understand the rabbinic lessons of the generation of the Flood, the destruction of Sodom, the near-destruction of the city of

---

[58] Ibid., 262.

Ninevah (prevented at the last moment by Yonah's unwilling intervention) were all due to *robbery*, or violation of the Noahide Law of
theft. The Noahide Law of theft[59] covers a broad range of laws in the
Torah: laws of business, commerce, property, buying and selling and
so forth—much of what we would view as the secular discipline of
economics. It should be pointed out, however, that in all the economic
theories such as Marx's theories of economics and class conflict, there
is one viewpoint that has been missing: the link between fossil fuel use
and the Industrial Revolution.

The only viable contingency plan we have is the Torah. In order for
our culture, our society, indeed, our civilization to survive is for us to
rid ourselves of the legal and economic system of Edom the way we rid
ourselves of the Greek and Roman gods such as Zeus, Apollo, Mars, and
Jupiter. We need a system to identify and remove the harmful elements in
our culture that hamper justice and morality. The destructive ideologies
such as patriotism and nationalism have joined forces with organized
religion to create much of the warfare[60] and misery that has flared across
the earth during the last century. Our worship of our man-made "Constitution" and our artificial nation based on this document is one of the
major obstacles for implementing the Noahide Law in our society. We
can thump our Bibles and say "God is with us," but that is no more a
guarantee than it was for the German soldiers who wore their *Gott mitt us*
belt buckles as they herded the Jews into the cattle cars. This is why it is
important to understand the broad scope of the Torah instead of the narrow individualistic view; a Noahide who boasts that they no longer worship Jesus, yet is imbued with patriotic fervor and loudly supports their
government to wage war on distant lands in order to secure the petroleum
lifeline to their consumerism, supporting a policy that has governments
in places such as Guatemala and Chile overthrown in order to supplant
freely elected leaders with despots and dictatorships loyal to American
business interests, is a Noahide guilty of idolatry.

---

[59] The famous "*Thou shall not steal*" from the Ten Commandments is a prohibition
of kidnapping.

[60] The Esavian viewpoint is expressed by Hellmuth von Moltke, who said that:
"Perpetual Peace is a dream—and not even a beautiful dream—and War is an integral
part [*ein Glied*] of God's ordering of the Universe [*Weltordnung*]. In War, Man's
noblest virtues come into play [*entfalten sich*]: courage and renunciation, fidelity to
duty and a readiness for sacrifice that does not stop short of offering up Life itself."
Helmuth von Moltke, quoted in Arnold J. Toynbee, *War and Civilization*. (New York:
Oxford University Press, 1950), 16.

There are those who protest against any criticism of America, pointing out that America was a haven for the Jews who were victims of European persecution. It is true that, in the late eighteenth century, America let the Jews enjoy a religious freedom which the nations of Europe had suppressed. But we should not forget the lessons of the Torah, that "a new king rose up over Mitzrayim, who knew nothing of Yosef,"[61] and however benevolent a nation's intentions are in the beginning, these attitudes of tolerance can quickly change, particularly if that nation's government is not based upon Torah.[62]

❧

THE AVARICE WHICH is so ubiquitous in Esavian society is not simply based on a desire for leisure and luxury; the turmoil in Western society stems from the Esavian relationship between justice and wealth, and that for the poor, there is no justice. In Edom, money is power, justice can be bought, and the "Golden Rule" for Esavian society is *he who has the Gold makes the Rules*. The solution for the ills of our society lies outside the paradigms of Greco-Roman culture and philosophy. It requires a serious reassessment of our foundational values and understanding of law, justice, and property.[63] It is to this solution we now turn.

---

[61] *Shemos* 1:8.

[62] "If they were to consider how, amidst the degeneration of ancient societies, the people of Israel had been given a law whose standards of justice, humanity and morality were so infinitely superior not only to the political systems existing at that time but also to those that have arisen since then, would such comparative studies not afford added documentary proof that this Law is indeed of Divine origin?" Hirsch, *Collected Writings*, Vol. VII, 97.

[63] "Judaism measures the worth of an individual not in terms of his material wealth or intellectual prowess but, above all, in terms of his obedience to the laws of morality... Judaism believes that a truly viable state cannot be founded solely on collective power or individual need; it must be based on a sense of duty shared by all and on a universal respect for human rights. Judaism sees spiritual enlightenment and moral ennoblement, resulting in personal and national lives founded on duty and mutual respect, as goals shared by all men and nations. Judaism views the course of history as a path upon which God guides all men and nations toward this ultimate goal... of course, an interpretation of history based on our Jewish perception of man and humanity would not find much favor with those whose personal or national motto is 'the survival of the fittest.' Originally applied to scientific phenomena in organic life, this slogan is often employed nowadays to justify the attitudes and actions of certain individuals and nations. Indeed, there are some who say that 'the survival of the fittest' describes the only realistic motivation for any action on the part of a person, a group or a nation. Carried to its logical conclusion, such an attitude would have to regard ruthlessness and the use of violence for selfish ends as the ideal of human greatness." Ibid., 270–71.

Part Three

❧

Lessons from Moriah

Overview

His ignorance was as remarkable as his knowledge. Of contemporary literature, philosophy and politics he appeared to know next to nothing. Upon my quoting Thomas Carlyle, he inquired in the naivest way who he might be and what he had done. My surprise reached a climax, however, when I found incidentally that he was ignorant of the Copernican Theory and of the composition of the Solar System. That any civilized human being in this nineteenth century should not be aware that the earth travelled round the sun appeared to me to be such an extraordinary fact that I could hardly realize it.

"You appear to be astonished," he said, smiling at my expression of surprise. "Now that I do know it I shall do my best to forget it."

"To forget it!"

"You see," he explained, "I consider that a man's brain originally is like a little empty attic, and you have to stock it with such furniture as you choose. A fool takes in all the lumber of every sort that he comes across, so that the knowledge which might be useful to him gets crowded out, or at best is jumbled up with a lot of other things, so that he has a difficulty in laying his hands upon it. Now the skillful workman is very careful indeed as to what he takes into his brain−attic. He will have nothing but the tools which may help him in doing his work, but of these he has a large assortment, and all in the most perfect order. It is a mistake to think that that little room has elastic walls and can distend to any extent. Depend upon it there comes a time when for every addition of knowledge you forget something that you knew before. It is of the highest importance, therefore, not to have useless facts elbowing out the useful ones."

"But the Solar System!" I protested.

"What the deuce is it to me?" he interrupted impatiently: "you say that we go round the sun. If we went round the moon it would not make a pennyworth of difference to me or to my work."

— Sir Arthur Conan Doyle[1]

Iɴ ᴛʜɪs ᴀᴍᴜsɪɴɢ ʙᴀɴᴛᴇʀ ʙᴇᴛᴡᴇᴇɴ Sʜᴇʀʟᴏᴄᴋ Hᴏʟᴍᴇs ᴀɴᴅ ʜɪs ɢᴏᴏᴅ friend Dr. Watson (from the beginning of Sir Arthur Conan Doyle's novel *A Study in Scarlet*), Holmes explains the principle of learning how to differentiate between the vital and the unnecessary, while his colleague Dr. Watson is astonished at Holmes's apparent lack of knowledge of certain facets of modern science. Yet, what the deuce does modern science have to do with the morality and ethics of the Torah?

---

[1] Sir Arthur Conan Doyle, *The Original Illustrated 'Strand' Sherlock Holmes*. (Ware, Hertfordshire: Wordsworth Editions, ltd., 2001), 15.

    Science is certainly an important subject, but intellectuals such as the
atheist Richard Dawkins, like the exasperated Dr. Watson, believe that
science is the ultimate in knowledge, and that religion "teaches us not to
change our minds, and not to want to know exciting things that are available to be known."[2] Yet Dawkins and his ilk do not seem to grasp that
there are more important things to learn other than how many molecules
of *RNA* can dance on the head of a pin. As Susan Jacoby explained,
"the job of higher education is not to instruct students in popular culture
but to expose them to something better,"[3] but Jacoby then myopically
states that our schools of higher education should "offer a course in
which students are required to read *Crime and Punishment* and *Wuthering Heights*, and they may come to understand why *Friday the 13th* and
Stephen King's novels are not worthy objects for deconstruction."[4]
From the Noahide point of view, courses in Rabbi S. R. Hirsch's commentary on the Torah and the *Séfer haHinnuch* are what should be required, and then students would see that make-believe fantasy novels of
modern Esavian popular culture, novels such as *Crime and Punishment*
and *Wuthering Heights*, are, by comparison, "not worthy objects for deconstruction." Esavian literature, no matter how entertaining or well-
written (as well as subjects such as mathematics and astronomy), are the
"condiments of wisdom," not the main course.[5] To suggest that we can
learn morality from bawdy sexual puns and innuendo, as Christopher
Hitchens claims ("Shakespeare has much more moral salience than the
Talmud")[6] shows a disturbing lack of understanding of the mores and
values of Torah. The dismissal of Torah because, according to Dawkins,
"it actively debauches the scientific enterprise"[7] is a misrepresentation
of Torah and of rabbinic logic, neither of which are "anti-science." The
modern intellectual's disdain of religion and of the Bible is that, in their
argument, religion is devoid of reason.[8]

                                    ౷

---

[2] Dawkins, *The God Delusion*, 321.

[3] Jacoby, *The Age of American Unreason*, 314.

[4] Ibid., 315.

[5] *Avot*, 3:23.

[6] Hitchens, *god is not Great*, 151.

[7] Dawkins, *The God Delusion*, 321.

[8] "The Enlightenment's insistence that reason be applied to all inherited dogmas and its plea
for toleration did not eradicate [anti-Semitism]." Marvin Perry and Frederick M. Schweitzer,

As Sir Arthur Conan Doyle's fictional character Sherlock Holmes pointed out, what difference does it make whether the sun goes round the earth or the earth goes around the sun in terms of how people can live together in a peaceful and just society?[9] It mattered not to the simple shepherds and farmers who lived over three thousand years ago, and the knowledge of modern astronomy gives no solace today to the young widow who has been laid off work and was kicked out of her apartment, wondering how she will care for and feed her children. What good is our knowledge of genetic biology that enables us to produce more productive strains of grain when children in Haiti are being fed "cookies" made from mud because the economy of Haiti has collapsed, and there is no food to buy, genetically modified or not? Exactly what use is the knowledge of the genetic differences between the North American wapiti and the European red deer for people in Ethiopia, Somalia, or Alabama who helplessly watch their children sicken and die because of the lack of some inexpensive medicine or nutritional supplements that are unavailable or denied them? It is not that science is unimportant, but we must put our priorities in order. It is not simply a matter of integrating the prodigious amount of secular knowledge that has been amassed into a Torah-based structure; if we do not use science for the betterment of the human condition, exactly what good does our scientific knowledge do for us? Our culture is deficient in justice and morality, not science.

The failure of our educational system to teach morality and its prioritizing of Esavian values[10] was explained by Rabbi S. R. Hirsch:

> Those who are truly concerned about human welfare are fully aware that the attainment of the human mind will not achieve its complete potential as long as it does not enjoy a substantial increase in human happiness. They will not permit exultation even over the most

---

Antisemitism: Myth and Hate from Antiquity to the Present. (New York: Palgrave Macmillian, 2002), 73.

[9] "Science teaches us that the earth goes around the sun, rather than the sun round the earth. Does it really matter which is the case?" Samuel, *You Gentiles,* 158.

[10] "Schooling through the eighteenth and nineteenth centuries (up until the last third of the nineteenth) heavily invested its hours with language, philosophy, art, and the life of the classical civilizations of Greece and Rome." Gatto, *The Underground History of American Education,* 11.

brilliant intellectual achievements of the present century to drown out the cries of distress from those who rightly feel cheated of their life's happiness. Those who are concerned about human welfare must surely have asked themselves certain questions, particularly about their schools, which should be the nursery of all man's hopes for the future. For instance: Is the educational work on behalf of our young, as carried on nowadays primarily by our schools, of such quality that it can truly help promote the welfare of the next generation? Do our schools give due attention to all the factors on which man's true happiness depends? Is it possible, perhaps, that our schools have put too much emphasis on practical skills and theoretical knowledge, on the physical and intellectual development of their students, while ignoring a fundamental component of education? Could it be that the ever-growing demands in the area of technical knowledge and skills are forcing our schools to concentrate almost exclusively on these fields, and that, as a result, our schools are in danger of losing sight of some basic elements, either permitting them to atrophy entirely or using teaching methods that will actually work against them? We are referring to elements which, irrespective of theoretical knowledge and practical skills, will indeed enable our sons and daughters to attain that measure of happiness which is the birthright of every human being by the Will of the merciful Father of all mankind. Is not the striving for morality at least as important as theoretical knowledge and practical abilities? In the final analysis, is not our life's happiness dependent on whether or not we use all our knowledge and skills for moral purposes?…What will become of our children if they are taught how to solve every conceivable practical problem they might face in life, but hardly any time in their course of studies is given to the problems of making the right moral choices?"[11]

It is clear that our educational system is designed to indoctrinate youth into the Esavian system and the Esavian mode of thinking, to substitute Torah values with those of greed and avarice, that *you, too, might acquire enough wealth and power to lord it over others as you live a life of sloth.* In his book *The Underground History of American Education*, John Taylor Gatto explained the development and priorities of how "public" education developed in America, based on the Prussian[12] system, and that "in the last third of the nineteenth century, a loud call for popular education arose from princes of industry, from comfortable clergy, professional humanists and academic scientists,

---

[11] Hirsch, *Collected Writings*, Vol. VII, 47–48.

[12] "The Americans were the first other people in modern history to follow the Prussian example in establishing free common-school systems." Hofstadter, *Anti-Intellectualism in American Life*, 299.

those who saw schooling as an instrument to achieve state and corporate purposes."[13] The leaders of the Esavian system decided to make it *public* education, which meant that the taxpayer would shoulder the costs of training the corporate workforce.

The first step in transforming our Esavian-based culture to a Torah-based one is to focus on education[14] from kindergarten on up to the graduate level. Structuring academic disciplines on the Torah would give all disciplines the proper moral and legal framework as "our Sages have declared: 'Without intellectual education there can be no moral education; without moral education there can be no intellectual education'" [*Pirke Avot* 3:21].[15] Our reluctance in implementing Torah in our present educational system comes from the intellectual resistance to anything "religious" in "secular" academics. Our public schools are based upon teaching the Esavian culture, and it is "an essential support system for a model of social engineering that condemns most people to be subordinate stones in a pyramid that narrows as it ascends to a terminal of control."[16]

ﻉ

THE EMPHASIS ON science and technology, the fruits of Greek and Roman culture, was a deliberate attempt at social control brought about through the creation of wealth due to the use of inexpensive fossil fuel energy, and as our schools turned towards science and technology to be used to create more wealth, money was diverted to schools that produced engineers and scientists rather than teachers of Torah.[17] Not only has our education system kept Torah off of the intellectual menu, they have tried to keep Jews themselves out

---

[13] Gatto, *The Underground History of American Education*, 141.

[14] "'Create schools! Improve the schools you already have!' This is the call we would pass from hamlet to hamlet, from village to village, from city to city; it is an appeal to the hearts, the minds and the conscience of our Jewish [and Noahide] brethren." Hirsch, *Collected Writings*, Vol. VII, 3.

[15] Ibid., 53.

[16] John Taylor Gatto, *Dumbing Us Down*. (Gabriola Island, British Columbia: New Society Publishers, 2005), 13.

[17] "After the Civil War, utopian speculative analysis regarding isolation of children in custodial compounds where they could be subjected to deliberate molding routines, began to be discussed seriously by the Northeastern policy elites of business, government, and university life." Gatto, *The Underground History of American Education*, 38.

of the educational system. In the 1920s the "big three" universities, Harvard, Yale, and Princeton, changed their admission policies and procedures to limit the number of Jews that were flooding into these top universities at an "alarming" rate.[18] In his book *The Chosen*, Jerome Karabel explained that "the centerpiece of the new policy would be 'character'—a quality thought to be in short supply among Jews but present in abundance among high-culture Protestants."[19] Excellent academic criteria alone was no longer enough; subjective considerations such as "social background," "sturdy character," and "an undergraduate who devoted his time to his club or his sports team[20] was the ideal."[21] The new policies were "constructed by the Protestant upper class in response to 'the Jewish problem,'" and "the new regime was a radical departure from traditional academic selection practices."[22] Abbot Lawrence Lowell, the president of Harvard University from 1909–1933, was a firm believer in "the superiority of Anglo-Saxon values and customs."[23] When Lowell was asked why he wanted to limit the number of Jews admitted to Harvard, his answer was "because Jews cheat. When a distinguished alumnus objected on the grounds that non-Jews also cheat, Lowell replied, 'You're changing the subject. I'm talking about Jews.'"[24] To Lowell and many others, there was a great gulf between Gentile and Jewish "character," which was "a shorthand for

---

[18] "At Harvard the proportion [of Jews] was seven percent in 1900 and twenty-one and a half percent in 1922." Arthur Hertzberg, *The Jews in America*. (New York: Columbia University Press, 1998), 234.

[19] Karabel, *The Chosen*, 2.

[20] "The contention of the majority of your educators, that the moral instinct is trained on the football and baseball field, in boxing, rowing, wrestling and other contests, is a true one, is truer, perhaps, than most of them realize. Your ideal morality is a sporting morality. The intense discipline of the game, the spirit of fair play, the qualities of endurance, of good humor, of conventionalized seriousness in effort, of loyalty, of struggle without malice or bitterness, of readiness to forget like a sport—all these are brought out in their sheerest and cleanest starkness in well-organized and closely regulated college sports. And on the experiences and lessons which these sports imply your entire spiritual life is inevitably founded." Samuel, *You Gentiles*, 42.

[21] Karabel, *The Chosen*, 4.

[22] Ibid., 9.

[23] Ibid., 48.

[24] Alan Dershowitz, *The Case for Israel*. (Hoboken: John Wiley & Sons, Inc., 2003), 2.

an entire ethos and way of being."[25] Resorting to subjective criteria in their admission policies meant that Harvard, Yale, and Princeton could "control over the composition of the freshman class[26]...constructed by the Protestant upper class in response to 'the Jewish problem.'"[27]

It has been observed that "what is influential in the higher intellectual circles always ends up in the schools."[28] Therefore, we must re-assess the paradigm of intellectual thought, as Rabbi S. R. Hirsch stated:

> Uniting timeless religious values and transient human ideas, specifically Jewish concepts and general human concepts to form a unified path for a harmonious intellectual education and character training; only of home and school can transmit the teachings of secular knowledge and learning from the vantage point of Jewish truth, and utilize the results of secular studies for a clearer and more complete understanding of the truths of Judaism; only if they will know how to relate specifically Jewish teachings, their concepts and methods, to secular knowledge.[29]

When it comes to the Torah, the intellectuals of Western Society are, in many ways, as narrow-minded as the theologians they so often ridicule. To quote Richard Dawkins, "I suspect that for many people the main reason they cling to religion is not that it is consoling, but that they have been let down by our educational system...I prefer to say that I believe in people, and people, when given the right encouragement to think for themselves about all the information now available, very often turn out *not* to believe in God."[30] It is true that we have been let down by our educational system;[31] as we have seen, it

---

[25] Karabel, *The Chosen*, 2.

[26] Ibid.

[27] Ibid., 9.

[28] Bloom, *The Closing of the American Mind*, 55.

[29] Hirsch, *Collected Writings*, Vol. VII, 295.

[30] Dawkins, *The God Delusion*, 22.

[31] "The 'University' is the church of the secular society, and no church can withstand its influence. The graduates of missionaries of the 'University' hold all the reigns of power: in government, in business, in the mass media. The 'University,' with its sciences and pseudo-sciences, its arts and technologies, its professional schools and humanities, is the heart of contemporary civilization. Its priests are for the most part secularized Christians, i.e., half-hearted atheists who preach the gospel of tolerance. Tolerance is obviously required in pluralistic societies where 'everything is relative,'

is they, the intellectuals, who have kept the Torah knowledge out of academic discussion. It is they, the intellectuals such as Dawkins, who have discouraged people to "think for themselves" by "limiting the information now available." It is they, the intellectuals, who are against the Torah because they disagree with concepts such as the prohibition of hedonism (which is often little more than the desire to have sex outside marriage) and is, along with idolatry, too often the reasoning behind the Constitution-thumper's constant yammering about "freedom," "equality,"[32] and "liberty" when confronted with the Torah.

∽

To UNDERSTAND THE uniqueness of the Noahide perspective on what constitutes "intellectualism" requires an understanding of the place of Noahide Law in Western thought. The consensus among many non-Jews and non-observant Noahides seems to be that *the academic attack on Judaism has been spearheaded by a hostile Christianity while at the same time tolerated by a benign and objective secular academic culture.* Yet the intellectual arguments against the Torah come not only from religion, but from philosophy, history, sociology, and to a lesser extent, economics and political science. The influence of Christian theology has had an effect on all Western academic disciplines, whether directly as in the case of the humanities and social sciences[33] or indirectly as with the "hard" sciences and how they are used and implemented in a Christian culture. It should also be understood that to

---

that is, where the true, the good, and the beautiful are nowhere to be found. The consequence is intellectual mediocrity, moral laxity, and vulgarity—all conspicuous in today's institutions of 'higher' education." Eidelberg, *Jerusalem vs. Athens*, 231.

[32] "Ironically, the colonists who had deprived most of the population—religious dissenters, women, slaves, and Indians—of legal rights and voices in governance based their Declaration of Independence on pious claims that 'all men are created equal' and that governments must drive 'their just powers from the consent of the governed.' Those who drafted and signed this solemn declaration in 1776 firmly believed in its principles and protestations, but they were all white men of property who simply did not comprehend that people unlike them had been equally 'endowed by their Creator' with the same 'inalienable rights' they claimed for themselves. And so, when another group of white men of property met in Philadelphia in 1787 to draft a constitution for the United States, they brought to this task the same lack of comprehension." Irons, *A People's History of the Supreme Court*, 16.

[33] "The most significant developments in the art or science of interpretation during the nineteenth and twentieth centuries have been the emergence of the social sciences, especially psychology and sociology." Robert Morgan and John Barton, *Biblical Interpretation*. (Oxford: Oxford University Press, 1988), 5.

keep Biblical interpretation in the sphere of "religion" is accepting the Enlightenment concept of the separation of "secular" and "religious."

At this point, we should have a broad historical narrative to provide a solid framework for such an expansive religious subject. It is here, however, that we run into our first snag. It is not that the Torah has been neglected due to some historical oversight; the problems with the West's dealings with the Torah go far beyond simple disinterest: it is a deliberate omission. Our institutions of higher learning, the institutions which educate and produce the professional teachers of our children, do not teach Torah because it is neither relevant nor interesting—the reasons go far deeper. Instead, these institutions teach a mixture of theological and Greco-Roman anti-Semitism where the Torah is concerned, and how "anti-Semitism...sits with equal grace on the grossest of your peasantry and the most refined of your aristocracy. In the one case it is fortified by superstition, in the other case by all the information that 'scientific' research into philosophy, history, ethnography and anthropology can accumulate."[34]

As we have seen, the power of intellectual ideas can be used to transform and define the political and economic[35] landscape of our society. After two and a half centuries of Enlightenment, of secular ideas and scientific superiority, our society—indeed our civilization—teeters on the brink.[36] For Yaphet to dwell in the tents of Shem means

---

[34] Samuel, *You Gentiles*, 25.

[35] "The intellectual is well aware of the elaborate apparatus which the businessman uses to mold our civilization to his purposes and adapt it to his standards. The businessman is everywhere; he fills the coffers of the political parties; he owns or controls the influential press and the agencies of mass culture; he sits on university boards of trustees and on local school boards; he mobilizes and finances cultural vigilantes; his voice dominates the rooms in which the real decisions are made" Hofstadter, *Anti-Intellectualism in American Life*, 234–35.

[36] "Even as he lies in the dust, with the Edomite foot of Rome upon his neck, Jacob has every right to look Rome firmly in the eye. Before conceding that he had been defeated and destroyed and that his oppressor was indeed the triumphant heir to his own mission to save the world, Jacob could ask Rome just how much peace and salvation, how much happiness and prosperity, her world domination had brought to mankind, how much freedom and right, how much enlightenment and edification her Church had bestowed upon the souls of men. Jacob could question her about the ruined cities, the incinerated hovels, the tortured bodies, the broken hearts, the enslaved peoples, the fallen nations, the despairing spirits and the duped minds that resulted from the rule of Rome. He could point to the fanaticism she hallowed, the truths she denied, the scorn she had heaped upon humanity, the insults she had dealt to human dignity, the crime, the desolation, the misery and the vice that ran rampant

that Yaphet is to freely incorporate his gifts of culture and his eye for
beauty in accord with Torah morality for the benefit of all mankind.
From the Western Edomite perspective, Shem's tent is to be burned to
the ground, hopefully with Shem inside. Shem is to play no part in the
development of Western Civilization. This is the message of "intellectuals" such as Dawkins, Hitchens, and Harris.

Our society, our culture, perhaps even our civilization, is coming to an end soon. Life as we have known it is about to change.
What will be left over after the peak curve of fossil fuel starts the
inevitable and inexorable downward spiral is anyone's guess. Will
we ditch the Constitution and go back to the Articles of Confederation—which were never repealed, by the way—and let the individual
states resume their autonomous sovereignty? Or will the President
issue Executive Orders for martial law (to preserve "law and order,"
of course) and toss the Constitution in the trash, treating it like the
worthless piece of parchment it actually is (again, as they did the
Articles of Confederation; cf. footnote 26 p. 492 in the Constitution's
Article VII in the Appendix below) and showing us how feeble the
promises of freedom, liberty, and equality truly are? This seems to
be the current course; we have the giant military machine in place,
our armies are camped out in Babylon, location of the second largest
petroleum reserves known, and all we need is a trigger—a natural or
man-made disaster (even if manufactured)—to turn the corner and
turn America into another Roman dictatorship. How easy it would
be for the government, in concert with the corporations, to take full
control of the media and the internet, and restrict travel and commu-
nications. Yes, there will be some who will resist; local militias who
bravely but foolishly go into battle with rifles against Abrams tanks,
Apache helicopters, cruise missiles, and nuclear weapons. Most of
the population (what is left, anyway) will complacently accept the
new arrangement, understanding that it is simply "human nature" that
has taken charge of affairs, the strong subjugating the weak and powerless. This is what happens in an Edomite society.

After all, Americans value and cherish their freedom. Freedom is
what made this country great, such as the freedom to move west into

---

under her dominion. Jacob could point to all these historical outrages and lodge the
most eloquent protest against the mad delusion that the Esau spirit of Rome had
brought happiness and salvation to the world." Hirsch, *Collected Writings,* Vol. II, 435.

lands that had been occupied by Native Americans for millennia, and kill them and drive them off the land. We valued the freedom to import black slaves to do our hard work, and, like Thomas Jefferson, to relive our pent up lusts whenever we wanted. We have had the freedom to take by force whatever we wanted from the nations of the world, particularly the weaker nations that we could economically, politically, and militarily bully. We have enjoyed the freedom to refuse to put any sort of moral restraints on our freedom of acquisition.[37] We are Edom, the destroyer of worlds.

It is those who want their freedom of idolatry and hedonism who rail loudest against establishing a "theocracy." Yet theocracies in the past and present have been based on organized religion, not Torah. It is theonomy, not theology, on which we should base our governmental structure. The rule should be of God's Law, a Law that was literally set in stone.[38] It is not the type of government we choose to have that is important; we could have a representative republic as we have now, or a Constitutional monarchy, or a Parliamentary system, or whatever sort of government we want. If we wish to keep our democracy, fine. It must be understood, however, that the Torah sets limits on democracy.[39]

The intellectuals of Western nations, both religious and secular, look to the heavens for salvation or answers. As *Devarim* 30:12 states, neither the answers nor salvation are in heaven. The answers are here, now, for us to understand and better the sorry lot of human existence, that there is a way to control human nature. We have a plan, a guide book on how to live with one another, that keeps the abuses of "the law of the jungle" in check instead of the anti-government, anti-law individualist hedonistic attitude, the "do whatever is good in your own eyes" sort of philosophy which has divided us to the point where we

---

[37] "The Romans talked loudly of liberty—for themselves. The word hardly applied to those who came under Rome's sway." Murphy, *Are We Rome?*, 139.

[38] Devarim 27:8, "And you shall write upon the stones all the words of this Teaching, so that they may be adequately understood." The Talmud, in *Sotah* 32a, explains that there was a translation of the Torah in the languages of the nations "so that all the other nations would be able to understand it also." Hirsch, *T'rumath Tzvi*, 774.

[39] "'Decide in accordance with the majority' (Ex. 23:2). But the passage immediately preceding warns us…'Do not follow the majority to do evil'…the law thus sets limits to the majority rule." Hirsch, *Collected Writings,* Vol. II, 237–38.

do not know or trust our own neighbor. Instead of a Gnostic religion that teaches the selfish salvation of the individual, we could have a moral code that is centered on the family and the community.[40] Instead of an Esavian legal system with its class-stratifying system of protecting the property of the wealthy, we could have a Law[41] that assures us that no one, be they rich or poor, powerful or weak, is treated unfairly. We can choose this path if we want—and this is the true freedom.[42]

---

[40] One of the reasons so many Noahides embrace the Kabbalah is because they have come out of Evangelical Christianity, a religion based on Gnostic mysticism. This has led to the support of many erroneous ideologies among Noahides, not the least of which is the belief in "individual salvation." As Rabbi Hirsch explained, "It is not with the Jewish individual but with the Jewish *community* that God made the covenant set forth in His Law and in His promises." Hirsch, *Collected Writings*, Vol. II, 174.

[41] "It is not faith, even the purest, that can consummate the deliverance of the world. The deliverance of the world lies in law. Faith can illumine the mind and comfort the heart. But to wed upon earth justice with love, sanctity with joy, life with peace, to bring Paradise back to earth and make men blessed already here below, this can be accomplished fully only by law." Hirsch, *Collected Writings*, Vol. I, 348.

[42] "The ultimate purpose of God's Scripture is not to orient us in the real of nature... rather, after its first chapter, Scripture closes the book of nature in order to open for us the book of the history of mankind, teaching us to behold the workings of God and God's nearness not only in the eternal harmony of all that is great and glorious in physical existence but also, indeed even more so, in the history of men and nations... Scripture sets before us the 'tree of the knowledge of good and evil' as representing the point of departure, and at the same time the basic problem, for the entire history of human civilization. The course of history can be described in simple terms as one lone series of free-willed decisions by men and nations that continues to this very day. Man has the freedom to choose. He can behave like a beast, judging 'good' or 'evil' in terms of what will best satisfy his physical appetites. Or, he can conduct himself in a manner worthy of a human being, electing to obey God, to do that which is morally good even though it may run counter to his momentary physical or material desires, and to shun evil though it may tempt his senses with promises of pleasure and personal gain." Hirsch, *Collected Writings*, Vol. VII, 94–95.

How Odd of God

Instead of seeking fulfillment in an ever-expanding personal material domain, which is bound to collide with other expanding domains and which is about to exhaust the world's resources, the Torah teaches us to see our fulfillment in a spiritual expansion. Not in physical strength; not in economic growth, which invariably generates conflicts; not even in intellectual virtuosity, which stacks the deck in favor of the gifted individual; but in developing our spiritual potential, a feat for which we are all equally qualified. This is the ultimate equality which revolutionaries have mouthed—and almost invariably have denied in practice— since the French revolution. They denied it because they sought it on the economic or intellectual plane where equality is impossible. The Torah makes it possible.

— Yehudah Levi[1]

NEARLY FOUR THOUSAND YEARS AGO AN OLD MAN, HIS WIFE, AND his nephew journeyed from Charan to the land of Canaan. They lived in tents in the wilderness, they had herds of sheep and goats, and there would seem to have been nothing remarkable about these people except that they set off a chain of events which would change the path of human history. The old man had two sons, *Yishmael* and *Yitzhak*, and although he would have other children later, these were the two that would turn the wheels of history. *Yitzhak* had two twin boys, *Ya'acov* and *Esau*. *Ya'acov*, or Israel, would become the father of the Jewish Nation, and from *Esau* would come the Edomites, and eventually Rome. From their uncle *Yishmael* would spring the Arabs. This extended family would create the three monotheistic religions of Judaism, Christianity, and Islam, the latter two comprising over half the population of the earth.

The Jewish historical view is unique. Unlike the history of Greece and Rome, the Jews taught that the universe had a beginning, that time and matter were created, that all humankind sprung from a single female, and although at the very beginning spiritually pure, there was something different about them that separated them from the other

---

[1] Levi, *Torah and Science*, 58.

living beings on Planet Earth: they were able to exercise free will, and man alone could disobey the Rules established by the Creator.

Although man knew the Rules, he would often disobey them, for as candy is sweet and vegetables such as broccoli and kale are not, man would often be swayed by his senses and emotion rather than his intellect and choose the sweet, even if it was harmful, over the non-sweet, even if it was healthy and beneficial. Eventually most of mankind forgot about the Rules altogether, even though the Creator severely punished them for violating His Rules. There arose a family, however, who kept the Rules, and the Creator chose them over all the families and peoples of the earth to keep and teach the Rules, even though they would often be persecuted by the rest of mankind, who, like children, wanted to gorge themselves on sweets rather than nourish themselves on what was good and healthy. In return, the Creator told this family that He would preserve them, and explained that they were the key element in history, for unlike the cyclical histories of the rest of mankind, their history would be linear, with a beginning, middle, and end. Their history would entail a constant striving towards a great goal: the redemption of mankind. Although they would often slip and fall, they would eventually reach their goal, even if all of mankind opposed them.[2] The descendants of this family only constituted a small fraction of the human race, they would break the natural historical cycles of the growth and entropy of the civilizations and cultures of the other nations, the people of whom would finally join them in their linear quest to bring mankind to its ultimate fulfillment, recognition, and observance of the Rules of the Creator of the Universe.

ॐ

ISRAEL'S LINEAR APPROACH to history—that history[3] had a beginning, middle, and an end—was different from the Greek understanding of

---

[2] "These enemies of Israel have not learned any lessons from history, have no understanding for the unseen Mover of events. In the downfall of Israel they would see only the overwhelming nature of their own power. Therefore Israel must remain—remain in the midst of the nations—remain despite all the hatred and opposition—so that out of the futility of their attempt to destroy Israel, an inkling of the Divine as it reveals itself in Israel's destiny as an eternal people might dawn upon the nations of the world." Hirsch, *Collected Writings*, Vol. I, 175.

[3] "What is history? However we may understand history, it is certainly the road to the fulfillment of human destiny by mankind as a whole...this, then, is how the Torah guides us to an understanding of Yisrael and its task: through recognition of God, the world and the purpose of man and of history." Hirsch, *The Nineteen Letters*, 27.

history; besides their world-historical role and the keepers and teachers of the Torah,[4] Israel was the nation of prophecy.[5] The historical view of Israel was tempered by the knowledge of not only what *was* but what *is* and *what will be*. It is this understanding of future events which makes the Jewish view of history different from all others, and it is this unique viewpoint which is ignored or dismissed in the secular interpretations, the world-historical importance given to many of the events in the Torah which affect all of mankind.

Of the many events in the Torah, particularly the events in *Bereishis* (Genesis), none is more salient to our understanding of current events than the power struggle and rivalry between Jacob and Esau. In *Bereishis* 25:23 it says that a prophecy was given to Rebecca, the wife of Isaac: "And H*ashem* said to her: 'Two nations [are] in your womb and two states; they will be divided from one another, starting from within you; one state shall become mightier than the other, and the mighty one shall serve the lesser.'" *Rashi* interpreted this struggle between Jacob and Esau as "They will never be both strong at the same time; when one falls, the other will rise." For Esau, it is this loss of power to his "weaker" brother Jacob that angers him. As explained by Rabbi Samson Raphael Hirsch:

> Rebecca was informed that she carried two nations in her womb who would represent two different forms of social government. The one state would build up its greatness on spirit and morals, on the humane in humans, the other would seek its greatness in cunning and strength. Spirit and strength, morality and violence oppose each other, and indeed, from birth onwards will they be in opposition to each other. One form of government will always be more powerful that the other. The scales will constantly sway from one to the other...the whole of history is nothing

---

[4] "The light is the Torah, which will emanate from Zion to the nations. Israel will ensure the existence of the nations in two ways: because of Israel, there will be peace throughout the world, as in [Isaiah] Chapter 2, and secondly, because of Israel all the nations will observe the Noachide commandments and will deal justly with one another, as above 2:3 (*Redak*)." Rosenberg, *Isaiah,* Vol. II, 339.

[5] The Talmud (*Megillah* 14a) explains that "through the course of history, twice as many prophets arose among the Jews as there were Israelites who left Egypt." Rabbi Matis Roberts, *Trei Asar*, Vol. I. (Brooklyn: Mesorah Publications, Ltd., 1995), xviii. Out of all of these, "only forty–eight men and seven women have been recorded in the Scriptures." [Ibid.] This was because "there was no need...to record all prophetic statements: 'Only such prophecy that was needed for later generations was written down' (*Megillah* 14a)...recorded because the respective prophets spoke to future generations, as well as their own." Ibid., xxix.

else than a struggle as to whether spirit or sword, or, as our sages put it, whether Caesarea or Jerusalem is to have the upper hand."[6]

It is important to note that Rabbi Hirsch explained that the nations of Jacob and Esau represented "two different forms of social government," or, alternatively, two different social systems. It is this difference which constitutes the basis of the disparity between the Western Esavian nations and Israel.[7] Much more than Jacob representing a new form of religion, Jacob represented a new ideal of social government, a legal system different from anything else then on the planet. To the Edomite nations, the Jews, because they "forsook Christ" or "denied Muhammad," have been consigned to the backwaters of history.[8]

The Sages linked the kingdom of Edom to the organized religion of Christianity (Islam, too, which was itself influenced deeply by Christianity[9]): "Abarbanel argues that Rome, as representative of

---

[6] Hirsch, commentary on *Bereishis* 25:23, 423.

[7] "As the receiver and preserver of this Divine Law, Israel occupies a unique position among the nations. The other nations lack the knowledge of the חקים, of those 'statues' which confine the physical, sensual aspects of the individual personality within the proper bounds of moral purity and sanctification. In fact, they are ignorant even of the משפטים, which govern the life of the community as such by and through the commandments of righteousness, which no group within the society of man can do without. To those nations, society is not at all the result of lawful order. Instead, they believe that any concept of law is determined by the views held at any given time and place concerning the needs of a society, and thus their laws are based on the premise of expediency. Hence their law and order are in a constant process of change, and their social conditions and relationships lack a firm basis. They have no concept of an eternal order of laws which was revealed by God, enjoys His protection and stands high and inviolable above all men and things. They know nothing of this supreme Law, the unreserved obedience to which will alone one day bring lasting peace and salvation to all the world, and for which God had placed Israel among the nations to act as its trustees." Hirsch, *The Hirsch Psalms*, §ii, 489.

[8] "Although God had commanded Israel, *"Do not despise an Edomite for he is your brother"* [see *Deuteronomy* 23:8], Edom harmed Israel at every opportunity and rejoiced at the destruction of their land and their Temple, forever incurring God's wrath (*Radak*)." *Trei Asar*, Vol. II. Rabbi Yitzchok Stavsky, Translation and Commentary. (Brooklyn: Mesorah Publications, ltd., 2009), 312.

[9] "There will be in all the land—the word of *HASHEM*—[that] two portions [of the population] will be cut off and perish, and the third will remain in it." (*Zechariah* 13:8). "Two thirds of the entire world population will perish at that time. The two thirds that will perish are the Edomites and Ishmaelites [Christians and Moslems]... (*Metzudos*)." Ibid., 294. It is sobering to realize that Christian and Muslim nations compromise close to two billion people each out of a world population of seven billion—close to two thirds of the entire population of mankind.

Christianity, is the spiritual heir of Edom. Just as Isaac had two sons, Jacob and Esau, so does the true belief in one God figuratively have two sons—Jacob, the Jewish faith, and Edom, representing variants of monotheism. Abarbanel cites many other parallels between Christianity and Edom."[10] As Samuel Huntington pointed out in his book *The Clash of Civilizations and the Remaking of World Order*, it is this clash between the two religions, Christianity and Islam, as well as Western political ideologies such as communism and democracy, which are the determining factors behind much of the world's turmoil today. Because most religious and secular interpretations of the *Tanach* give the prophecies Christological themes, the Jewish interpretation is largely unknown; in fact, many rabbinic interpretations have been censored by the Church because they deny the theological ramifications taught by Christianity.[11]

Even a casual reading shows the *Tanach* is clear about the attitude of *HASHEM* towards Edom:

Was not Esau the brother of Jacob—the word of *HASHEM* —yet I loved Jacob. But I hated Esau; I made his mountains a desolation and [gave] his heritage to the desert serpents. Though Edom will say, "We have become destitute, but we will return and rebuild the ruins," thus says *HASHEM*, Master of Legions; They may build, but I will tear down! They will be called "the boundary of wickedness" and "the people whom *HASHEM* has condemned forever."[12]

---

[10] Goldwurm, *Daniel*, 106.

[11] "Rambam saw this phrase [*Daniel* 11:14] as a strong allusion to the founder of Christianity as follows: 'Also about Yeshu the Nazarene who imagined himself to be the Messiah and was put to death by the court, it has already been prophesied by Daniel as is written, וּבְנֵי פָּרִיצֵי עַמְּךָ, *and the sons of the lawless of your people, will exalt themselves to set up vision and will stumble.* For is there a greater stumbling-block than this? All the prophets foretold that the Messiah will redeem the Jews, help them, gather in the exiles, and support their observance of the commandments. But he caused Jewry to be put to the sword; to have their remnants scattered; to be degraded; changed the Torah; and misled most of the world to serve a god other than *HASHEM*. But the thoughts of the Creator of the world are unfathomable to humans...' (*Rambam, Hilchos Melachim* 11:4). This passage, cited only in part, is missing in all recent editions. See Pardes edition which contains it as found in ancient manuscripts. See also *Rambam's Igeres Teman*. The same interpretation is held by *R'Saadiah Gaon* (quoted in *Me-gillas HaMegalleh* p. 98), *Ibn Ezra* (*Perush HaKatzer*), and perhaps *Rashi* (our versions are extremely ambiguous and have no doubt been tampered with by censors)." Goldwurm, *Daniel*, 292.

[12] Malachi, 1:2–4. "The principle of Esau-Edom is: — the worship of force, the laurel of blood is its highest ornament, plans for conquest of the world form the dream of the

With this harsh pronouncement, taken in context with Rabbi Hirsch's understanding of the nations of Jacob (Israel) and Edom being two distinctly different forms of social government, we can better understand the prophecies[13] concerning the future fate of Edom.[14] For instance, in Isaiah it states:

> For My sword has become sated in the heaven. Behold, it shall descend upon Edom and upon the nation with whom I contend, for judgment... for the Lord has a slaughter in Bozrah and a great slaughter in the land of Edom...for it is a day of vengeance for the Lord, a year of retribution for the plea of Zion. And its streams shall turn into pitch and its dust into sulfur, and its land shall become burning pitch. By night and by day, it shall not be extinguished; its smoke shall ascend forever and ever; from generation to generation it shall be waste, to eternity, no one passing through it.[15]

---

greatest of its world-historic great ones. With them the care and development of all the material, spiritual and moral forces and wealth of men stand in the service of this ideal. We know that our sages saw in the Roman Empire the strongest embodiment of this Edomite principle. But this Esau-principle is in complete contrast to the Divine order of the world. That fixes the rule of justice and right and love on the foundation of the sanctification of life as the highest, as the sole goal. In the service of this highest human goal the principle of the life of Jacob stands, in contrast to it that of Esau-Edom. It is on this contrast that the mighty kingdoms of Edom founder, however 'mountain-like' — הרי — they reach to the skies, and, to the contemporary outlook, seem established for ever. 'The Esau-principle is what God hates, the Jacob-principle is what He loves', that is what the downfall, the ruins of the empire of Edom teaches, that is what the survival of Israel teaches." Hirsch, commentary to *Malachi* 1:3–4, *Commentary on the Torah: Haftoroth.* Dr. Mendel Hirsch, trans. (London: The Judaica Press, 1966), 48.

[13] "*Rambam* (*Hilchos Melochim* 12:2) advises against a detailed study of the events which lead to the coming of the Messiah. Knowledge of these matters, he teaches, leads neither to fear [nor the] love of God." Eisemann, *Yechezkel*, 577.

[14] "Edom has two separate identities in the words of the prophets. Firstly, it is the Biblical nation of Edom, which bordered the Land of Israel and was often involved in the persecution of the Jewish nation (cf. *Amos* 1:11, 12). Biblical Edom was conquered and its inhabitants exiled by Nebuchadneszzar, king of Babylonia, around the time of the destruction of the First Temple. In addition, the city (and empire) of Rome is described by the Sages as having been originally settled by the people of Edom, and prophetic reference to Edom is often interpreted as referring to the Roman Empire. 'Rome' is considered to be perpetuated by Christian civilization which the empire made dominant in the world, and its final destruction will not occur until the times of Messiah." Roberts, *Trei Asar*, Vol. I, 268.

[15] Isaiah 34:5–6, 8–10. Rosenberg, *Isaiah*, Vol. 2, 278–79.

Throughout the *Tanach*, the fate of Edom is foretold.[16] It begins in *Bereishis*, where in chapter fourteen Abraham fights in the first recorded war, the war against the Four Kings. The symbolism[17] of the

---

[16] "The Sages speak of three separate wars which are to be fought (see *Midrash Tehillim* to *Psalms* 118). According to *Malbim*, the first two of these are the subject of our chapters in *Ezekiel*. The final war when Gog will actually break into Jerusalem, is described in *Zechariah* 14. [References to the wars of Gog and Magog abound in Scripture, overtly in the prophets and, according to the *Targumim* and *Midrashim*, by allusion in the Torah. However, the longest, most detailed, and most specific accounts are contained in the books of *Ezekiel, Zechariah, Joel,* and *Daniel*.]" Eisemann, *Yechezkel*, 578.

[17] There is an uncomfortable similarity between the rabbinic commentary to the prophecies in the *Tanach* and what the scientists are warning about today: the collapse of modern industrialized society, the end of the grid, of cheap travel by gasoline-powered automobiles, ships, air travel, and destructive war resulting in culling billions of the world's population down to a sustainable level. This is the best Edom can hope for. The worst-case scenario is that civilization will completely collapse, and we will have to start over from small pockets of hunter-gatherers, small farmers, and shepherds.

Although kabbalistic interpretations can be illuminating, the rabbis who teach Noahides the mysticism of kabbalah (in lieu of genuine *halakha*) too often ignore the unpleasant kabbalistic interpretations dealing with the fate of Edom. Real kabbalah is dangerous stuff, and three out of four rabbis that venture into *Gan Eden* (cf. *Hagigah* 14b) do not recommend the study of kabbalah to observant Jews, let alone Noahides. The Kabbalists of צפת (Tsfat) spoke of the Torah verses corresponding to each Jewish year. These verses allude to major events that occur in both Jewish and World history. As we go through the verses, lining them up with the years, we can better grasp the picture the Torah paints for us during the next two and a half decades. Since this is the Gregorian Calendar year 2011, the Jewish year 5771 (September 9, 2010, the first day of *Tishrei* or *Rosh Hashanah*), then the year 5771 corresponds with verse *Devarim* (Deuteronomy) 32:19, "*Hashem* will see and be provoked by the anger of His sons and daughters." This one verse does not mean much in itself; we need to look at it in the grim context of the rest of the passage (*Devarim* 32:19–43).

The Talmud speaks of the חבלי משיח as a time of great suffering. Drought, famine, and economic collapse (cf. *San.* 97a) will be severe. Fish stocks in our oceans and rivers will vanish, and the seas will become full of oil (ibid. 98a). The verse *Devarim* 32:24 speaks of "bloating of famine." This is alluding to the great famine that will strike the planet in the years preceding the coming of *HaMachiach. San.* 98a also says that "R' Chanina said: The son of David will not come until a fish will be sought for a sick person, and it will not be found, as it is stated: Then I will make their waters settle and cause their rivers to flow like oil" (from Ezekiel 32:14). A recent scientific study says that, if current trends continue, there will be a collapse of fish stocks such as cod and tuna worldwide in just one generation, and the recent oil spill in the Gulf of Mexico could be an portent of unpleasant things to come.

Also, "in a dissertation fundamental to the understanding of the stories of the Patriarchs recorded in the Torah, *Ramban* explains...'I will tell you a principle, which you should keep in mind throughout all the coming passages regarding the lives of Abraham, Isaac and Jacob...it is a major principle, which the Sages mentioned

Four Kingdoms is a recurring theme in the *Tanach*, particularly in the books of the Prophets.[18] In *Daniel* chapter Seven, it speaks of a vision of four "immense beasts" coming out of the sea. These four beasts symbolize the four kingdoms which would subjugate Israel: Babylonia, Persia/Media,[19] Greece, and Rome.[20] The last kingdom, Rome,

---

succinctly when they said (cf. *Midrash Taachuma, Lech Lecha* 9), "Everything that occurred to the Patriarchs is a sign (or *portent*) for their descendants."'" [*Ramban. Bereishis*, Vol. I, 293.] In other words, every incident that occurred in the lives of Abraham, Isaac, and Jacob was to foreshadow a parallel event that would affect the Jewish people in the future. Following the teaching that what happens to the Patriarchs happens to Israel, it is interesting to note that the birth of Abraham occurred in the Jewish year 1948, and the birth of the modern nation of Israel occurred in the year 1948 of the Common Era. Following this, could a major war in the Middle East—the War of Gog and Magog—be in 2023, the year of the War of the Four Kings in *Bereishis* 14? It is the nations that have harmed Israel, namely the nations of Edom and *Yishmael* (Christian and Muslim) who will be brought into the war of Gog and Magog. It will be a war between the Christian nations and the Arabs over Jerusalem. Or the *Akeida*, the Binding of Isaac, which will be in the year 2085, the same year that (coincidently?) signals the end of the number of Torah verses (there are 5845 verses in the Torah; the Jewish year 5845 coincides with the Gregorian year 2085). The year 5845 is also very close to the end of the 6000 year "cycle" (before the one-thousand year Sabbath) when you add in the 165 years that were "hidden" (cf. Yehudah Levi, *Torah and Science*, 172–73). According to many of the giants of Torah scholarship (including *Ramban*, *Rabbeinu Bachya*, *Radbaz*, Rabbi Eliyahu, the Gaon of Vilna, and Rabbi Isaac of Akko), our civilization runs in seven seven-thousand-year cycles. Six cycles for the "creation" of civilization; one cycle of a thousand year "Sabbath" when each cycle of civilization collapses. The Sages generally agree that we are not in the first cycle, but few of them believe we are in the last. Our civilization may soon crumble to give the planet a thousand years of "rest" from our mismanagement (cf. *Rabbeinu Bachya* to *Bamidbar* 10:35).

[18] E.g., *Daniel*, ch. 2 and *Zechariah*, ch. 6.

[19] In *Daniel*, the dream of *Nebuchadnezzar* interpreted by *Daniel* was that the head of gold represented Babylon, the breast and arms of silver represented *Persia* and *Media*, the thighs of copper represented Greece, and the legs of iron were Rome. These were the Four Kingdoms which subjugated Israel. (Persia פרס is mentioned with Media מדי throughout scripture (cf. Daniel 8:20), the Persians being the dominant partner of the two.) The feet in *Daniel* chapter 2:41 represent "the area occupied by the Roman empire [which] came to be dominated by two religions, Christianity and Islam. Both together comprise the latter day *fourth kingdom*. One is as strong as iron, the other as weak as pottery (*Mayenei HaYeshuah* 6:1; *Malbim*)." Goldwurm, *Daniel*, 107.

[20] "As interpreted by *Abarbanel*, the four species of locusts [*Yoel* 1:4] symbolize the four kingdoms which subsequently conquered the Land of Israel. *Gazam* refers to Babylonia, whose king, Nebuchadnezzar, was so noteworthy in both power and wickedness that [his description sounds like] an exaggeration (גוזמה). Alternatively, it relates to the word גזז, as he cut away all of the nations in existence. *Arbeh*—meaning many—represents the kingdom of Persia, which consisted of a great multitude of people since it included

will eventually be destroyed: "And saviors shall ascend Mt. Zion to wreak judgment upon the Mountain of Esau and dominion shall be *HASHEM'S*" (Obadiah 21).[21] Israel will emerge victorious: "At that time your people will escape" [*Daniel* 12:1].[22] At the culmination of history, there will be a great war in the Middle East[23] where the forces of *Yishmael*[24] and *Esau*[25] will come against Israel. The civilization and culture of Edom will be eradicated.

---

the nations of both Persia and Media. *Yelek* are the people of Greece, who lapped with their tongues like dogs. *Chasil*, the finishing locusts, symbolize the Roman Empire, which wreaked the final destruction upon the Jewish nation, destroying the Temple and exiling the inhabitants of the land." Roberts, *Trei Asar*, Vol. I, 150.

[21] According to the Noahide perspective, the "Dark Ages" did not end with the Enlightenment. "There is another dimension to Edom, one that carries it beyond its territorial boundaries and places it squarely at the century of world history. Edom is the last, and most vicious, of the Four Monarchies destined to subjugate Israel in its road through history…Israel's nadir was reached when the Second Temple fell to Rome's legions. That was the moment at which the final and darkest of all the exiles came upon it. This was Edom's moment in history, and the two millennia of suffering which its ascendancy brought upon mankind will not be relieved until the coming of the Messiah. At that time *saviors will go up on Mount Zion to punish Mount Esau. The kingship will be God's (Obidiah* v. 21)." Eisemann, *Yechezekel*, 542–43.

[22] "The fourth kingdom, Rome, will be destroyed and Israel will be saved (*Rashi*)." Goldwurm, *Daniel*, 319–20.

[23] In the *Midrash Rabbah, Bereishis* 76:6, it "comments on Daniel's visions of the four beasts (*Daniel* ch. 7) symbolizing the Four Kingdoms which are to subjugate Israel. The fourth and most terrible beast has ten horns from which an eleventh is seen to sprout. The Midrash comments that these ten horns symbolize ten kings of the Fourth Kingdom, and the eleventh horn is the final king whom Israel will confront. All these kings, the Midrash stresses, are to be descendants of Esau…the implication is that the king and initiator of the campaign against Israel will be from Esau-Edom. The fighting force, however, will be drawn from the ranks of Japheth and Ham (*v.* 5) and from Ishmael's descendants…this picture of Esau-Edom instigating other nations to fight Israel is entirely in consonance with the teachings of our Sages concerning the Fourth Kingdom. Its very essence, which distinguishes it from the other Kingdoms, is its ability to spread the poison of its hatred to other nations. (See *Ramban*, to Genesis 14:1; *Pachad Yitzchak*, Purim ch. 2; Artscroll *Bereishis* Vol. I, *The Four Monarchies*, 417). So it was in Esther's time, when the Amalekite Haman (descended from Esau) was the instigating force in the Persian (Japhethic) court, and so it will be in the wars of Gog and Magog, when the Edomite king Gog will lead the Japhethic nations to war." Eisemann, *Yechezkel*, 582.

[24] In *Abarbanel's* commentary to Isaiah 52:11 he states that the verse is "an indication that Jerusalem will be in the hands of the Ishmaelites when the Messiah reveals himself. They are referred to above (v. 1) as 'unclean.'" Rosenberg, *Isaiah*, Vol. 2, 421.

[25] The Arab/Muslim nations and the Western/Christian nations.

T HE DESCENDANTS OF *Ya'acov*, the Jewish people, wrote a series of books that the people of today call the Bible. For nearly two thousand years, the Hebrew Bible has been a major influence in Western Civilization. Its influence has gone far beyond the boundary of religion; the *Tanach* has influenced nearly all areas of social life including politics, economics, and science. Even today in our secular society the Bible has been influential in how people vote and whom they vote for, how Congress and the Supreme Court have created our laws and interpreted the Constitution, and how we spend our money.

Yet the *Tanach* has been misrepresented in Western Culture. The problem is the approach and interpretation of the *Tanach*; for too long the *Tanach* has been interpreted by its supporters and detractors alike from a Christian theological perspective. For most Americans, the Bible is about Jesus and his teachings, about heaven and hell, about being "saved." This approach has created more problems than it has solved. A plethora of pundits have written profusely about the problems of Western society—the "knife-and-fork-using nations," as James Kunstler calls them—and that these problems are mounting up faster than Western Civilization can solve them. Our standard of living is deteriorating rapidly, taking the middle and lower-classes along with it. The economy is crumbling, ecological disasters are mounting (such as oil spills in the Gulf of Mexico, global warming, the collapse of important food stocks such as fish, and the increasing scarcity of fresh water), and, perhaps most importantly, we are running out of the fossil-fuels that make everything work. Our intellectual pundits see Western Civilization as the Titanic—we have hit the iceberg, yet the ship is still afloat, the drinks at the bar are still cold, and the band keeps tooting merrily away. But if you look out the portholes, the First Class passengers are all in what few lifeboats there are, and have already left the stricken liner. The steerage passengers are locked below, out of sight, and there is a noticeable list that is getting worse by the minute.

Morris Berman, in his book *Dark Ages America*, observed that "what we are now seeing are the obvious characteristics of the West after the fall of Rome: the triumph of religion[26] over reason; the atrophy

---

[26] "We can begin by describing the role of religion in American politics and war with two words: *widely underestimated.*" Phillips, *American Theocracy*, 121.

of education and critical thinking."[27] Berman weaves a tale of woe, of how our society is breaking down, how the rich are getting richer at the expense of the shrinking middle class and the ever-expanding lower class of the working poor. "We are in a state of advanced cultural disintegration…it is hard to imagine where a recovery would come from."[28] Berman speaks of Toynbee's "process of decline" of a civilization, and brings up (once again) that "the decline of Rome…may be a more reliable guide to our future,"[29] and that the downfall of our culture has crossed a tipping point, as "Caesar's move across the Rubicon in 49 B.C. marked a major discontinuity, signaling as it did the death of the Republic and the emergence of the Empire."[30] Chalmers Johnson painted a more pessimistic picture, that "our current behavior is likely to lead" to the destruction of our democracy "and in the end produce a military dictatorship or its civilian equivalent."[31] With the demise of democracy and the destruction of our culture, we sail on to a dismal and indefinite shore. The question is: can we even make it to land before we sink into the abyss?

Although these intellectuals recognize the problems facing our culture and civilization, they rarely offer any viable solutions to the economic and political failures of Western culture which are opening up before us like a fiery pits of doom, that for the vast majority of our society, our standard of living is going to irreversibly decline. As a recent Arabic joke goes: "My father rode a camel. I ride a car. My son flies an airplane. His son will ride a camel."

How much longer will the rest of us be in denial? Western civilization glories in its culture, but its culture is starting to crumble. As the acetate dissolves, the mylar melts, and the plastic compact disks break down and separate from their thin aluminum backing, our movies and music will disappear. The deeds of the athletes at our "sporting events" in the coliseums will fade and be forgotten. Our marvelous technology that depends on cheap fossil-fuel will decay and become

---

[27] Berman, *Dark Ages America*, 2.

[28] Ibid., 302.

[29] Ibid., 304.

[30] Ibid.

[31] Johnson, *Nemesis*, 278.

useless as our extravagant lifestyle depletes the last of the hydrocarbons. Our glittering steel and glass cities will fall into disrepair and crumble into ruins as their citizens migrate out into what farmland we have not yet paved over with asphalt and concrete. This is the fate of our culture, our civilization, and there are many intellectuals who recognize the path of self-destruction we are treading upon even as they search for the answers which will deliver us from the pit of doom we have dug for ourselves.

As we have pointed out, the problem our modern society has in understanding the Torah is that it has been misrepresented by secular culture. To give an illustration, we turn to an old fable from India about a small group of blind men and an elephant. When the blind men came upon it, each man felt a different part of the elephant; one felt its leg, one its tail, one its side. Each of the blind men had a different idea of what an "elephant" was; the blind man who felt the elephant's leg thought it was like a trunk of a tree, the one who felt its tail thought it like a rope, the side like a wall, the tusk a spear, the trunk a snake, the ear a fan, and so on. Yet for those with sight, the elephant is all these things and more; the sighted can stand back and view the elephant as a whole. The legs of an elephant are like a tree trunk, the ears like a sail, the tail like a rope; it is the sum of its parts, a living, breathing animal.

For the majority of non-Jews, the Torah is like the elephant in the fable. The Torah, in its literal sense, comprises of the first five books of Moses: Genesis, Exodus, Leviticus, Numbers, and Deuteronomy. Although we tend to think of them as five different books, they are essentially one work. But the Torah (Hebrew for "teaching"), according to the rabbis, has two parts to it, the Written Torah, and the Oral Torah, which is called the Talmud. The Written Torah has long been analyzed, discussed, prodded, and picked apart by myriads of Gentile scholars, academics, and theologians. It has been discussed as a book of ancient history, a book of ancient philosophy, or of ancient geography, or of ancient laws and customs. Most of all, however, the Torah has been portrayed as a book of religion, the link between the physical and the metaphysical, the things which related to God. The Talmud, on the other hand, has been a mystery to the vast majority of non-Jews. It is not taught in any college, university, or even seminary. At best you might have a quote here and there, often taken out of context. Without the Talmud, however, we are like a blind man trying to understand the Torah. We grab hold of a verse or a chapter here or there, but we miss the big picture. Without the Talmud, we misunderstand many of the important teachings of the Written Torah, not the least of which is the relationship of the non-Jew to the Torah as well as his obligations to God.

That the Torah deserves serious academic study should be obvious to anyone, and not simply because of its historical, religious and literary value; the Torah's peerless legal and ethical code—as complex as any modern legal code, including our own—certainly deserves greater academic scrutiny. To pound the point home once again, the exclusion of the Torah from Western academic discourse is not an accident of history, but a deliberate attempt to exclude the relevant teachings of a complex system of law, morality, and ethics. The Torah was not overlooked because it was archaic, nor ignored because it was irrelevant. Western intellectual thought has been defined by the paradigms of its Western, i.e., its Greek/Roman/Christian teachings, and there is simply no excuse or logical rationale for its exclusion in intellectual thought. The failure of modern intellectuals to "think outside the box" when it comes to Torah is no more apparent than the sad fact that there is no academic institution (outside of the Jewish yeshivas) that teaches authentic Torah. At best, some colleges and universities have religion classes on the "Old Testament," but, as the name suggests, it deals with the *Tanach* from either a theological or literary viewpoint.

Our Western society, however, balks at any attempt to understand this problem.[32] The result of the lack of Torah study among our "secular" academic institutions means that there is no peer review for Noahide literature, no publishers willing to spend advertising dollars on Noahide books, much less to have them published, since there is little market for a subject that few have heard of, a subject that has been deliberately excised from academic dialogue.[33] Because of these problems, this is

---

[32] "The disease [of anti-Semitism] flows largely from the top, from those nominally responsible for maintaining the public health, government officials, educators, opinion makers, religious authorities and the like." Schoenfeld, *The Return of Anti-Semitism*, 141.

[33] The effects of Weber's *rationalization* on academics is explained by Carl Boggs: "The fragmented, professionalized, and insular character of established scholarly fields (and subfields) has the effect of blocking system analysis of the contemporary impasse; in fact, academic preoccupations more often obfuscate or distort rather than illuminate by chopping up social reality into manageable (and usually quantifiable) disciplinary texts, discourses, and 'methods.'" Boggs, *The End of Politics*, viii. Even

why we began our study of the Torah on this subject, on *why* the Torah was not a part of Western academic study as taught in our colleges and universities. This is why we explored the logic and reasoning on *how* the Torah has been ignored, even though, like the proverbial eight-hundred pound gorilla in the living room, everyone knew what the Torah was, and that everyone knew that it was there.

In our study of various academic disciplines, we viewed these condiments of wisdom through the lens of the Torah[34] and we discussed our secular ethical and moral foundations as well as how these principles were applied in our society, particularly in the economic and political spheres. We should now turn to the function of Torah in a modern, non-Jewish society, based on the works and commentary of the Sages both ancient and modern, touching on the application of Torah into our modern Western culture.

It should be obvious to all that there is no hope in creating a just and safe society within the Greek and Roman cultural paradigm as we have been doing for the past two millennia. The cyclic system of social failure, the constant warfare, and the grinding misery of the poor at the expense of a small percentage of the wealthy have caused centuries of unimaginable suffering. The triumph of science over religion was accomplished by dazzling the masses with our clever use of fossil-fueled energy and inventing new ways to manipulate it. Yet there will soon come a time when the batteries will die, the gas pumps will run dry, and the lights will dim and go out as the electrical grid fails. Our marvelous technology, which has held us in the thralldom of scientism, a technology dependant on cheap fossil fuel, will become useless, and civilization will sink back to a pre-industrial level.

◌

IRONICALLY, IT IS THE popular science-fiction series *Star Trek* that gives us what is perhaps our best-known example of a society based on rabbinic logic. In the *Star Trek* "universe," as their fans call it, there

---

before the academic disciplines became so fragmented, there was no discipline which dealt with Torah or Noahide Law.

[34] "The Sages advise the student to learn the basic substance of the Torah in terse outline form from only one teacher so that he should not become confused by the variations in the terms used by various instructors. However, one should go to more than one teacher in order to acquire the higher spirit of the Torah so that one may study each question from as many aspects as possible (*Avodah Zarah* 19a)." Hirsch, *Collected Writings,* Vol. VII, 201–02.

was an alien species called the "Vulcans" whose society was saved from constant war and violence by developing a system of logic and reason that was employed not only in dealing with interpersonal relationships but in all facets of their culture and society including government, law, and economics. This alien civilization and its system of logic was developed by one of the co-stars of the original series, an actor whose grandparents were Orthodox Jews who had immigrated from Ukraine, and who used his knowledge of rabbinic Judaism to help develop the cultural background of his character he played on the series.[35] This fictional culture based their philosophy on a system of logic which the actor, Leonard Nimoy, modeled on rabbinic logic, a system that was applicable to every situation in life, be it public or private.[36]

In order for our civilization to survive, we must embrace the system of rabbinic logic as did the fictional Vulcans of *Star Trek*. The path to our salvation is to be found down the road of reason, a road seldom traveled, even by our intellectuals. The beginning of this path has been strewn with emotional arguments about the Divine Nature of the Torah, or belief in the existence of a Supreme Being. As we have seen, the arguments against the Torah have been unreasonable and illogical, based on emotionalism from both the theologians as well as the secular intellectuals. The intellectual who studies the Torah will inevitably grasp the Divine nature of the Law, and realize that this legal system was not, and could not have been, devised by man.

Can humankind, as did the fictional Vulcans of *Star Trek*, save its civilization by adopting the logic and reason of the Torah? All other options have run out. It is time for mankind to face up to its failure in trying to mold a society using Greek philosophy and Roman law. It is time for the intellectuals of Western civilization to think outside the box. It is, as Mr. Spock would say, the logical thing to do.

---

[35] "Everywhere else law and religion are subservient to the social and religious needs of men and nations, but Jews are expected to subordinate their emotions, their wishes and desires to the Law." Hirsch, *Collected Writings*, Vol. II, 387.

[36] "Spock is a character we Jews can identify with: a highly intelligent intellectual who is justly proud of his own Vulcan heritage...the most Jewish of all Spock's characteristics is his extreme intellectualism. Spock's world is ruled by precise, disciplined, logical thinking, not fuzzy Human emotionalism." Rabbi Yonassan Gershom, *Jewish Themes in Star Trek*. (Earth: Lulu Press, Inc., 2009), pp. 34, 44.

CHAPTER SEVEN

How to be Sieved

There are four types among students who sit before the sages: A sponge, a funnel, a strainer and a sieve: a sponge, which absorbs everything; a funnel, which lets in from one end and lets out from the other; a strainer, which lets the wine flow through and retains the sediment; and a sieve, which allows the flour dust to pass through and retains the fine flour.

— *Pirkei Avot*[1]

THE TALMUD TEACHES A PRINCIPLE MUCH LIKE THE EXAMPLE OF Sherlock Holmes's "brain attic" mentioned above, to learn and retain what is vital and eschew the superfluous. According to the *mishna*, the "sponge," like the fool who "takes in all the lumber of every sort that he comes across," remembers everything whether it is important or nonessential, and often has trouble differentiating between the two, strewing his "brain attic" with so many non-essentials that the important material is buried. The "funnel" lets the lessons go in one ear and out the other, and the strainer only remembers the nonessential. The sieve, however, retains the vital parts of the lesson, the "fine flour." When studying the Noahide Law it is important to understand

---

[1] *Pirkei Avot,* 5:18.

that there is a great deal in the Torah that does not apply to the Noahide's service to God. Given the indefinite paradigms of Noahide Law
as taught by the Talmud and the rabbis, this has not always been an
easy task to separate the vital from the unnecessary, or the permitted
from the prohibited. This problem is compounded when we add the
vast knowledge of the secular world: science, biology, physics (the
laws that govern our physical universe), and the culture and literature
of civilizations both ancient and modern.

In April of 1835, Rabbi Samson Raphael Hirsch sent a letter to his
cousin Zvi Hirsch May asking him to help in finding a publisher for a
two-part work called *Moriah and Horeb*.[2] The first part of the work,
Moriah, was intended to be about "the theoretical foundation of the
Bible's teachings on God, the universe, man and Israel, whereas this
second part, *Horeb*, tries to describe Israel's duties in practical life."[3]
Although Rabbi Hirsch never got around to writing *Moriah*, he did
have an outline, published in his book *Nineteen Letters*, which was
written and published first to "test the waters" for *Horeb*. The success
of *Nineteen Letters* led to the publication of *Horeb*. Both *Nineteen Letters* and *Horeb* became instant classics; their popularity thrust Rabbi
Hirsch into the limelight, and he became the leader of Orthodox Judaism in Germany for the next half-century.

Although *Moriah* was never published as a finished work, the
outline can be found in Letters 3–9 of Hirsch's work *The Nineteen
Letters*.[4] These seven chapters deal with, respectively: God, Man,
Education, History, Israel's relationship to the nations, the founding
of the Jewish People, and the Exile of the Jews from *Eretz Yisrael*,

---

[2] "*Horeb* was originally intended to be the second part of a two-volume work, entitled
Moriah and Horeb. The first part was to be an exposition of the basics of Jewish
thought. It is unclear why Rabbi Hirsch never wrote *Moriah*." Rabbi Eliyahu Meir
Klugman, *Rabbi Samson Raphael Hirsch: Architect of Torah Judaism for the Modern
World*. (Brooklyn: Mesorah Publications, Ltd., 2003), 67, n. *g*.

[3] Hirsch, *Horeb*, cxli.

[4] "Events changed Hirsch's original plan: he felt constrained to write *Horeb*, the
practical part of his work, first. This change of plan was Hirsch's instinctive reaction
to the revolt against Jewish law which had begun with the French Revolution and the
consequent emancipation of European Jewry, and which had reached its climax in
the Reform movement of Hirsch's days—a revolt which had led in a comparatively
short time to an almost complete breakdown of Jewish religious observance and an
estrangement from the thought-world of the Torah among the overwhelming majority
of German Jews." Grunfeld, *Horeb*, xxxi.

or the Land of Israel. Although Rabbi Hirsch's work was written to a Jewish audience, one of the themes throughout his work was the duty and obligation of the non-Jew to keep the part of the Torah as well as the Jew's obligation to teach and be an example. As Rabbi Hirsch explained, the non-Jew's approach to the Torah is intrinsically different from the Jew. As the *Cohen* and *Levite* have laws that apply only to themselves and not to the general Jewish population, so too the non-Jew has restrictions on which parts of the Torah they are to observe.

The Noahide's view of Moriah is from the base of the mountain, not from the summit (cf. n. 19, p. 418). The Noahide's path to the Torah is fundamentally different, and the Noahide is only to observe a specific—although still substantial—part of the Torah. According to Rabbi Hirsch, these observances can be summed up into three general categories:

> An indication of a later revelation to the sons of No'ach was preserved for us in the seven No'achide commandments, from which we can deduce some basic principles, i.e.:
> 1. acknowledgment of God as the One Alone;
> 2. justice, as guided by the inner revelation of man's conscience;
> 3. control of bestial drives and self-protection against bestial degeneration.
> Demands based on the principle of lovingkindness are, however, missing (*Sanhedrin* 56a).[5]

Besides the omission of the principle of lovingkindness, there is also the omission of any sort of obligation of "religious" duties for the Noahide. There is no obligation for the Noahide to engage in formal prayer, group "worship," or any of the other tenets we associate with organized religion. This is because the "religious duty" of the Noahide is the creation of a moral and just society, not a "religion."[6] As Rabbi Joseph Elias, the translator, editor and commentator of Hirsch's *Nineteen Letters* explained, "Rabbi S. R. Hirsch saw the Torah as fixed (as

---

[5] Hirsch, *The Nineteen Letters*, 77.

[6] "From the time when men first drew breath on earth they have had a kind of religion. The heathen who prays to his fetish, the Aborigine who moulds his god of honey-dough and paints it with human blood, the Greek who carved his god of gold and ivory and ascribed to him the invention of his arts and indulgence to his own gallantries, and finally the adherents of those two world-religions which have come into existence by combining a few ideas from the Torah with various conceptions taken from the nations of the world—all these had, and continue to have some kind of religion. Even the atheist who despises religion has, perhaps, himself retained some sort of religion." Hirsch, *Collected Writings*, Vol. I, 184.

immutable as the Creator Whose Will it represents), and what evolved was history, the fate of mankind and of the Jew in particular—*shaped* by man's compliance (or non-compliance) with God's Will and His goal for the world."[7] It is the Torah which is to "guide us toward a proper understanding of nature and history and of our place in the world."[8]

As we have repeatedly pointed out, the Noahide Law is a legal and moral code. Although mention of the Noahide Law can be found sprinkled here and there throughout the Talmud, the main discussion is found in the tractate *Sanhedrin* 56a–60a, and the entire debate has to do with violations of Torah law; that is, which laws of the Torah a Noahide could be held liable for punishment.[9] The Sages concluded there were Seven Laws, or more specifically, Seven Categories of prohibitions for the non-Jew that were supported by the Written Torah. This was based on the seemingly superfluous[10] verse of 2:16:

ויצו יי אלקים על־האדם לאמר מכל עץ־הגן אכל תאכל

"And HASHEM God commanded the man, saying, 'Of every tree of the garden you may freely eat'"—which in the original Hebrew contained seven distinct concepts:[11]

---

[7] Joseph Elias, commentary to the Third Letter, *Nineteen Letters*, 35.

[8] Ibid., 40.

[9] One of the criticisms of the Noahide Law is that it is not specifically spelled out in Scripture. A perusal of the Torah will show that there was a moral code in place for mankind long before the Torah was given to Israel on Sinai: the punishment for murder: Genesis 4:10–11, 9:6 (murder); Genesis 6:11 (theft); Genesis 9:4 (limb of the living); Genesis 9:5 (courts of justice); the punishment meted out to Sodom, Canaan, and Egypt (illicit sex, idolatry, blasphemy, cf. Genesis 12:17, 19:13, 20:3, Exodus 5:2, Leviticus 18:24). It is illogical to assume God would have punished these people if they had not violated any laws. It should also be noted that during the time mentioned above the Law had not yet been written down; this moral and legal code was orally transmitted.

[10] No verse, word, or even letter in the Torah is superfluous. A verse that repeats something that has been said before, such as *Bereishis* 2:16 repeating 1:29, the rabbis taught that there was a reason, particularly since the wording in the two verses is different. Through rabbinic exegesis they concluded that there were seven specific prohibitions taught in verse 2:16.

[11] "Ever since God communicated His will to Adam, mankind has been guided by Divine pronouncements addressed to such outstanding personalities Noah, the Patriarchs, and Moses. Indeed, as Jewish philosophers (*Ikkarim* 3:12) have pointed out, it would have been inconceivable for God to have created the universe without providing the guidelines for man's mission on earth." *Trei Asar*, Vol. I. Rabbi Joseph Elias, Overview, xvii.

And commanded—God commands Adam, that is, He sets down rules of conduct (social justice).[12]

HASHEM—The Holy Name of God, which is known as the tetragrammaton. This Holy Name should not be spoken as spelt, thus the prohibition of blasphemy.[13]

Elokim—The Name of God which signifies justice (as the Name *HASHEM*—literally "The Name"—signifies mercy); this is a prohibition against idolatry.[14]

upon the man—upon the human being which God had created and given a living, speaking spirit. This is the prohibition of murder.[15]

saying—forbidden relationships always begin with speech; the prohibition of adultery.[16]

of every tree of the garden—but not of the one tree that does not belong to you. This is the prohibition of theft.[17]

you may freely eat—all herbage (save one) is given to you for sustenance, but not other living animals, for their blood contains their spirit. This is the prohibition of eating the limb of the living.[18]

---

[12] "We see from this verse [Genesis 18:19] that the term 'command' [ויצו] is used specifically for carrying out justice [משפט], and for reaching compromises between litigants [צדקה]. We can therefore infer that the term 'command' mentioned to Adam also alludes to carrying out justice [which also presupposes the existence of civil laws]." Rabbi Micheol Weiner, *The Schottenstein Talmud: Sanhedrin*, Vol. II. (Brooklyn: Mesorah Publications, ltd., 2005), 56a, n. 10.

[13] "Leviticus 24:16...the term '*HASHEM*' in the verse stated to Adam alludes to blasphemy." Ibid., n. 11.

[14] "Exodus 20:3. Thus, the term [אלקים] in the verse stated to Adam implies that only God should be worshiped, but not an idol." Ibid., n. 12.

[15] "Genesis 9:6. The term אדם alludes to murder." Ibid., n. 13.

[16] "Jeremiah 3:1. The term לאמר thus introduces the verse discussing a woman who leaves her husband for another man." Ibid., n. 14.

[17] "Since God found it necessary to permit Adam to partake of the trees in the Garden, giving him possession of them, this implies that the fruits of those trees that did not belong to Adam were prohibited (*Rashi*)." Ibid., n. 15.

[18] "The verse thus indicates that Adam was permitted to partake only of something that was designated for eating [such as fruits of a tree]. This excludes taking a limb from a live animal." Ibid., n. 16.

These are the Seven Categories[19] in which a Noahide could be prosecuted in a *beis din*, or court of Jewish (or Noahide) law, the prohibitions of which were incumbent on each and every non-Jew. It is no coincidence that the discussion of the Noahide Law is found in the book of *Sanhedrin*, the tractate which deals with courts of justice. This code is to be the basis of a legal system, not a religion. As Rabbi Hirsch explained:

> In view of Judaism, every human being is expected to recognize God and His attributes...only a purified awareness of God makes a man truly human. If I were gifted with the purest, most sublime perception of God and His attributes but had not crossed the threshold of Judaism, I would be nothing more (but also nothing less) than an ordinary human being. That kind of perception does not require a knowledge of the Torah. The very fact that this knowledge is expected of all men, including those who did not receive the Torah from God at Mount Sinai, is proof that such a knowledge about God does not require Torah study and that, through Judaism, the Torah was intended to give something additional and much more far-reaching to mankind as a whole...*la loi*, not *la foi*, law, not faith, is the motto of Judaism. It is obedience, not faith, or hope, or prayer, that makes the Jew a Jew.[20]

If it is obedience and not faith that makes a Jew a Jew, then it is also obedience and not faith that makes a Noahide a Noahide, for the Seven Laws are a part of Torah-observant Judaism, not a separate "religion." This is why the Noahide Law is only found in the Talmud, a book that has been long closed to the non-Jew. The Seven Laws of Noah are neither a "religion" nor should they be viewed simply as a list of commandments; the Noahide Code is the non-Jew's interface to the Torah.

In *Devarim* 27:8 it states "And you shall write upon the stones all the words of this Law very plainly." According to *Rashi*, this meant that the Torah was written in the seventy languages of man, intelligible to all, so that all mankind could learn the Torah. Far from being a closed book, the Torah was for all mankind, a guide for both the Jews and the non-Jews. As we have seen, the resistance in implementing this law is based on a combination of ignorance and hostility. There is

---

[19] Cf. *Rashi's* commentary *Sanhedrin* 74b. "Noahites are required to observe not only the seven basic Noahide laws but also the various regulations associated with them... thus, our Gemara uses the term אבזרייהו, *spices*, to describe mitzvos that strengthen or define other laws." Weiner, *The Schottenstein Talmud: Sanhedrin*, Vol. II, 74b, n. 20.

[20] Hirsch, *Collected Writings*, Vol. VII, 33–34.

a great deal of misinformation about Noahide Law; many of its opponents say that the Jews want to use it to "take over the world," or that if you steal a candy bar you will be decapitated, and other such nonsense from those who try to discredit the Torah.[21] It has been the Edomite nations who have been in control and have instituted harsh punishments. For example, in Britain, even as late as the eighteenth century, it was legal to torture defendants in order to obtain a "confession."[22]

For most of the past two thousand years, the Edomite legal systems had made it illegal—often under penalty of death—for Jews to teach the Noahide Law to non-Jews. This is the sort of tyranny which Allan Bloom[23] spoke of, the removal of alternate possibilities to the class-defining Roman/Edomite legal system. As long as the public was kept unaware of an alternative to the traditional Roman-based legal system, the Edomite law could reign supreme, and since there has not been any modern state or society that has adopted Noahide Law as the legal system, there is no precedent to go by.

~

OUR CULTURE HAS taught us that the Bible is about "religion." Many Noahides, having been raised in a Christian culture, shelve the Law in

---

[21] Both *Ravad* and *Ramban* were of the opinion that Israel cannot enforce the Noahide Law upon neighboring nations that Israel conquers militarily, let alone Gentile nations over which it has no control (cf. *Ravad* on *Malachim* 6:1 and Issura Beah 12:7–8; *Ramban's* commentary on *Bereishis* 26:5, *Devirim* 20:1, 11; *Tosafot Avoda Zara* 26b). The Jews are to lead by example, not by strength. "The nation which is to descend from him is to represent one entity to the outside world, but internally it is to be a multiplicity of elements united into one. Each tribe is to represent an ethnic individuality in its own right. The nation of Jacob, which, as 'Israel,' is to demonstrate to the other nations the power of God, triumphantly pervading and shaping all of mankind, should not present a one-sided image. As a model nation it should reflect the greatest possible variety of national characteristics in a microcosm. In its tribes it should represent variously the warrior nation, the merchant nation, the agricultural nation, the nation of scholars, etc. In this manner it will become clear to all the world that the consecration of human life to the covenant with the Law of God does not demand occupational restrictions, or depend on specific ethnic characteristics, but that all mankind in all its multiplicity is capable of accepting the concept of monotheism taught by Israel, and of fashioning the multiplicity of human and national individualities into one united kingdom of God." Hirsch, *T'rumath Tzvi*, 158.

[22] And as America has done recently in Guantanamo.

[23] "The most successful tyranny is not the one that uses forces to assure uniformity but the one that removes the awareness of other possibilities that makes it seem inconceivable that other ways are viable, that removes the sense that there is no outside." Bloom, *The Closing of the American Mind*, 249.

the pigeonhole of "religion" in their own minds, unaware of the limitations they are putting on the Torah:

> One is accustomed to call the Torah 'Religion' or Jewish Religion, because the word religion describes everywhere outside Israel the relationship of man to his God or gods; this word, too, is invested everywhere else with dignity and holiness; could one then have a holier and more impressive designation for the Torah than religion? And yet, it is exactly this term 'religion' which has made it so difficult to understand the essence of the Torah.[24]

This is a most difficult concept for the non-Jew to grasp; for the Noahide, the Torah is not about religion, at least not the way we understand the concept.

During the nineteenth century, when the Enlightenment opened the gates of the ghettos and allowed the Jews of Germany to enjoy many of the freedoms of their Christian neighbors, and when "Reform" Judaism threatened to snuff out traditional "Torah-true" Judaism, Rabbi Samson Raphael Hirsch,[25] the founder of modern Orthodox Judaism, became the bulwark against the flood of non-observant Judaism. Rabbi Hirsch often had harsh words for Reform Jews who spurned *halakha* in favor of the "religious" or "spiritual" elements of the Torah, of the "deplorable splitting-up of the single Law of God, a meaningless division of the indivisible Torah into…duties of man to God and of man to man, and the still more deplorable transference of this idea from theory into practice."[26] The teaching of Rabbi Hirsch has a special relevance today, for many who call themselves Noahides are, like their non-orthodox Jewish co-religionists, also non-observant. As with "Reform" Judaism, the non-observant[27] Noahides pick and choose the

---

[24] Hirsch, *Collected Writings*, Vol. I, 184.

[25] Rabbi Samson Raphael Hirsch (1808–1888) was one of the great commentators and structuralists of modern Judaism. Unlike previous Jewish sages, such as Maimonides or *Rashi* who lived in medieval Arabic or Christian cultures, Hirsch lived and wrote during the modern industrial age, and his life spanned the lives of such Enlightenment luminaries as Thomas Jefferson, James Madison, Georg Hegel, Karl Marx, John Stewart Mill, and Herbert Spencer. His commentary reflected the problems of *halakha* in dealing with modern industrial society as well as social and intellectual movements such as Reform Judaism and the Enlightenment.

[26] Hirsch, *Collected Writings*, Vol. II, 273.

[27] There is a difference between *non-believing* and *non-observant*. Even among non-observant (Reform) Jews, many of them still "believe" in HASHEM; in the *halakha*

mitzvot they want to keep, particularly the "spiritual"[28] or "religious" elements of the Torah that are specifically for the Jew's service to God and have nothing to do with the Seven Laws of Noah. (Examples of the Jewish service include organized prayer,[29] keeping the Sabbath and other Jewish festivals, eating kosher food and wearing *tallis* and *tefillin* while praying.) In the neglect of the legal and moral teachings[30] of the Noahide Law, the non-observant Noahides focus instead on the religious aspects, often using Christian terminology such as "worshiping" and "fellowshipping" as their main goals. Instead of performing their duty of establishing a just and moral society as God has instructed them, the non-observant Noahides do what is pleasing in their own eyes, turning the Noahide Law into an organized religion.

Rabbi Hirsch often commented on why keeping *halakha* was more important than prayer or "worship," and if, in Rabbi Hirsch's words, "Divine Service is not the focal point of Judaism…Temple and priests, offerings and prayers, are not the most important pillars of the Jewish way of life"[31] was a critique on the Reform Jew's attitude about

---

detailed in the Oral Law, however, they view simply as a matter of convenience, picking and choosing which *miztvot* they wish to observe.

[28] This is not to demean spirituality, but rather, the perception among Reform Noahides that being "spiritual" is similar to "dropping spiritual pennies into the Divine piggybank, magically saving up good deeds towards their investment in the Word-to-come." Weinberg, "The Torah of Life, as Understood by Rav. S. R. Hirsch", *The World of Hirschian Teachings: An Anthology on the Hirsch Chumash and the Haskafa of Rav Samson Raphael Hirsch*. (Jerusalem: Feldheim Publishers, 2008), 115.

[29] "The whole point in bringing sacrifices is that they inspire a person to rededicate himself to serving Me devoutly" (*Malbim*). Roberts, *Trei Asar*, 62. Since the destruction of the *Beis HaMikdash*, prayer has replaced sacrifice, but this teaching of *Malbim* can be applied to prayer as well. The service of the Noahide is primarily to establish a Torah-based government and legal system.

[30] "The tension between law and morals and the complexity of relations between them are part of our intellectual and institutional history…in the Hebrew Scriptures, the distinction between law and morals does not exist." Konvitz, *Torah & Constitution*, 69.

[31] Hirsch, *Collected Writings*, Vol. I, 312. In his commentary to Psalm 100, Hirsch elaborates: "It is regrettable that the concept of 'Divine Service' is understood to consist primarily of the ritual of prayer and sacrifice in the temple and synagogues. This is not in accordance with the Jewish idea of עבודת ד׳. This, the true 'service of the Lord,' is primarily and most truly performed in the process of day-to-day living… prayer and the offering of sacrifices are called 'Divine Service' only because through them we prepare and consecrate ourselves anew each time for that which is the actual service of the Lord…the earnestness of attitude and resolve with which the nations

prayer and worship—which the Jew is commanded to observe—then how much more so is it to the Noahide, who is *not* commanded to observe these things? Yet for the past few decades, the focus of the Noahide movement has been to form small religious groups in places such as Texas and Tennessee, groups that revolve around imitating the "religious" elements in the Jewish service to God. This has had the unfortunate effect of the general public's perception of the Noahide Law as the basis of a peculiar religious cult, another odd branch of Judeo-Christianity that has spawned other cults such as the Hebrew Christians and Nazarene Noahidism.

Much of the blame for this development can be put on the so-called Noahide "leadership" whose superficial[32] understanding of Torah and *hashkafa* (Jewish philosophy) has led to a focus on the "religious" elements of the Torah, on mysticism and kabbalah[33] instead of *halakha*.[34] What little study of Noahide *halakha* there has been is limited to Maimonides's *Mishna Torah*, particularly the three chapters of *Hilchot Melachim* which deal with the Noahide Laws. Ironically, the reliance on Rambam's *Mishna Torah* has been one of the reasons the Noahide movement has seen limited growth.

---

shall one day enter into the covenant of God and thus come into His presence…to serve the Lord with gladness, and to serve Him *outside* the confines of the Temple." Hirsch, *The Hirsch Psalms*, §ii, 195.

[32] "Our Sages have particularly harsh criticism for the arrogance of those whose knowledge is only superficial and for the memorizer who has learned only the letter of the discipline without understanding its spirit and the ideas that motivate the Law. (*Sotah* 22a)." Hirsch, *Collected Writings*, Vol. VII, 201.

[33] "Any religious ideology that soars upon the wings of the *seraphim* and the angels on high and abhors mortal man, flesh and blood, will, perforce, in the end (1) prove unfaithful to itself and be guilty of perpetrating a religious lie…(2) constrict itself to a narrow, dark corner, relinquish the public domain, and give rise to a concept of religious esotericism. A religiosity that centers upon the heavenly kingdom and not upon the earthy kingdom—that can be made to reflect the heavenly kingdom—gives rise to ecclesiastical tyranny, religious aristocracies, and charismatic personalities." [Examples of whom include Jesus, Sabbatai Tzvi, Jacob Frank, and most recently, Rabbi Menachem Mendel Schneerson—A.C.] Soloveitchik, *Halakhic Man*, 43.

[34] Using a mystical and kabbalistic approach to the decidedly legalistic Noahide Law has been one of the major problems with the modern Noahide movement, for it has been the *hasidim*, rather than the *mitnagdim*, who have been a major presence with teaching the Noahide Law. The volatile conflict between the *mitnagdim* and the *hasidim*, although it has cooled down considerably since the late nineteenth century, has flared up again with the messianification of Rabbi Menachem Mendel Schneerson, and this has affected the Noahide movement, although few Noahides are aware of this battle of Torah ideology between the two schools of Orthodox Judaism.

As with Jewish Law, the Noahide Law should grow and change to meet the times;[35] Noahide Law is not mummified in a twelfth century Egyptian sarcophagus. Modern nations and states have written codes of law and constitutions, and our civilization has moved beyond the ancient practice of having individual judges being the sole dispensers of legal justice. Opinions and views which were valid in Maimonides's time and place (Medieval Arabia) have changed, and though the *Mishna Torah* is important to the understanding and application of the Seven Laws, there has been some valid rabbinic criticism[36] about certain points of his work, particularly in Maimonides's interpretation of the Noahide law of social justice. This has posed a problem for the Noahide movement, getting it off on the wrong foot; the first two rabbinic works (in English) that dealt exclusively with the Noahide Law—Rabbi Aaron Lichtenstein's *The Seven Laws of Noah* (1981) and Rabbis Chaim Clorfene and Yakov Rogalsky's *The Path of the Righteous Gentile* (1987)—were based on Maimonides's *Mishna Torah* which was written in the late twelfth century in Egypt, and which focused on the individual observance of the Noahide Law, and, for the most part, ignoring the community aspect of Noahide observance. This lack of stressing the communal aspect of the Noahide law was the key issue in a major disagreement between Nachmonides and Maimonidies on the issue of the Noahide law of social justice.

﹏

---

[35] "Far from being static—the impression one may gain from a code of law—the Halakha is a dynamic and ever-expanding system of jurisprudence intrinsically capable of dealing with the ever-changing conditions of mankind—social, political, economic, and technological." Eidelberg, *Beyond the Secular Mind*, 59.

[36] "To the extent that the *Rambam* sought to resolve this conflict by reconciling Aristotelian philosophy with Torah, Rabbi S. R. Hirsch takes him to task...he [R. Hirsch] maintains that, overall, by accommodating non-Jewish philosophical views, it caused serious problems. The idea that man does not achieve perfection by doing mitzvot as such, and that they are only a means to attaining an understanding of God, of His providence, of how He guides the world—in line with Aristotelian thought—bore misleading and harmful results...The reader is bound to be taken aback by...[R. Hirsch's] boldness in putting forth such a forceful critique of the *Rambam*. We must remember, however, that he merely followed in the steps of earlier critics (and...was moved by the same considerations that prompted them)...Rabbi Me'ir Abulafia, the author of the Yad Rama...Rabbi Yehudah Alfacher...in particular, however, Rabbi S. R. Hirsch was guided by the Chasid Ya'avetz and by his response to those who saw philosophical speculation as the highest form of service to God." Elias, commentary to Rabbi S. R. Hirsch's *Nineteen Letters*, 284, 286–87.

NACHMONIDES, KNOWN BY the acronym *Ramban*, had a different perspective on the Noahide law of social justice than did Maimonides. In a lengthy commentary on the Noahide Law in *Bereishis* 34:13, *Ramban* said that Noahides were commanded by God:

> Concerning the laws of theft, overcharging, withholding wages, the laws of bailees and of the rapist or the seducer of minors, the various categories of damages, personal injury, the laws of creditors and debtors, the laws of buying and selling, etc., comparable to the civil laws about which Israel was commanded.[37]

Understanding this approach, we see that Noahide law should be the legal basis of our contract law, property law, trust law, tort law, criminal law, and international law.[38] *Ramban's* approach viewed the Noahide Law in a much broader context than did Maimonides; instead of the Noahide having to set up individual courts of justice (having judges who based their decisions on Noahide Law) as Maimonides taught, Nachmonides maintained that a Noahide society should develop a body of civil law based on the Torah. The Noahide law is not to be as exact either in strictness or in severity, but it should follow the halakha as closely as possible. According to *Ramban*, Noahide law should be the legal basis of our contract law, property law, trust law, tort law, criminal law, and international law—basically everything we consider our "secular" law. In the broader context of implementing Noahide Law in a society, the laws of idolatry and blasphemy are not simply prohibitions against the worship of false idols, but prohibitions against organized religion. This can be seen in the context of the discussion in *Sanhedrin* 56a–60a, where the focus of the discussion by the rabbis is on which *mitzvah* violation a non-Jew can be tried for in a court of law, *not* for setting up a "religion" for the Noahide.

There is no denying the stature of the *Rambam* as one of the giants of Torah scholarship,[39] and that his *Mishna Torah* is the only Code of

---

[37] Ramban, *Bereishis*, Vol II. (Brooklyn: Mesorah Publications, Ltd., 2005), 224; cf. Schottenstein Talmud, *Sanhedrin* 56b, n. 34.

[38] "The individual is held in check by his fear of society and its authorized spokesmen. But nations can be kept within the limits of correctness and propriety in their dealings with other nations only by the fear of a Higher Being, that is, God Himself." Hirsch, *The Hirsch Psalms*, §ii, 166–67.

[39] "It is to this great man [*Rambam*] alone that we owe the preservation of practical Judaism until the present day. By accomplishing this and yet, on the other hand, merely reconciling Judaism with the ideas from without, rather than developing it creatively

Jewish Law that deals with the Seven Laws of Noah. Yet, despite what many think, *Rambam* was not the final authority on Noahide Law. This has to do with the Torah (by which we include Oral Torah) being a living Law, not a static set of rules. The limiting effect of basing Noahide Law solely on the *Mishna Torah* has created problems in the Noahide community, affecting not only its growth but its effectiveness at producing a stable society.

A Noahide may be deeply "religious," believing in God and the Torah, rejecting all other man-made religions in favor of the Seven Laws. Yet if the focus of the Noahide is on the *mitzvot* that a Noahide is not commanded to observe (organized prayer, observing Jewish holidays, keeping kosher, etc.) while neglecting the *halakha* of the Seven Laws, then the Noahide is, by definition, non-observant. The view that the Noahide can embrace Jewish religious observances is based on a technicality; it should be pointed out that the Noahide is permitted to pray and to observe certain holy days such as Rosh Hashanna and Shavuot, but not at the expense of neglecting the responsibility of keeping the Seven Laws. The observance of the "religious" elements of the Torah is left to the discretion of the individual, and prayers and observance of Jewish holidays should be limited to the individual and the family; to encourage community worship and prayer (such as establishing a Noahide "synagogue") violates the commandment that Noahides are forbidden to establish organized religion. The observance of the Noahide law of Social Justice, on the other hand, can only be achieved by the community at large. Although Noahides think that they are fulfilling God's Will by observing the "religious" *mitzvot*, particularly the *mitzvot* that have to do with the Jew's service to God, they are instead fulfilling their own selfish desires, doing what they want to do rather than what God expects of them. Also, the Noahide should understand

---

from within, and by the way in which he effected this reconciliation, he gave rise to all the good that followed—as well as all the bad. His trend of thought was Arab-Greek, as was his concept of life. Approaching Judaism from without, he brought to it views that he had gained elsewhere, and these he reconciled with Judaism...mitzvos, then, were to him only guides...they were not understood as symbolic actions through which ideas were forever to be perpetuated. Nor did the interpretations offered for mitzvos explain them in their totality: he, the great systematic codifier of the practical conclusions of the Talmud, in the last part of his philosophical work advanced interpretations of the mitzvos which shed no light on their practical details, as defined in his code, and which, indeed, are often incompatible with them. This, these interpretations cannot serve as a complement to the mitzvos in practice, whether in life or in scholarly study." Hirsch, *Nineteen Letters*, 265–66.

that the reward for keeping a *mitzvah* that one is not commanded to perform is not as great as the reward for observing *mitzvot* that one has been commanded, and so the observance of non-obligatory *mitzvot* at the expense of the obligatory *mitzvot* detailed in the Noahide Law defeats the purpose of the Noahide wanting to draw nearer to God. The Talmud is emphatic about this point: "R. Meir used to say: Whence do we know that even a heathen who studies the Torah is as a High Priest? From the verse [Ye shall therefore keep My statutes, and My judgments:] which, if men do, he shall live in them. Priests, Levites, and Israelites are not mentioned, but men: hence thou mayest learn that even a heathen who studied the Torah is as a High Priest!—*That refers to their own seven laws*" (*Sanhedrin* 59a). In this oft-quoted verse, those last seven words are usually ignored (if they are quoted at all). The Talmud makes a point to explain that the Noahide is rewarded for keeping the Seven Laws and the Seven Laws only.[40] It is true that there is no prohibition for Noahides to observe many of the *mitzvot* that are not listed among the Seven Laws, and many rabbis teach that a Noahide can take on other *mitzvot* if he or she desires (as long as the Seven Laws are observed), but to think that just because one prays from a Noahide Siddur every day while ignoring the duty of ensuring a just and moral society by means of a Torah-based legal system shows a lack of understanding of Torah.[41]

---

[40] "Not all of the...duties of Jewish life...need be adopted by other nations. Theirs would be only those connected with the general nature of man and what he was meant to be, but not the tasks which are specifically part of the priestly calling of the Jewish nation. On the other hand...the duties of social life, the attitudes, relationships and obligations between man and man were to be common to all mankind." Hirsch, *Collected Writings*, Vol. IV, 228.

[41] "Unlike civil legal systems, Judaism's legal system was not established for the main purpose of preserving an orderly society; rather it was presented to the Jewish people as a legal framework in which a society recognizing G-d's rulership over the world can develop through implementation of the highest level of ethics. Therefore the principles of legality and ethics are closely intertwined in Judaism. In Judaism, generally acts that are legally permitted are ethical and acts that are not permitted are by definition considered unethical. This differentiation is important, since law does not always equal morality, and preachings of morality do not always translate themselves into a moral society. For example, in societies where law is not combined with ethics and morality, a legal system may develop that permits the most terrible acts such as is brought in the Ramban's commentary to Leviticus 19:2 who explains that the injunction to be "Holy" warns of areas of behavior where the law does not command a particular form of behavior. Thus it may be possible to be a law abiding Jew but over indulge in food and other physical pleasures. Such behavior would be deemed immoral because of the Torah's injunction to be "Holy." Alternatively, given the nature of people and the realities of life, mere ethical and moral slogans

There are many who believe that the teaching of keeping the Noa-hide Law "by chance" (such as having current secular laws approxi-mating Torah concepts)[42] should not be pursued. This teaching, that one must accept that the Torah was given to Moshe at Sinai as a prerequi-site for accepting the Noahide Law,[43] is a teaching that, as the one about the focus of the Noahide Law being "salvation in the World to Come," is based on the *Mishna Torah*: "If he [the Noahide] fulfills [the Seven Laws] out of intellectual conviction, he is not...of 'the pious among the gentiles,' **nor of** their wise men."[44] The Hebrew of the Vilna text reads "nor of their wise men," but the Yemenite version of the *Mishna Torah* (which was not subject to Christian censors) reads "**but rather**, of their wise men."[45] The Christian censors were the cause of this small but im-portant alteration; the Christians, not satisfied with altering their own books, had to alter the writings of the Sages as well. The difference in the wording of this teaching has created a problem in the approach to the Noahide Law; namely, should the non-Jews accept the Noahide Law on the basis that it is a logical and practical system of law? It all depends on whether one thinks our society should be "religious" or whether our society should be based on justice and righteousness as dictated by the Torah. The propagators of the view that the Noahide Law was a "religion" and look at creating a "religious society" disagree with teaching the Noahide Law to "unbelievers" because it was simply "a good idea," or that a Noahide could accept the Noahide Law through his own reason and understanding as Abraham had done.[46]

---

tend to be ineffective and even sometimes pernicious unless contained and enforced within a legal framework." Mark Schwartz, Meir Tamari and Daniel Schwab, "Ethical Investing from a Jewish Perspective." *Business and Society Review*. Vol. 112, Issue 1 (March 2007) 137–161.

[42] Cf. R. Hirsch's commentary to Lev. 26:21.

[43] "Maimonides does not state why he adds the proviso, and no basis for it has been found in the Talmud or other ancient Jewish sources." Konvitz, *Torah and Constitution*, 156.

[44] Yad, *Hilchot Melechim*, 8:11, 582.

[45] Chief Rabbi Abraham Isaac Kook said that "a gentile who observes the seven Noahide laws through the rational process—rather than through a belief that these commandments were 'given by God'—merits not only a share in the world-to-come but also recognition as being one 'of their wise men.'" Konvitz, *Torah & Constitution*, 115.

[46] "Man can and should achieve recognition of God through the use of his own rational, reasoning intellect...whenever the Holy Scriptures ask man to recognize God, they appeal not to man's faith but to his reason." Hirsch, *The Hirsch Psalms*, §i, 92.

Teaching the Noahide Law as a superior legal system based on logic and reason is not only a good idea, but a necessary idea, as explained in the *Séfer haHinnuch*:

> Know that a man is influenced in accordance with his actions. His heart and all his thoughts are always [drawn] after his deeds in which he is occupied, whether [they are] good or bad. Thus even a person who is thoroughly wicked in his heart, and every imagination of the thoughts of his heart is only evil the entire day—if he will arouse his spirit and set his striving and his occupation, with constancy, in the Torah and the mitzvoth, even if not for the sake of Heaven, he will veer at once toward the good, and with the power of his good deeds he will deaden his evil impulse. For after one's acts is the heart drawn.[47]

What the *Séfer haHinnuch* teaches in this passage is that, even if a person keeps the Torah for reasons such as social and peer pressure, that the Law is a "good idea" instead of for the sake of heaven, their behavior will eventually modify their character. As we have seen, the behavior of secular intellectuals such as Voltaire, Rousseau, Jefferson, and Marx left much to be desired. This is where the moral training in the Torah comes in, not just to do what is right but to understand why it is right. Yes, the great personalities in the Torah made mistakes, but the Torah points these out, as well as the consequences of their actions.

As the "wise of the nations"[48] learn more about the Torah and see the infinite wisdom in the Law as well as understand Israel's historic mission, they will be drawn to HASHEM, and even those who do not will recognize that the Noahide Law is a law based on reason and justice, that the Torah is the best of all possible legal systems, a legal system that has yet to be tried. To approach the Torah from a "non-religious" perspective is the problem non-observant Noahides share, for spirituality and mysticism are all that the non-observant Noahides (who have come out of Christianity or other organized religions) are interested in when they learn about the Noahide Law. As one would

---

[47] *Séfer haHinnuch*, Charles Wengrov, trans. (Jerusalem: Feldheim Publishers, 1992), 119.

[48] "As Psalm 147:10–11 has taught us, Israel's return to its ancient splendor will clearly prove that the true greatness of men and nations does not lie in political tyranny and power which men were wont to worship heretofore, but that man's genuine salvation, which is God's alone to give, can be built only upon loyalty to duty, founded upon trust in the Lord. Because this truth had not been generally accepted as such before, the חסידים of the non-Jewish nations also did not receive the recognition justly due them from their fellow-men." Hirsch, *The Hirsch Psalms*, §ii, 494.

not give a glass of wine to a recovering alcoholic, one should not delve into spirituality with a non-Jew just coming out of a spirituality-based religion such as Christianity.

By keeping a strict *halakhic* approach to the Noahide Law, it alleviates another fear as well—the fear of a non-Jew learning Torah in order to convert Jews to a religion such as Christianity. After all, in order to spread the knowledge of the Noahide Law among the nations we have to teach Torah, and what better place to start than the laws detailed by Nachmonides? By presenting the Noahide Law as a legal and moral code as it should be presented, and not a template for organized religion[49] as the non-observant Noahides have been doing, we can assuage the fears of the rabbis as well as quell the arguments about the "wall of separation" in teaching Noahide Law in our schools.[50]

Another problem, and one of the main reasons that Noahides base their observance of Torah strictly on the *Rambam's* paradigm, is the misconception that Maimonides wrote more about the Noahide Law than any other sage. It is true that the *Mishna Torah* is the only Code that deals with the Noahide Law, but there were many other rabbis who wrote about the Seven Laws, particularly Rabbi S. R. Hirsch, who wrote extensively about the Seven Laws and the duties of the Noahide in implementing these laws into their legal systems and governments. It was one of the major themes of his work; in fact, his entire approach to "modern orthodoxy" had to do in part with the Noahide Law. He wanted a Judaism that did not hide in the far corners of society, and for Jews not try to pretend they were still living in a sixteenth-century

---

[49] It should be pointed out that, in regard to the prohibition of organized religion, Judaism has always had a built-in obsolescence. "Judaism" was never meant to be permanent. The "religion" of Judaism was created by the rabbis to ensure the survival of Israel and the Torah until the End of Days when all Jews will return and once again dwell in *Eretz Yisrael*, and the entire Torah, all 613 *mitzvot*, would once again become the law of the land. When this occurs, "Judaism" as we know it will cease to be.

[50] "Meiri explains that R' Yochansan's prohibition refers to an idolater who learns the precepts of the Torah and the Talmud in order to mislead Israelites. That is, he wishes to use his knowledge of Israelite law to trick them into thinking that he is an Israelite and then influence them. A person is therefore fit to be punished for studying the Torah for such a purpose. However, if a Noahide studies the seven commandments that apply to him, he should be honored like a Kohen Gadol even if his investigations lead him to study most of the precepts of the Torah. Since his main purpose in studying is knowledge of the Noahide laws, there is no concern that he will influence Israelites (see also Chamra VeChayei)." Weiner, *Schottenstein Talmud, Sanhedrin* 59a, n. 10.

Polish ghetto, but that Jews could (and should) interact with gentile society in order to fulfill their ultimate world-historical mission: to be a nation of priests and a light unto the nations. As this was the primary purpose of the nation of Israel, the purpose of the Children of Noah was to observe the Noahide Laws, not simply to be the vehicle for individual salvation, but to create a safe, peaceful, and just society so Israel could do its job. This is why it is imperative that Noahides concentrate their efforts of observance on the *halakha* of the Seven Laws instead of spending their energy trying to imitate the Jews and the Jewish service to God.

⁓

ONLY THE CHILDREN of Israel can ascend to the top of Moriah. It is not because of any sort of spiritual inferiority with non-Jewish souls (as some Chabad teach) any more than an implicit superiority on why only the *Kohen Gadol* can enter the Holy of Holies; after all, a non-Jew can rise to the same spiritual level as the Jew, as the Talmud so clearly teaches. It all has to do with service, and for each of us accepting the laws given to us to follow. In the words of Rabbi Samson Raphael Hirsch:

> In the same manner God also needs in His kingdom of humanity both Jews and non-Jews. Jew and non-Jew each has been assigned his own calling and his own law, and God's sublime purpose will be attained only if each one, Jew and non-Jew, will gladly and faithfully carry out that calling and obey that law which God has set for him, and in so doing will make his own contribution to the common good as God expects him to do.[51]

Spirituality, on its own, will not lead the nations to the Torah. The spiritual approach has never worked. Even today, with millions of "spiritual" people, the nations are still in turmoil, and are still in denial. Spirituality, without a halakhic foundation, will not convince the nations to adopt the Torah as the basis for a legal foundation. This can be seen with the non-observant Noahides today who are mainly interested in mysticism and spirituality and show little interest in establishing a legal system based on Torah. The true path to spirituality will establish itself when the nations accept the Torah as the basis for government and law, when the "wise of the nations" see the Divine Wisdom of the Torah as the means for establishing a peaceful and just society.

---

[51] Hirsch, *T'rumath Tzvi*, 6.

Torah im Derech Eretz

Only when the teaching of the God of Shem in unabridged and unadulterated form becomes the property of all mankind will the shadows of error and delusion disappear and truly illuminate the minds and hearts of mankind...the teaching of Shem refrains from making demands on man that are beyond the capacity to comprehend. The teaching of Shem shows man the way to God, revealing only those attributes of God which will permit him to understand and fulfill his mission on earth. It does not expect of man to solve the enigma of God's divinity through an understanding of the world and mankind, but teaches him to understand the world and mankind through God. Thus, it opens a limitless field of ennobling truths that are accessible to all. Shem's teaching does not contain man's thoughts of 'God and the Divine' but God's thoughts of man and human endeavor. It therefore gives precedence to the Law and the establishment, development, and shaping of all human affairs according to God's Will.

— Rabbi Samson Raphael Hirsch[1]

T HE "SECULAR" NATURE OF THE NOAHIDE LAW CONFUSES MANY who think that the prohibitions of idolatry and blasphemy are strictly "religious" laws. In Torah Law, there is a much broader understanding of idolatry; the common (non-Jewish) view of worshiping false gods[2] is only part of what constitutes idolatry, for along with the worship of false gods there is also a prohibition concerning the worship of false ideas. Rabbi Aryeh Kaplan explained that "the Torah warns: 'Do not turn to the idols' (*Vayikra* 19:4), which the Gemara explains as a reference to conceptual idols,[3] ideologies not based

---

[1] Hirsch, *Collected Writings*, Vol. II, 205–06.

[2] The concept of God among Western Culture too often conjures up images of Michaelangelo's Santa Claus-like figure floating on a cloud, or more often, a dead man in a loincloth nailed to a cross.

[3] "The idea that the worship of man will be the last idolatry before the advent of the Mashiach is cited in the name of the Vilna Gaon...in putting forth this concept, Rabbi S. R. Hirsch of course had in mind the modern age, in which man and his reason and judgment have become the supreme arbiter and authority in the world. Secularism, naturalism and scientism (the belief that science and only science can furnish the answer to all questions) are some of the approaches that have replaced mankind's seeking of God's guidance. The failure of the twentieth century to solve any of the

on the Torah (*Shabbos* 149a)."[4] Examples of these idolatrous ideologies are the non-Jewish concept of nationalism,[5] or even the idea that the Noahides must form isolated communities and their own houses of "worship," both which are contrary to the Seven Laws. The *mitzvot* Rabbi Aaron Litchtenstein lists in his book *The Seven Laws of Noah* as incumbent upon the Noahide, particularly the prohibitions of idolatry, include "against turning to idolatry [in word, in thought, in deed, or by any observance that may draw us to its worship]"[6] as he does in *Shemos* 20:5, "against worshiping idols in any of their customary manners of worship."[7] This is the halakhaic basis for the prohibition of organized religion, for organized religion with its houses of "worship" is what pagan religions have used over the years to ensnare both Jews and non-Jews, to "draw us to its worship," i.e., using the "joys of fellowship" replete with group prayer and singing, and it is certainly their "customary manner of worship." The concept of creating a Noahide "congregation" that tries to emulate the Jewish service by things such as wearing *kippahs*, Noahide "*tallis*," chanting Hebrew prayers, and holding their services on Friday nights and Saturday mornings is a violation of *halakha*.[8] In fact, the closer a Noahide congregation

basic problems of humanity—achievement of international peace, agreement on accepted standards of morality and interpersonal relations, mental health requirements, alleviation of poverty and famine, protection of our environment, etc.—certainly justifies the author's remark about 'the havoc wrought by human violence and human folly.' Ultimately, the 'worship of man' is disastrous, because man's insight cannot arrive at a clear knowledge of moral law." Elias, *Nineteen Letters*, 101.

[4] Rabbi Aryeh Kaplan, *The Aryeh Kaplan Reader*. (Brooklyn: Mesorah Publications, Ltd., 1985), 70.

[5] "Rav S. R. Hirsch was vehemently opposed to a hollow, empty, *secular* nationalism based on race and shared historical accident...to the Jewish world-view, this 'nationalism' is none other than the worst example of idol worship." Rav Yaakov Yechiel Weinberg, "The Torah of Life, as Understood by Rav. S. R. Hirsch." *The World of Hirschian Teachings*, 99.

[6] Rabbi Aaron Litchtenstein, *The Seven Laws of Noah*. (New York: The Rabbi Jacob Joseph School Press, 1986), 66.

[7] Ibid., 67.

[8] Some Noahides say that, since Noah and Abraham offered sacrifices and prayer, they too should be able to do likewise. They miss the point of *Bamidbar* 3:4; where "Nadab and Abihu died before HASHEM when they offered alien fire before HASHEM in the Wilderness of Sinai." Even with the best intentions, one should neither invent nor emulate any "religious" modes of worship that the Torah does not specifically stipulate.

tries to mimic the Jewish service of God, the closer they get to *Chillul HASHEM*[9] which Rabbi Litchtenstein also lists as one of the Noahide prohibitions of blasphemy.[10]

These are the idolatrous ideologies that true Noahide observance must be wary of emulating, as well as following any Noahide "leader" who espouses ideas of organized Noahide "religion."[11] As Rabbi Kaplan explained, "he who leads others must be extremely firm in his faith. He must not follow his own whims, but must base his entire ideology on God's Torah. He…must not be misled by false ideologies or foreign methodologies."[12] Most Noahides who have come out of organized religion (particularly Christianity) have problems letting go of the theology, complaining about having to study "dry legalism" instead of "spirituality," and that the prime motivation is for "fellowship" and "worship" rather than the moral and legal stipulations of the Seven Laws. The non-observant or Reform Noahide, much like his Reform Jewish counterpart, is the Noahide who believes the Noahide Law constitutes a "religion," and focuses on the ceremonial and religious aspects of the Torah while ignoring the *halakha* of the Seven Laws. The observant Noahide, on the other hand, focuses on his or her obligation to observe the *halakha* of the Seven Laws. This is no doubt one of the major factors in the non-observant Noahide's exclusivity in basing the Noahide Law on Maimonides, and his focus on keeping the Noahide Law (as well as other non-obligatory mitzvot) for "rewards" and "everlasting life" in *Olam haBah*, the World to Come.[13]

---

[9] This would happen if someone saw a Noahide and mistook him for a Jew, then later seeing this same Noahide going into a non-kosher restaurant or exhibiting some other form of non-Jewish behavior.

[10] Litchtenstein, *The Seven Laws of Noah*, 87.

[11] "Judaism is not a religion solely for holidays and feast days; it embraces all aspects of life—workdays and festival days. Judaism, the most 'religious' of all religions has no word for 'religion.'" Hirsch, *Collected Writings*, Vol. VIII, 253.

[12] Kaplan, *The Aryeh Kaplan Reader*, 70.

[13] Maimonides begins his section in the *Mishna Torah* on the Noahide Law with the statement that "anyone who accepts upon himself the fulfillment of these seven mitzvot and is precise in their observance is considered one of 'the pious among the gentiles' and will merit a share in the world to come…this applies only when he accepts them and fulfills them because the Holy One…commanded them." (Yad, *Hilchot Melechim* 8:11). This has had the unfortunate effect of making correct beliefs more important than correct behavior as well as putting the Seven Laws into a "religious" context; many ex-Christians who have embraced the Noahide Laws focus on the "salvation" aspect of the Noahide Law. The problem is that, according to *Ramban*'s

Another problem with this strict adherence to the *Rambam*'s view of the Noahide Law has to do with disagreements between other rabbinic opinions as well as questions regarding the *Rambam's* sources[14] (such as Maimonides using the *Midrash* in formulating his opinions when listing the Seven Laws.)[15] There is also the question of focus. As noted above, in chapters eight through ten of *Hilchot Melachim*, the *Rambam* focused on the individual Noahide's responsibility at the expense of community observance.[16] In Rabbi Eliyahu Touger's commentary on the *Mishna Torah*, Rabbi Touger said "the mitzvot given [at Sinai] then differ, in purpose as well as in number, from the mitzvot given the gentiles. The gentiles' seven mitzvot are intended to establish a stable and moral society. The purpose of the 613 mitzvot is to establish a complete bond between God and every aspect of man's personality."[17] This is a point that is too-often lost on the non-observant Noahide, that there is a major difference between the Jewish service to God and the Noahide service to God.[18] The non-observant

---

commentary to *Bereishis* 34:13, the Seven Laws are not simply an individual means of salvation, but a communal one. "Apart from other serious questions that we have noted concerning the proviso, it should be obvious to persons familiar with Christian dogma that the proviso injected by Maimonides into the doctrine of the Noahide laws disturbingly looks very much like justification by faith...the Noahide laws are consistent with the ethical essence of Judaism...there is no positive commandment to believe in any dogma." Konvitz, *Torah & Constitution*, 107.

[14] Cf. *Sefer Shoftim*, Ch. 9, fn. 16 and 61. "As mentioned above, the *Rambam* uses the expression 'it appears to me' when he has no explicit proof for his statements in Talmudic sources." Rabbi Eliyahu Touger, *Mishneh Torah, Sefer Shoftim*, 607.

[15] *Hilchot Melachim*, 9:1. The *Rambam* follows the midrashic teaching that only six of the Seven Laws were given to Adam (the law of the "limb of the living" was, according to *Bereishis Rabbah* 16:6, given to Noah (*Bereishis* 9:4). This contradicts the teaching in the Talmud (*Sanhedrin* 56b) that all Seven were given to Adam.

[16] "God's Law does not deal with things that are supernatural, or not of this world; instead, it includes every aspect of a full life which can be lived here below...the prerequisite for the true fulfillment of the laws of the Lord is knowledge, as thorough as possible, of all the realities of human affairs on earth. For example, the writings of our Sages have preserved for us an immense treasury of such a variety of skills and arts as agriculture, cattle-breeding, industry, commerce, pharmacology, dietetics, etc." Hirsch, *The Hirsch Psalms*, §ii, 354.

[17] Maimonides, *Mishneh Torah, Sefer Shoftim*. Rabbi Eliyahu Touger, trans. and commentary. (Jerusalem: Monznaim Publishing Corporation, 2001), 585.

[18] "Here, at the foot of Moriah, comes the parting of the ways between זרע אברהם, the seed of Abraham, and בני נח, the sons of Noah. Only one within whose breast the Torah has stirred the response הנני ["Here I am!"] will be able, like Abraham, to

Noahide, more than likely a former Christian, still clings to the Christian ideology that the *halakha* in the Talmud is little more than "dry legalism" and stifling of their "faith" and desire to be close to God. To draw close to God by obeying the Seven Laws of Noah does not seem to enter into the mind of the non-observant Noahide; the non-observant Noahide's "observance" of the Torah is based on the "religious" parts of the Torah which deal with the Jew's service to God, and of their attempts to turn the Noahide Law into a sort of "Judaism Lite."

The Talmud (*Avodah Zarah* 3a) presents another problem with the interpretation of the Noahide Law, which explains that the reward for a Noahide keeping the *Sheva Mitzvot* is the reward for one who is not commanded certain *mitzvot* but keeps them anyway. According to Rashi in his commentary (cf. *Avodah Zarah* 6a and *Bava Kamma* 38a), Noahides only receive the reward (of fulfilling a *mitzvot* they have been commanded) for the positive performance of the precepts (although they are still under obligation—and punishment—for violating them). The *Tosafot* steps in here and explains that the *yetzer harah*—man's evil inclination—is much stronger against the performance of commandments one is obligated to perform, and thus the reward for doing the obligatory commandments is far greater than the reward for doing commandments one is not obligated to do. Therefore, according to the Talmud, even a *mamzer* who is a Torah scholar is held in higher regard than an unlearned Kohen Gadol (which, after the late Second Temple era, was too often the case). It is no accident that here in *Avodah Zara* 3a, a section of the Talmud that discusses the Noahide Law, is found the dictum that "he who is commanded and does stands higher than he who is not commanded and does."

∽

How does one understand the "conceptual idols, ideologies not based on the Torah" which the Talmud places in the category of idolatry? How do we identify these ideologies, and more importantly, weed them out? Luckily for us, there is a teaching on how to implement Noahide Law in a non-Jewish society, a system that we can use to facilitate the change of our legal system in compliance to Torah Law

---

abandon himself to the Divine will, with complete disregard of his own insights... using his energies for the fulfillment of the will of God...they can walk together with the בני נח as far as Moriah, for בני נח are also the children of God. But the בני נח can come only as far as the foot of the mountain. Further than that they cannot go." Hirsch, *T'rumath Tzvi*, 106.

and weed out the corrosive and destructive Edomite elements in our culture: *Torah im Derech Eretz,* or *Torah with the way of the land,* a philosophy developed by Rabbi Hirsch to continue Israel's work as "a nation of priests" and "a light unto the gentiles."

Rabbi Hirsch spent his adult life teaching an orthodox Jewish lifestyle that did not isolate Jews from modern society, of how to integrate Judaism with modern Gentile culture instead of isolating Jews and living a life pretending they were still shut up in sixteenth-century European ghettos. Hirsch fervently believed that Israel was to be "a light unto the Gentiles," and in order to teach the nations the Noahide Law, they had to interact with the nations as much as possible, to be timely and relevant in modern society without sacrificing either their Jewishness or a single *yud* of Torah. To understand this philosophy, we will take a passage from Rabbi Hirsch's essay *Religion Allied to Progress*:

> The more we understand that Judaism reckons with all of man's endeavors, and the more its declared mission includes the salvation of all mankind, the less can its views be confined to the four cubits of one room or one dwelling. The more the Jew is a Jew, the more universalist will be his views and aspirations, the less alien will he be to anything that is noble and good, true and upright in the arts and sciences, in civilization and culture. The more the Jew is a Jew, the more joyously will he hail everything that will shape human life so as to promote truth, right, peace and refinement among mankind, the more happily will he himself embrace every opportunity to prove his mission as a Jew on new, still untrodden grounds. The more the Jew is a Jew, the more gladly will he give himself to all that is true progress in civilization and culture—provided that in this new circumstance he will not only maintain his Judaism but will be able to bring it to ever more glorious fulfillment...he will not want to accomplish anything that he cannot accomplish as a Jew...any step that takes him away from Judaism is not progress.[19]

This is the essence of *Torah im Derech Eretz,* to take what is good and noble[20] from our Western culture and use it in tandem with Torah Law. By simply reversing the osmosis of Rabbi Hirsch's approach,

---

[19] Hirsch, *Collected Writings*, Vol. VI, 123.

[20] "The חכמה of a civilization is not only its science, but also its artistic and literary productions...the sum total of human thought and accomplishment throughout the ages down to our time. While a great deal of this, perhaps *even most of it*, must be rejected...there are some gems here and there that lend themselves to 'Toraization.'" Danziger, *The World of Hirschian Teachings*, 168.

Torah im Derech Eretz could be developed into an invaluable system for fine tuning Western culture to harmonize with the Torah—to put our culture through a Torah sieve,[21] to separate the flour dust from the fine flour, to weed out the destructive non-Torah elements in our society.[22] This was the role of Israel, to be the benchmark and example for non-Jewish society.[23]

The first step in instituting this program of *Torah im Derech Eretz* is a focus on education.[24] Because of the focus on "religion," there has been too little emphasis on Noahide education, and what planning there has been revolves around ideas such as Noahide home-schooling, Noahide "shuls," and Noahide "yeshivas," the sort of thinking analogous to the Christian or secular view of education,[25] of having

---

[21] "[The] educational philosophy of *Torah im Derech Eretz*, [is] the dominion of Torah over all of life, including all that the civilized world has to offer for Torah Judaism." Hirsch, *Collected Writings*, Vol. VI, xiii.

[22] "Torah im Derech Eretz does not mean that there are two independent sources of truth, Divine and human, that may conflect with each other and have to be reconciled. Torah cannot be compared to, or equated with, any other branch of knowledge or set of values. To no human knowledge did Rabbi Hirsch grant intrinsic value. The Torah is the only source of truth, and the yardstick by which any knowledge or idea must be measured...*derech eretz*, that is to say the material, social and economic world, is generally speaking, in itself, neither good nor bad. However, the Torah rejects certain forms and aspects of *derech eretz* as incompatible with its teachings and they are, as a result, unacceptable to the Torah-observant Jew [or Noahide]. The same holds true for human knowledge. We may allow other types of knowledge 'only so much entrance into our intellectual and emotional life as is exactly in accordance with these Divine Truths'" [Hirsch, *Collected Writings*, Vol. I, 304].
Or, as Isaac Breuer put it: "It is incorrect to speak of 'Torah *with*...anything else. There is no synthesis, there is no tension, there is no reconciliation, there is no balance; there is only domination.'" Klugman, *Rabbi Samson Raphael Hirsch*, 203–04.

[23] "God introduced Israel into history in order to refute the delusion that man's welfare depended upon a maximum show of human power and force. Israel was to be a group of men which, foregoing all warlike pomp and power, was to attain its own greatness simply by unfolding a blessed and pure humaneness...even the purely cultural achievements in the arts and sciences recorded by the other nations will have true and beneficial value only if they are coupled with the virtues taught and practiced by this נות בית, and only if they are used as means to the fulfillment of those ends that are part of the Divine plan for man's destiny. נוה...means 'a quiet, pleasant dwelling place.'" Hirsch, *The Hirsch Psalms*, §i, 459–60.

[24] "A Torah academy, unlike a secular university, synthesizes moral and intellectual discipline." Eidelberg, *Beyond the Secular Mind*, 146.

[25] As we have seen, our current academic disciplines interpret Torah with every conceivable non-Jewish system except the systems taught by the Torah itself. "One must turn instead to the authentic sources of Jewish thought, Tanach, Talmud, and the

separate "religious" and "secular" schools. This ideology is wrong for two reasons: first, the Noahide Law is not a "religious" law, and secondly, we already have an education system in place, paid for by our own tax dollars. Establishing the Noahide Law as an academic discipline in our existing education system is a more viable alternative than trying to build a Noahide educational system from scratch. The Noahide system is not meant to be separate from Noahide society as is the Jewish educational system; the teaching of the Noahide Law is meant to be integrated fully into our primary and secondary schools as well as into our colleges and universities. This is the first important step in establishing a Noahide society, and this should be the primary goal of every individual Noahide and Noahide group. Frittering away our time and resources on "worship" and "fellowship" is a serious dereliction of duty, for our society is sinking into the abyss of hedonism and idolatry.[26]

Today's intellectual climate is not conducive to the establishment of Torah in mainstream education and culture. The secular intellectual is not going to be swayed by spiritual arguments or kabbalistic teachings; only by the logical and practical arguments of Torah will we be able to change the minds of those who turn the wheels of government and economics, of those who produce the arts and sciences whose power and wealth wield great influence on culture and society. This is the historic function of the Noahide Law, to provide a Divine foundation for our social, economic, political, moral and legal Noahide communities and states.

One thing which cannot be over-emphasized is the fundamental difference in the viewpoint between Noahides and Jews. For the Noahide, he is on the outside of the Torah, looking in. For the Jew, he is

---

Midrashic literature, and learn, *from within*, the true Jewish view regarding God, the world, humanity, and Yisrael." Weinberg, *The World of Hirschian Teachings*, 107.

[26] "We have practically resigned ourselves to apathy with regard to the widespread contemporary non-compliance with God's Laws. We have become phlegmatic with regard to the spirit of irresponsibility—both in matters philosophical and practical—which entangles spirits and hearts. This attitude of laissez-fair [*sic*] governs us despite the fact that the phenomenon of dereliction of duty threatens to undermine our inner sanctuary almost to the point of destroying it. Not only is God's Law trodden under foot in the life of the present, but our future as well is being jeopardized by this spirit of godlessness which has already seized most of the spiritual seed-beds of the coming generation. This includes the educational establishments of our future teachers and leaders." Hirsch, *Collected Writings*, Vol. I, 291–92.

on the inside, looking out at secular culture. For the Jew, it is simply a matter of what elements of secular culture to let in, one at a time. For the Noahide, there is a tremendous amount of baggage they must leave behind, false ideologies which must be unlearned while learning "Torah-ideology, commonly known as *Torah im Derech Eretz*, which proclaims the mastery of Torah over every aspect of life."[27]

Unfortunately, what many rabbis are teaching Noahides today is a watered-down Torah, heavy on the mystical interpretations, light on *halakha*. As Maurice Samuel pointed out, there is a great gulf between the two nations. This is not to say that the Noahide's service to God is any less important or meaningful than the Jew's service. The Noahide's approach to the Law is simply different, and by fulfilling the laws given to them, the Noahide helps Israel fulfill its mission among the nations, "the perfection of mankind...the sublime historical calling of the House of Israel."[28] The Noahide must focus on the *halakha* of the Torah, not on the mystical or spiritual elements.

> What is the basic definition of *Torah im Derech Eretz* in the light of all this? Does it mean going to college? Does it mean becoming a professional? Does it mean becoming an artist, a novelist, a journalist, a musician, a physician, a scientist, a T.V. actor, etc.? Not so fast! Maybe yes and maybe no! The irreducible definition of *Torah im Derech Eretz* is Torah in relation to, in the context of, the world, the civilization, the raw material as it exists in time, in *our* time, in *this* time. Not as it existed in the sixteen hundreds, or the seventeen hundreds, or even the eighteen hundreds of Rav Hirsch's day in Germany, or in Poland, or in Lithuania. *But in relation to the raw material as it exists today.* What that relation should be, however, what form it should take, what must be rejected and what may be accepted, must be decided, as any other question, according to the halachic factors and the values of the Torah.[29]

The most pervasive idolatrous ideology is the idea that the Noahide Law is simply a vehicle for "salvation,"[30] i.e., the sort of

---

[27] Dr. Elliott Bondi, *The World of Hirschian Teachings*, 2.

[28] Hirsch, *Collected Writings*, Vol. I, 26.

[29] Danziger, *The World of Hirschian Teachings*, 160.

[30] The debate between *Rambam* and *Ramban* over the law of *Dinim* is one of the most well-known (and important) debates on the subject of the Noahide Law. Unfortunately, because of the narrow-minded focus on the *Mishna Torah* as the source for Noahide *halakha*, most Noahides are unaware of this debate, as they

Secular by Design

individual salvation taught in Christianity. The very structure of the Noahide Law—laws covering murder, theft, and illicit sex—show that it is about *community*, for these laws all deal with social interactions between two or more people. Even the "religious" laws of idolatry and blasphemy have a social context in that they prohibit any sort of organized religion. *Dinim*, not *emunah*, is the foundation of the Noahide Law.

⌒

BY UNDERSTANDING THE weaknesses in the intellectual arguments against the Torah as well as the inherent structural weaknesses in our present economic and political systems, by using Rabbi Hirsch's *Torah im Derech Eretz* to weed out the destructive pagan and idolatrous concepts that have infested our culture, we can begin our task to implement the Noahide Law into modern society.[31]

We must also come to grips with, contrary to the eloquent words of Jefferson, that, according to the Torah, all men are *not* created equal. Some are more intelligent, some are better at "people skills" and business, some are more dexterous with tools than others. We use words such as "equality" and "freedom" to boast about our way of life in America, but to be honest, who are the truly free? The poor? Is the poor man "free" to get a loan? To obtain medical care that he or she needs? Men are not created equal, but the Torah makes them equal under the law. The ultimate aim of *Torah im Derech Eretz* is to not only create a legal system, but to create an entire economic and political structure that is based on Torah instead of the self-destructive elements of Western Greco-Roman culture.

---

are about the great deal of rabbinic criticism on many of *Rambam's* rulings. [cf. n. 36 p. 407, n. 13 p. 417 above]. "*Lechem Mishneh (Hil. Melachim* 9:14) finds this Gemara problematic according to *Rambam's* view. As noted above (56a note 48 ['our commentary will follow the view of *Ramban*']), according to *Rambam* the commandment of דינין [Dinim—the Gemara is in Aramaic] includes only the obligation to establish courts to enforce the other six Noahide Laws. This Gemara, though, apparently assumes that actual laws are included in that commandment. We therefore follow *Ramban's* view here. This also appears to be the way *Rashi* understands the Gemara." R´ Weiner, *Schottenstein Talmud, Sanhedrin* 56b, n. 34.

[31] "No custom (*minhag*) which may have evolved in a community has any binding power if it is contrary to the Halacha." Eidelberg, *Beyond the Secular Mind*, 60.

The Master of Sinai

According to the outlook of Halakhah, the service of God (with the exception of the study of the Torah) can be carried out only through the implementation, the actualization of its principles in the real world. The ideal of righteousness is the guiding light of this world-view...the Halakhah is not hermetically enclosed within the confines of cult sanctuaries but penetrates into every nook and cranny of life. The marketplace, the street, the factory, the house, the meeting place, the banquet hall, all constitute the backdrop for the religious life.

— Rabbi Joseph B. Soloveitchik[1]

TO IMPLEMENT THE NOAHIDE LAW IN OUR SOCIETY AS COMMANDED by the Torah means to not simply have courts but courts of *justice*, and by that meaning justice according to Torah Law. To weed out the elements that are detrimental to Torah values, we must first identify the problems, to separate the flour dust from the fine flour, and to use Rabbi Hirsch's system of *Torah im Derech Eretz* to filter out the corrosive and harmful pagan elements in our culture and law.[2] For Noahides to have self-sufficient courts of law demands that Noahides learn to determine *halakha* for themselves. This has traditionally been the sticking point for rabbis who insist that non-Jews cannot study Torah and determine *halakha* on their own; rabbis often point to the disastrous results from Christians and other non-Jewish attempts to do so. For example, the problem with Christian interpretation of the *Tanach* had to do with their method of analysis, which was based on Christian theology, a system based on illogical Gnostic mysticism. As we have seen, the Torah can neither be correctly analyzed nor interpreted by any non-Jewish methodology. This has been the problem with the non-Jewish interpretations of the Law, and why the rabbis have traditionally been reluctant to teach the Talmud to non-Jews. For the Noahide to

---

[1] Soloveitchik, *Halakhic Man*, 94.

[2] The Talmud teaches us (*Megillah* 6a) that, in the Messianic age, the theaters and circuses of Edom will be turned into halls of study for the Torah. The time we waste on violent and sexually explicit movies, on gladiatorial "sporting" events, on mind-numbing corporate television, will instead be spent on studying Torah.

attempt to be able to study Torah and determine *halakha*, there has to be a system that will allow the Noahide to determine *halakha* in the Noahide courts as well as be able to self-govern effectively.[3]

The determination of *halakha* is not some random guessing game. There is a complex and ancient system of interpretation used by the rabbis to determine *halakha* using two different modes of analysis: *sevarah* and *pilpul*. *Pilpul* is the dialectical approach, "deducing positive from negative and vice versa; drawing inferences from what was omitted and from ostensibly superfluous material."[4] The other approach is *sevarah*, or "discovering the reason behind the halakhah, which enables us to compare and contrast different cases."[5] *Pilpul* is a system that takes intensive training as well as an "insiders" understanding of Torah; to determine the fine points of *halakha* using *pilpul* is difficult for even the most learned Noahide, and, although certain principles can be applied to Noahide Law, *pilpul* should be left to the rabbis.

Severah, on the other hand, is the logical understanding of *halakha*, and is certainly within the scope of the Noahide.[6] The Noahide Law is not meant to be as exact or as strict as Jewish Law, so there really is no need to wrestle every conclusion to the finer points of law using *pilpul*, and if a problem arises, one can always use the rabbis as a resource for arbitration.[7] As *Ramban* pointed out, the Noahide legal system should

---

[3] "Apart from its function as the Supreme Court of the Land, the Sanhedrin had legislative powers to enact laws, both religious and civil, which it considered to be necessary. It therefore operated in a dual capacity—as a judiciary and as a legislature, and as such was very much part of government in ancient Israel." Arnold Cohen, *An Introduction to Jewish Civil Law*. (Jerusalem: Feldheim Publishers, 2000), 20–21.

[4] Yehudah Levi, *Torah Study: A Survey of Classic Sources on Timely Issues*. (Jerusalem: Feldheim Publishers, Inc., 1990), 178.

[5] Ibid.

[6] "Can [a righteous gentile] use his intellect to arrive at the 'right reason' for the Noahide laws? Would that suffice or must he justify his observance of these laws by avowing his belief that they were enjoined by God's revelation to Moses? These questions are not addressed, but, it seems to me, they loom large as one reads Maimonides and is perplexed by what he says...Haim Cohn...considers the question of the source of the oral law when no scriptural text and no tradition, custom, or judicial precedent is available. In such a case, recourse is to 'independent reasons' (Sevara)." Konvitz, *Torah & Constitution*, 104–05.

[7] "דרכים are the main roads and ארחות are its branches...the nations will say, 'Although we have only been taught the דרכים — the fundamentals of the religion—nevertheless we will strive to learn its details on our own—ונלכה בארחתיו'" (*Malbim, Isaiah* 2:3). Stavsky, *Trei Asar*, Vol. II, 29.

be "comparable to the civil laws about which Israel was commanded;" that is, it does not need to be as severe or exact as Jewish law. Therefore, the Noahide can use the Codes (such as the *Shulchan Aruch*) and other resources to determine *halakha*. The logic employed in *sevarah* is rabbinic logic, not Greek philosophy or religious theology. In other words, a Noahide needs to understand the rabbinic point of view and approach to the Torah in all of its moral and legal aspects.

It also needs to be understood that "the object of the Jewish legal system is not to preserve a particular dynasty or certain form of government, but to establish social righteousness and to maintain thereby a close, constant, inseparable connection between ethics and law."[8] In place of our Constitutional system of Edomite law, we have an opportunity to rebuild a society based on the Torah's legal system. It is not the form of government that is important, but rather the legal system on which our society runs and operates.

Implementing and dispensing law is an important function, as can be seen in the amount of *mitzvot* in the Torah in dealing with courts of law. The task we face is made difficult by the lack of a systematic method of teaching gentiles Oral Law. Other than the rudimentary basics of the Seven Laws, the paltry number of books dealing with Noahide Law do not even begin to address dealing with implementing Torah justice in a non-Jewish society. This is not Israel's job. Israel is the keeper of the Torah as well as the example which the nations of the world should follow. This was the purpose of *Hashem* in scattering the Nation of Israel among the nations.[9]

We have had an opportunity to learn Torah from the *Kohenim* of mankind, not only by their teaching but their example, by their simply being in our midst, where even the everyday speech of the servants of God is instructive. Instead, we have squandered the opportunity by centuries of abuse, religious persecution, and social ostracization while at the same time giving aid and comfort to the enemies of God and Israel. The blame for Israel not successfully transmitting and

---

[8] Cohen, *An Introduction to Jewish Civil Law*, 14.

[9] In his commentary to *Devarim* 4:27, Rabbi Hirsch spoke of this mission, saying that "you will become scattered and spread amongst the nations...and (Israel) will be seeds of God, strewn about in the world, and *baamim*, in the midst of the social life of the nations will awake and nurture the idea of a different way of looking at the world and life and a different way of living one's life." Hirsch, *Devarim*, 66.

teaching the Noahide Code to mankind rests *baamim*, among the nations, and our punishment is not too far off.

That being said, let us turn to the Book of *Yonah* (Jonah). The story is no doubt familiar to us, how *Yonah* received a command to go to Ninevah, "a great city for God," to tell them to repent or else be destroyed. *Yonah* fled from the presence of *HASHEM*, thinking that once he was no longer on the holy soil of *Eretz Yisrael* he would not hear the instructions of the prophecy, and how *HASHEM* forced him to go anyway. After *Yonah* completed his mission, the Ninevites indeed repented, and avoided destruction. This upset *Yonah*, for he feared (and rightly so) that it would make Israel look bad in comparison since they themselves had ignored the warnings of numerous prophets and had not repented. The book ends with *HASHEM* pointing out to *Yonah* that he, *Yonah*, was more upset about the destruction of a *kikayon* (carob, according to many commentators) than he was about the immanent destruction of thousands of innocent children and animals.

One of the lessons to be gleaned from this amazing story is the power of *teshuvah*, or repentance.[10] It was not just the sackcloth and ashes or the fasting that all the Ninevites, from the king on down to the lowliest commoner subjected themselves to, but that "God saw their *deeds*, that they turned back from their evil ways." And as Rabbi Hirsch pointed out, this book teaches us that "mending one's ways is the sole nature of Teshuva, and it alone achieves the miracle of God's Grace." Kimchi (*Radak*) explained that it was, in particular, the Noahide prohibition of *hamas*, of robbery and oppression, that the Ninevites repented for. The other important lesson from *Yonah* is one that is rarely mentioned, that *Yonah* did not want the Ninevites to repent, because it would make Israel look bad by comparison. *Yonah* wanted to spare Israel the wrath of *HASHEM*, even if it meant giving up his own life. *HASHEM* forced *Yonah* to deliver his message, and then rebuked *Yonah* for caring more about a plant than the children and beasts of Ninevah.

It seems a bit odd that there is so little commentary for Noahides concerning *Sefer Yonah*, the Book of *Yonah*, the only book in the *Tanach* about a prophet who was sent to the *Bnai Noah*, a book about repentance, a book deemed worthy to be read every year in its entirety

---

[10] One important misconception is that Jews and Noahides are trying to "convert" those of other faiths to become observant Noahides. Becoming an observant Noahide is not about conversion, but *teshuvah*; since all non-Jews are under the Noahide Law, you do not "convert" to Noahidism, rather you *return*.

on *Yom Kippur*, the holiest day in the Hebrew calendar. It would seem that the relevance of this book would make it of great importance to the Noahide. This is, however, not the case; *Sefer Yonah* has been, for the most part, ignored.

As with the prophet *Yonah*, the main concerns of modern rabbis are for the people of Israel. For the past twenty years (when the rabbis started to get involved with the nascent Noahide movement), the rabbis have kept the Noahides on a tight leash, discouraging them from attacking the major idolatrous religion of our society or even studying the Talmud, the primary source of the Noahide Law, placating the Noahides instead with a steady diet of kabbalah and *Rambam's Mishna Torah* which presents the Noahide Law as a personal religion of salvation rather than a society-altering moral and legal code. The main fear of the rabbis—and it is a fear somewhat justified—is that if the Noahides rile up the Christians the blowback would be directed at the Jews themselves, and there are still many Jews still living who saw with their own eyes the armies of Edom marching with blood-red flags emblazoned with running crosses and tipped with Roman Eagles, being saluted with Roman salutes, and their ears still ring with the Edomite cries of *Alle Juden muss tot*. This can certainly happen here in Edomite America; in fact, as economic conditions worsen, you can count on the anti-Semitic memes in our Edomite culture coming to the fore,[11] blaming the Jews for the woes of society.

Misplacing our faith in the Constitution is one of the most important lessons we can learn from *Sefer Yonah*. Our Constitution has long been a legal *kikayon*, providing the Jews with comfort and protection. Yet the time will come when America, indeed all Western Civilization, will turn against Israel, and the *kikayon* will wither, and we will be overthrown unless we repent and fix our sick society (the reason presidential candidates cater to Jews is because of the large Jewish populations of voters in places such as New York and Florida; these two states comprise over one fifth of the electoral votes needed to win the presidency). Yet in their efforts to protect the Jewish population of our society, the rabbis are severely retarding the growth of the Noahide movement. As with the prophet *Yonah*, who tried to flee from

---

[11] "Economic crisis make people's antisemitism more manifest and *activate* it into open expression." Goldhagen, *Hitler's Willing Executioners*, 45.

HASHEM in order to protect Israel, the rabbis seem to be willing to sacrifice the Noahide movement in order to protect the Jews who have a
comfortable life living among the fleshpots of Edom. The rabbis say
they fear that the Noahides, if left rudderless, will steer the good ship
SS *Bnai Noah* into idolatrous waters, yet the rabbis continue to emphasize the religious elements of the Torah, teaching Noahides about Torah
mitzvot that pertain to Israel's service to God instead of the legal dicta
that *Ramban* said the Noahides should focus on, "the laws of theft,
overcharging, withholding wages, the laws of bailees and of the rapist
or the seducer of minors, the various categories of damages, personal
injury, the laws of creditors and debtors, the laws of buying and selling,
etc., comparable to the civil laws about which Israel was commanded."
It is our legal system we need to work on rather than create a "Noahide religion," and to be teaching things such as "Noahide prayers"
and "Noahide blessings" and allowing "Noahide tallis" and "Noahide
mezuzahs," things that do not pertain to the Noahide's service to God,
is steering the Noahide movement in the wrong direction. The millions
of people in our society who are in the grip of idolatry need our help to
lead them to *teshuvah*, and Noahides must change their focus.

The Rabbis are caught in a dilemma. Many rabbis actually want to
help the Noahide movement, but this conflict of interest—to help the
Noahides while at the same time protect Israel from Edom—is why the
rabbis need to take a more passive approach and disengage themselves
from trying to lead the Noahide movement. Too many of the rabbis have
been so focused on preserving the Jews that they have forgotten what
they were preserving the Jews *for*. By turning their backs on Gentile society in order to save the Jewish people they are forgetting their mission
in this world, which is to bring mankind back to the Torah.

In *Bava Metzia* 90b the Talmud applies the commandment §232
[as listed in the *Séfer haHinnuch*; cf. n. 85, p. 450 below] to a Noahide's observance of the Torah, "which prohibits causing another person to sin. It includes causing a non-Jew to violate one of the laws
commanded to him." Thus the Jews are prohibited from interfering
with the Noahide's observance of the Seven Laws, such as telling the
Noahide he or she is not to endeavor to eliminate an idolatrous religion such as Christianity from their society, or not to get involved in
political matters such as working to set up a legal system based on Torah. In the same vein, the rabbis cannot force the Noahide Law upon

Gentile society.[12] The Jews are to be the examples and the teachers of the Torah, not the leaders of the Noahide movement. This is a job we Noahides must do ourselves. The paranoia[13] the rabbis have about Noahides teaching themselves Torah is understandable to a point, but the fear of Noahides turning into "Noahidism" or some other organized religion[14] can be allayed by simply prohibiting the teaching of any sort of "religious" *halakha*.

We also have to deal with the Reform Noahide's problem with "rabbi worship." Yes, rabbis have had training—they spend their youth pouring over Torah, at ease in at least three languages, studying complicated texts at the age when our non-Jewish youth are playing video games. But the rabbis are not omniscient, and they have limits to what they know and understand of non-Jewish culture. The rabbinic teachings of *Dina DeMalchuta Dina* (the law of the land), treating other (idolatrous) religions respectfully, and the positive commandment to believe in *Hashem* are rabbinic teachings of Judaism, not of the Noahide Law. Because of the fundamental difference in Jewish and Noahide *hashkafa*, the rabbis are incapable of teaching the Noahide Law to non-Jews. The task of teaching, implementing, and executing *Torah im Derech Eretz* is the sole responsibility of the Noahide. To successfully weed out the alien ideologies is something that the Jews cannot teach the Noahides any more than they can teach us the proper way to cook shrimp scampi. Israel was commanded to be separate from the nations, but *we* are the nations. This land is *our* land. Establishing separate Noahide "communities" is counterproductive to the implementation of Torah Law as the basis of our legal system:

---

[12] "Abraham's attitude can serve as an example to his descendants whenever they dwell in a land not their own. The Jew must remain a Jew, but remain a moderate, not troubling the public order of his society." Munk, *The Call of the Torah: Bereishis*, 177.

[13] "We Jews are so frequently and so vigorously reminded, in all constitutionally governed and liberal countries, that we ought to be grateful for permission to live there, that we develop a gratitude which is not only disproportionate but occasionally grotesque. Our children, in schools and elsewhere, are taught, year in, year out, to contrast their present freedom and equality of opportunity with the oppression and bitterness which was the lot of their parents elsewhere. Frequently the contrast, as painted in their imagination, is not a duplicate of the reality. However this may be, these incessant and vehement reminders produce their effect. The child almost comes to believe that it was for the special benefit of oppressed foreigners that America became a 'free country' and, instead of accepting American forms of government level-headedly, with the proper degree of appreciation and criticism, he develops a suppressed hysteria of gratitude. This is not a healthy and natural feeling." Samuel, *You Gentiles*, 60–61.

[14] This is not an unreasonable fear, as seen by recent events among certain *Hasidim* who believe their recently departed *rebbe* is going to resurrect and become *haMashiach*.

As the rabbis will have to step aside and stop holding the Noahide movement back, so too will the non-observant Noahides have to overcome the Christian concept of "individual salvation" in their approach to the Noahide Law. The Talmud (*Rosh Hashanah* 17b) explains that, if the decree of punishment has not been sealed, an individual can still pray to be spared even if he or she lives in an evil community or society. As we have explained above, the "decree of punishment" for Edom was sealed long ago, and, unfortunately, the United States is the standard-bearer of Edom, the flagship of Gog and Magog. Our society is based on the Edomite principle of *hamas*, of robbery and oppression, the Edomite ideal of "what is mine is mine and what is yours is yours." The idea that our prayers and blessings sound sweet to HASHEM while living in a society whose legal system is based on the robbery and suppression of the poor is a delusional one. "For I am HASHEM, Who loves justice and hates a burnt-offering [bought] with robbery; and I will repay their deeds in truth" (Isaiah 61:8). It is highly doubtful that we, as Noahides, can achieve "individual salvation" living in a morally and legally corrupt Edomite culture.[15]

IF OUR BELEAGUERED society is to survive, our intellectuals are going to have to—in the parlance of our game-loving culture—"step up to the plate" and reassess the wisdom of structuring our legal and governmental system on Greek and Roman models. We must overcome the anti-Semitic memes which have kept Torah out of our academic institutions and implement a study of Torah.[16] We must use the Hirschian philosophy of *Torah im Derech Eretz* to weed out the destructive elements of our Edomite culture, and use the system of *severah* to develop *halakha* for the nations.

---

[15] "Through the implementation of the principles of righteousness, man fulfills the task of creation imposed upon him: the perfection of the world under the dominion of Halakhah and the renewal of the face of creation. No religious cult is of any worth if the laws and principles of righteousness are violated and trampled upon by the foot of pride. 'A precept that is fulfilled through a transgression,' attaining religious ends through unjust means, is of absolutely no value. 'For I the Lord love justice, I hate robbery with a burnt offering' (Isa. 61:8). Iniquity prevents man's prayer from being accepted on high. The anguish of the poor, the despair of the helpless and humiliated outweigh many many commandments." Soloveitchik, *Halakhic Man*, 91.

[16] "The Torah does not belong solely to those of Jewish descent. In fact, it is the universal law, indirectly addressed to all men...the Children of Israel were taught a valuable lesson regarding their relationship with the nations of the world. The fierce hatred of some is counterbalanced by admiration from others, and it is not always the kinsman who show the greatest understanding." Munk, *The Call of the Torah: Shemos*, 230.

Mitzvot Applicable to Noahide Law

The far removal of robbery from among people is of benefit to all; and the human intelligence is a trustworthy witness to this. There is no great length of laws about it, as all its content is clarified in the Writ. It is in force everywhere, at every time, for both man and woman. All humankind too is duty-bound by it, since it is a branch of the precept about robbery, which is one of the seven precepts that all in the world were commanded to keep...now, make no mistake, my son, in this reckoning of the seven precepts for the descendants of Noah, which is known and is mentioned in the Talmud. For in truth, those seven are in the nature of main categories, and they contain many details. Thus you will find that the ban on consanguineous, forbidden conjugal relations is reckoned in a general way as one precept; yet there are quite many details in it: for instance, the ban on a mother, the ban on a sister from the same mother, and the ban on a married woman and a father's wife, and on a male and an animal. So too, the entire matter of idol-worship is reckoned as one precept for them, yet there are many, many details in it—since they are equal to the Israelites about it, in regard to the fact that they are punishable for anything over which an Israelite beth din (court) would sentence to death. Then we likewise say that since they were abjured about robbery, they were equally adjured about all decrees to keep a person far away from it.

It is not my intention, though, to say that like us, they are adjured about this by a negative precept. For they were not cautioned about details of injunctions like the Israelites, but were rather adjured in a general way about those seven—as you might say by way of illustration, that Scripture cautioned them, No man shall come intimately close to anyone near of kin to him (Leviticus 18:6), to a mother, sister, and all the rest; and so likewise about idol-worship, equally in a general way. Then so too about robbery: it is as though they were told, "Do not commit robbery—but get utterly far away from it"; and included in getting far from it is the rule not to act covetously.

For Israelites, though, the matter is not so; the omnipresent God wished to make them meritorious, and He increased the precepts for them far beyond the number for them [the other nations], and even with those that [both] we and they were commanded, we merited that our orders about them are [often] through separate positive and negative commandments.

— *Séfer haHinnuch*, §4.416 [1]

TO BUILD A NOAHIDE LEGAL SYSTEM AS EXPLAINED BY *RAMBAN*, AND structuring it as a foundation for a moral government and society as Rabbi Hirsch expounded, we must use the system of *Torah im Derech Eretz* and apply the logic of *sevarah* to eliminate the Edomite memes from our culture and structure a legal system

---

[1] *Séfer haHinnuch*, Vol. IV, 247–49.

based on Torah. By using the broad categories of the Seven Laws, we can begin this task by identifying the *mitzvot* of the Torah needed to create a system of law "comparable to the civil laws about which Israel was commanded" as *Ramban* taught. As there are laws only for the *Kohenim*, and laws only for the Levites, so too there are many laws only for Israel, particularly laws that pertain to Eretz Yisrael and Israel's service to God.

The following is a list of the civil and moral laws that are applicable to the Noahide Code,[2] and these laws are based on the *Séfer haHinnuch's* enumeration as they appear in the Torah.[3] The first number is the volume of the *Séfer haHinnuch*, the second number is the *mitzvah*.

§1.25. *To believe in the Existence of God* [Shemos 20:2].[4]

---

[2] In *Sanhedrin* 74b, it states that "Noahites were given seven commandments…and all their ancillaries…Noahites are required to observe not only the seven basic Noahide laws but also the various regulations associated with them (see *Rashi* here and *Rashi* ms. to *Menachos* 73b ד"ה וכל אביזרא)…*Aruch* (see entry אבזר) and *Yad Ramah* interpret the word (אבזרייהו) to mean 'their spices.' Spices are generally added to food merely to enhance its flavor, but a spice is not considered a food in its own right. Thus, our Gemara uses the term אבזרייהו, *spices*, to describe mitzvos that strengthen or define other laws." Weiner, *The Schottenstein Talmud, Sanhedrin* 74b, n. 20.

[3] "To all the rest of the human race He also gave a pathway to separate them from the animal level. This way comprises the seven precepts which all the people in the world were together commanded." *Séfer haHinnuch*, Vol. I, 65.

[4] This *mitzvah*, considered by the Sages as the foundation of all other commandments, is problematic for those Noahides who do not have a religious background (unlike those who have come out of a religion such as Christianity), and the observance of this commandment epitomizes the great gulf between Israel and the nations, particularly in their understanding and approach to the Torah. The reason this commandment is problematic is that, unlike Israel, the nations were *not* there at Sinai. The Noahides were *not* released from bondage in Egypt. We did *not* experience the momentous events which have permanently engraved themselves on the Jewish psyche. All Noahides have to go by is the intellectual understanding of the miracle of Israel's survival through four millennia of tumultuous history and, more importantly, the logic and reason of the laws of the Torah.

For the Noahide, the acceptance of *Hashem* as the Divine Lawgiver and the true King of the Universe is the ideal which we all must strive for, yet halakhically it is not the pre-requisite for making God's Torah the basis of law for the nations. One of the themes we find in the *Séfer haHinnuch* is that "a person is influenced by his deeds; his actions leave their impression and effect on him as a human being." (Charles Wengrov, trans., *Séfer haHinnuch*, Vol. V, xv). It is through the study of Torah and by performing the precepts of its logical and rational laws that will bring the intellectual

§1.26. *To believe in no divinity but God* [Shemos 20:3].[5]

§1.27. *Not to make a graven image* [Shemos 20:4].[6]

---

to God. Rabbi S. R. Hirsch explains, "as this verse is not to be taken as a declaration, but as a mitzvah, as one of the commandments, it does not mean 'I, HASHEM am your God' but 'I, HASHEM am to be (should be) your God.' This makes the foundation of our whole relation to God to be that demand which our sages express in the term קבלת עול מלכות שמים (taking on oneself the duties which are involved by considering God as one's King)...the so-called 'belief in the existence of God,' as ancient and modern theological philosophers like to express the idea of 'the first commandment,' is miles away from what this fundamental verse of Jewish thought and Jewish existence demands from Jewish thought and Jewish life." Rabbi S. R. Hirsch, commentary to *Shemos* 20:2, 258.

[5] As the *Séfer haHinnuch* explains in the commentary to this *mitzvah*: "This precept is *the* great principle of the Torah, on which all depends...[it] is also one of the group of seven precepts which all people in the world generally were commanded to keep." *Séfer haHinnuch*, Vol. I, 145, 147. Contrary to what many might think, for the Noahide it is the *prohibition* of the belief in other gods that the non-Jews are commanded, *not* the positive commandment to believe in God. "[Hermann] Cohen finds great significance in the fact that belief in the Jewish God was not demanded of the Noahide." [Jehuda Melber, *Judaism: A Religion of Reason.* (Middle Village, NY: Jonathan David Publishers, Inc., 2003), 224.] Orthodox rabbis, having spent their entire lives living in insular orthodox communities, have an exceedingly difficult time coming to grips with the concept that, from the *halakhic* viewpoint, an atheist who faithfully keeps the Seven Laws could (technically) be an observant Noahide, since he or she does not violate the commandment prohibiting the worship of other gods. This is not meant to condone atheism; rather, it illustrates one of the fundamental differences between the Jewish and Noahide observance of the Torah, that the positive commandment of the belief in God is not a prerequisite for a non-Jew's observance of the Noahide Law, and why the Noahide Law is not a "religion." The understanding of this precept comes from *Bereishis*: the sages commented on the difference between the punishments for the generation of the flood—total annihilation—and the generation of the Tower of Babel, which only had their languages confused and were dispersed across the land. This was because the generation of the *dispersion*, although they had committed blasphemy against God, worked together peacefully and did not commit *hamas*, robbery and oppression, as did the generation of the flood. To further illustrate this, we turn again to the book of *Yonah*. The sin that the Ninevites were guilty of (*Yonah* 1:2) was that of *hamas*. Robbery, according to the sages, destroys social order and *shalom*, or peace. According to the commentators *Malbim* and *Abarbanel*, the Ninevites in *Yonah* were idolatrous, but it was their theft and oppression that caused God to send *Yonah* to make them repent and avoid destruction (which they succeed in doing), even though they were allowed to keep their idolatrous temples. This tells us something of the seriousness of theft and oppression, and why the law of social justice is so vitally important.

[6] "The error becomes greater when the idea of the existence of another god is given more concrete expression by making some pictorial representation or image of it." (Hirsch, *Shemos*, 260). One only has to remember all of the paintings, icons, and sculptures of Jesus to understand the problem with the violation of this commandment. Even for "secular" Noahides, there are obvious violations; for instance, in the American History Museum in Washington D.C., there is a giant marble statue of George Washington modeled after the famous statue of Zeus (that was one of the Seven "Wonders" of the ancient world), and Washington is decked out in Greek finery complete with toga and sandals.

§1.28. *Not to prostrate oneself in idol-worship* [Shemos 20:5].[7]

§1.29. *Not to worship an idol in its usual way of veneration* [Shemos 20:5].[8]

§1.34. *Not to put an innocent man to death* [Shemos 20:13].[9]

§1.35. *Not to be immoral with another's wife.* [Shemos 20:13][10]

§1.36. *Not to kidnap.* [Shemos 20:13][11]

§1.37. *Not to bear false witness.* [Shemos 20:13][12]

§1.38. *Not to covet what belongs to another.* [Shemos 20:14][13]

§1.42. *The law of the bondservant.* [Shemos 21:2][14]

---

[7] Prostrating oneself on the ground (as the Muhammadians do) is not a "prescribed procedure in the Mikdosh to show our allegiance to the One God" (Hirsch, *Shemos*, 261). Not only is it strictly prohibited to bow down to any other god, one should not prostrate one's self in worship for any reason.

[8] This is the meaning of "to serve them;" i.e., to serve other gods in the traditional manner for that particular god. Because Noahides do not have any commandment for organized worship, this prohibition includes any sort of organized religion, even one based on the Torah. Cf. *Vayikra* 10:1, *Bamidbar* 3:4.

[9] The prohibition against murder. This prohibition also includes things such as using abortion as a means of birth control and assisted suicide. ["Euthanasia, voluntary or otherwise, is in Jewish law tantamount to homicide." Lew, *The Humanity of Jewish Law*, 24] It is also why the Torah is so strict about the safeguards of the *beis din* meting out capital punishment; it is better to let a thousand guilty men go free than to put one innocent man to death.

[10] The prohibition against adultery. The importance of the family cannot be over-emphasized: "The family is the most important social institution. It has been the strongest stabilizing factor in society...the family provided the ideal background for justice and moral lessons." Ibid., 75.

[11] The prohibition of kidnapping is the meaning of *Shemos* 20:13; there are other commandments which cover general and specific laws of theft.

[12] The prohibition against giving false testimony.

[13] This prohibition means longing which leads to action, and "obtaining a coveted object my means of pressure [such as pestering someone by incessant importunity through friends or by other means), even if it is then obtained perfectly legally by purchase or otherwise, is prohibited" (Hirsch, *Shemos*, 279). Coveting is one of the prime motivators in the Esavian personality. Edomite states covet other lands for their wealth (oil, food, minerals), or simply to take slaves. This has been the prime motivator for warfare among the Western nations for centuries. "Only when God will become 'King over the whole world' and thereby His Will will become the Law for mankind, only then can prisons be closed and wretchedness disappear from the world" (ibid., 280).

[14] Here is an example of why, without the Oral Law, the Written Torah can be misunderstood. Right after the giving of the Ten Commandments and the construction of the altar, instead of teaching "religious" and "spiritual" concepts, the Torah delves into civil law. Chapter XXI of *Shemos* is especially problematic for those ignorant in

§1.43. *Marital designation of the maidservant.* [Shemos 21:8][15]

---

halakha, for the civil and criminal legislation begins with a man being sold into slavery, and a man selling his daughter. "Anyone whose heart is troubled with misgivings or qualms about these matters...by the simple, literal meaning of the verses of the Written Torah, without their interpretations and true traditions, we can never reach conclusions of truth...yet one who knows their true interpretation understands and sees that the ways of the Lord are right (Hosea 14:10)." *Séfer haHinnuch,* Vol. 1, 73. Yet there is probably no better example of the difference between Torah law and our "modern" Roman/Edomite law than this *mitzvah.*

The Oral Law explains that this case explicitly has to do with a man who had been convicted of theft. When we prosecute and incarcerate a man who has been convicted of theft, be it passing bad checks, shoplifting, stealing an automobile, how does our society treat the "criminal?" We separate him from his family, from his wife and children, toss him in a small bleak cell and strip him of every shred of dignity he has; even his name is taken away and replaced with a number. Contrast our "modern" system with the Torah, as explained by Rabbi S. R. Hirsch: "If we consider this law, which the Word of God has placed at the beginning of its social legislation...we shall see that there is hardly another law as eminently suited as this one to afford us an insight into the purpose of the Divine institutions of social justice and to show us how fundamentally different the character of Jewish Law is from all other legal systems. We have here [in the case of a thief] *the one sole instance* in which the Law of God imposes loss of freedom as a punishment (though we shall see that in fact even this is not to be construed as a punishment). And in what manner is this punishment to be carried out? The law specifies that the offender must be placed with a family, just as we today might place a juvenile delinquent into a family environment. Note, too, the precautions which the law enumerates for this procedure in order not to crush the offender's self-respect, so that, despite the degradation he has brought upon himself, he may still feel that he is treated and respected as a brother, capable of earning and giving love! *Note how the law makes sure that he can retain his contact with his family, and how it sees to it that his family should not suffer distress because of his offense!...*Prison sentence, with all the attendant despair and moral debasement behind prison bars, with all the woe and misery that imprisonment inflects upon the prisoner's wife and children, are unknown in God's Law. Where God's Law holds sway, prisons as an abode for criminals do not exist. Jewish Law provides only for detention pending trail, and even this can happen only in accordance with a judicial procedure set down in detail...hence loss of freedom is merely a consequence of the offender's legal obligation to make restitution for the theft he committed. Restitution is not to be made by the offender as a punishment for his offense; it is merely a way of canceling the effects of the crime that endure as long as the unlawful or felonious damage done to the victim's property has not been redressed" [i.e., he did not have the money to pay for the items stolen or damaged]. Rabbi S. R. Hirsch, *T'rumath Tzvi,* 288. To this the *Séfer haHinnuch* adds: "Sifra on Vayikra 25:40: 'Let him [the servant] be with you'—[equally] with you in regard to food, drink and bedding: that you should not eat refined bread and he coarse bread, you drink aged wine and he new wine; you sleep on soft cloth and he on straw." *Séfer haHinnuch,* 198.

[15] This law deals with the extreme circumstance of a man, out of desperate poverty, who sells his daughter to a man who will either marry her when she comes of age, or if he or his son does not marry her, finds her a suitable husband. As Rabbi Hirsch explained, "when in this way a...man sells his little immature daughter...can only be, that the extremest bitterest necessity can have brought him to it. And according to the Halacha really he must first have sold his house, home and land, even have sold

§1.44. *The redemption of the maidservant* [Shemos 21:8].[16]

§1.45. *The buyer of a maidservant may not sell her* [Shemos 21:8].[17]

§1.46. *Not to withhold from one's wife her rightful due* [Shemos 21:10].[18]

---

his last shirt before he may decide to take this step (Kiddushin 20a, Rambam Hilch. Abadim IV, 2)." We should understand that this is hardly the normal or desired state of affairs in Judaism; according to the Oral Law "in general, a father should not make use even of his legal authority to give his little daughter in marriage during her minority... it is forbidden for a man to give his daughter in marriage while she is a child, until she has grown up and declares: 'That is the man I want to marry.' This not only declares any forced marriage as sinful, but even the only too common practice of persuading a daughter into a marriage as equally so. (*Kiddushin* 41a)" (Hirsch).

Although it seems anachronistic in today's modern society to sell your young daughter to a prospective husband, we need to remember that most of the Third World is not a female-friendly place, and too often a poverty-stricken man's only opportunity for his daughter is to make sure she can be married to a man who has the means to take care of her. Places such as Sub-Saharan Africa, India, or Latin America are not locales carpeted with Macy's department stores, Victoria Secrets, Starbucks and other opportunities for employment. Those who scoff at this law should spend a day with the street urchins in places such as Rio de Janeiro in order to get a better understanding of what the world's truly poor face.

[16] There are over one hundred thousand adoptions in America each year, and nearly half are from foster homes. With all the horror stories about the abuse that foster children receive (acknowledging that there are many decent foster parents out there) as well as the stories about how children are forcibly taken from their parents by the Department of Family and Children Services, we can trace the attitude of raising our society's children back to Plato's *Republic*, where he said that children should be raised by the common, not knowing who their parents are. This is hardly surprising coming from a society that believed tossing unwanted babies down wells or leaving them out in the cold to die of exposure was an acceptable method of population control. "That...exposure and infanticide in other forms were not only practiced but also publicly recognized is clear not only from the evidence of Roman law, which has been mentioned, but also from Greek law, religion, and philosophy." (Cameron, *The Exposure of Children and Greek Ethics*, 108.)

Keeping the Greek and Roman attitude on children in mind, here we have a law that requires the actual father of the girl to redeem her as soon as he is able, and the "owner" of the girl actively helping to bring her back with her family. In fact, the Talmud (*Kiddushin* 18a) says that the courts can force the father to redeem the girl as soon as he is able, and if he is not financially able, then his family is responsible to do so.

[17] The subject is the father, who is not allowed to sell his daughter to any people whose culture she is unused to, nor to close family members whom she would not be allowed to wed.

[18] As Rabbi Hirsch points out, "This is the only place where the Torah speaks of the duties of a man towards his wife. When it wants to lay down the משפט בנות, the elementary rights of the daughters of its people, it picks out for its example a woman of the very lowest social grade, the child of a beggar, of a man who has had to sell the very shirt off his back, and then, to save his child and himself from starvation has to sell her as a slave!" Hirsch, *Shemos*, 301.

§1.48. *Not to strike one's father or mother* [Shemos 21:15].[19]

§1.49. *The laws of fines—penalties* [Shemos 21:18].[20]

§1.50. *The court should execute by decapitation anyone who deserves it.* [Shemos 21:20].[21]

§1.51. *That the court should judge damages by domestic animals* [Shemos 21:28].[22]

§1.53. *The obligation of the court to judge damages by a pit.* [Shemos 21:33].[23]

This girl is not to be mistreated by lack of food, or clothing, or (if she becomes married to the man who purchased her or his son) her conjugal rights. She cannot be treated any differently than his own daughter. In applying the law of קל וחמר, we see that if these laws apply to a maidservant, how much more would they apply to a freewoman. "Women…both historically and because of their nature, are the guardians of tradition, the molders of character, children, and family. Furthermore, women have often protected Judaism when the impetuosity and aggressiveness of the male nature led the men astray. The classic precedent was in the Wilderness when the men—not the women—worshiped the Golden Calf." Rabbi Nosson Scherman, *Siddur Eitz Chaim.* (Brooklyn: Mesorah Publications, Ltd., 1985), 21–22.

[19] If it is forbidden to strike any person (except in self-defense), how much more so to not strike one's parents out of anger. "To strike even without inflicting injury means to see in man only the body, to treat him as an animal and to dishonor him…even he, the Torah teaches, who only lifts his hands with the intention of striking his brother is called 'wicked.'" Hirsch, *Horeb*, 224.

[20] This deals with not only assault and battery, but laws of slander and libel.

[21] Again, the Torah gives the example with laws protecting the weakest and powerless of our society. It is forbidden for a master to kill his own slave; a slave owner can be put to death for the murder of a slave. Even causing a slave to lose an eye or a tooth requires that the slave be set free; this is a clear example of how different the "barbarous" Torah law is from American law of the early nineteenth century.

Despite what antagonists of Noahide law say, "capital punishment was rarely carried out and that it was a law in theory rather than in practice. Indeed, the Sages declared, 'A court that convicts one man in seven years is called a destructive court. R. Eleazar b. Azariah says one in even seventy years' [M. Makkoth 1, 10]…in Judaism punishment was designed neither as retribution nor as a deterrent. Its purpose was to teach the people that criminal conduct was a sin against God and man." Lew, *The Humanity of Jewish Law*, 68.

[22] The laws dealing with damages from domestic animals are found in the first six chapters of the tractate *Bava Kamma*. As an example, if a dog bites someone, the fines are determined by "which is a *mu'ad* (a habitually damaging animal) and which is a *tam* (a newly damaging animal)." *Séfer haHinnuch*, Vol. I, 219.

[23] "Our case here speaks primarily of…the uncovering or digging of a hole in the public thoroughfare i.e., of the responsibility for contriving a danger to the public… but at the same time this also declares responsibility for…any of one's property which may be dangerous to the public e.g., if anybody gives the public the right of access to a well on his private domain." Hirsch, commentary to *Shemos* 21:33, 324.

§1.54. *That the court should impose proper payment on a thief* [Shemos 21:37].[24]

§1.55. *The obligation of the court to judge damages by a domestic animal's grazing or trampling* [Shemos 22:4].[25]

§1.56. *The obligation of the court to judge damage by fire* [Shemos 22:5].[26]

§1.57. *That the court should judge cases involving an unpaid custodian* [Shemos 22:6].[27]

§1.58. *The court's obligation to judge the case of a plaintiff and a defendant* [Shemos 22:8].[28]

§1.59. *The court's obligation to judge cases involving a paid custodian or a hirer* [Shemos 22:9].[29]

§1.60. *The court's obligation to judge cases involving a man who borrows an object for use* [Shemos 22:13].[30]

§1.61. *The duty of the court to pass judgment on a seducer* [Shemos 22:15].[31]

---

[24] "Its laws are, for example, the payment of double value (Exodus 22:3) and four and five times the value (*ibid*. 21:37); the law on killing a thief who breaks in (*ibid*. 22:1); or selling him [into servitude] for his theft (*ibid*. 2)," etc. *Séfer haHinnuch*, Vol. I, 225.

[25] "Responsibility for damage done by an animal following his natural propensities is only incurred when the animal has no right to go there, and the damaged goods have the right to be there viz., in the premises of the plaintiff." Hirsch, commentary to *Shemos* 22:4, 344.

[26] "Fire, in the example given, and the legal term, for all damage done by inanimate property which is set in motion by ordinary natural forces and which does the damage while in motion. This would include e.g....a stone, a knife or anything that one has left on the roof, and which is blown down by an ordinary every-day wind, and which does damage as it falls." Hirsch, commentary to *Shemos* 22:5, 347.

[27] There are four kinds of custodians, as explained in *Bava Metzia* 94b: an unpaid custodian, a borrower, a paid custodian, and a renter. This mitzvoth deals with a שׁוֹמֵר חנם, an unpaid custodian. An unpaid custodian is not liable to damages through events outside his control (i.e., anything except פשיעה, gross negligence). For instance, if an unpaid custodian was asked to keep a shovel, and locked the shovel in his shed with his other tools and someone broke in and stole it, he is not liable. On the other hand, if he simply left it out on his porch, he would be liable.

[28] This is the obligation to hold trial for any person who sues someone for any matter.

[29] This law deals with the liability of a paid custodian, or one who receives payment as well as one who leases something.

[30] This is the opposite of the unpaid custodian, of the liability of someone who borrows something without payment.

[31] This is the law of what we call "statutory rape," of consensual intimacy with a minor. This law is different from the law regarding rape, or non-consensual intimacy, a crime of violence and theft (cf. §5.557).

§1.62. *Not to allow a sorcerer to live* [Shemos 22:17].[32]

§1.63. *Not to verbally oppress a convert to Judaism* [Shemos 22:20].[33]

§1.64. *Not to wrong a convert in matters of property* [Shemos 22:20].[34]

§1.65. *Not to afflict an orphan or widow* [Shemos 22:21].[35]

§1.66. *The mitzvah of lending to the poor* [Shemos 22:24].[36]

§1.67. *Not to dun a poor man unable to pay his debt* [Shemos 22:24].[37]

§1.68. *Not to help a borrower or a lender transact a loan at interest* [Shemos 22:24].[38]

---

[32] The death penalty only applies to the Land of Israel. For Noahides, it falls under the law of idolatry, forbidding any use of "magic" or any organized religion that uses magic, such as Wicca or Vodou.

[33] Although this is about shaming a *ger*, it can also apply to one who has become an observant Noahide, even if they had formally been a member of a religion such as Christianity by reminding them of their former idolatry.

[34] Not to wrong a *ger* in matters of monetary value. "By the juxtaposition of these two verses [Exodus 22:19–20], the great, oft-repeated in the Torah, basic law is laid down, that it is not race, not descent, not birth or country or property, altogether nothing external or due to chance, but simply and purely the inner spiritual and moral worth of a human being, which gives him all the rights of a man and of a citizen." Hirsch, commentary to *Shemos* 22:20, 373.

[35] This is a prohibition from oppressing by deed or word an orphan or widow, two types of people who lack anyone to stand up for their rights.

[36] In our Edomite society, the poorer one is, the more difficult it is to obtain a loan. The Torah teaches the exact opposite, that it is the poor man who we should endeavor to loan money to. "This religious duty of giving loans [to the poor] is a stronger and greater obligation than the *mitzvah* of giving charity." *Séfer haHinnuch*, Vol. I, 265.

[37] *Shemos* 22:24 also has the prohibition לא תהיה לו כנושה which means "to take legal proceedings against, or otherwise to bring pressure on, a debtor who is without means, or who is temporarily unable to meet his obligations. Hence, the instruction, even for the court itself, not to exact the very last penny which is legally due, but to leave the debtor the means for his daily existence, and for his clothing, bedding, and tools for his work…if anybody has a claim on a person, and knows that this latter is not in a position to meet it, he must go out of the way of that person, to avoid arousing the feeling of shame in his mind, for the Torah says לא תהיה לו כנושה 'you shall not appear to him as one demanding the payment of a debt.'" Hirsch, commentary to *Shemos* 22:24, 376–77. Under Torah Law, a man who fell behind on his automobile payments could not have his car repossessed indefinitely if he needs it for his work, or be subjected to hounding telephone calls demanding payment.

[38] Cf. mitzvah §3.343 n. 112 below. One of the greatest challenges Noahides face is dealing with the Edomite concept of money and materialism. "In areas of religious observance our Sages prescribed, 'And make a [protective] hedge for the Torah' (Avot 1:1), thus indicating that regulatory 'fences,' precautionary restrictions, be enacted around basic religious laws because man's attention is often distracted by

§1.69. *To utter no curse against a judge* [Shemos 22:27].[39]

§1.70. *The prohibition against cursing the name of the Eternal Lord* [Shemos 22:27].[40]

§1.71. *To utter no curse against a sovereign leader* [Shemos 22:27].[41]

§1.74. *Not to hear a litigant in court in his opponent's absence* [Shemos 23:1].[42]

§1.75. *That a sinner should not give testimony* [Shemos 23:1].[43]

§1.76. *Not to follow a majority of one among judges in a capital case* [Shemos 23:2].[44]

---

temptation." Rabbi Abraham R. Besdin, *Reflections of the Rav: Lessons in Jewish Thought*. Vol. I. (Hoboken: KTAV Publishing House, Inc., 1993), 49.

"The fact that the prohibition against interest on loans is not to be looked at simply from the concrete effect it has…on the whole structure of social life is incalculable. The preceding laws work against all the inequality of rights which birth and fate tend to bring, in ordinary social life. This law takes away the worst effect of the power of money, that most potent factor in causing social inequality. It breaks the too great power of capital. If this prohibition is strictly kept, all capital is in itself dead and unproductive, and can only be of use by wedding it to labour. It raises labour to the primary and essential factor of social well-being. Capital is forced to recognise [*sic*] the equality of labour. The rich man must either bring his otherwise dead capital to the power of labour of the poor man, share profit and loss with him, and in his own interests further the interests of labour. Every crisis of labour becomes to an even higher degree a crisis of capital, and capital can never make profit from the ruin of labour. The possibility of that shocking contrast, where the wretchedness of the labouring class is rampant right next to the most luxurious opulence, and the ground cut away from under its feet by this law." Hirsch, commentary to *Shemos* 22:24, 379.

[39] The prohibition against saying anything to a judge to instill fear in order to influence a verdict.

[40] This is about blaspheming the Holy Name HASHEM. Cf. *Sanhedrin* 56a.

[41] "At the root of the precept lies the reason that it is impossible for a settled community of human beings [to exist and function] without making one among them the head over the others, to obey his order and carry out his decrees." *Séfer haHinnuch*, Vol. I, 277.

[42] The first part of *Shemos* 23:1 is "a warning to the judges, not to listen to one party [in a criminal case] before the arrival of the other, opposing party (*Sanhedrin* 7b), so that no one-sided, partial impression of the facts of the case be formed beforehand." Hirsch, commentary to *Shemos* 23:1, 387.

[43] A man convicted in court of crimes such as robbery, and who is unrepentant, cannot be trusted as a witness.

[44] This is a trial of a capital case, with a twenty–three member Sanhedrin, and there is uncertainty about the verdict, and the guilty verdict is by one vote, and the presiding justice cannot follow the majority to vote for a guilty verdict by only one vote. The danger of putting an innocent man to death would be too great.

§1.77. *A judge who argues for innocence in a capital case should not argue for guilt afterward* [Shemos 23:2].[45]

§1.78. *The precept of following the majority in legal decisions* [Shemos 23:2].[46]

§1.79. *Not to take pity on a poor man in judgment* [Shemos 23:3].[47]

§1.80. *The mitzvah of unloading another person's burden* [Shemos 23:5].[48]

§1.81. *Not to pervert justice for a sinner on account of his wickedness* [Shemos 23:6].[49]

§1.82. *Not to decide a capital case on probability* [Shemos 23:7].[50]

§1.83. *A judge is not to take any bribe* [Shemos 23:8].[51]

§1.86. *Not to swear by any idol.* [Shemos 23:13].[52]

---

[45] "In this negative precept itself is included [the rule] that if someone argues to show the innocence [of the person on trial] he is not to turn about and argue to show his guilt." *Séfer haHinnuch*, Vol. I, 305.

[46] "The choice of this majority is evidently when the two contending groups know the wisdom of the Torah equally. For it cannot be said that a small group of Torah scholars should not outweigh a large group of ignoramuses." *Séfer haHinnuch*, Vol. I, 311.

[47] The prohibition not to corrupt justice for feelings of sympathy for the poor.

[48] This law is tied to the *Limb of the Living* (cf. §452); it is to show kindness in helping not only your fellow man, but for animals as well. The Torah gives the example of helping someone you hate; i.e., someone who you have seen willfully transgress the Torah, which you are allowed to hate. You are required to help someone you hate load their burden before helping a friend unload his. This is to conquer your evil inclination.

[49] Even if the man on trial is "poor in mitzvoth," he is to be tried with justice. "If, however, one was known to have committed murder but there were no valid witnesses he was imprisoned for life and was fed with a prison diet consisting of scant bread and scant water" [*Sanhedrin* 37b]. Lew, *The Humanity of Jewish Law*, 66.

[50] "This is the most comprehensive and far reaching sentence for the duties of a judge. It makes it his duty in general meticulously to avoid any and every thing by which there is the slightest possibility of the veracity of the judgment being affected." Hirsch, commentary to *Shemos* 23:7. Although circumstantial evidence is allowed in a Noahide *beis din*, a judge must be extremely careful not to sentence an innocent man to death, for the penalties are severe. "In Jewish law punishment has a moral objective, the restoration of the criminal to a good life and right conduct. It, indeed, reflects the attitude of Judaism to the weak and the fallen. The idea of punishment as retribution designed to inflict torment and humiliation is alien to Jewish legal notions." Ibid., 62.

[51] A judge must not take a bribe from either party, even if the outcome is to render a true judgment.

[52] "That we should not swear by the name of an idol, even to its worshippers, nor should we have a non-Jew swear by it." *Séfer haHinnuch*, Vol. I, 333. Merely saying

§1.87. *Not to lead Israelites astray into idolatry* [Shemos 23:13].[53]

§1.93. *To make no treaty with the seven nations to be extirpated, or with any idol-worshipper* [Shemos 23:32].[54]

§1.94. *Not to settle any idol-worshipper in our land* [Shemos 23:33].[55]

§1.111. *The ban on eating or drinking anything from an offering to an idol* [Shemos 34:12,15].[56]

§1.114. *That the court should not carry out any execution on the Sabbath* [Shemos 35:3].[57]

§2.122. *The obligation to bear witness in court* [Vayikra 5:1].[58]

§2.130. *The precept of returning property seized in robbery* [Vayikra 5:23].[59]

---

the name of an idol is not idolatry; what the Torah teaches is that we are to "put a fence" around the Torah, to guard ourselves against any sort of violation.

[53] This law should be self-explanatory. To entice a Jew to forsake the Torah and "convert" to a man-made idolatrous religion is prohibited.

[54] The prohibition of making international treaties with nations who do not have the Torah as their legal foundation.

[55] Idolators are not allowed to settle in Eretz Yisrael. Contrary to what many people think, Muhammadians are not observant Noahides. As with Esau, they may honor the Father, observing the prohibition of the Noahide Law of idolatry, but they certainly violate the other six laws, and their legal systems are not based on Torah.

[56] Part of this prohibition's relevance to the Noahide has to do with the festive meals that members of idolatrous organized religions often have, such as church dinners.

[57] Although Noahides are forbidden to observe the Sabbath as Jews are commanded to do, it would seem prudent not to go out of our way to profane it, particularly by putting someone to death. One of the problems with our culture is that, for the majority of non-Jews, the Sabbath (starting at sundown Friday night) is the time for revelry, merrymaking and even drunkenness, and typically Friday night to Saturday night is the time when the Torah is the furthest thing from Western minds.

[58] There is a difference between civil and capital cases; in a civil case, a person is not obligated to testify unless summoned, but in a capital case, if a person was a witness, they have a duty to testify. "Whenever there is a monetary dispute between people, there is a responsibility on witnesses to come forward if they are requested by one of the parties to do so. If a witness denies that he has any knowledge of the case, the party may ask him to swear, either inside or outside of the *beis din*, that he is telling the truth. Our verse deals with a witness who has taken such an oath, and then admits that he lied." Scherman and Goldwurm, *Vayikra*, Vol. I, 84.

[59] As explained in *Bava Kamma* 112a, if a person has the unaltered property of another that had been taken by force, he is to return it to the robbed man, even if he himself desired the item and wished to give the monetary value of the object. If the object is altered or damaged, then he is to give the monetary value of the object. "If the item

§2.152. *After drinking wine a kohen should not enter the sanctuary, and no one is to give a ruling* [Vayikra 10:9].[60]

§2.188. *The prohibition of pleasure with any woman ranked as 'ervah* [Vayikra 18:6].[61]

§2.189. *The prohibition on uncovering the nakedness of one's father* [Vayikra 18:7].[62]

§2.190. *The prohibition of uncovering one's mother's nakedness* [Vayikra 18:7].

§2.191. *The prohibition of conjugal intimacy with one's father's wife even if she is not his mother* [Vayikra 18:8].

§2.192. *Not to uncover a sister's nakedness, if she's one's sister in any way* [Vayikra 18:9].

§2.193. *The prohibition of conjugal intimacy with the daughter of a son* [Vayikra 18:10].

§2.194 *The prohibition of conjugal intimacy with a daughter's daughter* [Vayikra 18:10].

§2.195 *The prohibition of conjugal intimacy with a daughter* [Vayikra 18:10].

§2.196. *The prohibition of conjugal relations with a sister on the father's side who is the father's wife's daughter* [Vayikra 18:11].

§2.197. *The prohibition of conjugal intimacy with a father's sister* [Vayikra 18:12].

---

that he stole is still intact, he must return it as is, and it is forbidden for him to keep and pay for it. However, if he has changed the item significantly so that it is no longer the thing *that he robbed*, the robber may pay for it and keep the item. For example, if someone stole lumber and made a bookcase from it, he must pay for the lumber, but he may keep the bookcase, since it is not the item that he stole (*Bava Kamma* 66a, 93b)." Ibid., 94.

[60] A judge may not give a ruling when intoxicated or under the influence of any drug.

[61] The laws involving illicit sex are for the protection of the family, the building block of a peaceful and stable community. "When God led the first woman to the first man He did so in order that their union, based on free-willed morality (as opposed to the blind physical urges of the animal), might serve Him as a pillar on which to build all of human development—marriage, the family and society." Hirsch, *T'rumath Tzvi*, 446. "The commandment is expressed in the plural to teach that it applies equally to the male and the female (*Rashi, Sifra*)." Sherman and Goldwurm, *Vayikra*, Vol. II, 324.

[62] *Mitzvot* §2.189–206 should be self-explanatory. Although the *Mishna Torah* lists only six illicit relationships for a Noahide [his mother, father's wife (even if she is not his mother), a married woman, his maternal sister, a male, and an animal], it would seem prudent to follow Torah guidelines on all illicit relationships listed in *Vayikra* 18. For instance, although there is debate about a Noahide marrying his daughter in the Talmud, it is not listed as one of the prohibited relationships. This prohibition follows the dictum that just because something is not prohibited does not mean it should be allowed.

§2.198. *The prohibition of conjugal intimacy with a mother's sister* [Vayikra 18:13].

§2.199. *The prohibition of carnal relations with a father's brother* [Vayikra 18:14].

§2.200. *The prohibition of conjugal relations with the wife of a father's brother* [Vayikra 18:14].

§2.201. *The prohibition of conjugal relations with the wife of a son* [Vayikra 18:15].

§2.202. *The prohibition of conjugal relations with a brother's wife* [Vayikra 18:16].

§2.203. *The prohibition of conjugal relations with both a woman and her daughter* [Vayikra 18:17].

§2.204. *The prohibition of conjugal intimacy with both a woman and her son's daughter* [Vayikra 18:17].

§2.205. *The prohibition of conjugal intimacy with both a woman and her daughter's daughter* [Vayikra 18:17].

§2.206. *The prohibition of conjugal relations with two sisters while both are alive* [Vayikra 18:18].

§2.209. *The prohibition of carnal relations with any male* [Vayikra 18:22].[63]

---

[63] Homosexuality is one of the most divisive issues our society faces, and there is no greater foe of the Torah than the homosexual. Because the homosexual "movement" is only a few decades old, many perceive that homosexual "rights" is a new and progressive issue. Nothing could be further from the truth. The sages unanimously prohibited homosexuality, mainly because it led to the abominable practice of pederasty which the ancient Greeks honed to a fine art, a point that is rarely mentioned in recent debates over the issue. "There is a strong case to be made that overt male pederasty was a development of the years around 600 BCE in parallel with the rise of the sexually exclusive phenomena of the athletic *agon*, the *gymnasion* [from the Greek word meaning to "exercise naked"], *palaistra*, and *symposion*." Lynette G. Mitchell and P. J. Rhodes, *The Development of the Polis in Archaic Greece*. (London: New York Taylor & Francis, 1997), 90. That pederasty was supported by Platonic philosophy is one of the problems with attempting to defend homosexuality on logical or rational grounds; the homosexual argument is based on lust and emotion, not reason. "The ancient sources appear to take Plato's homoeroticism for granted. At the same time, they say nothing of Plato marrying a wife. Plato seems to write with personal experience of pederastic desire in several places, notable in the *Symposium*, with its heartfelt insistence of 'right pederasty'; in the *Phaedrus* (250e–252b, 253c–256d); in the *Republic* (474c–475a); and in the *Charmides* (155d)." James M. Rhodes, *Eros, Wisdom, and Silence: Plato's Erotic Dialogues*. (Columbia, Mo: University of Missouri Press, 2003), 116. Plato's own words leave little to the imagination; in *Charmides* (155d), Plato—sounding like a dirty old philosopher as he ogled a young boy—wrote: "I saw inside his cloak and caught on fire and was quite beside myself." *Plato: Complete Works*. John M. Cooper, ed. (Indianapolis: Hackett Publishing Company, 1997), 642.

The supporters of homosexuality insist that homosexuality is not detrimental to the family. Their protests sound similar to the tobacco company's decades-long

§2.210. *The prohibition of carnal relations with animals* [Vayikra 18:23].[64]

§2.211. *The prohibition on carnal intimacy by a woman with an animal* [Vayikra 18:23].[65]

§3.212. *The mitzvah of reverence for father and mother* [Vayikra 19:3].[66]

§3.213. *Not to turn astray after idol-worship in thought or word* [Vayikra 19:4].[67]

§3.214. *To make no idol, for oneself or for anyone else* [Vayikra 19:4].[68]

§3.216. *The mitzvah of leaving an edge of one's field unreaped, for the poor* [Vayikra 19:10].[69]

---

insistence that tobacco does not cause cancer. Like tobacco, not only is homosexuality damaging to the individual, but the second-hand sin spiritually affects our society like a malignant cancer. In condoning homosexuality, we slip down the slippery shaft of logic to the Greek practice of pederasty. "What is remarkable about ancient Greek homophilia is not so much that homoerotic relations existed, but that for several centuries they came to be so overt, and so positively and strongly reinforced by an institutional framework and semi-official ideology of mutual educational benefit." [Mark Griffith, '"Public" and "Private" in Early Greek Institutions of Education." *From Education in Greek and Roman Antiquity*. Yun Lee Too, ed. (Leiden: Boston Brill Academic Publishers, 2001), 62.] The homosexual lobby has organized itself into a powerful political force since so many people will cast their vote on this single issue alone—they love to coat their hedonism with slogans such as "freedom, liberty, equality, and democracy"—their homosexuality trumping any issue and all other societal concerns such as the welfare of the poor, children, and families.

[64] This prohibition includes any beast, wild or domestic.

[65] This prohibition is listed separately from §2.210, even though they are in the same category.

[66] As *Kiddushin* 31a teaches (about the Noahide Dama Ben-Netinah), it is a mitzvah for a Noahide to honor one's parents. "*Honor*, as mandated in the Ten Commandments, refers in general to caring for parents, such as feeding and dressing them, or assisting them if they find it difficult to walk (*Rashi, Sifra*)." Sherman and Goldwurm, *Vayikra*, Vol. II, 337.

[67] As Rabbi Aryeh Kaplan explained above (p. 415–16), this is about the idolatry of conceptual idols, not just the false gods such as the Nazarene. When a person puts conceptual idols over God and the Torah, such as the Constitution being more important than the Torah or ideals such as Nationalism and Patriotism being more important than the *mitzvot*, then that person is violating this important *mitzvah*.

[68] This is a prohibition for making any idol for yourself or anyone else, such as the figure of a dead Jew on a stick.

[69] The text in the Torah explicitly says ולגר, *to the gér*, or a full proselyte. However, the ruling in *Gittin* 59b, it says that even poor Noahides should be permitted to reap from the corners of the field, which makes the *mitzvot* from *Vayikra* 19:9–10 applicable

§3.217. *Not to reap the very last end of one's field* [Vayikra 19:9].[70]

§3.218. *The precept of leaving the gleanings of the harvest for the poor* [Vayikra 19:10].[71]

§3.219. *Not to gather stalks of grain that fell away during the harvest* [Vayikra 19:9].[72]

§3.220. *The precept of leaving a part of a vineyard unreaped, for the poor* [Vayikra 19:10].[73]

§3.221. *The prohibition of reaping absolutely all the fruit of a vineyard* [Vayikra 19:10].[74]

§3.222. *The precept of leaving fallen grapes in a vineyard, for the*

---

to Noahide Law. Although this is not a mandatory law, the fact the Torah has eight mitzvoth on these two verses shows the importance of helping the poor. People who build fences around their fields, putting NO TRESSPASSING signs everywhere, and chasing off the poor from gathering the gleanings have little or no understanding of Torah. As Rabbi Hirsch explained, "Even the poor man himself has to leave his [gleanings, forgotten sheaves, corners, unripe grapes, etc.] from his field to other poor people! It is clear that, at once at the harvest, at the moment when a person takes home that which Nature and his own own hard-work has yielded to him, and puts the proud and far-reaching word 'my own' in his mouth, these laws are to remind every member of the Nation, and to demand an act of recognition from him, of the fact that this 'my own' includes for everybody the duty of caring for others who are needy; that field and vineyard have not yielded their produce for his exclusive use, and that his hand is not to work exclusively for himself, that in God's holy State the care for the 'poor and the stranger without property' is not a matter which is left to the greater or lesser soft-hearted feelings of sympathy, or to the greater or lesser feeling of expediency, that the despair of the poor and needy classes may constitute a threatening danger to the property of the well-to-do, in short, not to be left to sympathy nor to policy, but is raised to a God-given right to the poor, and to a God-ordained duty to the owners of property from God, Who proclaims His *I, God, your God* over all of them, and thereby assures that each and every one of them is equally considered by Him, that each and every one of them is equally encompassed by His Love, and granted rights from Him, that they are all equally bound to give the same rights and the same love, and so to unite to form a community holy to God, and held together by respect for rights and for the duty of brotherly love." Hirsch, commentary to *Vayikra* 19:10, 510.

[70] The minimum one must leave is one-sixtieth of the field.

[71] This commandment is that the grains that have fallen on the ground must be left for the poor.

[72] Not simply the single grains, but the whole ears of grain, if they fall to the ground, must be left for the poor.

[73] That the single grapes that are not in bunches are to be left to the poor.

[74] The author of the *Séfer haHinnuch* points out a discrepancy between *Rambam's Séfer haMitzvoth* and the Talmud (although it was corrected in the *Mishna Torah*) that applied to this commandment, linking it to Devarim 24:20 prohibition of going back over the vineyard to gather the missed clusters.

poor [Vayikra 19:10].[75]

§3.223. *The prohibition of gathering the fallen grapes in a vineyard* [Vayikra 19:10].[76]

§3.224. *The prohibition on the theft of anything of value* [Vayikra 19:11].[77]

§3.225. *Not to deny it when something of value that belongs to another is on our possession* [Vayikra 19:11].[78]

§3.226. *Not to swear over a false denial about something of value* [Vayikra 19:11].[79]

§3.227. *The prohibition against swearing falsely* [Vayikra 19:12].[80]

§3.228. *Not to withhold another person's property wrongly* [Vayikra 19:13].[81]

---

[75] As with the grain, one must leave the fallen grapes for the poor.

[76] Not to gather the fallen grapes, such as putting a basket underneath the vine while you are picking the grapes.

[77] Immediately after the laws about leaving the corners of the fields and the gleanings to the poor, there is the admonition not to steal; if your neighbor lets you glean from his fields, you should not take advantage and steal unprotected property. When theft, dishonesty and swearing become so widespread that it becomes a national characteristic, the society is in trouble. There is nothing more destructive to a society than robbery. The Torah teaches that we should not steal even in jest as a practical joke, or even if we were wanting to pay four times the amount the object is worth. "Just as God gave a body to the human spirit as a tool for his human activities, and the body must be respected for the spirit within it; so He gave him the earth with all that is on it and that belongs to it so that he may freely acquire it and dispose of it according to his destiny...as soon, therefore, as a human being states that he has acquired something which belongs to the earth and comes within the realm of his body, it becomes his own as much as the body which God has allotted to him...therefore, just as it is God's command that thou shalt not kill or injure, that thou shalt respect the body for the Divine spirit within it, so also is it God's command that thy shalt not steal or rob." Hirsch, *Horeb*, 226–27.

[78] A person who lies about having something of value in his possession is disqualified as being a witness.

[79] This is a prohibition of a person swearing about his lie of having something in his possession.

[80] This has to do with swearing falsely about something the person has done in the past or will do in the future.

[81] This is the prohibition of keeping the property of another through "force or by procrastination and trickery...[also] anyone who owes his fellow a specific amount of money and he cheats him out of it." *Séfer haHinnuch*, Vol. III, 37.

§3.229. *The prohibition against committing robbery* [Vayikra 19:13].[82]

§3.230. *That payment of a hired man is not to be delayed* [Vayikra 19:13].[83]

§3.231. *The prohibition on cursing any Jew, man or woman* [Vayikra 19:14].[84]

§3.232. *Not to make a trusting person stumble through misleading advice* [Vayikra 19:14].[85]

§3.233. *Not to pervert justice in a civil judgment* [Vayikra 19:15].[86]

§3.234. *Not to honor an eminent person at a trial* [Vayikra 19:15].[87]

§3.235. *The precept that a judge should render judgment with rigteousness* [Vayikra 19:15].[88]

§3.236. *The prohibition on gossiping slanderously* [Vayikra19:16].[89]

§3.237. *Not to stand idly by when someone's blood is shed* [Vayikra 19:16].[90]

---

[82] The prohibition of taking something by force. "It is immaterial from whom you may steal, filch or withhold, be it an Israelite or a non-Israelite, a heathen or idolator, an adult or a minor, in every case you have transgressed against a Divine prohibition and are in sin until you have restored it." Hirsch, *Horeb*, 228.

[83] "The substance of this precept is that we should not delay the wages of a hired worker, but should pay him within a fixed period." *Séfer haHinnuch*, Vol. III, 47. According to *Rambam*, this law applies to Noahides.

[84] Not to curse anyone, even if they do not hear it.

[85] "*Leviticus* 19:14, which prohibits causing another person to stumble in sin. It includes causing a non-Jew to violate one of the laws commanded to him." Schottenstein Talmud, *Bava Metzia* 90b, n. 6.

[86] That a judge will do no injustice at a trial as explained in the Talmud. The laws regarding this precept are many, covering the conduct of judges, sentencing, and reaching a timely verdict, etc. "If the subject would not be so long, taking us beyond the framework of our task, we would proceed to explain at length all the instances when a verdict is overturned and the instances when it is not overturned, the *beth din* (court) then being obligated to pay out of its own funds [to the wronged party], and those circumstances where the verdict is not overturned." *Séfer haHinnuch*, Vol. III, 63. According to Rabbi Hirsch, "justice thus simply means allowing each creature all that it may expect as the portion allotted to it by God." Hirsch, *Horeb*, 217.

[87] Not to honor one over another, even if he is rich and respected.

[88] "Righteousness" here meaning according to Torah standards. For example, not to tell one that he could speak as long as he wanted, and tell the other to shorten his words, or if one is dressed in fine clothing and another in old work clothes, but to make sure they are dressed the same so as not to influence the decision.

[89] "[The Sages] taught distinctly that slander brings death to the one who says it, the one who receives it, and the one about whom it is told—but most of all to the one who receives it." *Séfer haHinnuch*, Vol. III, 71.

[90] Not to let anyone come to harm if it is within our power to help them. This also applies to testifying for someone who could lose their property if you have knowledge that could help them in a civil case.

§3.238. *The prohibition against hating one's brethren* [Vayikra 19:17].[91]

§3.239. *The duty to rebuke a fellow for improper behavior* [Vayikra 19:17].[92]

§3.240. *The prohibition against shaming a Jew* [Vayikra 19:17].[93]

§3.241. *The prohibition against taking revenge* [Vayikra 19:18].[94]

§3.242. *The prohibition against bearing a grudge* [Vayikra 19:18].[95]

§3.243. *The Prime Directive* [Vayikra 19:18].[96]

§3.244. *The prohibition on mating two animals of different species* [Vayikra 19:19].[97]

§3.248. *Not to eat or drink in the manner of a glutton or drunkard* [Vayikra 19:26].[98]

---

[91] This has to do with hating someone in your heart; that is, not letting the person you despise know how you feel (this precept is not violated if the person you hate knows your feelings.) This is the cause for slandering someone from the previous verse.

[92] Unlike some organized religions that foolishly teach "thou shalt not judge another," this commandment says that when someone sees a person violating the Torah in either affairs between man and man or man and God, he is to reprove them over and over, even to a hundred times if necessary (*Bava Metzia* 31a). To respect their feelings, you should first chide them in secret, that is, in private, using soft speech. If this does not work, and the person keeps violating the Torah, stronger language is used, even to the point of shaming him or her in public. If the person is adamant about violating the Torah, one is allowed to hate them. "On the hatred of wicked people...there is no prohibition; it is rather a religious duty to hate them after we reprove them many times about their sins and they yet do not wish to retract them; for it is stated, *Do I not hate those, O Lord, who hate Thee, and strive with those that rise against Thee?* (Psalms 139:21)." *Séfer haHinnuch*, Vol. III, 79.

[93] Not to shame anyone deliberately or needlessly.

[94] Not to take revenge; for example, telling someone they could not borrow your telephone because they did not let you borrow their telephone the previous day.

[95] If someone has wronged you, do not keep it festering in your heart. You are to forgive even if the other person has not apologized.

[96] The Prime Directive. It does not say to love the *person* of your neighbor, but rather the *well-being* of your neighbor; to rejoice in his well-being, and to grieve with him in his times of woe. The Noahide link to this commandment comes from the famous story in the Talmud (*Shabbat* 31a) that tells of a Noahide asking Rabbi Hillel to teach him the Torah while standing on one foot, or quickly. Hillel replied: "what is hateful to yourself, do not do to another. The rest is commentary; go study."

[97] This prohibition is found in a Baraisa in *Sanhedrin* 56b.

[98] "Not to overindulge in eating and drinking in the days of youth, under the conditions mentioned about the stubborn and rebellious son in Scripture (Deuteronomy 21:18)." *Séfer haHinnuch*, Vol. III, 111. In our culture, we follow the Roman custom

§3.249. *The prohibition against practicing augury* [Vayikra 19:26].[99]

§3.250. *The prohibition against the practice of conjuring* [Vayikra 19:26].[100]

§3.255. *The prohibition against acting as an 'ov—a medium* [Vayikra 19:31].[101]

§3.256. *Not to function as a yid'oni, a kind of wizard* [Vayikra 19:31].

§3.257. *The mitzvah of honoring wise scholars* [Vayikra 19:32].[102]

§3.258. *The prohibition against cheating with any kind of measure* [Vayikra 19:35].[103]

§3.259. *The precept that scales, weights and measures should be made correct* [Vayikra 19:36].[104]

§3.260. *The prohibition against cursing one's father or mother* [Vayikra 20:9].[105]

§3.262. *The prohibition against following customs and ways of the Amorites* [Vayikra 20:23].[106]

---

of celebrating youth with gluttony and drunkenness, such as college students are wont to do, and our penchant for junk-food and super-sized meals.

[99] The prohibition against superstitious nonsense, such as believing you will have seven years of bad luck if you break a mirror, or not taking some course of action just because a black cat crossed your path.

[100] The prohibition against determining set times, say such-and-such an hour is unlucky. Also prohibiting using slight-of-hand tricks to deceive people, such as magician can do, putting in a red handkerchief into his fist and turning it into an egg, etc.

[101] Both the *'ov* and the *yid'oni* [§3.256] are mediums who "talk" to the dead (*Sanhedrin* 65a, b). Palm-readers, soothsayers, etc. fall into this category.

[102] Unlike our modern society which idealizes the Greek "cult of youth" and its worship of athletic prowess and superficial attractiveness, the Torah teaches we should respect age and one with intellectual wisdom, i.e., Torah wisdom.

[103] The prohibition not to cheat with any sort of measure: dry goods, liquids, the measurement of land, cloth, etc.

[104] That the instruments of measuring are correct and working properly.

[105] You are not allowed to curse anyone (§3.231), especially your parents.

[106] "Not to follow the customs of the Amorites, and equally the customs of the heathen… the same law holds for all other nations, because the reason is that they turn away from following the Eternal Lord and worship idols…the substance of the precept is that we should not behave like them…that you should not follow their practices in matters that are established for them, such as theaters, circuses, and amphitheater spectacles. These are all forms of sport and entertainment that they enact in their mass gatherings, when they assemble to commit lunatic acts, immorality, and idol-worship." *Séfer haHinnuch*, Vol. III, 161. This has to do with everything from the Greek-influenced Olympic "games" (where people race each other down snow-covered mountains on thin slats

§3.295. *To do nothing by which the Divine Name will be profaned or desecrated among men* [Vayikra 22:32].[107]

§3.296. *The mitzvah of sanctifying the Almighty's Name* [Vayikra 22:32].[108]

§3.336. *The precept of effecting justice between buyer and seller* [Vayikra 25:14].[109]

§3.337. *The prohibition against wronging anyone in buying and selling* [Vayikra 25:14].[110]

---

of wood strapped to their feet and other foolish things) to "strip" joints and idolatrous tent "revival" meetings complete with "faith-healers," etc. (cf. *Avodah Zarah* 18b). "One might have argued that the various listed comedies employ sophisticated parody and allegory, and should be permitted as intellectual and artistic pursuits. Moreover, they cheer dejected hearts. The Tanna therefore adduces *Psalms* [Psalm 1:1–2; *The praises of Man are that he walked not in the counsel of the wicked, and stood not in the path of the sinful, and sat not in the session of scorners. But his desire is in the Torah of HASHEM, and in his Torah he meditates day and night*] to teach that on the contrary, such comedies *undermine* true wisdom and real joy. They lead to the cessation of the study of Torah." *Schottenstein Talmud, Avodah Zarah* 18b, n.18. In the tractate *Megillah* 6a, it states that in the future, the theaters and circuses of Edom will be transformed into halls of Torah study.

[107] "Anybody, by his knowledge of the Word of God, and by his position in the social world, is prominent as a 'bearer of the Name of God,' the sharper and the more imperative is the demand made to him: *And you shall not profane My Holy Name*, and all the more in his case is the slightest, even only a seemingly, deviation from the truthfulness and honesty, from the morality and by living from the justness, kindness and goodness which the Torah demands reckoned as a great crime (Yoma, 86b)." Hirsch, commentary to *Vayikra* 22:32, 641.

[108] There are three mitzvot which a Jew cannot transgress, even when faced with death: idolatry, adultery, and murder (*Sanhedrin* 74a). A Noahide does not have to go to this extreme, but a Noahide can sanctify the Divine Name nonetheless. "Every enhanced degree of mental or spiritual superiority demands a higher degree of conscientiousness, shows in what sense the intelligentsia and men of special gifts of the Jewish people regarding their position in relation to the laws of morality, and how far away they were from that deplorable erroneous opinion which is ready to grant every upward step of intellectual greatness a greater dispensation from having to keep the laws of morality." Hirsch, commentary to *Vayikra* 22:32, 641.

[109] That we should follow the laws in the Torah regarding purchasing and selling. For instance, the Torah forbids opportunistic raising of commodity prices during times of scarcity (*Bava Bathra* 89a, 90b). "The community was duty bound to regulate commodity prices." Lew, *The Humanity of Jewish Law*, 42.

[110] The prohibition against cheating anyone in buying or selling. "Every big or little fraud in buying or selling is forbidden. Do not give your goods a deceptive appearance so that they seem better than they really are. Do not mix bad with good merchandise, old with new. Things which can be tasted before they are bought and which each buyer tastes before he buys you may mix. Do not let the upper layer be better than those underneath…do not sell damaged goods as perfect, nor goods that are unsuited for their purpose as suitable." Hirsch, *Horeb*, 236.

§3.338. *The prohibition against oppressing anyone with words.* [Vayikra 25:17].[111]

§3.343. *The prohibition against lending at interest* [Vayikra 25:37][112]

---

[111] Not to hurt anyone's feelings in any way by means of speech. "If you seek pleasure in mocking the inexperienced and less intelligent, in deceiving and embarrassing him instead of teaching and correcting him; if you ridicule the unfortunate whose troubled mind is longing for comfort from your lips, and overwhelm him with useless reproaches; if you put your brother to shame in front of others even for the purpose of correcting him; if you degrade your brother's personality by calling him bad names; if with icy scorn and fiery disdain in your barbed words you shoot sharp arrows into your brother's heart and rejoice in his discomfiture—oh then, do not dare to look up to heaven!" Hirsch, *Horeb*, 257.

[112] Any *shiur* on the law of usury as applied to Noahide Law must take into account two factors: one, that there is no prohibition of usury for the *Bnai Noah*; two, the need for strict restrictions (fences) to temper the rampant abuses of capital we have seen in Edomite society, not the least of which is to finance wars of conquest and *hamas*. In order to use *severah* for the law of interest, we must explore the reasons behind the commandment.

Usury involves the concept of charity, as well as the way we look at money. "The Torah in no wise looks on interest on loans as anything which is morally wrong. Otherwise it would not forbid with equal solemnity the paying of interest as it does the taking of it, nor would it restrict the prohibition to Jews only. But it is rather a great act of acknowledgment, of recognizing God as the Lord and Owner of our moveable property…against this way of looking on interest on loans from the non-Jewish standpoint…our money is not absolutely our own property, it is only conditionally ours." [Hirsch, commentary on *Vayikra* 24:36, 766–67.] Of course, this flies in the face of our modern financial system's structure of "credit rating" and the bank's reluctance to give loans to the poor. "The concept of charity…includes the duty of lending to those in need…lending must be motivated by humanity and sympathy. The Biblical prohibition of interest made money-lending a non-profitable activity. Consequently lenders were unlikely to advance money with the risks attached to business transactions without the compensation of interest. There was clearly a need for measures that would safeguard the interest of creditors. Alive to the commercial needs of the people, needs often aggravated by political and economic conditions, the Rabbis evolved a legal instrument, known as עיסקא, literally business, occupation. Briefly, every sum involved in a loan, especially when advanced for trading purposes, was considered half as a loan and half as a trust on which the lender was entitled to the larger share of the profits [*Bava Metzia* 104b]. This legal instrument was introduced to meet the needs, within the framework of the Halachah, of an urban society with its commerce and industry. It was also, no doubt, to enable those in a position to practise [*sic*] this form of economic aid. To avoid the prohibition of usury the investor takes a greater share of the risk than of the profit; he receives, for example either half of the profit but bears two thirds of the loss or a third of the profit but bearing half of the loss. This arrangement was considered by the Rabbis to meet the problems both of the debtor and the creditor." Lew, *The Humanity of Jewish Law*, 43–44.

§3.346. *Not to work a manservant at hard labor* [Vayikra 25:43].[113]

§3.349. *The prohibition against prostrating ourselves on a figured stone* [Vayikra 26:1].[114]

§4.387. *Not to go straying after one's heart and eyes* [Bamidbar 15:39].[115]

§4.409. *Not to execute a guilty person who deserves death, before he stands trial* [Bamidbar 35:12].[116]

§4.411. *That a witness who testifies in a trial for a capital crime should not speak in judgment* [Bamidbar 35:30].[117]

§4.412. *To take no ransom to save a killer from his death sentence* [Bamidbar 35:31].[118]

§4.414. *Not to appoint any judge who is unlearned in the Torah, even if he is generally learned* [Devarim 1:17].[119]

§4.415. *That a judge presiding at a trial should not fear any man* [Devarim 1:17].[120]

§4.416. *Not to desire what belongs to our fellow [Noahides]* [Devarim 5:18].[121]

§4.417. *The precept of the oneness of the Eternal Lord* [Devarim 6:4].[122]

---

[113] This is a prohibition against crushing oppressive work that has no limit and no real need, such as how we make prisoners break rocks. You should not work a servant simply to keep them busy.

[114] You should not prostrate yourself on figured stone even to worship the Eternal Lord.

[115] "The substance of this injunction is that we were restricted not to devote our thoughts to entertain views that are opposed to the system of thought on which the Torah is constructed." *Séfer haHinnuch*, Vol. IV, 115.

[116] The prohibition of lynching, or putting a murderer to death before he has stood trial.

[117] The prohibition of a witness in a capital trial not to give judgment no matter how wise and learned he may be.

[118] The prohibition of taking a ransom to save the life of a convicted murderer as well as the prohibition of plea-bargining.

[119] The prohibition of a man of being a judge if he is unlearned in Torah no matter how wise or learned in other areas he might be.

[120] The prohibition of a judge to render a true judgment for fear of retribution from the accused.

[121] The prohibition for even longing for what belongs to another.

[122] This is what the *Séfer haHinnuch* calls the "core element" of faith in God for all mankind, both Jew and Noahide. Because there is no commandment for a Noahide to pray, or to have any sort of established prayers, one must still keep in mind that all prayer should be directed to the One and Only God.

§4.418. *The precept of love for the Eternal Lord* [Devarim 6:5].[123]

§4.419. *The precept of Torah study* [Devarim 6:7].[124]

§4.432. *The precept of reverent awe for the Eternal Lord* [Devarim 10:20].[125]

§4.434. *The mitzvah of associating with Torah scholars and adhering to them* [Devarim 11:22].[126]

§4.436. *The precept to destroy an idol and all that serves it* [Devarim 12:2].[127]

§4.437. *Not to erase Holy Writings or Written Names of the Holy One* [Devarim 12:4].[128]

§4.452. *Not to eat a limb or part taken from a living animal* [Devarim 12:23].[129]

§4.454. *The prohibition against adding to the precepts of the Torah* [Devarim 13:1].[130]

---

[123] "Everything that you think and feel, everything that you strive for and desire and everything that you possess, shall be unto you only the means, only have value to you, for getting near to God, for bringing God near to you." Hirsch, commentary to Devarim 6:5, 92.

[124] Since all mankind is obligated to keep the Torah, we are commanded to learn and to teach it.

[125] To be in awe of God. Not fear, but the awe one would have in the presence of a king or a president.

[126] To associate ourselves with Torah scholars in order to learn *halakha*.

[127] Since Noahides are prohibited to worship idols, part of the elimination of idolatry in our society is the total removal of all traces of the worship of other gods, their houses of worship, their feasts and festivals, etc. We are not commanded to "respect" other gods, we are commanded to eliminate them.

[128] This teaches respect for the Torah.

[129] One of the Seven Mitzvot given to Noah (*Bereishis* 9:4). "At the root of the precept lies the reason that we should not train our spirit in the quality of cruelty, which is a most reprehensible trait of character." *Séfer haHinnuch*, Vol. IV, 411.

[130] The prohibition to adding anything to the Written or Oral Torah. This is the grave mistake many of the Reform (religious) Noahides make, the mistake of Nadab and Abihu. In *Bamidbar* 3:4, it says that "Nadab and Abihu died before HASHEM when they offered alien fire before HASHEM in the Wilderness of Sinai." Noahides are not commanded to pray, or to have organized religious services, or to wear *kippahs* or "Noahide" *tallis*, or to keep the Sabbath or any of the Jewish festivals, or to say, "since Noah offered sacrifices, I will offer sacrifices." What Noahides are commanded to do is to create a safe and just society with laws based on the Torah. "Do not try to discover new ways of honouring God, and do not seek giving satisfaction to your God by any other means than those which He has prescribed for you. Only by faithfully,

§4.455. *Not to diminish the precepts of the Torah in any way* [Devarim 13:1].[131]

§4.456. *To pay no heed to anyone prophesying in the name of an idol or idolatry* [Devarim 13:4].[132]

§4.457. *To have no affection for an enticer to idolatry* [Devarim 13:9].[133]

§4.458. *Not to relinquish hatred for an enticer to idolatry* [Devarim 13:9].[134]

§4.459. *Not to rescue from death an enticer to idol-worship* [Devarim 13:9].[135]

§4.460. *That someone enticed to idolatry should not speak in favor of the enticer* [Devarim 13:9].[136]

§4.461. *That a person enticed to idol-worship should not refrain from speaking out against the enticer* [Devarim 13:9].[137]

---

conscientiously carrying out the commands He has given you do you render the homage He expects from you. The Mitzvas which He has commanded you, and precisely as He has commanded you, are the expression of His Will for you, and they tell you what He expects from you, and what you have to do to arrange your life on earth in accordance with His satisfaction. As they are not your own ideas of what is right and befitting but the dictates of your God, you have not got to try and improve them in any way, not to add to them or subtract from them. By doing more or less they would no longer be the dictates of your God." Hirsch, commentary on *Devarim* 13:1, 230–31.

[131] The prohibition of diminishing any of the precepts of the Torah.

[132] "The wording of this verse shows that it is not speaking only of being led into idolatry but equally so of being led into any disloyalty towards the Torah." Hirsch, commentary to *Devarim* 13:4, 233.

[133] Not only to ignore the message, but to dislike the enticer of idolatry.

[134] To hate the enticer of idolatry. The gooey and wrong-headed argument about "love," that "God loves everybody, so you should, too," is disproven by this mitzvah. Anyone who willfully tries to turn any Torah-observant Jew or Noahide from the Torah deserves our hate for the evil he or she is trying to do.

[135] "That the enticed person is forbidden to rescue the enticer [to idolatry] when he sees him in danger of death and perdition; for it is stated about this, *neither shall your eye pity him* (Deuteronomy 13:9). And so the Sages of blessed memory said [Sifre, Deuteronomy §89]: Since the rule was stated, *you shall not stand idly by the blood of your neighbor* (Leviticus 19:16), I might think you are not to stand idly by [the shedding of] this one's blood? Hence Scripture states, *neither shall your eye pity him*." *Séfer haHinnuch*, Vol. IV, 425.

[136] Not to argue in favor of the enticer.

[137] Not to hold back any evidence that the person was enticing people away from the Torah. "From the great number of these injunctions about an enticer, I can understand that it is permitted—nay, it is even a religious duty—for us to hate likewise even those

§4.462. *Not to entice an Israelite toward idol-worship* [Devarim 13:12].[138]

§4.463. *The precept of examining witnesses thoroughly* [Devarim 13:15].[139]

§4.467. *The prohibition against gashing oneself as idol-worshipers do* [Devarim 14:1].[140]

§4.468. *Not to cause baldness, tearing the hair in grief over the dead* [Devarim 14:1].[141]

§4.476. *The precept of exacting a loan rigorously from a heathen* [Devarim 15:3].[142]

§4.478. *Not to refrain from sustaining a poor man and giving him what he needs* [Devarim 15:7].[143]

§4.479. *The mitzvah of charity* [Devarim 15:8].[144]

§4.481. *Not to send away a manservant empty handed when he goes free* [Devarim 15:13].[145]

§5.491. *The precept of appointing judges and officers in every single community* [Devarim 16:18].[146]

---

who are wicked with other transgressions, after we see that they have corrupted and befouled their ways of action until there is no hope for them, and they will not listen to the voice of instructors but rather scorn their words, giving no heed to anyone who would teach them, their way being rather set to harm them." *Séfer haHinnuch*, Vol. IV, 427.

[138] It is a grave sin to try to entice any Jew to turn from the Torah, i.e., as missionaries are wont to do.

[139] To diligently and thoroughly examine a witness according to Torah law.

[140] Not to cut yourself in grieving for the dead.

[141] Not to tear out one's hair in grief over the dead.

[142] Not to have any pity on an idolater so you may be drawn into their idolatry.

[143] That we should not act miserly, but with kindness and charity to help a poor person, and certainly a relative.

[144] To make sure the poor man has what is sufficient for his need, not to enrich him. "He who does not help the poor to the utmost of his power commits a *sin*, and is guilty before God." Hirsch, commentary to *Devarim* 15:8, 272.

[145] Not to discharge empty handed a man who had been convicted of theft.

[146] "To appoint judges and officers that they should enforce the observance of the *mitzvoth* of the Torah, and should return to it, against their will, those who stray from the path of truth; they should ordain what is proper to do, and prevent reprehensible matters; and they should execute the punishments on the transgressors—until the commandments of the Torah and its restrictions should not need [be dependent on] the religious faith of each and every man." *Séfer haHinnuch*, Vol. V, 3.

§5.493. *The prohibition against erecting an idolatrous pillar* [Devarim 16:22].[147]

§5.502. *That the king should not amass gold and silver inordinately, but only what he needs* [Devarim 17:17].[148]

§5.510. *The prohibition against the practice of divination* [Devarim 18:10].[149]

§5.511. *Not to practice sorcery* [Devarim 18:10].[150]

§5.512. *The prohibition against employing charms* [Devarim 18:10–11].[151]

§5.513. *Not to consult an 'ov, a kind of medium* [Devarim 18:10–11].[152]

§5.514. *The prohibition against consulting a yid'oni, a kind of wizard* [Devarim 18:10–11].[153]

§5.515. *The prohibition against making any enquiry of the dead* [Devarim 18:10–11].[154]

§5.521. *To have no mercy in corporeal judgment on a person who has inflicted injury* [Devarim 19:21].[155]

§5.522. *The prohibition against overreaching a boundary* [Devarim 19:14].[156]

§5.524. *The precept to do to scheming witnesses as they intended to have done to their victim* [Devarim 19:19].[157]

---

[147] This is a prohibition to erect a pillar anywhere at all. In an example to our idolatrous worship of the Framers of the Constitution, we have the Washington Monument in Washington, D. C. The Washington Monument is modeled after the Egyptian obelisks that dot many Edomite capitals, and there are monuments to both Thomas Jefferson and Abraham Lincoln that are also modeled after pagan Greek temples.

[148] Although the leader of the state needs money "for carrying out his duties in the nation and also to ensure the independence of his position"…he "shall not gather gold and silver more than is necessary, shall guard himself against passion for riches. Of all the possible passions of a ruler 'avarice' is the most pernicious, and at the same time one that can never be satisfied…the gathering of riches is simply absolutely forbidden." Hirsch, commentary to *Devarim* 17:17, 341.

[149] The prohibition of "psychics."

[150] The prohibition of the "vapid nonsense" of using herbs and stones and such for "magic."

[151] The prohibitions of incantations for "luck" or "good or bad fortune."

[152] The prohibition to consult a necromancer.

[153] The prohibition to consult a wizard.

[154] The prohibition to consult someone who claims to speak with the dead.

[155] To punish those who have deliberately inflicted permanent bodily harm on another.

[156] The prohibition of shifting a landmark by force or theft.

[157] To punish a false witness by the same measure of the harm they wished on the one they testified against.

§5.529. *Not to destroy fruit-trees in setting siege—and so is any needless destruction included in the ban* [Devarim 20:19].[158]

§5.537. *The precept of burial for someone executed by court order, and so for every deceased person* [Devarim 21:13].[159]

§5.538. *The mitzvah of returning a lost object to its owner* [Devarim 22:1].[160]

§5.539. *Not to turn a blind eye to a lost object* [Devarim 22:3].[161]

§5.540. *Not to leave the beast of one's fellow-man lying under its burden* [Devarim 23:4].[162]

§5.542. *That a woman is not to wear a man's finery* [Devarim 22:5].[163]

§5.543. *That a man is not to wear a woman's finery* [Devarim 22:5].[164]

§5.546. *The duty of building a parapet* [Devarim 22:8].[165]

§5.547. *Not to leave a stumbling-block (keep a dangerous object) about* [Devarim 22:8].[166]

§5.556. *Not to punish anyone compelled to commit a transgression* [Devarim 22:26].[167]

§5.557. *The duty of a rapist to take his victim for a wife* [Devarim 22:29].[168]

---

[158] The prohibition of "total war" as well as the unnecessary destruction of anything which could lead to harming the environment.

[159] To bury that day one who was executed by the state.

[160] To return any lost object with identifying marks. This is the opposite of our "finders-keepers" philosophy.

[161] Not to dismiss a lost object because it would be "too much trouble."

[162] Not to ignore an animal in distress.

[163] The prohibition of cross-dressing for a female.

[164] The prohibition of cross-dressing for a man (transvestite).

[165] "To remove the obstacles and sources of harm from all our habitations." *Séfer haHinnuch*, Vol. V, 195.

[166] The prohibition of leaving dangerous objects about (such as a loaded gun or a knife around young children). "As a special commandment the Torah imposes the duty: Remove from your property all that is dangerous to life or by means of adequate protection render it harmless…generally speaking, whenever unlawfully you leave unprotected anything you own which is potentially dangerous to human life, you incur responsibility for any consequent accident. For instance, wells or holes in the ground without a fence…broken staircases, poison, weapons, knives, stones, etc." Hirsch, *Horeb*, 246.

[167] Not to punish any man who transgressed against his will.

[168] "At the root of the precept lies the purpose to chastise and restrain scoundrels from this evil deed…she will be bound to him and imposed on him all his days, for the

§5.558. *That a rapist is not ever to divorce his victim* [Devarim 22:29].[169]

§5.568. *Not to return a slave who fled from his master abroad* [Devarim 23:16].[170]

§5.569. *Not to oppress this slave who flees from his master abroad* [Devarim 23:17].[171]

§5.576. *Our duty to allow a hired worker to eat certain things while under hire* [Devarim 23:25].[172]

§5.577. *That a hired man should not raise a sickle to his fellow-man's standing grain* [Devarim 23:25].[173]

§5.578. *That a hired hand is forbidden to eat from his employer's crops during work* [Devarim 23:26].[174]

§5.579. *The precept that one who wants to divorce his wife should do so with a proper document* [Devarim 24:1].[175]

---

obligation of food [and] clothing...and even if he should become disgusted with her he will not have the right to divorce her ever." *Séfer haHinnuch*, Vol. V, 241. This does not mean the victim has to live with the rapist, but rather that the rapist will be forced to pay for his victim's livelihood for the rest of her days. He is also to pay a fine to the father of the victim if she is a minor, or to the victim herself if she is an adult (*K'thuboth* 46b). Any non-compliance on the part of the rapist and he is to be flogged; outright refusal to provide for his victim would mean the rapist is subject to decapitation.

[169] Cf. n. 168 above.

[170] "In Gittin 45a, the case discussed in our text here is explained to be...that of a non-Jewish slave who had fled from a Jewish master living outside the land of Israel." Hirsch, *Devarim*, 464. How different the *Dred Scott* decision would have been if Torah law had been followed.

[171] "In the language of the Midrash *Sifre*: 'you shall not wrong him'—this denotes wronging (oppressing) with words. This is to say that we are not to abuse him and humiliate him with words, and all the more certainly not by action." *Séfer haHinnuch*, Vol. V, 271.

[172] "That we are commanded that a hired man may eat during the time of work from the [edible] commodity with which he is working when that commodity is something that grows from the earth and its labor has not been finished." *Séfer haHinnuch*, Vol. V, 297.

[173] "That a hired worker is prohibited from taking out of [the produce] with which he is working more than what he eats." Ibid., 301.

[174] This clarifies the "certain things" which a hired worker can eat, and when he can eat them. A worker cannot eat produce that is still attached to the soil [grain, grapes], although he can eat the grapes after he finishes picking them. [God] makes it a duty for...landowners to allow the workers who are engaged on cutting and gathering the fruit in this orchards and vineyards to eat as much of the fruit as they please while working, and makes it a duty for such workers to keep strictly within the limits of this permission and to be careful not to misuse it." Hirsch, *Devarim*, 470–71.

[175] "Divorce proceedings must be supervised by a Beth Din...consisting of three rabbis [judges] competent in the laws of marriage and divorce." Rabbi Hayim Halevy Donin,

§5.581. *That a bridegroom is not to be taken from home for long during the entire first year of marriage* [Devarim 24:5].[176]

§5.582. *The precept that a bridegroom should rejoice with his wife in their first year* [Devarim 24:5].[177]

§5.585. *Not to take an object in pledge from a debtor by force* [Devarim 24:10].[178]

§5.586. *Not to withhold a pawned object from its owner when he needs it* [Devarim 24:12].[179]

§5.587. *The duty of returning a pledged object to its owner when he needs it* [Devarim 24:13].[180]

§5.588. *The precept of giving a hired man his due pay on his day— when he has earned it* [Devarim 24:15].[181]

§5.589. *That a near relation of a person in a court trial should not give testimony* [Devarim 24:16].[182]

To Be A Jew: A Guide to Jewish Observance in Contemporary Life. (New York: Basic Books, Inc., Publishers, 1972), 292. Also, according to *Rambam* (*Hilchot Ishut* 14:8), a woman who finds her husband "repulsive" (for example, if he becomes non-observant according to Torah Law) can have the court force the husband to divorce her.

[176] "The Torah looks on this duty of a husband for the happiness of the marriage as being such a high one, and lays such importance to it, not only for its individual happiness but also for the national well-being that, *for a whole year after marrying a wife, it frees him from all public services and duties, yea actually forbids him to undertake any of them so that he can give himself up entirely to his home life and to laying the foundation of his wife's happiness.*" Hirsch, *Devarim*, 481.

[177] "At the root of the precept lies the reason that it arose in conception before God, blessed is He, to create a world, and it was His desire that it should be settled by good human beings [each] born from a male and a female who form a couple under sanction; for immorality is an abomination before Him." *Séfer haHinnuch*, Vol. V, 327.

[178] "*Séfer haHinnuch* teaches that this prohibition is intended to discourage people from thinking that might makes right. The strong may not coerce the weak and take their security collateral without qualm. Likewise, the weak need not be afraid of the strong when they have a legal complaint against them. The law puts them both on an equal footing and ensures that the poor person can live without fear of being victimized." Munk, *The Call of the Torah: Devarim*, 255.

[179] Not to withhold a pawned object if it is needed by the debtor.

[180] "If the pledge is something a man needs by day, such as his work-tools, he should return it to him in the daytime, and the borrower is to bring it back to him at night." *Séfer haHinnuch*, Vol. V, 343.

[181] "Any wages done must not be withheld by the master beyond the time for payment, whether it be the hire for the man hired by the day, payment for hired animals or tools, or the wages of a craftsman when his task is completed. The time for payment is never later than the end of the day on which the wages are due." Hirsch, *Horeb*, 230.

[182] "What it means is that politically and socially no member of a family should be

§5.590. *Not to pervert justice in regard to a proselyte or an orphan* [Devarim 24:17].[183]

§5.591. *Not to take anything in pledge from a widow* [Devarim 24:17].[184]

§5.592. *The precept of leaving forgotten sheaves* [Devarim 24:19].[185]

§5.593. *Not to take a forgotten sheaf of grain or forgotten fruit of trees* [Devarim 24:19].[186]

§5.594. *The precept of whiplashes for the wicked* [Devarim 25:2].[187]

§5.595. *Not to add to the whiplashes due someone who merits flogging* [Devarim 25:3].[188]

§5.596. *Not to muzzle a domestic animal during its work* [Devarim 25:4].[189]

§5.600. *The duty to save a person pursued by a killer* [Devarim 25:12].[190]

---

made to suffer in any way even for capital crimes committed by a near or even nearest relative...there are probably no more unhappy people, who feel themselves more hardly dealt with socially than the children and parents of murderers and criminals, and the primary tendency of this proclamation is to keep their own social and political blamelessness independently clear and unaffected." Hirsch, *Devarim*, 489–90.

[183] This commandment deals with "the duty of considerate kindness towards socially depressed people." Hirsch, *Devarim*, 493.

[184] It is forbidden to take a pledge [pawn] from a widow, "whether she is poor or rich, no pledge is to be taken from her." *Séfer haHinnuch*, Vol. V, 359.

[185] "That we are commanded, when we forget a sheaf of grain in the field, to leave it there, and we should not go back to take it when the matter becomes known to us... at the root of the precept lies the reason that the poor and the needy in their want and their penury, set their eyes on the crops of grain when they see the owners of the fields binding sheaves in the field...and they think in their heart, 'If it were only granted me that it should be thus for me, to gather sheaves into my house! If only I could bring one [home] I would rejoice with it.'" *Séfer haHinnuch*, Vol. V, 361, 363.

[186] "That you may not greedily and jealously think that you must use the very last penny for yourself or that for which you have worked, that anything of that, which escapes you, you need not think lost, and therefore you have to have something standing in your fields and vineyards for the poor, and what escapes your cutting sickle and gathering yards for the poor." Hirsch, *Devarim*, 497.

[187] "That the *beth din*...was commanded to flog those who transgress certain precepts of the Torah." *Séfer haHinnuch*, Vol. V, 367.

[188] "That a justice is restricted from having a sinner beaten with great [severe] blows." Ibid., 369.

[189] "That we should not restrain an animal from eating of what it is working with, during its work." Ibid., 375.

[190] "That we were commanded to save a chased or hunted person from the hand of one who is pursuing him to kill him, even if by the life of the pursuer; in other words, we are commanded to kill the pursuer if we are unable to rescue the chased man unless we end the pursuer's life." Ibid., 399.

§5.601. *To have no mercy on a pursuer with intent to kill* [Devarim 25:12].[191]

§5.602. *That we should not keep deficient scales or weights with us, even if we will not use them in trading* [Devarim 25:13].[192]

§5.604. *The precept to eradicate the progeny of Amalek* [Devarim 25:18].[193]

§5.611. *The precept to emulate the good and right ways of the Eternal Lord* [Devarim 28:9].[194]

§5.612. *The precept to assemble the entire people to hear the Torah read, after the seventh year* [Devarim 31:12].[195]

⌒

T HESE 209 MITZVOT are the commandments which are covered by the categories of the Seven Noahide Laws, and they comprise a full one-third of the 613 of the *mitzvot* of the Torah. When one understands the amount of the *Talmud* these 209 *mitzvot* cover, one can better appreciate the depth of the Noahide Law, and that "the purpose of His Law is not only for the hallowing of the individual, but the perfection of the whole community upon the foundation of the holy will of God."[196] The Torah effectively balances the needs of both the individual and the community.

---

[191] "That we are restricted from having pity on the life of a pursuer." Ibid., 403.

[192] "The mere possession, the mere existence of inaccurate weights and measures in 'bag or house' is forbidden, and thereby the prevention of any misuse, yea, the very appearance of any such possibility, is assured." Hirsch, *Devarim*, 520.

[193] Amalek, or Rome/Edom. "The very opposite to…the national character of a people woven out of justice and the duties of love which only sees its power and its future in conscientious faithfulness to duty and through whose example the exclusive devotion to duty will ultimately in the future be participated in by the whole of mankind, is presented by a great nation, like Amalek, which only finds its strength in the might of its sword and its love of glory in treading down all unprepared weaker ones." Hirsch, *Devarim*, 523.

[194] "That we were commanded to perform all our actions in a way of honesty and goodness with all our power, and to channel all our matters that are between us and others in a way of kindness and compassion." *Séfer haHinnuch*, Vol. V, 427. This is why it is important to study Torah, to learn the ways of HASHEM.

[195] *Devarim* 31:12 states: *Gather together the people—the men, the women, and the small children, and your stranger who is in your cities—so that they will hear and so that they will learn, and they shall fear HASHEM, your God, and be careful to perform all the words of this Torah.* The words *and the stranger* refer to "a non-Jew who observes the Noahide laws." Rabbi Nosson Scherman, *The Stone Chumash*. (Brooklyn: Mesorah Publications, ltd., 1998), 1096.

[196] Hirsch, *Collected Writings*, Vol. II, 175.

It protects the property of the individual, facilitates free enterprise, yet at the same time allows the fullest amount of freedom for each and every person. It is a legal system that has been in development for thousands of years, and it has been ready for implementation into any and every society.

THE SOCIAL RESTRUCTURING it will take to implement the Noahide Law as the foundation of our legal system will be no small endeavor; it will take time and a great deal of effort. The most difficult part will be to let go of our Greco/Roman cultural foundation as it applies to social constructs. It will mean letting go of our irrational and illogical meme of antisemitism. It will mean letting go of our need for organized religion. Most importantly, however, it will mean that we must understand "that mankind's greatest problem is not economic, social, or political—it is essentially moral."[197] Despite all of its learning, its technological brilliance, its engineering and scientific accomplishments, mankind has not progressed morally in the past two millennia. The problems which had beset Greece and Rome—infanticide, sexual immorality, environmental destruction, class conflict, oppression of women and minorities, warfare—so many of the things that have produced human misery throughout the history of Western Civilization have had their root in the moral limitations of Ancient Greek and Roman culture. We can now answer Daniel Goldhagen's question (p. 49 above), "why did the most civilized, scientific, and cultured nation in the early twentieth century—a nation that led in the forefront of academics, reason, science, and philosophy—decide to mass-murder millions of innocent human beings?" by understanding that the Germans (as well as the British, French, Americans and every other Western society) ultimately based their morality on the teachings of the Greeks and Romans whether it was morality derived from secular philosophy or religion. The time has come in mankind's history for a change, a chance to better ourselves.

Surely, if you improve yourself, you will be forgiven. But if you do not improve yourself, sin rests at the door. Its desire is toward you, yet you can conquer it.
—Bereishis 4:7

סלה

---

[197] Munk, *The Call of the Torah: Bereishis*, 66.

Appendix

There are many who enjoin us to become active citizens once again, to try to fix our broken legal system,[1] yet it does not seem to occur to them that it is the legal system itself that is the problem and that it needs to be replaced. There has been little, if any, criticism of the Constitution itself;[2] most criticism has to do with dependant variables dealing with social and economic factors. You can criticize "big government," you can criticize "crooked politicians," but to criticize the Constitution is, to most people, treasonous.[3] Yet, we should ask ourselves, what is treason? The Torah's definition is that "treason" is going against God's Torah. In Article III, section 3 of the Constitution it states "Treason against the United States, shall consist only in levying War against them, or in adhering to their Enemies, giving them Aid and Comfort." When people get all bent out of shape when someone criticizes the "holy" and "sacred" Constitution, they forget that the Constitution was written by men themselves guilty of high treason, and these traitors produced a document that has become the benchmark apology for treason, a classic document which enumerated the reasons for freeing a society from a crooked and unjust government: The Declaration of Independence. — A. C.

&

The Declaration of Independence

WHEN IN THE COURSE OF HUMAN EVENTS IT BECOMES NECESSARY FOR one people to dissolve the political bands which have connected them with another and to assume among the powers of the earth, the separate and equal station to which the Laws of Nature and of Nature's

---

[1] "Our nation is in need of a transformation movement, one that combines the forces of healthy business, energized workers and unions, and newly activist citizens." Derber, *Corporation Nation*, 9–10.

[2] "Academics endlessly debate issues of constitutional interpretation, and almost never talk about the flaws inherent in the document itself." William N. Eskridge, *Constitutional Stupidities, Constitutional Tragedies*. (New York: New York University Press, 1998).

[3] "Since all new states originate in force, say rather in revolutionary violence, their founders are, and by definition must be, 'criminals.' Only after they have established new "orders" do they become "legitimate" and respectable." Eidelberg, *Beyond the Secular Mind*, 9.

God[4] entitle them, a decent respect to the opinions of mankind requires that they should declare the causes which impel them to the separation.[5]

We hold these truths[6] to be self-evident,[7] that all men[8] are created equal,[9] that they are endowed by their Creator with certain

---

[4] Contrary to popular belief, the references to God were "conspicuously missing in Jefferson's draft" and were later added by Congressional editors. Pauline Maier, *American Scripture: Making the Declaration of Independence*. (New York: Vintage Books, 1998), 148.

[5] Dissolving the bonds of government in the name of the "Laws of Nature's God" has usually been interpreted from a secular viewpoint. From a rabbinic viewpoint, this statement should have only one interpretation: the Divine Laws of the Torah. To imply that we are allowed to dissolve a government when it is in violation of Torah, then declare the reasons for doing so, is a logical step. "As long as the law governing men is determined by men, all of the effort of humanity will be expended in finding new definitions for what is true, what is right, what is noble and what is good. Every day will find a different right and a different truth; the next day will question that which was regarded as sacred only yesterday." Hirsch, *Collected Writings*, Vol. I, 156.

[6] "You non-Jews who in the Council of the nations have duly weighed and considered, or are on the point of duly weighing and considering, how much of the rights which are in themselves indivisible, and are holy for all or for none...no law is strong enough to withhold justice up to a certain point and then to resist injustice successfully when it oversteps this point. Take any man and declare him—even from the best motives—to be unworthy of any part of a single system of rights which is in itself indivisible, and you have thereby against your will and your purpose marked him out before hand as an object of blind hatred and fury, on whom these passions may vent themselves with impunity. Think of this, and do not forget, too, that the wretched position of the Jews in the past was not produced at one stroke. The denial of the very first right—in itself perhaps insignificant—to the Jew, held him up as an 'exception' who was not entitled to every right, and thus laid the foundation for all that followed. Or do you imagine that the 'enlightenment' of the preset day is a guarantee that such fanaticism will never be let loose again? Look around you—see the signs of the times—and be warned." Ibid., 119–20.

[7] In this sentence, arguably the most famous line Jefferson ever penned, we see the underlying concepts entailed in Jeffersonian Democracy that both rich and poor, liberals and conservatives, Democrats and Republicans tout enthusiastically from their soap-boxes. Jefferson's "certain unalienable Rights" that "are endowed by their Creator... that among these are Life, Liberty and the pursuit of Happiness" is a concept taken from English philosopher John Locke, who himself was influenced by the writings of John Selden. "Man being born, as has been proved, with a title to perfect freedom, and an uncontrolled enjoyment of all the rights and privileges of the law of nature, equally with any other man, or number of men in the world, hath by nature a power, not only to preserve his property, that is, his life, liberty and estate, against the injuries and attempts of other men." John Locke, *Two Treatises on Government, Chapter VII: Of Political of Civil Society*, section 87.

[8] According to the laws of the land, which were of course based on English Common Law, women were not created as equal as men. Unlike women in eighteenth century America, women in Ancient Israel could own property, buy and sell property, as well as make their own contracts. This is yet another example of how the "archaic" Torah was far advanced beyond even the laws of the "enlightened" Constitution.

[9] The Torah, of course, teaches otherwise: all men are *not* created equal. Some have greater intelligence; some are better at business, some are better at mathematics or art,

unalienable Rights,[10] that among these are Life, Liberty and the pursuit of Happiness.[11]

⌒ᴇᴏ

Note: However grand these concepts are, there is a problem with these truths being self-evident. "That these truths were not understood as self-evident in themselves, but functionally and politically self-evident only, is suggested by a variety of other facts. Neither Jefferson nor any other thinker of his generation referred to these propositions as self-evident in any other place...or so far as any other scholar of the period has shown, even though the members of the revolutionary generation frequently discoursed on the very truths outlined in the Declaration."[12] There were many who did view these truths as self-evident, such as the twenty-two black slaves of Thomas Jefferson who "took [Lord John Dunsmore] up on his offer"[13] on gaining their freedom if they joined the loyalist cause. The subjective concept of "happiness" is a bit of a problem as well. Owning female slaves and legally being allowed to rape them daily was a source of "happiness" to many Southern plantation owners, such as Thomas Jefferson. Obviously, there are problems with the self-evidence of what constitutes "life, liberty, and the pursuit of happiness."[14] — A. C.

⌒ᴇᴏ

---

and so on. It is true that all men (and women) are equal under Torah Law, but this was certainly not how the Framers saw things.

[10] "A new twist to the theory of natural law was made largely by John Locke when he translated natural law into natural rights...just as there has been a translation of natural law into natural rights, so too has there been a translation of natural rights into human rights." Konvitz, *Torah & Constitution*, 96.

[11] "Locke cites authorities sparingly; but in his Two Treatises on Government, his citations are almost entirely Calvinistic: Scripture seventy-nine times; seven Calvinists (Hooker, Cilson, James I., Milton, Hunton, Ainsworth, Selden); one ex-Calvinist, [and] the Dutch Remonstrant Grotius." Herbert D. Foster, "International Calvinism through Locke and the Revolution of 1688." *The American Historical Review*. Vol. 32, No. 3 (Apr., 1927), 476.

[12] Michael P. Zuckert, "Self-Evident Truth and the Declaration of Independence," *The Review of Politics*. Vol. 49, No. 3 (Summer, 1987), 327.

[13] Lazare, *The Velvet Coup*, 32.

[14] "As long as freedom, right, independence and human dignity are taught, demonstrated and defended only by men and from the standpoint of men, all chance of universal harmony will be demolished by the natural dissimilarity among men. The strong will continually say to the weak and the master to the servant: 'I am more than you. Otherwise I would not be your master!'" Hirsch, *Collected Writings*, Vol. I, 156.

That to secure these rights,[15] Governments are instituted among Men, deriving their just powers from the consent of the governed,— That whenever any Form of Government becomes destructive of these ends, it is the Right of the People to alter or to abolish it, and to institute new Government, laying its foundation on such principles and organizing its powers in such form, as to them shall seem most likely to effect their Safety and Happiness. Prudence, indeed, will dictate that Governments long established should not be changed for light and transient causes; and accordingly all experience hath shewn that mankind are more disposed to suffer, while evils are sufferable than to right themselves by abolishing the forms to which they are accustomed. But when a long train of abuses and usurpations, pursuing invariably the same Object evinces a design to reduce them under absolute Despotism, it is their right, it is their duty, to throw off such Government, and to provide new Guards for their future security.— Such has been the patient sufferance of these Colonies; and such is now the necessity which constrains them to alter their former Systems of Government. The history of the present King of Great Britain[16] is a history of repeated injuries and usurpations, all having in direct object the establishment of an absolute Tyranny[17] over these States. To prove this, let Facts be submitted to a candid world.[18]

---

[15] "As long as...bias and weakness, narrowness and passion, self-seeking and self-interest will dictate the laws of mankind...the vision of mankind will continually be blurred. And the only right which will be holy will be the one which men demand and which suits their desire. But the right that they should have appreciated and practiced all along, obscured in the glare of their self-seeking, is actually quite different from the general perception of 'right.'—That is how the annals of mankind come to be written with tears and blood." Ibid., 157.

[16] "To attack the King was, in short, a constitutional form. It was the way Englishmen announced revolution." [Pauline Maier, *American Scripture: Making the Declaration of Independence.* (New York: Vintage Books, 1998), 38.] This can be seen by the example of a previous "Declaration of Rights" that was "reenacted...on December 16, 1689...in thirteen clauses, it cited specific instances of the King's misconduct in an appropriately plain and certain manner. He was charged, for example, with raising money without the consent of Parliament, 'raiseing and keeping a standing army within this Kingdom in time of Peace without Consent of Parliament and quartering of Souldiers contrary to Law.'" Ibid., 53.

[17] "The grievances in the Declaration were not meant to identify...precisely which events had reconciled the Americans to separate nationhood. The grievances in the Declaration served a different purpose...to justify revolution by proving that George III was a tyrant." Maier, *American Scripture*, 115.

[18] "Most prominent modern studies have...[devoted] little serious attention to the charges against the King, whose origins too often lay in the obscure quarrels of

He has refused his Assent to Laws, the most wholesome and necessary for the public good.[19]

He has forbidden his Governors to pass Laws of immediate and pressing importance, unless suspended in their operation till his Assent should be obtained; and when so suspended, he has utterly neglected to attend to them.

He has refused to pass other Laws for the accommodation of large districts of people, unless those people would relinquish the right of Representation in the Legislature, a right inestimable to them and formidable to tyrants only.[20]

He has called together legislative bodies at places unusual, uncomfortable, and distant from the depository of their Public Records, for the sole purpose of fatiguing them into compliance with his measures.[21]

He has dissolved Representative Houses repeatedly, for opposing with manly firmness his invasions on the rights of the people.

He has refused for a long time, after such dissolutions, to cause others to be elected, whereby the Legislative Powers, incapable of Annihilation, have returned to the People at large for their exercise; the State remaining in the mean time exposed to all the dangers of invasion from without, and convulsions within.

He has endeavoured to prevent the population of these States; for that purpose obstructing the Laws for Naturalization of Foreigners; refusing to pass others to encourage their migrations hither, and raising the conditions of new Appropriations of Lands.

---

provincial politics, and focusing instead on the document's preface, or on words or phrases within it." Ibid., 123.

[19] "In his critique of the Declaration, [Thomas] Hutchinson noted that the first of these accusations was 'general...without any particulars to support it,' which made it 'fit enough to be placed at the head of a list of imaginary grievances.'" Ibid., 109.

[20] Thus said the slave-owner Thomas Jefferson. "The right to vote was linked to the ownership of property. For example, Delaware required a freeholder to have fifty acres of land with at least twelve acres cleared, worth at least forty pounds." [Beard, *An Economic Interpretation of the Constitution of the United States*, 68.] It is interesting to note that neither women nor slaves, nor the lower classes for that matter, had the right to vote in early America.

[21] "John Adams almost certainly suggested the fourth charge...[recalling] the royal governor's moving the Massachusetts House of Representatives to Cambridge in 1768." Maier, *American Scripture*, 110.

He has obstructed the Administration of Justice by refusing his Assent to Laws for establishing Judiciary Powers.[22]

He has made Judges dependent on his Will alone for the tenure of their offices, and the amount and payment of their salaries.

He has erected a multitude of New Offices, and sent hither swarms of Officers to harass our people and eat out their substance.[23]

He has kept among us, in times of peace, Standing Armies without the Consent of our legislatures.[24]

He has affected to render the Military independent of and superior to the Civil Power.[25]

---

[22] "There was good reason for referring to some of these cases in only the most oblique way. To examine them more closely confirms the adage that there are two sides to every story, and the colonists weren't always clearly on the side of the angels." Ibid., 110–111.

[23] This charge "was probably prompted by the American Board of Customs Commissioners, which was located in Boston, and its dependents—clerks, surveyors, tide waiters and the like—whom the Bible-reading folk of Massachusetts considered much like an Old Testament plague of locusts." Ibid., 110.

[24] The framers viewed the existence of a standing army as one of the greatest dangers to a republic. Today, for the first time in American history, we now have a "professional" standing army that has been developed over the past few decades. Unlike previous wars, when our military conscripted young men to fight and then had them demobilized, our new "professional army" is a permanent feature, and it is (for the most part) made up of the lower caste of our citizenry. Also, as Rome increasingly relied on conscripts and barbarians to fill its ranks, so are we also turning to the large immigrant population, promising citizenry to all who serve in the military. We are no doubt only an executive order away from martial law; it would only require one terrorist act such as a "dirty bomb" or a deliberately caused outbreak of a virulent disease such as smallpox to have our government suspend our beloved Bill of Rights in order to "protect" us from the "enemy." Eisenhower, in his final address to the nation as president, spoke of the "military-industrial complex," of how the corporate army could threaten our democracy. "Today there are only two million farms in the United States, only one-third of the number we had fifty years ago. Instead of the agricultural society that Jefferson hoped for, we have the military-industrial complex that President Eisenhower bewailed. Instead of a society in which swords are beaten into ploughshares, we are members of a society in which ploughshares are quite literally beaten into swords." Konvitz, *Torah & Constitution*, 25.

[25] "Unfortunately, after more than two centuries (about the same length of time that the Roman Republic was in its prime), this framework has almost completely disintegrated. For those who believe that the structure of government in Washington today bears some resemblance to that outlined in the Constitution of 1787, the burden of proof is on them. The president now dominates the government in a way no ordinary monarch possibly could. He has at his disposal the clandestine services of the CIA, a private army unaccountable to the Congress, the press, or the public because everything it does

He has combined with others to subject us to a jurisdiction foreign to our constitution, and unacknowledged by our laws; giving his Assent to their Acts of pretended Legislation: For quartering large bodies of armed troops among us:

For protecting them, by a mock Trial from punishment for any Murders which they should commit on the Inhabitants of these States:

For cutting off our Trade with all parts of the world:[26]

For imposing Taxes on us without our Consent:[27]

For depriving us in many cases, of the benefit of Trial by Jury:[28]

For transporting us beyond Seas to be tried for pretended offences:

For abolishing the free System of English Laws in a neighbouring Province, establishing therein an Arbitrary government, and enlarging its Boundaries so as to render it at once an example and fit instrument for introducing the same absolute rule into these Colonies.

For taking away our Charters, abolishing our most valuable Laws and altering fundamentally the Forms of our Governments:

For suspending our own Legislatures, and declaring themselves invested with power to legislate for us in all cases whatsoever.

---

is secret. No president since Harry Truman, having discovered what unlimited power the CIA affords him, has ever failed to use it." Johnson, *Nemisis*, 17.

[26] The destruction of our manufacturing base over the past few decades has not only resulted in a loss of jobs, it has caused the United States to develop a trade imbalance; instead of being a major exporter, we now are a major importer of manufactured goods.

[27] As mentioned above, most of the things we have in the way of public services come from local or state taxes; our roads are kept up by gasoline taxes, our schools are funded by property taxes, our garbage and waste disposal are from state and local taxes, and so on. The income tax is primarily used to fund military expenditures, social control (education), and broad social programs such as Social Security and Medicare, and allows the government to borrow vast sums of money from foreign banks by the promise of continual economic growth. Our consumeristic culture is encouraged to keep buying bigger houses, bigger cars, the latest gadgets and appliances, and to do so to earn more, borrow more, and thus fuel "economic growth" (or a larger tax base). As the "baby boomer" generation ages and retires, the amount of our expenditures to support these social programs will grow to unsustainable levels since we have stripped our manufacturing base, weakened or eliminated unions, and passed laws creating a massive flow of capital to the top one percent of the population. This will put added pressure on our diminishing middle class to provide the taxes we need to support our bloated corporate government. How much longer will our beleaguered citizenry acquiesce to the inevitable increase in taxation? When the majority of the people demand a cut in taxation, there will no doubt be cuts made in the Federal budget, and these cuts will greatly affect the poor and working classes as social programs, affecting programs such as public education.

[28] As we have recently done in Guantanamo.

He has abdicated Government here, by declaring us out of his Protection and waging War against us.

He has plundered our seas, ravaged our coasts, burnt our towns, and destroyed the lives of our people.

He is at this time transporting large Armies of foreign Mercenaries to compleat the works of death, desolation, and tyranny, already begun with circumstances of Cruelty & Perfidy scarcely paralleled in the most barbarous ages, and totally unworthy the Head of a civilized nation.

He has constrained our fellow Citizens[29] taken Captive on the high Seas to bear Arms against their Country, to become the executioners of their friends and Brethren, or to fall themselves by their Hands.

He has excited domestic insurrections amongst us,[30] and has endeavoured to bring on the inhabitants of our frontiers, the merciless Indian Savages whose known rule of warfare, is an undistinguished destruction of all ages, sexes and conditions.

In every stage of these Oppressions We have Petitioned for Redress in the most humble terms: Our repeated Petitions have been answered only by repeated injury. A Prince, whose character is thus marked by every act which may define a Tyrant, is unfit to be the ruler of a free people.

Nor have We been wanting in attentions to our British brethren. We have warned them from time to time of attempts by their legislature to extend an unwarrantable jurisdiction over us. We have reminded them of the circumstances of our emigration and settlement here. We have appealed to their native justice and magnanimity, and we have conjured them by the ties of our common kindred to disavow these usurpations, which would inevitably interrupt our connections and correspondence. They too have been deaf to the voice of justice and of consanguinity.[31] We must, therefore, acquiesce in the necessity, which denounces our Separation, and hold them, as we hold the rest of mankind, Enemies in War, in Peace Friends.

---

[29] In an early draft of the Declaration, which is in the Library of Congress, shows that Jefferson had originally written "subjects" before changing it to "citizens."

[30] This was a rebuke for King George III stirring up revolt amongst the black slaves; "In its final charge against George III—'He has excited domestic insurrections amongst us, and has endeavoured to bring on the inhabitants of our frontiers the merciless Indian Savages'—an indictment of the monarch for stirring up an enslaved and an oppressed people to seek their freedom from freedom-seeking revolutionaries—the Declaration is perhaps doubly flawed." Sidney Kaplan, "The 'Domestic Insurrections' of the Declaration of Independence." *The Journal of Negro History*. Vol. 61, No. 3 (Jul., 1976), 253.

[31] As we have seen, many of the same "injustices" committed by the British, which drove the Americans to revolution, have been committed by our own government.

We, therefore, the Representatives of the united States of America, in General Congress, Assembled, appealing to the Supreme Judge of the world for the rectitude of our intentions, do, in the Name, and by Authority of the good People of these Colonies, solemnly publish and declare, That these united Colonies are, and of Right ought to be Free and Independent States, that they are Absolved from all Allegiance to the British Crown, and that all political connection between them and the State of Great Britain, is and ought to be totally dissolved; and that as Free and Independent States, they have full Power to levy War, conclude Peace, contract Alliances, establish Commerce, and to do all other Acts and Things which Independent States may of right do. — And for the support of this Declaration, with a firm reliance on the protection of Divine Providence, we mutually pledge to each other our Lives, our Fortunes, and our sacred Honor.[32]

---

[32] The only part of the Declaration of Independence most people are familiar with is the stirring sentence at the beginning: "We hold these truths to be self-evident, that all men are created equal, that they are endowed by their Creator with certain unalienable Rights, that among these are Life, Liberty and the pursuit of Happiness." These ringing words seem discongruous with the rest of the Declaration, which mainly deals with political and economic issues. This famous phrase also has a disturbingly hollow tone to it when one realizes that the author, Thomas Jefferson, was an elitist white slaveowner.

Maurice Samuel had a different take on the concept of "Sacred Honor" spoken of by the signers of the Declaration: "This difference in behavior and reaction springs from something much more earnest and significant than a difference in beliefs...it is a difference in the taking of life which cannot be argued. You have your way of life, we ours. In your system of life we are essentially without 'honor.' In our system of life you are essentially without morality. In your system of life we must forever appear graceless; to us you must forever appear Godless." [Samuel, *You Gentiles*, 34.]

For those who think Samuel's view harsh and unfair, it should be pointed out that Maurice Samuel wrote *You Gentiles* in response to the passing of the Johnson-Reed Act of 1924, the "Anti-Immigration Act" which effectively slammed the door of escape on the tired, poor, homeless, huddled masses of tempest-tost Jews from the Old World who were yearning to breathe free on our teeming shore. Samuel well understood that the Signers of the Declaration of Independence were themselves descendents of immigrants who fled the Old World because of religious persecution, and these same White Christian immigrants who came to the New World took the land from the Native Americans by force of arms, killing the Native Americans and driving the rest into the arid deserts of the West, then hypocritically denying immigration to others suffering religious persecution, particularly the Jews, whom even Jefferson thought "repulsive and anti-social."

Seen in this light, Samuel's words would become chillingly prophetic in less than a decade: "The demand for racial homogeneity within the State has led, in America... to the exclusion of the immigrant, and particularly of the immigrant who will not lend himself to the type of assimilation—or self-destruction—which you demand...when the Jew migrates from one country to another, it is almost invariably under the pressure of persecution...he that refuses asylum to a victim fleeing from a murderer is, before God, a free and willing accomplice in the crime." [Ibid., 216–17.]

The Constitution of the United States

WE THE PEOPLE[1] OF THE UNITED STATES,[2] IN ORDER TO FORM A MORE perfect Union,[3] establish Justice,[4] insure domestic Tranquility,[5] provide for the common defence, promote the general Welfare,[6] and

---

[1] "The Constitution of the United States was written by fifty–five men—and one ghost...the ghost was that of Oliver Cromwell...who, in the course of defending Parliament...devised a tyranny worse than any that had ever existed under the English Kings. The Founders were terrified of a badly educated populace that could be duped by a Cromwell." Robert D. Kaplan, *The Coming Anarchy: Shattering the Dreams of the Post Cold War.* (New York: Vintage Books, 2000) 67–68.

[2] "The Constitution was ratified by a vote of probably not more than one-sixth of the adult males...the leaders who supported the Constitution in the ratifying conventions represented the same economic groups as the members of the Philadelphia Convention; and in a large number of instances they were also directly and personally interested in the outcome of their efforts...the Constitution was not created by 'the whole people' as the jurists have said...but it was the work of a consolidated group whose interests knew no state boundaries and were truly national in their scope." Beard, *An Economic Interpretation of the Constitution of the United States*, 325.

[3] "The builders of states, as well as the citizenry, helplessly scan the horizon for the arrival of the latest political messiah, who will come forward with new utopian solutions for the problems besetting the state. This messiah, they comfort themselves, will come, must come, or else everything is ruined. They wait for the political redeemer who will devise the formula for deliverance and the equation for what is most irrational: to secure through external institutions the well-being, peace, health, and prosperity of nations and men." Hirsch, *Collected Writings*, Vol. I, 269.

[4] "It is not true that everything is permitted for the sake of *salus publica* [promoting the general welfare]. It is not true that there are two standards of morality, one for communities and another for individuals. That which is forbidden for an individual is even less permissible for a community...attempts are often made to find excuses for all manner of abhorrent acts that undermine public morality but have been perpetrated in the name of such considerations as diplomacy, politics, or reasons of state. It is argued that the falsehood and fraud, plunder and robbery had, after all, not been motivated by self-interest but by concern for the interest of the community. This notion, which poisons both personal and communal life, has been outlawed for Israel from the very outset." Hirsch, *Collected Writings*, Vol. VI, 5.

[5] "Any efforts made in opposition to the principles hallowed by 'Zion' will fail. Injustice that one perpetrates will eventually turn against oneself; justice denied others cannot be appealed to for one's own protection...the future of a nation can be foretold from the way in which they treat the poor, the deprived, the strangers and the helpless of their society, those who have no strong representation among the mighty." Hirsch, *Collected Writings*, Vol. IV, 391.

[6] "Amid business dealings and the exchange of goods and products, the Law...forbids the strict carrying out of right where this could lead to oppression and cruelty, or even to the enslavement of free men who possess little or no wealth." Hirsch, *Collected Writings*, Vol. I, 219.

secure the Blessings of Liberty to ourselves[7] and our Posterity,[8] do ordain and establish this Constitution[9] for the United States of America.[10]

Article I

Section 1

All legislative Powers herein granted shall be vested in a Congress of the United States, which shall consist of a Senate and House of Representatives.[11]

Section 2

The House of Representatives shall be composed of Members chosen every second Year by the People of the several States, and the

---

[7] "The movement for the Constitution of the United States was originated and carried through principally by four groups of personality interests which had been adversely affected under the Articles of Confederation: money, public securities, manufactures, and trade and shipping. The first firm steps toward the formation of the Constitution were taken by a small and active group of men immediately interested through their personal possessions in the outcome of their labors. No popular vote was taken directly or indirectly on the proposition to call the Convention which drafted the Constitution. A large propertyless mass was, under the prevailing suffrage qualifications, excluded at the outset from participation (through representatives) in the work of framing the Constitution. The members of the Philadelphia Convention which drafted the Constitution were, with a few exceptions, immediately, directly, and personally interested in, and derived economic advantages from, the establishment of the new system. The Constitution was essentially an economic document based upon the concept that the fundamental private rights of property are anterior to government and morally beyond the reach of popular majorities." Beard, *An Economic Interpretation of the Constitution of the United States,* 324.

[8] "There is no double standard of the Law, one for nations and another for the individual; both can only achieve fulfillment by upholding the same moral Law. Obedience to God is incumbent not only on individuals but also, and first and foremost, on nations." Hirsch, *Collected Writings*, Vol. IV, 287.

[9] "Many Americans appear to believe that our constitution has been a model for the rest of the democratic world. Yet among the countries most comparable to the United States and where democratic institutions have long existed without breakdown, not one has adopted our American constitutional system." Dahl, *How Democratic is the American Constitution?,* 41.

[10] "The artificial structure of politics and human power which had been offered to the people as a substitute for...Torah." Hirsch, *Collected Writings*, Vol. IV, 110.

[11] "[The Torah] came to us from a Source outside us. It did not originate from us, or through us. This Law was not invented, devised, chosen or enacted by us so that, depending on our mood or our intellectual 'progress,' we could invent, devise, choose or enact other laws...precisely because it is God-given, this Law is inviolable; it cannot be altered according to our momentary whims." Ibid., 34.

Electors in each State shall have the Qualifications requisite for Electors of the most numerous Branch of the State Legislature.

No Person shall be a Representative who shall not have attained to the Age of twenty five Years, and been seven Years a Citizen of the United States, and who shall not, when elected, be an Inhabitant of that State in which he shall be chosen.[12]

Representatives and direct Taxes shall be apportioned among the several States which may be included within this Union, according to their respective Numbers, which shall be determined by adding to the whole Number of free Persons, including those bound to Service for a Term of Years, and excluding Indians not taxed, three fifths of all other Persons.[13] The actual Enumeration shall be made within three Years after the first Meeting of the Congress of the United States, and within every subsequent Term of ten Years, in such Manner as they shall by Law direct. The Number of Representatives shall not exceed one for every thirty Thousand, but each State shall have at Least one Representative; and until such enumeration shall be made, the State of New Hampshire shall be entitled to choose three, Massachusetts eight, Rhode Island and Providence Plantations one, Connecticut five, New York six, New Jersey four, Pennsylvania eight, Delaware one, Maryland six, Virginia ten, North Carolina five, South Carolina five and Georgia three.

When vacancies happen in the Representation from any State, the Executive Authority thereof shall issue Writs of Election to fill such Vacancies.

The House of Representatives shall choose their Speaker and other Officers; and shall have the sole Power of Impeachment.

Section 3

The Senate of the United States shall be composed of two Senators from each State, chosen by the Legislature thereof, for six Years; and each Senator shall have one Vote.

---

[12] As with all other gentile nations, "citizenship" is determined by the land of birth and residency. Israel became a nation before it had a native land; "citizenship" is determined through allegiance to the Torah and *HASHEM*, not real estate, kings, or a certain political system.

[13] The constitution's concern with "minority rights" was the concern with the protection of the Ruling Class from the much larger "bewildered herd" of the lower classes, thus following the pattern of Roman Law for safeguards in protecting the property of the wealthy and powerful; it certainly was not about rights for the poor, women, black slaves, or Native Americans.

Immediately after they shall be assembled in Consequence of the first Election, they shall be divided as equally as may be into three Classes. The Seats of the Senators of the first Class shall be vacated at the Expiration of the second Year, of the second Class at the Expiration of the fourth Year, and of the third Class at the Expiration of the sixth Year, so that one third may be chosen every second Year; and if Vacancies happen by Resignation, or otherwise, during the Recess of the Legislature of any State, the Executive thereof may make temporary Appointments until the next Meeting of the Legislature, which shall then fill such Vacancies.

No person shall be a Senator who shall not have attained to the Age of thirty Years, and been nine Years a Citizen of the United States, and who shall not, when elected, be an Inhabitant of that State for which he shall be chosen.

The Vice President of the United States shall be President of the Senate, but shall have no Vote, unless they be equally divided.

The Senate shall choose their other Officers, and also a President pro tempore, in the absence of the Vice President, or when he shall exercise the Office of President of the United States.

The Senate shall have the sole Power to try all Impeachments. When sitting for that Purpose, they shall be on Oath or Affirmation. When the President of the United States is tried, the Chief Justice shall preside: And no Person shall be convicted without the Concurrence of two thirds of the Members present.

Judgment in Cases of Impeachment shall not extend further than to removal from Office, and disqualification to hold and enjoy any Office of honor, Trust or Profit under the United States: but the Party convicted shall nevertheless be liable and subject to Indictment, Trial, Judgment and Punishment, according to Law.

Section 4

The Times, Places and Manner of holding Elections for Senators and Representatives, shall be prescribed in each State by the Legislature thereof; but the Congress may at any time by Law make or alter such Regulations, except as to the Place of Choosing Senators.

The Congress shall assemble at least once in every Year, and such Meeting shall be on the first Monday in December, unless they shall by Law appoint a different Day.

Section 5

Each House shall be the Judge of the Elections, Returns and Qualifications of its own Members, and a Majority of each shall constitute a Quorum to do Business; but a smaller number may adjourn from day to day, and may be authorized to compel the Attendance of absent Members, in such Manner, and under such Penalties as each House may provide.

Each House may determine the Rules of its Proceedings, punish its Members for disorderly Behavior, and, with the Concurrence of two-thirds, expel a Member.

Each House shall keep a Journal of its Proceedings, and from time to time publish the same, excepting such Parts as may in their Judgment require Secrecy;[14] and the Yeas and Nays of the Members of either House on any question shall, at the Desire of one fifth of those Present, be entered on the Journal.

Neither House, during the Session of Congress, shall, without the Consent of the other, adjourn for more than three days, nor to any other Place than that in which the two Houses shall be sitting.

Section 6

The Senators and Representatives shall receive a Compensation for their Services, to be ascertained by Law, and paid out of the Treasury of the United States. They shall in all Cases, except Treason, Felony and Breach of the Peace, be privileged from Arrest during their Attendance at the Session of their respective Houses, and in going to and returning from the same; and for any Speech or Debate in either House, they shall not be questioned in any other Place.

No Senator or Representative shall, during the Time for which he was elected, be appointed to any civil Office under the Authority of the United States which shall have been created, or the Emoluments whereof shall have been increased during such time; and no Person holding any Office under the United States, shall be a Member of either House during his Continuance in Office

Section 7

All bills for raising Revenue shall originate in the House of Representatives; but the Senate may propose or concur with Amendments as on other Bills.

Every Bill which shall have passed the House of Representatives and the Senate, shall, before it become a Law, be presented to the

---

[14] "Public life, the rule of the ruler...is never honoured by secrecy. Secret politics, according to the Jewish idea, are bad politics." Hirsch, *Bereishis*, 199.

President of the United States; If he approve he shall sign it, but if not he shall return it, with his Objections to that House in which it shall have originated, who shall enter the Objections at large on their Journal, and proceed to reconsider it. If after such Reconsideration two thirds of that House shall agree to pass the Bill, it shall be sent, together with the Objections, to the other House, by which it shall likewise be reconsidered, and if approved by two thirds of that House, it shall become a Law. But in all such Cases the Votes of both Houses shall be determined by Yeas and Nays, and the Names of the Persons voting for and against the Bill shall be entered on the Journal of each House respectively. If any Bill shall not be returned by the President within ten Days (Sundays excepted) after it shall have been presented to him, the Same shall be a Law, in like Manner as if he had signed it, unless the Congress by their Adjournment prevent its Return, in which Case it shall not be a Law.

Every Order, Resolution, or Vote to which the Concurrence of the Senate and House of Representatives may be necessary (except on a question of Adjournment) shall be presented to the President of the United States; and before the Same shall take Effect, shall be approved by him, or being disapproved by him, shall be repassed by two thirds of the Senate and House of Representatives, according to the Rules and Limitations prescribed in the Case of a Bill.

Section 8

The Congress shall have Power[15] To lay and collect Taxes, Duties, Imposts and Excises, to pay the Debts and provide for the common Defence and general Welfare of the United States; but all Duties, Imposts and Excises shall be uniform throughout the United States;

To borrow money on the credit of the United States;

To regulate Commerce with foreign Nations, and among the several States, and with the Indian Tribes;

To establish an uniform Rule of Naturalization, and uniform Laws on the subject of Bankruptcies[16] throughout the United States;

---

[15] "Congress was given that quintessential parliamentary power—control of the budget—without which it would be merely an ornamental body like the 'people's congress' in communist-dominated countries." Johnson, *Nemisis*, 16.

[16] To give an example of the control of the Ruling Class of our government and the relative impotence of our "democracy," in 2005 the banking corporations pushed through a bill [Public Law 109–8] in congress (and signed into law by President Bush on April twentieth of that year) which made it harder for the working poor to declare bankruptcy; these same banking corporations, themselves faced with bankruptcy a few

To coin Money, regulate the Value thereof, and of foreign Coin, and fix the Standard of Weights and Measures;

To provide for the Punishment of counterfeiting the Securities and current Coin of the United States;

To establish Post Offices and Post Roads;

To promote the Progress of Science and useful Arts, by securing for limited Times to Authors and Inventors the exclusive Right to their respective Writings and Discoveries;

To constitute Tribunals inferior to the supreme Court;

To define and punish Piracies and Felonies committed on the high Seas, and Offenses against the Law of Nations;

To declare War, grant Letters of Marque and Reprisal, and make Rules concerning Captures on Land and Water;

To raise and support Armies, but no Appropriation of Money to that Use shall be for a longer Term than two Years;

To provide and maintain a Navy;

To make Rules for the Government and Regulation of the land and naval Forces;

To provide for calling forth the Militia to execute the Laws of the Union, suppress Insurrections and repel Invasions;

To provide for organizing, arming, and disciplining the Militia, and for governing such Part of them as may be employed in the Service of the United States, reserving to the States respectively, the Appointment of the Officers, and the Authority of training the Militia according to the discipline prescribed by Congress;

To exercise exclusive Legislation in all Cases whatsoever, over such District (not exceeding ten Miles square) as may, by Cession of particular States, and the acceptance of Congress, become the Seat of the Government of the United States, and to exercise like Authority over all Places purchased by the Consent of the Legislature of the State in which the Same shall be, for the Erection of Forts, Magazines, Arsenals, dock-Yards, and other needful Buildings; And

To make all Laws which shall be necessary and proper for carrying into Execution the foregoing Powers, and all other Powers vested

---

years later, then pushed for (and attained) a nearly $800 billion bailout (the American Recovery and Reinvestment Act of 2009) footed by these same working poor taxpayers. Neither of these bills was supported by the general public, but their objections went unheard, silenced by the banking and finance industry. "An enactment based on the injunction to do 'what is right and good in the eyes of the Lord' [*Devarim* 6:18] concerns the case of a bankrupt. If his property was sold by order of the court, the buyer of the property was obliged to return it to the bankrupt whenever he was in a position to buy it back again" [*Bava Kamma* 15a]. Lew, *The Humanity of Jewish Law*, 35.

by this Constitution in the Government of the United States, or in any Department or Officer thereof.

Section 9

The Migration or Importation of such Persons as any of the States now existing shall think proper to admit, shall not be prohibited by the Congress prior to the Year one thousand eight hundred and eight, but a tax or duty may be imposed on such Importation, not exceeding ten dollars for each Person.

The privilege of the Writ of Habeas Corpus shall not be suspended, unless when in Cases of Rebellion or Invasion the public Safety may require it.[17]

No Bill of Attainder or ex post facto Law shall be passed.

No capitation, or other direct, Tax shall be laid, unless in Proportion to the Census or Enumeration herein before directed to be taken.

No Tax or Duty shall be laid on Articles exported from any State.

No Preference shall be given by any Regulation of Commerce or Revenue to the Ports of one State over those of another: nor shall Vessels bound to, or from, one State, be obliged to enter, clear, or pay Duties in another.

No Money shall be drawn from the Treasury, but in Consequence of Appropriations made by Law; and a regular Statement and Account of the Receipts and Expenditures of all public Money shall be published from time to time.

No Title of Nobility shall be granted by the United States: And no Person holding any Office of Profit or Trust under them, shall, without the Consent of the Congress, accept of any present, Emolument, Office, or Title, of any kind whatever, from any King, Prince or foreign State.

Section 10

No State shall enter into any Treaty, Alliance, or Confederation; grant Letters of Marque and Reprisal; coin Money; emit Bills of Credit; make any Thing but gold and silver Coin a Tender in Payment of Debts; pass any Bill of Attainder, ex post facto Law, or Law impairing the Obligation of Contracts, or grant any Title of Nobility.

---

[17] This fundamental right, which we inheirted from British Common Law, can be suspended at any time "when in Cases of Rebellion or Invasion the public Safety may require it." In fact, it has been suspended twice: first in the early part of the Civil War by Abraham Lincoln and recently by George W. Bush after the terrorist attacks on September 11, 2001. It could be suspended at any time at the whims of the President of the Ruling Class when "public Saftey may require it."

No State shall, without the Consent of the Congress, lay any Imposts or Duties on Imports or Exports, except what may be absolutely necessary for executing its inspection Laws: and the net Produce of all Duties and Imposts, laid by any State on Imports or Exports, shall be for the Use of the Treasury of the United States; and all such Laws shall be subject to the Revision and Control of the Congress.

No State shall, without the Consent of Congress, lay any duty of Tonnage, keep Troops, or Ships of War in time of Peace, enter into any Agreement or Compact with another State, or with a foreign Power, or engage in War, unless actually invaded, or in such imminent Danger as will not admit of delay.

Article II

Section 1

The executive Power shall be vested in a President of the United States of America. He shall hold his Office during the Term of four Years, and, together with the Vice-President chosen for the same Term, be elected, as follows:

Each State shall appoint, in such Manner as the Legislature thereof may direct, a Number of Electors,[18] *equal to the whole Number of Senators and Representatives to which the State may be entitled in the Congress: but no Senator or Representative, or Person holding an Office of Trust or Profit under the United States, sha*ll be appointed an Elector.

The Electors shall meet in their respective States, and vote by Ballot for two persons, of whom one at least shall not lie an Inhabitant of the same State with themselves. And they shall make a List of all the Persons voted for, and of the Number of Votes for each; which List they shall sign and certify, and transmit sealed to the Seat of the Government of the United States, directed to the President of the Senate. The President of the Senate shall, in the Presence of the Senate and House of Representatives, open all the Certificates, and the Votes shall

---

[18] "Americans…have no constitutional right to vote for the president of the United States. The framers of our Constitution did not trust all of the people to elect their president. Fearful of 'mobocracy,' they created a governmental structure under which elites would check and balance the rabble. These elites consisted of electors, chosen by whatever manner each state legislature designated who would select the president and vice president, senators, who would be chosen by state legislatures, and judges, appointed for life. Only the members of the House of Representatives were to be elected directly by the voters. Moreover, a relatively small percentage of people were deemed qualified to vote in any elections." Alan M. Dershowitz, *Supreme Injustice: How the High Court Hijacked Election 2000*. (New York: Oxford University Press, 2001), 17.

then be counted. The Person having the greatest Number of Votes shall be the President, if such Number be a Majority of the whole Number of Electors appointed; and if there be more than one who have such Majority, and have an equal Number of Votes, then the House of Representatives shall immediately choose by Ballot one of them for President; and if no Person have a Majority, then from the five highest on the List the said House shall in like Manner choose the President. But in choosing the President, the Votes shall be taken by States, the Representation from each State having one Vote; a quorum for this Purpose shall consist of a Member or Members from two-thirds of the States, and a Majority of all the States shall be necessary to a Choice. In every Case, after the Choice of the President, the Person having the greatest Number of Votes of the Electors shall be the Vice President. But if there should remain two or more who have equal Votes, the Senate shall choose from them by Ballot the Vice-President.

The Congress may determine the Time of choosing the Electors, and the Day on which they shall give their Votes; which Day shall be the same throughout the United States.

No person except a natural born Citizen, or a Citizen of the United States, at the time of the Adoption of this Constitution, shall be eligible to the Office of President; neither shall any Person be eligible to that Office who shall not have attained to the Age of thirty-five Years, and been fourteen Years a Resident within the United States.

In Case of the Removal of the President from Office, or of his Death, Resignation, or Inability to discharge the Powers and Duties of the said Office, the same shall devolve on the Vice President, and the Congress may by Law provide for the Case of Removal, Death, Resignation or Inability, both of the President and Vice President, declaring what Officer shall then act as President, and such Officer shall act accordingly, until the Disability be removed, or a President shall be elected.

The President shall, at stated Times, receive for his Services, a Compensation, which shall neither be increased nor diminished during the Period for which he shall have been elected, and he shall not receive within that Period any other Emolument from the United States, or any of them.

Before he enter on the Execution of his Office, he shall take the following Oath[19] or Affirmation: "I do solemnly swear (or affirm) that I will faithfully execute the Office of President of the United States,

---

[19] An example of misplaced loyalty is when a President takes the oath of office, he swears fealty to the man-made Constitution instead of the Torah.

and will to the best of my Ability, preserve, protect and defend the Constitution of the United States."

Section 2

The President shall be Commander in Chief of the Army and Navy of the United States, and of the Militia of the several States, when called into the actual Service of the United States; he may require the Opinion, in writing, of the principal Officer in each of the executive Departments, upon any subject relating to the Duties of their respective Offices, and he shall have Power to Grant Reprieves and Pardons for Offenses against the United States, except in Cases of Impeachment. He shall have Power, by and with the Advice and Consent of the Senate,[20]

---

[20] "Throughout U.S. history presidents have relied on their executive authority to make unilateral policy without interference from either Congress or the courts…presidents have used executive orders to make momentous policy choices." Kenneth R. Mayer, *With the Stroke of a Pen: Executive Orders and Presidential Power.* (Princeton: Princeton University Press, 2001), 4.

An example of this power is Executive Order 9066:

February 19, 1942

Authorizing the Secretary of War to Prescribe Military Areas

Whereas, The successful prosecution of the war requires every possible protection against espionage and against sabotage to national defense material, national defense premises and national defense utilities as defined in Section 4, Act of April 20, 1918, 40 Stat. 533 as amended by the Act of November 30, 1940, 54 Stat. 1220. and the Act of August 21, 1941. 55 Stat. 655 (U.S.C., Title 50, Sec. 104):

Now, therefore, by virtue of the authority vested in me as President of the United States, and Commander in Chief of the Army and Navy, I hereby authorize and direct the Secretary of War, and the Military Commanders whom he may from time to time designate, whenever he or any designated Commander deem such action necessary or desirable to prescribe military areas in such places and of such extent as he or the appropriate Military Commander may determine, from which any or all persons may be excluded, and with respect to which, the right of any person to enter, remain in, or leave shall be subject to whatever restriction the Secretary of War or the appropriate Military Commander may impose in his discretion. The Secretary of War is hereby authorized to provide for residents of any such area who are excluded there from. such transportation, food, shelter, and other accommodations as may be necessary, in the judgment of the Secretary of War or the said Military Commander and until other arrangements are made, to accomplish the purpose of this order. The designation of military areas in any region or locality shall supersede designation of prohibited and restricted areas by the Attorney General under the Proclamation of December 7 and 8, 1941, and shall supersede the responsibility and authority of the Attorney General under the said Proclamation in respect of such prohibited and restricted areas.

I hereby further authorize and direct the Secretary of War and the said Military Commanders to take such other steps as he or the appropriate Military Commander may deem advisable to enforce compliance with the restrictions applicable to each Military area herein above authorized to be designated. including the use of Federal

to make Treaties, provided two thirds of the Senators present concur; and he shall nominate, and by and with the Advice and Consent of the Senate, shall appoint Ambassadors, other public Ministers and Consuls, Judges of the supreme Court, and all other Officers of the United States, whose Appointments are not herein otherwise provided for, and which shall be established by Law: but the Congress may by Law vest the Appointment of such inferior Officers, as they think proper, in the President alone, in the Courts of Law, or in the Heads of Departments.

The President shall have Power to fill up all Vacancies that may happen during the Recess of the Senate, by granting Commissions which shall expire at the End of their next Session.

Section 3

He shall from time to time give to the Congress Information of the State of the Union, and recommend to their Consideration such Measures as he shall judge necessary and expedient; he may, on extraordinary Occasions, convene both Houses, or either of them, and in Case of Disagreement between them, with Respect to the Time of Adjournment, he may adjourn them to such Time as he shall think proper; he shall receive Ambassadors and other public Ministers; he shall take Care that the Laws be faithfully executed,[21] and shall Commission all the Officers of the United States.

---

troops and other Federal Agencies, with authority to accept assistance of state and local agencies.

I hereby further authorize and direct all Executive Department, independent establishments and other Federal Agencies, to assist the Secretary of War or the said Military Commanders in carrying out this Executive Order, including the furnishing of medical aid, hospitalization, food, clothing, transportation, use of land, shelter, and other supplies, equipment, utilities, facilities and service.

This order shall not be construed as modifying or limiting in any way the authority granted under Executive Order 8972. dated December 12.1941, nor shall it be construed as limiting or modifying the duty and responsibility of the Federal Bureau of Investigation, with response to the investigation of alleged acts of sabotage or duty and responsibility of the Attorney General and the Department of Justice under the Proclamation of December 7 and 8, 1941, prescribing regulations for the conduct and control of alien enemies, except as such duty and responsibility is superseded by the designation of military areas thereunder.
Franklin D. Roosevelt
The White House, February 19, 1942.

This order led to the internment of Japanese Americans. It is a sobering thought that a President could arrest and incarcerate an entire group of people (for example, Jews) in the name of "national security."

[21] This is the clause in the Constitution that the idea behind Presidential Executive Orders is based upon. Cf. *United States v. Eliason*, 41 U.S. 291, 301 (1842).

Section 4

The President, Vice President and all civil Officers of the United States, shall be removed from Office on Impeachment for, and Conviction of, Treason, Bribery, or other high Crimes and Misdemeanors.[22]

Article III

Section 1

The judicial Power of the United States, shall be vested in one supreme Court, and in such inferior Courts as the Congress may from time to time ordain and establish. The Judges, both of the supreme and inferior Courts, shall hold their Offices during good Behavior, and shall, at stated Times, receive for their Services a Compensation which shall not be diminished during their Continuance in Office.

Section 2

The judicial Power shall extend to all Cases, in Law and Equity, arising under this Constitution, the Laws of the United States, and Treaties made, or which shall be made, under their Authority; to all Cases affecting Ambassadors, other public Ministers and Consuls; to all Cases of admiralty and maritime Jurisdiction; to Controversies to which the United States shall be a Party; to Controversies between two or more States; between a State and Citizens of another State; between Citizens of different States; between Citizens of the same State claiming Lands under Grants of different States, and between a State, or the Citizens thereof, and foreign States, Citizens or Subjects.

In all Cases affecting Ambassadors, other public Ministers and Consuls, and those in which a State shall be Party, the supreme Court shall have original Jurisdiction. In all the other Cases before mentioned, the supreme Court shall have appellate Jurisdiction, both as to Law and Fact, with such Exceptions, and under such Regulations as the Congress shall make.

---

[22] The term "High Crimes and Misdemeanors" was "inserted into the Constitution by the Framers with no discussion of its meaning." The phrase came from "English common-law interpretation" which "encompassed political offenses as well as crimes" and that "political attacks on the British crown were criminal acts under the law of 'seditious libel,' which was incorporated into American law after the Revolution." Irons, *A People's History of the Supreme Court*, 109.

The Trial of all Crimes, except in Cases of Impeachment, shall be by Jury; and such Trial shall be held in the State where the said Crimes shall have been committed; but when not committed within any State, the Trial shall be at such Place or Places as the Congress may by Law have directed.

Section 3

Treason against the United States, shall consist only in levying War against them, or in adhering to their Enemies, giving them Aid and Comfort.[23] No Person shall be convicted of Treason unless on the Testimony of two Witnesses to the same overt Act, or on Confession in open Court.

The Congress shall have power to declare the Punishment of Treason, but no Attainder of Treason shall work Corruption of Blood, or Forfeiture except during the Life of the Person attainted.

Article IV

Section 1

Full Faith and Credit shall be given in each State to the public Acts, Records, and judicial Proceedings of every other State. And the Congress may by general Laws prescribe the Manner in which such Acts, Records and Proceedings shall be proved, and the Effect thereof.

---

[23] Treason is a tricky thing to define. On one hand, you have Jonathan Pollard, "who was accused of leaking top-secret satellite photos that aided Israel in its attack on Iraq's Osirak nuclear reactor" when the United States refused to give Israel the intelligence they needed to knock out Saddam Hussein's ability to make nuclear weapons. [John Loftus and Mark Aarons, *The Secret War Against the Jews*. (New York: St. Martin's Griffin, 1994), 401.] On the other hand, the word "treason" is not applied to men such as Allen and John Foster Dulles, two brothers who were lawyers and "international finance specialists for the powerful Wall Street law firm of Sullivan & Cromwell" [*ibid.*, 55], and both represented German firms such as I. G. Farben, the company that not only "held the patent for the poison gas used at Auschwitz and for working thousands of Jews to death as slave laborers" [ibid., 56] but was also the second largest shareholder in Standard Oil, the oil company which had also "provided Farben with its synthetic rubber patents and technical knowledge" [ibid., 64] during World War II. The Dulles brothers' Vatican contacts were instrumental in smuggling out the Reichsbank gold at the end of the war, as well as smuggling many of the top Nazis (such as Adolf Eichmann) out of Europe. After giving the Nazis "Aid and Comfort," John Foster Dulles would later become Secretary of State under Eisenhower, and his brother Allen would become director of the CIA. Pollard is still serving a life sentence in prison.

Section 2

The Citizens of each State shall be entitled to all Privileges and Immunities of Citizens in the several States.

A Person charged in any State with Treason, Felony, or other Crime, who shall flee from Justice, and be found in another State, shall on demand of the executive Authority of the State from which he fled, be delivered up, to be removed to the State having Jurisdiction of the Crime.

No Person held to Service or Labour in one State, under the Laws thereof, escaping into another, shall, in Consequence of any Law or Regulation therein, be discharged from such Service or Labour, But shall be delivered up on Claim of the Party to whom such Service or Labour may be due.

Section 3

New States may be admitted by the Congress into this Union; but no new States shall be formed or erected within the Jurisdiction of any other State; nor any State be formed by the Junction of two or more States, or parts of States, without the Consent of the Legislatures of the States concerned as well as of the Congress.

The Congress shall have Power to dispose of and make all needful Rules and Regulations respecting the Territory or other Property belonging to the United States; and nothing in this Constitution shall be so construed as to Prejudice any Claims of the United States, or of any particular State.

Section 4

The United States shall guarantee to every State in this Union a Republican Form of Government, and shall protect each of them against Invasion; and on Application of the Legislature, or of the Executive (when the Legislature cannot be convened) against domestic Violence.

Article V[24]

The Congress, whenever two thirds of both Houses shall deem it necessary, shall propose Amendments to this Constitution, or, on the

---

[24] This is the "imperfect Constitution" article, giving Congress the ability to "fix" the Constitution. Unlike the Torah, the man-made Constitution is forever in need of revising.

Application of the Legislatures of two thirds of the several States, shall call a Convention for proposing Amendments, which, in either Case, shall be valid to all Intents and Purposes, as part of this Constitution, when ratified by the Legislatures of three fourths of the several States, or by Conventions in three fourths thereof,[25] as the one or the other Mode of Ratification may be proposed by the Congress; Provided that no Amendment which may be made prior to the Year One thousand eight hundred and eight shall in any Manner affect the first and fourth Clauses in the Ninth Section of the first Article; and that no State, without its Consent, shall be deprived of its equal Suffrage in the Senate.[26]

Article VI

All Debts contracted and Engagements entered into, before the Adoption of this Constitution, shall be as valid against the United States under this Constitution, as under the Confederation.

This Constitution, and the Laws of the United States which shall be made in Pursuance thereof; and all Treaties made, or which shall be made, under the Authority of the United States, shall be the supreme Law of the Land; and the Judges in every State shall be bound thereby, any Thing in the Constitution or Laws of any State to the Contrary notwithstanding.

The Senators and Representatives before mentioned, and the Members of the several State Legislatures, and all executive and judicial Officers, both of the United States and of the several States, shall be bound by Oath or Affirmation, to support this Constitution; but no religious Test shall ever be required as a Qualification to any Office or public Trust under the United States.

---

[25] Because of this clause, any Amendment to the Constitution can be blocked by "thirty-four senators from the seventeen smallest states with a total population of 20,495,878, or 7.28 percent of the population of the United States [as of the year 2000]. If miraculously the amendment were to pass the Senate it could then be blocked by thirteen state legislatures in the smallest states with a total population of 10,904,895, or 3.87 percent of the population of the United States." Dahl, *How Democratic is the American Constitution?*, 161.

[26] California, which has sixty-nine times the population of Wyoming, has the same number of Senators: two. The top five states in population: California, Texas, New York, Florida, and Illinois have over a third of the population of the United States, yet have only ten Senators out of one hundred.

Article VII

The Ratification of the Conventions of nine States, shall be sufficient for the Establishment of this Constitution between the States so ratifying the Same.[27]

Done in Convention by the Unanimous Consent of the States present the Seventeenth Day of September in the Year of our Lord one thousand seven hundred and Eighty seven and of the Independence of the United States of America the Twelfth. In Witness whereof We have hereunto subscribed our Names.[28]

George Washington
President and deputy from Virginia
New Hampshire: John Langdon, Nicholas Gilman
Massachusetts: Nathaniel Gorham, Rufus King
Connecticut: William Samuel Johnson, Roger Sherman.
New York: Alexander Hamilton
New Jersey: William Livingston, David Brearley, William Paterson, Jonathan Dayton
Pennsylvania: Benjamin Franklin, Thomas Mifflin, Robert Morris, George Clymer, Thomas Fitzsimons, Jared Ingersoll, James Wilson, Gouvernour Morris
Delaware: George Read, Gunning Bedford Jr., John Dickinson, Richard Bassett, Jacob Broom
Maryland: James McHenry, Daniel of St Thomas Jenifer, Daniel Carroll
Virginia: John Blair, James Madison Jr.

---

[27] This was in direct violation of the Articles of Confederation, which was still the law of the land when the Constitution was drafted. Article XIII of the Articles of Confederation stated that "Every State shall abide by the determination of the United States in Congress assembled, on all questions which by this confederation are submitted to them. And the Articles of this Confederation shall be inviolably observed by **every State,** and the Union shall be perpetual; nor shall any alteration at any time hereafter be made in any of them; unless such alteration be agreed to in a Congress of the United States, and be afterwards confirmed by the legislatures of **every State**." How could the Framers violate this law? James Madison, in Federalist number 40, explained that: "The forbearance can only have proceeded from an irresistible conviction of the absurdity of subjecting the fate of twelve States to the perverseness or corruption of a thirteenth...as this objection, therefore, has been in a manner waived by those who have criticised [*sic*] the powers of the convention, I dismiss it without further observation." Obviously, we could, according to Madison's logic, dismiss the Constitution the same way, "without further observation." Cf. Lazare, *The Frozen Republic*, 290–91.

[28] These "framers" represented the "American economic and social elite" Ibid., 37.

North Carolina: William Blount, Richard Dobbs Spaight, Hugh Williamson

South Carolina: John Rutledge, Charles Cotesworth Pinckney, Charles Pinckney, Pierce Butler

Georgia: William Few, Abraham Baldwin

Attest: William Jackson, Secretary

AMENDMENTS TO THE CONSTITUTION OF THE UNITED STATES

Amendment I[29]

Congress shall make no law respecting an establishment[30] of religion,[31] or prohibiting the free exercise thereof; or abridging the freedom of speech,[32] or of the press;[33] or the right of the people

---

[29] The First Amendment (the "establishment" clause) gives the citizens of the United States the legal right to be idolaters as well as the right to have organized religion, both of which are prohibited under Noahide Law. According to the Torah, Noahides are supposed to create a body of law *prohibiting* idolatry and blasphemy. It should be noted that, under Noahide Law, a "Bill of Rights" would be unnecessary (cf. p. 506 below).

[30] The famous phrase of "a wall of separation between Church and State" came not from the Constitution but from a letter Jefferson wrote to the Danbury Baptist Association in 1802. It should also be noted that two items of Jefferson's "original intent" did not make it into the Bill of Rights: freedom from monopolies and freedom from standing armies. In a letter Jefferson wrote to Francis Hopkinson in March of 1789, Jefferson said that "What I disapproved from the first moment also was the want of a bill of rights to guard liberty against the legislative as well as executive branches of the government, that is to say to secure freedom in religion, freedom of the press, freedom from monopolies, freedom from unlawful imprisonment, freedom from a permanent military, and a trial by jury in all cases determinable by the laws of the land." If the "intent of the framers" was so important in interpreting the Constitution, why were these two "intents"—freedom from monopolies and standing armies—repeatedly ignored?

[31] "The religions of mankind are...human products—creations of the mind and spirit of man; and there exists consequently a genesis, a history of the development of religion and religions, just as there exists a history of languages, arts and sciences. The religion of a people rises and falls together with the other manifestations of its culture. Religion is only part of the cultural life of a nation, and is conditioned by it." Hirsch, *Collected Writings*, Vol. I, 184.

[32] This gives Americans the "freedom" of blasphemy. Also, "claiming the First Amendment right of all 'persons' to free speech, corporate lawsuits against the government successfully struck down laws that prevented them from lobbying or giving money to politicians and political candidates. " Hartmann, *Unequal Protection*, 120.

[33] American scripturalization of the Constitution and the near-deification of democracy have been barriers to true social change. In statements such as "the First Amendment belongs to all Americans, not just the billionaire investors in a handful of giant media firms, and it is based on the notion that democracy demands a press that serves us all"

peaceably to assemble, and to petition the Government for a redress of grievances.[34]

Amendment II

A well regulated Militia,[35] being necessary to the security of a free State, the right of the people to keep and bear Arms, shall not be infringed.[36]

(Nichols and McChesney, *It's the Media, Stupid!*, 43), the critics of corporate control of our media understand that there is something seriously wrong with a system that "is the result of government laws and regulations that have made it possible for massive private concerns to play such a significant role in our media's affairs. These laws—such as the Telecommunications Act of 1996—are usually written by and for the media firms with almost no public participation" (ibid., 43–44). The same people who call for "reforms" in the system (in lieu of real change) admit that reforms so far have been grossly inadequate, and that "the system seems almost impervious to change" (ibid., 49). Few seem to understand that it is the Constitution itself—a Constitution that supports and enforces an Edomite legal system—that is the problem, and that it is our "democracy" which enables tyrannical corporate control. Because speaking out against the Constitution and our democracy is considered blasphemous, our intellectuals are unable to think outside the box, and the "reforms" they suggest would be bound by the paradigm of our Edomite legal system and Constitutional government and therefore ineffective.

[34] It should be noted that the Bill of Rights was only ratified by ten of the original thirteen colonies; Massachusetts, Georgia, and Connecticut did not ratify the Bill of Rights until 1939—one hundred and fifty years after it had been written.

[35] The problem with the interpretation of the second amendment is that when the Constitution was framed both citizens and soldiers had, more or less, the same weaponry: muzzle loading rifles. Yes, the military could have artillery, but it was not too difficult to procure cannons (or even produce them, as the Confederacy did during the Civil War). Nowadays, a "militia" that aspires to protect itself against the government would be so badly outgunned it would be practically useless (you pull a Glock or an AK-47, they pull a M1 Abrams tank. Or an Apache helicopter with Hellfire missiles.) Any attempt to create a "militia" to "protect" a group against the "government" would be doomed to failure since that militia would be hopelessly outgunned by Federal military forces.

[36] "In recent years, advocates on both sides of the 'gun control' issue have debated the 'original intent' of those who framed the Second Amendment. Elbridge Gerry... offered this defense of the proposed amendment: 'What, sir, is the use of a militia? It is to prevent the establishment of a standing army, the bane of liberty.' Arming the citizens who belonged to state militias, Gerry argued, would deter Congress from establishing a federal army that might oppress or invade the states. Those who now advocate the constitutional 'right' of every citizen to 'bear arms' of any kind—from cheap handguns to assault rifles—are well advised to read the debates that led to adoption of the Second Amendment. Not a single member countered Gerry's argument that the 'right to bear arms' was limited to members of a state militia.

Amendment III

No Soldier shall, in time of peace be quartered in any house, without the consent of the Owner, nor in time of war, but in a manner to be prescribed by law.[37]

Amendment IV

The right of the people to be secure in their persons, houses, papers, and effects, against unreasonable searches and seizures, shall not be violated, and no Warrants shall issue, but upon probable cause, supported by Oath or affirmation, and particularly describing the place to be searched, and the persons or things to be seized.[38]

Amendment V

No person shall be held to answer for a capital, or otherwise infamous crime, unless on a presentment or indictment of a Grand Jury, except in cases arising in the land or naval forces, or in the Militia, when in actual service in time of War or public danger; nor shall any person be subject for the same offense to be twice put in jeopardy of life or limb; nor shall be compelled in any criminal case to be a witness against himself, nor be deprived of life, liberty, or property, without due process of law; nor shall private property be taken for public use, without just compensation.[39]

The current opponents of gun control legislation pay little heed to the Framer who spoke most clearly to the 'intent' of Congress on this controversial issue." Irons, *A People's History of the Supreme Court*, 75.

[37] This anachronistic Amendment has not been an issue since the Revolution.

[38] "The Fourth Amendment, instituted to prevent soldiers from bursting into homes and unreasonably searching and seizing property, has been used by corporations to avoid government regulators as if they were British dragoons." Hartmann, *Unequal Protection*, 158.

[39] "Like the Fourth Amendment, the Fifth Amendment was written to prevent a recurrence of government abuses from colonial days...today the shoe is on the other foot: Business, the more powerful party, is claiming protection, again to avoid government investigation of its alleged misdoings. Convicted once of *criminal* misdoing in an anti-trust case, a textile supply company used Fifth Amendment protections and barred retrial." Ibid., 159.

Amendment VI

In all criminal prosecutions, the accused shall enjoy the right to a speedy and public trial, by an impartial jury of the State and district wherein the crime shall have been committed, which district shall have been previously ascertained by law, and to be informed of the nature and cause of the accusation; to be confronted with the witnesses against him; to have compulsory process for obtaining witnesses in his favor, and to have the Assistance of Counsel for his defence.[40]

Amendment VII

In Suits at common law, where the value in controversy shall exceed twenty dollars, the right of trial by jury shall be preserved, and no fact tried by a jury, shall be otherwise re-examined in any Court of the United States, than according to the rules of the common law.

Amendment VIII

Excessive bail shall not be required, nor excessive fines imposed, nor cruel and unusual punishments inflicted.

Amendment IX

The enumeration in the Constitution, of certain rights, shall not be construed to deny or disparage others retained by the people.

Amendment X

The powers not delegated to the United States by the Constitution, nor prohibited by it to the States, are reserved to the States respectively, or to the people.

---

[40] If two men go to trial over a specific claim, a poor man who cannot hire an expensive lawyer is at a decided disadvantage; for example, a farmer going up against a "person" such as Monsanto or General Electric. Under Torah law, it is forbidden to rule in favor of the poor because you feel sympathy for their plight, and it is equally forbidden to rule in favor of the rich or powerful because of respect or fear. The very concept of the modern "lawyer" who argues the case before a judge came from the Greek and Roman court system. According to the Torah, there should be no "lawyers" or legal advocates. In fact, the *Tanach* calls such men wicked—legal advocates who try to sway the opinion of the judge in favor of their client, or a prosecutor who does the same. Cf. Rabbi Yisrael Meir Lau, *Rav Lau on Pirkei Avos*, (Brooklyn: Mesorah Publications, ltd., 2006), 71.

Amendment XI

The Judicial power of the United States shall not be construed to extend to any suit in law or equity, commenced or prosecuted against one of the United States by Citizens of another State, or by Citizens or Subjects of any Foreign State.

Amendment XII

The Electors shall meet in their respective states, and vote by ballot for President and Vice-President, one of whom, at least, shall not be an inhabitant of the same state with themselves; they shall name in their ballots the person voted for as President, and in distinct ballots the person voted for as Vice-President, and they shall make distinct lists of all persons voted for as President, and of all persons voted for as Vice-President and of the number of votes for each, which lists they shall sign and certify, and transmit sealed to the seat of the government of the United States, directed to the President of the Senate; the President of the Senate shall, in the presence of the Senate and House of Representatives, open all the certificates and the votes shall then be counted; the person having the greatest Number of votes for President, shall be the President, if such number be a majority of the whole number of Electors appointed; and if no person have such majority, then from the persons having the highest numbers not exceeding three on the list of those voted for as President, the House of Representatives shall choose immediately, by ballot, the President. But in choosing the President, the votes shall be taken by states, the representation from each state having one vote; a quorum for this purpose shall consist of a member or members from two-thirds of the states, and a majority of all the states shall be necessary to a choice. And if the House of Representatives shall not choose a President whenever the right of choice shall devolve upon them, before the fourth day of March next following, then the Vice-President shall act as President, as in the case of the death or other constitutional disability of the President. The person having the greatest number of votes as Vice-President, shall be the Vice-President, if such number be a majority of the whole number of Electors appointed, and if no person have a majority, then from the two highest numbers on the list, the Senate shall choose the Vice-President; a quorum for the purpose shall consist of two-thirds of the whole number of Senators, and a majority of the whole number shall be necessary to a choice. But no person constitutionally ineligible to the office of President shall be eligible to that of Vice-President of the United States.

Amendment XIII   ·

Section 1

Neither slavery nor involuntary servitude, except as a punishment for crime whereof the party shall have been duly convicted, shall exist within the United States, or any place subject to their jurisdiction.[41]

Section 2.

Congress shall have power to enforce this article by appropriate legislation.

Amendment XIV[42]

Section 1

All persons born or naturalized in the United States, and subject to the jurisdiction thereof, are citizens of the United States and of the State wherein they reside. No State shall make or enforce any law which shall abridge the privileges or immunities of citizens of the United States; nor shall any State deprive any person[43] of life, liberty, or property, without due process of law; nor deny to any person within its jurisdiction the equal protection of the laws.

---

[41] Mississippi finally ratified the thirteenth Amendment prohibiting slavery on the sixteenth of March, 1995, but since they failed to notify the United States Archivist, its ratification is not official.

[42] "Claiming the Fourteenth Amendment protection against discrimination (granting persons equal protection), the J. C. Penny chain store successfully sued the state of Florida, ending a law designed to help small, local business by charging chain stores a higher business license fee than locally owned stores." Hartmann, *Unequal Protection*, 121. [Cf. below in "Supreme Court Decision," p. 521.]

[43] The language of the Fourteenth Amendment was crafted by "Senator (and railroad lawyer) Roscoe Conking and…congressman (and railroad lawyer) John A. Bingham… Conkling, when he was part of the Senate committee that wrote the Fourteenth Amendment back in 1868, had intentionally inserted the word 'person' instead of the correct legal phrase 'natural person' to describe who would get the protections of the amendment. Bingham similarly worked in the House of Representatives to get the language passed." Ibid., 110.

Section 2

Representatives shall be apportioned among the several States according to their respective numbers, counting the whole number of persons in each State, excluding Indians not taxed. But when the right to vote at any election for the choice of electors for President and Vice-President of the United States, Representatives in Congress, the Executive and Judicial officers of a State, or the members of the Legislature thereof, is denied to any of the male inhabitants of such State, being twenty-one years of age, and citizens of the United States, or in any way abridged, except for participation in rebellion, or other crime, the basis of representation therein shall be reduced in the proportion which the number of such male citizens shall bear to the whole number of male citizens twenty-one years of age in such State.

Section 3

No person shall be a Senator or Representative in Congress, or elector of President and Vice-President, or hold any office, civil or military, under the United States, or under any State, who, having previously taken an oath, as a member of Congress, or as an officer of the United States, or as a member of any State legislature, or as an executive or judicial officer of any State, to support the Constitution of the United States, shall have engaged in insurrection or rebellion against the same, or given aid or comfort to the enemies thereof. But Congress may by a vote of two-thirds of each House, remove such disability.

Section 4

The validity of the public debt of the United States, authorized by law, including debts incurred for payment of pensions and bounties for services in suppressing insurrection or rebellion, shall not be questioned. But neither the United States nor any State shall assume or pay any debt or obligation incurred in aid of insurrection or rebellion against the United States, or any claim for the loss or emancipation of any slave; but all such debts, obligations and claims shall be held illegal and void.

Section 5

The Congress shall have power to enforce, by appropriate legislation, the provisions of this article.

Amendment XV

Section 1

The right of citizens of the United States to vote shall not be denied or abridged by the United States or by any State on account of race, color, or previous condition of servitude.

Section 2

The Congress shall have power to enforce this article by appropriate legislation.

Amendment XVI

The Congress shall have power to lay and collect taxes on incomes, from whatever source derived, without apportionment among the several States, and without regard to any census or enumeration.[44]

Amendment XVII

The Senate of the United States shall be composed of two Senators from each State, elected by the people thereof, for six years; and each Senator shall have one vote. The electors in each State shall have the qualifications requisite for electors of the most numerous branch of the State legislatures. When vacancies happen in the representation of any State in the Senate, the executive authority of such State shall issue writs of election to fill such vacancies: Provided, That the legislature of any State may empower the executive thereof to make temporary appointments until the people fill the vacancies by election as the legislature may direct. This amendment shall not be so construed as to affect the election or term of any Senator chosen before it becomes valid as part of the Constitution.

---

[44] "By what right and under what law should I therefore be compelled to make financial contributions to a community and its institution whose principles and objectives are diametrically opposed to my own, whose principles and objectives I feel duty-bound to fight with my heart's blood? I believe that to accord formal recognition to the legitimacy of these principles and objectives by contributing even a penny for their perpetuation would be a most grievous sin on my part, an open denial and mockery of all that is sacred to me. Such a sin would weigh heavily on my conscience forever." Hirsch, *Collected Writings*, Vol. VI, 89.

Amendment XVIII

Section 1

After one year from the ratification of this article the manufacture, sale, or transportation of intoxicating liquors within, the importation thereof into, or the exportation thereof from the United States and all territory subject to the jurisdiction thereof for beverage purposes is hereby prohibited.

Section 2

The Congress and the several States shall have concurrent power to enforce this article by appropriate legislation.

Section 3

This article shall be inoperative unless it shall have been ratified as an amendment to the Constitution by the legislatures of the several States, as provided in the Constitution, within seven years from the date of the submission hereof to the States by the Congress.

Amendment XIX

The right of citizens of the United States to vote shall not be denied or abridged by the United States or by any State on account of sex. Congress shall have power to enforce this article by appropriate legislation.

Amendment XX

Section 1

The terms of the President and Vice President shall end at noon on the 20th day of January, and the terms of Senators and Representatives at noon on the 3d day of January, of the years in which such terms would have ended if this article had not been ratified; and the terms of their successors shall then begin.

Section 2

The Congress shall assemble at least once in every year, and such meeting shall begin at noon on the 3d day of January, unless they shall by law appoint a different day.

Section 3

If, at the time fixed for the beginning of the term of the President, the President elect shall have died, the Vice President elect shall become President. If a President shall not have been chosen before the time fixed for the beginning of his term, or if the President elect shall have failed to qualify, then the Vice President elect shall act as President until a President shall have qualified; and the Congress may by law provide for the case wherein neither a President elect nor a Vice President elect shall have qualified, declaring who shall then act as President, or the manner in which one who is to act shall be selected, and such person shall act accordingly until a President or Vice President shall have qualified.

Section 4

The Congress may by law provide for the case of the death of any of the persons from whom the House of Representatives may choose a President whenever the right of choice shall have devolved upon them, and for the case of the death of any of the persons from whom the Senate may choose a Vice President whenever the right of choice shall have devolved upon them.

Section 5

Sections 1 and 2 shall take effect on the 15th day of October following the ratification of this article.

Section 6

This article shall be inoperative unless it shall have been ratified as an amendment to the Constitution by the legislatures of three-fourths of the several States within seven years from the date of its submission.

Amendment XXI

Section 1

The eighteenth article of amendment to the Constitution of the United States is hereby repealed.[45]

---

[45] The main reason for repealing the nineteenth amendment was money; in 1933, the United States was in the middle of the Great Depression, and tax revenue had sunk to its lowest point in nearly two decades. In just three years (1936), excise tax revenue on the sale of alcohol attributed to thirteen percent of all federal tax revenues.

Section 2

The transportation or importation into any State, Territory, or possession of the United States for delivery or use therein of intoxicating liquors, in violation of the laws thereof, is hereby prohibited.

Section 3

The article shall be inoperative unless it shall have been ratified as an amendment to the Constitution by conventions in the several States, as provided in the Constitution, within seven years from the date of the submission hereof to the States by the Congress.

Amendment XXII

Section 1

No person shall be elected to the office of the President more than twice, and no person who has held the office of President, or acted as President, for more than two years of a term to which some other person was elected President shall be elected to the office of the President more than once. But this Article shall not apply to any person holding the office of President, when this Article was proposed by the Congress, and shall not prevent any person who may be holding the office of President, or acting as President, during the term within which this Article becomes operative from holding the office of President or acting as President during the remainder of such term.

Section 2

This article shall be inoperative unless it shall have been ratified as an amendment to the Constitution by the legislatures of three-fourths of the several States within seven years from the date of its submission to the States by the Congress.

Amendment XXIII

Section 1

The District constituting the seat of Government of the United States shall appoint in such manner as the Congress may direct: A number of electors of President and Vice President equal to the whole number of Senators and Representatives in Congress to which the District would be entitled if it were a State, but in no event more than the least populous State; they shall be in addition to those appointed by the States, but they shall be considered, for the purposes of the election of President and Vice President, to be electors appointed by a State; and they shall meet in the District and perform such duties as provided by the twelfth article of amendment.

Section 2

The Congress shall have power to enforce this article by appropriate legislation.

Amendment XXIV

Section 1

The right of citizens of the United States to vote in any primary or other election for President or Vice President, for electors for President or Vice President, or for Senator or Representative in Congress, shall not be denied or abridged by the United States or any State by reason of failure to pay any poll tax or other tax.

Section 2

The Congress shall have power to enforce this article by appropriate legislation.

Amendment XXV

Section 1

In case of the removal of the President from office or of his death or resignation, the Vice President shall become President.

Section 2

Whenever there is a vacancy in the office of the Vice President, the President shall nominate a Vice President who shall take office upon confirmation by a majority vote of both Houses of Congress.

Section 3

Whenever the President transmits to the President pro tempore of the Senate and the Speaker of the House of Representatives his written declaration that he is unable to discharge the powers and duties of his office, and until he transmits to them a written declaration to the contrary, such powers and duties shall be discharged by the Vice President as Acting President.

Section 4

Whenever the Vice President and a majority of either the principal officers of the executive departments or of such other body as Congress may by law provide, transmit to the President pro tempore of the Senate and the Speaker of the House of Representatives their written declaration that the President is unable to discharge the powers and duties of his office, the Vice President shall immediately assume the powers and duties of the office as Acting President. Thereafter, when the President transmits to the President pro tempore of the Senate and the Speaker of the House of Representatives his written declaration that no inability exists, he shall resume the powers and duties of his office unless the Vice President and a majority of either the principal officers of the executive department or of such other body as Congress may by law provide, transmit within four days to the President pro tempore of the Senate and the Speaker of the House of Representatives their written declaration that the President is unable to discharge the powers and duties of his office. Thereupon Congress shall decide the issue, assembling within forty eight hours for that purpose if not in session. If the Congress, within twenty one days after receipt of the latter written declaration, or, if Congress is not in session, within twenty one days after Congress is required to assemble, determines by two thirds vote of both Houses that the President is unable to discharge the powers and duties of his office, the Vice President shall continue to discharge the same as Acting President; otherwise, the President shall resume the powers and duties of his office.

Amendment XXVI

Section 1

The right of citizens of the United States, who are eighteen years of age or older, to vote shall not be denied or abridged by the United States or by any State on account of age.

Section 2

The Congress shall have power to enforce this article by appropriate legislation.

Amendment XXVII

No law, varying the compensation for the services of the Senators and Representatives, shall take effect, until an election of Representatives shall have intervened.[46]

AS WE HAVE SEEN, the Constitution is merely a structure for government. Jefferson's "Certain Unalienable Rights" came from Locke's "Natural Rights," the idea which itself was influenced by Selden's thesis of "Natural Law" being based on Noahide Law. With a legal system and government based on Torah, i.e., Noahide Law, a "Bill of Rights" would be unnecessary[47] since the concepts of freedom and liberty we seem to hold dear are already laid out in the Torah.[48]

---

[46] An excellent example of how swiftly the Constitution accepts change; this amendment was passed in 1992 after it had been submitted in 1789. As we have seen [*McGowan v. Maryland, Braunfeld v. Brown*], the protection of minority rights from the "tyranny of the majority" did not apply to Jews. As we have pointed out above, the "intent of the Framers" was that the "minority rights" were those of the Upper Class, and the Constitution has been traditionally interpreted by the Supreme Court to protect the rights of the Ruling Class. As the economy crumbles, we will see more of our ephemeral "Constitutional Rights" lost while, at the same time, the primary function of the Constitution will become more apperant as the top one percent of the population acquires most of the wealth. We will also see the inevitable and unavoidable shift towards a more blatant anti-Semitism until one day a President arises who did not know Joseph.

[47] "In the end a democratic country cannot depend on its constitutional systems for the preservation of its liberties. It can depend only on the beliefs and cultures shared by its political, legal, and cultural elites." Dahl, *How Democratic is the American Constitution?*, 99.

[48] "What has been a long and arduous struggle for freedom in Western constitutional law was clearly established at the very origins of Jewish law over three thousand years ago. Jewish law is rooted in an appreciation for and a deep understanding of freedom as one of the basic pillars of human society. One of the cornerstones of Jewish law is that every human being is created 'in the image of God.' This means that every person has within him a God-given soul and that it is this soul that invests a person with significance and greatness...any affront to a human being, including a restriction of his freedom, is an affront to God. Jewish law, therefore, has a problem with one person being subjected to the authority of another, as it restricts the freedom of the subject and constitutes a denial of the 'image of God' within that person. From the perspective of Jewish law, only God Himself has the moral right to impose His authority on people. Thus, Jewish law is inherently uncomfortable with any form of political authority." Goldstein, *Defending the Human Spirit*, 34.

Declaration and Resolves of the
First Continental Congress, October 1774

WHEREAS, SINCE THE CLOSE OF THE LAST WAR, THE BRITISH PARLIAMENT, claiming a power of right to bind the people of America by statute in all cases whatsoever, hath, in some acts expressly imposed taxes on them, and in others, under various pretenses, but in fact for the purpose of raising a revenue, hath imposed rates and duties payable in these colonies, established a board of commissioners with unconstitutional powers, and extended the jurisdiction of courts of Admiralty not only for collecting the said duties, but for the trial of causes merely arising within the body of a country.[1]

And whereas, in consequence of other statutes, judges who before held only estates at will in their offices, have been made dependent on the Crown alone for their salaries, and standing armies kept in times of peace. And it has lately been resolved in Parliament, that by force of a statute made in the 35th year of the reign of king Henry the Eighth, colonists may be transported to England, and tried there upon accusations for treasons and misprisions, or concealments of treasons committed in the colonies; and by a late statute, such trials have been directed in cases therein mentioned.

And whereas, in the last session of Parliament, three statutes were made; one entitled "An act to discontinue, in such manner and for such time as are therein mentioned, the landing and discharging, lading, or shipping of goods, wares and merchandise, at the town, and within the harbor of Boston in the province of Massachusetts-bay, in North America;" another, entitled "An act for the better regulating the government of the province of the Massachusetts-bay in New England;" and another, entitled "An act for the impartial administration of justice, in the cases of persons questioned for any act done by them in the execution of the law, or for the suppression of riots and tumults, in the province of the Massachusetts-bay, in New England." And another statute was then made, "for making more effectual provision for the government of the province of Quebec, etc." All which statutes are impolitic, unjust, and cruel, as well as unconstitutional, and most dangerous and destructive of American rights.

---

[1] Devoid of the flowery rhetoric of Jefferson's "unalienable rights," this declaration gets to the heart of the matter, the economic reasons for revolution.

And whereas, Assemblies have been frequently dissolved, contrary to the rights of the people, when they attempted to deliberate on grievances; and their dutiful, humble, loyal, and reasonable petitions to the crown for redress, have been repeatedly treated with contempt, by His Majesty's ministers of state:

The good people of the several Colonies of New Hampshire, Massachusetts bay, Rhode Island and Providence plantations, Connecticut, New York, New Jersey, Pennsylvania, Newcastle, Kent and Sussex on Delaware, Maryland, Virginia, North Carolina, and South Carolina, justly alarmed at these arbitrary proceedings of parliament and administration, have severally elected, constituted, and appointed deputies to meet, and sit in general Congress, in the city of Philadelphia, in order to obtain such establishment, as that their religion, laws, and liberties, may not be subverted:

Whereupon the deputies so appointed being now assembled, in a full and free representation of these Colonies, taking into their most serious consideration the best means of attaining the ends aforesaid, do in the first place, as Englishmen their ancestors in like cases have usually done, for asserting and vindicating their rights and liberties, declare,

That the inhabitants of the English Colonies in North America, by the immutable laws of nature, the principles of the English constitution, and the several charters or compacts, have the following Rights:

1. That they are entitled to life, liberty, and property,[2] and they have never ceded to any sovereign power whatever, a right to dispose of either without their consent.

2. That our ancestors, who first settled these colonies, were at the time of their emigration from the mother country, entitled to all the rights, liberties, and immunities of free and natural born subjects within in the realm of England.

3. That by such emigration they by no means forfeited, surrendered, or lost any of those rights, but that they were, and their descendants now are entitled to the exercise and enjoyment of all such of them, as their local and other circumstances enable them to exercise and enjoy.

---

[2] Locke's original version before Jefferson changed "property" to "happiness." "The uniqueness of biblical law lay in its...consideration for the poor and underprivileged, respect for human life, freedom, and dignity, and concern for justice. 'It is not the protection of property, but the protection of humanity, that is the aim of the Mosaic code. Its sanctions are not directed to securing the strong in heaping up wealth so much as to preventing the weak from being crowded to the wall.'" Sivan, *The Bible and Civilization*, 109.

4. That the foundation of English liberty, and of all free government, is a right in the people to participate in their legislative council: and as the English colonists are not represented, and from their local and other circumstances, cannot properly be represented in the British parliament, they are entitled to a free and exclusive power of legislation in their several provincial legislatures, where their right of representation can alone be preserved, in all cases of taxation and internal polity, subject only to the negative of their sovereign, in such manner as has been heretofore used and accustomed. But, from the necessity of the case, and a regard to the mutual interest of both countries, we cheerfully consent to the operation of such acts of the British parliament, as are bona fide restrained to the regulation of our external commerce, for the purpose of securing the commercial advantages of the whole empire to the mother country, and the commercial benefits of its respective members excluding every idea of taxation, internal or external, for raising a revenue on the subjects in America without their consent.

5. That the respective colonies are entitled to the common law of England, and more especially to the great and inestimable privilege of being tried by their peers of the vicinage, according to the course of that law.[3]

6. That they are entitled to the benefit of such of the English statutes, as existed at the time of their colonization; and which they have, by experience, respectively found to be applicable to their several local and other circumstances.

7. That these, his majesty's colonies, are likewise entitled to all the immunities and privileges granted and confirmed to them by royal charters, or secured by their several codes of provincial laws.

8. That they have a right peaceably to assemble, consider of their grievances, and petition the King; and that all prosecutions, prohibitory proclamations, and commitments for the same, are illegal.

9. That the keeping a Standing army in these colonies, in times of peace, without the consent of the legislature of that colony in which such army is kept, is against law.[4]

---

[3] The men who made up the Continental Congress did not intend to change English Common law, only the government.

[4] Having a standing army makes it much easier to declare Martial Law in the interests of "national security." As pointed out above, our economy is based upon the "Pentagon Model," the "military-industrial complex" spoken of by President Eisenhower. Our massive military expenditures, in the name of "national security," are funded by the income tax which every American is forced to pay.

10. It is indispensably necessary to good government, and rendered essential by the English constitution, that the constituent branches of the legislature be independent of each other; that, therefore, the exercise of legislative power in several colonies, by a council appointed during pleasure, by the crown, is unconstitutional, dangerous, and destructive to the freedom of American legislation.

All and each of which the aforesaid deputies, in behalf of themselves, and their constituents, do claim, demand, and insist on, as their indubitable rights and liberties; which cannot be legally taken from them, altered or abridged by any power whatever, without their own consent, by their representatives in their several provincial legislatures.

In the course of our inquiry, we find many infringements and violations of the foregoing rights, which, from an ardent desire that harmony and mutual intercourse of affection and interest may be restored, we pass over for the present, and proceed to state such acts and measures as have been adopted since the last war, which demonstrate a system formed to enslave America.

Resolved, That the following acts of Parliament are infringements and violations of the rights of the colonists; and that the repeal of them is essentially necessary, in order to restore harmony between Great Britain and the American colonies, viz:

The several Acts of 4 Geo. 3, chapter 15 and chapter 34; 5 Geo. 3, chapter 25; 6 Geo. 3, chapter 52; 7 Geo. 3, chapter 41 and 46; 8 Geo. 3, chapter 22; which impose duties for the purpose of raising a revenue in America, extend the powers of the admiralty courts beyond their ancient limits, deprive the American subject of trial by jury, authorize the judges' certificate to indemnify the prosecutor from damages that he might otherwise be liable to, requiring oppressive security from a claimant of ships and goods seized before he shall be allowed to defend his property; and are subversive of American rights.

Also the 12 Geo. 3, chapter 24, entitled "An act for the better preserving his Majesty's dockyards, magazines, ships, ammunition, and stores," which declares a new offense in America, and deprives the American subject of a constitutional trial by jury of the vicinage, by authorizing the trial of any person charged with the committing any offense described in the said act, out of the realm, to be indicted and tried for the same in any shire or county within the realm.

Also the three acts passed in the last session of parliament, for stopping the port and blocking up the harbor of Boston, for altering the charter and government of the Massachusetts bay, and that which is entitled "An Act for the better administration of Justice," etc.

Also the act passed the same session for establishing the Roman Catholic Religion in the province of Quebec, abolishing the equitable system of English laws, and erecting a tyranny there, to the great danger, from so great a dissimilarity of Religion, law, and government, of the neighboring British colonies by the assistance of whose blood and treasure the said country was conquered from France.[5]

Also the act passed the same session for the better providing suitable quarters for officers and soldiers in his Majesty's service in North America.

Also, that the keeping a standing army in several of these colonies, in time of peace, without the consent of the legislature of that colony in which the army is kept, is against law.

To these grievous acts and measures Americans cannot submit, but in hopes that their fellow subjects in Great Britain will, on a revision of them, restore us to that state in which both countries found happiness and prosperity, we have for the present only resolved to pursue the following peaceable measures:

1. To enter into a non-importation, non-consumption, and non-exportation agreement or association.

2. To prepare an address to the people of Great Britain, and a memorial to the inhabitants of British America, and

3. To prepare a loyal address to his Majesty, agreeable to resolutions already entered into.

---

[5] The establishment of the Catholic Church in Quebec was a concern for the Congress.

The Articles of Confederation

Agreed to by Congress November 15, 1777; ratified and in force,
March 1, 1781.

Preamble

TO ALL TO WHOM THESE PRESENTS SHALL COME, WE THE UNDERSIGNED
Delegates of the States affixed to our Names send greeting.

Articles of Confederation[1] and perpetual Union between the States of
New Hampshire, Massachusetts bay, Rhode Island and Providence
Plantations, Connecticut, New York, New Jersey, Pennsylvania, Delaware, Maryland, Virginia, North Carolina, South Carolina and Georgia.

Article I. The Stile of this Confederacy shall be "The United States
of America."

Article II. Each state retains its sovereignty, freedom, and independence, and every power, jurisdiction, and right, which is not by this Confederation expressly delegated to the United States, in Congress assembled.

---

[1] The Articles of Confederation, the original social contract and framework for American
government, was the original "Constitution" which has never been repealed (cf. n. 26,
p. 492 above). Although the Articles of Confederation has been viewed historically
as "ineffective" and "weak," the real problem with the Articles of Confederation was
that it was much too democratic for the nascent Nation's elite Ruling Class who feared
the "tyranny of the majority" (i.e., the poor) and the subsequent threat to the wealthy
merchants and landowners who had supported the Revolution for economic reasons:
"Along with New England merchants and professionals, officials in the middle and
southern states feared that the insurgents sought a general redistribution of property."
David P. Szatmary. *Shays' Rebellion: The Making of an Agrarian Insurrection.*
(Amherst: The University of Massachusetts Press, 1980), 124 (cf. Shays's rebellion
283–85 above). This supports Charles A. Beard's thesis that the framers of the
Constitution were guided by economic self-interest: "According to some prominent
Americans, the Shaysite turmoil had hurt the prospects of merchants engaged in
international trade...British merchants, they warned, eventually would withdraw all
credit and would completely cut commercial ties with their American counterparts due
to fears of property loss at the hands of the rebels." Ibid., 128–29.
　　Much to the chagrin of many of the revolutionary leaders, the Articles of
Confederation were tossed aside in favor of a stronger national government designed
to protect the property of the Ruling Class. "Antifederalists feared what Patrick Henry
termed the 'consolidated government' proposed by the new Constitution. They saw
in Federalist hopes for commercial growth and international prestige only the lust
of ambitious men for a 'splendid empire' that, in the time-honored way of empires,
would oppress the people with taxes, conscription, and military campaigns." Ralph
Ketcham, "Antifederalist Essays and Speeches: 1787–1788" *Roots of the Republic:
American Founding Documents Interpreted.* Stephen L. Schechter, ed. (Madison:
Madison House Publishers, Inc., 1990), 383.

Article III. The said States hereby severally enter into a firm league of friendship with each other, for their common defense, the security of their liberties, and their mutual and general welfare, binding themselves to assist each other, against all force offered to, or attacks made upon them, or any of them, on account of religion, sovereignty, trade, or any other pretense whatever.

Article IV. The better to secure and perpetuate mutual friendship and intercourse among the people of the different States in this Union, the free inhabitants of each of these States, paupers, vagabonds, and fugitives from justice excepted,[2] shall be entitled to all privileges and immunities of free citizens in the several States; and the people of each State shall free ingress and regress to and from any other State, and shall enjoy therein all the privileges of trade and commerce, subject to the same duties, impositions, and restrictions as the inhabitants thereof respectively, provided that such restrictions shall not extend so far as to prevent the removal of property imported into any State, to any other State, of which the owner is an inhabitant; provided also that no imposition, duties or restriction shall be laid by any State, on the property of the United States, or either of them.

If any person guilty of, or charged with, treason, felony, or other high misdemeanor in any State, shall flee from justice, and be found in any of the United States, he shall, upon demand of the Governor or executive power of the State from which he fled, be delivered up and removed to the State having jurisdiction of his offense.

Full faith and credit shall be given in each of these States to the records, acts, and judicial proceedings of the courts and magistrates of every other State.

Article V. For the most convenient management of the general interests of the United States, delegates shall be annually appointed in such manner as the legislatures of each State shall direct, to meet in Congress on the first Monday in November, in every year, with a power reserved to each State to recall its delegates, or any of them, at any time within the year, and to send others in their stead for the remainder of the year.

No State shall be represented in Congress by less than two, nor more than seven members; and no person shall be capable of being a

---

[2] Here we see the influence of Western Law in regard to the weakest and most disadvantaged of society, the poor and homeless who are reduced to begging. The attitude of Western Culture since Rome has been that beggars are society's outcasts, and are fit for punishment. Throughout the Middle Ages and up to modern times Western society has passed laws punishing those reduced to begging and homelessness. The Torah approaches this subject quite differently than Western law; instead of punishing the poor, we are commanded to help them. The right for a destitute person to beg has always been recognized in Torah Law.

delegate for more than three years in any term of six years; nor shall any person, being a delegate, be capable of holding any office under the United States, for which he, or another for his benefit, receives any salary, fees or emolument of any kind.

Each State shall maintain its own delegates in a meeting of the States, and while they act as members of the committee of the States.

In determining questions in the United States in Congress assembled, each State shall have one vote.

Freedom of speech and debate in Congress shall not be impeached or questioned in any court or place out of Congress, and the members of Congress shall be protected in their persons from arrests or imprisonments, during the time of their going to and from, and attendance on Congress, except for treason, felony, or breach of the peace.

Article VI. No State, without the consent of the United States in Congress assembled, shall send any embassy to, or receive any embassy from, or enter into any conference, agreement, alliance or treaty with any King, Prince or State; nor shall any person holding any office of profit or trust under the United States, or any of them, accept any present, emolument, office or title of any kind whatever from any King, Prince or foreign State; nor shall the United States in Congress assembled, or any of them, grant any title of nobility.

No two or more States shall enter into any treaty, confederation or alliance whatever between them, without the consent of the United States in Congress assembled, specifying accurately the purposes for which the same is to be entered into, and how long it shall continue.

No State shall lay any imposts or duties, which may interfere with any stipulations in treaties, entered into by the United States in Congress assembled, with any King, Prince or State, in pursuance of any treaties already proposed by Congress, to the courts of France and Spain.

No vessel of war shall be kept up in time of peace by any State, except such number only, as shall be deemed necessary by the United States in Congress assembled, for the defense of such State, or its trade; nor shall any body of forces be kept up by any State in time of peace, except such number only, as in the judgement of the United States in Congress assembled, shall be deemed requisite to garrison the forts necessary for the defense of such State; but every State shall always keep up a well-regulated and disciplined militia, sufficiently armed and accoutered, and shall provide and constantly have ready for use, in public stores, a due number of filed pieces and tents, and a proper quantity of arms, ammunition and camp equipage.

No State shall engage in any war without the consent of the United States in Congress assembled, unless such State be actually invaded by enemies, or shall have received certain advice of a resolution being formed by some nation of Indians to invade such State, and the danger is so imminent as not to admit of a delay till the United States in Congress assembled can be consulted; nor shall any State grant commissions to any ships or vessels of war, nor letters of marque or reprisal, except it be after a declaration of war by the United States in Congress assembled, and then only against the Kingdom or State and the subjects thereof, against which war has been so declared, and under such regulations as shall be established by the United States in Congress assembled, unless such State be infested by pirates, in which case vessels of war may be fitted out for that occasion, and kept so long as the danger shall continue, or until the United States in Congress assembled shall determine otherwise.

Article VII. When land forces are raised by any State for the common defense, all officers of or under the rank of colonel, shall be appointed by the legislature of each State respectively, by whom such forces shall be raised, or in such manner as such State shall direct, and all vacancies shall be filled up by the State which first made the appointment.

Article VIII. All charges of war, and all other expenses that shall be incurred for the common defense or general welfare, and allowed by the United States in Congress assembled, shall be defrayed out of a common treasury, which shall be supplied by the several States in proportion to the value of all land within each State, granted or surveyed for any person, as such land and the buildings and improvements thereon shall be estimated according to such mode as the United States in Congress assembled, shall from time to time direct and appoint.

The taxes for paying that proportion shall be laid and levied by the authority and direction of the legislatures of the several States within the time agreed upon by the United States in Congress assembled.

Article IX. The United States in Congress assembled, shall have the sole and exclusive right and power of determining on peace and war, except in the cases mentioned in the sixth article — of sending and receiving ambassadors — entering into treaties and alliances, provided that no treaty of commerce shall be made whereby the legislative power of the respective States shall be restrained from imposing such imposts and duties on foreigners, as their own people are subjected to, or from prohibiting the exportation or importation of any species of goods or commodities whatsoever — of establishing rules for deciding in all cases, what captures on land or water shall be legal, and in what manner prizes taken by land or naval forces in the service of the United States shall be divided or appropriated — of granting letters of marque and reprisal in times of peace — appointing courts for the trial of piracies and felonies committed on the high seas and establishing courts for receiving and determining finally appeals in all cases of captures, provided that no member of Congress shall be appointed a judge of any of the said courts.

The United States in Congress assembled shall also be the last resort on appeal in all disputes and differences now subsisting or that hereafter may arise between two or more States concerning boundary, jurisdiction or any other causes whatever; which authority shall always be exercised in the manner following. Whenever the legislative or executive authority or lawful agent of any State in controversy with another shall present a petition to Congress stating the matter in question and praying for a hearing, notice thereof shall be given by order of Congress to the legislative or executive authority of the other State in controversy, and a day assigned for the appearance of the parties by their lawful agents, who shall then be directed to appoint by joint consent, commissioners or judges to constitute a court for hearing and determining the matter in question: but if they cannot agree, Congress shall name three persons out of each of the United States, and from the list of such persons each party shall alternately strike out one, the petitioners beginning, until the number shall be reduced to thirteen; and from that number not less than seven, nor more than nine names as Congress shall direct, shall in the presence of Congress be drawn out by lot, and the persons whose names shall be so drawn or any five of them, shall be commissioners or judges, to hear and finally determine the controversy, so always as a major part of the judges who shall hear the cause shall agree in the determination: and if either party shall neglect to attend at the day appointed, without showing reasons, which Congress shall judge sufficient, or being present shall refuse to strike, the Congress shall proceed to nominate three persons out of each State, and the secretary of Congress shall strike in behalf of such party absent or refusing; and the judgement and sentence of the court to be appointed, in the manner before prescribed, shall be final and conclusive; and if any of the parties shall refuse to submit to the authority of such court, or to appear or defend their claim or cause, the court shall nevertheless proceed to pronounce sentence, or judgement, which shall in like manner be final and decisive, the judgement or sentence and other proceedings being in either case transmitted to Congress, and lodged among the acts of Congress for the security of the parties concerned: provided that every commissioner, before he sits in judgement, shall take an oath to be administered by one of the judges of the supreme or superior court of the State, where the cause shall be tried, 'well and truly to hear and determine the matter in question, according to the best of his judgement, without favor, affection or hope of reward': provided also, that no State shall be deprived of territory for the benefit of the United States.

All controversies concerning the private right of soil claimed under different grants of two or more States, whose jurisdictions as they may respect such lands, and the States which passed such grants are adjusted, the said grants or either of them being at the same time claimed to have originated antecedent to such settlement of jurisdiction, shall on the petition of either party to the Congress of the United States, be finally determined as near as may be in the same manner as is before prescribed for deciding disputes respecting territorial jurisdiction between different States.

The United States in Congress assembled shall also have the sole and exclusive right and power of regulating the alloy and value of coin struck by their own authority, or by that of the respective States — fixing the standards of weights and measures throughout the United States — regulating the trade and managing all affairs with the Indians, not members of any of the States, provided that the legislative right of any State within its own limits be not infringed or violated — establishing or regulating post offices from one State to another, throughout all the United States, and exacting such postage on the papers passing through the same as may be requisite to defray the expenses of the said office — appointing all officers of the land forces, in the service of the United States, excepting regimental officers — appointing all the officers of the naval forces, and commissioning all officers whatever in the service of the United States — making rules for the government and regulation of the said land and naval forces, and directing their operations.

The United States in Congress assembled shall have authority to appoint a committee, to sit in the recess of Congress, to be denominated 'A Committee of the States', and to consist of one delegate from each State; and to appoint such other committees and civil officers as may be necessary for managing the general affairs of the United States under their direction — to appoint one of their members to preside, provided that no person be allowed to serve in the office of president more than one year in any term of three years; to ascertain the necessary sums of money to be raised for the service of the United States, and to appropriate and apply the same for defraying the public expenses — to borrow money, or emit bills on the credit of the United States, transmitting every half-year to the respective States an account of the sums of money so borrowed or emitted — to build and equip a navy — to agree upon the number of land forces, and to make requisitions from each State for its quota, in proportion to the number of white inhabitants in such State; which requisition shall be binding, and thereupon the legislature of each State shall appoint the regimental officers, raise the men and cloath, arm and equip them in a solid- like manner, at the expense of the United States; and the officers and men so cloathed, armed and equipped shall march to the place appointed, and within the time agreed on by the United States in Congress assembled. But if the United States in Congress assembled shall, on consideration of circumstances judge proper that any State should not raise men, or should raise a smaller number of men than the quota thereof, such extra number shall be raised, officered, cloathed, armed and equipped in the same manner as the quota of each State, unless the legislature of such State shall judge that such extra number cannot be safely spread out in the same, in which case they shall raise, officer, cloath, arm and equip as many of such extra number as they judge can be safely spared. And the officers and men so cloathed, armed, and equipped, shall march to the place appointed, and within the time agreed on by the United States in Congress assembled.

The United States in Congress assembled shall never engage in a war, nor grant letters of marque or reprisal in time of peace, nor enter into any treaties or alliances, nor coin money, nor regulate the value thereof, nor ascertain the sums and expenses necessary for the defense and welfare of the United States, or any of them, nor emit bills, nor borrow money on the credit of the United States, nor appropriate money, nor agree upon the number of vessels of war, to be built or purchased, or the number of land or sea forces to be raised, nor appoint a commander in chief of the army or navy, unless nine States assent to the same: nor shall a question on any other point, except for adjourning from day to day be determined, unless by the votes of the majority of the United States in Congress assembled.

The Congress of the United States shall have power to adjourn to any time within the year, and to any place within the United States, so that no period of adjournment be for a longer duration than the space of six months, and shall publish the journal of their proceedings monthly, except such parts thereof relating to treaties, alliances or military operations, as in their judgement require secrecy; and the yeas and nays of the delegates of each State on any question shall be entered on the journal, when it is desired by any delegates of a State, or any of them, at his or their request shall be furnished with a transcript of the said journal, except such parts as are above excepted, to lay before the legislatures of the several States.

Article X. The Committee of the States, or any nine of them, shall be authorized to execute, in the recess of Congress, such of the powers of Congress as the United States in Congress assembled, by the consent of the nine States, shall from time to time think expedient to vest them with; provided that no power be delegated to the said Committee, for the exercise of which, by the Articles of Confederation, the voice of nine States in the Congress of the United States assembled be requisite.

Article XI. Canada acceding to this confederation, and adjoining in the measures of the United States, shall be admitted into, and entitled to all the advantages of this Union; but no other colony shall be admitted into the same, unless such admission be agreed to by nine States.

Article XII. All bills of credit emitted, monies borrowed, and debts contracted by, or under the authority of Congress, before the assembling of the United States, in pursuance of the present confederation, shall be deemed and considered as a charge against the United States, for payment and satisfaction whereof the said United States, and the public faith are hereby solemnly pledged.

Article XIII. Every State shall abide by the determination of the United States in Congress assembled, on all questions which by this confederation are submitted to them. And the Articles of this Confederation shall be inviolably observed by every State, and the Union shall be perpetual; nor shall any alteration at any time hereafter be made in any of them; unless such alteration be agreed to in a Congress of the United States, and be afterwards confirmed by the legislatures of every State.

And Whereas it hath pleased the Great Governor of the World to incline the hearts of the legislatures we respectively represent in Congress, to approve of, and to authorize us to ratify the said Articles of Confederation and perpetual Union. Know Ye that we the undersigned delegates, by virtue of the power and authority to us given for that purpose, do by these presents, in the name and in behalf of our respective constituents, fully and entirely ratify and confirm each and every of the said Articles of Confederation and perpetual Union, and all and singular the matters and things therein contained: And we do further solemnly plight and engage the faith of our respective constituents, that they shall abide by the determinations of the United States in Congress assembled, on all questions, which by the said Confederation are submitted to them. And that the Articles thereof shall be inviolably observed by the States we respectively represent, and that the Union shall be perpetual.

In Witness whereof we[3] have hereunto set our hands in Congress. Done at Philadelphia in the State of Pennsylvania the ninth day of July

---

[3] On the part and behalf of the State of New Hampshire: Josiah Bartlett, John Wentworth Junr. August 8th 1778. On the part and behalf of The State of Massachusetts Bay: John Hancock, Samuel Adams, Elbridge Gerry, Francis Dana, James Lovell. Samuel Holten. On the part and behalf of the State of Rhode Island and Providence Plantations: William Ellery, Henry Marchant, John Collins. On the part and behalf of the State of Connecticut: Roger Sherman, Samuel Huntington, Oliver Wolcott, Titus Hosmer, Andrew Adams. On the Part and Behalf of the State of New York: James Duane, Francis Lewis, Wm Duer, Gouv Morris. On the Part and in Behalf of the State of New Jersey, November 26, 1778. Jno Witherspoon, Nath. Scudder. On the part and behalf of the State of Pennsylvania: Robt Morris, Daniel Roberdeau, John Bayard Smith. William Clingan, Joseph Reed 22nd July 1778. On the part and behalf of the State of Delaware: Tho Mckean February 12, 1779, John Dickinson May 5th 1779. Nicholas Van Dyke. On the part and behalf of the State of Maryland: John Hanson March 1 1781, Daniel Carroll, On the Part and Behalf of the State of Virginia: Richard Henry Lee, John Banister, Thomas Adams, Jno Harvie, Francis Lightfoot Lee, On the part and Behalf of the State of No Carolina: John Penn July 21st 1778, Corns Harnett, Jno Williams, On the part and behalf of the State of South Carolina: Henry Laurens, William Henry Drayton, Jno Mathews, Richd Hutson, Thos Heyward Junr. On the part and behalf of the State of Georgia: Jno Walton 24th July 1778, Edwd Telfair, Edwd Langworthy.

in the Year of our Lord One Thousand Seven Hundred and Seventy-Eight, and in the Third Year of the independence of America.[4]

---

[4] With a bit of tweaking, the Articles of Confederation, which has never been repealed, could still be the template for government along with the Noahide Law and a Noahide court system. A Noahide "Sanhedrin," as the Great Sanhedrin in Israel, would be the judicial and legislative body which could enforce taxation and regulate the economy. "In the realm of the national administration, there is no special function for [a king]. The organization that is needed to implement our national task is fully provided for by means of the Courts of Justice and the Houses of Learning and those invested with judiciary and executive powers." [Hirsch, Collected Writings, Vol. IV, 276.] As far as the Constitution is concerned, we could, in the words of James Madison, "dismiss it without further observation." Cf. n. 26, p. 492.

Louis K. Liggett Co. v. Lee

IN A RARE DISPLAY OF AN ANTI-CORPORATE OPINION, JUSTICE LOUIS Brandeis (who, perhaps not incidentally, was the first Jew ever on the Supreme Court) wrote in his dissent to the 1933 case of *Louis K. Liggett Co. v. Lee*:

∞

"In my opinion, the judgment of the Supreme Court of Florida should be affirmed.[1] Florida Laws 1931, Chapter 15624, is legislation of the type popularly called Anti-Chain Store Laws. The statute provides for the licensing of retail stores by the state, the counties, and the municipalities—a system under which large revenues may be raised. But the raising of revenue is obviously not the main purpose of the legislation. Its chief aim is to protect the individual, independently owned retail stores from the competition of chain stores. The statute seeks to do this by subjecting the latter to financial handicaps which may conceivably compel their withdrawal from the state. An injunction against its enforcement is sought on the ground that the law violates rights guaranteed by the Federal Constitution.

The Florida law is general in its terms. It prohibits the operation, after September 30, 1931, of any retail store without securing annually a license, and provides, among other things, for annual fees which are in part graduated. If the owner operates only one store, the state fee is $5; if more than one, the fee for the additional stores rises by step increases, dependent upon both the number operated and whether all operated are located in a single county. The highest fee is for a store in excess of 75. If all of the stores are located in a single county, the fee for each store in excess of 75 is $40; if all are not located in the same county, the fee is $50. Under this law, the owner of 100 stores not located in a single county pays for each store operated, on the average, $33.65, and if they were located in a single county, the owner would

---

[1] The Supreme Court overturned a 1931 law passed by the Florida Legislature which "imposed annual license fees" on all state retail business. "The new law provided that the fee per store was to rise in proportion to the number of units owned, so that each chain store branch would pay a higher license fee than an individually owned business." This law was challenged by the Liggett Company, which claimed it violated its rights under the fourteenth amendment. The court ruled in Liggett's favor by a 5 to 4 vote. Diana Klebanow and Franklin L. Jonas, *People's Lawyers: Crusaders for Justice in American History.* (Armonk, NY: M. E. Sharpe, 2003), 97.

pay for each store, on the average, $25.20. If the 100 stores were independently owned (although operated cooperatively as a so-called "voluntary chain"), the annual fee for each would be only $5. The statute provides that the licenses shall issue to expire on September 30th of each calendar year. This suit was begun September 30, 1931. The first license year had expired before the case was heard in this Court. In its main features, this statute resembles the Indiana law discussed in State Board of Tax Commissioners v. Jackson, 283 U. S. 527. For the reasons there stated, the Court sustains like provisions in the Florida statute. But it declares arbitrary, and hence invalid, the novel provision imposing heavier license fees where the multiple stores of a single owner are located in more than one county because it is "unable to discover any reasonable basis for this classification." There is nothing in the record to show affirmatively that the provision may not be a reasonable one in view of conditions prevailing in Florida. Since the presumption of constitutionality must prevail in the absence of some factual foundation of record for overthrowing the statute, its validity should, in my opinion, be sustained...there is, however, another ground on which this provision should be, and the whole statute could be, sustained—a ground not considered in the Jackson case and not pertinent there. Jackson was an individual. The plaintiffs here are all corporations. Though the provisions of the statutes in the two states are similar, certain rules of law applicable to the parties to the litigation are different.

The plaintiffs are thirteen corporations which engage in Florida exclusively in intrastate commerce. Each (except one) owns and operates a chain of retail stores within the state, and some operate stores in more than one county. Several of the plaintiffs are organized under the laws of Florida; the rest under the laws of other states. No claim of discrimination as between the foreign and domestic corporations is made, compare Southern Ry. Co. v. Greene, 216 U. S. 400; Hanover Fire Insurance Co. v. Harding, 272 U. S. 494; nor could it be, since the statute affects both classes of corporations alike. The suit is brought as a class suit, for the benefit of all merchants similarly situated who may desire to avail themselves thereof. From certain allegations in the bill, it may be inferred that there are at least two natural persons within the state who own and operate more than one store. But, as no such person has intervened in the cause, we have no occasion to inquire whether the discrimination complained of would be fatal as applied to natural persons. The plaintiffs can succeed only if the discrimination is unconstitutional as applied to them—that is, as applied to corporations. One who would strike down a statute must show not only that he is affected by it, but that, as applied to him, it exceeds the power of the state. This rule, acted upon as early as 74 U. S. 314, has been consistently followed since that time...for the reasons to be stated, the discrimination complained of, and held arbitrary by the court, is, in my opinion, valid as applied to corporations.

First. The federal Constitution does not confer upon either domestic or foreign corporations the right to engage in intrastate commerce in Florida. The privilege of engaging in such commerce in corporate form is one which the state may confer or may withhold as it sees fit... Florida might grant the privilege to one set of persons and deny it to others; might grant it for some kinds of business and deny it for others; might grant the privilege to corporations with a small capital while denying it for those whose capital or resources are large. Or it might grant the privilege to private corporations whose shares are owned mainly by those who manage them and to corporations engaged in co-operative undertakings, while denying the privilege to other concerns called private, but whose shares are listed on a stock exchange—corporations financed by the public, largely through the aid of investment bankers. It may grant the privilege broadly, or restrict its exercise to a single county, city, or town, and to a single place of business within any such subdivision of the state.

Whether the corporate privilege shall be granted or withheld is always a matter of state policy. If granted, the privilege is conferred in order to achieve an end which the state deems desirable. It may be granted as a means of raising revenue, or in order to procure for the community a public utility, a bank, or a desired industry not otherwise obtainable; or the reason for granting it may be to promote more generally the public welfare by providing an instrumentality of business which will facilitate the establishment and conduct of new and large enterprises deemed of public benefit. Similarly, if the privilege is denied, it is denied because incidents of like corporate enterprise are deemed inimical to the public welfare and it is desired to protect the community from apprehended harm.[2]

Second. The prevalence of the corporation in America has led men of this generation to act, at times, as if the privilege of doing business in corporate form were inherent in the citizen, and has led them to accept the evils attendant upon the free and unrestricted use of the corporate mechanism as if these evils were the inescapable price of

---

[2] Cf. n. 20, p. 320–21 above.

civilized life, and, hence to be borne with resignation. Throughout the greater part of our history, a different view prevailed. Although the value of this instrumentality in commerce and industry was fully recognized, incorporation for business was commonly denied long after it had been freely granted for religious, educational, and charitable purposes. It was denied because of fear. Fear of encroachment upon the liberties and opportunities of the individual. Fear of the subjection of labor to capital. Fear of monopoly. Fear that the absorption of capital by corporations, and their perpetual life, might bring evils similar to those which attended mortmain. There was a sense of some insidious menace inherent in large aggregations of capital, particularly when held by corporations...

Able, discerning scholars have pictured for us the economic and social results of thus removing all limitations upon the size and activities of business corporations and of vesting in their managers vast powers once exercised by stockholders—results not designed by the states and long unsuspected. They show that size alone gives to giant corporations a social significance not attached ordinarily to smaller units of private enterprise. Through size, corporations, once merely an efficient tool employed by individuals in the conduct of private business, have become an institution—an institution which has brought such concentration of economic power that so-called private corporations are sometimes able to dominate the state. The typical business corporation of the last century, owned by a small group of individuals, managed by their owners, and limited in size by their personal wealth, is being supplanted by huge concerns in which the lives of tens or hundreds of thousands of employees and the property of tens or hundreds of thousands of investors are subjected, through the corporate mechanism, to the control of a few men. Ownership has been separated from control, and this separation has removed many of the checks which formerly operated to curb the misuse of wealth and power. And, as ownership of the shares is becoming continually more dispersed, the power which formerly accompanied ownership is becoming increasingly concentrated in the hands of a few. The changes thereby wrought in the lives of the workers, of the owners, and of the general public are so fundamental and far-reaching as to lead these scholars to compare the evolving "corporate system" with the feudal system, and to lead other men of insight and experience to assert that this "master institution of civilized life" is committing it to the rule of a plutocracy.

The data submitted in support of these conclusions indicate that, in the United States, the process of absorption has already advanced so far that perhaps two-thirds of our industrial wealth has passed from individual possession to the ownership of large corporations whose shares are dealt in on the stock exchange; that 200 nonbanking corporations, each with assets in excess of $90,000,000, control directly about one-fourth of all our national wealth, and that their influence extends far beyond the assets under their direct control; that these 200 corporations, while nominally controlled by about 2,000 directors, are actually dominated by a few hundred persons—the negation of industrial democracy. Other writers have shown that, coincident with the growth of these giant corporations, there has occurred a marked concentration of individual wealth, and that the resulting disparity in incomes is a major cause of the existing depression. *Such is the Frankenstein monster which states have created by their corporation laws* [emphasis added].

There is a widespread belief that the existing unemployment is the result, in large part, of the gross inequality in the distribution of wealth and income which giant corporations have fostered; that, by the control which the few have exerted through giant corporations, individual initiative and effort are being paralyzed, creative power impaired, and human happiness lessened; that the true prosperity of our past came not from big business, but through the courage, the energy, and the resourcefulness of small men; that only by releasing from corporate control the faculties of the unknown many, only by reopening to them the opportunities for leadership, can confidence in our future be restored and the existing misery be overcome, and that only through participation by the many in the responsibilities and determinations of business can Americans secure the moral and intellectual development which is essential to the maintenance of liberty. If the citizens of Florida share that belief, I know of nothing in the Federal Constitution which precludes the state from endeavoring to give it effect and prevent domination in intrastate commerce by subjecting corporate chains to discriminatory license fees. To that extent, the citizens of each state are still masters of their destiny…"

Bibliography

〜

Abraham, Gary A. *Max Weber and the Jewish Question*. Chicago: University of Illinois Press, 1992.

Adler, Michael. "The Emperor Julian and the Jews." *The Jewish Quarterly Review*. Vol. 5, No. 4 (Jul., 1893), 592.

Aland, Kurt. "The Greek New Testament: Its Present and Future Editions." *Journal of Biblical Literature*. Vol. 87, No. 2 (June 1968).

Aland, Kurt and Barbara Aland. *The Text of the New Testament*. Erroll G. Rhodes, trans. Grand Rapids, MI: William B. Eerdmans, 1987.

Arendt, Hanna. *Responsibility and Judgment*, ed. Jerome Kohn. New York: Schocken Books, 2003.

Armitage, David. "The Declaration of Independence and International Law." *The William and Mary Quarterly*. Third Series, Vol. 59, No. 1 (January 2002).

Aron, Raymond. *Main Currents in Sociological Thought*, Vol. 2. Richard Howard and Helen Weaver, trans. New York: Basic Books Inc., 1967.

Bakan, Joel. *The Corporation: The Pathological Pursuit of Profit and Power*. New York: Free Press, 2004.

Barash, Jeffery Andrew. *Martin Heidegger and the Problem of Historical Meaning*. New York: Fordham University Press, 2003.

Barbour, Reid. *John Selden*. Toronto: University of Toronto Press, 2003.

Baugh, Albert C. and Thomas Cable. *A History of the English Language*. Englewood Cliffs: Prentice-Hall, Inc., 1993.

Bauman, Zygmunt. "Sociology after the Holocaust." *The British Journal of Sociology*. Vol. 39, No. 4 (December 1988).

Beard, Charles A. *An Economic Interpretation of the Constitution of the United States*. New Brunswick, N.J.: Transaction Publishing, 1998.

Bellah, Robert N. "Max Weber and World-Denying Love: A Look at the Historical Sociology of Religion." *Journal of the American Academy of Religion*. Vol. 67, No. 2 (June 1999).

Belz, Herman. *A Living Constitution or Fundamental Law?: American Constitutionalism in Historical Perspective*. Lanham, Md.: Rowman & Littlefield, 1998.

Berman, Bruce J. "Nationalism, Ethnicity, and Modernity: The Paradox of Mau Mau." *Canadian Journal of African Studies/Revue Canadienne des Études Africaines*. Vol. 25, No. 2 (1991).

Berman, Harold J. "The Origins of Historical Jurisprudence: Coke, Selden, Hale." *The Yale Law Journal*. Vol. 103, No. 7 (May 1994).

Berman, Morris. *Dark Ages America: The Final Phase of Empire*. New York: W. W. Norton & Company, 2006.

Besdin, Rabbi Abraham R. *Reflections of the Rav: Lessons in Jewish Thought*. Vol. I. Hoboken: KTAV Publishing House, Inc., 1993.

Blackmore, Susan. *The Meme Machine*. Oxford: Oxford University Press, 1999.

Bloom, Allan. *The Closing of the American Mind*. New York: Simon & Schuster Inc., 1987.

Bober, M. M. *Karl Marx's Interpretation of History*. New York: Norton, 1965.

Boggs, Carl. *The End of Politics: Corporate Power and the Decline of the Public Sphere*. New York: The Guilford Press, 2000.

Boyarin, Daniel. *Carnal Israel: Reading Sex in Talmudic Culture*. Berkeley: University of California Press, 1995.

Breuer, Edward. *The Limits of Enlightenment*. Cambridge, Massachusetts: Harvard University Press, 1996.

Brewer, Anthony. *Marxist Theories of Imperialism: A Critical Survey*. Second edition. London: New York Taylor & Francis Routledge, 1990

Bultmann, Rudolf. *Theology of the New Testament*. New York: Charles Scribner's Sons, 1951.

Cameron, A. "The Exposure of Children and Greek Ethics." *The Classical Review*. Vol. 46, No. 3 (July 1932).

Carr, Edward Hallett. *What is History?* New York: Vintage Books, 1961.

Cassuto, Rabbi Umberto. *The Documentary Hypothesis*. Jerusalem, Shalem Press, 2006.

Cecil, Alan W. *The Noahide Code*. Aventura: Academy of Shem Press, 2006.

———. *The Noahide Guide to Matthew*. Estero: Academy of Shem Press, 5769/2009.

Chomsky, Noam. *Media Control: The Spectacular Achievements of Propaganda*. New York: Seven Stories Press, 1997.

Clark, William R. *Petrodollar Warfare: Oil, Iraq and the Future of the Dollar*. Gabriola Island, BC: New Society Publishers, 2005.

Clarke, W. K. Lowther. *Concise Bible Commentary*. London: SPCK, 1952.

Cohen, Arnold. *An Introduction to Jewish Civil Law*. Jerusalem: Feldheim Publishers, 2000.

Cohen, Martin. *Political Philosophy: From Plato to Mao*. London: Pluto Press, 2001.

Cornelius, Steven. *Music of the Civil War Era: American History Through Music*. Westport, Conn: Greenwood Publishing Group, 2004.

Dahl, Robert Alan. *Democracy and Its Critics*. New Haven: Yale University Press, 1989.

———. *How Democratic is the American Constitution?* New Haven: Yale University Press, 2003.

Danziger, Rabbi Shelomoh. *The World of Hirschian Teachings: An Anthology on the Hirsch Chumash and the Haskafa of Rav Samson Raphael Hirsch*. Jerusalem: Feldheim Publishers, 2008.

Dawkins, Richard. *The God Delusion*. New York: Mariner Books, 2008.

———. *The Selfish Gene*. New York: Oxford University Press, 2006.

Dennett, Daniel C. "Memes and the Exploitation of Imagination." *The Journal of Aesthetics and Art Criticism*. Vol. 48, No. 2 (Spring, 1990).

Denson, John V. *The Costs of War: America's Pyrrhic Victories*. New Brunswick: Transaction Publishing, 1999.

Derber, Charles. *Corporation Nation: How Corporations are Taking Over our Lives and What We Can Do About It*. New York: St. Martin's Griffin, 1998.

Dershowitz, Alan M. *Supreme Injustice: How the High Court Hijacked Election 2000*. New York: Oxford University Press, 2001.

———. *The Case for Israel*. Hoboken: John Wiley & Sons, Inc., 2003.

Diamond, Jared. *Collapse*. New York: Viking, 2005.

———. *Guns, Germs, and Steel*. New York: W. W. Norton & Company, 1999.

Donin, Rabbi Hayim Halevy. *To Be A Jew: A Guide to Jewish Observance in Contemporary Life.* New York: Basic Books, Inc., Publishers, 1972.

Doyle, Sir Arthur Conan. *The Original Illustrated 'Strand' Sherlock Holmes* Ware, Hertfordshire: Wordsworth Editions, ltd., 2001.

Drutman, Lee and Charlie Cray. *The People's Business: Controlling Corporations and Restoring Democracy.* San Francisco: Berrett-Koehler Publishers, Inc., 2004.

Dudley, Will. *Hegel, Nietzsche, and Philosophy: Thinking Freedom.* Cambridge: Cambridge University Press, 2004.

Dyke, C. "Collective Decision Making in Rousseau, Kant, Hegel, and Mill." *Ethics,* Vol. 80, No. 1, (Oct., 1969).

Eidelberg, Paul. *Beyond the Secular Mind: A Judaic Response to the Problems of Modernity.* New York: Greenwood Press, 1989.

———. *Demophrenia: Israel and the Malaise of Democracy.* Columbia: Prescott Press, Inc., 1994.

———. *Jerusalem vs. Athens: In Quest of a General Theory of Existence.* Lanham: University Press of America, Inc., 1983.

———. *The Philosophy of the American Constitution.* Lanham, MD: University Press of America, 1986.

Ekstrand, Thomas. *Max Weber in a Theological Perspective.* Leuven, Belgium: Peeters, 2000.

Elgar Encyclopedia of Comparative Law. Jan M. Smits, ed. Cheltenham, UK: Edward Elgar Publishing Limited, 2006.

Elkins, Caroline. *Imperial Reckoning: The Untold Story of Britain's Gulag in Kenya.* New York: Henry Hold and Company, 2005.

Eskridge, William N. *Constitutional Stupidities, Constitutional Tragedies.* New York: New York University Press, 1998.

Evans, Richard J. *In Defense of History.* New York: W. W. Norton & Company, 1999.

Fahey, Tony. "Max Weber's Ancient Judaism." *The American Journal of Sociology.* Vol. 88, No. 1 (July 1982).

Farrand, Max. "The Federal Constitution and the Defects of The Confederation." *The American Political Science Review.* Vol. 2, No. 4 (November 1908).

Finley, Moses I. "Was Greek Civilization Based on Slave Labor?" Moses I. Finley, ed. *Slavery in Classical Antiquity: Views and Controversies.* Cambridge: W. Heffer, 1960.

Fischman, Dennis K. *Discourse in Exile: Karl Marx and the Jewish Question.* Amherst, Mass. University of Massachusetts Press, 1991.

Foster, Herbert D. "International Calvinism through Locke and the Revolution of 1688." *The American Historical Review.* Vol. 32, No. 3 (April 1927).

Freedman, Johathan. *The Temple of Culture: Assimilation and Anti-Semitism in Literary Anglo-America.* New York: Oxford University Press, 2000.

Freund, Julian. *The Sociology of Max Weber.* New York: Vintage Books, 1969.

Fukuyama, Francis. *The End of History and the Last Man.* New York: Free Press, 2006.

Gatto, John Taylor. *The Underground History of American Education.* New York: The Oxford Village Press, 2006.

———. *Dumbing Us Down.* Gabriola Island, British Columbia: New Society Publishers, 2005.

Gay, Ruth. *The Jews of Germany.* New Haven: Yale University Press, 1992.

Gershom, Rabbi Yonassan. *Jewish Themes in Star Trek.* Eretz Goyim: Lulu Press, Inc., 2009.

Gibbon, Edward. *The Decline and Fall of the Roman Empire.* New York: The Modern Library, 1995.

Gilderhus, Mark T. *History and Historians: A Historiographical Introduction.* Upper Saddle River, New Jersey: Prentice Hall, 2003.

Goethe, Johann Wolfgang Von. *Conversations of Goethe.* Whitefish, MT: Kessinger Publishing, 2005.

Goldhagen, Daniel Jonah. *Hitler's Willing Executioners: Ordinary Germans and the Holocaust.* New York: Vintage Books, 1997.

Goldstein, Rabbi Dr. Warren. *Defending the Human Spirit: Jewish Law's Vision for a Moral Society.* Jerusalem: Feldheim Publishers, 2006.

Goldwurm, Rabbi Hersh. *Daniel.* Brooklyn: Mesorah Publications, Ltd., 1998.

Gordis, Robert. *Judaic Ethics For a Lawless World.* New York: The Jewish Theological Seminary of America, 1986.

Gouldner, Alvin W. *The Coming Crisis in Western Sociology.* New York: Equinox Books, 1970.

Graber, Mark A. "Our (Im)Perfect Constitution." *The Review of Politics.* Vol. 51, No. 1 (Winter 1989).

Grayzel, Solomon. *A History of the Jews.* Philadelphia: The Jewish Publication Society of America, 1984.

Green, Maia. "Mau Mau Oathing Rituals and Political Ideology in Kenya: A Re-Analysis." *Journal of the International African Institute.* Vol. 60, No. 1 (1990).

Griffith, Mark. "'Public' and 'Private' in Early Greek Institutions of Education." *From Education in Greek and Roman Antiquity.* Yun Lee Too, ed. Leiden: Boston Brill Academic Publishers, 2001.

Haakonssen, Knud. *Natural Law and Moral Philosophy: From Grotius to the Scottish Enlightenment.* Cambridge: Cambridge University Press, 1996.

Harris, Sam. *The End of Faith: Religion, Terror, and the Future of Reason.* New York: W. W. Norton & Company, 2004.

Hartmann, Thom. *Unequal Protection.* New York: Rodale, 2004.

Hegel, Georg Wilhelm Friedrich. *On Art, Religion, and the History of Philosophy: Introductory Lectures* J. Glenn Gray, ed. New York: Harper & Row, 1970.

Heinberg, Richard. *The Party's Over: Oil, War and the Fate of Industrial Societies.* Gabriola Island, BC: New Society Publishers, 2003.

Hertzberg, Arthur. *The French Enlightenment and the Jews.* New York: Columbia University Press, 1968/5728.

———. *The Jews in America.* New York: Columbia University Press, 1998.

Herzog, Rabbi Isaac. "John Selden and Jewish Law." *Journal of Comparative Legislation and International Law.* 3rd Ser., Vol. 13, No. 4 (1931).

Highet, Gilbert. *The Classical Tradition.* New York: Oxford University Press, 1957.

Hirsch, Rabbi Samson Raphael. *Collected Writings.* Jerusalem: Phillip Feldheim, Inc., 1997.

———. *Commentary on the Torah.* London: The Judaica Press, Inc., 1966.

———. *Horeb.* Dayan Dr. I. Grunfeld, trans. New York: The Soncino Press, 1994.

———. *Nineteen Letters.* Rabbi Joseph Elias, trans. and commentary. Jerusalem: Feldheim Publishers, 1996.

———. *The Hirsch Chumash: Bereishis.* Daniel Haberman, trans. Jerusalem: Feldheim Publishers, 2006.

———. *The Hirsch Psalms.* Jerusalem: Feldheim Publishers, 1997.

———. *T'rumath Tzvi.* New York: The Judaica Press, 1986.

Hitchens, Christopher. *god is not Great.* New York: Twelve, 2007.

Hofstadter, Richard. *Anti-Intellectualism in American Life.* New York: Vintage Books, 1963.

———. *Social Darwinism in American Thought.* Boston: Beacon Press, 1992.

Holdcroft, David and Harry Lewis. "Memes, Minds and Evolution." *Philosophy*. Vol. 75, No. 292 (Apr., 2000).

Hook, La Rue van. "The Exposure of Infants at Athens." *Transactions and Proceedings of the American Philological Association*. Vol. 51 (1920).

Hubbert, M. King. "Nuclear Energy and the Fossil Fuels." *Drilling and Production Practice*. Publication no. 95 (1956).

Huntington, Samuel P. *The Clash of Civilizations and the Remaking of World Order*. New York: Simon & Schuster Paperbacks, 1996.

Irons, Peter H. *A People's History of the Supreme Court*. New York: Viking, 1999.

Isaiah, Rabbi Abraham Ben. and Rabbi Benjamin Sharfman, *The Pentateuch and Rashi's Commentary: Vayikra*. Brooklyn: S. S. & R. Publishing Company, Inc., 1977.

The Israeli-Arab Reader: A Documentary History of the Middle East Conflict. Walter Laqueur and Barry Rubin, ed. New York: Penguin Books, 1984.

Jacoby, Susan. *The Age of American Unreason*. New York: Pantheon Books, 2008.

Jevons, William Stanley. *The Coal Question: An Inquiry Concerning the Progress of the Nation, and the Probable Exhaustion of Our Coal-Mines*. A. W. Flux, ed. London: Macmillan and Co, Limited, 1906.

Johnson, Chalmers. *Nemesis: The Last Days of the American Republic*. New York: Metropolitan Books/Henry Holt and Company, 2006.

Johnson, Paul. *Intellectuals*. New York: HarpePerennial, 1990.

Johnston, David Cay. *Free Lunch: How the Wealthiest Americans Enrich Themselves at Government Expense (and Stick You With the Bill)*. New York: Portfolio, 2007.

———. *Perfectly Legal: The Covert Campaign to Rig Our Tax System to Benefit the Super Rich— and Cheat Everybody Else*. New York: Portfolio, 2005.

Johnston, David. *Roman Law in Context*. Cambridge: Cambridge University Press, 1999.

Kahaner, Larry. *Values, Prosperity and the Talmud: Business Lessons From the Ancient Rabbis*. Hoboken: John Wiley & Sons, Inc., 2003.

Kant, Immanuel. *Kant: Political Writings*. H. S. Reiss, ed. Cambridge: Cambridge University Press, 2005.

———. *Of the Different Races of Man. Race and the Enlightenment: A Reader*. Emmanuel Chukwudi Eze, ed. Oxford: Blackwell Publishers, Ltd., 2000.

———. *The Conflict of the Faculties*. Lincoln: University of Nebraska Press, 1992.

———. Kaplan, Rabbi Aryeh. *The Aryeh Kaplan Reader*. Brooklyn: Mesorah Publications, Ltd., 1985.

———. *Immortality, Resurrection and the Age of the Universe*. New York: KTAV Publishing House, Inc., 1993.

Kaplan, Jeffrey. *Radical Religion in America: Millenarian Movements from the Far Right to the Children of Noah*. (Syracuse: Syracuse University Press, 1997

Kaplan, Robert D. *The Coming Anarchy: Shattering the Dreams of the Post Cold War*. New York: Vintage Books, 2000.

Kaplan, Sidney. "The 'Domestic Insurrections' of the Declaration of Independence." *The Journal of Negro History*. Vol. 61, No. 3 (Jul., 1976).

Karabel, Jerome. *The Chosen: The Hidden History of Admission and Exclusion at Harvard, Yale, and Princeton*. New York: Houghton Mifflin Company, 2005

Kapustin, Max. "Biblical Criticism: A Traditionalist View." *Challenge*. Aryeh Carmell and Cyril Domb, eds. Jerusalem: Feldheim Publishers, 2000.

Karsh, Efrain. *Islamic Imperialism*. New Haven: Yale University Press, 2007.

Katz, Samuel. *Battleground: Fact & Fantasy in Palestine*. New York: Taylor Productions, Ltd., 2002.

Kelemen, R. Daniel and Eric C. Sibbitt, "The Globalization of American Law." *International Organization*. Vol. 58, No. 1 (Winter 2004).

Ketcham, Ralph. "Antifederalist Essays and Speeches, 1787–1788" *Roots of the Republic: American Founding Documents Interpreted*. Stephen L. Schechter, ed. Madison: Madison House Publishers, Inc., 1990.

Kinzer, Bruce L. *England's Disgrace?: J.S. Mill and the Irish Question*. Toronto: University of Toronto Press, 2001.

Klebanow, Diana and Franklin L. Jonas, *People's Lawyers: Crusaders for Justice in American History*. Armonk, NY: M. E. Sharpe, 2003.

Klugman, Rabbi Eliyahu Meir. *Rabbi Samson Raphael Hirsch: Architect of Torah Judaism for the Modern World*. Brooklyn: Mesorah Publications, Ltd., 2003.

Konvitz, Milton R. *Torah & Constitution: Essays in American Jewish Thought*. Syracuse: Syracuse University Press, 1998.

Krieger, Leonard. "Kant and the Crisis of Natural Law." *Journal of the History of Ideas*. Vol. 26, No. 2 (April–June 1965).

Knoles, George Harmon. "The Religious Ideas of Thomas Jefferson." *The Mississippi Valley Historical Review*. Vol. 30, No. 2 (September 1943).

Kunstler, James Howard. *The Long Emergency*. New York: Atlantic Monthly Press, 2005.

Kuttner, Robert. *The End of Laissez-Faire: National Purpose and the Global Economy After the Cold War*. New York: Alfred A. Knoff, 1991.

Lapide, Pinchas E. *Hebrew in the Church*. Errol F. Rhodes, trans. Grand Rapids: William B. Eerdmans Publishing Company, 1984.

Lau, Rabbi Yisrael Meir. *Rav Lau on Pirkei Avos*. Brooklyn: Mesorah Publications, ltd., 2006.

Lazare, Daniel. *The Frozen Republic: How the Constitution is Paralyzing Democracy*. New York: Harcourt Brace & Company, 1998.

———. *The Velvet Coup: The Constitution, the Supreme Court, and the Decline of American Democracy*. London: Verso, 2001.

Lazonick, William. "Industrial Organization and Technological Change: The Decline of the British Cotton Industry." *The Business History Review*. Vol. 57, No. 2 (Summer, 1983).

Lee, R. W. "The Civil Law and the Common Law: A World Survey." *Michigan Law Review*, Vol. 14, No. 2 (December 1915).

Levi, Yehudah. *Torah and Science: Their Interplay in the World Scheme*. Jerusalem: Feldheim Publishers, 2006.

———. *Torah Study: A Survey of Classic Sources on Timely Issues*. Jerusalem: Feldheim Publishers, Inc., 1990.

Levine, Aaron. *Moral Issues of the Marketplace in Jewish Law*. Brooklyn: Yashar Books Inc., 2006.

Lew, Dayan Dr. Myer S. *The Humanity of Jewish Law*. London: The Soncino Press, 1985.

Lewis, Mark Edward. *The Flood Myths of Early China*. Albany: State University of New York Press, 2006.

Liberles, Robert. *Salo Wittmayer Baron: Architect of Jewish History*. New York: New York University Press, 1995.

Litchtenstein, Rabbi Aaron. *The Seven Laws of Noah*. New York: The Rabbi Jacob Joseph School Press, 1986.

Loftus, John and Mark Aarons, *The Secret War Against the Jews*. New York: St. Martin's Griffin, 1994.

Lonsdale, John. "Mau Maus of the Mind: Making Mau Mau and Remaking Kenya." *The Journal of African History*. Vol. 31, No. 3 (1990).

Maccoby, Hyam. *Antisemitism and Modernity: Innovation and Continuity*. London: Taylor & Francis Routledge, 2006.

Maier, Pauline. *American Scripture: Making the Declaration of Independence*. New York: Vintage Books, 1998.

Maimonides. *Mishneh Torah, Sefer Shoftim*. Rabbi Eliyahu Touger, trans. and commentary. Jerusalem: Monznaim Publishing Corporation, 2001.

Maletz, Donald J. "History in Hegel's 'Philosophy of Right.'" *The Review of Politics*. Vol. 45, No. 2 (April 1983).

Marx, Karl. *Capital*. London: Penguin Books, 1990.

Marx, Karl and Friedrich Engels. *The Communist Manifesto*. New York: Pocket Books, 1964.

Mayer, Kenneth R. *With the Stroke of a Pen: Executive Orders and Presidential Power*. Princeton: Princeton University Press, 2001.

McCorkle, Pope. "The Historian as Intellectual: Charles Beard and the Constitution Reconsidered." *The American Journal of Legal History*. Vol. 28, No. 4 (October 1984).

McGuire, Robert A. and Robert L. Ohsfeldt. "Economic Interests and the American Constitution: A Quantitative Rehabilitation of Charles A. Beard." *The Journal of Economic History*. Vol. 44, No. 2 (June 1984).

McLellan, David. *Karl Marx: His Life and Thought*. New York: Harper & Row, Publishers, 1973.

Melber, Jehuda. *Judaism: A Religion of Reason*. Middle Village, NY: Jonathan David Publishers, Inc., 2003.

Mendes-Flohr, Paul R. and Jehuda Reinharz, ed., *The Jew in the Modern World*. New York: Oxford University Press, 1995.

Metzger, Bruce. *The Canon of the New Testament*. Oxford: Clarendon Press, 1992.

———. *A Textual Commentary on the Greek New Testament*. Stuttgart: Deutsche Bibelgesellschaft, 2000.

Mill, John Stuart. *On Liberty and Other Essays*. Oxford: Oxford University Press, 1991.

Mills, C. Wright. *The Power Elite*. New York: Oxford University Press, 1956.

———. *The Sociological Imagination*. New York: Oxford University Press, 1959.

Mitchell, Lynette G. and P. J. Rhodes. *The Development of the Polis in Archaic Greece*. London, New York Taylor & Francis, 1997.

Momigliano, Arnaldo. "A Note on Max Weber's Definition of Judaism as a Pariah-Religion." *History and Theory*. Vol. 19, No. 3 (October 1980).

———. "Two Types of Universal History: The Cases of E. A. Freeman and Max Weber." *The Journal of Modern History*. Vol. 58, No. 1 (March 1986).

Mommsen, Wolfgang J. *Max Weber and German Politics 1890—1920*. Michael S. Steinberg, trans. Chicago: The University of Chicago Press, 1990.

Montgomery, Henry C. "Thomas Jefferson and Roman Law." *The Classical Weekly*. Vol. 37, No. 15 (Mar. 6, 1944).

Morgan, Robert. and John Barton. *Biblical Interpretation*. Oxford: Oxford University Press, 1988.

Munk, Rabbi Elie. *The Call of the Torah*. E. S. Mazer, trans. Brooklyn: Mesorah Publications, Ltd., 1994.

Murphy, Cullen. *Are We Rome?* New York: Houghton Mifflin Company, 2007.

Narrett, Eugene. *Israel and the Endtimes: Writings on the Logic and Surface Turbulence of History*. Bloomington: AuthorHouse, 2006.

Nichols, John and Robert W. McChesney. *It's the Media, Stupid*. New York: Seven Stories Press, 2000.

Novick, Peter. *That Noble Dream*. Cambridge: Cambridge University Press, 1988.

Ober, Josiah. *Mass and Elite in Democratic Athens: Rhetoric, Ideology, and the Power of the People*. Princeton: Princeton University Press, 1989.

The Oxford Guide to United States Supreme Court Decisions. Kermit L. Hall, ed. New York: Oxford University Press, Inc., 1999.

Pagels, Elaine. *The Gnostic Paul*. Philadelphia: Trinity Press International, 1992.

Parenti, Michael. *The Assassination of Julius Caesar: A People's History of Ancient Rome*. New York: The New Press, 2003.

Parker, Rachel R. "Shays' Rebellion: An Episode in American State-Making." *Sociological Perspectives*. Vol. 34, No. 1 (Spring 1991).

Parkin, Frank. *Max Weber*. New York: Routledge, 1991.

Paterson, W. Romaine. *The Nemesis of Nations*. New York: E. P. Dutton & Co., 1907.

Patterson, Orlando. *Freedom: Freedom in the Making of Western Culture*. New York: BasicBooks, 1991.

Pennington, Kenneth. *The Prince and the Law, 1200–1600: Sovereignty and Rights in the Western Legal Tradition*. Berkeley: University of California Press, 1993.

Perry, Marvin and Frederick M. Schweitzer. *Antisemitism: Myth and Hate from Antiquity to the Present*. New York: Palgrave Macmillian, 2002,

Phillips, Kevin. *American Theocracy*. New York: Viking, 2006.

Plato. *Plato: Complete Works*. John M. Cooper, ed. Indianapolis: Hackett Publishing Company, 1997.

———. *The Republic*. Allan Bloom, trans. New York: Basic Books, 1991.

Poliakoff, Michael B. *Combat Sports in the Ancient World*. New Haven: Yale University Press, 1987.

Popovic, Milan. *The Life and Letters of Mileva Marić*. Baltimore: The Johns Hopkins University Press, 2003.

Portis, Edward Bryan. *Reconstructing the Classics: Political Theory From Plato to Marx*. Chatham: Chatham House, 1998.

Potok, Chaim. *Wanderings: Chaim Potok's History of the Jews*. New York: Fawcett Crest, 1978.

Prager, Dennis and Joseph Telushkin. *Why the Jews?* New York: Touchstone, 2003.

Rabinovitch, Nachum L. "Torah and Science: Conflict or Compliment?" *Challenge*. Aryeh Crmell and Cyril Domb, eds. Jerusalem: Feldheim Publishers, 1976.

Ramban. *Bereishis*. Rabbi Yaakov Blinder and Rabbi Yoseph Kamenetsky, trans. Brooklyn: Mesorah Publications, Ltd., 2005.

———. *The Book of Redemption*. Rabbi Dr. Charles B. Chavel, trans. New York: Shilo Publishing House, Inc., 1986.

Raymond, Robert. *Out of the Fiery Furnace: The Impact of Metals on the History of Mankind*. University Park, PA: Penn State Press, 1986.

Reich, Charles A. *Opposing the System*. New York: Crown Publishers, Inc., 1995.

Rhodes, James M., *Eros, Wisdom, and Silence: Plato's Erotic Dialogues*. Columbia, Mo: University of Missouri Press, 2003.

Roberts, Rabbi Matis. *Trei Asar*. Brooklyn: Mesorah Publications, Ltd., 1995.

Roberts, Paul. *The End of Oil*. New York: Mariner/Houghton Mifflin Company, 2004.

Robertson, Roland. "On the Analysis of Mysticism: Pre-Weberian, Weberian and Post-Weberian Perspectives." *Sociological Analysis*. Vol. 36, No. 3 (Autumn 1975).

Rosenberg, Rabbi A. J. *Isaiah*. Brooklyn: The Judaica Press, Inc., 2004.

Rosenblatt, Jason P. *Renaissance England's Chief Rabbi: John Selden*. Oxford: Oxford University Press, 2006.

Roth, Guenther. "Political Critiques of Max Weber: Some Implications for Political Sociology" *American Sociological Review*. Vol. 30, No. 2 (April 1965).

Runciman, W. G. *A Critique of Max Weber's Philosophy of Social Science*. Cambridge: Cambridge University Press, 2002.

Samuel, Maurice. *The Professor and the Fossil*. New York: Alfred A. Knopf, 1956.

———. *You Gentiles*. New York: Harcourt, Brace and Company, 1924.

Scherman, Rabbi Nosson. *Bereishis*. Brooklyn: Mesorah Publications, Ltd., 2002.

———. *Siddur Eitz Chaim*. Brooklyn: Mesorah Publications, Ltd., 1985.

———. *The Stone Chumash*. Brooklyn: Mesorah Publications, Ltd., 1994.

Scherman, Rabbi Nosson and Rabbi Hersh Goldwurm, *Vayikra*. Brooklyn: Mesorah Publications, Ltd., 1989.

Schoenfeld, Gabriel. *The Return of Anti-Semitism*. San Francisco: Encounter Books, 2004.

Schonfield, Dr. Hugh J. *Those Incredible Christians*. New York: Bantam Books, 1969.

Schwartz, Mark, Meir Tamari and Daniel Schwab. "Ethical Investing from a Jewish Perspective." *Business and Society Review*. Vol. 112, Issue 1 (March 2007).

Schwartz, Nancy L. "Communitarian Citizenship: Marx & Weber on the City." *Polity*. Vol. 17, No. 3 (Spring 1985).

Schwartz, Rabbi Yoel. *Kosher Money*, David Weiss, trans. Jerusalem: Feldheim Publishers, 2004.

Séfer haHinnuch. Charles Wengrov, trans. Jerusalem: Feldheim Publishers, 1992.

Seidman, Steven. "Weber's Turn to Sociology: A Reply to Horst Helle." *Canadian Journal of Sociology/Cahiers canadiens de sociologie*. Vol. 10, No. 2 (Spring 1985).

———. *The Postmodern Turn: New Perspectives on Social Theory*. Cambridge: Cambridge University Press, 1998.

———. "The End of Sociological Theory: The Postmodern Hope." *Sociological Theory*. Vol. 9, No. 2 (1991).

Sherer, F. M. "Invention and Innovation in the Watt-Boulton Steam-Engine Venture." *Technology and Culture*. Vol. 6, No. 2 (Spring 1965).

Simmons, Matthew R. *Twilight in the Desert: The Coming Saudi Oil Shock and the World Economy*. Hoboken: John Wiley & Sons, Inc., 2005.

Sivan, Gabriel. *The Bible and Civilization*. New York: Quadrangle/The New York Times Book Co., 1973.

Smith, Adam. *An Inquiry Into the Nature and Causes of the Wealth of Nations*. Washington, D.C.: Regnery Publishing, Inc., 1998.

Smith, Steven B. *Spinoza, Liberalism, and the Question of Jewish Identity*. New Haven: Yale University Press, 1997.

Soloveitchik, Rabbi Joseph B. *Halakhic Man*. Philadelphia: The Jewish Publication Society, 1991.

Sombart, Werner. *The Jews and Modern Capitalism*. Brunswick, NJ: Transaction Books, 2006.

Sowell, Thomas. *Marxism: Philosophy and Economics*. New York: William Morrow and Company, Inc., 1985.

Spengler, Oswald. *The Decline of the West*. New York: Knopf, 1932.

Stalley, R. F. "Plato's Doctrine of Freedom." *Proceedings of the Aristotelian Society, New Series*. Vol. 98 (1998).

Stavsky, Rabbi Yitzchok. *Trei Asar*, Vol. II. Brooklyn: Mesorah Publications, ltd., 2009.

Steele, E. D. "J. S. Mill and the Irish Question: The Principles of Political Economy, 1848–1865." *The Historical Journal*. Vol. 13, No. 2 (June 1970).

Stein, Peter. *Roman Law in European History*. Cambridge: Cambridge University Press, 2005.

Steinsaltz, Rabbi Adin. *Bava Metzia*. New York: Random House, 1989.

Swatos, William H. Jr. and Peter Kivisto. "Max Weber as 'Christian Sociologist.'" *Journal for the Scientific Study of Religion*. Vol. 30, No. 4 (December 1991).

Szatmary, David P. *Shays' Rebellion: The Making of an Agrarian Insurrection*. Amherst: The University of Massachusetts Press, 1980.

Tehillim. Rabbi Avrohom Chaim Feuer, trans. and commentary. Brooklyn: Mesorah Publications, Inc., 1995.

Toynbee, Arnold J. *Hellenism: The History of a Civilization*. Westport, Connecticut: Greenwood Press, Publishers, 1981.

———. *A Study of History*. London: Oxford University Press, 1963.

———. *War and Civilization*. (New York: Oxford University Press, 1950).

Tuchman, Barbara W. *The March of Folly*. New York: Ballantine Books, 1984.

Twain, Mark. *The Complete Essays of Mark Twain*. New York: Doubleday & Co., 1963.

Voltaire. *The Works of Voltaire: A Contemporary Version*. William F. Fleming, trans. New York: E.R. DuMont, 1901.

Warren, Elizabeth & Amelia Warren Tyagi. *The Two-Income Trap: Why Middle-Class Parents are Going Broke*. New York: Basic Books, 2003.

Weber, Max. *Ancient Judaism*. Hans H. Gerth and Don Martindale, trans. New York: The Free Press, 1952.

———. *Economy and Society*. Guenther Roth and Claus Wittich, eds. Berkeley: University of California Press, 1978.

———. *From Max Weber: Essays in Sociology*. Translated and edited by H. H. Gerth and C. Wright Mills. New York: Oxford University Press, 1946.

———. *The Protestant Ethic and the Spirit of Capitalism*. New York: Charles Scribner's Sons, 1958.

———. *The Sociology of Religion*. Ephraim Fischoff, trans. Boston: Beacon Press, 1991.

Weinberg, Rav Yaakov Yechiel. *The World of Hirschian Teachings: An Anthology on the Hirsch Chumash and the Haskafa of Rav Samson Raphael Hirsch*. Jerusalem: Feldheim Publishers, 2008.

Weiner, Rabbi Michoel. *The Schottenstein Talmud*. Brooklyn: Mesorah Publications, Ltd., 2005.

Wellhausen, Julius. *Prolegomena to the History of Ancient Israel*. Cleveland: The World Publishing Company, 1965.

Welter, Rush. "Anti-intellectualism in American Life by Richard Hofstadter." *The Journal of American History*. Vol. 51, No. 3, (Dec., 1964).

Wistrich, Robert S. *Laboratory for World Destruction: Germans and Jews in Central Europe*. Lincoln: University of Nebraska Press, 2007.

Wright, Louis B. "Thomas Jefferson and the Classics." *Proceedings of the American Philosophical Society*. Vol. 87, No. 3 (July 14, 1943).

Woodham-Smith, Cecil. *The Great Hunger: Ireland 1845–1849*. London: Penguin Books, 1962.

Woodward, Bob and Scott Armstrong. *The Brethren*. New York: Simon and Schuster, 1979.

Wouk, Herman. *This is My God*. New York: Little, Brown and Company, 1988.

Yechezkel. Rabbi Moshe Eisemann, translation and commentary. Brooklyn: Mesorah Publications, Ltd., 1994.

Zeitlin, Irving M. *Ancient Judaism: Biblical Criticism from Max Weber to the Present*. Oxford: Polity Press, 1984.

———. *Jesus and the Judaism of His Time*. Cambridge: Polity Press, 1988.

Ziskind, Martha A. "John Selden: Criticism and Affirmation of the Common Law Tradition." *The American Journal of Legal History*. Vol. 19, No. 1 (January 1975).

Zuckert, Michael P. "Self-Evident Truth and the Declaration of Independence." *The Review of Politics*. Vol. 49, No. 3 (Summer 1987).

Index

Recessional

God of our fathers, known of old—
Lord of our far-flung battle line—
Beneath whose awful hand we hold
Dominion over palm and pine—
Lord God of Hosts, be with us yet,
Lest we forget, lest we forget!

The tumult and the shouting dies—
The captains and the kings depart—
Still stands Thine ancient sacrifice,
An humble and a contrite heart.
Lord God of Hosts, be with us yet,
Lest we forget, lest we forget!

Far-called, our navies melt away—
On dune and headland sinks the fire—
Lo, all our pomp of yesterday
Is one with Nineveh and Tyre!
Judge of the Nations, spare us yet,
Lest we forget, lest we forget!

If, drunk with sight of power, we loose
Wild tongues that have not Thee in awe—
Such boasting as the Gentiles use
Or lesser breeds without the Law—
Lord God of Hosts, be with us yet,
Lest we forget, lest we forget!

For heathen heart that puts her trust
In reeking tube and iron shard—
All valiant dust that builds on dust,
And guarding, calls not Thee to guard—
For frantic boast and foolish word,
Thy mercy on Thy people, Lord!

Rudyard Kipling